Late Modern Philosophy

Blackwell Readings in the History of Philosophy

Series Editors: *Fritz Allhoff and Anand Jayprakash Vaidya*

The volumes in this series provide concise and representative selections of key texts from the history of philosophy. Expertly edited and introduced by established scholars, each volume represents a particular philosophical era, replete with important selections of the most influential work in metaphysics, epistemology, moral and political philosophy, and the philosophy of science and religion.

1. *Ancient Philosophy: Essential Readings with Commentary*
Edited by Nicholas Smith with Fritz Allhoff and Anand Jayprakash Vaidya

2. *Medieval Philosophy: Essential Readings with Commentary*
Edited by Gyula Klima with Fritz Allhoff and Anand Jayprakash Vaidya

3. *Early Modern Philosophy: Essential Readings with Commentary*
Edited by A. P. Martinich with Fritz Allhoff and Anand Jayprakash Vaidya

4. *Late Modern Philosophy: Essential Readings with Commentary*
Edited by Elizabeth S. Radcliffe and Richard McCarty with Fritz Allhoff and Anand Jayprakash Vaidya

Late Modern Philosophy

Essential Readings with Commentary

Edited by

Elizabeth S. Radcliffe and Richard McCarty
with Fritz Allhoff and Anand Jayprakash Vaidya

Blackwell
Publishing

Editorial material and organization © 2007 by Blackwell Publishing Ltd

BLACKWELL PUBLISHING
350 Main Street, Malden, MA 02148-5020, USA
9600 Garsington Road, Oxford OX4 2DQ, UK
550 Swanston Street, Carlton, Victoria 3053, Australia

The right of Elizabeth S. Radcliffe, Richard McCarty, Fritz Allhoff, and Anand Jayprakash Vaidya to be identified as the Authors of the Editorial Material in this Work has been asserted in accordance with the UK Copyright, Designs, and Patents Act 1988.

First published 2007 by Blackwell Publishing Ltd

1   2007

Library of Congress Cataloging-in-Publication Data

Late modern philosophy : essential readings with commentary / edited by Elizabeth S. Radcliffe and Richard McCarty ; with Fritz Allhoff and Anand Jayprakash Vaidya. — 1st ed.
    p. cm.
    Includes index.
    ISBN-13: 978-1-4051-4688-3 (hardcover : alk. paper)
    ISBN-10: 1-4051-4688-5 (hardcover : alk. paper)
    ISBN-13: 978-1-4051-4689-0 (pbk. : alk. paper)
    ISBN-10: 1-4051-4689-3 (pbk. : alk. paper)   1. Philosophy, Modern.   I. Radcliffe, Elizabeth Schmidt, 1955–   II. McCarty, Richard, 1947–   III. Allhoff, Fritz.   IV. Vaidya, Anand.

    B791.L36 2006
    190—dc22

                                                                        2006017114

A catalogue record for this title is available from the British Library.

Set in 10/12.5pt Dante
by Graphicraft Limited, Hong Kong
Printed and bound in Singapore
by COS Printers Pte Ltd

The publisher's policy is to use permanent paper from mills that operate a sustainable forestry policy, and which has been manufactured from pulp processed using acid-free and elementary chlorine-free practices. Furthermore, the publisher ensures that the text paper and cover board used have met acceptable environmental accreditation standards.

For further information on
Blackwell Publishing, visit our website:
www.blackwellpublishing.com

Contents

Acknowledgments

We should like to thank the Provost's Office at Santa Clara University for funding the compilation of an index.

Text Credits

The editors and publisher gratefully acknowledge the permission granted to reproduce the copyright material in this book:

1: John Locke, pp. 48–52, 104–6, 119–22, 127–30, 134–8, 139–41, 163–4, 233–8, 240–1, 244–7, 295–9, 335–7, 340–3, 345–7, 525–8, 530–2, 538–40, 618, 619–21, 630–1 from P. H. Nidditch (ed.), *Essay concerning Human Understanding* (Oxford: Clarendon Press, 1975). © 1975 by Clarendon Press. Reprinted by permission of Oxford University Press.

2: George Berkeley, "The First Dialogue; The Second Dialogue; The Third Dialogue," pp. 7–21, 23–30, 35–6, 43, 45–7, 50–3, 61–71 from Robert M. Adams (ed.), *Three Dialogues between Hylas and Philonous in Opposition to Sceptics and Atheists* (Indianapolis: Hackett Publishing Company, 1979). © 1979 by Hackett Publishing Company, Inc. Reprinted by permission of Hackett Publishing Company, Inc. All rights reserved.

3: David Hume, pp. 96–9, 101–2, 108–11, 113–17, 120–9, 135–41, 143–7, 169–74, 183–5 from Tom L. Beauchamp (ed.), *An Enquiry concerning Human Understanding* (Oxford: Oxford University Press, 1999). © 1999 by Oxford University Press. Reprinted by permission of Oxford University Press.

4: David Hume, "Book 1, Part 4, Sect. 5. Of the Immateriality of the Soul, Sect. 6. Of Personal Identity; Book 2, Part 3, Section 1. Of Liberty and Necessity; Section 2. The same subject continu'd," pp. 152–4, 164–71, 257–62, 262–4 from David Fate Norton and Mary J. Norton (eds.), *A Treatise of Human Nature* (Oxford: Oxford University Press, 2000). © 2000 by Oxford University Press. Reprinted by permission of Oxford University Press.

5: Gottfried Wilhelm Leibniz, pp. 53–8, 66–8 from Peter Remnant and Jonathan Bennett (eds.), *New Essays concerning Human Understanding* (Cambridge: Cambridge University Press, viii

1981). © 1981 by Cambridge University Press. Reprinted by permission of the editors and publisher.

6: Gottfried Wilhelm Leibniz and Samuel Clarke, "Mr. Leibniz's First Paper; Dr. Clarke's First Reply; Mr. Leibniz's Third Paper; Mr. Leibniz's Fourth Paper; Dr. Clarke's Fifth Reply," pp. 11–12, 12–14, 25–8, 36–7, 97–9, 114–20 from H. G. Alexander (ed.), *The Leibniz–Clarke Correspondence* (Manchester, UK: Manchester University Press, 1996). © 1956 by Manchester University Press. Reprinted by permission of the publisher.

7: Thomas Reid, "Ch. VII: Conclusion," pp. 203–4, 208–10, 212–17 from Derek R. Brookes (ed.), *An Inquiry into the Human Mind on the Principles of Common Sense* (University Park, Pennsylvania: Pennsylvania State University Press, 1997).

8: Immanuel Kant, "Preface; Preamble; Main Transcendental Question, First Part; Main Transcendental Question, Second Part; Main Transcendental Question, Third Part," pp. 54–8, 62–7, 77–88, 89–101, 103–6, 110–12, 119–20, 122–40 from Gary Hatfield (ed.), *Prolegomena to Any Future Metaphysics* (Cambridge: Cambridge University Press, 2002). © 1997 by Cambridge University Press. This selection is taken from the first edition and has been revised by the author especially for Blackwell's edition. A fully revised and updated version was published as a second edition in 2004. Revised by permission of the editor and publisher.

9: Samuel Clarke, "Section III. A Demonstration of the Being and Attributes of God," pp. 12–17 from Ezio Vailati (ed.), *A Demonstration of the Being and Attributes of God* (Cambridge: Cambridge University Press, 1998). © 1998 by Cambridge University Press. Reprinted by permission of the editor and publisher.

10: William Paley, "Chapter I – State of the Argument; Chapter II – State of the Argument Continued," pp. 1–6, 8–17 from *Natural Theology*, 12 (Charlottesville: Lincoln-Rembrandt Publishing, 1997).

11: David Hume, "Part II, Part III, Part V, Part IX," pp. 15–20, 23–7, 34–7, 54–7 from Richard H. Popkin (ed.), *Dialogues concerning Natural Religion*, first edition (Indianapolis: Hackett Publishing Company, 1988). © 1988 by Hackett Publishing Company, Inc. Reprinted by permission of Hackett Publishing Company, Inc. All rights reserved.

12: Immanuel Kant, "On the Impossibility of an Ontological Proof of God's Existence," pp. 564–9, 677–80, 682, 684 from Paul Guyer and Allen W. Wood (eds.), *Critique of Pure Reason* (Cambridge: Cambridge University Press, 1998). © 1998 by Cambridge University Press. Reprinted by permission of the editors and publisher.

13: John Locke, selections from *Second Treatise of Government*, pp. 262–3, 263–8, 269–71, 271–2, 274–5, 276–7, 284–6, 304, 306–7, 309–11, 322–4 from David Wootton (ed.), *John Locke, Political Writings* (Indianapolis: Hackett Publishing Company, 2003). Originally published by Penguin Books © 1993. Reprinted in 2003 by Hackett Publishing Company, Inc. Reprinted by permission of Hackett Publishing Company, Inc. All rights reserved.

14: David Hume, "Of the Original Contract," pp. 467–71, 474–5, 479–82, 486–7 from Eugene F. Miller (ed.), *Essays Moral, Political, Literary* (Indianapolis: Hackett Publishing Company, 1987).

15: Jean-Jacques Rousseau, "On the Social Contract," pp. 17, 19–27, 31–5, 49–52, 66–7, 76–7 from Donald A. Cress (ed.), *On the Social Contract* (Indianapolis: Hackett Publishing Company,

1987). © 1987 by Hackett Publishing Company, Inc. Reprinted by permission of Hackett Publishing Company, Inc. All rights reserved.

16: Samuel Clarke, "Section I," pp. 192–4, 198–201 from D. D. Raphael (ed.), *Discourse concerning the Unchangeable Obligations of Natural Religion*, British Moralists vol. 1 (Oxford: Clarendon, 1969). © 1969 by D. D. Raphael. Reprinted by permission of Professor D. D. Raphael.

17: David Hume, pp. 265–8, 293–302, 302–6, 307–11, 311–15, 320–1, 367–74 from David Fate Norton and Mary J. Norton (eds.), *A Treatise of Human Nature* (Oxford: Oxford University Press, 2000). © 2000 by Oxford University Press. Reprinted by permission of Oxford University Press.

18: Richard Price, "Chapter I. Section 1. The Question Stated Concerning the Foundation of Morals; Section II. Of the Origin of Our Ideas in General; Section III. Of the Origin of Our Ideas of Moral Right and Wrong; Chapter IV. Of Our Ideas of Good and Ill Desert," pp. 131–3, 134–7, 141–7, 154–7 from D. D. Raphael (ed.), *A Review of the Principal Questions in Morals*, British Moralists vol. 2 (Oxford: Clarendon, 1969). © 1969 by D. D. Raphael. Reprinted by permission of Professor D. D. Raphael.

19: Adam Smith, "Chapter 1. Of Sympathy; Chapter 4. The same subject continued; Chapter 6. In what cases the Sense of Duty ought to be the sole Principle of our Conduct," pp. 47–52, 63–9, 203–7, 284–5, 287–90, 292–3 from E. G. West (ed.), *The Theory of Moral Sentiments* (Indianapolis: Liberty Classics, 1976).

20: Immanuel Kant, "Of the Principle of Morality; The Supreme Principle of Morality," pp. 11–14, 36–47 from Louis Infield (ed.), *Lectures on Ethics* (Indianapolis: Hackett Publishing Company, 1963). © 1963 by Routledge. Reproduced by permission of Taylor & Francis Books UK.

21: Immanuel Kant, "Section II. Transition from Popular Moral Philosophy to Metaphysics of Morals," pp. 34–9 from Mary Gregor (ed.), *Groundwork of the Metaphysics of Morals* (Cambridge: Cambridge University Press, 1997). © 1997 by Cambridge University Press. Reprinted by permission of the Estate of M. J. Gregor and the publisher.

22: Thomas Reid, pp. 201–3, 222–5, 231–3, 387–91, 393–7 from *Essays on the Active Powers of the Human Mind* (Cambridge, MA: MIT Press, 1969).

23: Jeremy Bentham, "Chapter I. Of the Principle of Utility; Chapter II. Of the Principles Adverse to that of Utility; Chapter IV. Value of a Lot of Pleasure or Pain, How to be Measured; Chapter X. Different senses of the word motive," pp. 1–6, 13–14, 20–36, 49–54, 161–9 from *An Introduction to the Principles of Morals and Legislation* (London: E. Wilson, 1823).

24: Mary Wollstonecraft, "Chapter 9. Of the Pernicious Effects Which Arise from the Unnatural Distinctions Established in Society," pp. 230–41 from Sylvana Tomaselli (ed.), *A Vindication of the Rights of Woman* (Cambridge: Cambridge University Press, 1995). © 1995 by Cambridge University Press. Reprinted by permission of the editor and publisher.

Every effort has been made to trace copyright holders and to obtain their permission for the use of copyright material. The publisher apologizes for any errors or omissions in the above list and would be grateful if notified of any corrections that should be incorporated in future reprints or editions of this book.

General Introduction

The best way to learn about the ideas of the greatest minds in the history of philosophy is by reading firsthand what they wrote. In using this volume, the reader will be doing just that. The story of modern philosophy taught in just about every English-language college and university is dominated by developments in the theory of knowledge, starting with René Descartes and moving eventually through three eighteenth-century figures of British empiricism: John Locke, George Berkeley, and David Hume. Here we introduce *Late Modern Philosophy* with this trio of venerable empiricists because we present them as initiating a new epoch in the philosophy of the modern era.

Why a new epoch? These empiricist philosophers writing at the start of the eighteenth century argued against their rationalist opponents, who thought that reason was the only capacity by which we could attain certainty. Influenced by the early modern scientific method, the empiricists emphasized the role of sensory observation and experiment in acquiring the elements necessary for knowledge. All knowledge, they agreed, *must* begin with experience. They breathed new life into the perspective of "naturalism," approaching inquiries about the human mind, knowledge, action, and morality as systems in nature subject to scientific explanation. Among the questions they explored were: How do our sense perceptions represent the objects in the world that cause them? What is the nature of the reality we perceive? Can we experience ourselves in the way we experience the rest of the world? If we are part of nature and subject to the same natural laws, how can we be free?

The empiricist influence pervaded the first half of the eighteenth century, until sometime just after its midpoint, when we encounter in Germany (East Prussia) one of the most famous of all philosophical "awakenings." Immanuel Kant claimed, in his *Prolegomena to Any Future Metaphysics* (1783), that it was Hume, the most extreme of the British empiricists, who had earlier roused him from "dogmatic slumber." Hume and Kant, the giants of eighteenth-century philosophy, presented fascinating and opposing views on how we justify our beliefs about the causal structure of the natural world. Although Kant rejected Hume's empiricism, his philosophy is sometimes called a "synthesis" of the techniques of rationalism and empiricism. Since his reply to Hume on the subject of cause and effect is central to the story of modern philosophy, we have happily extended the range of *Late Modern Philosophy* at least through the most productive years of Kant's career, which ended with the eighteenth century.

For many decades the classroom chronicle of modern philosophy has been dominated to a fault by controversies in the philosophy of knowledge and reality – in epistemology and metaphysics. But this narrow focus is disappointing. In this volume we have endeavored to integrate these traditional topics of study with the eighteenth century's moral and political philosophy, and with some disputes in religious philosophy as well. In ethics we include debates about the possibility of a "moral sense" that detects virtue and vice, and opposing views on the appropriateness of the "sense of duty" as a motive for moral action. In political philosophy we consider questions surrounding the source of political authority and its creation in a social contract, a tradition of political theorizing popularized in the seventeenth century by Thomas Hobbes. Through our inclusion of reading selections in these areas we attempt here to present the philosophy of the late modern period as an even foundation for the intellectual development of succeeding centuries.

The reading selections in this volume are arranged in six parts: Empiricism, Critics of Empiricism, Kant's Critique of Rationalism and Empiricism, Arguments for the Existence of God, Political Philosophy, and Moral Philosophy. In the following pages of this General Introduction we outline some of the more central controversies encountered within the readings we have selected.

Innatism vs. Empiricism

John Locke initiated the philosophy of the late modern period with a sharp attack on the doctrine of "innate ideas." Knowledge or ideas are "innate" when they are considered to be among the original equipment of the human mind. If we go back in the history of philosophy as far as Plato we find the doctrine that to learn or acquire knowledge is really just to remember. Human knowledge advances, according to this view, through recovery of the innate contents of our minds: through remembering ideas better known by the soul in a previous existence, but now obscured by the sensory "noise" of human experience. St. Augustine carried the doctrine of innatism into scholastic philosophy, with his view that the human memory is like a "cave" that is furnished by God with all the ideas human beings can know – including, of course, the idea of God himself.

For René Descartes, at the beginning of modern philosophy, the innateness of the idea of God was to serve prominently in his proof of God's existence. He said in one of his famous arguments that because the idea of God has the highest degree of "objective reality," it could not exist in the human mind unless caused to exist there by nothing less than God himself. Hence, God must exist. By this idea's supreme "objective reality" Descartes appears to have meant something like this: the idea that we have of God, as an omnipotent creator and sustainer of the world, as all-knowing, and as infinite in time and present all throughout infinite space, is beyond comparison to any other object we can imagine. Descartes concluded, therefore, that it is absurd to think that anything less grand, certainly not any of the finite things we see or hear around us, nor any combination of them, could possibly be the cause of such an idea. It could come only from an infinite substance, God himself, and be impressed upon our minds as he created us, like a seal impressed in wax: our maker's mark.

The doctrine of innate ideas is the stalwart tradition in the theory of human knowledge that Locke set out to undo in his *Essay concerning Human Understanding*. The slogan of Locke and subsequent empiricists, which reaches all the way back to Aristotle, was that "There is nothing in the intellect that does not first appear in sensation." Locke accordingly maintained, against the likes of Plato, Augustine, and Descartes, that prior to birth and sense experience the human mind is a blank page, a *tabula rasa*. "Empiricism," as opposed to "innatism," is the doctrine that the source of human knowledge lies exclusively in sense experience. Anyone who would demonstrate how she *knows* something, according to the empiricists, must trace the origin of her knowledge ultimately to what can be experienced through the senses. Locke and other eighteenth-century empiricists were duly impressed by the tremendous advances of modern science, in which older, often superstitious beliefs taken for scientific knowledge were overturned by disciplined observation of the world. Hadn't the observation-based experiments of Galileo refuted ancient physics based on supposedly innate ideas? Hadn't Newton's research on gravity and experiments with light conclusively demonstrated that observation is the sole path to knowledge?

How, then, would Locke proceed to argue against the philosophical tradition of innate ideas? Well . . . how else but by observation? If there is innate knowledge, such as the idea that "the whole is greater than the part," then every human being would know it. But do they? Aren't there children and mentally challenged adults who do not know such things? Does every human being, not just every educated European, but *every* human being in the world, have in his or her head Descartes's image of the sole, omnipotent, omniscient, omnipresent creator and sustainer of the world? Look for yourself! You'll see that there are no innate ideas.

It was not part of Locke's attack on the doctrine of innate ideas to deny that *anything* is innate in human beings. Of course, some elements of our humanity, of what makes us biologically human, are innate. We undoubtedly have innate patterns of behavior, called instincts. Newborn babies know how to cry, obviously, and this is not something they must learn from experience. But Locke's opposition to innate *ideas* is directed only toward those who think that there are conceptual truths in the human mind that are not achieved by experience and observation. What Locke is denying is that there is anything innate in the human mind that counts as *true*. He would admit that newborns know, innately, how to cry; but he would say that in knowing how to cry babies do not know anything that is *true*. It is true that if a baby cries she will often get the attention of a nearby adult. But babies are not born knowing this truth. Newborns do not cry because they know, innately, that crying is the way to get the attention they need.

We have included in this volume some of the later writings of Gottfried Wilhelm Leibniz who, though he contributed to the philosophy of the earlier century, reacted also to the philosophy of Locke. Leibniz was thoroughly entrenched in the tradition of innate ideas that Locke set out to criticize. On a plausible reading of Leibniz's philosophy, in fact, there are no ideas that are *not* innate. In defending his innatism against Locke's attack he posed an ingenious objection: if, as Locke said, the original content of all human minds is exactly the same; if we all begin with the same blank page, then there can be only one human mind! His argument here makes use of what has come to be known in metaphysics as Leibniz's Law, or "the identity of indiscernibles." Imagine, if you can, two objects that have all the same qualities, and so are exactly alike in every respect. Not even God could tell them apart because, by hypothesis, every quality even *he* might use to distinguish them is common to both, in exactly the same way. According to Leibniz's Law, these two things exactly alike would have to be the very same object. He held this view because he was convinced that God would not, even could not, create two or more things with exactly the same qualities: He would have no reason to do so, and without a sufficient reason, Leibniz thought, God cannot do anything. It follows, then, that every individual God creates has to be different in at least some respect from every other. Yet if we follow Locke, Leibniz says, then every human soul or mind is just like every other; for if there are no innate ideas, then no soul has anything that can distinguish it from another. All of these indiscernible, blank-page human minds Locke imagines must therefore be the same! The only way that God can make you a distinct individual, according to Leibniz's way of thinking, is to create your soul with some uniqueness in the innate contents of your mind.

Idealism vs. Realism

In metaphysics and epistemology, an "idealist" is someone who thinks of existing things as found only in the mind. But a "realist" is someone who disagrees, thinking that at least some of what exists is located outside the mind. A good way to highlight the difference between them is to observe that, for an idealist, if there were no minds, then nothing could exist; whereas for a realist, things could exist even if no minds existed.

In explaining and organizing the kinds of things we can know about the world we experience, Locke expressed a realist view when he made the following, commonsense observation. He distinguished the qualities that exist in objects and that "resemble" our perceptions of them (*primary qualities*) from qualities that do not exist in objects in the way that we perceive them (*secondary qualities*). Our perceptions of the latter qualities, that is, do not resemble anything in the objects. Descartes had made a similar distinction earlier, but not quite in these terms. Shape and weight are examples of the primary qualities of things; color, odor, and taste are examples of their secondary qualities. The primary qualities, Locke says, are in objects, no matter whether and under what conditions we perceive them. It makes sense to think that a billiard ball will be round whether we perceive it or not, whether we see it on a bright sunny day rolling along a city sidewalk, or at night, in the dim light of a pool hall. But a ball that appears yellow in broad daylight can look beige or even gray in subdued light. Is the noonday sun the only true light, so that the ball is "really" the color it appears to be in that light? If not, then what color is the ball "really"? Locke's suggestion is that the perception of the color of the ball, like the perception of its other secondary qualities (sound, smell, feel, etc.), always depends partly on the conditions under which we perceive it; and this means in turn that objects have no "real," objective color. By contrast, the shape of the ball, like its other primary qualities (size, movement, weight, etc.), is objective.

Locke thought of the "matter" of an object as the bearer of its primary qualities and of the power to cause its perceived, secondary qualities in our minds. He characterized matter here in terms introduced by the modern scientist Robert Boyle, who offered an atomistic theory of physical reality. On Locke's view, the real billiard ball is formed of matter existing outside our minds, which has in the configuration of its minute particles the power to cause our sensory images of it. Locke's is the perspective of realists, who suppose that even if there were no minds to perceive them, material, physical things like billiard balls could still exist. However, in admitting that physical reality is separate from mind, that matter is composed of imperceptibly small parts, and that our experience of some qualities may be very different from the actual causes in the objects of those experiences, Locke opens the door to doubt about our ability to know the world around us. We can perceive only the apparent qualities of objects, not their real essences: their constituent particles. One lesson Locke's philosophy has taught us is that commonsense realism leads to skepticism about the nature of physical reality.

Berkeley, writing in response to Locke, pointed out that the supposed difference Locke described between the primary qualities and secondary qualities is not supportable. Berkeley observed, for example, that the movement of the billiard ball on the table might be slow to one observer and fast to another; that the same ball's size could be small or large, depending on the context of observation. The conclusion he drew from this was that the very same reasons that lead us to think of *some* experienced qualities of objects as existing only in the mind should lead us to think of *all* experienced qualities of objects as existing only in the mind. This is the idealist perspective.

Several arguments led Berkeley to think of "matter" as an illusory, even nonsensical, idea. If we take just the empiricist's principle that there is nothing in the mind that was not first in the senses, we do not have any basis even for thinking that matter exists. For what sense experience of "matter" do we have? We experience colors, hardness, and sizes and shapes of objects, of course. But these are no more than *qualities* of matter; they are not perceptions of matter itself. Berkeley would not deny that the qualities of things we perceive are in the mind; but how, he asked, would the idea of "matter" itself get into the mind? If it cannot get into the mind through the senses, as it evidently cannot, then it is not in the mind at all. So someone who says that "matter exists" cannot possibly know what he is saying! Do not be misled about Berkeley, however. He did not say that the chairs, tables, and billiard balls in our sense perceptions are not real. He said rather that to be real is not to be made out of matter. To be real is nothing other than to be perceived.

The Active Powers Theory vs. the Regularity Theory of Causation

Philosophers are interested in understanding causation because applying this concept is crucial not only for knowing how things got to be they way they are now, but also for predicting what will happen next. Scientific progress depends on nothing more basic than understanding the connections between the world's causes and effects. But empiricism, as Hume pointed out well into the eighteenth century, leads to a radical revision in the accepted theory of causation. Philosophers prior to Hume had assumed that a cause is some object or set of objects active in the world through the exertion of power. They had assumed, further, that objects' exertions of their causal powers are lawful, meaning that they can be described in law-like statements of the form: "When events like A happen, then, *necessarily*, events like B will happen." For example, when a rolling billiard ball strikes another ball at rest, then, *necessarily*, the second ball will begin to roll. It simply cannot remain at rest when struck by the first ball, unless its movement is somehow restricted. In another case, when fire exerts its burning, consuming power on wood, then, *necessarily*, the wood will become charred and smoke will rise. The impacting billiard balls and the fire and smoke of these examples stand in what Hume will call a causal relation of "necessary connection."

Yet what do we find when we apply the empiricist slogan to these ideas of "power" and "necessary connection"? In observing the first billiard ball's approach to the second, do we actually sense its moving force, its so-called "momentum"? When we experience the fire, and then the rising smoke, do we in any way experience the "power" through which the fire acts, or the "necessity" of the smoke's rising from the burning wood? Here is the orange fire, there is the gray smoke; but what does the *power* of the fire look or sound like? How do we sense the presumed *necessity* of their connection: the sheer *impossibility* of the fire's burning without the resulting smoke? Locke had struggled with this problem earlier, and had offered the following explanation. There is no way, he admitted, to experience or feel the power of the fire. If the fire warms or burns us, we feel only the effects of its power, not the power itself. *But*, said Locke, we do get the experience of power in experiencing our own activity, and then we legitimately transfer this idea from our self-experience to our experience of the fire. I know what it is like to move my body willfully, said Locke; and, in a similar way, the rolling billiard ball exerts its momentum on the one at rest; the fire likewise exerts effort, although not willful effort, in burning wood and emitting smoke.

Hume was not satisfied with Locke's explanation of causal power, however. Isn't it true, he asked, that the connection between the mind and the body is one of the most mysterious of all? How, then, can we expect to make any progress in explaining our knowledge of the active powers of other things in terms of this great conundrum? Without being able to experience even our own power to move our bodies, we have no basis for learning the laws of operations of other powers in the world, or for making causal judgments. Obviously, though, we do make causal judgments, and we feel we have every right to rely on them when we judge in the right ways. Hume therefore says, in effect, let us not trouble ourselves to explain any unobservable powers of causes. Let us instead explain what makes us feel we are right in relying on our causal judgments. If we can merely explain where we get the idea of the "necessary connection" between the cause and the effect, or why we are justified in expecting the occurrence of an effect like smoke every time a cause like fire occurs, we will then have a secure, philosophical basis for causal judgment, and for our scientific knowledge of the world.

Hume did not think that we can experience the *necessity* by which a cause produces its effect. But he pointed out that there is something else we can experience that is, arguably, exactly what has always been meant by the idea of that *necessity*. Consider the fact that if a sequence of events is repeated often enough human beings become accustomed to experiencing these events together. We become so used to the regularity of the sequence that we cannot help but expect the next occurring sequence to match the same pattern as every one before. Imagine Adam, in the Garden of Eden, cue-stick in hand, watching the amazing spectacle of billiard balls rolling around on a table. Their movements must at first seem entirely random to him, since he has no experience of the laws of nature. But then at some point he begins to notice that, so far, every time one ball has struck another, the second one has moved. As Adam continues watching he begins to notice an exceptionless regularity in the movements of balls that are struck by other balls. Then something remarkable happens. After sufficient experience of this regularity he has noticed, Adam begins to expect it to continue!

Perhaps human beings were created so that we would develop these kinds of expectations from observing our environment; or maybe we just evolved this way. In any case, countless observations will show that human beings go about usually expecting things to happen in roughly the same ways they always have. We expect the leaves of trees to come out in the spring and to fall off later in the autumn. When we heat a pot of water at sea level to 212°, we expect it to boil. It has always happened that way. From commonplace observations like these Hume drew the conclusion that the causal relation, characterized by a necessary connection between the cause-event and the effect-event, is based on nothing more than our own habituated feelings of expectation. What many have imagined to be the *power* that a cause like fire exerts when it burns wood and produces smoke is really only our own force of habit. We feel ourselves expecting smoke as an effect of fire, and we mistakenly attribute the force of our feeling to the fire, in the form of a power to consume wood and produce smoke. The force of our expectation of smoke from fire is so strong that it is almost impossible for us to imagine flame without fume. That is just how we establish the necessary connection between fire, the cause, and smoke, its effect.

In summary, Hume's view of causation is that we are right or justified in our belief that fire causes smoke, for no other reason than that we so strongly expect fire to be followed by smoke, owing to the regularity of our past experience. If we tried somehow to identify the active power that fire is presumed to exert, we would never be able to do so: for, again, there is no sense experience of *power*, and hence it is a fictitious idea. The force through which fire is presumed to cause its effects is really the force of our feelings of expectation. In Hume's terminology, after human beings become accustomed to observing a regular or "constant conjunction" of an object like fire (A), and a subsequent object like smoke (B), we cannot help but associate A and B in our minds as a natural sequence of events. The force of habit that arises in our minds from such regular event sequences is precisely what forms the "necessary connection" between causes and effects. This is Hume's "regularity theory" of causation, which says that the necessary connection between causes and effects in the world is something we attribute to objects, based on regularities we have observed, and expect to continue.

So is Hume actually saying that all causal laws, indeed, all laws of nature, are founded on nothing but operations of the human mind, so that if there were no minds there would be no causes? Most scholars today think this is exactly what Hume is saying. This would mean also, for instance, that before Adam becomes habituated by observing numerous instances of moving billiard balls setting others in motion, there really are no causal connections between them. For causal connections and their laws are based on human expectations; and humans do not develop expectations until after we experience "constant conjunctions." Hence, in the view of most scholars, Hume is saying that no causal laws, and no laws of nature, can exist in the initial stages of human experience, prior to the development of human habits of expectation. But others think that Hume is saying only that *our knowledge* of the laws of nature can be founded on nothing but operations of the human mind. They think Hume agreed that there are *powers*, unknowable to us, which explain the regularity of nature. But since we cannot possibly experience them, we must rely on "constant conjunction" and our expectations in order to discover the laws of their operations. So, these scholars say, there really is a cause explaining the regularity of the movement of the billiard balls that Adam observes before he develops habits of expectation. Nature is regular in its processes even apart from human beings; all Hume is saying, they think, is that human beings have no way of knowing this without experiencing nature's regularity, and developing expectations. We may leave this debate to Hume's scholarly interpreters. Here it is sufficient that we indicate two quite different prospects for understanding what Hume meant about causal relations and necessity.

Synthetic vs. Analytic Judgments

Hume claimed that there are only two broad classes of human knowledge. He said we can know "matters of fact" and "relations of ideas." Statements expressing the latter kind of knowledge seem always to be true by definition. "Bachelors are unmarried" is a classic statement expressing a relation of ideas. But it is not something known through experience. Our knowledge that bachelors are unmarried was not derived from observing a sample of the world's bachelors and finding that none had a wife. That bachelors are unmarried is not a piece of knowledge Hume would call a "matter of fact," like the knowledge expressed in statements such as: "Fire causes smoke," "Snow is white," or "Paris is the capital of France." Someone knowing just the definition of "bachelor" does not need further experience to recognize that the classic statement about bachelors just above is true. But merely by knowing the definitions of words like "fire," "snow," and "Paris," no one can tell whether those next three statements are true. Hume once explained the difference this way: for relations of ideas, their "contraries" are always logical contradictions, and therefore impossible; but the contrary of any matter of fact is always possible. Hence, the thought of a married bachelor involves a logical contraction; it expresses something impossible. Yet the thought of Marseilles as the capital of France does not express a logical contradiction or impossibility. Paris happens to be the capital of France; but it is not the capital *by definition*. Only through experience can we tell that Paris is the capital and Marseilles is not.

The difference in these types of knowledge that Hume was getting at is expressed classically in the distinction between *a priori* knowledge and *a posteriori* knowledge, or between what we know prior to or independent of experience, and what we can know only after experience. Others would express it as a distinction between *analytic* knowledge and *synthetic* knowledge, or between claims we can know to be true just by analyzing the meanings of terms like "bachelor," and knowledge claims that join together (synthesize) terms that are unrelated through analysis or definition: statements that join terms like "Paris" with terms like "capital of France." But Immanuel Kant would say, not so fast! There remains an important difference between *how we know* statements or judgments (the *a priori* and the *a posteriori*), and the *logical form* of statements (the analytic and the synthetic). If we do not bear this difference in mind, we will miss something very important, Kant claimed. He admitted that Hume was certainly correct in thinking that all of the matters of fact we know are known *a posteriori*, through experience. He said it is correct likewise to express all of those facts in synthetic statements. So statements known *a posteriori* are always synthetic. He agreed also that all analytic statements are known *a priori*. In order for us to know what is true by definition (analytic) it is not necessary for us to experience it. But Kant argued, in opposition to Hume, that there seems to be yet another class of human knowledge, besides the class of (analytic) knowledge of relations of ideas and the class of (synthetic) knowledge of matters of fact. This additional class of knowledge consists of synthetic statements that we know *a priori*. Kant's suggestion is that, independent of experience, we seem capable of knowing some things that are not simply matters of definition.

One of Kant's famous examples of such *a priori* knowledge is this synthetic statement: "Every event has a cause." This statement does not say that every *effect* has a cause. That would be an analytic statement, because "effect" just *means* something caused. Neither does this statement say that every event *so far* has had a cause. No, the statement means that there haven't been any uncaused happenings or events, and furthermore, that there won't be any uncaused happenings or events, because there can't be any. Kant claimed that we know that every event has a cause, even though we could not have gotten this knowledge through experience. We have obviously not experienced every event, so there is no way our limited experience could show us that every event has a cause. Hence, the statement that "Every event has a cause" is what Kant called an example of a "synthetic *a priori* judgment." It is known *a priori*, independent of experience; but it is not analytic, not true by definition.

Empiricism would tell us that the only way we can know that every event has a cause is through sense experience. But Kant claimed that sense experience simply is not rich enough to be the source of our certainty that every event has a cause. So empiricism seems to be refuted. On the other hand, "innatism," usually connected with "rationalism," would say that our knowledge that every event has a cause must be an innate idea, since it could not come from experience. But as Locke pointed out, and as Kant agreed, there is no reason to assume that even young children and the mentally challenged know that every event has a cause. In order to know that every event has a cause someone needs to know what an event is, and what a cause is; and it is doubtful that anyone can know about these things without adequate experience of the world. So rationalism seems as ill suited as empiricism to explain our knowledge of synthetic *a priori* judgments like "Every event has a cause." The central puzzle that Kant set for himself in his weighty *Critique of Pure Reason* (1781) is therefore "How are synthetic *a priori* judgments possible?" He returned to the same question later, with a more streamlined presentation of his arguments in his *Prolegomena to Any Future Metaphysics* (1783), from which the reading selections in part III below are taken.

"Every event has a cause" is just one example of a synthetic *a priori* judgment; for Kant found many other examples, like "The shortest distance between two points is a straight line." He even considered most mathematical statements to be synthetic *a priori*, like, for example, "Five plus seven equals twelve." Although Hume would have said that this statement expresses a relation of ideas, Kant pointed out that in the idea of "sum of five plus seven" we do not *think* the idea of "twelve"; that is not what "sum of five plus seven" *means*, by definition. Perhaps we cannot help thinking "twelve" when someone says "sum of five plus seven," but this is only because we had that sum drilled into our heads in our early math education. What sum do you think when you read: "twenty-three thousand four hundred sixty-one plus one thousand nine hundred fifty-five"? The fact that you'll have to work out that sum shows that the two sides of your equation (these numbers and their sum) are synthetically connected; yet you would probably not claim to know *by experience* that your sum is correct. If all mathematical judgments are synthetic *a priori*, then, as Kant said, this shows that a vast field of human knowledge cannot be adequately explained by empiricism. So someone needs to explain how this kind of knowledge is even possible.

Kant found the beginning of the answer to his question – "How are synthetic *a priori* judgments possible?" – in his arguments that time and space are only "ideal," not "real." We might think of time as a kind of "container" in which all the events of the world happen. We could think of space, likewise, as a universe-size empty box containing all the world's physical objects. But if time and space are real containers as we are imagining them here, then it should be meaningful to ask "How long will time last?" or "How wide is space?" But these are not meaningful questions. Only events that happen in time are of longer or shorter duration; the time-container in which all events happen has no duration. For if time itself "lasts," then it is conceivable that it began at some point and that it will eventually end. But it is impossible to make sense of the idea of the beginning of time. There is no beginning of something unless there was a prior time in which it did not exist. So the only way there could be a beginning of time is if there were a time before time began. But this is absurd. Similar arguments work also for space. There is no edge, no border of space without some space on the other side. There could be nothing "beyond space" but, of course, more space. That is why it is absurd to think of space itself as a box-like container of every physical thing that exists.

Through arguments like these, and others, Kant showed that we must think of time and space as very different from the events and objects that we encounter within them. He therefore called time and space *"a priori* forms of intuition," and "conditions of the possibility of sense experience." By these phrases he meant that time and space are not objects of experience, but ways in which the human mind orders and organizes what it encounters in experience. Time and space are not *real*, he claimed; they are *ideal*. There might be beings on this planet, or even on other planets, who do not have any sense of time or space at all. God, as Kant imagined him, would not know things in time and space the way we do. God would presumably see everything that is to happen in the whole span of time in just an instant, or in some timeless way. From God's perspective on reality, nothing "takes time" or "takes up space."

Recognizing that time and space are only ideal prepares us to see how synthetic *a priori* judgments could be possible. Suppose it were that, because of the way the human mind organizes its experience in time, no event could be experienced by a human being without being connected with some prior event as its cause. In that case, every event must have a cause, since humans could not experience any event if it lacked a cause. Again, what if it were true that, because of the way the human mind organizes things spatially, nothing could be experienced by human beings as an area of space without its appearing in such a way that the shortest distance between any two points in that area is a straight line? If these suppositions were so, then we could claim to know that every event has a cause, and that the shortest distance between any two points is a straight line, just because of our understanding of human perceptual experience itself. These two examples, presented here only as suppositions or "What ifs", do not by themselves provide all that is needed to show how synthetic *a priori* knowledge is possible. Establishing the "ideality" of time and space is only the first step. The complete explanation involves what Kant called "categories" or "pure concepts of the understanding," which are better explained later (see the introduction to Part III, "Kant's Critique of Rationalism and Empiricism").

Power vs. Authority: The Social Contract

The central questions of political philosophy focus on the relation between "might" and "right." Where do those with governing *power* get their governing *authority*? What makes the monarch or sovereign assembly *right* in imposing taxes and in punishing those who do not obey its laws and commands? "The consent of the governed" is a standard reply. Locke's political philosophy is in the social-contract tradition of his seventeenth-century countryman Thomas Hobbes. At the same time, Locke's views of human nature and the origin of rights are very different from Hobbes's. Whereas Hobbes thought all people are self-interested by nature and observe no rules of justice in the absence of government, Locke believed that people could live by self-evident rules of natural justice prior to the emergence of governments and civil society. Prior to civic life, in the so-called "State of Nature," everyone would have an equal right to punish the violators of these natural rules, said Locke. But they would eventually need to agree with one another to set up a civil authority over themselves, so that judgments and sentences for violators of the rules of justice would be impartial. The "mechanism" for this kind of agreement is what is known as a "social contract." It is a kind of promise that each person in a society makes, to everyone else in the society, that he or she will follow the rules, or suffer the consequences at the hands of civil authorities. So, as Locke saw it, the role of political authority is primarily as an impartial "umpire" in the social game of justice. The people grant their chosen government the right to enact legislation, and authorize its punishing violations of enacted laws.

However appealing Locke's presentation of the motives behind this "original contract" may be, Hume would later point out that as an explanation of politics in the real world it is not very well informed. The empiricist method demands that we seek the origin of ideas like "power" and "authority," "government" and "governed," in experience. So to learn about politics we must look at history. But, Hume asks, how often in human history do we find a free people contracting together for the purpose of setting up a government to serve as their social umpire? Moreover, if Locke's views on political authority were correct, then why did he have to delay publication of his *Second Treatise on Government* for fear of imprisonment or even death at the hands of English political authority? History shows, contrary to Locke's idealization, that the original basis for the political authority of kings and princes lies almost always in brutal demonstrations of their power to enforce their arbitrary will. Only after years, sometimes even generations, of habitual submission to raw political power do people begin to regard the constant threat they live under as legitimate authority. As Hume sees it, therefore, it is not that might *makes* right. It is rather that might *tends to become* right, as people get used to yielding to it. (Notice here how Hume's philosophy of political power resembles his regularity theory of causation. Just as our causal judgments are right or justified as we become accustomed to regular sequences in experience, so the government's power over us is right or justified as we become used to living under its control.)

Jean-Jacques Rousseau's contribution to the theory of the social contract in the late eighteenth century was nothing short of brilliant. With Rousseau we begin to encounter a significant challenge to empiricist methodology, at least in political philosophy. If the questions of political philosophy are questions related to *political* authority and power, and not to the intimidating might of thugs, "strong men," and bullies, then they are questions about *government of the people*. There is accordingly no politics without *the people*; and for this reason also there is no political power unless individuals join themselves together to create it. The first political act is therefore the mutual, usually tacit consent of individual persons to form a governable people. Then the second political act, as Rousseau sees it, is always the people's choice to submit themselves, as a governable entity, to a governor. By virtue of this second act they at once confer authority and power upon their chosen leader, joining right with might. The methodological lesson of Rousseau's thinking is this: empirical observations of political behavior tend to ignore the tacit, intellectual conditions that make it an object of possible experience. Just as there can be no empirical observation of a government without a people, so there can be no observation of a people governed without their consent. If you're observing a people, Rousseau would say, then you're observing subjects who have chosen to make themselves governable.

Liberty vs. Necessity

Locke and Hume agreed in thinking that terms like "liberty" or "free will" apply to human behavior just when our actions stem from our own, settled, desires. When you act on such desires, each explained, you act voluntarily, and you can be held responsible for your conduct. On the other hand, if someone bumps your arm and you spill your drink on the hostess, this is not something for which you can be held accountable. In both kinds of case, nevertheless, we act by "necessity." Locke and Hume presumed that desires are the causes of our actions, and so that whatever a person desires most, that she is bound to do, by the law of nature. The force of desire, as they saw it, is like the force of gravity or of the wind.

It is just another causal force of nature. Consider Hume's regularity theory of causation once again. The "necessity" of the connection between any cause and its effect is based on our habituated expectations. Causes in the mind are no different from physical causes in this respect. Hume wrote, "There is a general course of nature in human actions, as well as in the operations of the sun and the climate." Our knowledge of each "is founded on the observation of an uniformity in the actions, that flow from them; and this unity forms the very essence of necessity." Neither Locke nor Hume would deny that the desires that cause our actions are caused in turn by prior events and circumstances, and that those events are likewise the necessary effects of still prior events that are well beyond our control. To say otherwise would admit sheer chance and random occurrence into the system of nature; and who could be held responsible for chance happenings?

Empiricists typically do not admit the existence of human "free choice," where this means a deliberate and responsible choice to act contrary to our strongest, settled desires. Neither do they find anything meaningful or sensible in the prospect that we freely choose the desires that causally necessitate our actions. We might expect Kant to agree here also, since after all, he maintained that we know *a priori* that every event in the world has a cause, and our choices and actions are events in the world. But here Kant's philosophy opposes empiricism again, although in complicated and confusing ways. For even though Kant insisted that every event has a cause in a prior time, so that the causes of each of our actions could be traced, theoretically, even back to ancient times, he still believed we have "free choice." How is this possible? How is it even meaningful? Kant's answer to this question requires us to recognize two, radically different, perspectives on things.

Above we introduced Kant's arguments suggesting that time and space are not real, but ideal. From these arguments he concluded also that there is a difference between the way objects appear to us, and the way they are in themselves, apart from space and time. Kant's technical terms for these distinct entities are *phenomenon*, or appearance, and *noumenon*, or thing in itself. This distinction, Kant says, allows us to consider the world around us from one perspective as a world of phenomena (in time and space), and from another perspective as a timeless, spaceless world of noumena, or things in themselves. But let us observe now that we can also view *ourselves* as belonging both to the phenomenal world of sense experience and to the noumenal world of things in themselves. For we ourselves also, as minds, appear at least in time: we have one idea or perception after another; we desire this thing now, and that thing later. There is presumably "more" to our existence as persons than what we experience of ourselves through the course of time, however. We, too, are timeless, spaceless things in ourselves.

We explained above also how Kant claimed that we can know, a priori, that every event has a cause. That explanation involved seeing that human experience of temporal events could be structured so that no event could appear to a human mind in time without a connection to some prior event as its cause. But notice how this prospect could be true only of a world *in time*. In the space-time world of phenomena it could be true that every event has a prior cause, including every human action. Yet in the timeless, noumenal world, this law would not apply. This proves, Kant said, that it is at least possible that human beings have free choice, considered as noumena, even though, considered as phenomena, every one of our actions is caused by prior events. He later went on to explain, in his moral philosophy, how we can be confident that human beings, considered as timeless, noumenal beings, have free choice.

Scholars of Kant's philosophy today are divided on the question of how Kant's thoughts of noumena and phenomena should be understood. Sometimes his writings suggest that he thought of them as entities somehow making up two different worlds. Other times, what he wrote seems to imply that he treated them merely as terms indicating two different perspectives we can take on things. Some scholars say, for instance, that every person exists and acts freely in a timeless, noumenal world, but somehow appears as a flesh-and-blood human being in the separate, phenomenal world of time and space, where all his or her actions are caused by prior events. Others believe Kant meant only that we can consider any human being either as she is in herself, as a person with free choice wholly responsible for her actions, or as she appears in time and space, as just another cog in the great machine of nature. However we are to interpret Kant's noumena/phenomena distinction, the promise of eventually understanding how to see ourselves as both causally determined and yet free to choose is one of the driving forces that sustains scholars in the difficult study of Kant's philosophy.

Sense vs. Reason in Moral Judgment

According to a long tradition in Western philosophy, we distinguish between right and wrong, virtue and vice, by means of reason. Reason tells us what we ought to do, and desire often leads us to stray from doing it; so the moral life is a constant contest between the command of reason and the contrary pull of desire. But in opposition to this venerable tradition of "moral rationalism," Hume posed the following, highly persuasive argument.

Hume pointed out, first, that almost everyone observes that moral judgments of right and wrong have an influence on our feelings, desires, and actions. We do not always *do* what we judge we ought to do, of course. But still, when we recognize something as the right thing to do, we are at least "inclined" to do it; we feel the pull of the obligation. Philosophers today refer to this observation as "moral internalism," by which they mean that it is impossible for a person to judge that she ought, morally, to do something without experiencing some motivation to do it.

Next Hume showed that the faculty of reason is "motivationally inert." That is, although reason is competent to tell us in logic what is true or false, and in mathematics what is equal or unequal, reason is simply not in the business of inclining us to act. If we first have a desire, Hume said, then we can use reason to discover how to act in order to satisfy our desire. But in that case we will be inclined to do what reason will tell us to do only because of our prior desire. Reason by itself will not incline us to act; it at most only discovers the means to our ends, or truths about how to act in order to satisfy our desires. For these reasons Hume claimed, famously, that "Reason is, and ought only to be, the slave of the passions."

When we therefore combine Hume's two observations, moral internalism plus the motivational inertness of reason, the result is that the difference between right and wrong, virtue and vice, is not something we can know by reason. Whatever faculty of the mind tells us what we ought to do, must also incline us to do it (moral internalism); and reason, as we said, cannot incline us to act (motivational inertness). What *can* incline us, according to Hume, is sensibility or feeling. So, he argued, the difference between right and wrong, good and bad, must ultimately be traced to some difference in human sensation. Following an earlier British philosopher, Francis Hutcheson, Hume suggested that people distinguish right from wrong based on a special "moral sense," through which pleasant sensations indicate that actions or character traits are right or virtuous, and painful sensations indicate the opposite.

To Hume's theory of the moral sense Richard Price would later object that it makes right and wrong, good and bad, dependent upon human perception. Actions and characters would then have no rightness or virtue *in themselves*, protested Price, any more than objects in themselves are colored. But it was Thomas Reid who would later point out that Hume must simply be mistaken about reason's motivational inertness. For there are two ways reason itself guides us to act, without leading us to satisfy any of our pre-existing desires. The first motivational role of reason arises when it identifies what is "good on the whole." The second arises when it tells us what is our moral "duty." Even if Hume were correct in thinking that we judge moral goodness by a moral sense, the senses could never indicate what is good on the whole, or good in general. For sensation is always excited only by particular objects. It is our intellect and reason that give us general ideas, such as good overall, or on the whole. So if we can be inclined to prefer one good action to another because of its overall goodness for our circumstances, then this inclination or motive can only arise through reason. Further, Reid claimed, there is a clear difference between what we ought to do because it is in our interest, and what we ought to do because it is our duty. Reason can tell us what is in our interest, by comparing various available means to our existing sense-based desires, and determining the most satisfactory course of action for us, on the whole. In this way we can be prompted by reason to take actions for the sake of our interest, even when we have no pre-existing desire for these actions. But besides this inclination of interest we sometimes also feel the pull of duty. If we can be motivated by judging that we ought, morally, to do something, something that may require even sacrificing what is in our interest, then this judgment can be nothing other than a judgment of reason, and the resulting motive can be nothing but an inclining force of reason.

Yet Hume would reply: what can possibly oppose or compete with the force of passion or desire but another passion or desire? A judgment of reason about good on the whole will give us, at most, a truth. But how can we expect a truth of reason to be as strong as or stronger than an opposing desire? The only way to understand a desire as standing in opposition to a judgment of reason is to suppose the judgment true and the desire false. But what sense can it make to say that a desire is *false*?

Deontology vs. Consequentialism

Although the terms "Deontology" and "Consequentialism" are of later origin, the modern debate over these opposing perspectives in ethics began in the late eighteenth century. Deontological theories present moral principles in the form of commands, which find their authority or justification in their source. But consequentialist theories seek the justification of moral principles not in their provenance, but in their promise; not in where they came from, that is, but in where they lead.

Religion provides a clear example of deontological morality when its principles of conduct are said to be the right ones to live by because they are commanded by God. Depending on the religion, its principles of right conduct may or may not be expected also to lead to a happy or rewarding life, or to a better society. What makes the principles correct and compelling for us, the religious deontologist says, is only the fact that they originate with God. The rest, if there is more, may be just a bonus. But the religious deontologist believes we are obligated to follow the commands of God even if there is no heavenly reward for doing so. For rationalist moral theorists like Reid and Kant, similarly, the principles of *duty* are said to obligate us because they are commands originating in *practical reason*. Reason can tell us what is in our private interest, they say, as well as what is our moral duty; and these two are plainly different. What makes a policy or "maxim" of action in our interest is only its promise of leading to personal happiness. But what makes some way of acting our moral duty, these deontologists say, is not a matter of its leading to happiness or satisfaction of our desires. Consider the famous *golden rule*: "Do unto others as you would have them do unto you." This policy of conduct is not recommended to us because it will ultimately lead to some desired result. Rather, we see the rationality or wisdom of this policy in the equality and reciprocity it expresses. It is still right to treat others as you wish to be treated, the rationalist deontologist says, even if we might all be better off behaving differently.

At this point, however, the consequentialist objects. What would be *the point* of following a system of moral duties if we would all be better off behaving differently? If a different system of conduct benefited everyone, or humanity *on the whole*, wouldn't our living by that system make more sense? The consequentialist claims, therefore, that the justification of moral principles has nothing to do with whoever may have commanded them or thought of them. The point of morality is to improve human life.

In developing a moral theory known as "utilitarianism," the moral empiricist and social reformer Jeremy Bentham settled on the feeling or sensation of pleasure as the origin of our idea of goodness. There would be no goodness, no preference for one thing rather than another, he thought, in a world without the feeling of pleasure. From this he concluded that moral principles are therefore correct just insofar as following them will lead to the maximum overall pleasure (goodness), assuming everyone's pleasure counts the same. But in opposition to visions of morality like Bentham's, Price pointed out that it makes a difference who ends up being pleased or happy. The utilitarian theory said that principles or policies are right if they produce the greatest overall happiness when everyone, or at least most people, follow them. But Price said, let us imagine two different worlds containing exactly the same amount of human happiness. In the one, all the virtuous people are happy, while all the vicious people are not. In the other world, it is just the opposite. Price observed that no one will agree that these two worlds are equally good; and yet, according to utilitarianism, there cannot be any moral difference between them. Insofar as all that matters in utilitarian thinking is just the overall happiness of human beings, two equally happy worlds must be considered to be two equally good worlds. What utilitarians (consequentialists) always overlook, it seems, is the happiness that people *deserve* for being good. It seems morally right for good people to be happier than bad people, whether this leads to better consequences or not.

On the other hand, utilitarians point out that the real power of their theory lies in its ability to settle conflicts between competing moral goods. Deontologists see moral principles as expressions of sacred duty, with each principle having the justifying endorsement of the moral commander, be it God or reason. But what can the deontologist be expected to do when two different moral principles conflict, each commanding a different action in the same situation? One moral command is: *Thou shalt not lie!* Another is *Love thy neighbor as thyself!* But what if the only way to save the life of a neighbor is to tell a lie? A classic objection often raised to Kant's moral theory involves this scenario: a murderer is on the loose, intending to kill your friend. To protect her you've hidden her in your house. But then there's a knock at the door. It's the murderer, and he's asking if you've hidden his intended victim in your house. If you say "No," you tell a lie. If you say "Yes," you contribute to your friend's demise, perhaps to yours as well. If you do neither, if you stutter and try to stall, you will tip off the murderer that you're hiding your friend, which the same as saying "Yes." So here you are caught in a conflict of duties. You ought to tell the truth, and you ought to protect your friend; but you cannot do both. Here the utilitarian offers what seems to many to be the only reasonable resolution of the difficulty: the right thing to do is to bring about the best consequence. Lie!

Each of the preceding debates or controversies we have considered in this General Introduction has its roots in centuries prior to 1700. Alfred North Whitehead, a twentieth-century American philosopher, was guilty only of exaggeration when he said that the history of Western philosophy has been just a series of footnotes to Plato. Yet the eighteenth century stands out for us today as an especially noteworthy period of philosophical progress. Locke's ideas about "essences" and qualities continue to attract attention in contemporary metaphysics and philosophy of language. Recent philosophies of causation, and of human motivation, owe a great debt to Hume, while new work in epistemology looks back to Reid. Contractarian thinking today is still inspired by the ideas of Locke and the genius of Rousseau; and deontological thinking in ethics is dominated by the moral philosophy of Kant. It would be rash, however, to characterize the philosophy of the present day as just so many footnotes to the eighteenth century. Still, the philosophers of the twenty-first century will find no finer models for their own contributions to the history of philosophy than are presented in the reading selections that follow.

Part I

Empiricism

Introduction

Locke, Berkeley, and Hume are the British philosophers who represent the golden age of empiricism. In the modern period, their principal methodological opponents are the philosophers called "rationalists," including Descartes and his disciples in France, Spinoza, and Leibniz and his followers in Germany. Both modern rationalists and modern empiricists were impressed by the scientific method, which employs both reason and experience, but the rationalist school took mathematics to be the paradigm of knowledge, while the empiricists favored the experimental methods of natural science.

What classifies philosophers as rationalists is this: that they believed philosophical progress can be made in science, morality, politics, and religion just by reasoning. Here we may recall, for example, how Descartes presented himself as uncertain even of his own existence until he hit upon a fine rational argument to demonstrate it: "I think, therefore I am." He would not conclude that he existed just from the fact that he could see and feel his own body, for he knew that sometimes he saw and felt nonexistent things just as clearly in his dreams. Some rationalist philosophers say that we cannot know or be certain about anything other than what we can demonstrate entirely by rational argument. So one implication of their philosophical approach is that there are innate ideas or truths in the mind. Reason alone can help us discover new information only if there is already some material in our minds for reason to work with.

The empiricists' approach, on the other hand, can be defined by negating the key claims of rationalism: there are no innate ideas, and reason on its own cannot provide us with knowledge about the world outside the mind. The empiricists did not doubt that reason is an important capacity for confirming some truths. But they saw reason as showing us logical relationships among concepts, presenting only necessary truths like "A triangle is a three-sided figure." Empiricist philosophers are often described in terms of the vocabulary introduced in the beginning of this volume, by saying that empiricists deny that there is synthetic *a priori* knowledge, or (synthetic) truths about the world that are known (*a priori*) by reason alone. But this may be an oversimplification. Locke, for example, believed that *moral* principles can be known purely by reason (for instance, that it is wrong to take property that does not belong to you), and whether this is an exception to the above description depends on whether one sees moral principles as "about the world." One thing Locke, Berkeley, and Hume agreed upon is that all of our concepts get their meaning from sense experience; so, even for Locke, the idea of property would mean nothing to someone without experience. It seems best therefore to think of the empiricists with the dictum, "No contents in the mind not first in experience." This principle later gets spelled out in Hume as a crucial test for the very meaningfulness of an idea.

Locke, Berkeley, and Hume shared an interest in the questions of how our mind knows the natural world, how we identify the self or subject of perception, and how we can understand human freedom in a world governed by causal necessity. These are relatively easy questions for rationalists to answer, since they think it legitimate to go beyond nature for the answers, and so they purport to ground human knowledge in the certainty of reason and view the self and its actions as outside the natural world, not subject to causal laws. Since the empiricists want to explain human knowledge and action within the confines of ordinary experimental science, however, these questions pose genuine problems for them.

Knowledge of the natural world. Locke's philosophy was largely influenced by leading theoretical scientists of the seventeenth century, Robert Boyle, Isaac Newton, and Francis Bacon. He subscribed to the theory of Boyle, who said the world is made of moving matter composed of imperceptibly small corpuscles. He was noncommittal about whether the mind is material or immaterial, since he supposed that God could, if he wished, make matter think. He believed that the human mind is a blank slate at birth, and thus that there are no innate ideas, so that only experience – either sensation or reflection on the operations of our minds – can give meaning to the terms we use. Locke attempted to follow empiricism to its logical conclusions. He argued that the senses can give us knowledge that there exists a world of objects outside the mind and knowledge of what the perceivable or apparent qualities of those objects are, but they cannot tell us about the ultimate nature of reality, and why we experience the world in the way we do. It is logically impossible to extend our sense perception beyond the perceivable qualities of objects, where the essences that cause our perceptions of the qualities lie.

Berkeley later circumvented these skeptical conclusions of Locke's by arguing that there is no reason to suppose a reality beyond perceptual experience. If we start with sense perceptions as our evidence, we find that the additional supposition of material substance leads to contradictions. Perceptions of the world vary from perceiver to perceiver or perspective to perspective, but surely physical objects do not possess contrary qualities according to these variations. If we try to give a physical explanation of our perceptions – for instance that sound is particles in motion – we always end up with further absurdities, such as that we cannot hear a sound (wave), but only feel it. Furthermore, any attempt to explain how inert matter can cause a change in mind is incoherent. The only plausible conclusion, said Berkeley, is that reality is composed of nothing other than perceptions and the minds that perceive them. Hence, the mind is directly in contact with reality and we have no cause to hold any skepticism about our ability to know what the natural universe is.

Hume, on the other hand, thought that neither Locke nor Berkeley had worked out the full implications of empiricism. He showed that empiricists making no assumptions beyond what is given in experience should be driven to conclude not only that we cannot know the nature of reality (whether it is mental or physical, or how it causes perceptions), but also that we cannot know that external objects, or even minds, exist. These skeptical conclusions actually opened a new area of inquiry for Hume, however. He took it as his task to explain how we naturally form beliefs about the world, even if we cannot know whether our beliefs correspond to reality. How do we come to believe that there is a world of continually existing objects, despite the fact that our perceptions of objects are constantly interrupted? How do we come to believe that external objects cause changes in each other, and cause perceptions in our minds? Empiricism may lead to doubt, but it also leads to rich psychological enquiries into the operations of the human understanding. This is what Hume's contemporary interpreters refer to as his "naturalistic" project.

Identity of the self. Non-living things that are complexes of atoms, Locke said, are identified by the parts they contain. Living complexes are identified by the functional organization of their parts. So, a member of the biological species "man," Locke argued, is identified by a body organized in a particular way. A person, however, is different: each of us is identified by a consciousness over time. Locke proposed the following thought experiment to support his claims. Imagine that the soul of a prince, with all of his thoughts, is transferred from the prince's body to the lifeless body of a cobbler. Would the person remaining after this transfer be the prince or the cobbler? Locke explained that the resulting person will identify himself as the prince, since he has the consciousness and the memories of the prince, despite finding himself in an altogether different body. What this experiment shows, according to Locke, is that the person or self consists in a mental history.

Although Berkeley acknowledged that minds or spirits cannot be perceived through the senses, he believed that each of us nevertheless has an immediate intuition of ourselves, and that this conscious awareness of the self is enough to ground an idea of an enduring self. But Hume pressed the question: How do we *experience* the self? The self, after all, is supposedly that which persists throughout all the changes in the perceptions of a person, the possessor of the sensations, feelings, desires, thoughts, and other experiences. Try as hard as we might, we can never find a continuing, changeless perception from which we derive such an idea; all we find when we turn inward is a parade of varied perceptions. Hume therefore explained how we are led to invent an idea of the self, as a useful "fiction," and to imagine that there is a continuing ground for our varied experiences.

Free will. How is it that human beings are subject to the same causal forces as the rest of nature, and yet also held responsible for what they do? Many suppose that the will must be free if we are to make sense of moral responsibility, and that our having a free will is incompatible with our being subject to natural causal laws. But the modern empiricists are said to be "compatibilists" on this question. They believed that all our actions are caused, and that we can still hold people responsible for what they do.

Locke began his discussion of free will in the context of his analysis of the idea of power. Power is the ability to make or receive change, according to Locke. So the will is the power of preferring one option to another; I will to go for a walk instead of to stay at my desk, for instance. Freedom, he maintained, is the power to act on our willing or preferring without any external compulsion or restraint. If I will to walk and nothing inhibits me from doing so (I'm not paralyzed, I'm not in chains), then I am a free agent with respect to that action. It is the agent who is free, said Locke, not the will. To call the will free is to attribute the power of acting to the power of willing (to attribute a power to a power, which is absurd); so talk of a "free will" is nonsense and we should not even ask about it. Nothing in Locke's explanation says that the will cannot be caused. In fact, he believed that what we will is always caused by our desires. Hume not only agreed that moral responsibility and subjection to causal laws are compatible, but argued that the former requires the latter. I must be able to see an action as caused by the motives of a person in order to attribute responsibility for the action to the person. An uncaused action would be a matter of chance, and attributable to nothing; so it makes no sense to see actions as uncaused events in order to save human responsibility.

The question of human freedom takes a different turn for Berkeley. In Berkeley's idealist universe, the ideas we have are somehow caused by the mind of God. So the problem of freedom becomes a problem about how minds can be responsible for what they think and perceive, in light of divine causality. Berkeley's answer seems to be (although interpreters disagree) that while God's mind is ultimately the cause of all the perceptions we have, God allows our intentions and willings to be the occasions of the ideas he produces in us.

Critics of the empiricists have questioned their approach, often arguing that knowledge does not begin in discrete perceptual experiences. Others point out that empiricist accounts of responsibility are questionable: If my desires are determined by features of my nature for which I am not responsible, and my desires necessitate my will and my actions, then am I really ultimately responsible for what I do? Despite these criticisms, empiricist accounts of knowledge, the self, and freedom have been very influential in the history of philosophy. Many contemporary philosophers who practice the methods of natural science still work on refining the theories of the classic empiricists. Locke's empiricist theory of meaning and Hume's account of causality are just two examples of contributions by the modern empiricists that continue to inspire contemporary theorists.

1

John Locke, *Essay concerning Human Understanding* (1690)

John Locke was the first great empiricist of the modern period. His philosophy in the *Essay*, written in four "books," is a rejection of many of the key elements of rationalist thought. His aim there is to show what the human mind can understand and know, given the capacities it possesses.

For Locke, the term "idea" covers all the contents of the mind; that is, all that it can be occupied with, including sensations, emotions, desires, etc. Locke argues that there are no innate ideas at birth and that all the materials for knowledge must first originate in experience. Found within his meticulous classification of the elements of experience is his famous formulation of the distinction between primary and secondary qualities, mentioned in the general introduction to this volume. Recall: the primary qualities (shape, weight, motion, etc.) are those that are presumed to exist in objects no matter how they are perceived, while the secondary qualities (color, taste, smell, etc.) seem to be defined relative to perceivers. The distinction is a tricky one, however, since it appears to treat primary qualities as features or powers in objects to produce ideas in perceivers, and secondary qualities as ideas in perceivers' minds. If Locke had treated both types of quality in the same way – i.e., both as powers or both as ideas – the distinction would not have been so easy to formulate.

Locke is concerned to explain how our ideas can represent a material world, given his unquestioned assumption that there is such a world and that is it made of imperceptibly tiny parts (atoms or corpuscles). How can the senses access the ultimate reality of such a world? He concludes that the real essences of objects are closed off to our limited senses. But even more devastating is his conclusion that whatever qualities we sense, they must be qualities of some substance that binds them together; and this means that we never can sense the underlying substance that possesses the qualities. Our experience is necessarily of the qualities only!

Even though Locke argues that all ideas or concepts must begin in experience, knowledge is more than simply having ideas. He defines knowledge as "the perception of the connexion and agreement or disagreement and repugnancy of any of our Ideas." Some might see him as an inconsistent empiricist, however, since he allows that the perception of some of the connections that constitute knowledge can be gotten by intuition or reason. In Book IV of his *Essay*, for example, he concludes that (1) knowledge of the self is intuited; (2) knowledge of God is demonstrated (proven by reason); and (3) knowledge of the existence of finite things is known by the senses. What we cannot know, alas, is what causes the objects in the world to have the qualities they appear to have.

Born in Britain, Locke (1632–1704) was a physician and medical researcher who became politically active during one of the most tumultuous times in British history. Under Charles II, he was involved in the writing of a constitution for the American Carolinas, but later became a rebel who supported the Glorious Revolution of 1688, when the balance of power passed from the king to the parliament.

Book I
Of Innate Notions

Chapter II
No Innate Principles in the Mind

§1. It is an established Opinion amongst some Men, That there are in the Understanding certain innate Principles; some primary Notions, κοιναὶ ἔννοιαι, Characters, as it were stamped upon the Mind of Man, which the Soul receives in its very first Being; and brings into the World with it. It would be sufficient to convince unprejudiced Readers of the falseness of this Supposition, if I should only shew (as I hope I shall in the following Parts of this Discourse) how Men, barely by the Use of their natural Faculties, may attain to all the Knowledge they have, without the help of any innate Impressions; and may arrive at Certainty, without any such Original Notions or Principles. For I imagine any one will easily grant, That it would be impertinent to suppose, the Ideas of Colours innate in a Creature, to whom God hath given Sight, and a Power to receive them by the Eyes from external Objects: and no less unreasonable would it be to attribute several Truths, to the Impressions of Nature, and innate Characters, when we may observe in our selves Faculties, fit to attain as easie and certain Knowledge of them, as if they were Originally imprinted on the Mind.

But because a Man is not permitted without Censure to follow his own Thoughts in the search of Truth, when they lead him ever so little out of the common Road: I shall set down the Reasons, that made me doubt of the Truth of that Opinion, as an Excuse for my Mistake, if I be in one, which I leave to be consider'd by those, who, with me, dispose themselves to embrace Truth, where-ever they find it.

§2. There is nothing more commonly taken for granted, than that there are certain Principles both Speculative and Practical (for they speak of both) universally agreed upon by all Mankind: which therefore they argue, must needs be the constant Impressions, which the Souls of Men receive in their first Beings, and which they bring into the World with them, as necessarily and really as they do any of their inherent Faculties.

§3. This Argument, drawn from Universal Consent, has this Misfortune in it, That if it were true in matter of Fact, that there were certain Truths, wherein all Mankind agreed, it would not prove them innate, if there can be any other way shewn, how Men may come to that Universal Agreement, in the things they do consent in; which I presume may be done.

§4. But, which is worse, this Argument of Universal Consent, which is made use of, to prove innate Principles, seems to me a Demonstration that there are none such: Because there are none to which all Mankind give an Universal Assent. I shall begin with the

Speculative, and instance in those magnified Principles of Demonstration, Whatsoever is, is; and 'Tis impossible for the same thing to be, and not to be, which of all others I think have the most allow'd Title to innate. These have so setled a Reputation of Maxims universally received, that 'twill, no doubt, be thought strange, if any one should seem to question it. But yet I take liberty to say, That these Propositions are so far from having an universal Assent, that there are a great Part of Mankind, to whom they are not so much as known.

§5. For, first 'tis evident, that all Children, and Ideots, have not the least Apprehension or Thought of them: and the want of that is enough to destroy that universal Assent, which must needs be the necessary concomitant of all innate Truths: it seeming to me near a Contradiction, to say, that there are Truths imprinted on the Soul, which it perceives or understands not; imprinting, if it signify any thing, being nothing else, but the making certain Truths to be perceived. For to imprint any thing on the Mind without the Mind's perceiving it, seems to me hardly intelligible. If therefore Children and Ideots have Souls, have Minds, with those Impressions upon them, they must unavoidably perceive them, and necessarily know and assent to these Truths, which since they do not, it is evident that there are no such Impressions. For if they are not Notions naturally imprinted, How can they be innate? And if they are Notions imprinted, How can they be unknown? To say a Notion is imprinted on the Mind, and yet at the same time to say, that the mind is ignorant of it, and never yet took notice of it, is to make this Impression nothing. No Proposition can be said to be in the Mind, which it never yet knew, which it was never yet conscious of. For if any one may; then, by the same Reason, all Propositions that are true, and the Mind is capable ever of assenting to, may be said to be in the Mind, and to be imprinted: Since if any one can be said to be in the Mind, which it never yet knew, it must be only because it is capable of knowing it; and so the Mind is of all Truths it ever shall know. Nay, thus Truths may be imprinted on the Mind, which it never did, nor ever shall know: for a Man may live long, and die at last in Ignorance of many Truths, which his Mind was capable of knowing, and that with Certainty. So that if the Capacity of knowing be the natural Impression contended for, all the Truths a Man ever comes to know, will, by this Account, be, every one of them, innate; and this great Point will amount to no more, but only to a very improper way of speaking; which whilst it pretends to assert the contrary, says nothing different from those, who deny innate Principles. For no Body, I think, ever denied, that the Mind was capable of knowing several Truths. The Capacity, they say, is innate, the Knowledge acquired. But then to what end such contest for certain innate Maxims? If Truths can be imprinted on the Understanding without being perceived, I can see no difference there can be, between any Truths the Mind is capable of knowing in respect of their Original: They must all be innate, or all adventitious: In vain shall a Man go about to distinguish them. He therefore that talks of innate Notions in the Understanding, cannot (if he intend thereby any distinct sort of Truths) mean such Truths to be in the Understanding, as it never perceived, and is yet wholly ignorant of. For if these Words (to be in the Understanding) have any Propriety, they signify to be understood. So that, to be in the Understanding, and, not to be understood; to be in the Mind, and, never to be perceived, is all one, as to say, any thing is, and is not, in the Mind or Understanding. If therefore these two Propositions, Whatsoever is, is; and, It is impossible for the same thing to be, and not to be, are by Nature imprinted, Children cannot be ignorant of them: Infants, and all that have Souls must necessarily have them in their Understandings, know the Truth of them, and assent to it.

§6. To avoid this, 'tis usually answered, that all Men know and *assent* to them, when they come to the use of Reason, and this is enough to prove them innate. I answer,

§7. Doubtful Expressions, that have scarce any signification, go for clear Reasons to those, who being prepossessed, take not the pains to examine even what they themselves say. For to apply this Answer with any tolerable Sence to our present Purpose, it must signify one of these two things; either, That as soon as Men come to the use of Reason, these supposed native Inscriptions come to be known, and observed by them: Or else, that the Use and Exercise of Men's Reasons assists them in the Discovery of these Principles, and certainly makes them known to them.

§8. If they mean that by the Use of Reason Men may discover these Principles; and that this is sufficient to prove them innate; their way of arguing will stand thus, (viz.) That whatever Truths Reason can certainly discover to us, and make us firmly assent to, those are all naturally imprinted on the Mind; since that universal Assent, which is made the Mark of them, amounts to no more but this; That by the use of Reason, we are capable to come to a certain Knowledge of, and assent to them; and by this Means there will be no difference between the Maxims of the Mathematicians, and Theorems they deduce from them: All must be equally allow'd innate, they being all Discoveries made by the use of Reason, and Truths that a rational Creature may certainly come to know, if he apply his Thoughts rightly that Way.

§9. But how can these Men think the Use of Reason necessary to discover Principles that are supposed innate, when Reason (if we may believe them) is nothing else, but the Faculty of deducing unknown Truths from Principles or Propositions, that are already known? That certainly can never be thought innate, which we have need of Reason to discover, unless as I have said, we will have all the certain Truths, that Reason ever teaches us, to be innate. We may as well think the use of Reason necessary to make our Eyes discover visible Objects, as that there should be need of Reason, or the Exercise thereof, to make the Understanding see, what is Originally engraven in it, and cannot be in the Understanding, before it be perceived by it. So that to make Reason discover those Truths thus imprinted, is to say, that the use of Reason discovers to a Man, what he knew before; and if Men have these innate, impressed Truths Originally, and before the use of Reason, and yet are always ignorant of them, till they come to the use of Reason, 'tis in effect to say, that Men know, and know them not at the same time.

[...]

Book II
Of Ideas

Chapter I
Of Ideas in General, and their Original

§1. Every Man being conscious to himself, That he thinks, and that which his Mind is employ'd about whilst thinking, being the *Ideas*, that are there, 'tis past doubt, that Men have in their Minds several *Ideas*, such as are those expressed by the words, *Whiteness, Hardness, Sweetness, Thinking, Motion, Man, Elephant, Army, Drunkenness*, and others: It is in the first place then to be enquired, How he comes by them? I know it is a received Doctrine, That Men have native *Ideas*, and original Characters stamped upon their Minds, in their very first Being. This Opinion I have at large examined already; and, I suppose, what I have said in the fore-going Book, will be much more easily admitted, when I have shewn, whence the Understanding may get all the *Ideas* it has, and by what ways and degrees they may come into the Mind; for which I shall appeal to every one's own Observation and Experience.

§2. Let us then suppose the Mind to be, as we say, white Paper, void of all Characters, without any *Ideas*; How comes it to be furnished? Whence comes it by that vast store, which the busy and boundless Fancy of Man has painted on it, with an almost endless variety? Whence has it all the materials of Reason and Knowledge? To this I answer, in one word, From *Experience*: In that, all our Knowledge is founded; and from that it ultimately derives it self. Our Observation employ'd either about *external, sensible Objects; or about the internal operations of our Minds, perceived and reflected on by our selves, is that, which supplies our Understandings with all the materials of thinking*. These two are the Fountains of Knowledge, from whence all the *Ideas* we have, or can naturally have, do spring.

§3. First, *Our Senses*, conversant about particular sensible Objects, do *convey into the Mind*, several distinct *Perceptions* of things, according to those various ways, wherein those Objects do affect them: And thus we come by those *Ideas*, we have of *Yellow, White, Heat, Cold, Soft, Hard, Bitter, Sweet*, and all those which we call sensible qualities, which when I say the senses convey into the mind, I mean, they from external Objects convey into the mind what produces there those *Perceptions*. This great Source, of most of the *Ideas* we have, depending wholly upon our Senses, and derived by them to the Understanding, I call *SENSATION*.

§4. Secondly, The other Fountain, from which Experience furnisheth the Understanding with *Ideas*, is the *Perception of the Operations of our own Minds* within us, as it is employ'd about the *Ideas* it has got; which Operations, when the Soul comes to reflect on, and consider, do furnish the Understanding with another set of *Ideas*, which could not be had from things without: and such are, *Perception, Thinking, Doubting, Believing, Reasoning, Knowing, Willing*, and all the different actings of our own Minds; which we being conscious of, and observing in our selves, do from these receive into our Understandings, as distinct *Ideas*, as we do from Bodies affecting our Senses. This Source of *Ideas*, every Man has wholly in himself: And though it be not Sense, as having nothing to do with external Objects; yet it is very like it, and might properly enough be call'd internal Sense. But as I call the other *Sensation*, so I call this *REFLECTION*, the *Ideas* it affords being such only, as the Mind gets by reflecting on its own Operations within it self. By *REFLECTION* then, in the following part of this Discourse, I would be understood to mean, that notice which the Mind takes of its own Operations, and the manner of them, by reason whereof, there come to be *Ideas* of these Operations in the Understanding. These two, I say, *viz.* External, Material things, as the Objects of *SENSATION*; and the Operations of our own Minds within, as the Objects of *REFLECTION*, are, to me, the only Originals, from whence all our *Ideas* take their beginnings. The term *Operations* here, I use in a large sence, as comprehending not barely the Actions of the Mind about its *Ideas*, but some sort of Passions arising sometimes from them, such as is the satisfaction or uneasiness arising from any thought.

§5. The Understanding seems to me, not to have the least glimmering of any *Ideas*, which it doth not receive from one of these two. *External Objects furnish the Mind with the* Ideas *of sensible qualities*, which are all those different perceptions they produce in us: And the *Mind furnishes the Understanding with* Ideas *of its own Operations*.

These, when we have taken a full survey of them, and their several Modes, Combinations, and Relations, we shall find to contain all our whole stock of *Ideas*; and that we have nothing in our Minds, which did not come in, one of these two ways. Let any one examine his own Thoughts, and throughly search into his Understanding, and then let him tell me, Whether all the original *Ideas* he has there, are any other than of the Objects of his *Senses*; or of the Operations of his Mind, considered as Objects of his *Reflection*: and how great a mass of Knowledge soever he imagines to be lodged there, he will, upon taking a strict view, see, that he has *not any* Idea *in his Mind, but what one of these two have imprinted*; though, perhaps, with infinite variety compounded and enlarged by the Understanding, as we shall see hereafter.

[. . .]

Chapter II
Of Simple Ideas

§1. The better to understand the Nature, Manner, and Extent of our Knowledge, one thing is carefully to be observed, concerning the *Ideas* we have; and that is, That *some* of them are *simple*, and *some complex*.

Though the Qualities that affect our Senses, are, in the things themselves, so united and blended, that there is no separation, no distance between them; yet 'tis plain, the *Ideas* they produce in the Mind, enter by the Senses simple and unmixed. For though the Sight and Touch often take in from the same Object, at the same time, different *Ideas*; as a Man sees at once Motion and Colour; the Hand feels Softness and Warmth in the same piece of Wax: Yet the simple *Ideas* thus united in the same Subject, are as perfectly distinct, as those that come in by different Senses. The coldness and hardness, which a Man feels in a piece of *Ice*, being as distinct *Ideas* in the Mind, as the Smell and Whiteness of a Lily; or as the taste of Sugar, and smell of a Rose: And there is nothing can be plainer to a Man, than the clear and distinct Perception he has of those simple *Ideas*; which being each in it self uncompounded, contains in it nothing but *one uniform Appearance*, or Conception in the mind, and is not distinguishable into different *Ideas*.

§2. These simple *Ideas*, the Materials of all our Knowledge, are suggested and furnished to the Mind, only by those two ways above mentioned, *viz. Sensation* and *Reflection*. When the Understanding is once stored with these simple *Ideas*, it has the Power to repeat, compare, and unite them even to an almost infinite Variety, and so can make at Pleasure new complex *Ideas*. But it is not in the Power of the most exalted Wit, or enlarged Understanding, by any quickness or variety of Thought, to *invent or frame one new simple* Idea in the mind, not taken in by the ways before mentioned: nor can any force of the Understanding, *destroy* those that are there. The Dominion of Man, in this little World of his own Understanding, being muchwhat the same, as it is in the great World of visible things; wherein his Power, however managed by Art and Skill, reaches no farther, than to compound and divide the Materials, that are made to his Hand; but can do nothing towards the making the least Particle of new Matter, or destroying one Atome of what is already in Being. The same inability, will every one find in himself, who shall go about to fashion in his Understanding any simple *Idea*, not received in by his Senses, from external Objects; or by reflection from the Operations of his own mind about them. I would have any one try to fancy any Taste, which had never affected his Palate; or frame the *Idea* of a Scent, he had never smelt: And when he can do this, I will also conclude, that a blind Man hath *Ideas* of Colours, and a deaf Man true distinct Notions of Sounds.

§3. This is the Reason why, though we cannot believe it impossible to God, to make a Creature with other Organs, and more ways to convey into the Understanding the notice of Corporeal things, than those five, as they are usually counted, which he has given to Man: Yet I think, it is *not possible*, for any one *to imagine* any other *Qualities* in Bodies, howsoever constituted, whereby they can be taken notice of, besides Sounds, Tastes, Smells, visible and tangible Qualities. And had Mankind been made with but four Senses, the Qualities then, which are the object of the Fifth Sense, had been as far from our Notice, Imagination, and Conception, as now any *belonging to a Sixth, Seventh, or Eighth Sense*, can possibly be: which, whether yet some other Creatures, in some other Parts of this vast, and stupendious Universe, may not have, will be a great Presumption to deny. He that will not set himself proudly at the top of all things; but will consider the Immensity of this Fabrick, and the great variety, that is to be found in this little and inconsiderable part of it, which he has to do with, may be apt to think, that in other Mansions of it, there may be other, and different intelligent Beings, of whose Faculties, he has as little Knowledge or Apprehension, as a Worm shut up in one drawer of a Cabinet, hath of the Senses or Understanding of a Man; Such Variety and Excellency, being suitable to the Wisdom and Power of the Maker. I have here followed the common Opinion of Man's having but five Senses; though, perhaps, there may be justly counted more; but either Supposition serves equally to my present purpose.

Chapter III
Of Ideas of One Sense

§1. The better to conceive the *Ideas*, we receive from Sensation, it may not be amiss for us to consider them, in reference to the different ways, whereby they make their Approaches to our minds, and make themselves perceivable by us.

First then, There are some, which come into our minds *by one Sense* only.
Secondly, There are others, that convey themselves into the mind *by more Senses than one*.
Thirdly, Others that are had from *Reflection* only.
Fourthly, There are some that make themselves way, and are suggested to the mind *by all the ways of Sensation and Reflection*.
We shall consider them apart under these several Heads.

First, There are *some* Ideas, *which have admittance only through one Sense*, which is peculiarly adapted to receive them. Thus Light and Colours, as white, red, yellow, blue; with their several Degrees or Shades, and Mixtures, as Green, Scarlet, Purple, Sea-green, and the rest, come in only by the Eyes: All kinds of Noises, Sounds, and Tones only by the Ears: The several Tastes and Smells, by the Nose and Palate. And if these Organs, or the Nerves which are the Conduits, to convey them from without to their Audience in the Brain, the mind's Presence-room (as I may so call it) are any of them so disordered, as not to perform their Functions, they have no Postern to be admitted by; no other way to bring themselves into view, and be perceived by the Understanding.

The most considerable of those, belonging to the Touch, are Heat and Cold, and Solidity; all the rest, consisting almost wholly in the sensible Configuration, as smooth and rough; or else more, or less firm adhesion of the Parts, as hard and soft, tough and brittle, are obvious enough.

[. . .]

Chapter V
Of Simple Ideas of Divers Senses

The *Ideas* we get by more than one Sense, are of *Space*, or *Extension*, *Figure*, *Rest*, and *Motion*: For these make perceivable impressions, both on the Eyes and Touch; and we can receive and convey into our Minds the *Ideas* of the Extension, Figure, Motion, and Rest of Bodies, both by seeing and feeling. But having occasion to speak more at large of these in another place, I here only enumerate them.

Chapter VI
Of Simple Ideas of Reflection

§1. The Mind receiving the *Ideas*, mentioned in the foregoing Chapters, from without, when it turns its view inward upon it self, and observes its own Actions about those *Ideas* it has, takes from thence other *Ideas*, which are as capable to be the Objects of its Contemplation, as any of those it received from foreign things.

§2. The two great and principal Actions of the Mind, which are most frequently considered, and which are so frequent, that everyone that pleases, may take notice of 'em in himself, are these two:

> *Perception*, or *Thinking*, and
> *Volition*, or *Willing*.

The Power of Thinking is called the *Understanding*, and the Power of Volition is called the *Will*, and these two Powers or Abilities in the Mind are denominated *Faculties*. Of some of the Modes of these simple *Ideas* of Reflection, such as are *Remembrance*, *Discerning*, *Reasoning*, *Judging*, *Knowledge*, *Faith*, etc. I shall have occasion to speak hereafter.

Chapter VII
Of Simple Ideas of Both Sensation and Reflection

§1. There be other simple *Ideas*, which convey themselves into the Mind, by all the ways of Sensation and Reflection, *viz.*

> *Pleasure*, or *Delight*, and its opposite.
> *Pain*, or *Uneasiness*.
> *Power*.
> *Existence*.
> *Unity*.

§2. *Delight*, or *Uneasiness*, one or other of them join themselves to almost all our *Ideas*, both of Sensation and Reflection: And there is scarce any affection of our Senses from without, any retired thought of our Mind within, which is not able to produce in us *pleasure* or *pain*. By *Pleasure* and *Pain*, I would be understood to signifie, whatsoever delights or molests us; whether it arises from the thoughts of our Minds, or any thing operating on our Bodies. For whether we call it Satisfaction, Delight, Pleasure, Happiness, *etc.* on the one side; or Uneasiness, Trouble, Pain, Torment, Anguish, Misery, *etc.* on the other, they are still but different degrees of the same thing, and belong to the *Ideas* of *Pleasure* and *Pain*, Delight or Uneasiness; which are the Names I shall most commonly use for those two sorts of *Ideas*.

§3. The infinite Wise Author of our being, having given us the power over several parts of our Bodies, to move or keep them at rest, as we think fit; and also by the motion of them, to move our selves, and other contiguous Bodies, in which consists all the Actions of our Body: Having also given a power to our Minds, in several Instances, to chuse, amongst its *Ideas*, which it will think on, and to pursue the enquiry of this or that Subject with consideration and attention, to excite us to these Actions of thinking and motion, that we are capable of, has been pleased to join to several Thoughts, and several Sensations, a *perception* of *Delight*. If this were wholly separated from all our outward Sensations, and inward Thoughts, we should have no reason to preferr one Thought or Action, to another; Negligence, to Attention; or Motion, to Rest. And so we should neither stir our Bodies, nor employ our Minds; but let our Thoughts (if I may so call it) run a drift, without any direction or design; and suffer the *Ideas* of our Minds, like unregarded shadows, to make their appearances there, as it happen'd, without attending to them. In which state Man, however furnished with the Faculties of Understanding and Will, would be a very idle unactive Creature, and pass his time only in a lazy lethargick Dream. It has therefore pleased our Wise Creator, to annex to several Objects, and to the *Ideas* which we receive from them, as also to several of our Thoughts, a concomitant pleasure, and that in several Objects, to several degrees, that those Faculties which he had endowed us with, might not remain wholly idle, and unemploy'd by us.

§4. *Pain* has the same efficacy and use to set us on work, that Pleasure has, we being as ready to employ our Faculties to avoid that, as to pursue this: Only this is worth our consideration, That *Pain is often produced by the same Objects and* Ideas, *that produce Pleasure* in us. This their near Conjunction, which makes us often feel pain in the sensations where we expected pleasure, gives us new occasion of admiring the Wisdom and Goodness of our Maker, who designing the preservation of our Being, has annexed Pain to the application of many things to our Bodies, to warn us of the harm that they will do; and as advices to withdraw from them. But he, not designing our preservation barely, but the preservation of every part and organ in its perfection, hath, in many cases, annexed pain to those very *Ideas*, which delight us. Thus Heat, that is very agreeable to us in one degree, by a little greater increase of it, proves no ordinary torment: and the most pleasant of all sensible Objects, Light it self, if there be too much of it, if increased beyond a due proportion to our Eyes, causes a very painful sensation. Which is wisely and favourably so ordered by Nature, that when any Object does, by the vehemency of its operation, disorder the instruments of Sensation, whose Structures cannot but be very nice and delicate, we might by the pain, be warned to withdraw, before the Organ be quite put out of order, and so be unfitted for its proper Functions for the future. The consideration of those Objects that produce it, may well perswade us, That this is the end or use of pain. For though great light be insufferable to our Eyes, yet the highest degree of darkness does not at all disease them: because that causing no disorderly motion in it, leaves that curious Organ unharm'd, in its natural state. But yet excess of Cold, as well as Heat, pains us: because it is equally destructive to that temper, which is necessary to the preservation of life, and the exercise of the several functions of the Body, and which consists in a moderate degree of warmth; or, if you please, a motion of the insensible parts of our Bodies, confin'd within certain bounds.

[. . .]

Chapter VIII
Some Farther Considerations Concerning our Simple Ideas

[. . .]

§7. To discover the nature of our *Ideas* the better, and to discourse of them intelligibly, it will be convenient to distinguish them, as they are *Ideas* or Perceptions in our Minds; and as they are modifications of matter in the Bodies that cause such Perceptions in us: that so we *may not* think (as perhaps usually is done) that they are exactly the Images and *Resemblances* of something inherent in the subject; most of those of Sensation being in the Mind no more the likeness of something existing without us, than the Names, that stand for them are the likeness of our *Ideas*, which yet upon hearing, they are apt to excite in us.

§8. Whatsoever the Mind perceives in it self, or is the immediate object of Perception, Thought, or Understanding, that I call *Idea*; and the Power to produce any *Idea* in our mind, I call *Quality* of the Subject wherein that power is. Thus a Snow-ball having the power to produce in us the *Ideas* of *White*, *Cold*, and *Round*, the Powers to produce those *Ideas* in us, as they are in the Snow-ball, I call *Qualities*; and as they are Sensations, or Perceptions, in our Understandings, I call them *Ideas*: which *Ideas*, if I speak of sometimes, as in the things themselves, I would be understood to mean those Qualities in the Objects which produce them in us.

§9. Qualities thus considered in Bodies are, First such as are utterly inseparable from the Body, in what estate soever it be; such as in all the alterations and changes it suffers, all the force can be used upon it, it constantly keeps; and such as Sense constantly finds in every particle of Matter, which has bulk enough to be perceived, and the Mind finds inseparable from every particle of Matter, though less than to make it self singly be perceived by our Senses. *v.g.* Take a grain of Wheat, divide it into two parts, each part has still *Solidity, Extension, Figure*, and *Mobility*; divide it again, and it retains still the same qualities; and so divide it on, till the parts become insensible, they must retain still each of them all those qualities. For division (which is all that a Mill, or Pestel, or any other Body, does upon another, in reducing it to insensible parts) can never take away either Solidity, Extension, Figure, or Mobility from any Body, but only makes two, or more distinct separate masses of Matter, of that which was but one before, all which distinct masses, reckon'd as so many distinct Bodies, after division make a certain Number. These I call *original* or *primary Qualities* of Body, which I think we may observe to produce simple *Ideas* in us, viz. Solidity, Extension, Figure, Motion, or Rest, and is Number.

§10. *2dly*, Such *Qualities*, which in truth are nothing in the Objects themselves, but Powers to produce various Sensations in us by their *primary Qualities*, *i.e.* by the Bulk, Figure, Texture, and Motion of their insensible parts, as Colours, Sounds, Tasts, *etc.* These I call *secondary Qualities*. To these might be added a third sort which are allowed to be barely Powers though they are as much real Qualities in the Subject, as those which I to comply with the common way of speaking call *Qualities*, but for distinction *secondary Qualities*. For the power in Fire to produce a new Colour, or consistency in Wax or Clay by its primary Qualities, is as much a quality in Fire, as the power it has to produce in me a new *Idea* or Sensation of warmth or burning, which I felt not before, by the same primary Qualities, *viz*. The Bulk, Texture, and Motion of its insensible parts.

§11. The next thing to be consider'd, is how *Bodies* produce *Ideas* in us, and that is manifestly *by impulse*, the only way which we can conceive Bodies operate in.

§12. If then external Objects be not united to our Minds, when they produce *Ideas* in it; and yet we perceive *these original Qualities* in such of them as singly fall under our Senses, 'tis evident, that some motion must be thence continued by our Nerves, or animal Spirits, by some parts of our Bodies, to the Brains or the seat of Sensation, there to *produce in our Minds the particular* Ideas *we have of them.* And since the Extension, Figure, Number, and Motion of Bodies of an observable bigness, may be perceived at a distance *by* the sight, 'tis evident some singly imperceptible Bodies must come from them to the Eyes, and thereby convey to the Brain some *Motion*, which produces these *Ideas*, which we have of them in us.

§13. After the same manner, that the *Ideas* of these original Qualities are produced in us, we may conceive, that the *Ideas of secondary Qualities* are also *produced, viz. by the operation of insensible particles on our Senses.* For it being manifest, that there are Bodies, and good store of Bodies, each whereof is so small, that we cannot, by any of our Senses, discover either their bulk, figure, or motion, as is evident in the Particles of the Air and Water, and other extremely smaller than those, perhaps, as much smaller than the Particles of Air, or Water, as the Particles of Air or Water, are smaller than Pease or Hail-stones. Let us suppose at present, that the different Motions and Figures, Bulk, and Number of such Particles, affecting the several Organs of our Senses, produce in us those different Sensations, which we have from the Colours and Smells of Bodies, *v.g.* that a Violet, by the impulse of such insensible particles of matter of peculiar figures, and bulks, and in different degrees and modifications of their Motions, causes the *Ideas* of the blue Colour, and sweet Scent of that Flower to be produced in our Minds. It being no more impossible, to conceive, that God should annex such *Ideas* to such Motions, with which they have no similitude; than that he should annex the *Idea* of Pain to the motion of a piece of Steel dividing our Flesh, with which that *Idea* hath no resemblance.

§14. What I have said concerning *Colours* and *Smells*, may be understood also of *Tastes* and *Sounds, and other the like sensible Qualities*; which, whatever reality we, by mistake, attribute to them, are in truth nothing in the Objects themselves, but Powers to produce various Sensations in us, and *depend on those primary Qualities, viz.* Bulk, Figure, Texture, and Motion of parts; as I have said.

§15. From whence I think it is easie to draw this Observation, That the *Ideas of primary Qualities* of Bodies, *are Resemblances* of them, and their Patterns do really exist in the Bodies themselves; but the *Ideas, produced* in us *by* these *Secondary Qualities, have no resemblance* of them at all. There is nothing like our *Ideas*, existing in the Bodies themselves. They are in the Bodies, we denominate from them, only a Power to produce those Sensations in us: And what is Sweet, Blue, or Warm in *Idea*, is but the certain Bulk, Figure, and Motion of the insensible Parts in the Bodies themselves, which we call so.

§16. *Flame* is denominated *Hot* and *Light*; *Snow White* and *Cold*; and *Manna White* and *Sweet*, from the *Ideas* they produce in us. Which Qualities are commonly thought to be the same in those Bodies, that those *Ideas* are in us, the one the perfect resemblance of the other, as they are in a Mirror; and it would by most Men be judged very extravagant, if one should say otherwise. And yet he, that will consider, that *the same Fire*, that at one distance *produces* in us the Sensation of *Warmth*, does at a nearer approach, produce in us the far different Sensation of *Pain*, ought to bethink himself, what Reason he has to say, That his *Idea* of *Warmth*, which was produced in him by the Fire, is actually *in the Fire*; and his *Idea* of *Pain*, which the same Fire produced in him the same way, is *not* in the *Fire*. Why is Whiteness and Coldness in Snow, and Pain not, when it produces the one and the other *Idea* in us; and can do neither, but by the Bulk, Figure, Number, and Motion of its solid Parts?

§17. The particular *Bulk, Number, Figure, and Motion of the parts of Fire, or Snow, are really in them*, whether any ones Senses perceive them or no: and therefore they may be called *real Qualities*, because they really exist in those Bodies. But *Light, Heat, Whiteness, or Coldness, are no more really in them, than Sickness or Pain is in* Manna. Take away the Sensation of them; let not the Eyes see Light, or Colours, nor the Ears hear Sounds; let the Palate not Taste, nor the Nose Smell, and all Colours, Tastes, Odors, and Sounds, as they are such particular *Ideas*, vanish and cease, and are reduced to their Causes, *i.e.* Bulk, Figure, and Motion of Parts.

[. . .]

§21. *Ideas* being thus distinguished and understood, we may be able to give an Account, how the same Water, at the same time, may produce the *Idea* of Cold by one Hand, and of Heat by the other: Whereas it is impossible, that the same Water, if those *Ideas* were really in it, should at the same time be both Hot and Cold. For if we imagine *Warmth, as it is in our Hands*, to be *nothing but a certain sort and degree of Motion in the minute Particles of our Nerves, or animal Spirits*, we may understand, how it is possible, that the same Water may at the same time produce the Sensation of Heat in one Hand, and Cold in the other; which yet Figure never does, that never producing the *Idea* of a square by one Hand, which has produced the *Idea* of a Globe by another. But if the Sensation of Heat and Cold, be nothing but the increase or diminution of the motion of the minute Parts of our Bodies, caused by the Corpuscles of any other Body, it is easie to be understood, That if that motion be greater in one Hand, than in the other; if a Body be applied to the two Hands, which has in its minute Particles a greater motion, than in those of one of the Hands, and a less, than in those of the other, it will increase the motion of the one Hand, and lessen it in the other, and so cause the different Sensations of Heat and Cold, that depend thereon.

§22. I have in what just goes before, been engaged in Physical Enquiries a little farther than, perhaps, I intended. But it being necessary, to make the Nature of Sensation a little understood, and to make the *difference between the Qualities in Bodies, and the* Ideas *produced by them in the Mind*, to be distinctly conceived, without which it were impossible to discourse intelligibly of them; I hope, I shall be pardoned this little Excursion into Natural Philosophy, it being necessary in our present Enquiry, to distinguish the *primary*, and *real Qualities* of Bodies, which are always in them, (*viz.* Solidity, Extension, Figure, Number, and Motion, or Rest; and are sometimes perceived by us, *viz.* when the Bodies they are in, are big enough singly to be discerned) from those *secondary* and *imputed Qualities*, which are but the Powers of several Combinations of those primary ones, when they operate, without being distinctly discerned; whereby we also may come to know what *Ideas* are, and what are not Resemblances of something really existing in the Bodies, we denominate from them.

§23. The *Qualities* then that are in *Bodies* rightly considered, are of *Three sorts*.

First, The *Bulk, Figure, Number, Situation*, and *Motion, or Rest* of their solid Parts; those are in them, whether we perceive them or no; and when they are of that size, that we can discover them, we have by these an *Idea* of the thing, as it is in it self, as is plain in artificial things. These I call *primary Qualities*.

Secondly, The *Power* that is in any Body, *by* Reason of *its* insensible *primary Qualities*, to operate after a peculiar manner on any of our Senses, and thereby *produce in us* the *different Ideas* of several Colours, Sounds, Smells, Tasts, *etc*. These are usually called sensible Qualities.

Thirdly, The *Power* that is in any Body, *by* Reason of the particular Constitution of *its primary Qualities, to* make such a *change* in the *Bulk, Figure, Texture, and Motion of another Body,* as to make it operate on our Senses, differently from what it did before. Thus the Sun has a Power to make Wax white, and Fire to make Lead fluid. These are usually called Powers.

The First of these, as has been said, I think, may be properly called *real Original*, or *primary Qualities*, because they are in the things themselves, whether they are perceived or no: and upon their different Modifications it is, that the secondary Qualities depend.

The other two, are only Powers to act differently upon other things, which Powers result from the different Modifications of those primary Qualities.

[. . .]

Chapter XII
Of Complex Ideas

§1. We have hitherto considered those *Ideas*, in the reception whereof, the Mind is only passive, which are those simple ones received from *Sensation* and *Reflection* before-mentioned, whereof the Mind cannot make any one to it self, nor have any *Idea* which does not wholly consist of them. But as the Mind is wholly Passive in the reception of all its simple *Ideas*, so it exerts several acts of its own, whereby out of its simple *Ideas*, as the Materials and Foundations of the rest, the other are framed. The Acts of the Mind wherein it exerts its Power over its simple *Ideas* are chiefly these three, 1. Combining several simple *Ideas* into one compound one, and thus all Complex *Ideas* are made. 2. The 2*d*. is bringing two *Ideas*, whether simple or complex, together; and setting them by one another, so as to take a view of them at once, without uniting them into one; by which way it gets all its *Ideas* of Relations. 3. The 3*d*. is separating them from all other *Ideas* that accompany them in their real existence; this is called *Abstraction*: And thus all its General *Ideas* are made. This shews Man's Power and its way of Operation to be muchwhat the same in the Material and Intellectual World. For the Materials in both being such as he has no power over, either to make or destroy, all that Man can do is either to unite them together, or to set them by one another, or wholly separate them. I shall here begin with the first of these in the consideration of Complex *Ideas*, and come to the other two in their due places. As simple *Ideas* are observed to exist in several Combinations united together; so the Mind has a power to consider several of them united together, as one *Idea*; and that not only as they are united in external Objects, but as it self has join'd them. *Ideas* thus made up of several simple ones put together, I call *Complex*; such as are *Beauty, Gratitude, a Man, an Army, the Universe*; which though complicated of various simple *Ideas*, or *complex Ideas* made up of simple ones, yet are, when the Mind pleases, considered each by it self, as one entire thing, and signified by one name.

[. . .]

Chapter XXI
Of Power

§1. The Mind, being every day informed, by the Senses, of the alteration of those simple *Ideas*, it observes in things without; and taking notice how one comes to an end, and ceases to be, and another begins to exist, which was not before; reflecting also on what passes within it self, and observing a constant change of its *Ideas*, sometimes by the impression of outward Objects on the Senses, and sometimes by the Determination of its own choice; and concluding from what it has so constantly observed to have been, that the like Changes will for the future be made, in the same things, by like Agents, and by the like ways, considers in one thing the possibility of having any of its simple *Ideas* changed, and in another the possibility of making that change; and so comes by that *Idea* which we call *Power*. Thus we say, Fire has a *power* to melt Gold, *i.e.* to destroy the consistency of its insensible parts, and consequently its hardness, and make it fluid; and Gold has a *power* to be melted; That the Sun has a *power* to blanch Wax, and Wax a *power* to be blanched by the Sun, whereby the Yellowness is destroy'd, and Whiteness made to exist in its room. In which, and the like Cases, the *Power* we consider is in reference to the change of perceivable *Ideas*. For we cannot observe any alteration to be made in, or operation upon any thing, but by the observable change of its sensible *Ideas*; nor conceive any alteration to be made, but by conceiving a Change of some of its *Ideas*.

§2. *Power* thus considered is twofold, *viz.* as able to make, or able to receive any change: The one may be called *Active*, and the other *Passive Power*. Whether Matter be not wholly destitute of *active Power*, as its Author GOD is truly above all *passive Power*; and whether the intermediate state of created Spirits be not that alone, which is capable of both *active* and *passive Power*, may be worth consideration. I shall not now enter into that Enquiry, my present Business being not to search into the original of Power, but how we come by the *Idea* of it. But since *active Powers* make so great a part of our complex *Ideas* of natural Substances, (as we shall see hereafter,) and I mention them as such, according to common apprehension; yet they being not, perhaps, so truly *active Powers*, as our hasty Thoughts are apt to represent them, I judge it not amiss, by this intimation, to direct our Minds to the consideration of GOD and Spirits, for the clearest *Idea* of active Power.

§3. I confess *Power includes in it some kind of relation*, (a relation to Action or Change,) as indeed which of our *Ideas*, of what kind soever, when attentively considered, does not? For our *Ideas* of Extension, Duration, and Number, do they not all contain in them a secret relation of the Parts? Figure and Motion have something relative in them much more visibly: And sensible Qualities, as Colours and Smells, *etc.* what are they but the *Powers* of different Bodies, in relation to our Perception, *etc.* And if considered in the things themselves, do they not depend on the Bulk, Figure, Texture, and Motion of the Parts? All which include some kind of relation in them. Our *Idea* therefore of *Power*, I think, may well have a place amongst other simple *Ideas*, and be considered as one of them, being one of those, that make a principal Ingredient in our complex *Ideas* of Substances, as we shall hereafter have occasion to observe.

§4. We are abundantly furnished with the *Idea* of *passive Power*, by almost all sorts of sensible things. In most of them we cannot avoid observing their sensible Qualities, nay their very Substances to be in a continual flux: And therefore with reason we look on them as liable still to the same Change. Nor have we of *active Power* (which is the more proper signification of the word *Power*) fewer instances. Since whatever Change is observed, the Mind must collect a Power somewhere, able to make that Change, as well as a possibility in the thing it self to receive it. But yet, if we will consider it attentively, Bodies, by our Senses, do not afford us so clear and distinct an *Idea* of *active Power*, as we have from reflection on the Operations of our Minds. For all *Power* relating to Action, and there being but two sorts of Action, whereof we have any *Idea*, *viz.* Thinking and Motion, let us consider whence we have the clearest *Ideas* of the *Powers*, which produce these Actions. 1. Of Thinking, Body affords us no *Idea* at all, it is only from Reflection that we have that: 2. Neither have we from Body any *Idea* of the beginning of Motion. A Body at rest affords us no *Idea* of any *active Power* to move; and when it is set in motion it self, that Motion is rather a Passion, than an Action in it. For when the Ball obeys the stroke of a Billiard-stick, it is not any action of the Ball, but bare passion: Also when by impulse it sets another Ball in motion, that lay in its way, it only communicates the motion it had received from another, and loses in it self so much, as the other received; which gives us but a very obscure *Idea* of an *active Power* of moving in Body, whilst we observe it only to transfer, but not produce any motion. For it is but a very obscure *Idea* of *Power*, which reaches not the Production of the Action, but the Continuation of the Passion. For so is motion in a Body impelled by another: The continuation of the Alteration made in it from rest to motion being little more an Action, than the continuation of the Alteration of its Figure by the same blow is an Action. The *Idea* of the beginning of motion, we have only from reflection on what passes in our selves, where we find by Experience, that barely by willing it, barely by a thought of the Mind, we can move the parts of our Bodies, which were before at rest. So that it seems to me, we have from the observation of the operation of Bodies by our Senses, but a very imperfect obscure *Idea* of *active Power*, since they afford us not any *Idea* in themselves of the *Power* to begin any Action, either motion or thought. But if, from the Impulse Bodies are observed to make one upon another, any one thinks he has a clear *Idea* of *Power*, it serves as well to my purpose, *Sensation* being one of those ways, whereby the mind comes by its *Ideas*: Only I thought it worth while to consider here by the way, whether the mind doth not receive its *Idea* of *active Power* clearer from reflection on its own Operations, than it doth from any external Sensation.

§5. This at least I think evident, That we find in our selves a *Power* to begin or forbear, continue or end several actions of our minds, and motions of our Bodies, barely by a thought or preference of the mind ordering, or as it were commanding the doing or not doing such or such a particular action. This *Power* which the mind has, thus to order the consideration of any *Idea*, or the forbearing to consider it; or to prefer the motion of any part of the body to its rest, and *vice versâ* in any particular instance is that which we call the *Will*. The actual exercise of that power, by directing any particular action, or its forbearance is that which we call *Volition* or *Willing*. The forbearance or performance of that action, consequent to such order or command of the mind is called *Voluntary*. And whatsoever action is performed without such a thought of the mind is called *Involuntary*. The power of Perception is that which we call the *Understanding*. Perception, which we make the act of the Understanding, is of three sorts: 1. The Perception of *Ideas* in our Minds. 2. The Perception of the signification of Signs. 3. The Perception of the Connexion or Repugnancy, Agreement or Disagreement, that there is between any of our *Ideas*. All these are attributed to the *Understanding*, or perceptive Power, though it be the two latter only that use allows us to say we understand.

§6. These Powers of the Mind, *viz.* of *Perceiving*, and of *Preferring*, are usually call'd by another Name: And the ordinary way of Speaking is, That the *Understanding* and *Will* are two *Faculties* of the mind; a word proper enough, if it be used as all Words should be, so as not to breed any confusion in Mens Thoughts, by being supposed (as I suspect it has been) to stand for some real Beings in the Soul, that performed those Actions of Understanding and Volition. For when we say the *Will* is the commanding and superior Faculty of the Soul; that it is, or is not free; that it determines the inferior Faculties; that it follows the Dictates of the *Understanding*, etc. though these, and the like Expressions, by those that carefully attend to their own *Ideas*, and conduct their Thoughts more by the evidence of Things, than the sound of Words, may be understood in a clear and distinct sense: Yet I suspect, I say, that this way of Speaking of *Faculties*, has misled many into a confused Notion of so many distinct Agents in us, which had their several Provinces and Authorities, and did command, obey, and perform several Actions, as so many distinct Beings; which has been no small occasion of wrangling, obscurity, and uncertainty in Questions relating to them.

§7. Every one, I think, finds in himself a *Power* to begin or forbear, continue or put an end to several Actions in himself. From the consideration of the extent of the power of the mind over the actions of the Man, which every one finds in himself, arise the *Ideas* of *Liberty* and *Necessity*.

§8. All the Actions, that we have any *Idea* of, reducing themselves, as has been said, to these two, *viz.* Thinking and Motion, so far as a Man has a power to think, or not to think; to move, or not to move, according to the preference or direction of his own mind, so far is a Man *Free*. Where-ever any performance or forbearance are not equally in a Man's power; where-ever doing or not doing, will not equally follow upon the preference of his mind directing it, there he is not *Free*, though perhaps the Action may be voluntary. So that the *Idea* of *Liberty*, is the *Idea* of a Power in any Agent to do or forbear any particular Action, according to the determination or thought of the mind, whereby either of them is preferr'd to the other; where either of them is not in the Power of the Agent to be produced by him according to his *Volition*, there he is not at *Liberty*, that Agent is under *Necessity*. So that *Liberty* cannot be, where there is no Thought, no Volition, no Will; but there may be Thought, there may be Will, there may be Volition, where there is no *Liberty*. A little Consideration of an obvious instance or two may make this clear.

§9. A Tennis-ball, whether in motion by the stroke of a Racket, or lying still at rest, is not by any one taken to be a *free Agent*. If we enquire into the Reason, we shall find it is, because we conceive not a Tennis-ball to think, and consequently not to have any Volition, or preference of Motion to rest, or *vice versâ*; and therefore has not *Liberty*, is not a free Agent; but all its both Motion and Rest, come under our *Idea* of *Necessary*, and are so call'd. Likewise a Man falling into the Water, (a Bridge breaking under him,) has not herein liberty, is not a free Agent. For though he has Volition, though he prefers his not falling to falling; yet the forbearance of that Motion not being in his Power, the Stop or Cessation of that Motion follows not upon his Volition; and therefore therein he is not *free*. So a Man striking himself, or his Friend, by a Convulsive motion of his Arm, which it is not in his Power, by Volition or the direction of his Mind to stop, or forbear; no Body thinks he has in this *Liberty*; every one pities him, as acting by Necessity and Constraint.

§10. Again, suppose a Man be carried, whilst fast asleep, into a Room, where is a Person he longs to see and speak with; and be there locked fast in, beyond his Power to get out: he awakes, and is glad to find himself in so desirable Company, which he stays willingly in, *i.e.* preferrs his stay to going away. I ask, Is not this stay voluntary? I think, no Body will doubt it: and yet being locked fast in, 'tis evident he is not at liberty not to stay, he has not freedom to be gone. So that *Liberty is not an* Idea *belonging to Volition*, or preferring; but to the Person having the Power of doing, or forbearing to do, according as the Mind shall chuse or direct. Our *Idea* of Liberty reaches as far as that Power, and no farther. For where-ever restraint comes to check that Power, or compulsion takes away that Indifference of Ability on either side to act, or to forbear acting, there *liberty*, and our Notion of it, presently ceases.

[. . .]

§14. If this be so, (as I imagine it is,) I leave it to be considered, whether it may not help to put an end to that long agitated, and, I think, unreasonable, because unintelligible, Question, viz. *Whether Man's Will be free, or no.* For if I mistake not, it follows, from what I have said, that the Question it self is altogether improper; and it is as insignificant to ask, whether Man's *Will* be free, as to ask, whether his Sleep be Swift, or his Vertue square: *Liberty* being as little applicable to the *Will*, as swiftness of Motion is to Sleep, or squareness to Vertue. Every one would laugh at the absurdity of such a Question, as either of these: because it is obvious, that the modifications of motion belong not to sleep, nor the difference of Figure to Vertue: and when any one well considers it, I think he will as plainly perceive, that *Liberty*, which is but a power, belongs only to Agents, and cannot be an attribute or modification of the *Will*, which is also but a Power.

[. . .]

§16. 'Tis plain then, That the *Will* is nothing but one Power or Ability, and *Freedom* another Power or Ability: So that to ask, whether the *Will has Freedom*, is to ask, whether one Power has another Power, one Ability another Ability; a Question at first sight too grosly absurd to make a Dispute, or need an Answer. For who is it that sees not, that *Powers* belong only to *Agents*, and *are Attributes only of Substances, and not of Powers* themselves? So that this way of putting the Question, viz. whether the *Will be free*, is in effect to ask, whether the *Will* be a Substance, an Agent, or at least to suppose it, since Freedom can properly be attributed to nothing else. If Freedom can with any propriety of Speech be applied to Power, it may be attributed to the Power, that is in a Man, to produce, or forbear producing Motion in parts of his Body, by choice or preference; which is that which denominates him free, and is Freedom it self. But if any one should ask, whether Freedom were free, he would be suspected, not to understand well what he said; and he would be thought to deserve *Midas*'s Ears, who knowing that Rich was a denomination from the possession of Riches, should demand whether Riches themselves were rich.

[. . .]

§21. To return then to the Enquiry about Liberty, I think *the Question is not proper, whether the Will be free, but whether a Man be free.* Thus, I think,

1. That so far as any one can, by the direction or choice of his Mind, preferring the existence of any Action, to the non-existence of that Action, and, *vice versâ*, make it to exist, or not exist, so far he is *free*. For if I can, by a thought, directing the motion of my Finger, make it move, when it was at rest, or *vice versâ*, 'tis evident, that in respect of that, I am free: and if I can, by a like thought of my Mind, preferring one to the other, produce either words, or silence, I am at liberty to speak, or hold my peace: and *as far as this Power reaches, of acting, or not acting, by the determination of his own Thought preferring either, so far is a Man free.* For how can we think any one freer than to have the power to do what he will? And so far as any one can, by preferring any Action to its not being, or Rest to any Action, produce that Action or Rest, so far can he do what he will. For such a preferring of Action to its absence, is the *willing* of it: and we can scarce tell how to imagine any *Being* freer, than to be able to do what he *wills*. So that in respect of Actions, within the reach of such a power in him, a Man seems as free, as 'tis possible for Freedom to make him.

§22. But the inquisitive Mind of Man, willing to shift off from himself, as far as he can, all thoughts of guilt, though it be by putting himself into a worse state, than that of fatal Necessity, is not content with this: Freedom, unless it reaches farther than this, will not serve the turn: And it passes for a good Plea, that a Man is not free at all, if he be not as free to will, as he is to act, what he wills. Concerning a Man's Liberty there yet therefore is raised this farther Question, *Whether a Man be free to will*; which, I think, is what is meant, when it is disputed, Whether the *will* be free. And as to that I imagine,

§23. 2. That *Willing*, or *Volition* being an Action, and Freedom consisting in a power of acting, or not acting, *a Man in respect of willing, or the Act of Volition, when any Action in his power is once proposed to his Thoughts, as presently to be done, cannot be free.* The reason whereof is very manifest: For it being unavoidable that the Action depending on his *Will*, should exist, or not exist; and its existence, or not existence, following perfectly the determination, and preference of his *Will*, he cannot avoid willing the existence, or not existence, of that Action; it is absolutely necessary that he *will* the one, or the other, *i.e. prefer* the one to the other: since one of them must necessarily follow; and that which does follow, follows by the choice and determination of his Mind, that is, by his *willing it*: for if he did not *will* it, it would not be. So that in respect of the act of *willing*, a Man in such a case is not free: Liberty consisting in a power to act, or not to act, which, in regard of Volition, a Man, upon such a proposal, has not. For it is unavoidably necessary to prefer the doing, or forbearance, of an Action in a Man's power, which is once so proposed to his thoughts; a Man must necessarily *will* the one, or the other of them, upon which preference, or volition, the action, or its forbearance, certainly follows, and is truly voluntary: But the act of volition, or preferring one of the two, being that which he cannot avoid, a Man in respect of that act of *willing*, is under a necessity, and so cannot be free; unless Necessity and Freedom can consist together, and a Man can be Free and Bound at once.

§24. This then is evident, That in all proposals of present Action, *a Man is not at liberty to will, or not to will, because he cannot forbear willing*: Liberty consisting in a power to act, or to forbear acting, and in that only. For a Man that sits still, is said yet to be at liberty, because he can walk if he *wills* it. A Man that walks is at liberty also, not because he walks, or moves; but because he can stand still if he *wills* it. But if a Man sitting still has not a power to remove himself, he is not at liberty; so likewise a Man falling down a precipice, though in motion, is not at liberty, because he cannot stop that motion, if he would. This being so, 'tis plain that a Man that is walking, to whom it is proposed to give off walking, is not at liberty, whether he *will* determine himself to walk, or give off walking, or no: He must necessarily prefer one, or t'other of them; walking or not walking: and so it is in regard of all other Actions in our power so proposed, which are the far greater number. For considering the vast number of voluntary Actions, that succeed one another every moment that we are awake, in the course of our Lives, there are but few of them that are thought on or proposed to the *Will*, 'till the time they are to be done: And in all such Actions, as I have shewn, the Mind in respect of *willing* has not a power to act, or not to act, wherein consists Liberty: The Mind in that case has not a power to forbear *willing*; it cannot avoid some determination concerning them, let the Consideration be as short, the Thought as quick, as it will, it either leaves the Man in the state he was before thinking, or changes it; continues the Action, or puts an end to it. Whereby it is manifest, that it orders and directs one in preference to, or with neglect of the other, and thereby either the continuation, or change becomes unavoidably voluntary.

§25. Since then it is plain, that in most cases a Man is not at liberty, whether he will *Will*, or no; the next thing demanded is, *Whether a Man be at liberty to will which of the two he pleases,*

Motion or Rest. This Question carries the absurdity of it so manifestly in it self, that one might thereby sufficiently be convinced, that Liberty concerns not the Will. For to ask, whether a Man be at liberty to will either Motion, or Rest; Speaking, or Silence; which he pleases, is to ask, whether a Man can *will*, what he *wills*; or be pleased with what he is pleased with. A Question, which, I think, needs no answer: and they, who can make a Question of it, must suppose one Will to determine the Acts of another, and another to determinate that; and so on *in infinitum.*

[. . .]

Chapter XXIII
Of our Complex Ideas of Substances

§1. The Mind being, as I have declared, furnished with a great number of the simple *Ideas*, conveyed in by the *Senses*, as they are found in exteriour things, or by *Reflection* on its own Operations, takes notice also, that a certain number of these simple *Ideas* go constantly together; which being presumed to belong to one thing, and Words being suited to common apprehensions, and made use of for quick dispatch, are called so united in one subject, by one name; which by inadvertency we are apt afterward to talk of and consider as one simple *Idea*, which indeed is a complication of many *Ideas* together; Because, as I have said, not imagining how these simple *Ideas* can subsist by themselves, we accustom our selves, to suppose some *Substratum*, wherein they do subsist, and from which they do result, which therefore we call *Substance.*

§2. So that if any one will examine himself concerning his *Notion of pure Substance in general*, he will find he has no other *Idea* of it at all, but only a Supposition of he knows not what support of such Qualities, which are capable of producing simple *Ideas* in us; which Qualities are commonly called Accidents. If any one should be asked, what is the subject wherein Colour or Weight inheres, he would have nothing to say, but the solid extended parts: And if he were demanded, what is it, that that Solidity and Extension inhere in, he would not be in a much better case, than the *Indian* before mentioned; who, saying that the World was supported by a great Elephant, was asked, what the Elephant rested on; to which his answer was, a great Tortoise: But being again pressed to know what gave support to the broad-back'd Tortoise, replied, something, he knew not what. And thus here, as in all other cases, where we use Words without having clear and distinct *Ideas*, we talk like Children; who, being questioned, what such a thing is, which they know not, readily give this satisfactory answer, That it is *something*; which in truth signifies no more, when so used, either by Children or Men, but that they know not what; and that the thing they pretend to know, and talk of, is what they have no distinct *Idea* of at all, and so are perfectly ignorant of it, and in the dark. The *Idea* then we have, to which we give the general name Substance, being nothing, but the supposed, but unknown support of those Qualities, we find existing, which we imagine cannot subsist, *sine re substante*, without something to support them, we call that Support *Substantia*; which, according to the true import of the Word, is in plain *English*, *standing under*, or *upholding.*

§3. An obscure and relative *Idea* of Substance in general being thus made, we come to have the *Ideas of particular sorts of Substances*, by collecting such Combinations of simple *Ideas*, as are by Experience and Observation of Men's Senses taken notice of to exist together, and are therefore supposed to flow from the particular internal Constitution, or unknown

Essence of that Substance. Thus we come to have the *Ideas* of a Man, Horse, Gold, Water, *etc.* of which Substances, whether any one has any other clear *Idea*, farther than of certain simple *Ideas* coexisting together, I appeal to every one's own Experience. 'Tis the ordinary Qualities, observable in Iron, or a Diamond, put together, that make the true complex *Idea* of those Substances, which a Smith, or a Jeweller, commonly knows better than a Philosopher; who, whatever substantial forms he may talk of, has no other *Idea* of those Substances, than what is framed by a collection of those simple *Ideas* which are to be found in them; only we must take notice, that our complex *Ideas* of Substances, besides all these simple *Ideas* they are made up of, have always the confused *Idea* of *something* to which they belong, and in which they subsist: and therefore when we speak of any sort of Substance, we say it is a *thing* having such or such Qualities, as Body is a *thing* that is extended, figured, and capable of Motion; a Spirit a *thing* capable of thinking; and so Hardness, Friability, and Power to draw Iron, we say, are Qualities to be found in a Loadstone. These, and the like fashions of speaking intimate, that the Substance is supposed always *something* besides the Extension, Figure, Solidity, Motion, Thinking, or other observable *Ideas*, though we know not what it is.

§4. Hence when we talk or think of any particular sort of corporeal Substances, as *Horse, Stone, etc.* though the *Idea*, we have of either of them, be but the Complication, or Collection of those several simple *Ideas* of sensible Qualities, which we use to find united in the thing called *Horse* or *Stone*, yet because we cannot conceive, how they should subsist alone, nor one in another, we suppose them existing in, and supported by some common subject; *which Support we denote by the name Substance*, though it be certain, we have no clear, or distinct *Idea* of that *thing* we suppose a Support.

§5. The same happens concerning the Operations of the Mind, *viz.* Thinking, Reasoning, Fearing, *etc.* which we concluding not to subsist of themselves, nor apprehending how they can belong to Body, or be produced by it, we are apt to think these the Actions of some other *Substance*, which we call *Spirit*; whereby yet it is evident, that having no other *Idea* or Notion, of Matter, but *something* wherein those many sensible Qualities, which affect our Senses, do subsist; by supposing a Substance, wherein *Thinking, Knowing, Doubting*, and a power of Moving, *etc.* do subsist, *We have as clear a Notion of the Substance of Spirit, as we have of Body*; the one being supposed to be (without knowing what it is) the *Substratum* to those simple *Ideas* we have from without; and the other supposed (with a like ignorance of what it is) to be the *Substratum* to those Operations, which we experiment in our selves within. 'Tis plain then, that the *Idea* of corporeal *Substance* in Matter is as remote from our Conceptions, and Apprehensions, as that of Spiritual *Substance*, or *Spirit*; and therefore from our not having any notion of the *Substance* of Spirit, we can no more conclude its non-Existence, than we can, for the same reason, deny the Existence of Body: It being as rational to affirm, there is no Body, because we have no clear and distinct *Idea* of the *Substance* of Matter; as to say, there is no Spirit, because we have no clear and distinct *Idea* of the *Substance* of a Spirit.

§6. Whatever therefore be the secret and abstract Nature of *Substance* in general, all *the* Ideas *we have of particular distinct sorts of Substances*, are nothing but several Combinations of simple *Ideas*, co-existing in such, though unknown, Cause of their Union, as makes the whole subsist of itself. 'Tis by such Combinations of simple *Ideas* and nothing else, that we represent particular sorts of *Substances* to our selves; such are the *Ideas* we have of their several species in our Minds; and such only do we, by their specifick Names, signify to others, *v.g. Man, Horse, Sun, Water, Iron*, upon hearing which Words, every one who understands the Language, frames in his Mind a Combination of those several simple *Ideas*, which he has usually observed, or fancied to exist together under that denomination; all which he supposes to rest in, and be, as it were, adherent to that unknown common Subject, which inheres not in any thing else. Though in the mean time it be manifest, and every one upon Enquiry into his own thoughts, will find that he has no other *Idea* of any *Substance*, *v.g.* let it be *Gold*, *Horse*, *Iron*, *Man*, *Vitriol*, *Bread*, but what he has barely of those sensible Qualities, which he supposes to inhere, with a supposition of such a *Substratum*, as gives as it were a support to those Qualities, or simple *Ideas*, which he has observed to exist united together. Thus the *Idea* of the *Sun*, What is it, but an aggregate of those several simple *Ideas*, Bright, Hot, Roundish, having a constant regular motion, at a certain distance from us, and, perhaps, some other: as he who thinks and discourses of the *Sun*, has been more or less accurate, in observing those sensible Qualities, *Ideas*, or Properties, which are in that thing, which he calls the *Sun*.

[. . .]

Chapter XXVII
Of Identity and Diversity

[. . .]

§9. This being premised to find wherein *personal Identity* consists, we must consider what *Person* stands for; which, I think, is a thinking intelligent Being, that has reason and reflection, and can consider it self as it self, the same thinking thing in different times and places; which it does only by that consciousness, which is inseparable from thinking, and as it seems to me essential to it: It being impossible for any one to perceive, without perceiving, that he does perceive. When we see, hear, smell, taste, feel, meditate, or will any thing, we know that we do so. Thus it is always as to our present Sensations and Perceptions: And by this every one is to himself, that which he calls *self*: It not being considered in this case, whether the same *self* be continued in the same, or divers Substances. For since consciousness always accompanies thinking, and 'tis that, that makes every one to be, what he calls *self*; and thereby distinguishes himself from all other thinking things, in this alone consists *personal Identity*, *i.e.* the sameness of a rational Being: And as far as this consciousness can be extended backwards to any past Action or Thought, so far reaches the Identity of that *Person*; it is the same *self* now it was then; and 'tis by the same *self* with this present one that now reflects on it, that that Action was done.

§10. But it is farther enquir'd whether it be the same Identical Substance. This few would think they had reason to doubt of, if these Perceptions, with their consciousness, always remain'd present in the Mind, whereby the same thinking thing would be always consciously present, and, as would be thought, evidently the same to it self. But that which seems to make the difficulty is this, that this consciousness, being interrupted always by forgetfulness, there being no moment of our Lives wherein we have the whole train of all our past Actions before our Eyes in one view: But even the best Memories losing the sight of one part whilst they are viewing another; and we sometimes, and that the greatest part of our Lives, not reflecting on our past selves, being intent on our present Thoughts, and in sound sleep, having no Thoughts at all, or at least none with that consciousness, which remarks our waking Thoughts. I say, in all these cases, our consciousness being interrupted, and we losing the sight of our past *selves*, doubts are raised whether we are the same thinking thing; *i.e.* the same substance or no. Which however reasonable, or unreasonable, concerns not *personal*

Identity at all. The Question being what makes the same *Person*, and not whether it be the same Identical Substance, which always thinks in the same *Person*, which in this case matters not at all. Different Substances, by the same consciousness (where they do partake in it) being united into one Person; as well as different Bodies, by the same Life are united into one Animal, whose *Identity* is preserved, in that change of Substances, by the unity of one continued Life. For it being the same consciousness that makes a Man be himself to himself, *personal Identity* depends on that only, whether it be annexed only to one individual Substance, or can be continued in a succession of several Substances. For as far as any intelligent Being can repeat the *Idea* of any past Action with the same consciousness it had of it at first, and with the same consciousness it has of any present Action; so far it is the same *personal self*. For it is by the consciousness it has of its present Thoughts and Actions, that it is *self* to it *self* now, and so will be the same *self* as far as the same consciousness can extend to Actions past or to come; and would be by distance of Time, or change of Substance, no more two *Persons* than a Man be two Men, by wearing other Cloaths to Day than he did Yesterday, with a long or short sleep between: The same consciousness uniting those distant Actions into the same *Person*, whatever Substances contributed to their Production.

§11. That this is so, we have some kind of Evidence in our very Bodies, all whose Particles, whilst vitally united to this same thinking conscious self, so that we feel when they are touch'd, and are affected by, and conscious of good or harm that happens to them, are a part of our *selves*: *i.e.* of our thinking conscious *self*. Thus the Limbs of his Body is to every one a part of *himself*: He sympathizes and is concerned for them. Cut off an hand, and thereby separate it from that consciousness, we had of its Heat, Cold, and other Affections; and it is then no longer a part of that which is *himself*, any more than the remotest part of Matter. Thus we see the *Substance*, whereof *personal self* consisted at one time, may be varied at another, without the change of personal *Identity*: There being no Question about the same Person, though the Limbs, which but now were a part of it, be cut off.

[. . .]

§15. And thus we may be able without any difficulty to conceive, the same Person at the Resurrection, though in a Body not exactly in make or parts the same which he had here, the same consciousness going along with the Soul that inhabits it. But yet the Soul alone in the change of Bodies, would scarce to any one, but to him that makes the Soul the *Man*, be enough to make the same *Man*. For should the Soul of a Prince, carrying with it the consciousness of the Prince's past Life, enter and inform the Body of a Cobler as soon as deserted by his own Soul, every one sees, he would be the same Person with the Prince, accountable only for the Prince's Actions: But who would say it was the same Man? The Body too goes to the making the Man, and would, I guess, to every Body determine the Man in this case, wherein the Soul, with all its Princely Thoughts about it, would not make another Man: But he would be the same Cobler to every one besides himself. I know that in the ordinary way of speaking, the same Person, and the same Man, stand for one and the same thing. And indeed every one will always have a liberty to speak, as he pleases, and to apply what articulate Sounds to what *Ideas* he thinks fit, and change them as often as he pleases. But yet when we will enquire, what makes the same *Spirit, Man,* or *Person*, we must fix the *Ideas* of *Spirit, Man,* or *Person*, in our Minds; and having resolved with our selves what we mean by them, it will not be hard to determine, in either of them, or the like, when it is the *same*, and when not.

§16. But though the same immaterial Substance, or Soul does not alone, where-ever it be, and in whatsoever State, make the same Man; yet 'tis plain consciousness, as far as ever it can be extended, should it be to Ages past, unites Existences, and Actions, very remote in time, into the same Person, as well as it does the Existence and Actions of the immediately preceding moment: So that whatever has the consciousness of present and past Actions, is the same Person to whom they both belong. Had I the same consciousness, that I saw the Ark and *Noah's* Flood, as that I saw an overflowing of the *Thames* last Winter, or as that I write now, I could no more doubt that I, that write this now, that saw the *Thames* overflow'd last Winter, and that view'd the Flood at the general Deluge, was the same *self*, place that *self* in what Substance you please, than that I that write this am the same *my self* now whilst I write (whether I consist of all the same Substance, material or immaterial, or no) that I was Yesterday. For as to this point of being the same *self*, it matters not whether this present *self* be made up of the same or other Substances, I being as much concern'd, and as justly accountable for any Action was done a thousand Years since, appropriated to me now by this self-consciousness, as I am, for what I did the last moment.

§17. *Self* is that conscious thinking thing, (whatever Substance, made up of whether Spiritual, or Material, Simple, or Compounded, it matters not) which is sensible, or conscious of Pleasure and Pain, capable of Happiness or Misery, and so is concern'd for it *self*, as far as that consciousness extends. Thus every one finds, that whilst comprehended under that consciousness, the little Finger is as much a part of it *self*, as what is most so. Upon separation of this little Finger, should this consciousness go along with the little Finger, and leave the rest of the Body, 'tis evident the little Finger would be the *Person*, the *same Person*; and *self* then would have nothing to do with the rest of the Body. As in this case it is the consciousness that goes along with the Substance, when one part is separated from another, which makes the same *Person*, and constitutes this inseparable *self*: so it is in reference to Substances remote in time. That with which the *consciousness* of this present thinking thing can join it self, makes the same *Person*, and is one *self* with it, and with nothing else; and so attributes to it *self*, and owns all the Actions of that thing, as its own, as far as that consciousness reaches, and no farther; as every one who reflects will perceive.

§18. In this *personal Identity* is founded all the Right and Justice of Reward and Punishment; Happiness and Misery, being that, for which every one is concerned for *himself*, not mattering what becomes of any Substance, not joined to, or affected with that consciousness. For as it is evident in the instance I gave but now, if the consciousness went along with the little Finger, when it was cut off, that would be the same *self* which was concerned for the whole Body Yesterday, as making a part of it *self*, whose Actions then it cannot but admit as its own now. Though if the same Body should still live, and immediately from the separation of the little Finger have its own peculiar consciousness, whereof the little Finger knew nothing, it would not at all be concerned for it, as a part of it *self*, or could own any of its Actions, or have any of them imputed to him.

§19. This may shew us wherein *personal Identity* consists, not in the Identity of Substance, but, as I have said, in the Identity of *consciousness*, wherein, if *Socrates* and the present Mayor of *Quinborough* agree, they are the same Person: If the same *Socrates* waking and sleeping do not partake of the same *consciousness*, *Socrates* waking and sleeping is not the same Person. And to punish *Socrates* waking, for what sleeping *Socrates* thought, and waking *Socrates* was never conscious of, would be no more of Right, than to punish one Twin for what his Brother-Twin did, whereof he knew nothing, because their outsides were so like, that they could not be distinguished; for such Twins have been seen.

§20. But yet possibly it will still be objected, suppose I wholly lose the memory of some parts of my Life, beyond a possibility of retrieving them, so that perhaps I shall never be conscious of them again; yet am I not the same Person, that did those Actions, had those Thoughts, that I was once conscious of, though I have now forgot them? To which I answer, that we must here take notice what the Word *I* is applied to, which in this case is the Man only. And the same Man being presumed to be the same Person, *I* is easily here supposed to stand also for the same Person. But if it be possible for the same Man to have distinct incommunicable consciousness at different times, it is past doubt the same Man would at different times make different Persons; which, we see, is the Sense of Mankind in the solemnest Declaration of their Opinions, Humane Laws not punishing the *Mad Man* for the *Sober Man's* Actions, nor the *Sober Man* for what the *Mad Man* did, thereby making them two Persons; which is somewhat explained by our way of speaking in *English*, when we say such an one *is not himself*, or is *besides himself*; in which Phrases it is insinuated, as if those who now, or, at least, first used them, thought, that *self* was changed, the *self* same Person was no longer in that Man.

[. . .]

§25. I agree the more probable Opinion is, that this consciousness is annexed to, and the Affection of one individual immaterial Substance.

But let Men according to their divers Hypotheses resolve of that as they please. This every intelligent Being, sensible of Happiness or Misery, must grant, that there is something that is *himself*, that he is concerned for, and would have happy; that this *self* has existed in a continued Duration more than one instant, and therefore 'tis possible may exist, as it has done, Months and Years to come, without any certain bounds to be set to its duration; and may be the same *self*, by the same consciousness, continued on for the future. And thus, by this consciousness, he finds himself to be the *same self* which did such or such an Action some Years since, by which he comes to be happy or miserable now. In all which account of *self*, the same numerical Substance is not considered, as making the same *self*: But the same continued consciousness, in which several Substances may have been united, and again separated from it, which, whilst they continued in a vital union with that, wherein this consciousness then resided, made a part of that same *self*. Thus any part of our Bodies vitally united to that, which is conscious in us, makes a part of our *selves*: But upon separation from the vital union, by which that consciousness is communicated, that, which a moment since was part of our *selves*, is now no more so, than a part of another Man's *self* is a part of me; and 'tis not impossible, but in a little time may become a real part of another Person. And so we have the same numerical Substance become a part of two different Persons; and the same Person preserved under the change of various Substances. Could we suppose any Spirit wholly stripp'd of all its memory or consciousness of past Actions, as we find our Minds always are of a great part of ours, and sometimes of them all, the union or separation of such a Spiritual Substance would make no variation of personal Identity, any more than that of any Particle of Matter does. Any Substance vitally united to the present thinking Being, is a part of that very *same self* which now is: Any thing united to it by a consciousness of former Actions makes also a part of the *same self*, which is the same both then and now.

§26. *Person*, as I take it, is the name for this *self*. Where-ever a Man finds, what he calls *himself*, there I think another may say is the same *Person*. It is a Forensick Term appropriating Actions and their Merit; and so belongs only to intelligent Agents capable of a Law, and Happiness and Misery. This personality extends it *self* beyond present Existence to what is past, only by consciousness, whereby it becomes concerned and accountable, owns and imputes to it *self* past Actions, just upon the same ground, and for the same reason, that it does the present. All which is founded in a concern for Happiness the unavoidable concomitant of consciousness, that which is conscious of Pleasure and Pain, desiring, that that *self*, that is conscious, should be happy. And therefore whatever past Actions it cannot reconcile or appropriate to that present *self* by consciousness, it can be no more concerned in, than if they had never been done: And to receive Pleasure or Pain; *i.e.* Reward or Punishment, on the account of any such Action, is all one, as to be made happy or miserable in its first being, without any demerit at all. For supposing a Man punish'd now, for what he had done in another Life, whereof he could be made to have no consciousness at all, what difference is there between that Punishment, and being created miserable? And therefore conformable to this, the Apostle tells us, that at the Great Day, when every one shall *receive according to his doings, the secrets of all Hearts shall be laid open.* The Sentence shall be justified by the consciousness all Persons shall have, that they *themselves* in what Bodies soever they appear, or what Substances soever that consciousness adheres to, are the *same*, that committed those Actions, and deserve that Punishment for them.

[. . .]

Book IV
Of Knowledge and Opinion

Chapter I
Of Knowledge in General

§1. *Since the Mind*, in all its Thoughts and Reasonings, hath no other immediate Object but its own *Ideas*, which it alone does or can contemplate, it is evident, that our Knowledge is only conversant about them.

§2. *Knowledge* then seems to me to be nothing but *the perception of the connexion and agreement, or disagreement and repugnancy of any of our Ideas*. In this alone it consists. Where this Perception is, there is Knowledge, and where it is not, there, though we may fancy, guess, or believe, yet we always come short of Knowledge. For when we know that *White is not Black*, what do we else but perceive, that these two *Ideas* do not agree? When we possess our selves with the utmost security of the Demonstration, that *the three Angles of a Triangle are equal to two right ones*, What do we more but perceive, that Equality to two right ones, does necessarily agree to, and is inseparable from the three Angles of a Triangle?

§3. But to understand a little more distinctly, wherein this agreement or disagreement consists, I think we may reduce it all to these four sorts:

1. *Identity*, or *Diversity*.
2. *Relation*.
3. *Co-existence*, or *necessary connexion*.
4. *Real Existence*.

§4. *First*, As to the first sort of Agreement or Disagreement, *viz. Identity*, or *Diversity*. 'Tis the first Act of the Mind, when it has any Sentiments or *Ideas* at all, to perceive its *Ideas*, and so far as it perceives them, to know each what it is, and thereby also to perceive their difference, and that one is not another. This is so absolutely necessary, that without it there could be no Knowledge, no Reasoning, no Imagination, no distinct Thoughts at all. By this the Mind clearly and infallibly perceives each *Idea* to agree with it self, and to be what it is; and all distinct *Ideas* to disagree, *i.e.* the one not to be the other: And this it does without any pains, labour, or deduction; but at first view, by its natural power of Perception and Distinction. And though Men of Art have reduced this into those general Rules, *What is, is; and it is impossible for the same thing to be, and not to be,* for ready application in all cases, wherein there may be occasion to reflect on it; yet it is certain, that the first exercise of this Faculty, is about particular *Ideas*. A Man infallibly knows, as soon as ever he has them in his Mind that the *Ideas* he calls *White* and *Round,* are the very *Ideas* they are, and that they are not other *Ideas* which he calls *Red* or *Square.* Nor can any Maxim or Proposition in the World make him know it clearer or surer than he did before, and without any such general Rule. This then is the first agreement, or disagreement, which the Mind perceives in its *Ideas;* which it always perceives at first sight: And if there ever happen any doubt about it, 'twill always be found to be about the Names, and not the *Ideas* themselves, whose Identity and Diversity will always be perceived, as soon and as clearly as the *Ideas* themselves are, nor can it possibly be otherwise.

§5. *Secondly,* The next sort of Agreement, or Disagreement, the Mind perceives in any of its *Ideas,* may, I think, be called *Relative,* and is nothing but *the Perception of the Relation between any two Ideas,* of what kind soever, whether Substances, Modes, or any other. For since all distinct *Ideas* must eternally be known not to be the same, and so be universally and constantly denied one of another, there could be no room for any positive Knowledge at all, if we could not perceive any Relation between our *Ideas,* and find out the Agreement or Disagreement, they have one with another, in several ways the Mind takes of comparing them.

§6. *Thirdly,* The third sort of Agreement, or Disagreement to be found in our *Ideas,* which the Perception of the Mind is employ'd about, is *Co-existence,* or *Non-co-existence* in the same Subject; and this belongs particularly to Substances. Thus when we pronounce concerning *Gold,* that it is fixed, our Knowledge of this Truth amounts to no more but this, that fixedness, or a power to remain in the Fire unconsumed, is an *Idea,* that always accompanies, and is join'd with that particular sort of Yellowness, Weight, Fusibility, Malleableness, and Solubility in *Aqua Regia,* which make our complex *Idea,* signified by the word *Gold.*

§7. *Fourthly,* The fourth and last sort is, that of *actual real Existence* agreeing to any *Idea.* Within these four sorts of Agreement or Disagreement, is, I suppose contained all the Knowledge we have, or are capable of: For all the Enquiries that we can make, concerning any of our *Ideas,* all that we know, or can affirm concerning any of them, is, That it is, or is not the same with some other; that it does, or does not always co-exist with some other *Idea* in the same Subject; that it has this or that Relation to some other *Idea;* or that it has a real existence without the Mind. Thus *Blue is not Yellow,* is of Identity. *Two Triangles upon equal Basis, between two Parallels are equal,* is of Relation. *Iron is susceptible of magnetical Impressions,* is of Co-existence, *GOD is,* is of real Existence. Though Identity and Co-existence are truly nothing but Relations, yet they are so peculiar ways of Agreement, or Disagreement of our *Ideas,* that they deserve well to be considered as distinct Heads, and not under Relation in general; since they are so different grounds of Affirmation and Negation, as will easily appear to any one, who will but reflect on what is said in several places of this Essay. I should now proceed to examine the several degrees of our Knowledge, but that it is necessary first, to consider the different acceptations of the word *Knowledge.*

§8. There are several ways wherein the Mind is possessed of Truth; each of which is called *Knowledge*.

1. There is *actual Knowledge*, which is the present view the Mind has of the Agreement, or Disagreement of any of its *Ideas*, or of the Relation they have one to another.

2. A Man is said to know any Proposition, which having been once laid before his Thoughts, he evidently perceived the Agreement, or Disagreement of the *Ideas* whereof it consists; and so lodg'd it in his Memory, that whenever that Proposition comes again to be reflected on, he, without doubt or hesitation, embraces the right side, assents to, and is certain of the Truth of it. This, I think, one may call *habitual Knowledge*: And thus a Man may be said to know all those Truths, which are lodg'd in his Memory, by a foregoing clear and full perception, whereof the Mind is assured past doubt, as often as it has occasion to reflect on them. For our finite Understandings being able to think, clearly and distinctly, but on one thing at once, if Men had no Knowledge of any more than what they actually thought on, they would all be very ignorant: And he that knew most, would know but one Truth, that being all he was able to think on at one time.

[. . .]

Chapter II
Of the Degrees of our Knowledge

§1. All our Knowledge consisting, as I have said, in the view the Mind has of its own *Ideas*, which is the utmost Light and greatest Certainty, we with our Faculties, and in our way of Knowledge are capable of, it may not be amiss, to consider a little the degrees of its Evidence. The different clearness of our Knowledge seems to me to lie in the different way of Perception, the Mind has of the Agreement, or Disagreement of any of its *Ideas*. For if we will reflect on our own ways of Thinking, we shall find, that sometimes the Mind perceives the Agreement or Disagreement of two *Ideas* immediately by themselves, without the intervention of any other: And this, I think, we may call *intuitive Knowledge*. For in this, the Mind is at no pains of proving or examining, but perceives the Truth, as the Eye doth light, only by being directed toward it. Thus the Mind perceives, that *White* is not *Black*, That a *Circle* is not a *Triangle*, That *Three* are more than *Two*, and equal to *One* and *Two*. Such kind of Truths, the Mind perceives at the first sight of the *Ideas* together, by bare *Intuition*, without the intervention of any other *Idea*; and this kind of Knowledge is the clearest, and most certain, that humane Frailty is capable of. This part of Knowledge is irresistible, and like the bright Sun-shine, forces it self immediately to be perceived, as soon as ever the Mind turns its view that way; and leaves no room for Hesitation, Doubt, or Examination, but the Mind is presently filled with the clear Light of it. 'Tis on this *Intuition*, that depends all the Certainty and Evidence of all our Knowledge, which Certainty every one finds to be so great, that he cannot imagine, and therefore not require a greater: For a Man cannot conceive himself capable of a greater Certainty, than to know that any *Idea* in his Mind is such, as he perceives it to be; and that two *Ideas*, wherein he perceives a difference, are different, and not precisely the same. He that demands a greater Certainty than this, demands he knows not what, and shews only that he has a Mind to be a Sceptick, without being able to be so. Certainty depends so wholly on this Intuition, that in the next degree of *Knowledge*, which I call *Demonstrative*, this intuition is necessary in all the Connexions of the intermediate *Ideas*, without which we cannot attain Knowledge and Certainty.

§2. The next degree of Knowledge is, where the Mind perceives the Agreement or Disagreement of any *Ideas*, but not immediately. Though where-ever the Mind perceives the Agreement or Disagreement of any of its *Ideas*, there be certain Knowledge; Yet it does not always happen, that the Mind sees that Agreement or Disagreement, which there is between them, even where it is discoverable; and in that case, remains in Ignorance, and at most, gets no farther than a probable conjecture. The Reason why the Mind cannot always perceive presently the Agreement or Disagreement of two *Ideas* is, because those *Ideas*, concerning whose Agreement or Disagreement the Enquiry is made, cannot by the Mind be so put together, as to shew it. In this Case then, when the Mind cannot so bring its *Ideas* together, as by their immediate Comparison, and as it were Juxta-position, or application one to another, to perceive their Agreement or Disagreement, it is fain, by the Intervention of other *Ideas* (one or more, as it happens) to discover the Agreement or Disagreement, which it searches; and this is that which we call *Reasoning*. Thus the Mind being willing to know the Agreement or Disagreement in bigness, between the three Angles of a Triangle, and two right ones, cannot by an immediate view and comparing them, do it: Because the three Angles of a Triangle cannot be brought at once, and be compared with any other one, or two Angles; and so of this the Mind has no immediate, no intuitive Knowledge. In this Case the Mind is fain to find out some other Angles, to which the three Angles of a Triangle have an Equality; and finding those equal to two right ones, comes to know their Equality to two right ones.

§3. Those intervening *Ideas*, which serve to shew the Agreement of any two others, are called *Proofs*; and where the Agreement or Disagreement is by this means plainly and clearly perceived, it is called *Demonstration*, it being *shewn* to the Understanding, and the Mind made see that it is so. A quickness in the Mind to find out these intermediate *Ideas*, (that shall discover the Agreement or Disagreement of any other,) and to apply them right, is, I suppose, that which is called *Sagacity*.

§4. *This Knowledge by intervening Proofs*, though it be certain, yet the evidence of it is *not* altogether *so clear* and bright, nor the assent so ready, *as in intuitive* Knowledge. For though in *Demonstration*, the Mind does at last perceive the Agreement or Disagreement of the *Ideas* it considers; yet 'tis not without pains and attention: There must be more than one transient view to find it. A steddy application and pursuit is required to this Discovery: And there must be a Progression by steps and degrees, before the Mind can in this way arrive at Certainty, and come to perceive the Agreement or Repugnancy between two *Ideas* that need Proofs and the Use of Reason to shew it.

[. . .]

Chapter III
Of the Extent of Humane Knowledge

§1. Knowledge, as has been said, lying in the Perception of the Agreement, or Disagreement, of any of our *Ideas*, it follows from hence, That,

First, We can have *Knowledge* no farther than we have *Ideas*.

§2. *Secondly*, That we can have no *Knowledge* farther, than we can have Perception of that Agreement, or Disagreement: Which Perception being, 1. Either by *Intuition*, or the immediate comparing any two Ideas; or, 2. By *Reason*, examining the Agreement, or Disagreement of two *Ideas*, by the Intervention of some others: Or, 3. By *Sensation*, perceiving the Existence of particular Things. Hence it also follows,

§3. *Thirdly*, That we cannot have an *intuitive Knowledge*, that shall extend it self to all our *Ideas*, and all that we would know about them; because we cannot examine and perceive all the Relations they have one to another by *juxta*-position, or an immediate comparison one with another. Thus having the *Ideas* of an obtuse, and an acute angled Triangle, both drawn from equal Bases, and between Parallels, I can by intuitive Knowledge, perceive the one not to be the other; but cannot that way know, whether they be equal, or no; because their Agreement, or Disagreement in equality, can never be perceived by an immediate comparing them: The difference of Figure makes their parts uncapable of an exact immediate application; and therefore there is need of some intervening Quantities to measure them by, which is Demonstration, or rational Knowledge.

§4. *Fourthly*, It follows also, from what is above observed, that our *rational Knowledge*, cannot reach to the whole extent of our *Ideas*. Because between two different *Ideas* we would examine, we cannot always find such *Mediums*, as we can connect one to another with an intuitive Knowledge, in all the parts of the Deduction; and where-ever that fails, we come short of Knowledge and Demonstration.

§5. *Fifthly, Sensitive Knowledge* reaching no farther than the Existence of Things actually present to our Senses, is yet much narrower than either of the former.

§6. From all which it is evident, that *the extent of our Knowledge* comes not only short of the reality of Things, but even of the extent of our own *Ideas*. Though our Knowledge be limited to our *Ideas*, and cannot exceed them either in extent, or perfection; and though these be very narrow bounds, in respect of the extent of Allbeing, and far short of what we may justly imagine to be in some even created understandings, not tied down to the dull and narrow Information, is to be received from some few, and not very acute ways of Perception, such as are our Senses.

[. . .]

Chapter IX
Of our Knowledge of Existence

§1. Hither to we have only considered the Essences of Things, which being only abstract *Ideas*, and thereby removed in our Thoughts from particular Existence, (that being the proper Operation of the Mind, in Abstraction, to consider an *Idea* under no other Existence, but what it has in the Understanding,) gives us no Knowledge of real Existence at all. Where by the way we may take notice, that *universal Propositions*, of whose Truth or Falshood we can have certain Knowledge, concern not *Existence*; and farther, that all *particular Affirmations or Negations*, that would not be certain if they were made general, are only concerning *Existence*; they declaring only the accidental Union or Separation of *Ideas* in Things existing, which in their abstract Natures, have no known necessary Union or Repugnancy.

[. . .]

Chapter X
Of our Knowledge of the Existence of a God

§1. Though God has given us no innate *Ideas* of himself; though he has stamped no original Characters on our Minds, wherein we may read his Being: yet having furnished us with those

Faculties, our Minds are endowed with, he hath not left himself without witness: since we have Sense, Perception, and Reason, and cannot want a clear proof of him, as long as we carry our selves about us. Nor can we justly complain of our Ignorance in this great Point, since he has so plentifully provided us with the means to discover, and know him, so far as is necessary to the end of our Being, and the great concernment of our Happiness. But though this be the most obvious Truth that Reason discovers; and though its Evidence be (if I mistake not) equal to mathematical Certainty: yet it requires Thought and Attention; and the Mind must apply it self to a regular deduction of it from some part of our intuitive Knowledge, or else we shall be as uncertain, and ignorant of this, as of other Propositions, which are in themselves capable of clear Demonstration. To shew therefore, that we are capable of *knowing*, i.e. *being certain that there is a* GOD, and how we may come by this certainty, I think we need go no farther than our selves, and that undoubted Knowledge we have of our own Existence.

§2. I think it is beyond Question, that *Man has a clear Perception of his own Being*; he knows certainly, that he exists, and that he is something. He that can doubt, whether he be any thing, or no, I speak not to, no more than I would argue with pure nothing, or endeavour to convince Non-entity, that it were something. If any one pretends to be so sceptical, as to deny his own Existence, (for really to doubt of it, is manifestly impossible,) let him for me enjoy his beloved Happiness of being nothing, until Hunger, or some other Pain convince him of the contrary. This then, I think, I may take for a Truth, which every ones certain Knowledge assures him of, beyond the liberty of doubting, *viz.* that he is something that actually exists.

§3. In the next place, Man knows by an intuitive Certainty, that bare *nothing can no more produce any real Being, than it can be equal to two right Angles*. If a Man knows not that Non-entity, or the Absence of all Being cannot be equal to two right Angles, it is impossible he should know any demonstration in *Euclid*. If therefore we know there is some real Being, and that Non-entity cannot produce any real Being, it is an evident demonstration, that from Eternity there has been something; Since what was not from Eternity, had a Beginning; and what had a Beginning, must be produced by something else.

§4. Next, it is evident, that what had its Being and Beginning from another, must also have all that which is in, and belongs to its Being from another too. All the Powers it has, must be owing to, and received from the same Source. This eternal Source then of all being must also be the Source and Original of all Power; and so *this eternal Being must be also the most powerful*.

§5. Again, a Man finds in himself *Perception*, and *Knowledge*. We have then got one step farther; and we are certain now, that there is not only some Being, but some knowing intelligent Being in the World.

There was a time then, when there was no knowing Being, and when Knowledge began to be; or else, there has been also *a knowing Being from Eternity*. If it be said, there was a time when no Being had any Knowledge, when that eternal Being was void of all Understanding. I reply, that then it was impossible there should ever have been any Knowledge. It being as impossible, that Things wholly void of Knowledge, and operating blindly, and without any Perception, should produce a knowing Being, as it is impossible, that a Triangle should make it self three Angles bigger than two right ones. For it is as repugnant to the *Idea* of senseless Matter, that it should put into it self Sense, Perception, and Knowledge, as it is repugnant to the *Idea* of a Triangle, that it should put into it self greater Angles than two right ones.

§6. Thus from the Consideration of our selves, and what we infallibly find in our own Constitutions, our Reason leads us to the Knowledge of this certain and evident Truth, That *there is an eternal, most powerful, and most knowing Being;* which whether any one will please to call *God,* it matters not. The thing is evident, and from this *Idea* duly considered, will easily be deduced all those other Attributes, which we ought to ascribe to this eternal Being.

[. . .]

Chapter XI
Of our Knowledge of the Existence of other Things

§1. The Knowledge of our own Being, we have by intuition. The Existence of a GOD, Reason clearly makes known to us, as has been shewn.

The *Knowledge of the Existence* of any other thing we can have only by *Sensation*: For there being no necessary connexion of *real Existence,* with any *Idea* a Man hath in his Memory, nor of any other Existence but that of GOD, with the Existence of any particular Man; no particular Man can know the *Existence* of any other Being, but only when by actual operating upon him, it makes it self perceived by him. For the having the *Idea* of any thing in our Mind, no more proves the Existence of that Thing, than the picture of a Man evidences his being in the World, or the Visions of a Dream make thereby a true History.

§2. 'Tis therefore the actual receiving of *Ideas* from without, that gives us notice of the *Existence* of other Things, and makes us know, that something doth exist at that time without us, which causes that *Idea* in us, though perhaps we neither know nor consider how it does it: For it takes not from the certainty of our Senses, and the *Ideas* we receive by them, that we know not the manner wherein they are produced: *v.g.* whilst I write this, I have, by the Paper affecting my Eyes, that *Idea* produced in my Mind, which whatever Object causes, I call *White*; by which I know, that that Quality or Accident (*i.e.* whose appearance before my Eyes, always causes that *Idea*) doth really exist, and hath a Being without me. And of this, the greatest assurance I can possibly have, and to which my Faculties can attain, is the Testimony of my Eyes, which are the proper and sole Judges of this thing, whose Testimony I have reason to rely on, as so certain, that I can no more doubt, whilst I write this, that I see White and Black, and that something really exists, that causes that Sensation in me, than that I write or move my Hand; which is a Certainty as great, as humane Nature is capable of, concerning the Existence of any thing, but a Man's self alone, and of GOD.

§3. *The notice we have by our Senses, of the existing of Things without* us, though it be not altogether so certain, as our intuitive Knowledge, or the Deductions of our Reason, employ'd about the clear abstract *Ideas* of our own Minds; yet it is an assurance that *deserves the name of Knowledge.* If we persuade our selves, that our Faculties act and inform us right, concerning the existence of those Objects that affect them, it cannot pass for an ill-grounded confidence: For I think no body can, in earnest, be so sceptical, as to be uncertain of the Existence of those Things which he sees and feels. At least, he that can doubt so far, (whatever he may have with his own Thoughts) will never have any Controversie with me; since he can never be sure I say any thing contrary to his Opinion. As to my self, I think GOD has given me assurance enough of the Existence of Things without me: since by their different application, I can produce in my self both Pleasure and Pain, which is one great Concernment of my present state. This is certain, the confidence that our Faculties do not herein deceive us, is the greatest assurance we are capable of, concerning the Existence of material Beings. For we cannot act any thing, but by our Faculties; nor talk of Knowledge it self, but by the help of those Faculties, which are fitted to apprehend even what Knowledge is.

2

George Berkeley, *Three Dialogues between Hylas and Philonous in Opposition to Sceptics and Atheists* (1713)

Berkeley's *Dialogues* involve two characters, Hylas and Philonous, whose names are of great significance. "Hylas" means "matter," and "Philonous" means "lover of mind." Berkeley uses the *Dialogues* as a vehicle for a defense of idealism, the theory that the universe is composed only of ideas and minds that have them. He thinks idealism is the only plausible metaphysics for an empiricist.

At the beginning of their discussion, Hylas and Philonous agree to call a philosophical position true or acceptable when it meets two conditions: (a) it is far from skepticism (it does not require suspense of belief) and (b) it is consistent with common sense (it preserves the ordinary appearances). This agreement on their part is important, since Berkeley's strategy in the *Dialogues* is to show that idealism meets each of these conditions, while belief in a world of physical matter does not.

Philonous presents several arguments for idealism in the *Dialogues*, each of which is supposed to stand on its own, without the others. Among his key arguments are the following. (1) The immediate objects of perception are made of the qualities we sense. We sense only sensations – colors, shapes, sounds, etc. So, all objects we perceive are made of sensations, which exist only in minds. (2) Perceptions are relative. An object – like a pail of water – can feel hot to one hand and cold to another. It is absurd for a physical object to be both hot and cold at the same time. Therefore, the qualities of the object are not in physical matter but in the mind. (3) No one can conceive of an object existing outside of all minds. For as soon as you or I try to think of such a thing – such as a tree in a forest with no one to perceive it – it is existing as conceived in our minds. Therefore, objects cannot exist outside of minds.

After Berkeley has established idealism in the First Dialogue, he raises an important question in the Second: If the world is composed of ideas, why do I not control all of the ideas I experience? Why can I not make the world appear to me in the way I want it to appear? Furthermore, why do the ideas that are not under my control, such as my perceptions of my room, come to me in about the same way each time I have the experience of entering the room? Philonous contends that the best explanation of these phenomena is the existence of a mind or spirit that contains all of the perceptions I experience, and causes them to occur in me. In this way, Berkeley, in the mouth of Philonous, argues for the existence of God.

Berkeley was born in Ireland in 1685, and died in 1753. After his marriage in 1728 he spent three years in America, attempting to establish a college in Bermuda. The funding collapsed, however, and he returned to Ireland, where he later become the Anglican bishop of Cloyne.

The First Dialogue

Philonous. Good morrow, Hylas: I did not expect to find you abroad so early.

Hylas. It is indeed something unusual; but my thoughts were so taken up with a subject I was discoursing of last night, that finding I could not sleep, I resolved to rise and take a turn in the garden.

Phil. It happened well, to let you see what innocent and agreeable pleasures you lose every morning. Can there be a pleasanter time of the day, or a more delightful season of the year? That purple sky, these wild but sweet notes of birds, the fragrant bloom upon the trees and flowers, the gentle influence of the rising sun, these and a thousand nameless beauties of nature inspire the soul with secret transports; its faculties too being at this time fresh and lively, are fit for those meditations, which the solitude of a garden and tranquillity of the morning naturally dispose us to. But I am afraid I interrupt your thoughts: for you seemed very intent on something.

[. . .]

Hyl. You were represented in last night's conversation, as one who maintained the most extravagant opinion that ever entered into the mind of man, to wit, that there is no such thing as *material substance* in the world.

Phil. That there is no such thing as what philosophers call *material substance*, I am seriously persuaded: but if I were made to see anything absurd or sceptical in this, I should then have the same reason to renounce this, that I imagine I have now to reject the contrary opinion.

Hyl. What! Can anything be more fantastical, more repugnant to common sense, or a more manifest piece of scepticism, than to believe there is no such thing as *matter*?

[. . .]

Phil. Pray, Hylas, what do you mean by a *sceptic*?

Hyl. I mean what all men mean, one that doubts of everything.

[. . .]

Phil. How comes it then, Hylas, that you pronounce me a *sceptic*, because I deny what you affirm, to wit, the existence of matter? Since, for aught you can tell, I am as peremptory in my denial, as you in your affirmation.

Hyl. Hold, Philonous, I have been a little out in my definition; but every false step a man makes in discourse is not to be insisted on. I said indeed, that a *sceptic* was one who doubted of everything; but I should have added, or who denies the reality and truth of things.

Phil. What things? Do you mean the principles and theorems of sciences? But these you know are universal intellectual notions, and consequently independent of matter; the denial therefore of this doth not imply the denying them.

Hyl. I grant it. But are there no other things? What think you of distrusting the senses, of denying the real existence of sensible things, or pretending to know nothing of them. Is not this sufficient to denominate a man a *sceptic*?

Phil. Shall we therefore examine which of us it is that denies the reality of sensible things, or professes the greatest ignorance of them; since, if I take you rightly, he is to be esteemed the greatest *sceptic*?

Hyl. That is what I desire.

Phil. What mean you by sensible things?

Hyl. Those things which are perceived by the senses. Can you imagine that I mean anything else?

Phil. Pardon me, Hylas, if I am desirous clearly to apprehend your notions, since this may much shorten our inquiry. Suffer me then to ask you this farther question. Are those things only perceived by the senses which are perceived immediately? Or, may those things properly be said to be *sensible*, which are perceived mediately, or not without the intervention of others?

[. . .]

Hyl. To prevent any more questions of this kind, I tell you once for all, that by *sensible things* I mean those only which are perceived by sense, and that in truth the senses perceive nothing which they do not perceive immediately: for they make no inferences. The deducing therefore of causes or occasions from effects and appearances, which alone are perceived by sense, entirely relates to reason.

Phil. This point then is agreed between us, that *sensible things are those only which are immediately perceived by sense*. You will farther inform me, whether we immediately perceive by sight anything beside light, and colors, and figures: or by hearing anything but sounds: by the palate, anything beside tastes: by the smell, beside odors: or by the touch, more than tangible qualities.

Hyl. We do not.

Phil. It seems therefore, that if you take away all sensible qualities, there remains nothing sensible.

Hyl. I grant it.

Phil. Sensible things therefore are nothing else but so many sensible qualities, or combinations of sensible qualities.

Hyl. Nothing else.

Phil. Heat then is a sensible thing.

Hyl. Certainly.

Phil. Does the reality of sensible things consist in being perceived? Or, is it something distinct from their being perceived, and that bears no relation to the mind?

Hyl. To *exist* is one thing, and to be *perceived* is another.

Phil. I speak with regard to sensible things only: and of these I ask, whether by their real existence you mean a subsistence exterior to the mind, and distinct from their being perceived?

Hyl. I mean a real absolute being, distinct from, and without any relation to, their being perceived.

Phil. Heat therefore, if it be allowed a real being, must exist without the mind.

Hyl. It must.

Phil. Tell me, Hylas, is this real existence equally compatible to all degrees of heat, which we perceive: or is there any reason why we should attribute it to some, and deny it to others? And if there be, pray let me know that reason.

Hyl. Whatever degree of heat we perceive by sense, we may be sure the same exists in the object that occasions it.

Phil. What, the greatest as well as the least?

Hyl. I tell you, the reason is plainly the same in respect of both: they are both perceived by sense; nay, the greater degree of heat is more sensibly perceived; and consequently, if there is any difference, we are more certain of its real existence than we can be of the reality of a lesser degree.

Phil. But is not the most vehement and intense degree of heat a very great pain?

Hyl. No one can deny it.

Phil. And is any unperceiving thing capable of pain or pleasure?

Hyl. No, certainly.

Phil. Is your material substance a senseless being, or a being endowed with sense and perception?

Hyl. It is senseless, without doubt.

Phil. It cannot therefore be the subject of pain.

Hyl. By no means.

Phil. Nor consequently of the greatest heat perceived by sense, since you acknowledge this to be no small pain.

Hyl. I grant it.

Phil. What shall we say then of your external object; is it a material substance, or no?

Hyl. It is a material substance with the sensible qualities inhering in it.

Phil. How then can a great heat exist in it, since you own it cannot in a material substance? I desire you would clear this point.

Hyl. Hold, Philonous, I fear I was out in yielding intense heat to be a pain. It should seem rather, that pain is something distinct from heat, and the consequence or effect of it.

Phil. Upon putting your hand near the fire, do you perceive one simple uniform sensation, or two distinct sensations?

Hyl. But one simple sensation.

Phil. Is not the heat immediately perceived?

Hyl. It is.

Phil. And the pain?

Hyl. True.

Phil. Seeing therefore they are both immediately perceived at the same time, and the fire affects you only with one simple, or uncompounded idea, it follows that this same simple idea is both the intense heat immediately perceived, and the pain; and consequently, that the intense heat immediately perceived, is nothing distinct from a particular sort of pain.

Hyl. It seems so.

[. . .]

Phil. And is not warmth, or a more gentle degree of heat than what causes uneasiness, a pleasure?

Hyl. What then?

Phil. Consequently it cannot exist without the mind in any unperceiving substance, or body.

Hyl. So it seems.

Phil. Since therefore, as well those degrees of heat that are not painful, as those that are, can exist only in a thinking substance; may we not conclude that external bodies are absolutely incapable of any degree of heat whatsoever?

Hyl. On second thoughts, I do not think it so evident that warmth is a pleasure, as that a great degree of heat is a pain.

Phil. I do not pretend that warmth is as great a pleasure as heat is a pain. But if you grant it to be even a small pleasure, it serves to make good my conclusion.

Hyl. I could rather call it an *indolence*. It seems to be nothing more than a privation of both pain and pleasure. And that such a quality or state as this may agree to an unthinking substance, I hope you will not deny.

Phil. If you are resolved to maintain that warmth, or a gentle degree of heat, is no pleasure, I know not how to convince you otherwise than by appealing to your own sense. But what think you of cold?

Hyl. The same that I do of heat. An intense degree of cold is a pain; for to feel a very great cold, is to perceive a great uneasiness: it cannot therefore exist without the mind; but a lesser degree of cold may, as well as a lesser degree of heat.

Phil. Those bodies, therefore, upon whose application to our own, we perceive a moderate degree of heat, must be concluded to have a moderate degree of heat or warmth in them: and those, upon whose application we feel a like degree of cold, must be thought to have cold in them.

Hyl. They must.

Phil. Can any doctrine be true that necessarily leads a man into an absurdity?

Hyl. Without doubt it cannot.

Phil. Is it not an absurdity to think that the same thing should be at the same time both cold and warm?

Hyl. It is.

Phil. Suppose now one of your hands hot, and the other cold, and that they are both at once put into the same vessel of water, in an intermediate state; will not the water seem cold to one hand, and warm to the other?

Hyl. It will.

Phil. Ought we not therefore by your principles to conclude, it is really both cold and warm at the same time, that is, according to your own concession, to believe an absurdity?

Hyl. I confess it seems so.

Phil. Consequently, the principles themselves are false, since you have granted that no true principle leads to an absurdity.

Hyl. But after all, can anything be more absurd than to say, *there is no heat in the fire*?

Phil. To make the point still clearer; tell me, whether in two cases exactly alike, we ought not to make the same judgment?

Hyl. We ought.

Phil. When a pin pricks your finger, does it not rend and divide the fibres of your flesh?

Hyl. It does.

Phil. And when a coal burns your finger, does it any more?

Hyl. It does not.

Phil. Since therefore you neither judge the sensation itself occasioned by the pin, nor anything like it to be in the pin; you should not, conformably to what you have now granted, judge the sensation occasioned by the fire, or anything like it, to be in the fire.

Hyl. Well, since it must be so, I am content to yield this point, and acknowledge, that heat and cold are only sensations existing in our minds: but there still remain qualities enough to secure the reality of external things.

Phil. But what will you say, Hylas, if it shall appear that the case is the same with regard to all other sensible qualities, and that they can no more be supposed to exist without the mind, than heat and cold?

Hyl. Then indeed you will have done something to the purpose; but that is what I despair of seeing proved.

Phil. Let us examine them in order. What think you of tastes, do they exist without the mind, or no?

Hyl. Can any man in his senses doubt whether sugar is sweet, or wormwood bitter?

Phil. Inform me, Hylas. Is a sweet taste a particular kind of pleasure or pleasant sensation, or is it not?

Hyl. It is.

Phil. And is not bitterness some kind of uneasiness or pain?

Hyl. I grant it.

Phil. If therefore sugar and wormwood are unthinking corporeal substances existing without the mind, how can sweetness and bitterness, that is, pleasure and pain, agree to them?

Hyl. Hold, Philonous, I now see what it was deluded me all this time. You asked whether heat and cold, sweetness and bitterness, were not particular sorts of pleasure and pain; to which I answered simply, that they were. Whereas I should have thus distinguished: those qualities, as perceived by us, are pleasures or pains, but not as existing in the external objects. We must not therefore conclude absolutely, that there is no heat in the fire, or sweetness in the sugar, but only that heat or sweetness, as perceived by us, are not in the fire or sugar. What say you to this?

Phil. I say it is nothing to the purpose. Our discourse proceeded altogether concerning sensible things, which you defined to be the things we *immediately perceived by our senses*. Whatever other qualities therefore you speak of, as distinct from these, I know nothing of them, neither do they at all belong to the point in dispute. You may indeed pretend to have discovered certain qualities which you do not perceive, and assert those insensible qualities exist in fire and sugar. But what use can be made of this to your present purpose, I am at a loss to conceive. Tell me then once more, do you acknowledge that heat and cold, sweetness and bitterness, (meaning those qualities which are perceived by the senses) do not exist without the mind?

Hyl. I see it is to no purpose to hold out, so I give up the cause as to those mentioned qualities. Though I profess it sounds oddly, to say that sugar is not sweet.

[. . .]

Phil. Then as to sounds, what must we think of them: are they accidents really inherent in external bodies, or not?

Hyl. That they inhere not in the sonorous bodies, is plain from hence; because a bell struck in the exhausted receiver of an air-pump, sends forth no sound. The air therefore must be thought the subject of sound.

Phil. What reason is there for that, Hylas?

Hyl. Because when any motion is raised in the air, we perceive a sound greater or lesser, to the air's motion; but without some motion in the air, we never hear any sound at all.

Phil. And granting that we never hear a sound but when some motion is produced in the air, yet I do not see how you can infer from thence, that the sound itself is in the air.

Hyl. It is this very motion in the external air, that produces in the mind the sensation of *sound.* For, striking on the drum of the ear, it causes a vibration, which by the auditory nerves being communicated to the brain, the soul is thereupon affected with the sensation called *sound.*

Phil. What! Is sound then a sensation?

Hyl. I tell you, as perceived by us, it is a particular sensation in the mind.

Phil. And can any sensation exist without the mind?

Hyl. No certainly.

Phil. How then can sound, being a sensation, exist in the air, if by the *air* you mean a senseless substance existing without the mind?

Hyl. You must distinguish, Philonous, between sound as it is perceived by us, and as it is in itself; or (which is the same thing) between the sound we immediately perceive and that which exists without us. The former indeed is a particular kind of sensation, but the latter is merely a vibrative or undulatory motion in the air.

Phil. I thought I had already obviated that distinction by the answer I gave when you were applying it in a like case before. But to say no more of that; are you sure then that sound is really nothing but motion?

Hyl. I am.

Phil. Whatever therefore agrees to real sound, may with truth be attributed to motion.

Hyl. It may.

Phil. It is then good sense to speak of *motion,* as of a thing that is *loud, sweet, acute,* or *grave.*

Hyl. I see you are resolved not to understand me. Is it not evident, those accidents or modes belong only to sensible sound, or *sound* in the common acceptation of the word, but not to *sound* in the real and philosophic sense, which, as I just now told you, is nothing but a certain motion of the air?

Phil. It seems then there are two sorts of sound, the one vulgar, or that which is heard, the other philosophical and real.

Hyl. Even so.

Phil. And the latter consists in motion.

Hyl. I told you so before.

Phil. Tell me, Hylas, to which of the senses, think you, the idea of motion belongs: to the hearing?

Hyl. No certainly, but to the sight and touch.

Phil. It should follow then, that according to you, real sounds may possibly be *seen* or *felt,* but never *heard.*

Hyl. Look you, Philonous, you may if you please make a jest of my opinion, but that will not alter the truth of things. I own indeed, the inferences you draw me into, sound something oddly; but common language, you know, is framed by, and for the use of, the vulgar: we must not therefore wonder, if expressions adapted to exact philosophic notions, seem uncouth and out of the way.

Phil. Is it come to that? I assure, you, I imagine myself to have gained no small point, since you make so light of departing from common phrases and opinions; it being a main part of our inquiry, to examine whose notions are widest of the common road, and most repugnant to the general sense of the world. But can you think it no more than a philosophical paradox, to say that *real sounds are never heard*, and that the idea of them is obtained by some other sense. And is there nothing in this contrary to nature and the truth of things?

Hyl. To deal ingenuously, I do not like it. And after the concessions already made, I had as well grant that sounds too have no real being without the mind.

Phil. And I hope you will make no difficulty to acknowledge the same of colors.

Hyl. Pardon me: the case of colors is very different. Can anything be plainer, than that we see them on the objects?

Phil. The objects you speak of are, I suppose, corporeal substances existing without the mind.

Hyl. They are.

Phil. And have true and real colors inhering in therm?

Hyl. Each visible object has that color which we see in it.

Phil. How! Is there anything visible but what we perceive by sight.

Hyl. There is not.

Phil. And do we perceive anything by sense, which we do not perceive immediately?

Hyl. How often must I be obliged to repeat the same think? I tell you, we do not.

Phil. Have patience, good Hylas; and tell me once more, whether there is anything immediately perceived by the senses, except sensible qualities. I know you asserted there was not: but I would now be informed, whether you still persist in the same opinion.

Hyl. I do.

Phil. Pray, is your corporeal substance either a sensible quality, or made up of sensible qualities?

Hyl. What a question that is! Who ever thought it was?

Phil. My reason for asking was, because in saying, *Each visible object has that color which we see in it*, you make visible objects to be corporeal substances; which implies either that corporeal substances are sensible qualities, or else that there is something beside sensible qualities perceived by sight: but as this point was formerly agreed between us, and is still maintained by you, it is a clear consequence, that your corporeal substance is nothing distinct from sensible qualities.

Hyl. You may draw as many absurd consequences as you please, and endeavor to perplex the plainest things; but you shall never persuade me out of my senses. I clearly understand my own meaning.

Phil. I wish you would make me understand it too. But since you are unwilling to have your notion of corporeal substance examined, I shall urge that point no farther. Only be pleased to let me know, whether the same colors which we see, exist in external bodies, or some other.

Hyl. The very same.

Phil. What! Are then the beautiful red and purple we see on yonder clouds, really in them? Or do you imagine they have in themselves any other form, than that of a dark mist or vapor?

Hyl. I must own, Philonous, those colors are not really in the clouds as they seem to be at this distance. They are only apparent colors.

Phil. Apparent call you them? How shall we distinguish these apparent colors from real?

Hyl. Very easily. Those are to be thought apparent, which appearing only at a distance, vanish upon a nearer approach.

Phil. And those I suppose are to be thought real, which are discovered by the most near and exact survey.

Hyl. Right.

Phil. Is the nearest and exactest survey made by the help of a microscope, or by the naked eye?

Hyl. By a microscope, doubtless.

Phil. But a microscope often discovers colors in an object different from those perceived by the unassisted sight. And in case we had microscopes magnifying to any assigned degree; it is certain, that no object whatsoever, viewed through them, would appear in the same color which it exhibits to the naked eye.

Hyl. And what will you conclude from all this? You cannot argue that there are really and naturally no colors on objects: because by artificial managements they may be altered, or made to vanish.

Phil. I think it may evidently be concluded from your own concessions, that all the colors we see with our naked eyes, are only apparent as those on the clouds, since they vanish upon a more close and accurate inspection, which is afforded us by a microscope. Then as to what you say by way of prevention: I ask you, whether the real and natural state of an object is better discovered by a very sharp and piercing sight, or by one which is less sharp?

Hyl. By the former without doubt.

Phil. Is it not plain from *Dioptrics*, that microscopes make the sight more penetrating, and represent objects as they would appear to the eye in case it were naturally endowed with a most exquisite sharpness?

Hyl. It is.

Phil. Consequently the microscopical representation is to be thought that which best sets forth the real nature of the thing, or what it is in itself. The colors, therefore, by it perceived, are more genuine and real, than those perceived otherwise.

Hyl. I confess there is something in what you say.

Phil. Besides, it is not only possible but manifest, that there actually are animals, whose eyes are by nature framed to perceive those things, which by reason of their minuteness escape our sight. What think you of those inconceivably small animals perceived by glasses? Must we suppose they are all stark blind? Or, in case they see, can it be imagined their sight has not the same use in preserving their bodies from injuries, which appears in that of all other animals? And if it hath, is it not evident, they must see particles less than their own bodies, which will present them with a far different view in each object, from that which strikes our senses? Even our own eyes do not always represent objects to us after the same manner. In the *jaundice*, everyone knows that all things seem yellow. Is it not therefore highly probable, those animals in whose eyes we discern a very different texture from that of ours, and whose bodies abound with different humors, do not see the same colors in every object that we do? From all which, should it not seem to follow, that all colors are equally apparent, and that none of those which we perceive are really inherent in any outward object?

[. . .]

Hyl. I frankly own, Philonous, that it is in vain to stand out any longer. Colors, sounds, tastes, in a word, all those termed *secondary qualities*, have certainly no existence without the mind. But by this acknowledgment I must not be supposed to derogate anything from the reality of matter or external objects, seeing it is no more than several philosophers maintain, who nevertheless are the farthest imaginable from denying matter. For the clearer understanding of this, you must know sensible qualities are by philosophers divided into *primary* and *secondary*. The former are extension, figure, solidity, gravity, motion, and rest. And these they hold exist really in bodies. The latter are those above enumerated; or briefly, all sensible qualities beside the primary, which they assert are only so many sensations or ideas existing nowhere but in the mind. But all this, I doubt not, you are already apprised of. For my part, I have been a long time sensible there was such an opinion current among philosophers, but was never thoroughly convinced of its truth till now.

Phil. You are still then of opinion that extension and figures are inherent in external unthinking substances.

Hyl. I am.

Phil. But what if the same arguments which are brought against secondary qualities, will hold good against these also?

Hyl. Why then I shall be obliged to think, they too exist only in the mind.

Phil. Is it your opinion, the very figure and extension which you perceive by sense, exist in the outward object or material substance?

Hyl. It is.

Phil. Have all other animals as good grounds to think the same of the figure and extension which they see and feel?

Hyl. Without doubt, if they have any thought at all.

Phil. Answer me, Hylas. Think you the senses were bestowed upon all animals for their preservation and well-being in life? Or were they given to men alone for this end?

Hyl. I make no question but they have the same use in all other animals.

Phil. If so, is it not necessary they should be enabled by them to perceive their own limbs, and those bodies which are capable of harming them?

Hyl. Certainly.

Phil. A mite therefore must be supposed to see his own foot, and things equal or even less than it, as bodies of some considerable dimension; though at the same time they appear to you scarce discernible, or at best as so many visible points.

Hyl. I cannot deny it.

Phil. And to creatures less than the mite they will seem yet larger.

Hyl. They will.

Phil. Insomuch that what you can hardly discern, will to another extremely minute animal appear as some huge mountain.

Hyl. All this I grant.

Phil. Can one and the same thing be at the same time in itself of different dimensions?

Hyl. That were absurd to imagine.

Phil. But from what you have laid down it follows, that both the extension by you perceived, and that perceived by the mite itself, as likewise all those perceived by lesser animals, are each of them the true extension of the mite's foot; that is to say, by your own principles you are led into an absurdity.

Hyl. There seems to be some difficulty in the point.

Phil. Again, have you not acknowledged that no real inherent property of any object can be changed, without some change in the thing itself?

Hyl. I have.

Phil. But as we approach to or recede from an object, the visible extension varies, being at one distance ten or a hundred times greater than at another. Does it not therefore follow from hence likewise, that it is not really inherent in the object?

Hyl. I own I am at a loss what to think.

Phil. Your judgment will soon be determined, if you will venture to think as freely concerning this quality, as you have done concerning the rest. Was it not admitted as a good argument, that neither heat nor cold was in the water, because it seemed warm to one hand, and cold to the other?

Hyl. It was.

Phil. Is it not the very same reasoning to conclude, there is no extension or figure in an object, because to one eye it shall seem little, smooth, and round, when at the same time it appears to the other, great, uneven, and angular?

Hyl. The very same. But does this latter fact ever happen?

Phil. You may at any time make the experiment, by looking with one eye bare, and with the other through a microscope.

Hyl. I know not how to maintain it, and yet I am loath to give up *extension*, I see so many odd consequences following upon such a concession.

Phil. Odd, say you? After the concessions already made, I hope you will stick at nothing for its oddness. [But on the other hand should it not seem very odd, if the general reasoning which includes all other sensible qualities did not also include extension? If it be allowed that no idea nor anything like an idea can exist in an unperceiving substance, then surely it follows, that no figure or mode of extension, which we can either perceive or imagine, or have any idea of, can be really inherent in matter; not to mention the peculiar difficulty there must be, in conceiving a material substance, prior to and distinct from extension, to be the *substratum* of extension. Be the sensible quality what it will, figure, or sound, or color; it seems alike impossible it should subsist in that which doth not perceive it.]

Hyl. I give up the point for the present, reserving still a right to retract my opinion, in case I shall hereafter discover any false step in my progress to it.

Phil. That is a right you cannot be denied. Figures and extension being dispatched, we proceed next to *motion*. Can a real motion in any external body be at the same time both very swift and very slow?

Hyl. It cannot.

Phil. Is not the motion of a body swift in a reciprocal proportion to the time it takes up in describing any given space? Thus a body that describes a mile in an hour, moves three times faster than it would in case it described only a mile in three hours.

Hyl. I agree with you.

Phil. And is not time measured by the succession of ideas in our minds?

Hyl. It is.

Phil. And is it not possible ideas should succeed one another twice as fast in your mind, as they do in mine, or in that of some spirit of another kind.

Hyl. I own it.

Phil. Consequently the same body may to another seem to perform its motion over any space in half the time that it does to you. And the same reasoning will hold as to any other proportion: that is to say, according to your principles (since the motions perceived are both really in the object) it is possible one and the same body shall be really moved the same way at once, both very swift and very slow. How is this consistent either with common sense, or with what you just now granted?

Hyl. I have nothing to say to it.

Phil. Then as for *solidity*; either you do not mean any sensible quality by that word, and so it is beside our inquiry: or if you do, it must be either hardness or resistance. But both the one and the other are plainly relative to our senses: it being evident, that what seems hard to one animal, may appear soft to another, who hath greater force and firmness of limbs. Nor is it less plain, that the resistance I feel is not in the body.

Hyl. I own the very sensation of resistance, which is all you immediately perceive, is not in the *body*; but the cause of that sensation is.

Phil. But the causes of our sensations are not things immediately perceived, and therefore not sensible. This point I thought had been already determined.

Hyl. I own it was; but you will pardon me if I seem a little embarrassed: I know not how to quit my old notions.

Phil. To help you out, do but consider that if extension be once acknowledged to have no existence without the mind, the same must necessarily be granted of motion, solidity, and gravity, since they all evidently suppose extension. It is therefore superfluous to inquire particularly concerning each of them. In denying extension, you have denied them all to have any real existence.

[. . .]

Hyl. It is just come into my head, Philonous, that I have somewhere heard of a distinction between absolute and sensible extension. Now though it be acknowledged that *great* and *small*, consisting merely in the relation which other extended beings have to the parts of our own bodies, do not really inhere in the substances themselves; yet nothing obliges us to hold the same with regard to *absolute extension*, which is something abstracted from *great* and *small*, from this or that particular magnitude or figure. So likewise as to motion, *swift* and *slow* are altogether relative to the succession of ideas in our own minds. But it does not follow, because those modifications of motion exist not without the mind, that therefore absolute motion abstracted from them does not.

Phil. Pray what is it that distinguishes one motion, or one part of extension, from another? Is it not something sensible, as some degree of swiftness or slowness, some certain magnitude or figure peculiar to each?

Hyl. I think so.

Phil. These qualities, therefore, stripped of all sensible properties, are without all specific and numerical differences, as the schools call them.

Hyl. They are.

Phil. That is to say, they are extension in general, and motion in general.

Hyl. Let it be so.

Phil. But it is a universally received maxim, that *everything which exists, is particular*. How then can motion in general, or extension in general, exist in any corporeal substance?

Hyl. I will take time to solve your difficulty.

Phil. But I think the point may be speedily decided. Without doubt you can tell, whether you are able to frame this or that idea. Now I am content to put our dispute on this issue. If you can frame in your thoughts a distinct abstract idea of motion or extension, divested of all those sensible modes, as swift and slow, great and small, round and square, and the like, which are acknowledged to exist only in the mind, I will then yield the point you contend for. But if you cannot, it will be unreasonable on your side to insist any longer upon what you have no notion of.

Hyl. To confess ingenuously, I cannot.

Phil. Can you even separate the ideas of extension and motion, from the ideas of all those qualities which they who make the distinction, term *secondary*.

Hyl. What! Is it not an easy matter, to consider extension and motion by themselves, abstracted from all other sensible qualities? Pray how do the mathematicians treat of them?

Phil. I acknowledge, Hylas, it is not difficult to form general propositions and reasonings about those qualities, without mentioning any other; and in this sense to consider or treat of them abstractedly. But how does it follow that because I can pronounce the word *motion* by itself, I can form the idea of it in my mind exclusive of body? Or because theorems may be made of extension and figures, without any mention of *great* or *small*, or any other sensible mode or quality; that therefore it is possible such an abstract idea of extension, without any particular [size or figure, or sensible quality], should be distinctly formed, and apprehended by the mind? Mathematicians treat of quantity, without regarding what other sensible qualities it is attended with, as being altogether indifferent to their demonstrations. But when laying aside the words, they contemplate the bare ideas, I believe you will find, they are not the pure abstracted ideas of extension.

Hyl. But what say you to *pure intellect?* May not abstracted ideas be framed by that faculty?

Phil. Since I cannot frame abstract ideas at all, it is plain, I cannot frame them by the help of *pure intellect*, whatsoever faculty you understand by those words. Besides, not to inquire into the nature of pure intellect and its spiritual objects, as *virtue, reason, God*, or the like; thus much seems manifest, that sensible things are only to be perceived by sense, or represented by the imagination. Figures, therefore, and extension, being originally perceived by sense, do not belong to pure intellect. But for your farther satisfaction, try if you can frame the idea of any figure, abstracted from all particularities of size, or even from other sensible qualities.

Hyl. Let me think a little – I do not find that I can.

Phil. And can you think it possible, that should really exist in nature, which implies a repugnancy in its conception?

Hyl. By no means.

Phil. Since therefore it is impossible even for the mind to disunite the ideas of extension and motion from all other sensible qualities, does it not follow, that where the one exist, there necessarily the other exist likewise?

Hyl. It should seem so.

Phil. Consequently the very same arguments which you admitted, as conclusive against the secondary qualities, are, without any farther application of force, against the primary too.

[. . .]

Hyl. [. . .] But still I fear there is some fallacy or other. Pray what think you of this? It is just come into my head, that the ground of all our mistake lies in your treating of each quality by itself. Now, I grant that each quality cannot singly subsist without the mind. Color cannot without extension, neither can figure without some other sensible quality. But as the several qualities united or blended together form entire sensible things, nothing hinders why such things may not be supposed to exist without the mind.

Phil. Either, Hylas, you are jesting, or have a very bad memory. Though indeed we went through all the qualities by name one after another; yet my arguments, or rather your concessions, nowhere tended to prove, that the secondary qualities did not subsist each alone by itself; but that they were not *at all* without the mind. Indeed in treating of figure and motion, we concluded they could not exist without the mind, because it was impossible even in thought to separate them from all secondary qualities, so as to conceive them existing by themselves. But then this was not the only argument made use of upon that occasion. But (to pass by all that hath been hitherto said, and reckon it for nothing, if you will have it so) I am content to put the whole upon this issue. If you can conceive it possible for any mixture or combination of qualities, or any sensible object whatever, to exist without the mind, then I will grant it actually to be so.

Hyl. If it comes to that, the point will soon be decided. What more easy than to conceive a tree or house existing by itself, independent of, and unperceived by, any mind whatsoever? I do at this present time conceive them existing after that manner.

Phil. How say you, Hylas, can you see a thing which is at the same time unseen?

Hyl. No, that were a contradiction.

Phil. Is it not as great a contradiction to talk of *conceiving* a thing which is *unconceived*?

Hyl. It is.

Phil. The tree or house therefore which you think of, is conceived by you.

Hyl. How should it be otherwise?

Phil. And what is conceived is surely in the mind.

Hyl. Without question, that which is conceived is in the mind.

Phil. How then came you to say, you conceived a house or tree existing independent and out of all minds whatsoever?

Hyl. That was I own an oversight; but stay, let me consider what led me into it. – It is a pleasant mistake enough. As I was thinking of a tree in a solitary place, where no one was present to see it, methought that was to conceive a tree as existing unperceived or unthought of, not considering that I myself conceived it all the while. But now I plainly see, that all I can do is to frame ideas in my own mind. I may indeed conceive in my own thoughts the idea of a tree, or a house, or a mountain, but that is all. And this is far from proving, that I can conceive them *existing out of the minds of all spirits*.

Phil. You acknowledge then that you cannot possibly conceive, how any one corporeal sensible thing should exist otherwise than in a mind.

Hyl. I do.

[. . .]

The Second Dialogue

Hyl. I beg your pardon, Philonous, for not meeting you sooner. All this morning my head was so filled with our late conversation, that I had not leisure to think of the time of the day, or indeed of anything else.

Phil. I am glad you were so intent upon it, in hopes if there were any mistakes in your concessions, or fallacies in my reasonings from them, you will now discover them to me.

Hyl. I assure you, I have done nothing ever since I saw you, but search after mistakes and fallacies, and with that view have minutely examined the whole series of yesterday's discourse: but all in vain, for the notions it led me into, upon review, appear still more clear and evident; and the more I consider them, the more irresistibly do they force my assent.

[. . .]

Phil. Look! Are not the fields covered with a delightful verdure? Is there not something in the woods and groves, in the rivers and clear springs, that soothes, that delights, that transports the soul? At the prospect of the wide and deep ocean, or some huge mountain whose top is lost in the clouds, or of an old gloomy forest, are not our minds filled with a pleasing horror? Even in rocks and deserts, is there not an agreeable wildness? How sincere a pleasure is it to behold the natural beauties of the earth!

[. . .]

What treatment then do those philosophers deserve, who would deprive these noble and delightful scenes of all reality? How should those principles be entertained, that lead us to think all the visible beauty of the creation a false imaginary glare? To be plain, can you expect this scepticism of yours will not be thought extravagantly absurd by all men of sense?

Hyl. Other men may think as they please: but for your part you have nothing to reproach me with. My comfort is, you are as much a *sceptic* as I am.

Phil. There, Hylas, I must beg leave to differ from you.

Hyl. What! Have you all along agreed to the premises, and do you now deny the conclusion, and leave me to maintain those paradoxes by myself which you led me into? This surely is not fair.

Phil. I deny that I agreed with you in those notions that led to scepticism. You indeed said, the reality of sensible things consisted in an *absolute existence* out of the minds of spirits, or distinct from their being perceived. And pursuant to this notion of reality, you are obliged to deny sensible things any real existence: that is, according to your own definition, you profess yourself a *sceptic*. But I neither said nor thought the reality of sensible things was to be defined after that manner. To me it is evident, for the reasons you allow of, that sensible things cannot exist otherwise than in a mind or spirit. Whence I conclude, not that they have no real existence, but that seeing they depend not on my thought, and have an existence distinct from being perceived by me, *there must be some other mind wherein they exist.* As sure therefore as the sensible world really exists, so sure is there an infinite omnipresent spirit who contains and supports it.

Hyl. What! This is no more than I and all Christians hold; nay, and all others too who believe there is a God, and that he knows and comprehends all things.

Phil. Aye, but here lies the difference. Men commonly believe that all things are known or perceived by God, because they believe the being of a God, whereas I, on the other side, immediately and necessarily conclude the being of a God, because all sensible things must be perceived by him.

Hyl. But so long as we all believe the same thing, what matter is it how we come by that belief?

Phil. But neither do we agree in the same opinion. For philosophers, though they acknowledge all corporeal beings to be perceived by God, yet they attribute to them an absolute subsistence distinct from their being perceived by any mind whatever, which I do not. Besides, is there no difference between saying, *There is a God, therefore he perceives all things*: and saying, *Sensible things do really exist: and if they really exist, they are necessarily perceived by an infinite mind: therefore there is an infinite mind, or God.* This furnishes you with a direct and immediate demonstration, from a most evident principle, of the *being of a God.* Divines and philosophers had proved beyond all controversy, from the beauty and usefulness of the several parts of the creations that it was the workmanship of God. But that setting aside all help of astronomy and natural philosophy, all contemplation of the contrivance, order, and adjustment of things, an infinite mind should be necessarily inferred from the bare existence of the sensible world, is an advantage peculiar to them only who have made this easy reflection: that the sensible world is that which we perceive by our several senses; and that nothing is perceived by the senses beside ideas; and that no idea or archetype of an idea can exist otherwise than in a mind.

[. . .]

Hyl. I think I understand you very clearly; and own the proof you give of a deity seems no less evident, than it is surprising. But allowing that God is the supreme and universal cause of all things, yet may not there be still a third nature besides spirits and ideas? May we not admit a subordinate and limited cause of our ideas? In a word, may there not for all that be *matter*?

Phil. How often must I inculcate the same thing? You allow the things immediately perceived by sense to exist nowhere without the mind: but there is nothing perceived by sense, which is not perceived immediately: therefore there is nothing sensible that exists without the mind. The matter therefore which you still insist on, is something intelligible, I suppose; something that may be discovered by reason, and not by sense.

Hyl. You are in the right.

Phil. Pray let me know what reasoning your belief of matter is grounded on; and what this matter is in your present sense of it.

Hyl. I find myself affected with various ideas, whereof I know I am not the cause; neither are they the cause of themselves, or of one another, or capable of subsisting by themselves, as being altogether inactive, fleeting, dependent beings. They have therefore some cause distinct from me and them: of which I pretend to know no more, than that it is *the cause of my ideas*. And this thing, whatever it be, I call matter.

Phil. Tell me, Hylas, has every one a liberty to change the current proper signification annexed to a common name in any language? For example, suppose a traveller should tell you, that in a certain country men might pass unhurt through the fire; and, upon explaining himself, you found he meant by the word *fire* that which others call *water*: or if he should assert there are trees which walk upon two legs, meaning men by the term *trees*. Would you think this reasonable?

Hyl. No; I should think it very absurd. Common custom is the standard of propriety in language. And for any man to affect speaking improperly, is to pervert the use of speech, and can never serve to a better purpose, than to protract and multiply disputes where there is no difference in opinion.

Phil. And does not *matter*, in the common current acceptation of the word, signify an extended, solid, moveable, unthinking, inactive substance?

Hyl. It does.

Phil. And, has it not been made evident, that no such substance can possibly exist? And though it should be allowed to exist, yet how can that which is *inactive* be a *cause*; or that which is *unthinking* be a *cause of thought*? You may indeed, if you please, annex to the word *matter* a contrary meaning to what is vulgarly received; and tell me you understand by it an unextended, thinking, active being, which is the cause of our ideas. But what else is this, than to play with words, and run into that very fault you just now condemned with so much reason? I do by no means find fault with your reasoning, in that you collect a cause from the *phenomena*: but I deny that the cause deducible by reason can properly be termed matter.

Hyl. There is indeed something in what you say. But I am afraid you do not thoroughly comprehend my meaning. I would by no means be thought to deny that God or an infinite spirit is the supreme cause of all things. All I contend for, is, that subordinate to the supreme agent there is a cause of a limited and inferior nature, which concurs in the production of our ideas, not by any act of will or spiritual efficiency, but by that kind of action which belongs to matter, *viz. motion.*

Phil. I find, you are at every turn relapsing into your old exploded conceit, of a moveable and consequently an extended substance existing without the mind. What! Have you already forgot you were convinced, or are you willing I should repeat what has been said on that head? In truth this is not fair dealing in you, still to suppose the being of that which you have so often acknowledged to have no being. But not to insist farther on what has been so largely handled, I ask whether all your ideas are not perfectly passive and inert, including nothing of action in them?

Hyl. They are.

Phil. And are sensible qualities anything else but ideas?

Hyl. How often have I acknowledged that they are not?

Phil. But is not motion a sensible quality?

Hyl. It is.

Phil. Consequently it is no action.

Hyl. I agree with you. And indeed it is very plain, that when I stir my finger, it remains passive; but my will which produced the motion, is active.

Phil. Now I desire to know in the first place, whether motion being allowed to be no action, you can conceive any action besides volition: and in the second place, whether to say something and conceive nothing be not to talk nonsense: and lastly, whether having considered the premises, you do not perceive that to suppose any efficient or active cause of our ideas, other than *spirit*, is highly absurd and unreasonable?

Hyl. I give up the point entirely. But though matter may not be a cause, yet what hinders its being an *instrument* subservient to the supreme agent in the production of our ideas?

Phil. An instrument, say you; pray what may be the figure, springs, wheels, and motions of that instrument?

Hyl. Those I pretend to determine nothing of, both the substance and its qualities being entirely unknown to me.

Phil. What? You are then of opinion, it is made up of unknown parts, that it bath unknown motions, and an unknown shape.

Hyl. I do not believe that it hath any figure or motion at all, being already convinced, that no sensible qualities can exist in an unperceiving substance.

Phil. But what notion is it possible to frame of an instrument void of all sensible qualities, even extension itself?

Hyl. I do not pretend to have any notion of it.

Phil. And what reason have you to think, this unknown, this inconceivable Somewhat does exist? Is it that you imagine God cannot act as well as without it, or that you find by experience the use of some such thing, when you form ideas in your own mind?

Hyl. You are always teasing me for reasons of my belief. Pray what reasons have you not to believe it?

Phil. It is to me a sufficient reason not to believe the existence of anything, if I see no reason for believing it. But not to insist on reasons for believing, you will not so much as let me know what it is you would have me believe, since you say you have no manner of notion of it. After all, let me entreat you to consider whether it be like a philosopher, or even like a man of common sense, to pretend to believe you know not what, and you know not why.

Hyl. Hold, Philonous. When I tell you matter is an *instrument*, I do not mean altogether nothing. It is true, I know not the particular kind of instrument; but however I have some notion of *instrument in general*, which I apply to it.

Phil. But what if it should prove that there is something, even in the most general notion of *instrument*, as taken in a distinct sense from *cause*, which makes the use of it inconsistent with the divine attributes?

Hyl. Make that appear, and I shall give up the point.

Phil. What mean you by the general nature or notion of *instrument*?

Hyl. That which is common to all particular instruments composeth the general notion.

Phil. Is it not comon to all instruments, that they are applied to the doing those things only, which cannot be performed by the mere act of our wills? Thus for instance, I never use an instrument to move my finger, because it is done by a volition. But I should use one, if I were to remove part of a rock, or tear up a tree by the roots. Are you of the same mind? Or can you show any example where an instrument is made use of in producing an effect immediately depending on the will of the agent?

Hyl. I own, I cannot.

Phil. How therefore can you suppose, that an all-perfect spirit, on whose will all things have an absolute and immediate dependence, should need an instrument in his operations, or not needing it make use of it? Thus it seems to me that you are obliged to own the use of a lifeless inactive instrument, to be incompatible with the infinite perfection of God; that is, by your own confession, to give up the point.

Hyl. It does not readily occur what I can answer you.

[...]

The Third Dialogue

Phil. Tell me, Hylas, what are the fruits of yesterday's meditation? Has it confirmed you in the same mind you were in at parting? Or have you since seen cause to change your opinion?

Hyl. Truly my opinion is, that all our opinions are alike vain and uncertain. What we approve to-day, we condemn tomorrow. We keep a stir about knowledge, and spend our lives in the pursuit of it, when, alas! we know nothing all the while: nor do I think it possible for us ever to know anything in this life. Our faculties are too narrow and too few. Nature certainly never intended us for speculation.

Phil. What! Say you we can know nothing, Hylas?

Hyl. There is not that single thing in the world, whereof we can know the real nature, or what it is in itself.

Phil. Will you tell me I do not really know what fire or water is?

Hyl. You may indeed know that fire appears hot, and water fluid: but this is no more than knowing what sensations are produced in your own mind, upon the application of fire and water to your organs of sense. Their internal constitution, their true and real nature, you are utterly in the dark as to *that*.

[. . .]

Phil. But are you all this while in earnest, Hylas; and are you seriously persuaded that you know nothing real in the world? Suppose you are going to write, would you not call for pen, ink, and paper, like another man; and do you not know what it is you call for?

Hyl. How often must I tell you, that I know not the real nature of any one thing in the universe? I may indeed upon occasion make use of pen, ink, and paper. But what any one of them is in its own true nature, I declare positively I know not. And the same is true with regard to every other corporeal thing. And, what is more, we are not only ignorant of the true and real nature of things, but even of their existence. It cannot be denied that we perceive such certain appearances or ideas; but it cannot be concluded from thence that bodies really exist. Nay, now I think on it, I must agreeably to my former concessions farther declare, that it is impossible any real corporeal thing should exist in nature.

Phil. You amaze me. Was ever anything more wild and extravagant than the notions you now maintain: and is it not evident you are led into all these extravagancies by the belief of *material substance*? This makes you dream of those unknown natures in everything. It is this occasions your distinguishing between the reality and sensible appearances of things. It is to this you are indebted for being ignorant of what everybody else knows perfectly well. Nor is this all: you are not only ignorant of the true nature of everything, but you know not whether anything really exists, or whether there are any true natures at all; forasmuch as you attribute to your material beings an absolute or external existence, wherein you suppose their reality consists. And as you are forced in the end to acknowledge such an existence means either a direct repugnancy, or nothing at all, it follows that you are obliged to pull down your own hypothesis of material substance, and positively to deny the real existence of any part of the universe. And so you are plunged into the deepest and most deplorable *scepticism* that ever man was. Tell me, Hylas, is it not as I say?

Hyl. I agree with you. *Material substance* was no more than an hypothesis, and a false and groundless one too. I will no longer spend my breath in defence of it. But whatever hypothesis you advance, or whatsoever scheme of things you introduce in its stead, I doubt not it will appear every whit as false: let me but be allowed to question you upon it. That is, suffer me to serve you in your own kind, and I warrant it shall conduct you through as many perplexities and contradictions, to the very same state of scepticism that I myself am in at present.

Phil. I assure you, Hylas, I do not pretend to frame any hypothesis at all. I am of a vulgar cast, simple enough to believe my senses, and leave things as I find them. To be plain, it is my opinion, that the real things are those very things I see and feel, and perceive by my senses. These I know, and finding they answer all the necessities and purposes of life, have no reason to be solicitous about any other unknown beings. A piece of sensible bread, for instance, would stay my stomach better than ten thousand times as much of that insensible, unintelligible, real bread you speak of. It is likewise my opinion, that colors and other sensible qualities are on the objects. I cannot for my life help thinking that snow is white, and fire hot. You indeed, who by *snow* and *fire* mean certain external, unperceived, unperceiving substances, are in the right to deny whiteness or heat to be affections inherent in them. But I, who understand by those words the things I see and feel, am obliged to think like other folks. And as I am no sceptic with regard to the nature of things, so neither am I as to their existence. That a thing should be really perceived by my senses, and at the same time not really exist, is to me a plain contradiction; since I cannot prescind or abstract, even in thought, the existence of a sensible thing from its being perceived. Wood, stones, fire, water, flesh, iron, and the like things, which I name and discourse of, are things that I know; [otherwise I should never have thought of them, or named them]. And I should not have known them, but that I perceived them by my senses; and things perceived by the senses are immediately perceived; and things immediately perceived are ideas; and ideas cannot exist without the mind; their existence therefore consists in being perceived; when therefore they are actually perceived, there can be no doubt of their existence. Away then with all that scepticism, all those ridiculous philosophical doubts. What a jest is it for a philosopher to question the existence of sensible things, till he has it proved to him from the veracity of God: or to pretend our knowledge in this point falls short of intuition or demonstration? I might as well doubt of my own being, as of the being of those things I actually see and feel.

Hyl. Not so fast, Philonous: you say you cannot conceive how sensible things should exist without the mind. Do you not?

Phil. I do.

Hyl. Supposing you were annihilated, cannot you conceive it possible, that things perceivable by sense may still exist?

Phil. I can; but then it must be in another mind. When I deny sensible things an existence out of the mind, I do not mean my mind in particular, but all minds. Now it is plain they have an existence exterior to my mind, since I find them by experience to be independent of it. There is therefore some other mind wherein they exist, during the intervals between the times of my perceiving them: as likewise they did before my birth, and would do after my supposed annihilation. And as the same is true, with regard to all other finite created spirits; it necessarily follows, there is an *omnipresent eternal mind*, which knows and comprehends all things, and exhibits them to our view in such a manner, and according to such rules as he himself has ordained, and are by us termed the *laws of nature*.

Hyl. Answer me, Philonous. Are all our ideas perfectly inert beings? Or have they any agency included in them?

Phil. They are altogether passive and inert.

Hyl. And is not God an agent, a being purely active?

Phil. I acknowledge it.

Hyl. No idea therefore can be like unto, or represent the nature of God.

Phil. It cannot.

Hyl. Since therefore you have no idea of the mind of God, how can you conceive it possible, that things should exist in his mind? Or, if you can conceive the mind of God without having an idea of it, why may not I be allowed to conceive the existence of matter, notwithstanding that I have no idea of it?

Phil. As to your first question; I own I have properly no idea, either of God or any other spirit; for these being active, cannot be represented by things perfectly inert, as our ideas are. I do nevertheless know, that I, who am a spirit or thinking substance, exist as certainly, as I know my ideas exist. Farther, I know what I mean by the terms *I* and *myself*; and I know this immediately, or intuitively, though I do not perceive it as I perceive a triangle, a color, or a sound. The mind, spirit, or soul, is that indivisible unextended thing, which thinks, acts, and perceives. I say *indivisible*, because unextended; and *unextended*, because extended, figured, moveable things, are ideas; and that which perceives ideas, which thinks and wills, is plainly itself no idea, nor like an idea. Ideas are things inactive, and perceived: and spirits a sort of beings altogether different from them. I do not therefore say my soul is an idea, or like an idea. However, taking the word *idea* in a large sense, my soul may be said to furnish me with an idea, that is, an image, or likeness of God, though indeed extremely inadequate. For all the notion I have of God, is obtained by reflecting on my own soul, heightening its powers, and removing its imperfections. I have therefore, though not an inactive idea, yet in myself some sort of an active thinking image of the Deity. And though I perceive him not by sense, yet I have a notion of him, or know him by reflection and reasoning. My own mind and my own ideas I have an immediate knowledge of; and by the help of these, do mediately apprehend the possibility of the existence of other spirits and ideas. Farther, from my own being, and from the dependency I find in myself and my ideas, I do, by an act of reason, necessarily infer the existence of a God, and of all created things in the mind of God. So much for your first question. For the second: I suppose by this time you can answer it yourself. For you neither perceive matter objectively, as you do an inactive being or idea, nor know it, as you do yourself, by a reflex act: neither do you mediately apprehend it by similitude of the one or the other: nor yet collect it by reasoning from that which you know immediately. All which makes the case of *matter* widely different from that of the *Deity*.

[. . .]

Hyl. I own myself satisfied in this point. But do you in earnest think, the real existence of sensible things consists in their being actually perceived? If so; how comes it that all mankind distinguish between them? Ask the first man you meet, and he shall tell you, *to be perceived* is one thing, and *to exist* is another.

Phil. I am content, Hylas, to appeal to the common sense of the world for the truth of my notion. Ask the gardener, why he thinks yonder cherry tree exists in the garden, and he shall tell you, because he sees and feels it; in a word, because he perceives it by his senses. Ask him why he thinks an orange tree not to be there, and he shall tell you, because he does not perceive it. What he perceives by sense, that he terms a real being, and saith it *is*, or *exists*; but that which is not perceivable, the same, he saith, has no being.

Hyl. Yes, Philonous, I grant the existence of a sensible thing consists in being perceivable, but not in being actually perceived.

Phil. And what is perceivable but an idea? And can an idea exist without being actually perceived? These are points long since agreed between us.

Hyl. But be your opinion never so true, yet surely you will not deny it is shocking, and contrary to the common sense of men. Ask the fellow, whether yonder tree has an existence out of his mind: what answer think you he would make?

Phil. The same that I should myself, to wit, that it does exist out of his mind. But then to a Christian it cannot surely be shocking to say, the real tree existing without his mind is truly known and comprehended by (that is, *exists in*) the infinite mind of God. Probably he may not at first glance be aware of the direct and immediate proof there is of this, inasmuch as the very being of a tree, or any other sensible thing, implies a mind wherein it is. But the point itself he cannot deny. The question between the materialists and me is not, whether things have a real existence out of the mind of this or that person, but whether they have an absolute existence, distinct from being perceived by God, and exterior to all minds. This indeed some heathens and philosophers have affirmed, but whoever entertains notions of the Deity suitable to the Holy Scriptures, will be of another opinion.

Hyl. But according to your notions, what difference is there between real things, and chimeras formed by the imagination, or the visions of a dream, since they are all equally in the mind?

Phil. The ideas formed by the imagination are faint and indistinct; they have, besides, an entire dependence on the will. But the ideas perceived by sense, that is, real things, are more vivid and clear, and being imprinted on the mind by a spirit distinct from us, have not a like dependence on our will. There is therefore no danger of confounding these with the foregoing: and there is as little of confounding them with the visions of a dream, which are dim, irregular, and confused. And though they should happen to be never so lively and natural, yet by their not being connected, and of a piece with the preceding and subsequent transactions of our lives, they might easily be distinguished from realities. In short, by whatever method you distinguish *things* from *chimeras* on your own scheme, the same, it is evident, will hold also upon mine. For it must be, I presume, by some perceived difference, and I am not for depriving you of any one thing that you perceive.

Hyl. But still, Philonous, you hold, there is nothing in the world but spirits and ideas. And this, you must needs acknowledge, sounds very oddly.

Phil. I own the word *idea*, not being commonly used for *thing*, sounds something out of the way. My reason for using it was, because a necessary relation to the mind is understood to be implied by that term; and it is now commonly used by philosophers, to denote the immediate objects of the understanding. But however oddly the proposition may sound in words, yet it includes nothing so very strange or shocking in its sense, which in effect amounts to no more than this, to wit, that there are only things perceiving, and things perceived; or that every unthinking being is necessarily, and from the very nature of its existence, perceived by some mind; if not by any finite created mind, yet certainly by the infinite mind of God, in whom *we live, and move, and have our being*. Is this as strange as to say, the sensible qualities are not on the objects: or, that we cannot be sure of the existence of things, or know anything of their real natures, though we both see and feel them, and perceive them by all our senses?

Hyl. And in consequence of this, must we not think there are no such things as physical or corporeal causes; but that a spirit is the immediate cause of all the *phenomena* in nature? Can there be anything more extravagant than this?

Phil. Yes, it is infinitely more extravagant to say, a thing which is inert, operates on the mind, and which is unperceiving, is the cause of our perceptions, [without any regard either to consistency, or the old known axiom: *Nothing can give to another that which it hath not itself*]. Besides, that which to you, I know not for what reason, seems so extravagant, is no more than the Holy Scriptures assert in a hundred places. In them God is represented as the sole and immediate author of all those effects, which some heathens and philosophers are wont to ascribe to nature, matter, fate, or the like unthinking principle. This is so much the constant language of Scripture, that it were needless to confirm it by citations.

Hyl. You are not aware, Philonous, that in making God the immediate author of all the motions in nature, you make him the author of murder, sacrilege, adultery, and the like heinous sins.

Phil. In answer to that, I observe first, that the imputation of guilt is the same, whether a person commits an action with or without an instrument. In case therefore you suppose God to act by the mediation of an instrument, or occasion, called *matter*, you as truly make him the author of sin as I, who think him the immediate agent in all those operations vulgarly ascribed to nature. I farther observe, that sin or moral turpitude does not consist in the outward physical action or motion, but in the internal deviation of the will from the laws of reason and religion. This is plain, in that the killing an enemy in a battle, or putting a criminal legally to death, is not thought sinful, though the outward act be the very same with that in the case of murder. Since therefore sin does not consist in the physical action, the making God an immediate cause of all such actions, is not making him the author of sin. Lastly, I have nowhere said that God is the only agent who produces all the motions in bodies. It is true, I have denied there are any other agents beside spirits: but this is very consistent with allowing to thinking rational beings, in the production of motions, the use of limited powers, ultimately indeed derived from God, but immediately under the direction of their own wills, which is sufficient to entitle them to all the guilt of their actions.

Hyl. But the denying matter, Philonous, or corporeal substance; there is the point. You can never persuade me that this is not repugnant to the universal sense of mankind. Were our dispute to be determined by most voices, I am confident you would give up the point, without gathering the votes.

Phil. I wish both our opinions were fairly stated and submitted to the judgment of men who had plain common sense, without the prejudices of a learned education. Let me be represented as one who trusts his senses, who thinks he knows the things he sees and feels, and entertains no doubts of their existence; and you fairly set forth with all your doubts, your paradoxes, and your scepticism about you, and I shall willingly acquiesce in the determination of any indifferent person. That there is no substance wherein ideas can exist beside spirit, is to me evident. And that the objects immediately perceived are ideas, is on all hands agreed. And that sensible qualities are objects immediately perceived, no one can deny. It is therefore evident there can be no *substratum* of those qualities but spirit, in which they exist, not by way of mode or property, but as a thing perceived in that which perceives it. I deny therefore that there is any unthinking *substratum* of the objects of sense, and in that acceptation that there is any material substance. But if by *material substance* is meant only sensible body, that which is seen and felt, (and the unphilosophical part of the world, I dare say, mean no more) then I am more certain of matter's existence than you, or any other philosopher, pretend to be. If there be anything which makes the generality of mankind averse from the notions I espouse, it is a misapprehension that I deny the reality of sensible things: but as it is you who are guilty of that and not I, it follows that in truth their aversion is against your notions, and not mine. I do therefore assert that I am as certain as of my own being, that there are bodies or corporeal substances, (meaning the things I perceive by my senses) and that granting this, the bulk of mankind will take no thought about, nor think themselves at all concerned in the fate of those unknown natures, and philosophical quiddities, which some men are so fond of.

David Hume, *An Enquiry concerning Human Understanding* (1748)

Hume's *Enquiry* re-presents some of the ideas introduced in his *A Treatise of Human Nature* (1739). The reception of the *Treatise* disappointed Hume, and he decided to make his ideas more accessible to a wider audience. He started the *Enquiry* with a distinction among mental contents called "perceptions." Impressions are the forceful and lively experiences we have, and ideas are less lively and less vivid perceptions, usually faded copies of impressions. Hume here is talking about the difference between, say, the feeling of being cut by a knife, and just imagining being cut, or remembering. The key principle of Hume's theory of knowledge is that all meaningful ideas must be traced to preceding impressions. If we have an idea that is not a copy of an impression, we cannot possibly understand it, since it did not originate in an experience of ours.

Hume's most famous contribution from the *Enquiry* is his analysis of the idea of causation (see also the general introduction to this volume). He first shows us that every belief about a fact in the world is based on a causal connection the believer makes. If I believe that snow is cold, I have connected the stuff I call "snow" with a quality it causes – coldness. If I believe that my mother will answer the phone when I call her number, it is because I causally connect the dialing of her number with her phone's ringing, and I causally connect her phone's ringing with her voice on my receiver. Hume then shows that all causal connections employ an idea that cannot be traced to a preceding impression. The difference between a mere correlation between two events and a real causal connection lies in our thinking that the two events are *necessarily* connected, and our thinking that the two are necessarily connected simply means we think that the second will *always* occur when we experience the first. However, Hume asks, to what impression is the idea of necessary connection traced? He argues that we can find no such impression; we only find one event followed by another, a sequence that happens over and over again, to the point that we *expect* the one to follow upon the other. The idea of necessity, Hume maintains, is not founded in experience, but something we imagine is there, due to a habit of association of events. Hume's remarkable conclusion is that every belief in a matter of fact is based on an idea we cannot understand.

Hume was born in Scotland in 1711. His family expected him to be a lawyer, but he wrote that the study of law made him nauseous. Despite the fact that he was a very amiable man, Hume's purported skeptical views and anti-religiosity were deemed too intellectually dangerous to allow him a university position. He held respected appointments, including Secretary to the British embassy in Paris, but is best known as a historian, and as the most influential empiricist in the history of philosophy. Hume died in 1776.

Section 2
Of the Origin of Ideas

Every one will readily allow, that there is a considerable difference between the perceptions of the mind, when a man feels the pain of excessive heat, or the pleasure of moderate warmth, and when he afterwards recalls to his memory this sensation, or anticipates it by his imagination. These faculties may mimic or copy the perceptions of the senses; but they never can entirely reach the force and vivacity of the original sentiment. The utmost we say of them, even when they operate with greatest vigour, is, that they represent their object in so lively a manner, that we could *almost* say we feel or see it: But, except the mind be disordered by disease or madness, they never can arrive at such a pitch of vivacity, as to render these perceptions altogether undistinguishable. All the colours of poetry, however splendid, can never paint natural objects in such a manner as to make the description be taken for a real landscape. The most lively thought is still inferior to the dullest sensation.

We may observe a like distinction to run through all the other perceptions of the mind. A man, in a fit of anger, is actuated in a very different manner from one who only thinks of that emotion. If you tell me, that any person is in love, I easily understand your meaning, and form a just conception of his situation; but never can mistake that conception for the real disorders and agitations of the passion. When we reflect on our past sentiments and affections, our thought is a faithful mirror, and copies its objects truly; but the colours which it employs are faint and dull, in comparison of those in which our original perceptions were clothed. It requires no nice discernment or metaphysical head to mark the distinction between them.

Here therefore we may divide all the perceptions of the mind into two classes or species, which are distinguished by their different degrees of force and vivacity. The less forcible and lively are commonly denominated THOUGHTS or IDEAS. The other species want a name in our language, and in most others; I suppose, because it was not requisite for any, but philosophical purposes, to rank them under a general term or appellation. Let us, therefore, use a little freedom, and call them IMPRESSIONS; employing that word in a sense somewhat different from the usual. By the term *impression*, then, I mean all our more lively perceptions, when we hear, or see, or feel, or love, or hate, or desire, or will. And impressions are distinguished from ideas, which are the less lively perceptions, of which we are conscious, when we reflect on any of those sensations or movements above-mentioned.

Nothing, at first view, may seem more unbounded than the thought of man, which not only escapes all human power and authority, but is not even restrained within the limits of nature and reality. To form monsters, and join incongruous shapes and appearances, costs the imagination no more trouble than to conceive the most natural and familiar objects. And while the body is confined to one planet, along which it creeps with pain and difficulty; the thought can in an instant transport us into the most distant regions of the universe; or even beyond the universe, into the unbounded chaos, where nature is supposed to lie in total confusion. What never was seen, or heard of, may yet be conceived; nor is any thing beyond the power of thought, except what implies an absolute contradiction.

But though our thought seems to possess this unbounded liberty, we shall find, upon a nearer examination, that it is really confined within very narrow limits, and that all this creative power of the mind amounts to no more than the faculty of compounding, transposing, augmenting, or diminishing the materials afforded us by the senses and experience. When we think of a golden mountain, we only join two consistent ideas, *gold*, and *mountain*, with which we were formerly acquainted. A virtuous horse we can conceive; because, from our own feeling, we can conceive virtue; and this we may unite to the figure and shape of a horse, which is an animal familiar to us. In short, all the materials of thinking are derived either from our outward or inward sentiment: The mixture and composition of these belongs alone to the mind and will. Or, to express myself in philosophical language, all our ideas or more feeble perceptions are copies of our impressions or more lively ones.

To prove this, the two following arguments will, I hope, be sufficient. *First*, When we analyze our thoughts or ideas, however compounded or sublime, we always find, that they resolve themselves into such simple ideas as were copied from a precedent feeling or sentiment. Even those ideas, which, at first view, seem the most wide of this origin, are found, upon a nearer scrutiny, to be derived from it. The idea of God, as meaning *an infinitely intelligent, wise, and good Being*, arises from reflecting on the operations of our own mind, and augmenting, without limit, those qualities of goodness and wisdom. We may prosecute this enquiry to what length we please; where we shall always find, that every idea which we examine is copied from a similar impression. Those who would assert, that this position is not universally true nor without exception, have only one, and that an easy method of refuting it; by producing that idea, which, in their opinion, is not derived from this source. It will then be incumbent on us, if we would maintain our doctrine, to produce the impression or lively perception, which corresponds to it.

Secondly, If it happen, from a defect of the organ, that a man is not susceptible of any species of sensation, we always find, that he is as little susceptible of the correspondent ideas. A blind man can form no notion of colours; a deaf man of sounds. Restore either of them that sense, in which he is deficient; by opening this new inlet for his sensations, you also open an inlet for the ideas; and he finds no difficulty in conceiving these objects. The case is the same, if the object, proper for exciting any sensation, has never been applied to the organ. A Laplander or Negroe has no notion of the relish of wine. And though there are few or no instances of a like deficiency in the mind, where a person has never felt or is wholly incapable of a sentiment or passion, that belongs to his species; yet we find the same observation to take place in a less degree. A man of mild manners can form no idea of inveterate revenge or cruelty; nor can a selfish heart easily conceive the heights of friendship and generosity. It is readily allowed, that other beings may possess many senses, of which we can have no conception; because the ideas of them have never been introduced to us, in the only manner, by which an idea can have access to the mind, to wit, by the actual feeling and sensation.

There is, however, one contradictory phænomenon, which may prove, that it is not absolutely impossible for ideas to arise, independent of their correspondent impressions. I believe it will readily be allowed, that the several distinct ideas of colour, which enter by the eye, or those of sound, which are conveyed by the ear, are really different from each other; though, at the same time, resembling. Now if this be true of different colours, it must be no less so of the different shades of the same colour; and each shade produces a distinct idea, independent of the rest. For if this should be denied, it is possible, by the continual gradation of shades, to run a colour insensibly into what is most remote from it; and if you will not allow any of the means to be different, you cannot, without absurdity, deny the extremes to be the same. Suppose, therefore, a person to have enjoyed his sight for thirty years, and to have become perfectly acquainted with colours of all kinds, except one particular shade of blue, for instance, which it never has been his fortune to meet with. Let all the different shades of that colour, except that single one, be placed before him, descending gradually from the deepest to the lightest; it is plain, that he will perceive a blank, where that shade is wanting, and will be sensible, that there is a greater distance in that place between the contiguous colours than in any other. Now I ask, whether it be possible for him, from his own imagination, to supply this deficiency, and raise up to himself the idea of that particular shade, though it had never been conveyed to him by his senses? I believe there are few but will be of opinion that he can: And this may serve as a proof, that the simple ideas are not always, in every instance, derived from the correspondent impressions; though this instance is so singular, that it is scarcely worth our observing, and does not merit, that for it alone we should alter our general maxim.

Here, therefore, is a proposition, which not only seems, in itself, simple and intelligible; but, if a proper use were made of it, might render every dispute equally intelligible, and banish all that jargon, which has so long taken possession of metaphysical reasonings, and drawn disgrace upon them. All ideas, especially abstract ones, are naturally faint and obscure: The mind has but a slender hold of them: They are apt to be confounded with other resembling ideas; and when we have often employed any term, though without a distinct meaning, we are apt to imagine it has a determinate idea, annexed to it. On the contrary, all impressions, that is, all sensations, either outward or inward, are strong and vivid: The limits between them are more exactly determined: Nor is it easy to fall into any error or mistake with regard to them. When we entertain, therefore, any suspicion, that a philosophical term is employed without any meaning or idea (as is but too frequent), we need but enquire, *from what impression is that supposed idea derived*? And if it be impossible to assign any, this will serve to confirm our suspicion. By bringing ideas into so clear a light, we may reasonably hope to remove all dispute, which may arise, concerning their nature and reality.

Section 3
Of the Association of Ideas

It is evident, that there is a principle of connexion between the different thoughts or ideas of the mind, and that, in their appearance to the memory or imagination, they introduce each other with a certain degree of method and regularity. In our more serious thinking or discourse, this is so observable, that any particular thought, which breaks in upon the regular tract or chain of ideas, is immediately remarked and rejected. And even in our wildest and most wandering reveries, nay in our very dreams, we shall find, if we reflect, that the imagination ran not altogether at adventures, but that there was still a connexion upheld among the different ideas, which succeeded each other. Were the loosest and freest conversation to be transcribed, there would immediately be observed something, which connected it in all its transitions. Or where this is wanting, the person, who broke the thread of discourse, might still inform you, that there had secretly revolved in his mind a succession of thought, which had gradually led him from the subject of conversation. Among different languages, even where we cannot suspect the least connexion or communication, it is found, that the words, expressive of ideas, the most compounded, do yet nearly correspond to each other:

A certain proof, that the simple ideas, comprehended in the compound ones, were bound together by some universal principle, which had an equal influence on all mankind.

Though it be too obvious to escape observation, that different ideas are connected together; I do not find, that any philosopher has attempted to enumerate or class all the principles of association; a subject, however, that seems worthy of curiosity. To me, there appear to be only three principles of connexion among ideas, namely, *Resemblance, Contiguity* in time or place, and *Cause* or *Effect*.

That these principles serve to connect ideas will not, I believe, be much doubted. A picture naturally leads our thoughts to the original: The mention of one apartment in a building naturally introduces an enquiry or discourse concerning the others: And if we think of a wound, we can scarcely forbear reflecting on the pain which follows it. But that this enumeration is compleat, and that there are no other principles of association, except these, may be difficult to prove to the satisfaction of the reader, or even to a man's own satisfaction. All we can do, in such cases, is to run over several instances, and examine carefully the principle, which binds the different thoughts to each other, never stopping till we render the principle as general as possible. The more instances we examine, and the more care we employ, the more assurance shall we acquire, that the enumeration, which we form from the whole, is compleat and entire.

[. . .]

Section 4
Sceptical Doubts Concerning the Operations of the Understanding

Part 1

All the objects of human reason or enquiry may naturally be divided into two kinds, to wit, *Relations of Ideas* and *Matters of Fact*. Of the first kind are the sciences of Geometry, Algebra, and Arithmetic; and in short, every affirmation, which is either intuitively or demonstratively certain. *That the square of the hypothenuse is equal to the square of the two sides*, is a proposition, which expresses a relation between these figures. *That three times five is equal to the half of thirty*, expresses a relation between these numbers. Propositions of this kind are discoverable by the mere operation of thought, without dependence on what is any where existent in the universe. Though there never were a circle or triangle in nature, the truths, demonstrated by EUCLID, would for ever retain their certainty and evidence.

Matters of fact, which are the second objects of human reason, are not ascertained in the same manner; nor is our evidence of their truth, however great, of a like nature with the foregoing. The contrary of every matter of fact is still possible; because it can never imply a contradiction, and is conceived by the mind with the same facility and distinctness, as if ever so conformable to reality. *That the sun will not rise to-morrow* is no less intelligible a proposition, and implies no more contradiction, than the affirmation, *that it will rise*. We should in vain, therefore, attempt to demonstrate its falsehood. Were it demonstratively false, it would imply a contradiction, and could never be distinctly conceived by the mind.

It may, therefore, be a subject worthy of curiosity, to enquire what is the nature of that evidence, which assures us of any real existence and matter of fact, beyond the present testimony of our senses, or the records of our memory. This part of philosophy, it is observable, has been little cultivated, either by the ancients or moderns; and therefore our doubts and errors, in the prosecution of so important an enquiry, may be the more excusable; while we march through such difficult paths, without any guide or direction. They may even prove useful, by exciting curiosity, and destroying that implicit faith and security, which is the bane of all reasoning and free enquiry. The discovery of defects in the common philosophy, if any such there be, will not, I presume, be a discouragement, but rather an incitement, as is usual, to attempt something more full and satisfactory, than has yet been proposed to the public.

All reasonings concerning matter of fact seem to be founded on the relation of *Cause* and *Effect*. By means of that relation alone we can go beyond the evidence of our memory and senses. If you were to ask a man, why he believes any matter of fact, which is absent; for instance, that his friend is in the country, or in FRANCE; he would give you a reason; and this reason would be some other fact; as a letter received from him, or the knowledge of his former resolutions and promises. A man, finding a watch or any other machine in a desert island, would conclude, that there had once been men in that island. All our reasonings concerning fact are of the same nature. And here it is constantly supposed, that there is a connexion between the present fact and that which is inferred from it. Were there nothing to bind them together, the inference would be entirely precarious. The hearing of an articulate voice and rational discourse in the dark assures us of the presence of some person: Why? Because these are the effects of the human make and fabric, and closely connected with it. If we anatomize all the other reasonings of this nature, we shall find, that they are founded on the relation of cause and effect, and that this relation is either near or remote, direct or collateral. Heat and light are collateral effects of fire, and the one effect may justly be inferred from the other.

If we would satisfy ourselves, therefore, concerning the nature of that evidence, which assures us of matters of fact, we must enquire how we arrive at the knowledge of cause and effect.

I shall venture to affirm, as a general proposition, which admits of no exception, that the knowledge of this relation is not, in any instance, attained by reasonings *a priori*; but arises entirely from experience, when we find, that any particular objects are constantly conjoined with each other. Let an object be presented to a man of ever so strong natural reason and abilities; if that object be entirely new to him, he will not be able, by the most accurate examination of its sensible qualities, to discover any of its causes or effects. ADAM, though his rational faculties be supposed, at the very first, entirely perfect, could not have inferred from the fluidity and transparency of water, that it would suffocate him, or from the light and warmth of fire, that it would consume him. No object ever discovers, by the qualities which appear to the senses, either the causes, which produced it, or the effects, which will arise from it; nor can our reason, unassisted by experience, ever draw any inference concerning real existence and matter of fact.

This proposition, *that causes and effects are discoverable, not by reason, but by experience*, will readily be admitted with regard to such objects, as we remember to have once been altogether unknown to us; since we must be conscious of the utter inability, which we then lay under, of foretelling, what would arise from them. Present two smooth pieces of marble to a man, who has no tincture of natural philosophy; he will never discover, that they will adhere together, in such a manner as to require great force to separate them in a direct line, while they make so small a resistance to a lateral pressure. Such events, as bear little analogy to the common course of nature, are also readily confessed to be known only by experience; nor does any man imagine that the explosion of gunpowder, or the attraction of a loadstone, could ever be discovered by arguments *a priori*. In like manner, when an effect is supposed to depend upon an intricate machinery or secret structure of parts, we make no difficulty in attributing all our knowledge of it to experience. Who will assert, that he can give the ultimate reason, why milk or bread is proper nourishment for a man, not for a lion or a tyger?

But the same truth may not appear, at first sight, to have the same evidence with regard to events, which have become familiar to us from our first appearance in the world, which bear a close analogy to the whole course of nature, and which are supposed to depend on the simple qualities of objects, without any secret structure of parts. We are apt to imagine, that we could discover these effects by the mere operation of our reason, without experience. We fancy, that were we brought, on a sudden, into this world, we could at first have inferred, that one billiard-ball would communicate motion to another upon impulse; and that we needed not to have waited for the event, in order to pronounce with certainty concerning it. Such is the influence of custom, that, where it is strongest, it not only covers our natural ignorance, but even conceals itself, and seems not to take place, merely because it is found in the highest degree.

But to convince us, that all the laws of nature, and all the operations of bodies without exception, are known only by experience, the following reflections may, perhaps, suffice. Were any object presented to us, and were we required to pronounce concerning the effect, which will result from it, without consulting past observation; after what manner, I beseech you, must the mind proceed in this operation? It must invent or imagine some event, which it ascribes to the object as its effect; and it is plain that this invention must be entirely arbitrary. The mind can never possibly find the effect in the supposed cause, by the most accurate scrutiny and examination. For the effect is totally different from the cause, and consequently can never be discovered in it. Motion in the second billiard-ball is a quite distinct event from motion in the first; nor is there any thing in the one to suggest the smallest hint of the other. A stone or piece of metal raised into the air, and left without any support, immediately falls: But to consider the matter *a priori*, is there any thing we discover in this situation, which can beget the idea of a downward, rather than an upward, or any other motion, in the stone or metal?

And as the first imagination or invention of a particular effect, in all natural operations, is arbitrary; where we consult not experience; so must we also esteem the supposed tye or connexion between the cause and effect, which binds them together, and renders it impossible, that any other effect could result from the operation of that cause. When I see, for instance, a billiard-ball moving in a straight line towards another; even suppose motion in the second ball should by accident be suggested to me, as the result of their contact or impulse; may I not conceive, that a hundred different events might as well follow from that cause? May not both these balls remain at absolute rest? May not the first ball return in a straight line, or leap off from the second in any line or direction? All these suppositions are consistent and conceivable. Why then should we give the preference to one, which is no more consistent or conceivable than the rest? All our reasonings *a priori* will never be able to show us any foundation for this preference.

In a word, then, every effect is a distinct event from its cause. It could not, therefore, be discovered in the cause, and the first invention or conception of it, *a priori*, must be entirely arbitrary. And even after it is suggested, the conjunction of it with the cause must appear equally arbitrary; since there are always many other effects, which, to reason, must seem fully as consistent and natural. In vain, therefore, should we pretend to determine any single event, or infer any cause or effect, without the assistance of observation and experience.

[. . .]

Part 2

But we have not, as yet, attained any tolerable satisfaction with regard to the question first proposed. Each solution still gives rise to a new question as difficult as the foregoing, and leads us on to farther enquiries. When it is asked, *What is the nature of all our reasonings concerning matter of fact?* the proper answer seems to be, that they are founded on the relation of cause and effect. When again it is asked, *What is the foundation of all our reasonings and conclusions concerning that relation?* it may be replied in one word, EXPERIENCE. But if we still carry on our sifting humour, and ask, *What is the foundation of all conclusions from experience?* this implies a new question, which may be of more difficult solution and explication. Philosophers, that give themselves airs of superior wisdom and sufficiency, have a hard task, when they encounter persons of inquisitive dispositions, who push them from every corner, to which they retreat, and who are sure at last to bring them to some dangerous dilemma. The best expedient to prevent this confusion, is to be modest in our pretensions; and even to discover the difficulty ourselves before it is objected to us. By this means, we may make a kind of merit of our very ignorance.

I shall content myself, in this section, with an easy task, and shall pretend only to give a negative answer to the question here proposed. I say then, that, even after we have experience of the operations of cause and effect, our conclusions from that experience are *not* founded on reasoning, or any process of the understanding. This answer we must endeavour, both to explain and to defend.

It must certainly be allowed, that nature has kept us at a great distance from all her secrets, and has afforded us only the knowledge of a few superficial qualities of objects; while she conceals from us those powers and principles, on which the influence of these objects entirely depends. Our senses inform us of the colour, weight, and consistence of bread; but neither sense nor reason can ever inform us of those qualities, which fit it for the nourishment and support of a human body. Sight or feeling conveys an idea of the actual motion of bodies; but as to that wonderful force or power, which would carry on a moving body for ever in a continued change of place, and which bodies never lose but by communicating it to others; of this we cannot form the most distant conception. But notwithstanding this ignorance of natural powers and principles, we always presume, when we see like sensible qualities, that they have like secret powers, and expect, that effects, similar to those, which we have experienced, will follow from them. If a body of like colour and consistence with that bread, which we have formerly eat, be presented to us, we make no scruple of repeating the experiment, and foresee, with certainty, like nourishment and support. Now this is a process of the mind or thought, of which I would willingly know the foundation. It is allowed on all hands, that there is no known connexion between the sensible qualities and the secret powers; and consequently, that the mind is not led to form such a conclusion concerning their constant and regular conjunction, by any thing which it knows of their nature. As to past *Experience*, it can be allowed to give *direct* and *certain* information of those precise objects only, and that precise period of time, which fell under its cognizance: But why this experience should be extended to future times, and to other objects, which, for aught we know, may be only in appearance similar; this is the main question on which I would insist. The bread, which I formerly eat, nourished me; that is, a body of such sensible qualities, was, at that time, endowed with such secret powers: But does it follow that other bread must also nourish me at another time, and that like sensible qualities must always be attended with like secret powers? The consequence seems nowise necessary. At least, it must be acknowledged, that there is here a consequence drawn by the mind; that there is a certain step taken; a process of thought, and an inference, which wants to be explained. These two propositions are far from being the same, *I have found that such an object has always been attended with such an effect*, and *I foresee, that other objects, which are, in appearance, similar, will be attended with similar effects*. I shall allow, if you please, that the one proposition may justly be inferred from the other: I know in fact, that it always is inferred. But if you insist, that the inference is made by a chain of reasoning, I desire you to produce that reasoning. The connexion between these propositions is not intuitive. There is required a medium, which may enable the mind to draw such an inference, if indeed it be drawn by reasoning and argument. What that medium is, I must confess, passes *my* comprehension; and it is incumbent on those to produce it, who assert, that it really exists, and is the origin of all our conclusions concerning matter of fact.

This negative argument must certainly, in process of time, become altogether convincing, if many penetrating and able philosophers shall turn their enquiries this way; and no one be ever able to discover any connecting proposition or intermediate step, which supports the understanding in this conclusion. But as the question is yet new, every reader may not trust so far to his own penetration, as to conclude, because an argument escapes his enquiry, that therefore it does not really exist. For this reason it may be requisite to venture upon a more difficult task; and enumerating all the branches of human knowledge, endeavour to show, that none of them can afford such an argument.

All reasonings may be divided into two kinds, namely, demonstrative reasoning, or that concerning relations of ideas, and moral reasoning, or that concerning matter of fact and existence. That there are no demonstrative arguments in the case, seems evident; since it implies no contradiction, that the course of nature may change, and that an object, seemingly like those which we have experienced, may be attended with different or contrary effects. May I not clearly and distinctly conceive, that a body, falling from the clouds, and which, in all other respects, resembles snow, has yet the taste of salt or feeling of fire? Is there any more intelligible proposition than to affirm, that all the trees will flourish in DECEMBER and JANUARY, and decay in MAY and JUNE? Now whatever is intelligible, and can be distinctly conceived, implies no contradiction, and can never be proved false by any demonstrative argument or abstract reasoning *a priori*.

If we be, therefore, engaged by arguments to put trust in past experience, and make it the standard of our future judgment, these arguments must be probable only, or such as regard matter of fact and real existence, according to the division above-mentioned. But that there is no argument of this kind, must appear, if our explication of that species of reasoning be admitted as solid and satisfactory. We have said, that all arguments concerning existence are founded on the relation of cause and effect; that our knowledge of that relation is derived entirely from experience; and that all our experimental conclusions proceed upon the supposition, that the future will be conformable to the past. To endeavour, therefore, the proof of this last supposition by probable arguments, or arguments regarding existence, must be evidently going in a circle, and taking that for granted, which is the very point in question.

In reality, all arguments from experience are founded on the similarity, which we discover among natural objects, and by which we are induced to expect effects similar to those, which we have found to follow from such objects. And though none but a fool or madman will ever pretend to dispute the authority of experience, or to reject that great guide of human life; it may surely be allowed a philosopher to have so much curiosity at least, as to examine the principle of human nature, which gives this mighty authority to experience, and makes us draw advantage from that similarity, which nature has placed among different objects. From causes, which appear *similar*, we expect similar effects. This is the sum of all our experimental conclusions. Now it seems evident, that, if this conclusion were formed by reason, it would be as perfect at first, and upon one instance, as after ever so long a course of experience. But the case is far otherwise. Nothing so like as eggs; yet no one, on account of this appearing similarity, expects the same taste and relish in all of them. It is only after a long course of uniform experiments in any kind, that we attain a firm reliance and security with regard to a particular event. Now where is that process of reasoning, which, from one instance, draws a conclusion, so different from that which it infers from a hundred instances, that are nowise different from that single one? This question I propose as much for the sake of information, as with an intention of raising difficulties. I cannot find, I cannot imagine any such reasoning. But I keep my mind still open to instruction, if any one will vouchsafe to bestow it on me.

Should it be said, that, from a number of uniform experiments, we *infer* a connexion between the sensible qualities and the secret powers; this, I must confess, seems the same difficulty, couched in different terms. The question still recurs, on what process of argument this *inference* is founded? Where is the medium, the interposing ideas, which join propositions so very wide of each other? It is confessed, that the colour, consistence, and other sensible qualities of bread appear not, of themselves, to have any connexion with the secret powers of nourishment and support. For otherwise we could infer these secret powers from the first appearance of these sensible qualities, without the aid of experience; contrary to the sentiment of all philosophers, and contrary to plain matter of fact. Here then is our natural state of ignorance with regard to the powers and influence of all objects. How is this remedied by experience? It only shows us a number of uniform effects, resulting from certain objects, and teaches us, that those particular objects, at that particular time, were endowed with such powers and forces. When a new object, endowed with similar sensible qualities, is produced, we expect similar powers and forces, and look for a like effect. From a body of like colour and consistence with bread, we expect like nourishment and support. But this surely is a step or progress of the mind, which wants to be explained. When a man says, *I have found, in all past instances, such sensible qualities conjoined with such secret powers*: And when he says, *similar sensible qualities will always be conjoined with similar secret powers*; he is not guilty of a tautology, nor are these propositions in any respect the same. You say that the one proposition is an inference from the other. But you must confess, that the inference is not intuitive, neither is it demonstrative: Of what nature is it then? To say it is experimental, is begging the question. For all inferences from experience suppose, as their foundation, that the future will resemble the past, and that similar powers will be conjoined with similar sensible qualities. If there be any suspicion, that the course of nature may change, and that the past may be no rule for the future, all experience becomes useless, and can give rise to no inference or conclusion. It is impossible, therefore, that any arguments from experience can prove this resemblance of the past to the future; since all these arguments are founded on the supposition of that resemblance. Let the course of things be allowed hitherto ever so regular; that alone, without some new argument or inference, proves not, that, for the future, it will continue so. In vain do you pretend to have learned the nature of bodies from your past experience. Their secret nature, and consequently, all their effects and influence, may change, without any change in their sensible qualities. This happens sometimes, and with regard to some objects: Why may it not happen always, and with regard to all objects? What logic, what process of argument secures you against this supposition? My practice, you say, refutes my doubts. But you mistake the purport of my question. As an agent, I am quite satisfied in the point; but as a philosopher, who has some share of curiosity, I will not say scepticism, I want to learn the foundation of this inference. No reading, no enquiry has yet been able to remove my difficulty; or give me satisfaction in a matter of such importance. Can I do better than propose the difficulty to the public, even though, perhaps, I have small hopes of obtaining a solution? We shall at least, by this means, be sensible of our ignorance, if we do not augment our knowledge.

Section 5
Sceptical Solution of These Doubts

Part 1

[. . .]

Suppose a person, though endowed with the strongest faculties of reason and reflection, to be brought on a sudden into this world; he would, indeed, immediately observe a continual succession of objects, and one event following another; but he would not be able to discover any thing farther. He would not, at first, by any reasoning, be able to reach the idea of cause and effect; since the particular powers, by which all natural operations are performed, never appear to the senses; nor is it reasonable to conclude, merely because one event, in one instance, precedes another, that therefore the one is the cause, the other the effect. Their conjunction may be arbitrary and casual. There may be no reason to infer the existence of one from the appearance of the other. And in a word, such a person, without more experience, could never employ his conjecture or reasoning concerning any matter of fact, or be assured of any thing beyond what was immediately present to his memory and senses.

Suppose again, that he has acquired more experience, and has lived so long in the world as to have observed similar objects or events to be constantly conjoined together; what is the consequence of this experience? He immediately infers the existence of one object from the appearance of the other. Yet he has not, by all his experience, acquired any idea or knowledge of the secret power, by which the one object produces the other; nor is it, by any process of reasoning, he is engaged to draw this inference. But still he finds himself determined to draw it: And though he should be convinced, that his understanding has no part in the operation, he would nevertheless continue in the same course of thinking. There is some other principle, which determines him to form such a conclusion.

This principle is CUSTOM or HABIT. For wherever the repetition of any particular act or operation produces a propensity to renew the same act or operation, without being impelled by any reasoning or process of the understanding; we always say, that this propensity is the effect of *Custom*. By employing that word, we pretend not to have given the ultimate reason of such a propensity. We only point out a principle of human nature, which is universally acknowledged, and which is well known by its effects. Perhaps, we can push our enquiries no farther, or pretend to give the cause of this cause; but must rest contented with it as the ultimate principle, which we can assign, of all our conclusions from experience. It is sufficient satisfaction, that we can go so far; without repining at the narrowness of our faculties, because they will carry us no farther. And it is certain we here advance a very intelligible proposition at least, if not a true one, when we assert, that, after the constant conjunction of two objects, heat and flame, for instance, weight and solidity; we are determined by custom alone to expect the one from the appearance of the other. This hypothesis seems even the only one, which explains the difficulty, why we draw, from a thousand instances, an inference, which we are not able to draw from one instance, that is, in no respect, different from them. Reason is incapable of any such variation. The conclusions, which it draws from considering one circle, are the same which it would form upon surveying all the circles in the universe. But no man, having seen only one body move after being impelled by another, could infer, that every other body will move after a like impulse. All inferences from experience, therefore, are effects of custom, not of reasoning.

Custom, then, is the great guide of human life. It is that principle alone, which renders our experience useful to us, and makes us expect, for the future, a similar train of events with those which have appeared in the past. Without the influence of custom, we should be entirely ignorant of every matter of fact, beyond what is immediately present to the memory and senses. We should never know how to adjust means to ends, or to employ our natural powers in the production of any effect. There would be an end at once of all action, as well as of the chief part of speculation.

But here it may be proper to remark, that though our conclusions from experience carry us beyond our memory and senses, and assure us of matters of fact, which happened in the most distant places and most remote ages; yet some fact must always be present to the senses or memory, from which we may first proceed in drawing these conclusions. A man, who should find in a desert country the remains of pompous buildings, would conclude, that the country had, in ancient times, been cultivated by civilized inhabitants; but did nothing of this nature occur to him, he could never form such an inference. We learn the events of former ages from history; but then we must peruse the volumes, in which this instruction is contained, and thence carry up our inferences from one testimony to another, till we arrive at the eye-witnesses and spectators of these distant events. In a word, if we proceed not upon some fact, present to the memory or senses, our reasonings would be merely hypothetical; and however the particular links might be connected with each other, the whole chain of inferences would have nothing to support it, nor could we ever, by its means, arrive at the knowledge of any real existence. If I ask, why you believe any particular matter of fact, which you relate, you must tell me some reason; and this reason will be some other fact, connected with it. But as you cannot proceed after this manner, *in infinitum*, you must at last terminate in some fact, which is present to your memory or senses; or must allow that your belief is entirely without foundation.

What then is the conclusion of the whole matter? A simple one; though, it must be confessed, pretty remote from the common theories of philosophy. All belief of matter of fact or real existence is derived merely from some object, present to the memory or senses, and a customary conjunction between that and some other object. Or in other words; having found, in many instances, that any two kinds of objects, flame and heat, snow and cold, have always been conjoined together; if flame or snow be presented anew to the senses, the mind is carried by custom to expect heat or cold, and to *believe*, that such a quality does exist, and will discover itself upon a nearer approach. This belief is the necessary result of placing the mind in such circumstances. It is an operation of the soul, when we are so situated, as unavoidable as to feel the passion of love, when we receive benefits; or hatred, when we meet with injuries. All these operations are a species of natural instincts, which no reasoning or process of the thought and understanding is able, either to produce, or to prevent.

At this point, it would be very allowable for us to stop our philosophical researches. In most questions, we can never make a single step farther; and in all questions, we must terminate here at last, after our most restless and curious enquiries. But still our curiosity will be pardonable, perhaps commendable, if it carry us on to still farther researches, and make us examine more accurately the nature of this *belief*, and of the *customary conjunction*, whence it is derived. By this means we may meet with some explications and analogies, that will give satisfaction; at least to such as love the abstract sciences, and can be entertained with speculations, which, however accurate, may still retain a degree of doubt and uncertainty. As to readers of a different taste; the remaining part of this section is not calculated for them, and the following enquiries may well be understood, though it be neglected.

Part 2

Nothing is more free than the imagination of man; and though it cannot exceed that original stock of ideas, furnished by the internal and external senses, it has unlimited power of mixing, compounding, separating, and dividing these ideas, in all the varieties of fiction and vision. It can feign a train of events, with all the appearance of reality, ascribe to them a particular time and place, conceive them as existent, and paint them out to itself with every circumstance, that belongs to any historical fact, which it believes with the greatest certainty. Wherein, therefore, consists the difference between such a fiction and belief? It lies not merely in any peculiar idea, which is annexed to such a conception as commands our assent, and which is wanting to every known fiction. For as the mind has authority over all its ideas, it could voluntarily annex this particular idea to any fiction, and consequently be able to believe whatever it pleases; contrary to what we find by daily experience. We can, in our conception, join the head of a man to the body of a horse; but it is not in our power to believe, that such an animal has ever really existed.

It follows, therefore, that the difference between *fiction* and *belief* lies in some sentiment or feeling, which is annexed to the latter, not to the former, and which depends not on the will, nor can be commanded at pleasure. It must be excited by nature, like all other sentiments; and must arise from the particular situation, in which the mind is placed at any particular juncture. Whenever any object is presented to the memory or senses, it immediately, by the force of custom, carries the imagination to conceive that object, which is usually conjoined to it; and this conception is attended with a feeling or sentiment, different from the loose reveries of the fancy. In this consists the whole nature of belief. For as there is no matter of fact which we believe so firmly, that we cannot conceive the contrary, there would be no difference between the conception assented to, and that which is rejected, were it not for some sentiment, which distinguishes the one from the other. If I see a billiard-ball moving towards another, on a smooth table, I can easily conceive it to stop upon contact. This conception implies no contradiction; but still it feels very differently from that conception, by which I represent to myself the impulse, and the communication of motion from one ball to another.

Were we to attempt a *definition* of this sentiment, we should, perhaps, find it a very difficult, if not an impossible task; in the same manner as if we should endeavour to define the feeling of cold or passion of anger, to a creature who never had any experience of these sentiments. *Belief* is the true and proper name of this feeling; and no one is ever at a loss to know the meaning of that term; because every man is every moment conscious of the sentiment represented by it. It may not, however, be improper to attempt a *description* of this sentiment; in hopes we may, by that means, arrive at some analogies, which may afford a more perfect explication of it. I say then, that belief is nothing but a more vivid, lively, forcible, firm, steady conception of an object, than what the imagination alone is ever able to attain. This variety of terms, which may seem so unphilosophical, is intended only to express that act of the mind, which renders realities, or what is taken for such, more present to us than fictions, causes them to weigh more in the thought, and gives them a superior influence on the passions and imagination. Provided we agree about the thing, it is needless to dispute about the terms. The imagination has the command over all its ideas, and can join and mix and vary them, in all the ways possible. It may conceive fictitious objects with all the circumstances of place and time. It may set them, in a manner, before our eyes, in their true colours, just as they might have existed. But as it is impossible, that this faculty of imagination can ever, of itself, reach belief, it is evident, that belief consists not in the peculiar nature or order of ideas, but in the *manner* of their conception, and in their *feeling* to the mind. I confess, that it is impossible perfectly to explain this feeling or manner of conception. We may make use of words, which express something near it. But its true and proper name, as we observed before, is *belief*; which is a term, that every one sufficiently understands in common life. And in philosophy, we can go no farther than assert, that *belief* is something felt by the mind, which distinguishes the ideas of the judgment from the fictions of the imagination. It gives them more weight and influence: makes them appear of greater importance; enforces them in the mind; and renders them the governing principle of our actions. I hear at present, for instance, a person's voice, with whom I am acquainted; and the sound comes as from the next room. This impression of my senses immediately conveys my thought to the person, together with all the surrounding objects. I paint them out to myself as existing at present, with the same qualities and relations, of which I formerly knew them possessed. These ideas take faster hold of my mind, than ideas of an enchanted castle. They are very different to the feeling, and have a much greater influence of every kind, either to give pleasure or pain, joy or sorrow.

Let us, then, take in the whole compass of this doctrine, and allow, that the sentiment of belief is nothing but a conception more intense and steady than what attends the mere fictions of the imagination, and that this *manner* of conception arises from a customary conjunction of the object with something present to the memory or senses: I believe that it will not be difficult, upon these suppositions, to find other operations of the mind analogous to it, and to trace up these phænomena to principles still more general.

We have already observed, that nature has established connexions among particular ideas, and that no sooner one idea occurs to our thoughts than it introduces its correlative, and carries our attention towards it, by a gentle and insensible movement. These principles of connexion or association we have reduced to three, namely, *Resemblance, Contiguity,* and *Causation;* which are the only bonds, that unite our thoughts together, and beget that regular train of reflection or discourse, which, in a greater or less degree, takes place among all mankind. Now here arises a question, on which the solution of the present difficulty will depend. Does it happen, in all these relations, that, when one of the objects is presented to the senses or memory, the mind is not only carried to the conception of the correlative, but reaches a steadier and stronger conception of it than what otherwise it would have been able to attain? This seems to be the case with that belief, which arises from the relation of cause and effect. And if the case be the same with the other relations or principles of association, this may be established as a general law, which takes place in all the operations of the mind.

We may, therefore, observe, as the first experiment to our present purpose, that, upon the appearance of the picture of an absent friend, our idea of him is evidently enlivened by the *resemblance*, and that every passion, which that idea occasions, whether of joy or sorrow, acquires new force and vigour. In producing this effect, there concur both a relation and a present impression. Where the picture bears him no resemblance, or at least was not intended for him, it never so much as conveys our thought to him: And where it is absent, as well as the person; though the mind may pass from the thought of the one to that of the other; it feels its idea to be rather weakened than enlivened by that transition. We take a pleasure in viewing the picture of a friend, when it is set before us; but when it is removed, rather choose to consider him directly, than by reflection in an image, which is equally distant and obscure.

The ceremonies of the ROMAN CATHOLIC religion may be considered as instances of the same nature. The devotees of that superstition usually plead in excuse for the mummeries, with which they are upbraided, that they feel the good effect of those external motions, and postures, and actions, in enlivening their devotion and quickening their fervour, which otherwise would decay, if directed entirely to distant and immaterial objects. We shadow out the objects of our faith, say they, in sensible types and images, and render them more present to us by the immediate presence of these types, than it is possible for us to do, merely by an intellectual view and contemplation. Sensible objects have always a greater influence on the fancy than any other; and this influence they readily convey to those ideas, to which they are related, and which they resemble. I shall only infer from these practices, and this reasoning, that the effect of resemblance in enlivening the ideas is very common; and as in every case a resemblance and a present impression must concur, we are abundantly supplied with experiments to prove the reality of the foregoing principle.

We may add force to these experiments by others of a different kind, in considering the effects of *contiguity* as well as of *resemblance*. It is certain, that distance diminishes the force of every idea, and that, upon our approach to any object; though it does not discover itself to our senses; it operates upon the mind with an influence, which imitates an immediate impression. The thinking on any object readily transports the mind to what is contiguous; but it is only the actual presence of an object, that transports it with a superior vivacity. When I am a few miles from home, whatever relates to it touches me more nearly than when I am two hundred leagues distant; though even at that distance the reflecting on any thing in the neighbourhood of my friends or family naturally produces an idea of them. But as in this latter case, both the objects of the mind are ideas; notwithstanding there is an easy transition between them; that transition alone is not able to give a superior vivacity to any of the ideas, for want of some immediate impression.

No one can doubt but causation has the same influence as the other two relations of resemblance and contiguity. Superstitious people are fond of the relicts of saints and holy men, for the same reason, that they seek after types or images, in order to enliven their devotion, and give them a more intimate and strong conception of those exemplary lives, which they desire to imitate. Now it is evident, that one of the best relicts, which a devotee could procure, would be the handywork of a saint; and if his cloaths and furniture are ever to be considered in this light, it is because they were once at his disposal, and were moved and affected by him; in which respect they are to be considered as imperfect effects, and as connected with him by a shorter chain of consequences than any of those, by which we learn the reality of his existence.

Suppose, that the son of a friend, who had been long dead or absent, were presented to us; it is evident, that this object would instantly revive its correlative idea, and recall to our thoughts all past intimacies and familiarities, in more lively colours than they would otherwise have appeared to us. This is another phænomenon, which seems to prove the principle above-mentioned.

We may observe, that, in these phænomena, the belief of the correlative object is always presupposed; without which the relation could have no effect. The influence of the picture supposes, that we *believe* our friend to have once existed. Contiguity to home can never excite our ideas of home, unless we *believe* that it really exists. Now I assert, that this belief, where it reaches beyond the memory or senses, is of a similar nature, and arises from similar causes, with the transition of thought and vivacity of conception here explained. When I throw a piece of dry wood into a fire, my mind is immediately carried to conceive, that it augments, not extinguishes the flame. This transition of thought from the cause to the effect proceeds not from reason. It derives its origin altogether from custom and experience. And as it first begins from an object, present to the senses, it renders the idea or conception of flame more strong and lively than any loose, floating reverie of the imagination. That idea arises immediately. The thought moves instantly towards it, and conveys to it all that force of conception, which is derived from the impression present to the senses. When a sword is levelled at my breast, does not the idea of wound and pain strike me more strongly, than when a glass of wine is presented to me, even though by accident this idea should occur after the appearance of the latter object? But what is there in this whole matter to cause such a strong conception, except only a present object and a customary transition to the idea of another object, which we have been accustomed to conjoin with the former? This is the whole operation of the mind, in all our conclusions concerning matter of fact and existence; and it is a satisfaction to find some analogies, by which it may be explained. The transition from a present object does in all cases give strength and solidity to the related idea.

[. . .]

Section 7
Of the Idea of Necessary Connexion

Part 1

[. . .]

There are no ideas, which occur in metaphysics, more obscure and uncertain, than those of *power*, *force*, *energy*, or *necessary connexion*, of which it is every moment necessary for us to treat in all our disquisitions. We shall, therefore, endeavour, in this section, to fix, if possible, the precise meaning of these terms, and thereby remove some part of that obscurity, which is so much complained of in this species of philosophy.

It seems a proposition, which will not admit of much dispute, that all our ideas are nothing but copies of our impressions, or, in other words, that it is impossible for us to *think* of any thing, which we have not antecedently *felt*, either by our external or internal senses. I have endeavoured [see section 2 above] to explain and prove this proposition, and have expressed my hopes, that, by a proper application of it, men may reach a greater clearness and precision in philosophical reasonings, than what they have hitherto been able to attain. Complex ideas may, perhaps, be well known by definition, which is nothing but an enumeration of those parts or simple ideas, that compose them. But when we have pushed up definitions to the most simple ideas, and find still some ambiguity and obscurity; what resource are we then possessed of? By what invention can we throw light upon these ideas, and render them altogether precise and determinate to our intellectual view? Produce the impressions or original sentiments, from which the ideas are copied. These impressions are all strong and sensible. They admit not of ambiguity. They are not only placed in a full light themselves, but may throw light on their correspondent ideas, which lie in obscurity. And by this means, we may, perhaps, attain a new microscope or species of optics, by which, in the moral sciences, the most minute, and most simple ideas may be so enlarged as to fall readily under our apprehension, and be equally known with the grossest and most sensible ideas, that can be the object of our enquiry.

To be fully acquainted, therefore, with the idea of power or necessary connexion, let us examine its impression; and in order to find the impression with greater certainty, let us search for it in all the sources, from which it may possibly be derived.

When we look about us towards external objects, and consider the operation of causes, we are never able, in a single instance, to discover any power or necessary connexion; any quality, which binds the effect to the cause, and renders the one an infallible consequence of the other. We only find, that the one does actually, in fact, follow the other. The impulse of one billiard-ball is attended with motion in the second. This is the whole that appears to the *outward* senses. The mind feels no sentiment or *inward* impression from this succession of objects: Consequently, there is not, in any single, particular instance of cause and effect, any thing which can suggest the idea of power or necessary connexion.

From the first appearance of an object, we never can conjecture what effect will result from it. But were the power or energy of any cause discoverable by the mind, we could foresee the effect, even without experience; and might, at first, pronounce with certainty concerning it, by the mere dint of thought and reasoning.

In reality, there is no part of matter, that does ever, by its sensible qualities, discover any power or energy, or give us ground to imagine, that it could produce any thing, or be followed by any other object, which we could denominate its effect. Solidity, extension, motion; these qualities are all compleat in themselves, and never point out any other event which may result from them. The scenes of the universe are continually shifting, and one object follows another in an uninterrupted succession; but the power or force, which actuates the whole machine, is entirely concealed from us, and never discovers itself in any of the sensible qualities of body. We know, that, in fact, heat is a constant attendant of flame; but what is the connexion between them, we have no room so much as to conjecture or imagine. It is impossible, therefore, that the idea of power can be derived from the contemplation of bodies, in single instances of their operation; because no bodies ever discover any power, which can be the original of this idea.

Since, therefore, external objects, as they appear to the senses, give us no idea of power or necessary connexion, by their operation in particular instances, let us see, whether this idea be derived from reflection on the operations of our own minds, and be copied from any internal impression. It may be said, that we are every moment conscious of internal power; while we feel, that, by the simple command of our will, we can move the organs of our body, or direct the faculties of our mind. An act of volition produces motion in our limbs, or raises a new idea in our imagination. This influence of the will we know by consciousness. Hence we acquire the idea of power or energy; and are certain, that we ourselves and all other intelligent beings are possessed of power. This idea, then, is an idea of reflection, since it arises from reflecting on the operations of our own mind, and on the command which is exercised by will, both over the organs of the body and faculties of the soul.

We shall proceed to examine this pretension; and first with regard to the influence of volition over the organs of the body. This influence, we may observe, is a fact, which, like all other natural events, can be known only by experience, and can never be foreseen from any apparent energy or power in the cause, which connects it with the effect, and renders the one an infallible consequence of the other. The motion of our body follows upon the command of our will. Of this we are every moment conscious. But the means, by which this is effected; the energy, by which the will performs so extraordinary an operation; of this we are so far from being immediately conscious, that it must for ever escape our most diligent enquiry.

For *first*, is there any principle in all nature more mysterious than the union of soul with body; by which a supposed spiritual substance acquires such an influence over a material one, that the most refined thought is able to actuate the grossest matter? Were we empowered, by a secret wish, to remove mountains, or controul the planets in their orbit; this extensive authority would not be more extraordinary, nor more beyond our comprehension. But if by consciousness we perceived any power or energy in the will, we must know this power; we must know its connexion with the effect; we must know the secret union of soul and body, and the nature of both these substances; by which the one is able to operate, in so many instances, upon the other.

Secondly, We are not able to move all the organs of the body with a like authority; though we cannot assign any reason besides experience, for so remarkable a difference between one and the other. Why has the will an influence over the tongue and fingers, not over the heart or liver? This question would never embarrass us, were we conscious of a power in the former case, not in the latter. We should then perceive, independent of experience, why the authority of will over the organs of the body is circumscribed within such particular limits. Being in that case fully acquainted with the power or force, by which it operates, we should also know, why its influence reaches precisely to such boundaries, and no farther.

[...]

Thirdly, We learn from anatomy, that the immediate object of power in voluntary motion, is not the member itself which is moved, but certain muscles, and nerves, and animal spirits, and, perhaps, something still more minute and more unknown, through which the motion is successively propagated, ere it reach the member itself whose motion is the immediate object of volition. Can there be a more certain proof, that the power, by which this whole operation is performed, so far from being directly and fully known by an inward sentiment or consciousness, is, to the last degree, mysterious and unintelligible? Here the mind wills a certain event: Immediately another event, unknown to ourselves, and totally different from the one intended, is produced: This event produces another, equally unknown: Till at last, through a long succession, the desired event is produced. But if the original power were felt, it must be known: Were it known, its effect must also be known; since all power is relative to its effect. And *vice versa*, if the effect be not known, the power cannot be known nor felt. How indeed can we be conscious of a power to move our limbs, when we have no such power; but only that to move certain animal spirits, which, though they produce at last the motion of our limbs, yet operate in such a manner as is wholly beyond our comprehension?

We may, therefore, conclude from the whole, I hope, without any temerity, though with assurance; that our idea of power is not copied from any sentiment or consciousness of power within ourselves, when we give rise to animal motion, or apply our limbs to their proper use and office. That their motion follows the command of the will is a matter of common experience, like other natural events: But the power or energy by which this is effected, like that in other natural events, is unknown and inconceivable.

Shall we then assert, that we are conscious of a power or energy in our own minds, when, by an act or command of our will, we raise up a new idea, fix the mind to the contemplation of it, turn it on all sides, and at last dismiss it for some other idea, when we think that we have surveyed it with sufficient accuracy? I believe the same arguments will prove, that even this command of the will gives us no real idea of force or energy.

First, It must be allowed, that, when we know a power, we know that very circumstance in the cause, by which it is enabled to produce the effect: For these are supposed to be synonimous. We must, therefore, know both the cause and effect, and the relation between them. But do we pretend to be acquainted with the nature of the human soul and the nature of an idea, or the aptitude of the one to produce the other? This is a real creation; a production of something out of nothing: Which implies a power so great, that it may seem, at first sight, beyond the reach of any being, less than infinite. At least it must be owned, that such a power is not felt, nor known, nor even conceivable by the mind. We only feel the event, namely, the existence of an idea, consequent to a command of the will: But the manner, in which this operation is performed; the power, by which it is produced; is entirely beyond our comprehension.

Secondly, The command of the mind over itself is limited, as well as its command over the body; and these limits are not known by reason, or any acquaintance with the nature of cause and effect; but only by experience and observation, as in all other natural events and in the operation of external objects. Our authority over our sentiments and passions is much weaker than that over our ideas; and even the latter authority is circumscribed within very narrow boundaries. Will any one pretend to assign the ultimate reason of these boundaries, or show why the power is deficient in one case and not in another.

Thirdly, This self-command is very different at different times. A man in health possesses more of it, than one languishing with sickness. We are more master of our thoughts in the morning than in the evening: Fasting, than after a full meal. Can we give any reason for these variations, except experience? Where then is the power, of which we pretend to be conscious? Is there not here, either in a spiritual or material substance, or both, some secret mechanism or structure of parts, upon which the effect depends, and which, being entirely unknown to us, renders the power or energy of the will equally unknown and incomprehensible?

[. . .]

Part 2

But to hasten to a conclusion of this argument, which is already drawn out to too great a length: We have sought in vain for an idea of power or necessary connexion, in all the sources from which we could suppose it to be derived. It appears, that, in single instances of the operation of bodies, we never can, by our utmost scrutiny, discover any thing but one event following another; without being able to comprehend any force or power, by which the cause operates, or any connexion between it and its supposed effect. The same difficulty occurs in contemplating the operations of mind on body; where we observe the motion of the latter to follow upon the volition of the former; but are not able to observe or conceive the tye, which binds together the motion and volition, or the energy by which the mind produces this effect. The authority of the will over its own faculties and ideas is not a whit more comprehensible: So that, upon the whole, there appears not, throughout all nature, any one instance of connexion, which is conceivable by us. All events seem entirely loose and separate. One event follows another; but we never can observe any tye between them. They seem *conjoined*, but never *connected*. And as we can have no idea of any thing, which never appeared to our outward sense or inward sentiment, the necessary conclusion *seems* to be, that we have no idea of connexion or power at all, and that these words are absolutely without any meaning, when employed either in philosophical reasonings, or common life.

But there still remains one method of avoiding this conclusion, and one source which we have not yet examined. When any natural object or event is presented, it is impossible for us, by any sagacity or penetration, to discover, or even conjecture, without experience, what event will result from it, or to carry our foresight beyond that object, which is immediately present to the memory and senses. Even after one instance or experiment, where we have observed a particular event to follow upon another, we are not entitled to form a general rule, or foretel what will happen in like cases; it being justly esteemed an unpardonable temerity to judge of the whole course of nature from one single experiment, however accurate or certain. But when one particular species of event has always, in all instances, been conjoined with another, we make no longer any scruple of foretelling one upon the appearance of the other, and of employing that reasoning, which can alone assure us of any matter of fact or existence. We then call the one object, *Cause*; the other, *Effect*. We suppose, that there is some connexion between them; some power in the one, by which it infallibly produces the other, and operates with the greatest certainty and strongest necessity.

It appears, then, that this idea of a necessary connexion among events arises from a number of similar instances, which occur, of the constant conjunction of these events; nor can that idea ever be suggested by any one of these instances, surveyed in all possible lights and positions. But there is nothing in a number of instances, different from every single instance, which is supposed to be exactly similar; except only, that after a repetition of similar instances, the mind is carried by habit, upon the appearance of one event, to expect its usual attendant, and to believe, that it will exist. This connexion, therefore, which we *feel* in the mind, this customary transition of the imagination from one object to its usual attendant, is the sentiment or impression, from which we form the idea of power or necessary connexion. Nothing farther is in the case. Contemplate the subject on all sides; you will never find any other origin of that idea. This is the sole difference between one instance, from which we can never receive the idea of connexion, and a number of similar instances, by which it is suggested. The first time a man saw the communication of motion by impulse, as by the shock of two billiard-balls, he could not pronounce that the one event was *connected*; but only that it was *conjoined* with the other. After he has observed several instances of this nature, he then pronounces them to be *connected*. What alteration has happened to give rise to this new idea of *connexion*? Nothing but that he now *feels* these events to be *connected* in his imagination, and can readily foretel the existence of one from the appearance of the other. When we say, therefore, that one object is connected with another, we mean only, that they have acquired a connexion in our thought, and give rise to this inference, by which they become proofs of each other's existence: A conclusion, which is somewhat extraordinary; but which seems founded on sufficient evidence. Nor will its evidence be weakened by any general diffidence of the understanding, or sceptical suspicion concerning every conclusion, which is new and extraordinary. No conclusions can be more agreeable to scepticism than such as make discoveries concerning the weakness and narrow limits of human reason and capacity.

And what stronger instance can be produced of the surprizing ignorance and weakness of the understanding, than the present? For surely, if there be any relation among objects, which it imports to us to know perfectly, it is that of cause and effect. On this are founded all our reasonings concerning matter of fact or existence. By means of it alone we attain any assurance concerning objects, which are removed from the present testimony of our memory and senses. The only immediate utility of all sciences, is to teach us, how to controul and regulate future events by their causes. Our thoughts and enquiries are, therefore, every moment, employed about this relation. Yet so imperfect are the ideas which we form concerning it, that it is impossible to give any just definition of *cause*, except what is drawn from something extraneous and foreign to it. Similar objects are always conjoined with similar. Of this we have experience. Suitably to this experience, therefore, we may define a cause to be *an object, followed by another, and where all the objects, similar to the first, are followed by objects similar to the second.* Or in other words, *where, if the first object had not been, the second never had existed.* The appearance of a cause always conveys the mind, by a customary transition, to the idea of the effect. Of this also we have experience. We may, therefore, suitably to this experience, form another definition of *cause*; and call it, *an object followed by another, and whose appearance always conveys the thought to that other.* But though both these definitions be drawn from circumstances foreign to the cause, we cannot remedy this inconvenience, or attain any more perfect definition, which may point out that circumstance in the cause, which gives it a connexion with its effect. We have no idea of this connexion; nor even any distinct notion what it is we desire to know, when we endeavour at a conception of it. We say, for instance, that the vibration of this string is the cause of this particular sound. But what do we mean by that affirmation? We either mean, *that this vibration is followed by this sound, and that all similar vibrations have been followed by similar sounds*: Or, *that this vibration is followed by this sound, and that upon the appearance of one, the mind anticipates the senses, and forms immediately an idea of the other.* We may consider the relation of cause and effect in either of these two lights; but beyond these, we have no idea of it.

To recapitulate, therefore, the reasonings of this section: Every idea is copied from some preceding impression or sentiment; and where we cannot find any impression, we may be certain that there is no idea. In all single instances of the operation of bodies or minds, there is nothing that produces any impression, nor consequently can suggest any idea, of power or necessary connexion. But when many uniform instances appear, and the same object is always followed by the same event; we then begin to entertain the notion of cause and connexion. We then *feel* a new sentiment or impression, to wit, a customary connexion in the thought or imagination between one object and its usual attendant; and this sentiment is the original of that idea which we seek for. For as this idea arises from a number of similar instances, and not from any single instance; it must arise from that circumstance, in which the number of instances differ from every individual instance. But this customary connexion or transition of the imagination is the only circumstance, in which they differ. In every other particular they are alike. The first instance which we saw of motion, communicated by the shock of two billiard-balls (to return to this obvious illustration) is exactly similar to any instance that may, at present, occur to us; except only, that we could not, at first, *infer* one event from the other; which we are enabled to do at present, after so long a course of uniform experience. I know not, whether the reader will readily apprehend this reasoning. I am afraid, that, should I multiply words about it, or throw it into a greater variety of lights, it would only become more obscure and intricate. In all abstract reasonings, there is one point of view, which, if we can happily hit, we shall go farther towards illustrating the subject, than by all the eloquence and copious expression in the world. This point of view we should endeavour to reach, and reserve the flowers of rhetoric for subjects which are more adapted to them.

Section 10
Of Miracles

Part 1

[. . .]

Though experience be our only guide in reasoning concerning matters of fact; it must be acknowledged, that this guide is not altogether infallible, but in some cases is apt to lead us into errors. One, who, in our climate, should expect better weather in any week of JUNE than in one of DECEMBER, would reason justly, and conformably to experience; but it is certain, that he may happen, in the event, to find himself mistaken. However, we may observe, that, in such a case, he would have no cause to complain of experience; because it commonly informs us before-hand of the uncertainty, by that contrariety of events, which we may learn from a diligent observation. All effects follow not with like certainty from their supposed causes. Some events are found, in all countries and all ages, to have been constantly conjoined together: Others are found to have been more variable, and sometimes to disappoint our expectations; so that, in our reasonings concerning matter of fact, there are all imaginable degrees of assurance, from the highest certainty to the lowest species of moral evidence.

A wise man, therefore, proportions his belief to the evidence. In such conclusions as are founded on an infallible experience, he expects the event with the last degree of assurance, and regards his past experience as a full *proof* of the future existence of that event. In other cases, he proceeds with more caution: He weighs the opposite experiments: He considers which side is supported by the greater number of experiments: To that side he inclines, with doubt and hesitation; and when at last he fixes his judgment, the evidence exceeds not what we properly call *probability*. All probability, then, supposes an opposition of experiments and observations; where the one side is found to overbalance the other, and to produce a degree of evidence, proportioned to the superiority. A hundred instances or experiments on one side, and fifty on another, afford a doubtful expectation of any event; though a hundred uniform experiments, with only one that is contradictory, reasonably beget a pretty strong degree of assurance. In all cases, we must balance the opposite experiments, where they are opposite, and deduct the smaller number from the greater, in order to know the exact force of the superior evidence.

To apply these principles to a particular instance; we may observe, that there is no species of reasoning more common, more useful, and even necessary to human life, than that which is derived from the testimony of men, and the reports of eye-witnesses and spectators. This species of reasoning, perhaps, one may deny to be founded on the relation of cause and effect. I shall not dispute about a word. It will be sufficient to observe, that our assurance in any argument of this kind is derived from no other principle than our observation of the veracity of human testimony, and of the usual conformity of facts to the reports of witnesses. It being a general maxim, that no objects have any discoverable connexion together, and that all the inferences, which we can draw from one to another, are founded merely on our experience of their constant and regular conjunction; it is evident, that we ought not to make an exception to this maxim in favour of human testimony, whose connexion with any event seems, in itself, as little necessary as any other. Were not the memory tenacious to a certain degree; had not men commonly an inclination to truth and a principle of probity; were they not sensible to shame, when detected in a falsehood: Were not these, I say, discovered by *experience* to be qualities, inherent in human nature, we should never repose the least confidence in human testimony. A man delirious, or noted for falsehood and villany, has no manner of authority with us.

And as the evidence, derived from witnesses and human testimony, is founded on past experience, so it varies with the experience, and is regarded either as a *proof* or a *probability*, according as the conjunction between any particular kind of report and any kind of object has been found to be constant or variable. There are a number of circumstances to be taken into consideration in all judgments of this kind; and the ultimate standard, by which we determine all disputes, that may arise concerning them, is always derived from experience and observation. Where this experience is not entirely uniform on any side, it is attended with an unavoidable contrariety in our judgments, and with the same opposition and mutual destruction of argument as in every other kind of evidence. We frequently hesitate concerning the reports of others. We balance the opposite circumstances, which cause any doubt or uncertainty; and when we discover a superiority on any side, we incline to it; but still with a diminution of assurance, in proportion to the force of its antagonist.

This contrariety of evidence, in the present case, may be derived from several different causes; from the opposition of contrary testimony; from the character or number of the witnesses; from the manner of their delivering their testimony; or from the union of all these circumstances. We entertain a suspicion concerning any matter of fact, when the witnesses contradict each other; when they are but few, or of a doubtful character; when they have an interest in what they affirm; when they deliver their testimony with hesitation, or on the contrary, with too violent asseverations. There are many other particulars of the same kind, which may diminish or destroy the force of any argument, derived from human testimony.

Suppose, for instance, that the fact, which the testimony endeavours to establish, partakes of the extraordinary and the marvellous; in that case, the evidence, resulting from the testimony, admits of a diminution, greater or less, in proportion as the fact is more or less unusual. The reason, why we place any credit in witnesses and historians, is not derived from any *connexion*, which we perceive *a priori*, between testimony and reality, but because we are accustomed to find a conformity between them. But when the fact attested is such a one as has seldom fallen under our observation, here is a contest of two opposite experiences; of which the one destroys the other, as far as its force goes, and the superior can only operate on the mind by the force, which remains. The very same principle of experience, which gives us a certain degree of assurance in the testimony of witnesses, gives us also, in this case, another degree of assurance against the fact, which they endeavour to establish; from which contradiction there necessarily arises a counterpoise, and mutual destruction of belief and authority.

I should not believe such a story were it told me by CATO; was a proverbial saying in ROME, even during the lifetime of that philosophical patriot. The incredibility of a fact, it was allowed, might invalidate so great an authority.

The INDIAN prince, who refused to believe the first relations concerning the effects of frost, reasoned justly; and it naturally required very strong testimony to engage his assent to facts, that arose from a state of nature, with which he was unacquainted, and which bore so little analogy to those events, of which he had had constant and uniform experience. Though they were not contrary to his experience, they were not conformable to it.

But in order to encrease the probability against the testimony of witnesses, let us suppose, that the fact, which they affirm, instead of being only marvellous, is really miraculous; and suppose also, that the testimony, considered apart and in itself, amounts to an entire proof; in that case, there is proof against proof, of which the strongest must prevail, but still with a diminution of its force, in proportion to that of its antagonist.

A miracle is a violation of the laws of nature; and as a firm and unalterable experience has established these laws, the proof against a miracle, from the very nature of the fact, is as entire as any argument from experience can possibly be imagined. Why is it more than probable, that all men must die; that lead cannot, of itself, remain suspended in the air; that fire consumes wood, and is extinguished by water; unless it be, that these events are found agreeable to the laws of nature, and there is required a violation of these laws, or in other words, a miracle to prevent them? Nothing is esteemed a miracle, if it ever happen in the common course of nature. It is no miracle that a man, seemingly in good health, should die on a sudden; because such a kind of death, though more unusual than any other, has yet been frequently observed to happen. But it is a miracle, that a dead man should come to life; because that has never been observed, in any age or country. There must, therefore, be a uniform experience against every miraculous event, otherwise the event would not merit that appellation. And as a uniform experience amounts to a proof, there is here a direct and full *proof*, from the nature of the fact, against the existence of any miracle; nor can such a proof be destroyed, or the miracle rendered credible, but by an opposite proof, which is superior.

The plain consequence is (and it is a general maxim worthy of our attention), "That no testimony is sufficient to establish a miracle, unless the testimony be of such a kind, that its falsehood would be more miraculous, than the fact, which it endeavours to establish: And even in that case, there is a mutual destruction of arguments, and the superior only gives us an assurance suitable to that degree of force, which remains, after deducting the inferior." When any one tells me, that he saw a dead man restored to life, I immediately consider with myself, whether it be more probable, that this person should either deceive or be deceived, or that the fact, which he relates, should really have happened. I weigh the one miracle against the other; and according to the superiority, which I discover, I pronounce my decision, and always reject the greater miracle. If the falsehood of his testimony would be more miraculous, than the event which he relates; then, and not till then, can he pretend to command my belief or opinion.

Part 2

[. . .]

Upon the whole, then, it appears, that no testimony for any kind of miracle has ever amounted to a probability, much less to a proof; and that, even supposing it amounted to a proof, it would be opposed by another proof; derived from the very nature of the fact, which it would endeavour to establish. It is experience only, which gives authority to human testimony; and it is the same experience, which assures us of the laws of nature. When, therefore, these two kinds of experience are contrary, we have nothing to do but subtract the one from the other, and embrace an opinion, either on one side or the other, with that assurance which arises from the remainder. But according to the principle here explained, this subtraction, with regard to all popular religions, amounts to an entire annihilation; and therefore we may establish it as a maxim, that no human testimony can have such force as to prove a miracle, and make it a just foundation for any such system of religion.

I beg the limitations here made may be remarked, when I say, that a miracle can never be proved, so as to be the foundation of a system of religion. For I own, that otherwise, there may possibly be miracles, or violations of the usual course of nature, of such a kind as to admit of proof from human testimony; though, perhaps, it will be impossible to find any such in all the records of history. Thus, suppose, all authors, in all languages, agree, that, from the first of JANUARY 1600, there was a total darkness over the whole earth for eight days: Suppose that the tradition of this extraordinary event is still strong and lively among the people: That all travellers, who return from foreign countries, bring us accounts of the same tradition, without the least variation or contradiction: It is evident, that our present philosophers, instead of doubting the fact, ought to receive it as certain, and ought to search for the causes whence it might be derived. The decay, corruption, and dissolution of nature, is an event rendered probable by so many analogies, that any phænomenon, which seems to have a tendency towards that catastrophe, comes within the reach of human testimony, if that testimony be very extensive and uniform.

But suppose, that all the historians, who treat of ENGLAND, should agree, that, on the first of JANUARY 1600, Queen ELIZABETH died; that both before and after her death she was seen by her physicians and the whole court, as is usual with persons of her rank; that her successor was acknowledged and proclaimed by the parliament; and that, after being interred a month, she again appeared, resumed the throne, and governed ENGLAND for three years: I must confess that I should be surprized at the concurrence of so many odd circumstances, but should not have the least inclination to believe so miraculous an event. I should not doubt of her pretended death, and of those other public circumstances that followed it: I should only assert it to have been pretended, and that it neither was, nor possibly could be real. You would in vain object to me the difficulty, and almost impossibility of deceiving the world in an affair of such consequence; the wisdom and solid judgment of that renowned queen; with the little or no advantage which she could reap from so poor an artifice: All this might astonish me; but I would still reply, that the knavery and folly of men are such common phænomena, that I should rather believe the most extraordinary events to arise from their concurrence, than admit of so signal a violation of the laws of nature.

But should this miracle be ascribed to any new system of religion; men, in all ages, have been so much imposed on by ridiculous stories of that kind, that this very circumstance would be a full proof of a cheat, and sufficient, with all men of sense, not only to make them reject the fact, but even reject it without farther examination. Though the Being, to whom the miracle is ascribed, be, in this case, Almighty; it does not, upon that account, become a whit more probable; since it is impossible for us to know the attributes or actions of such a Being, otherwise than from the experience which we have of his productions, in the usual course of nature. This still reduces us to past observation, and obliges us to compare the instances of the violations of truth in the testimony of men with those of the violation of the laws of nature by miracles, in order to judge which of them is most likely and probable. As the violations of truth are more common in the testimony concerning religious miracles, than in that concerning any other matter of fact; this must diminish very much the authority of the former testimony, and make us form a general resolution, never to lend any attention to it, with whatever specious pretence it may be covered.

4

David Hume, *A Treatise of Human Nature* (1739–40)

Hume's *Treatise*, consisting of three "books," covers a range of topics on human nature from a scientific perspective. Book I, from which the following discussions "Of the Immateriality of the Soul" and "Of Personal Identity" are excerpted, includes subjects in epistemology. His discussion "Of Liberty and Necessity," on free will, is taken from Book II, which concerns human passions.

Hume attempted to show that the modern debate over whether the soul is a material or an immaterial substance is misguided. "Substance," among scholastic and modern philosophers, was taken to refer to something that can exist on its own, as opposed to a quality that can exist only as a property of something else. But Hume argued (1) that because we have no impressions (experience) of substance we can have no idea of it; and (2) that the traditional definition of substance applies even to the perceptions of the mind.

In the section, "Of Personal Identity," Hume observed that all we find when we search for an impression of the self is a series of changing perceptions, like the shifting scenes and actors on a theater stage. We cannot experience the "stage" itself, the unifying, enduring ground of the perceptions. Hume asks: "What then gives us so great a propension to ascribe an identity to these successive perceptions, and to suppose ourselves possest of an invariable and uninterrupted existence thro' the whole course of our lives?" His answer is that we appeal to the relations we find among some perceptions. Some perceptions resemble others: memories, for example, resemble experiences. Some perceptions are causally related to others: impressions cause ideas, and ideas cause other ideas and passions. The imagination "bundles" these related perceptions together into the idea of a self and creates what Hume calls a "fiction" – an idea originated naturally by the imagination, but not derived from experience.

In the selection taken from "Of Liberty and Necessity," Hume argues that if our actions are not caused, then they are chance events and we cannot be held responsible for them. Hume also reminds us, however, that to say one event is caused by another means only that we are able to infer (because of a constant conjunction of such events) that the one will happen when the other does. Thus, to say that my actions are caused by my desires or motives merely means that someone who knows the motives that constitute my character can predict what I will do. Just because we can predict that a known thief will steal, that is no reason not to hold him responsible when he does.

Hume's *Treatise* covers issues in moral philosophy in Book III, from which several selections are taken below, in part VI of this volume. The striking fact about the *Treatise* is that Hume completed it by the age of 28. Rarely do we find so much philosophical genius in such a young author.

Book I
Part 4
Of the Sceptical and Other Systems of Philosophy

Section 5
Of the Immateriality of the Soul

Having found such contradictions and difficulties in every system concerning external objects, and in the idea of matter, which we fancy so clear and determinate, we shall naturally expect still greater difficulties and contradictions in every hypothesis concerning our internal perceptions, and the nature of the mind, which we are apt to imagine so much more obscure, and uncertain. But in this we shou'd deceive ourselves. The intellectual world, tho' involv'd in infinite obscurities, is not perplex'd with any such contradictions, as those we have discover'd in the natural. What is known concerning it, agrees with itself; and what is unknown, we must be contented to leave so.

'Tis true, wou'd we hearken to certain philosophers, they promise to diminish our ignorance; but I am afraid 'tis at the hazard of running us into contradictions, from which the subject is of itself exempted. These philosophers are the curious reasoners concerning the material or immaterial substances, in which they suppose our perceptions to inhere. In order to put a stop to these endless cavils on both sides, I know no better method, than to ask these philosophers in a few words, *What they mean by substance and inhesion?* And after they have answer'd this question, 'twill then be reasonable, and not till then, to enter seriously into the dispute.

This question we have found impossible to be answer'd with regard to matter and body: But besides that in the case of the mind, it labours under all the same difficulties, 'tis burthen'd with some additional ones, which are peculiar to that subject. As every idea is deriv'd from a precedent impression, had we any idea of the substance of our minds, we must also have an impression of it; which is very difficult, if not impossible, to be conceiv'd. For how can an impression represent a substance, otherwise than by resembling it? And how can an impression resemble a substance, since, according to this philosophy, it is not a substance, and has none of the peculiar qualities or characteristics of a substance?

But leaving the question of *What may or may not be?* for that other *What actually is?* I desire those philosophers, who pretend that we have an idea of the substance of our minds, to point out the impression that produces it, and tell distinctly after what manner that impression operates, and from what object it is deriv'd. Is it an impression of sensation or of reflection? Is it pleasant, or painful, or indifferent? Does it attend us at all times, or does it only return at intervals? If at intervals, at what times principally does it return, and by what causes is it produc'd?

If instead of answering these questions, any one shou'd evade the difficulty, by saying, that the definition of a substance is *something which may exist by itself*; and that this definition ought to satisfy us: Shou'd this be said, I shou'd observe, that this definition agrees to every thing, that can possibly be conceiv'd; and never will serve to distinguish substance from accident, or the soul from its perceptions. For thus I reason. Whatever is clearly conceiv'd may exist;

and whatever is clearly conceiv'd, after any manner, may exist after the same manner. This is one principle, which has been already acknowledg'd. Again, every thing, which is different, is distinguishable, and every thing which is distinguishable, is separable by the imagination. This is another principle. My conclusion from both is, that since all our perceptions are different from each other, and from every thing else in the universe, they are also distinct and separable, and may be consider'd as separately existent, and may exist separately, and have no need of any thing else to support their existence. They are, therefore, substances, as far as this definition explains a substance.

Thus neither by considering the first origin of ideas, nor by means of a definition are we able to arrive at any satisfactory notion of substance; which seems to me a sufficient reason for abandoning utterly that dispute concerning the materiality and immateriality of the soul, and makes me absolutely condemn even the question itself. We have no perfect idea of any thing but of a perception. A substance is entirely different from a perception. We have, therefore, no idea of a substance. Inhesion in something is suppos'd to be requisite to support the existence of our perceptions. Nothing appears requisite to support the existence of a perception. We have, therefore, no idea of inhesion. What possibility then of answering that question, *Whether perceptions inhere in a material or immaterial substance*, when we do not so much as understand the meaning of the question?

[. . .]

Section 6
Of Personal Identity

There are some philosophers, who imagine we are every moment intimately conscious of what we call our SELF; that we feel its existence and its continuance in existence; and are certain, beyond the evidence of a demonstration, both of its perfect identity and simplicity. The strongest sensation, the most violent passion, say they, instead of distracting us from this view, only fix it the more intensely, and make us consider their influence on *self* either by their pain or pleasure. To attempt a farther proof of this were to weaken its evidence; since no proof can be deriv'd from any fact, of which we are so intimately conscious; nor is there any thing, of which we can be certain, if we doubt of this.

Unluckily all these positive assertions are contrary to that very experience, which is pleaded for them, nor have we any idea of *self*, after the manner it is here explain'd. For from what impression cou'd this idea be deriv'd? This question 'tis impossible to answer without a manifest contradiction and absurdity; and yet 'tis a question, which must necessarily be answer'd, if we wou'd have the idea of self pass for clear and intelligible. It must be some one impression, that gives rise to every real idea. But self or person is not any one impression, but that to which our several impressions and ideas are suppos'd to have a reference. If any impression gives rise to the idea of self, that impression must continue invariably the same, thro' the whole course of our lives; since self is suppos'd to exist after that manner. But there is no impression constant and invariable. Pain and pleasure, grief and joy, passions and sensations succeed each other, and never all exist at the same time. It cannot, therefore, be from any of these impressions, or from any other, that the idea of self is deriv'd; and consequently there is no such idea.

But farther, what must become of all our particular perceptions upon this hypothesis? All these are different, and distinguishable, and separable from each other, and may be separately consider'd, and may exist separately, and have no need of any thing to support their exist-ence. After what manner, therefore, do they belong to self; and how are they connected with it? For my part, when I enter most intimately into what I call *myself*, I always stumble on some particular perception or other, of heat or cold, light or shade, love or hatred, pain or pleasure. I never can catch *myself* at any time without a perception, and never can observe any thing but the perception. When my perceptions are remov'd for any time, as by sound sleep; so long am I insensible of *myself*, and may truly be said not to exist. And were all my perceptions remov'd by death, and cou'd I neither think, nor feel, nor see, nor love, nor hate after the dissolution of my body, I shou'd be entirely annihilated, nor do I conceive what is farther requisite to make me a perfect non-entity. If any one upon serious and unprejudic'd reflection, thinks he has a different notion of *himself*, I must confess I can reason no longer with him. All I can allow him is, that he may be in the right as well as I, and that we are essentially different in this particular. He may, perhaps, perceive something simple and continu'd, which he calls *himself*; tho' I am certain there is no such principle in me.

But setting aside some metaphysicians of this kind, I may venture to affirm of the rest of mankind, that they are nothing but a bundle or collection of different perceptions, which succeed each other with an inconceivable rapidity, and are in a perpetual flux and move-ment. Our eyes cannot turn in their sockets without varying our perceptions. Our thought is still more variable than our sight; and all our other senses and faculties contribute to this change; nor is there any single power of the soul, which remains unalterably the same, per-haps for one moment. The mind is a kind of theatre, where several perceptions successively make their appearance; pass, re-pass, glide away, and mingle in an infinite variety of pos-tures and situations. There is properly no *simplicity* in it at one time, nor *identity* in differ-ent; whatever natural propension we may have to imagine that simplicity and identity. The comparison of the theatre must not mislead us. They are the successive perceptions only, that constitute the mind; nor have we the most distant notion of the place, where these scenes are represented, or of the materials, of which it is compos'd.

What then gives us so great a propension to ascribe an identity to these successive per-ceptions, and to suppose ourselves possest of an invariable and uninterrupted existence thro' the whole course of our lives? In order to answer this question, we must distinguish betwixt personal identity, as it regards our thought or imagination, and as it regards our passions or the concern we take in ourselves. The first is our present subject; and to explain it perfectly we must take the matter pretty deep, and account for that idendtity, which we attribute to plants and animals; there being a great analogy betwixt it, and the identity of a self or person.

We have a distinct idea of an object, that remains invariable and uninterrupted thro' a suppos'd variation of time; and this idea we call that of *identity* or *sameness*. We have also a distinct idea of several different objects existing in succession, and connected together by a close relation; and this to an accurate view affords as perfect a notion of *diversity*, as if there was no manner of relation among the objects. But tho' these two ideas of identity, and a succession of related objects be in themselves perfectly distinct, and even contrary, yet 'tis certain, that in our common way of thinking they are generally confounded with each other. That action of the imagination, by which we consider the uninterrupted and invariable object, and that by which we reflect on the succession of related objects, are almost the same to the feeling, nor is there much more effort of thought requir'd in the latter case than in the former. The relation facilitates the transition of the mind from one object to another, and renders its passage as smooth as if it contemplated one continu'd object. This resemblance is the cause of the confusion and mistake, and makes us substitute the notion of identity, instead of that of related objects. However at one instant we may consider the related succession as variable or interrupted, we are sure the next to ascribe to it a perfect identity, and regard it as invariable and uninterrupted. Our propensity to this mistake is so great from the resemblance above-mention'd, that we fall into it before we are aware; and tho' we incessantly correct ourselves by reflection, and return to a more accurate method of thinking, yet we cannot long sustain our philosophy, or take off this biass from the imagination. Our last resource is to yield to it, and boldly assert that these different related objects are in effect the same, however interrupted and variable. In order to justify to ourselves this absurdity, we often feign some new and unintelligible principle, that connects the objects together, and prevents their interruption or variation. Thus we feign the continu'd existence of the perceptions of our senses, to remove the interruption; and run into the notion of a *soul*, and *self*, and *substance*, to disguise the variation. But we may farther observe, that where we do not give rise to such a fiction, our propension to confound identity with relation is so great, that we are apt to imagine something unknown and mysterious, connecting the parts, beside their relation; and this I take to be the case with regard to the identity we ascribe to plants and vegetables. And even when this does not take place, we still feel a propensity to confound these ideas, tho' we are not able fully to satisfy ourselves in that particular, nor find any thing invariable and uninterrupted to justify our notion of identity.

Thus the controversy concerning identity is not merely a dispute of words. For when we attribute identity, in an improper sense, to variable or interrupted objects, our mistake is not confin'd to the expression, but is commonly attended with a fiction, either of something invariable and uninterrupted, or of something mysterious and inexplicable, or at least with a propensity to such fictions. What will suffice to prove this hypothesis to the satisfaction of every fair enquirer, is to show from daily experience and observation, that the objects, which are variable or interrupted, and yet are suppos'd to continue the same, are such only as consist of a succession of parts, connected together by resemblance, contiguity, or causation. For as such a succession answers evidently to our notion of diversity, it can only be by mistake we ascribe to it an identity; and as the relation of parts, which leads us into this mistake, is really nothing but a quality, which produces an association of ideas, and an easy transition of the imagination from one to another, it can only be from the resemblance, which this act of the mind bears to that, by which we contemplate one continu'd object, that the error arises. Our chief business, then, must be to prove, that all objects, to which we ascribe identity, without observing their invariableness and uninterruptedness, are such as consist of a succession of related objects.

In order to this, suppose any mass of matter, of which the parts are contiguous and connected, to be plac'd before us; 'tis plain we must attribute a perfect identity to this mass, provided all the parts continue uninterruptedly and invariably the same, whatever motion or change of place we may observe either in the whole or in any of the parts. But supposing some very *small* or *inconsiderable* part to be added to the mass, or substracted from it; tho' this absolutely destroys the identity of the whole, strictly speaking; yet as we seldom think so accurately, we scruple not to pronounce a mass of matter the same, where we find so trivial an alteration. The passage of the thought from the object before the change to the object after it, is so smooth and easy, that we scarce perceive the transition, and are apt to imagine, that 'tis nothing but a continu'd survey of the same object.

There is a very remarkable circumstance, that attends this experiment; which is, that tho' the change of any considerable part in a mass of matter destroys the identity of the whole, yet we must measure the greatness of the part, not absolutely, but by its *proportion* to the whole. The addition or diminution of a mountain wou'd not be sufficient to produce a diversity in a planet; tho' the change of a very few inches wou'd be able to destroy the identity of some bodies. 'Twill be impossible to account for this, but by reflecting that objects operate upon the mind, and break or interrupt the continuity of its actions not according to their real greatness, but according to their proportion to each other: And therefore, since this interruption makes an object cease to appear the same, it must be the uninterrupted progress of the thought, which constitutes the imperfect identity.

This may be confirm'd by another phænomenon. A change in any considerable part of a body destroys its identity; but 'tis remarkable, that where the change is produc'd *gradually* and *insensibly* we are less apt to ascribe to it the same effect. The reason can plainly be no other, than that the mind, in following the successive changes of the body, feels an easy passage from the surveying its condition in one moment to the viewing of it in another, and at no particular time perceives any interruption in its actions. From which continu'd perception, it ascribes a continu'd existence and identity to the object.

But whatever precaution we may use in introducing the changes gradually, and making them proportionable to the whole, 'tis certain, that where the changes are at last observ'd to become considerable, we make a scruple of ascribing identity to such different objects. There is, however, another artifice, by which we may induce the imagination to advance a step farther; and that is, by producing a reference of the parts to each other, and a combination to some *common end* or purpose. A ship, of which a considerable part has been chang'd by frequent reparations, is still consider'd as the same; nor does the difference of the materials hinder us from ascribing an identity to it. The common end, in which the parts conspire, is the same under all their variations, and affords an easy transition of the imagination from one situation of the body to another.

But this is still more remarkable, when we add a *sympathy* of parts to their *common end*, and suppose that they bear to each other, the reciprocal relation of cause and effect in all their actions and operations. This is the case with all animals and vegetables; where not only the several parts have a reference to some general purpose, but also a mutual dependance on, and connexion with each other. The effect of so strong a relation is, that tho' every one must allow, that in a very few years both vegetables and animals endure a *total* change, yet we still attribute identity to them, while their form, size, and substance are entirely alter'd. An oak, that grows from a small plant to a large tree, is still the same oak; tho' there be not one particle of matter, or figure of its parts the same. An infant becomes a man, and is sometimes fat, sometimes lean, without any change in his identity.

[. . .]

We now proceed to explain the nature of *personal identity*, which has become so great a question in philosophy, especially of late years in *England*, where all the abstruser sciences are study'd with a peculiar ardour and application. And here 'tis evident, the same method of reasoning must be continu'd, which has so successfully explain'd the identity of plants, and animals, and ships, and houses, and of all the compounded and changeable productions either of art or nature. The identity, which we ascribe to the mind of man, is only a fictitious one, and of a like kind with that which we ascribe to vegetables and animal bodies. It cannot, therefore, have a different origin, but must proceed from a like operation of the imagination upon like objects.

[. . .]

The only question, therefore, which remains, is, by what relations this uninterrupted progress of our thought is produc'd, when we consider the successive existence of a mind or thinking person? And here 'tis evident we must confine ourselves to resemblance and causation, and must drop contiguity, which has little or no influence in the present case.

To begin with *resemblance*; suppose we cou'd see clearly into the breast of another, and observe that succession of perceptions, which constitutes his mind or thinking principle, and suppose that he always preserves the memory of a considerable part of past perceptions; 'tis evident, that nothing cou'd more contribute to the bestowing a relation on this succession amidst all its variations. For what is the memory but a faculty, by which we raise up the images of past perceptions? And as an image necessarily resembles its object, must not the frequent placing of these resembling perceptions in the chain of thought, convey the imagination more easily from one link to another, and make the whole seem like the continuance of one object? In this particular, then, the memory not only discovers the identity, but also contributes to its production, by producing the relation of resemblance among the perceptions. The case is the same whether we consider ourselves or others.

As to *causation*; we may observe, that the true idea of the human mind, is to consider it as a system of different perceptions or different existences, which are link'd together by the relation of cause and effect, and mutually produce, destroy, influence, and modify each other. Our impressions give rise to their correspondent ideas; and these ideas in their turn produce other impressions. One thought chaces another, and draws after it a third, by which it is expell'd in its turn. In this respect, I cannot compare the soul more properly to any thing than to a republic or commonwealth, in which the several members are united by the reciprocal ties of government and subordination, and give rise to other persons, who propagate the same republic in the incessant changes of its parts. And as the same individual republic may not only change its members, but also its laws and constitutions; in like manner the same person may vary his character and disposition, as well as his impressions and ideas, without losing his identity. Whatever changes he endures, his several parts are still connected by the relation of causation. And in this view our identity with regard to the passions serves to corroborate that with regard to the imagination, by the making our distant perceptions influence each other, and by giving us a present concern for our past or future pains or pleasures.

As memory alone acquaints us with the continuance and extent of this succession of perceptions, 'tis to be consider'd, upon that account chiefly, as the source of personal identity. Had we no memory, we never shou'd have any notion of causation, nor consequently of that chain of causes and effects, which constitute our self or person. But having once acquir'd this notion of causation from the memory, we can extend the same chain of causes, and consequently the identity of our persons beyond our memory, and can comprehend times, and circumstances, and actions, which we have entirely forgot, but suppose in general to have existed. For how few of our past actions are there, of which we have any memory? Who can tell me, for instance, what were his thoughts and actions on the first of *January* 1715, the 11th of *March* 1719, and the 3d of *August* 1733? Or will he affirm, because he has entirely forgot the incidents of these days, that the present self is not the same person with the self of that time; and by that means overturn all the most establish'd notions of personal identity? In this view, therefore, memory does not so much *produce* as *discover* personal identity, by showing us the relation of cause and effect among our different perceptions. 'Twill be incumbent on those, who affirm that memory produces entirely our personal identity, to give a reason why we can thus extend our identity beyond our memory.

[. . .]

Book II
Part 3
Of the Will and Direct Passions

Section 1
Of Liberty and Necessity

[. . .]

Of all the immediate effects of pain and pleasure, there is none more remarkable than the WILL; and tho', properly speaking, it be not comprehended among the passions, yet as the full understanding of its nature and properties, is necessary to the explanation of them, we shall here make it the subject of our enquiry. I desire it may be observ'd, that by the *will*, I mean nothing but *the internal impression we feel and are conscious of, when we knowingly give rise to any new motion of our body, or new perception of our mind.* This impression, like the preceding ones of pride and humility, love and hatred, 'tis impossible to define, and needless to describe any farther; for which reason we shall cut off all those definitions and distinctions, with which philosophers are wont to perplex rather than clear up this question; and entering at first upon the subject, shall examine that long disputed question concerning *liberty and necessity*; which occurs so naturally in treating of the will.

'Tis universally acknowledg'd, that the operations of external bodies are necessary, and that in the communication of their motion, in their attraction, and mutual cohesion, there are not the least traces of indifference or liberty. Every object is determin'd by an absolute fate to a certain degree and direction of its motion, and can no more depart from that precise line, in which it moves, than it can convert itself into an angel, or spirit, or any superior substance. The actions, therefore, of matter are to be regarded as instances of necessary actions; and whatever is in this respect on the same footing with matter, must be acknowledg'd to be necessary. That we may know whether this be the case with the actions of the mind, we shall begin with examining matter, and considering on what the idea of a necessity in its operations is founded, and why we conclude one body or action to be the infallible cause of another.

It has been observ'd already, that in no single instance the ultimate connexion of any objects is discoverable, either by our senses or reason, and that we can never penetrate so far into the essence and construction of bodies, as to perceive the principle, on which their mutual influence depends. 'Tis their constant union alone, with which we are acquainted; and 'tis from the constant union the necessity arises. If objects had not an uniform and regular conjunction with each other, we shou'd never arrive at any idea of cause and effect; and even after all, the necessity, which enters into that idea, is nothing but a determination of the mind to pass from one object to its usual attendant, and infer the existence of one from that of the other. Here then are two particulars, which we are to consider as essential to necessity, *viz.* the constant *union* and the *inference* of the mind; and wherever we discover these we must acknowledge a necessity. As the actions of matter have no necessity, but what is deriv'd from these circumstances, and it is not by any insight into the essence of bodies we discover their connexion, the absence of this insight, while the union and inference remain, will never, in any case, remove the necessity. 'Tis the observation of the union, which produces the inference; for which reason it might be thought sufficient, if we prove a constant union in the actions of the mind, in order to establish the inference, along with the necessity of these actions. But that I may bestow a greater force on my reasoning, I shall examine these particulars apart, and shall first prove from experience, that our actions have a constant union with our motives, tempers, and circumstances, before I consider the inferences we draw from it.

To this end a very slight and general view of the common course of human affairs will be sufficient. There is no light, in which we can take them, that does not confirm this principle. Whether we consider mankind according to the difference of sexes, ages, governments, conditions, or methods of education; the same uniformity and regular operation of natural principles are discernible. Like causes still produce like effects; in the same manner as in the mutual action of the elements and powers of nature.

[. . .]

We must now show, that as the *union* betwixt motives and actions has the same constancy, as that in any natural operations, so its influence on the understanding is also the same, in *determining* us to infer the existence of one from that of another. If this shall appear, there is no known circumstance, that enters into the connexion and production of the actions of matter, that is not to be found in all the operations of the mind; and consequently we cannot, without a manifest absurdity, attribute necessity to the one, and refuse it to the other.

There is no philosopher, whose judgment is so riveted to this fantastical system of liberty, as not to acknowledge the force of *moral evidence*, and both in speculation and practice proceed upon it, as upon a reasonable foundation. Now moral evidence is nothing but a conclusion concerning the actions of men, deriv'd from the consideration of their motives, temper and situation. Thus when we see certain characters or figures describ'd upon paper, we infer that the person, who produc'd them, wou'd affirm such facts, the death of *Cæsar*, the success of *Augustus*, the cruelty of *Nero*; and remembring many other concurrent testimonies we conclude, that those facts were once really existent, and that so many men, without any interest, wou'd never conspire to deceive us; especially since they must, in the attempt, expose themselves to the derision of all their contemporaries, when these facts were asserted to be recent and universally known. The same kind of reasoning runs thro' politics, war, commerce, œconomy, and indeed mixes itself so entirely in human life, that 'tis impossible to act or subsist a moment without having recourse to it. A prince, who imposes a tax upon his subjects, expects their compliance. A general, who conducts an army, takes account of a certain degree of courage. A merchant looks for fidelity and skill in his factor or super-cargo. A man, who gives orders for his dinner, doubts not of the obedience of his servants. In short, as nothing more nearly interests us than our own actions and those of others, the greatest part of our reasonings is employ'd in judgments concerning them. Now I assert, that whoever reasons after this manner, does *ipso facto* believe the actions of the will to arise from necessity, and that he knows not what he means, when he denies it.

[. . .]

According to my definitions, necessity makes an essential part of causation; and consequently liberty, by removing necessity, removes also causes, and is the very same thing with chance. As chance is commonly thought to imply a contradiction, and is at least directly contrary to experience, there are always the same arguments against liberty or free-will. If any one alters the definitions, I cannot pretend to argue with him, till I know the meaning he assigns to these terms.

Section 2
The Same Subject Continu'd

I believe we may assign the three following reasons for the prevalence of the doctrine of liberty, however absurd it may be in one sense, and unintelligible in any other. *First*, After we have perform'd any action; tho' we confess we were influenc'd by particular views and motives; 'tis difficult for us to perswade ourselves we were govern'd by necessity, and that 'twas utterly impossible for us to have acted otherwise; the idea of necessity seeming to imply something of force, and violence, and constraint, of which we are not sensible. [. . .]

Secondly, There is a *false sensation* or *experience* even of the liberty of indifference; which is regarded as an argument for its real existence. The necessity of any action, whether of matter or of the mind, is not properly a quality in the agent, but in any thinking or intelligent being, who may consider the action, and consists in the determination of his thought to infer its existence from some preceding objects: As liberty or chance, on the other hand, is nothing but the want of that determination, and a certain looseness, which we feel in passing or not passing from the idea of one to that of the other. Now we may observe, that tho' in reflecting on human actions we seldom feel such a looseness or indifference, yet it very commonly happens, that in performing the actions themselves we are sensible of something like it: And as all related or resembling objects are readily taken for each other, this has been employ'd as a demonstrative or even an intuitive proof of human liberty. We feel that our actions are subject to our will on most occasions, and imagine we feel that the will itself is subject to nothing; because when by a denial of it we are provok'd to try, we feel that it moves easily every way, and produces an image of itself even on that side, on which it did not settle. [. . .]

A *third* reason why the doctrine of liberty has generally been better receiv'd in the world, than its antagonist, proceeds from *religion*, which has been very unnecessarily interested in this question. There is no method of reasoning more common, and yet none more blameable, than in philosophical debates to endeavour to refute any hypothesis by a pretext of its dangerous consequences to religion and morality. When any opinion leads us into absurdities, 'tis certainly false; but 'tis not certain an opinion is false, because 'tis of dangerous consequence. Such topics, therefore, ought entirely to be foreborn, as serving nothing to the discovery of truth, but only to make the person of an antagonist odious. This I observe in general, without pretending to draw any advantage from it. I submit myself frankly to an examination of this kind, and dare venture to affirm, that the doctrine of necessity, according to my explication of it, is not only innocent, but even advantageous to religion and morality.

I define necessity two ways, conformable to the two definitions of *cause*, of which it makes an essential part. I place it either in the constant union and conjunction of like objects, or in the inference of the mind from the one to the other. Now necessity, in both these senses, has universally, tho' tacitly, in the schools, in the pulpit, and in common life, been allow'd to belong to the will of man, and no one has ever pretended to deny, that we can draw inferences concerning human actions, and that those inferences are founded on the experienc'd union of like actions with like motives and circumstances. The only particular in which any one can differ from me, is either, that perhaps he will refuse to call this *necessity*. But as long as the meaning is understood, I hope the word can do no harm. Or that he will maintain there is something else in the operations of matter. Now whether it be so or not is of no consequence to religion, whatever it may be to natural philosophy. I may be mistaken in asserting, that we have no idea of any other connexion in the actions of body, and shall be glad to be farther instructed on that head: But sure I am, I ascribe nothing to the actions of the mind, but what must readily be allow'd of. Let no one, therefore, put an invidious construction on my words, by saying simply, that I assert the necessity of human actions, and place them on the same footing with the operations of senseless matter. I do not ascribe to the will that unintelligible necessity, which is suppos'd to lie in matter. But I ascribe to matter, that intelligible quality, call it necessity or not, which the most rigorous orthodoxy does or must allow to belong to the will. I change, therefore, nothing in the receiv'd systems, with regard to the will, but only with regard to material objects.

Nay I shall go farther, and assert, that this kind of necessity is so essential to religion and morality, that without it there must ensue an absolute subversion of both, and that every other supposition is entirely destructive to all laws both *divine* and *human*. 'Tis indeed certain, that as all human laws are founded on rewards and punishments, 'tis suppos'd as a fundamental principle, that these motives have an influence on the mind, and both produce the good and prevent the evil actions. We may give to this influence what name we please; but as 'tis usually conjoin'd with the action, common sense requires it shou'd be esteem'd a cause, and he look'd upon as an instance of that necessity, which I wou'd establish.

This reasoning is equally solid, when apply'd to *divine* laws, so far as the deity is consider'd as a legislator, and is suppos'd to inflict punishment and bestow rewards with a design to produce obedience. But I also maintain, that even where he acts not in his magisterial capacity, but is regarded as the avenger of crimes merely on account of their odiousness and deformity, not only 'tis impossible, without the necessary connexion of cause and effect in human actions, that punishments cou'd be inflicted compatible with justice and moral equity; but also that it cou'd ever enter into the thoughts of any reasonable being to inflict them. The constant and universal object of hatred or anger is a person or creature endow'd with thought and consciousness; and when any criminal or injurious actions excite that passion, 'tis only by their relation to the person or connexion with him. But according to the doctrine of liberty or chance, this connexion is reduc'd to nothing, nor are men more accountable for those actions, which are design'd and premeditated, than for such as are the most casual and accidental. Actions are by their very nature temporary and perishing; and where they proceed not from some cause in the characters and disposition of the person, who perform'd them, they infix not themselves upon him, and can neither redound to his honour, if good, nor infamy, if evil. The action itself may be blameable; it may be contrary to all the rules of morality and religion: But the person is not responsible for it; and as it proceeded from nothing in him, that is durable or constant, and leaves nothing of that nature behind it, 'tis impossible he can, upon its account, become the object of punishment or vengeance. According to the hypothesis of liberty, therefore, a man is as pure and untainted, after having committed the most horrid crimes, as at the first moment of his birth, nor is his character any way concern'd in his actions; since they are not deriv'd from it, and the wickedness of the one can never be us'd as a proof of the depravity of the other. 'Tis only upon the principles of necessity, that a person acquires any merit or demerit from his actions, however the common opinion may incline to the contrary.

But so inconsistent are men with themselves, that tho' they often assert, that necessity utterly destroys all merit and demerit either towards mankind or superior powers, yet they continue still to reason upon these very principles of necessity in all their judgments concerning this matter. Men are not blam'd for such evil actions as they perform ignorantly and casually, whatever may be their consequences. Why? But because the causes of these actions are only momentary, and terminate in them alone. Men are less blam'd for such evil actions, as they perform hastily and unpremeditately, than for such as proceed from thought and deliberation. For what reason? But because a hasty temper, tho' a constant cause in the mind, operates only by intervals, and infects not the whole character. Again, repentance wipes off every crime, especially if attended with an evident reformation of life and manners. How is this to be accounted for? But by asserting that actions render a person criminal, merely as they are proofs of criminal passions or principles in the mind; and when by any alteration of these principles they cease to be just proofs, they likewise cease to be criminal. But according to the doctrine of *liberty* or *chance* they never were just proofs, and consequently never were criminal.

Part II

Critics of Empiricism

Introduction

One guiding principle of empiricist philosophy was that nothing can be found in the mind that has not entered originally through the senses. Locke confirmed this principle through his arguments against innate ideas; Berkeley held firmly to it in his denial of the reality of material substance; and Hume affirmed it in maintaining that the ideas of the mind are one and all copies of sense impressions.

A second, equally important, influence on the empiricist movement in Britain was the impressive success of Sir Isaac Newton's explanation of motion in the physical world. Newton had described a small set of laws governing the behavior of all material bodies in space, including, of course, human bodies. Convinced as they were that the behavior of material bodies is wholly determined by the forces of their environment, the empiricists could hardly resist attempting similar explanations of the behavior of the human mind. Some would even think it an at least plausible hypothesis that the human soul is material, and therefore mortal: susceptible, like any material object, to division and disintegration. Quite naturally then, the empiricist philosophy was considered dangerous to religion, despite the anti-materialist arguments of Berkeley. But not all of empiricism's critics attacked it on religious grounds.

It remained unclear to many philosophers that the thinking behavior and capacities of the human mind could be adequately explained using only the input of sense experience. Leibniz, as mentioned in this volume's introduction, objected to Locke's description of the inexperienced, newly created mind as a "blank page." Leibniz's powerful law of the *identity of indiscernibles* would imply that there can be no more than one "blank page" mind. Another of Leibniz's objections to empiricism applied his *law of continuity*. There are no sudden "leaps" in the universe, he claimed, because there are no "gaps"; all transitions are gradual. We always emerge from sleep or unconsciousness by degrees, for example. Hence, there would be no sudden "start" to experience, as Locke's "blank page" hypothesis seems to imply. It was Leibniz's view, instead, that a lifetime of ideas or perceptions is already in the human soul at the moment of creation, and these emerge progressively into the clarity of our consciousness, in a pre-established order.

Our ideas of time and space are also difficult to explain within the empiricist framework. Leibniz pointed out, as Kant would also, that time and space themselves cannot be known through sense experience, because it is not a rich enough source of knowledge. We can of course sense the duration of a leaf's fall from a tree, and the extension of its descent. But these temporal and spatial properties occupy only parts of time and space: parts that we could not understand at all unless we had some prior idea of their respective wholes. For every part of time and of space is defined by its relation to every other part; yet there is no way any human being can sense all of time, and the whole of space. It was Leibniz's view, in fact, that time and space are unreal, and hence insensible. The argument he provided for the unreality or "insubstantiality" of time and space in his correspondence with Samuel Clarke made use of his fundamental *principle of sufficient reason*. He said that if time and space were real, eternal entities, then, since every point of time must be just like every other point of time, and since every point of space must be just like every other point of space, God would have had no reason for choosing to create the world at any point in time, and no reason for locating his Creation at any point in space. That is, God cannot choose from among the exactly equal or "indifferent" alternatives presented by the parts of empty time and space. Leibniz's argument here recalls St. Augustine's reply to those who asked, "What was God doing before Creation?" Augustine answered: there was no time before Creation, since God created time along with the world by giving us memory for things past, attention for things present, and expectation for things future.

But Clarke objects to Leibniz's limiting God's ability to choose between indifferent alternatives. Isn't freedom of choice the ability to choose, by an act of sheer will, even when we are presented with exactly equal alternatives? If we say otherwise, then this must mean that the difference between the alternatives from which we choose is what determines our choice, and not our free will itself. Consider a simple balance scale. When the weights on either side are exactly the same, the balance bar cannot incline either way. Only when the weights are different do we see an inclination in the balance; and the inclination always follows the heaviest weight. So what Leibniz is saying, according to Clarke, is that the will is like a simple balance scale, never able to incline *itself* in conditions of equilibrium, and so always inclined only by forces acting upon it. This, surely, is not what we expect from the will of God; and not even from our own free will.

Did Leibniz then deny that the will is truly, metaphysically free, in the same way as Locke and Hume? Scholars generally agree that he sided with the empiricists on this point, at least in broad outline. Leibniz's view was that the will is always inclined by a sufficient reason, by which he meant the greatest perceived good. But the will's choice is not "necessitated" by that reason, or by that perception of goodness. In other words, though our will is always causally determined to choose as it does, it is not logically necessary that we so choose. Hence, we are free. But as Kant would later complain, this gives us nothing more than the "freedom of a turnspit"!

Thomas Reid posed another line of objection to the empiricists, one he saw as undermining also the rationalist philosophy of Descartes. According to Reid, the path upon which Descartes embarked led inevitably to the skepticism of Hume. Despite the striking differences between the methods of Descartes and the empiricists, they all accepted as a fundamental principle something Reid found problematic. It is the principle that knowledge of objects requires *resemblance* between the real qualities of objects and the perceptions or ideas in the mind. This is why both Descartes and Locke concluded that the reality of the so-called secondary qualities of objects – color, sound, taste, smell, warmth – cannot be known. Our perceptions – of redness, for example – bear no resemblance to any feature of external objects that causes us to perceive them as red. This is also why Berkeley and Hume later concluded that neither can we know the reality of the so-called primary qualities of objects: extension, shape, movement, number. If the mind is not a spatial entity, then how can there be any perception in the mind resembling the extension, shape, or movement of external objects? Hume pushed the point one step further, pointing out that since all sense impressions are fleeting, neither can there be any perception in the mind resembling an enduring internal object: the mind itself. Hence, we are just as incapable of knowing ourselves as we are incapable of knowing the external world. Skepticism is the inevitable result of this principle that knowledge of objects requires resemblance between object and perception. But in Reid's view the common sense of human kind simply cannot embrace the prospect that we have no knowledge of objects or of ourselves: a prospect Reid dismissed as "metaphysical lunacy." He therefore concluded that, since the resemblance principle adopted by Descartes and the empiricists leads us to metaphysical lunacy, it cannot be correct.

A further charge Reid leveled focuses on the over-simplicity of the empiricists' model of the human mind. Newton had over-simplified the powers or forces explaining motion in the material world, he thought; and in their admiration for the elegance of Newton's system the empiricists had similarly over-simplified the active powers of the human mind. Implicit in every perception of the mind, Reid claimed, is a distinct mental act of "judgment" that cannot be reduced to a comparison of sense perceptions. We do not merely *sense* the objects of our environment, we at the same time *judge* that they are real, by an act of mind that cannot arise from sense experience. This mental power of judgment, by which we actively form beliefs, is in Reid's view part of our creator's original endowment to the human mind. The correct use of this power, and of others like it, is what Reid called "common sense."

Following this section on the critics of empiricism we turn to explore the philosophy of another of empiricism's critics, Immanuel Kant. Kant's contribution to the theory of knowledge will provide an opportunity to extend this final line of criticism suggested here by Reid. For Kant will also emphasize the mind's native activity in "processing" or "conceptualizing" the material passively received through sensation. He will additionally identify a set of innate ideas or concepts required in order for our processing of sense experience to take place. The mind's activity in sense experience, Kant will explain, is the process of making "judgments of experience" held to be "objectively valid" for all possible observers of the world. But this activity requires the assumption of both a law-governed natural world common to all possible observers, and a common set of concepts these observers apply in understanding their world. Reid, who knew nothing of Kant's philosophy as he developed his own, would have applauded Kant's finding the basis for objectivity in that which is common to humankind, even if Kant would refuse to base objectivity, as Reid did, on "common sense."

5

Gottfried Wilhelm Leibniz, *New Essays concerning Human Understanding* (1704)

The title of Leibniz's *New Essays* refers to Locke's *Essay concerning Human Understanding* (1690). The main body of the work is written in dialogue form, with one character virtually quoting from Locke's *Essay*, and another character, representing Leibniz, responding now and again with enthusiastic agreement, though more often with compelling criticism. Written in French, the manuscript appears to have been completed by 1704, but was not published until 1765, almost half a century after the death of Leibniz. One of the author's intentions in writing the *New Essays* seems have been to provoke Locke into a dialogue on substantive points of disagreement between the two. But after learning of Locke's death in November 1704, Leibniz evidently lost his chief motivation to publish the text. He later remarked also that he considered it unfair to publish criticism of an author unable to defend himself.

The relatively short selection reproduced here comes from Leibniz's Preface to the *New Essays*. It refers to some implications of the central tenets of his philosophy, including:

(a) *The doctrine of insensible perceptions*: the assumption that every soul ("monad") constantly perceives the entire universe, while the sense experience of every soul always differs from every other owing to its unique perspective. It follows from this doctrine that the vast majority of our perceptions are too obscure to be sensible. Leibniz sometimes compared the insensible perceptions to the confusing multitude of sounds of crashing waves that can be heard while walking along the beach, and which all together constitute the roar of the surf.

(b) *The pre-established harmony of soul and body*, according to which our minds and bodies do not causally interact. Changes in the mind merely correspond with changes in the body – for example, willful intention and bodily action – because this is how God originally set up the created universe. The mind and body harmonize like two separate clocks marking the same time.

(c) *The law of continuity*: the doctrine that "nature never makes leaps." All changes in the created world, including changes of perception and thought, come into being by degree. All apparently sudden or instantaneous events like, say, the shattering of a glass, are in reality gradual processes. Time-lapse photography can make this clear in many cases.

(d) *The identity of indiscernibles*, also known as "Leibniz's Law." This is the assumption in metaphysics that no two existing things could be exactly alike in all respects.

Leibniz was born in Leipzig, Germany, in 1646. He spent most of his adult life in service to the Hanover family of the European nobility, while finding time to contribute significantly to a wide number of academic disciplines and sciences, including law, religion, mathematics, physics, geology, and, of course, philosophy. Though many of Leibniz's philosophical ideas were widely known, he produced no systematic statement of his philosophy. Most of his philosophical writings were published after his death, in 1716.

Our gifted author seems to claim that there is nothing *implicit* in us, in fact nothing of which we are not always actually aware. But he cannot hold strictly to this; otherwise his position would be too paradoxical, since, again, we are not always aware of our acquired dispositions [*habitude*] or of the contents of our memory, and they do not even come to our aid whenever we need them, though often they come readily to mind when some idle circumstance reminds us of them, as when hearing the opening words of a song is enough to bring back the rest. So on other occasions he limits his thesis to the statement that there is nothing in us of which we have not at least previously been aware. But no one can establish by reason alone how far our past and now perhaps forgotten awarenesses may have extended, especially if we accept the Platonists' doctrine of recollection which, though sheer myth, is entirely consistent with unadorned reason. And furthermore, why must we acquire everything through awareness of outer things and not be able to unearth anything from within ourselves? Is our soul in itself so empty that unless it borrows images from outside it is nothing? I am sure that our judicious author could not approve of such a view. Where could tablets be found which were completely uniform? Will a perfectly homogeneous and even surface ever be seen? So why could we not also provide ourselves with objects of thought from our own depths, if we take the trouble to dig there? Which leads me to believe that fundamentally his view on this question is not different from my own or rather from the common view, especially since he recognizes two sources of our knowledge, the senses and reflection.

I doubt if it will be so easy to make him agree with us and with the Cartesians when he maintains that the mind does not think all the time, and in particular that it has no perceptions during dreamless sleep, arguing that since bodies can be without movement souls can just as well be without thought. But my response to this is a little different from the usual one. For I maintain that in the natural course of things no substance can lack activity, and indeed that there is never a body without movement. Experience is already on my side, and to be convinced one need only consult the distinguished Mr Boyle's book attacking absolute rest. But I believe that reason also supports this, and that is one of my proofs that there are no atoms. Besides, there are hundreds of indications leading us to conclude that at every moment there is in us an infinity of perceptions, unaccompanied by awareness or reflection; that is, of alterations in the soul itself, of which we are unaware because these impressions are either too minute and too numerous, or else too unvarying, so that they are not sufficiently distinctive on their own. But when they are combined with others they do nevertheless have their effect and make themselves felt, at least confusedly, within the whole. This is how we become so accustomed to the motion of a mill or a waterfall, after living beside it for a while, that we pay no heed to it. Not that this motion ceases to strike on our sense-organs, or that something corresponding to it does not still occur in the soul because of the harmony between the soul and the body; but these impressions in the soul and the body, lacking the appeal of novelty, are not forceful enough to attract our attention and our memory, which are applied only to more compelling objects. Memory is needed for attention: when we are not alerted, so to speak, to pay heed to certain of our own present perceptions, we allow them to slip by unconsidered and even unnoticed. But if someone alerts us to them straight away, and makes us take note, for instance, of some noise which we have just heard, then we remember it and are aware of just having had some sense of it. Thus, we were not straight away aware of these perceptions, and we became aware of them only because we were alerted to them after an interval, however brief. To give a clearer idea of these minute perceptions which we are unable to pick out from the crowd, I like to use the example of the roaring noise of the sea which impresses itself on us when we are standing on the shore. To hear this noise as we do, we must hear the parts which make up this whole, that is the noise of each wave, although each of these little noises makes itself known only when combined confusedly with all the others, and would not be noticed if the wave which made it were by itself. We must be affected slightly by the motion of this wave, and have some perception of each of these noises, however faint they may be; otherwise there would be no perception of a hundred thousand waves, since a hundred thousand nothings cannot make something. Moreover, we never sleep so soundly that we do not have some feeble and confused sensation; and the loudest noise in the world would never waken us if we did not have some perception of its start, which is small, just as the strongest force in the world would never break a rope unless the least force strained it and stretched it slightly, even though that little lengthening which is produced is imperceptible.

These minute perceptions, then, are more effective in their results than has been recognized. They constitute that *je ne sais quoi*, those flavours, those images of sensible qualities, vivid in the aggregate but confused as to the parts; those impressions which are made on us by the bodies around us and which involve the infinite; that connection that each being has with all the rest of the universe. It can even be said that by virtue of these minute perceptions the present is big with the future and burdened with the past, that all things harmonize – *sympnoia panta*, as Hippocrates put it – and that eyes as piercing as God's could read in the lowliest substance the universe's whole sequence of events – 'What is, what was, and what will soon be brought in by the future' [Virgil].

These insensible perceptions also indicate and constitute the same individual, who is characterized by the vestiges or expressions which the perceptions preserve from the individual's former states, thereby connecting these with his present state. Even when the individual himself has no sense of the previous states, i.e. no longer has any explicit memory of them, they could be known by a superior mind. But those perceptions also provide the means for recovering this memory at need, as a result of successive improvements which one may eventually undergo. That is why death can only be a sleep, and not a lasting one at that: the perceptions merely cease to be sufficiently distinct; in animals they are reduced to a state of confusion which puts awareness into abeyance but which cannot last for ever; and I shall not here discuss the case of man, who must in this regard have special prerogatives for safeguarding his personhood.

It is also through insensible perceptions that I account for that marvellous pre-established harmony between the soul and the body, and indeed amongst all the monads or simple substances, which takes the place of an untenable influence of one on another and, in the opinion of the author of the finest of dictionaries [Bayle], exalts the greatness of divine perfection beyond anything previously conceived. It would not be adding much to that if I said that it is these minute perceptions which determine our behaviour in many situations without our thinking of them, and which deceive the unsophisticated with an appearance of *indifference of equilibrium* – as if it made no difference to us, for instance, whether we turned left or right. I need not point out here, since I have done so in the work itself, that they cause that disquiet which I show to consist in something which differs from suffering only as small from large, and yet which frequently causes our desire and even our pleasure, to which it gives a dash of spice. They are also the insensible parts of our sensible perceptions, which bring it about that those perceptions of colours, warmth and other sensible qualities are related to the motions in bodies which correspond to them; whereas the Cartesians (like our author, discerning as he is), regard it as arbitrary what perceptions we have of these qualities, as if God had given them to the soul according to his good pleasure, without concern for any essential relation between perceptions and their objects. This is a view which surprises me and appears unworthy of the wisdom of the author of things, who does nothing without harmony and reason.

In short, insensible perceptions are as important to pneumatology as insensible corpuscles are to natural science, and it is just as unreasonable to reject the one as the other on the pretext that they are beyond the reach of our senses. Nothing takes place suddenly, and it is one of my great and best confirmed maxims that *nature never makes leaps*. I called this the Law of Continuity when I discussed it formerly in the *Nouvelles de la république des lettres* ['Letter on a general principle useful in explaining the laws of nature']. There is much work for this law to do in natural science. It implies that any change from small to large, or vice versa, passes through something which is, in respect of degrees as well as of parts, in between; and that no motion ever springs immediately from a state of rest, or passes into one except through a lesser motion; just as one could never traverse a certain line or distance without first traversing a shorter one. Despite which, until now those who have propounded the laws of motion have not complied with this law, since they have believed that a body can instantaneously receive a motion contrary to its preceding one. All of which supports the judgment that noticeable perceptions arise by degrees from ones which are too minute to be noticed. To think otherwise is to be ignorant of the immeasurable fineness of things, which always and everywhere involves an actual infinity.

I have also pointed out that in consequence of imperceptible variations no two individual things could be perfectly alike, and that they must always differ more than numerically. This puts an end to the blank tablets of the soul, a soul without thought, a substance without action, empty space, atoms, and even to portions of matter which are not actually divided, and also to absolute rest, completely uniform parts of time or place or matter, perfect spheres of the second element which take their origin from perfect cubes, and hundreds of other fictions which have arisen from the incompleteness of philosophers' notions. They are something which the nature of things does not allow of. They escape challenge because of our ignorance and our neglect of the insensible; but nothing could make them acceptable, short of their being confined to abstractions of the mind, with a formal declaration that the mind is not denying what it sets aside as irrelevant to some present concern. On the other hand if we meant literally that things of which we are unaware exist neither in the soul nor in the body, then we would fail in philosophy as in politics, because we would be neglecting *to mikron*, imperceptible changes. Whereas abstraction is not an error as long as one knows that what one is pretending not to notice, is *there*. This is what mathematicians are doing when they ask us to consider perfect lines and uniform motions and other regular effects, although matter (i.e. the jumble of effects of the surrounding infinity) always provides some exception. This is done so as to separate one circumstance from another and, as far as we can, to trace effects back to their causes and to foresee some of their results; the more care we take not to overlook any circumstance that we can control, the more closely practice corresponds to theory. But only the supreme Reason, who overlooks nothing, can distinctly grasp the entire infinite and see all the causes and all the results. All we can do with infinities is to know them confusedly and at least to know distinctly that they are there. Otherwise we shall not only judge quite wrongly as to the beauty and grandeur of the universe, but will be unable to have a sound natural science which explains the nature of things in general, still less a sound pneumatology, comprising knowledge of God, souls and simple substances in general.

This knowledge of insensible perceptions also explains why and how two souls of the same species, human or otherwise, never leave the hands of the Creator perfectly alike, each of them having its own inherent relationship to the point of view which it will have in the universe. But that follows from what I have already said about two individuals, namely that the difference between them is always more than numerical. There is another significant point on which I must differ, not only from our author, but from most of the moderns: I agree with most of the ancients that every Spirit, every soul, every created simple substance is always united with a body and that no soul is ever entirely without one. I have *a priori* reasons for this doctrine, but it will be found to have the further merit of solving all the philosophical difficulties about the state of souls, their perpetual preservation, their immortality, and their mode of operation. Their changes of state never are and never were anything but changes from more to less sensible, from more perfect to less perfect, or the reverse, so that their past and future states are just as explicable as their present one. Even the slightest reflection shows that this is reasonable, and that a leap from one state to an infinitely different one cannot be natural.

[. . .]

As for thought, it is certain, as our author more than once acknowledges, that it cannot be an intelligible modification of matter and be comprehensible and explicable in terms of it. That is, a sentient or thinking being is not a mechanical thing like a watch or a mill: one cannot conceive of sizes and shapes and motions combining mechanically to produce something which thinks, and senses too, in a mass where [formerly] there was nothing of the kind – something which would likewise be extinguished by the machine's going out of order. So sense and thought are not something which is natural to matter, and there are only two ways in which they could occur in it: through God's combining it with a substance to which thought is natural, or through his putting thought into it by a miracle. On this topic I am therefore entirely in agreement with the Cartesians, except that I include the beasts and believe that they too have sense, and souls which are properly described as immaterial and are as imperishable as atoms are according to Democritus and Gassendi; whereas the Cartesians have been needlessly perplexed over the souls of beasts. Not knowing what to do about them if they are preserved (since they have failed to hit on the idea of the preservation of the animal in miniature), they have been driven to deny – contrary to all appearances and to the general opinion of mankind – that beasts even have sense. But if someone said that God could at least join the faculty of thought to a machine which was made ready [for it], I should reply that if that were done, and if God added this faculty to matter without at the same time infusing into it a substance in which this same faculty inhered (which is how I conceive it) – i.e. without joining an immaterial soul to it – the matter would have had to be miraculously exalted in order to receive a power of which it is not naturally capable. Similarly some Scholastics claim that God exalts fire to the point where it is able, without any intermediary, to burn spirits separated from bodies, which would be a sheer miracle. Suffice it to say that we cannot maintain that matter thinks unless we put into it either an imperishable soul or a miracle; and thus that the immortality of our souls follows from what is natural, since we can only maintain their extinction by means of a miracle, whether through the exaltation of matter or through the annihilation of the soul. For we know very well that although our souls are immaterial and, in the ordinary course of nature, immortal, God's omnipotence could make them mortal since he can annihilate them.

Now, there is no doubt that this truth about the immateriality of the soul is important. For in our day especially, when many people have scant respect for pure revelation and miracles, it is infinitely more useful to religion and morality to show that souls are naturally immortal, and that it would be miraculous if they were not, than to maintain that it is of their nature to die but that, thanks to a miraculous grace resting solely on God's promise, they will not die. It has long been known that those who have sought to destroy natural religion and reduce everything to revelation, as if reason had nothing to teach us in this area, have been under suspicion, and not always without reason. But our author is not one of these; he upholds the demonstration of the existence of God and he accords the immateriality of the soul a 'probability in the highest degree', which can therefore be regarded as a *moral certainty*. Therefore, since his sincerity is as great as his insight, I should think he could thoroughly accommodate himself to the doctrine which I have just set forth and which is fundamental in any rational philosophy. Otherwise I do not see how one could keep from relapsing into philosophy which is either fanatical, like Fludd's *Mosaicall Philosophy* which saves all the phenomena by ascribing them immediately and miraculously to God, or barbarous, like that of certain philosophers and physicians of the past, who still reflected the barbarism of their own times and are today rightly scorned; these saved the appearances by fabricating faculties or occult qualities, just for the purpose, and fancying them to be like little demons or imps which can without ado perform whatever is wanted, as though pocket watches told the time by a certain horological faculty without needing wheels, or as though mills crushed grain by a fractive faculty without needing anything in the way of millstones. As for the difficulty which some nations have had in conceiving an immaterial substance: this will simply disappear (in large part at least) when it stops being a question of substance separated from matter; and indeed I do not believe that such substances ever occur naturally among created things. There are still other subjects on which the author of the *Essay* and I agree and disagree, such as infinity and freedom.

Gottfried Wilhelm Leibniz and Samuel Clarke, *The Leibniz–Clarke Correspondence* (1717)

In the last years of Leibniz's life he initiated a correspondence with the English clergyman Samuel Clarke, which was mediated by Princess Caroline of Wales. The complete correspondence consists of five papers by Leibniz and as many replies by Clarke. Leibniz had earlier entered what turned out to be a bitter controversy with some disciples of Newton over which one of them had invented calculus, and over the merits of the latter's theory of gravity. The correspondence with Clarke began subsequently, after Caroline showed Clarke a letter she had received from Leibniz that was critical of Newton's view of space. That letter is "Mr. Leibnitz's First Paper" as reproduced below.

In their correspondence, both Leibniz and Clarke are critical of Locke's empiricist theory of knowledge, which allowed that, for all we can know, material substances might be capable of thought. Locke had written in his *Essay* that "We have the *Ideas* of *Matter* and *Thinking*, but possibly shall never be able to know, whether any mere material Being thinks, or no; it being impossible for us, by the contemplation of our own *Ideas*, without revelation, to discover, whether Omnipotency has not given to some Systems of Matter fitly disposed, a power to perceive and think." It should be no more difficult for God to add a faculty of thinking to a material substance than for him to add to the material human body a spiritual substance capable of thought; or so Locke suggests. But conjectures like this displeased Leibniz and Clarke, in equal measure, since both were convinced that materialism is incompatible with the Christian religion.

The material from the *Correspondence* reproduced below highlights chiefly Leibniz's views on space and time. But his argument for the relativity of space and time here relies on his controversial theory of freedom of the will, with God's ability to choose under conditions of *indifference* or *equilibrium* in the objects of his choice being the central issue. We have seen in the introduction to this section how Leibniz held that there can be no free choice without a *sufficient reason*, and how this places him on the side of Locke and Hume in his theory of the freedom of the will. But Clarke argues here in reply that the sufficient reason for a free choice must always come from the will, from the free will of God in this case, and never from the alternative objects of that will.

Samuel Clarke (1675–1729) was a minister in the Church of England with philosophical talent sufficient to establish his fame as an advocate of religion against the claims of modern science. He might have become archbishop of Canterbury, had his views on the Trinity not been considered unorthodox. Of his philosophical works, the best known in his lifetime was a set of lectures given in 1704–5, on God's existence and our moral obligations. He is known today principally through his correspondence with Leibniz, which he prepared for publication in 1717, after Leibniz's death.

Mr. Leibnitz's First Paper being An Extract of a Letter Written in November, 1715

1. Natural religion itself, seems to decay (in England) very much. Many will have human souls to be material: others make God himself a corporeal being.

2. Mr. Locke, and his followers, are uncertain at least, whether the soul be not material, and naturally perishable.

3. Sir Isaac Newton says, that space is an organ, which God makes use of to perceive things by. But if God stands in need of any organ to perceive things by, it will follow, that they do not depend altogether upon him, nor were produced by him.

4. Sir Isaac Newton, and his followers, have also a very odd opinion concerning the work of God. According to their doctrine, God Almighty wants to wind up his watch from time to time: otherwise it would cease to move. He had not, it seems, sufficient foresight to make it a perpetual motion. Nay, the machine of God's making, is so imperfect, according to these gentlemen; that he is obliged to clean it now and then by an extraordinary concourse, and even to mend it, as a clockmaker mends his work; who must consequently be so much the more unskilful a workman, as he is oftener obliged to mend his work and to set it right. According to my opinion, the same force and vigour remains always in the world, and only passes from one part of matter to another, agreeably to the laws of nature, and the beautiful pre-established order. And I hold, that when God works miracles, he does not do it in order to supply the wants of nature, but those of grace. Whoever thinks otherwise, must needs have a very mean notion of the wisdom and power of God.

Dr. Clarke's First Reply

1. That there are some in England, as well as in other countries, who deny or very much corrupt even natural religion itself, is very true, and much to be lamented. But (next to the vicious affections of men) this is to be principally ascribed to the false philosophy of the materialists, to which the mathematical principles of philosophy are the most directly repugnant. That some make the souls of men, and others even God himself to be a corporeal being; is also very true: but those who do so, are the great enemies of the mathematical principles of philosophy; which principles, and which alone, prove matter, or body, to be the smallest and most inconsiderable part of the universe.

2. That Mr. Locke doubted whether the soul was immaterial or no, may justly be suspected from some parts of his writings: but herein he has been followed only by some materialists, enemies to the mathematical principles of philosophy; and who approve little or nothing in Mr. Locke's writings, but his errors.

3. Sir Isaac Newton doth not say, that space is the organ which God makes use of to perceive things by; nor that he has need of any medium at all, whereby to perceive things: but on the contrary, that he, being omnipresent, perceives all things by his immediate presence to them, in all space wherever they are, without the intervention or assistance of any organ or medium whatsoever. In order to make this more intelligible, he illustrates it by a similitude: that as the mind of man, by its immediate presence to the pictures or images of things, form'd in the brain by the means of the organs of sensation, sees those pictures as if they were the things themselves; so God sees all things, by his immediate presence to them; he being actually present to the things themselves, to all things in the universe; as the mind of man is present to all the pictures of things formed in his brain. Sir Isaac Newton considers the brain and organs of sensation, as the means by which those pictures are formed: but not as the means by which the mind sees or perceives those pictures, when they are so formed. And in the universe, he doth not consider things as if they were pictures, formed by certain means, or organs; but as real things, form'd by God himself, and seen by him in all places wherever they are, without the intervention of any medium at all. And this similitude is all that he means, when he supposes infinite space to be (as it were) the *sensorium* of the Omnipresent Being.

4. The reason why, among men, an artificer is justly esteemed so much the more skilful, as the machine of his composing will continue longer to move regularly without any farther interposition of the workman; is because the skill of all human artificers consists only in composing, adjusting, or putting together certain movements, the principles of whose motion are altogether independent upon the artificer: such as are weights and springs, and the like; whose forces are not made, but only adjusted, by the workman. But with regard to God, the case is quite different; because he not only composes or puts things together, but is himself the author and continual preserver of their original forces or moving powers: and consequently 'tis not a diminution, but the true glory of his workmanship, that nothing is done without his continual government and inspection. The notion of the world's being a great machine, going on without the interposition of God, as a clock continues to go without the assistance of a clockmaker; is the notion of materialism and fate, and tends, (under pretence of making God a *supra-mundane intelligence*,) to exclude providence and God's government in reality out of the world. And by the same reason that a philosopher can represent all things going on from the beginning of the creation, without any government or interposition of providence; a sceptic will easily argue still farther backwards, and suppose that things have from eternity gone on (as they now do) without any true creation or original author at all, but only what such arguers call all-wise and eternal nature. If a king had a kingdom, wherein all things would continually go on without his government or interposition, or without his attending to and ordering what is done therein; it would be to him, merely a nominal kingdom; nor would he in reality deserve at all the title of king or governor. And as those men, who pretend that in an earthly government things may go on perfectly well without the king himself ordering or disposing of any thing, may reasonably be suspected that they would like very well to set the king aside: so whosoever contends, that the course of the world can go on without the continual direction of God, the Supreme Governor; his doctrine does in effect tend to exclude God out of the world.

[. . .]

Mr. Leibnitz's Third Paper

1. According to the usual way of speaking, mathematical principles concern only mere mathematics, viz. numbers, figures, arithmetic, geometry. But metaphysical principles concern more general notions, such as are cause and effect.

2. The author grants me this important principle; that nothing happens without a sufficient reason, why it should be so, rather than otherwise. But he grants it only in words, and in reality denies it. Which shows that he does not fully perceive the strength of it. And therefore he makes use of an instance, which exactly falls in with one of my demonstrations against real absolute space, which is an idol of some modern Englishmen. I call it an idol, not in a theological sense, but in a philosophical one; as Chancellor Bacon says, that there are *idola tribus, idola specus.*

3. These gentlemen maintain therefore, that space is a real absolute being. But this involves them in great difficulties; for such a being must needs be eternal and infinite. Hence some have believed it to be God himself, or, one of his attributes, his immensity. But since space consists of parts, it is not a thing which can belong to God.

4. As for my own opinion, I have said more than once, that I hold space to be something merely relative, as time is that I hold it to be an order of coexistences, as time is an order of successions. For space denotes, in terms of possibility, an order of things which exist at the same time, considered as existing together; without enquiring into their manner of existing. And when many things are seen together, one perceives that order of things among themselves.

5. I have many demonstrations, to confute the fancy of those who take space to be a substance, or at least an absolute being. But I shall only use, at the present, one demonstration, which the author here gives me occasion to insist upon. I say then, that if space was an absolute being, there would something happen for which it would be impossible there should be a sufficient reason. Which is against my axiom. And I prove it thus. Space is something absolutely uniform; and, without the things placed in it, one point of space does not absolutely differ in any respect whatsoever from another point of space. Now from hence it follows, (supposing space to be something in itself, besides the order of bodies among themselves,) that 'tis impossible there should be a reason, why God, preserving the same situations of bodies among themselves, should have placed them in space after one certain particular manner, and not otherwise; why every thing was not placed the quite contrary way, for instance, by changing East into West. But if space is nothing else, but that order or relation; and is nothing at all without bodies, but the possibility of placing them; then those two states, the one such as it now is, the other supposed to be the quite contrary way, would not at all differ from one another. Their difference therefore is only to be found in our chimerical supposition of the reality of space in itself. But in truth the one would exactly be the same thing as the other, they being absolutely indiscernible; and consequently there is no room to enquire after a reason of the preference of the one to the other.

6. The case is the same with respect to time. Supposing any one should ask, why God did not create every thing a year sooner; and the same person should infer from thence, that God has done something, concerning which 'tis not possible there should be a reason, why he did it so, and not otherwise: the answer is, that his inference would be right, if time was any thing distinct from things existing in time. For it would be impossible there should be any reason, why things should be applied to such particular instants, rather than to others, their succession continuing the same. But then the same argument proves, that instants,

consider'd without the things, are nothing at all; and that they consist only in the successive order of things: which order remaining the same, one of the two states, viz. that of a supposed anticipation, would not at all differ, nor could be discerned from, the other which now is.

7. It appears from what I have said, that my axiom has not been well understood; and that the author denies it, tho' he seems to grant it. 'Tis true, says he, that there is nothing without a sufficient reason why it is, and why it is thus, rather than otherwise: but he adds, that this sufficient reason, is often the simple or mere will of God: as, when it is asked why matter was not placed otherwhere in space; the same situations of bodies among themselves being preserved. But this is plainly maintaining, that God wills something, without any sufficient reason for his will: against the axiom, or the general rule of whatever happens. This is falling back into the loose indifference, which I have confuted at large, and showed to be absolutely chimerical even in creatures, and contrary to the wisdom of God, as if he could operate without acting by reason.

8. The author objects against me, that if we don't admit this simple and mere will, we take away from God the power of choosing, and bring in a fatality. But the quite contrary is true. I maintain that God has the power of choosing, since I ground that power upon the reason of a choice agreeable to his wisdom. And 'tis not this fatality, (which is only the wisest order of providence) but a blind fatality or necessity, void of all wisdom and choice, which we ought to avoid.

[. . .]

Mr. Leibnitz's Fourth Paper

1. In things absolutely indifferent, there is no [foundation for] choice; and consequently no election, nor will; since choice must be founded on some reason, or principle.

2. A mere will without any motive, is a fiction, not only contrary to God's perfection, but also chimerical and contradictory; inconsistent with the definition of the will, and sufficiently confuted in my Theodicy.

3. 'Tis a thing indifferent, to place three bodies, equal and perfectly alike, in any order whatsoever; and consequently they will never be placed in any order, by him who does nothing without wisdom. But then he being the author of things, no such things will be produced by him at all; and consequently there are no such things in nature.

4. There is no such thing as two individuals indiscernible from each other. An ingenious gentleman of my acquaintance, discoursing with me, in the presence of Her Electoral Highness the Princess Sophia, in the garden of Herrenhausen; thought he could find two leaves perfectly alike. The Princess defied him to do it, and he ran all over the garden a long time to look for some; but it was to no purpose. Two drops of water, or milk, viewed with a microscope, will appear distinguishable from each other. This is an argument against atoms; which are confuted, as well as a vacuum, by the principles of true metaphysics.

5. Those great principles of a *sufficient reason*, and of the *identity of indiscernibles*, change the state of metaphysics. That science becomes real and demonstrative by means of these principles; whereas before, it did generally consist in empty words.

6. To suppose two things indiscernible, is to suppose the same thing under two names. And therefore to suppose that the universe could have had at first another position of time

and place, than that which it actually had; and yet that all the parts of the universe should have had the same situation among themselves, as that which they actually had; such a supposition, I say, is an impossible fiction.

7. The same reason, which shows that extramundane space is imaginary, proves that all empty space is an imaginary thing; for they differ only as greater and less.

8. If space is a property or attribute, it must be the property of some substance. But what substance will that bounded empty space be an affection or property of, which the persons I am arguing with, suppose to be between two bodies?

9. If infinite space is immensity, finite space will be the opposite to immensity, that is, 'twill be mensurability, or limited extension. Now extension must be the affection of some thing extended. But if that space be empty, it will be an attribute without a subject, an extension without any thing extended. Wherefore by making space a property, the author falls in with my opinion, which makes it an order of things, and not any thing absolute.

10. If space is an absolute reality; far from being a property or an accident opposed to substance, it will have a greater reality than substances themselves. God cannot destroy it, nor even change it in any respect. It will be not only immense in the whole, but also immutable and eternal in every part. There will be an infinite number of eternal things besides God.

[. . .]

[Dr. Clarke's Final Reply*]

As multitudes of words are neither an argument of clear ideas in the writer, nor a proper means of conveying clear notions to the reader; I shall endeavour to give a distinct answer to this Fifth Paper, as briefly as I can.

1–20. There is no (§3) similitude between a balance being moved by weights or impulse, and a mind moving itself, or acting upon the view of certain motives. The difference is, that the one is entirely passive; which is being subject to absolute necessity: the other not only is acted upon, but acts also; which is the essence of liberty. To (§14) suppose that an equal apparent goodness in different ways of acting, takes away from the mind all power of acting at all, as an equality of weights keeps a balance necessarily at rest; is denying the mind to have in itself a principle of action; and is confounding the power of acting, with the impression made upon the mind by the motive, wherein the mind is purely passive. The motive, or thing considered as in view, is something extrinsic to the mind: the impression made upon the mind by that motive, is the perceptive quality, in which the mind is passive: the doing of any thing, upon and after, or in consequence of, that perception; this is the power of self-motion or action: which in all animate agents, is spontaneity; and, in moral agents, is what we properly call liberty. The not carefully distinguishing these things, but confounding (§15) the motive with the principle of action, and denying the mind to have any principle of action besides the motive, (when indeed in receiving the impression of the motive, the mind is purely passive;) this, I say, is the ground of the whole error; and leads men to think that the mind

---

* The following selections are from Clarke's reply to Leibniz's fifth and final contribution to the correspondence. Numbers scattered throughout refer to individually numbered paragraphs in Leibniz's Fifth Paper, and sometimes to longer passages of multiple numbered paragraphs.

is no more active, than a balance would be with the addition of a power of perception: which is wholly taking away the very notion of liberty. A balance pushed on both sides with equal force, or pressed on both sides with equal weights, cannot move at all: and supposing the balance endued with a power of perception, so as to be sensible of its own incapacity to move; or so as to deceive itself with an imagination that it moves itself, when indeed it is only moved; it would be exactly in the same state, wherein this learned author supposes a free agent to be in all cases of absolute indifference. But the fallacy plainly lies here: the balance, for want of having in itself a principle or power of action, cannot move at all when the weights are equal: but a free agent, when there appear two, or more, perfectly alike reasonable ways of acting, has still within itself, by virtue of its self-motive principle, a power of acting: and it may have very strong and good reasons, not to forbear acting at all; when yet there may be no possible reason to determine one particular way of doing the thing, to be better than another. To affirm therefore, (§§16–19, 69) that supposing two different ways of placing certain particles of matter were equally good and reasonable, God could neither wisely nor possibly place them in either of those ways, for want of a sufficient weight to determine him which way he should choose; is making God not an active, but a passive being: which is, not to be a God, or governor, at all. And for denying the possibility of the supposition, that there may be two equal parts of matter, which may with equal fitness be transposed in situation; no other reason can be alleged, but this (§20) *petitio principii*, that then this learned writer's notion of a sufficient reason would not be well-grounded. For otherwise, how can any man say, that 'tis (§§16, 17, 69, 66) impossible for God to have wise and good reasons to create many particles of matter exactly alike in different parts of the universe? In which case, the parts of space being alike, 'tis evident there can be no reason, but mere will, for not having originally transposed their situations. And yet even this cannot be reasonably said to be a (§§16, 69) will without motive; for as much as the wise reasons God may possibly have to create many particles of matter exactly alike, must consequently be a motive to him to take (what a balance could not do,) one out of two absolutely indifferents; that is, to place them in one situation, when the transposing of them could not but have been exactly alike good.

[. . .]

107–109. I affirmed, that, with regard to God, no one possible thing is more miraculous than another; and that therefore a miracle does not consist in any difficulty in the nature of the thing to be done, but merely in the unusualness of God's doing it. The terms, *nature*, and *powers of nature*, and *course of nature*, and the like, are nothing but empty words; and signify merely, that a thing usually or frequently comes to pass. The raising of a human body out of the dust of the earth, we call a miracle; the generation of a human body in the ordinary way, we call natural; for no other reason, but because the power of God effects one usually, the other unusually. The sudden stopping of the sun (or earth,) we call a miracle; the continual motion of the sun (or earth,) we call natural; for the very same reason only, of the one's being usual and the other unusual. Did man usually arise out of the grave, as corn grows out of seed sown, we should certainly call that also natural; and did the sun (or earth,) constantly stand still, we should then think that to be natural, and its motion at any time would be miraculous. Against these evident reasons, (ces (§108) *grandes raisons*) this learned writer offers nothing at all; but continues barely to refer us to the vulgar forms of speaking of certain philosophers and divines: which (as I before observed) is not the matter in question.

110–116. It is here very surprising, that, in a point of reason and not of authority, we are still again (§110) remitted to the opinions of certain philosophers and divines. But, to omit this: what does this learned writer mean by a (§110) *real internal difference* between what is miraculous, and not miraculous; or between (§111) operations natural, and not natural; absolutely, and with regard to God? Does he think there are in God two different and really distinct principles or powers of acting, and that one thing is more difficult to God than another? If not: then either a *natural* and a *super-natural action* of God, are terms whose signification is only relative to us; we calling an usual effect of God's power, *natural*; and an unusual one, *supernatural*; the (§112) *force of nature* being, in truth, nothing but an empty word: or else, by the one must be meant that which God does immediately himself; and by the other, that which he does mediately by the instrumentality of second causes. The former of these distinctions, is what this learned author is here professedly opposing: the latter is what he expressly disclaims, (§117) where he allows that angels may work true miracles. And yet besides these two, I think no other distinction can possibly be imagined.

It is very unreasonable to call (§113) attraction a miracle, and an unphilosophical term; after it has been so often distinctly declared that by that term we do not mean to express the cause of bodies tending towards each other, but barely the effect, or the phenomenon itself, and the laws or proportions of that tendency discovered by experience; whatever be or be not the cause of it. And it seems still more unreasonable, not to admit gravitation or attraction in this sense, in which it is manifestly an actual phenomenon of nature; and yet at the same time to expect that there should be admitted so strange an hypothesis, as the (§§109, 92, 87, 89, 90) *harmonia praestabilita*; which is, that the soul and body of a man have no more influence upon each other's motions and affections, than two clocks, which, at the greatest distance from each other, go alike, without at all affecting each other. It is alleged indeed that God, (§92) foreseeing the inclinations of every man's soul, so contrived at first the great machine of the material universe, as that by the mere necessary laws of mechanism, suitable motions should be excited in human bodies, as parts of that great machine. But is it possible, that such kinds of motion, and of such variety, as those in human bodies are; should be performed by mere mechanisms, without any influence of will and mind upon them? Or is it credible, that when a man has it in his power to resolve and know a month before-hand, what he will do upon such a particular day or hour to come; is it credible, I say, that his body shall by the mere power of mechanism, impressed originally upon the material universe at its creation, punctually conform itself to the resolutions of the man's mind at the time appointed? According to this hypothesis, all arguments in philosophy, taken from phenomena and experiments, are at an end. For, if the *harmonia praestabilita* be true, a man does not indeed see, nor hear, nor feel any thing, nor moves his body; but only dreams that he sees, and hears, and feels, and moves his body. And if the world can once be persuaded, that a man's body is a mere machine; and that all his seemingly voluntary motions are performed by the mere necessary laws of corporeal mechanism, without any influence, or operation, or action at all of the soul upon the body; they will soon conclude, that this machine is the whole man; and that the harmonical soul, in the hypothesis of an *harmonia praestabilita*, is merely a fiction and a dream. Besides: what difficulty is there avoided, by so strange an hypothesis? This only; that it cannot be conceived (it seems) how immaterial substance should act upon matter. But is not God an immaterial substance? And does not he act upon matter? And what greater difficulty is there in conceiving how an immaterial substance should act upon matter, than in conceiving how matter acts upon matter? Is it not as easy to conceive, how certain parts of matter may be obliged to follow the motions and affections of the soul, without corporeal contact; as that certain portions of matter should be obliged to follow each other's motions by the adhesion of parts, which no mechanism can account for; or that rays of light should reflect regularly from a surface which they never touch? Of which, Sir Isaac Newton in his *Opticks* has given us several evident and ocular experiments.

Nor is it less surprising, to find this assertion again repeated in express words, that, after the first creation of things, (§§115–16) the continuation of the motions of the heavenly bodies, and the formation of plants and animals, and every motion of the bodies both of men and all other animals, is as mechanical as the motions of a clock. Whoever entertains this opinion, is (I think) obliged in reason to be able to explain particularly, by what laws of mechanism the planets and comets can continue to move in the orbs they do, thro' unresisting spaces; and by what mechanical laws, both plants and animals are formed; and how the infinitely various spontaneous motions of animals and men, are performed. Which, I am fully persuaded, is as impossible to make out, as it would be to show how a house or city could be built, or the world itself have been at first formed by mere mechanism, without any intelligent and active cause. That things could not be at first produced by mechanism, is expressly allowed: and, when this is once granted; why, after that, so great concern should be shown, to exclude God's actual government of the world, and to allow his providence to act no further than barely in concurring (as the phrase is) to let all things do only what they would do of themselves by mere mechanism; and why it should be thought that God is under any obligation or confinement either in nature or wisdom, never to bring about any thing in the universe, but what is possible for a corporeal machine to accomplish by mere mechanic laws, after it is once set a going; I can no way conceive.

117. This learned author's allowing in this place, that there is greater and less in true miracles, and that angels are capable of working some true miracles; is perfectly contradictory to that notion of the nature of a miracle, which he has all along pleaded for in these papers.

118–123. That the sun attracts the earth, through the intermediate void space; that is, that the earth and sun gravitate towards each other, or tend (whatever be the cause of that tendency) towards each other, with a force which is in a direct proportion to their masses, or magnitudes and densities together, and in an inverse duplicate proportion of their distances; and that the space betwixt them is void, that is, hath nothing in it which sensibly resists the motion of bodies passing transversely through: all this, is nothing but a phenomenon, or actual matter of fact, found by experience. That this phenomenon is not produced (§118) *sans moyen*, that is without some cause capable of producing such an effect; is undoubtedly true. Philosophers therefore may search after and discover that cause, if they can; be it mechanical, or not mechanical. But if they cannot discover the cause; is therefore the effect itself, the phenomenon, or the matter of fact discovered by experience, (which is all that is meant by the words attraction and gravitation,) ever the less true? Or is a manifest quality to be called (§122) *occult*, because the immediate efficient cause of it (perhaps) is occult, or not yet discovered? When a body (§123) moves in a circle, without flying off in the tangent; 'tis certain there is something that hinders it: but if in some cases it be not mechanically (§123) explicable, or be not yet discovered, what that something is; does it therefore follow, that the phenomenon itself is false? This is very singular arguing indeed.

124–130. The phenomenon itself, the attraction, gravitation, or tendency of bodies towards each other, (or whatever other name you please to call it by;) and the laws, or proportions, of that tendency, are now sufficiently known by observations and experiments. If this or any other learned author can by (§124) the laws of mechanism explain these phenomena, he will not only not be contradicted, but will moreover have the abundant thanks of the learned world. But, in the mean time, to (§128) compare gravitation, (which is a phenomenon or actual matter of fact,) with Epicurus's declination of atoms, (which, according to his corrupt and atheistical perversion of some more ancient and perhaps better philosophy, was an hypothesis or fiction only, and an impossible one too, in a world where no intelligence was supposed to be present;) seems to be a very extraordinary method of reasoning.

As to the grand principle of a (§125) sufficient reason; all that this learned writer here adds concerning it, is only by way of affirming and not proving, his conclusion; and therefore needs no answer. I shall only observe, that the phrase is of an equivocal signification; and may either be so understood, as to mean necessity only, or so as to include likewise will and choice. That in general there (§125) is a sufficient reason why every thing is, which is; is undoubtedly true, and agreed on all hands. But the question is, whether, in some cases, when it may be highly reasonable to act, yet different possible ways of acting may not possibly be equally reasonable; and whether, in such cases, the bare will of God be not itself a sufficient reason for acting in this or the other particular manner; and whether in cases where there are the strongest possible reasons altogether on one side, yet in all intelligent and free agents, the principle of action (in which I think the essence of liberty consists,) be not a distinct thing from the motive or reason which the agent has in his view. All these are constantly denied by this learned writer. And his (§§20, 25, etc.) laying down his grand principle of a sufficient reason in such a sense as to exclude all these; and expecting it should be granted him in that sense, without proof; this is what I call his *petitio principii*, or begging of the question: than which, nothing can be more unphilosophical.

Thomas Reid, *An Inquiry into the Human Mind on the Principles of Common Sense* (1764)

It is fair to say that Thomas Reid's philosophy took its starting point from that of David Hume, whom he knew and admired, despite disagreeing with many of his views. Reid considered Hume's views to be the inevitable consequence of a problematic doctrine adopted with Descartes's initiation of modern philosophy: the doctrine, affirmed by all empiricists, that our awareness of things reaches only as far as the ideas of them in our minds. This doctrine leads ultimately to hopeless skepticism, according to Reid, and he credits Hume with being the first philosopher to have understood this. Both Descartes and Locke assumed that we can know external objects when we can be assured that our ideas resemble them. But Berkeley's attack on the reality of the so-called "primary" qualities caused trouble for the assumption that ideas in the mind could resemble anything other than ideas. Hume subsequently argued that, since there should be no way to have an idea of something existing independently of our sensing it, it must be sheer nonsense even to ask whether our ideas resemble any thing as it really is, apart from of our idea of it. Reid found Hume's reasoning here to be exactly right, and concluded that there must therefore be something wrong with one of modern philosophy's principal doctrines: that consciousness extends only to ideas.

Reid's positive contribution to the history of philosophy is as the founder of the Scottish school of "common sense." He held, first, that the mind must be active in interpreting the sensory data delivered to consciousness through a native intellectual power of "judgment." Second, he maintained that the set of basic principles or standards by which we judge the reliability of our sense experience forms the common sense of humankind. As the most basic principles of human knowledge, these cannot be confirmed through either reasoning or experience; but to doubt them is "lunacy."

The reading selections below come from the concluding chapter of Reid's first major work, published in 1764. He distinguished here between a time-honored method in philosophy he called the *method of analogy*, and the new, more promising procedure of Descartes, called the *method of reflection*. In regard to our knowledge of external objects, Reid distinguished also between the ancient, "peripatetic" philosophy and the new philosophy since Descartes. Aristotle ranks among the Peripatetics, who relied on the method of analogy and who assumed without question that objects of knowledge exist outside the mind. The

Peripatetics explained that an external object is represented within the mind by imprinting merely its form, not its matter.

Reid (1710–96) spent nearly fifteen years as a Presbyterian minister in northern Scotland before becoming a professor of philosophy at King's College in Aberdeen, and later at the University of Glasgow. Along with Adam Smith and Immanuel Kant, he is one of very few modern philosophers recognized today who held university teaching posts.

Chapter VII
Conclusion

There are two ways in which men may form their notions and opinions concerning the mind, and concerning its powers and operations. The first is the only way that leads to truth; but it is narrow and rugged, and few have entered upon it. The second is broad and smooth, and hath been much beaten, not only by the vulgar, but even by philosophers: it is sufficient for common life, and is well adapted to the purposes of the poet and orator: but, in philosophical disquisitions concerning the mind, it leads to error and delusion.

We may call the first of these ways, *the way of reflection*. When the operations of the mind are exerted, we are conscious of them; and it is in our power to attend to them, and to reflect upon them, until they become familiar objects of thought. This is the only way in which we can form just and accurate notions of those operations. But this attention and reflection is so difficult to man, surrounded on all hands by external objects which constantly solicit his attention, that it has been very little practised, even by philosophers. In the course of this inquiry, we have had many occasions to show, how little attention hath been given to the most familiar operations of the senses.

The second, and the most common way, in which men form their opinions concerning the mind and its operations, we may call *the way of analogy*. There is nothing in the course of nature so singular, but we can find some resemblance, or at least some analogy, between it and other things with which we are acquainted. The mind naturally delights in hunting after such analogies, and attends to them with pleasure. From them, poetry and wit derive a great part of their charms; and eloquence, not a little of its persuasive force.

Besides the pleasure we receive from analogies, they are of very considerable use, both to facilitate the conception of things, when they are not easily apprehended without such a handle, and to lead us to probable conjectures about their nature and qualities, when we want the means of more direct and immediate knowledge. When I consider that the planet Jupiter, in like manner as the earth, rolls round his own axis, and revolves round the sun, and that he is enlightened by several secondary planets, as the earth is enlightened by the moon; I am apt to conjecture from analogy, that as the earth by these means is fitted to be the habitation of various orders of animals, so the planet Jupiter is, by the like means, fitted for the same purpose; and having no argument more direct and conclusive to determine me in this point, I yield, to this analogical reasoning, a degree of assent proportioned to its strength. When I observe, that the potatoe plant very much resembles the *solanum* in its flower and fructification, and am informed, that the last is poisonous, I am apt from analogy to have some suspicion of the former: but in this case, I have access to more direct and certain evidence; and therefore ought not to trust to analogy, which would lead me into an error.

[. . .]

1. It may be observed, That the method which Des Cartes pursued, naturally led him to attend more to the operations of the mind by accurate reflection, and to trust less to analogical reasoning upon this subject, than any philosopher had done before him. Intending to build a system upon a new foundation, he began with a resolution to admit nothing but what was absolutely certain and evident. He supposed that his senses, his memory, his reason, and every other faculty to which we trust in common life, might be fallacious; and resolved to disbelieve every thing, until he was compelled by irresistible evidence to yield assent.

In this method of proceeding, what appeared to him, first of all, certain and evident, was, That he thought, that he doubted, that he deliberated. In a word, the operations of his own mind, of which he was conscious, must be real, and no delusion; and though all his other faculties should deceive him, his consciousness could not. This therefore he looked upon as the first of all truths. This was the first firm ground upon which he set his foot, after being tossed in the ocean of scepticism; and he resolved to build all knowledge upon it, without seeking after any more first principles.

As every other truth, therefore, and particularly the existence of the objects of sense, was to be deduced by a train of strict argumentation from what he knew by consciousness, he was naturally led to give attention to the operations of which he was conscious, without borrowing his notions of them from external things.

It was not in the way of analogy, but of attentive reflection, that he was led to observe, That thought, volition, remembrance, and the other attributes of the mind, are altogether unlike to extension, to figure, and to all the attributes of body; that we have no reason, therefore, to conceive thinking substances to have any resemblance to extended substances; and that, as the attributes of the thinking substance are things of which we are conscious, we may have a more certain and immediate knowledge of them by reflection, than we can have of external objects by our senses.

These observations, as far as I know, were first made by Des Cartes; and they are of more importance, and throw more light upon the subject, than all that had been said upon it before. They ought to make us diffident and jealous of every notion concerning the mind and its operations, which is drawn from sensible objects in the way of analogy, and to make us rely only upon accurate reflection, as the source of all real knowledge upon this subject.

2. I observe, That as the Peripatetic system has a tendency to materialize the mind, and its operations; so the Cartesian has a tendency to spiritualize body, and its qualities. One error, common to both systems, leads to the first of these extremes in the way of analogy, and to the last, in the way of reflection. The error I mean is, That we can know nothing about body, or its qualities, but as far as we have sensations which resemble those qualities. Both systems agreed in this: but according to their different methods of reasoning, they drew very different conclusions from it; the Peripatetic drawing his notions of sensation from the qualities of body; the Cartesian, on the contrary, drawing his notions of the qualities of body from his sensations.

The Peripatetic, taking it for granted that bodies and their qualities do really exist, and are such as we commonly take them to be, inferred from them the nature of his sensations, and reasoned in this manner: Our sensations are the impressions which sensible objects make upon the mind, and may be compared to the impression of a seal upon wax; the impression is the image or form of the seal, without the matter of it: in like manner, every sensation is the image or form of some sensible quality of the object. This is the reasoning of Aristotle, and it has an evident tendency to materialize the mind, and its sensations.

The Cartesian, on the contrary, thinks, that the existence of body, or of any of its qualities, is not to be taken as a first principle; and that we ought to admit nothing concerning it, but what, by just reasoning, can be deduced from our sensations; and he knows, that by reflection we can form clear and distinct notions of our sensations, without borrowing our notions of them by analogy from the objects of sense. The Cartesians, therefore, beginning to give attention to their sensations, first discovered that the sensations corresponding to secondary qualities, cannot resemble any quality of body. Hence Des Cartes and Locke inferred, that sound, taste, smell, colour, heat, and cold, which the vulgar took to be qualities of body, were not qualities of body, but mere sensations of the mind. Afterwards the ingenious Berkeley, considering more attentively the nature of sensation in general, discovered, and demonstrated, that no sensation whatever could possibly resemble any quality of an insentient being, such as body is supposed to be: and hence he inferred, very justly, that there is the same reason to hold extension, figure, and all the primary qualities, to be mere sensations, as there is to hold the secondary qualities to be mere sensations. Thus, by just reasoning upon the Cartesian principles, matter was stript of all its qualities; the new system, by a kind of metaphysical sublimation, converted all the qualities of matter into sensations, and spiritualized body, as the old had materialized spirit.

[. . .]

That the natural issue of this system is scepticism with regard to every thing except the existence of our ideas, and of their necessary relations which appear upon comparing them, is evident: for ideas being the only objects of thought, and having no existence but when we are conscious of them, it necessarily follows, that there is no object of our thought which can have a continued and permanent existence. Body and spirit, cause and effect, time and space, to which we were wont to ascribe an existence independent of our thought, are all turned out of existence by this short dilemma: Either these things are ideas of sensation or reflection, or they are not: if they are ideas of sensation or reflection, they can have no existence but when we are conscious of them; if they are not ideas of sensation or reflection, they are words without any meaning.

Neither Des Cartes nor Locke perceived this consequence of their system concerning ideas. Bishop Berkeley was the first who discovered it. And what followed upon this discovery? Why, with regard to the material world, and with regard to space and time, he admits the consequence, That these things are mere ideas, and have no existence but in our minds: but with regard to the existence of spirits or minds, he does not admit the consequence; and if he had admitted it, he must have been an absolute sceptic. But how does he evade this consequence with regard to the existence of spirits? The expedient which the good Bishop uses on this occasion is very remarkable, and shows his great aversion to scepticism. He maintains, that we have no ideas of spirits; and that we can think, and speak, and reason about them, and about their attributes, without having any ideas of them. If this is so, my Lord, what should hinder us from thinking and reasoning about bodies, and their qualities, without having ideas of them? The Bishop either did not think of this question, or did not think fit to give any answer to it. However, we may observe, that in order to avoid scepticism, he fairly starts out of the Cartesian system, without giving any reason why he did so in this instance, and in no other. This indeed is the only instance of a deviation from Cartesian principles which I have met with in the successors of Des Cartes; and it seems to have been only a sudden start, occasioned by the terror of scepticism; for in all other things Berkeley's system is founded upon Cartesian principles.

Thus we see, that Des Cartes and Locke take the road that leads to scepticism, without knowing the end of it; but they stop short for want of light to carry them farther. Berkeley, frighted at the appearance of the dreadful abyss, starts aside, and avoids it. But the author of the *Treatise of human nature*, more daring and intrepid, without turning aside to the right hand or to the left, like Virgil's Alecto, shoots directly into the gulf [. . .]

4. We may observe, That the account given by the new system, of that furniture of the human understanding which is the gift of nature, and not the acquisition of our own reasoning faculty, is extremely lame and imperfect.

The natural furniture of the human understanding is of two kinds; First, The *notions* or simple apprehensions which we have of things; and, Secondly, The *judgments* or the belief which we have concerning them. As to our notions, the new system reduces them to two classes; *ideas of sensation*, and *ideas of reflection*: the first are conceived to be copies of our sensations, retained in the memory or imagination; the second, to be copies of the operations of our minds whereof we are conscious, in like manner retained in the memory or imagination: and we are taught, that these two comprehend all the materials about which the human understanding is, or can be employed. As to our judgment of things, or the belief which we have concerning them, the new system allows no part of it to be the gift of nature, but holds it to be the acquisition of reason, and to be got by comparing our ideas, and perceiving their agreements or disagreements. Now I take this account, both of our notions, and of our judgments or belief, to be extremely imperfect; and I shall briefly point out some of its capital defects.

The division of our notions into ideas of sensation, and ideas of reflection, is contrary to all rules of logic; because the second member of the division includes the first. For, can we form clear and just notions of our sensations any other way than by reflection? Surely we cannot. Sensation is an operation of the mind of which we are conscious; and we get the notion of sensation, by reflecting upon that which we are conscious of. In like manner, doubting and believing are operations of the mind whereof we are conscious; and we get the notion of them by reflecting upon what we are conscious of. The ideas of sensation, therefore, are ideas of reflection, as much as the ideas of doubting, or believing, or any other ideas whatsoever.

But to pass over the inaccuracy of this division, it is extremely incomplete. For, since sensation is an operation of the mind, as well as all the other things of which we form our notions by reflection; when it is asserted, that all our notions are either ideas of sensation, or ideas of reflection, the plain English of this is, That mankind neither do, nor can think of any thing but of the operations of their own minds. Nothing can be more contrary to truth, or more contrary to the experience of mankind. I know that Locke, while he maintained this doctrine, believed the notions which we have of body and of its qualities, and the notions which we have of motion and of space, to be ideas of sensation. But why did he believe this? Because he believed those notions to be nothing else but images of our sensations. If therefore the notions of body and its qualities, of motion and space, be not images of our sensations, will it not follow, that those notions are not ideas of sensation? Most certainly.

There is no doctrine in the new system which more directly leads to scepticism than this. And the author of the *Treatise of human nature* knew very well how to use it for that purpose: for, if you maintain that there is any such existence as body or spirit, time or place, cause or effect, he immediately catches you between the horns of this dilemma: Your notions of these existences are either ideas of sensation, or ideas of reflection; if of sensation, from what sensation are they copied? if of reflection, from what operation of the mind are they copied?

It is indeed to be wished, that those who have written much about sensation, and about the other operations of the mind, had likewise thought and reflected much, and with great care, upon those operations: but is it not very strange, that they will not allow it to be possible for mankind to think of any thing else?

The account which this system gives of our judgment and belief concerning things, is as far from the truth as the account it gives of our notions or simple apprehensions. It represents our senses as having no other office, but that of furnishing the mind with notions or simple apprehensions of things; and makes our judgment and belief concerning those things to be acquired by comparing our notions together, and perceiving their agreements or disagreements.

We have shown, on the contrary, that every operation of the senses, in its very nature, implies judgment or belief, as well as simple apprehension. Thus, when I feel the pain of the gout in my toe, I have not only a notion of pain, but a belief of its existence, and a belief of some disorder in my toe which occasions it; and this belief is not produced by comparing ideas, and perceiving their agreements and disagreements; it is included in the very nature of the sensation. When I perceive a tree before me, my faculty of seeing gives me not only a notion or simple apprehension of the tree, but a belief of its existence, and of its figure, distance, and magnitude; and this judgment or belief is not got by comparing ideas, it is included in the very nature of the perception. We have taken notice of several original principles of belief in the course of this inquiry; and when other faculties of the mind are examined, we shall find more, which have not occurred in the examination of the five senses.

Such original and natural judgments are therefore a part of that furniture which nature hath given to the human understanding. They are the inspiration of the Almighty, no less than our notions or simple apprehensions. They serve to direct us in the common affairs of life, where our reasoning faculty would leave us in the dark. They are a part of our constitution, and all the discoveries of our reason are grounded upon them. They make up what is called *the common sense of mankind*; and what is manifestly contrary to any of those first principles, is what we call *absurd*. The strength of them is *good sense*, which is often found in those who are not acute in reasoning. A remarkable deviation from them, arising from a disorder in the constitution, is what we call *lunacy*; as when a man believes that he is made of glass. When a man suffers himself to be reasoned out of the principles of common sense, by metaphysical arguments, we may call this *metaphysical lunacy*; which differs from the other species of the distemper in this, that it is not continued, but intermittent: it is apt to seize the patient in solitary and speculative moments; but when he enters into society, Common Sense recovers her authority. A clear explication and enumeration of the principles of common sense, is one of the chief *desiderata* in logic. We have only considered such of them as occurred in the examination of the five senses.

5. The last observation that I shall make upon the new system is, That, although it professes to set out in the way of reflection, and not of analogy, it hath retained some of the old analogical notions concerning the operations of the mind; particularly, That things which do not now exist in the mind itself, can only be perceived, remembered, or imagined, by means of ideas or images of them in the mind, which are the immediate objects of perception, remembrance, and imagination. This doctrine appears evidently to be borrowed from the old system; which taught, that external things make impressions upon the mind, like the impressions of a seal upon wax; that it is by means of those impressions that we perceive, remember, or imagine them; and that those impressions must resemble the things from which they are taken. When we form our notions of the operations of the mind by

analogy, this way of conceiving them seems to be very natural, and offers itself to our thoughts: for as every thing which is felt must make some impression upon the body, we are apt to think, that every thing which is understood must make some impression upon the mind.

From such analogical reasoning, this opinion of the existence of ideas or images of things in the mind, seems to have taken its rise, and to have been so universally received among philosophers. It was observed already, that Berkeley, in one instance, apostatizes from this principle of the new system, by affirming, that we have no ideas of spirits, and that we can think of them immediately, without ideas. But I know not whether in this he has had any followers. There is some difference likewise among modern philosophers, with regard to the ideas or images by which we perceive, remember, or imagine sensible things. For, though all agree in the existence of such images, they differ about their place; some placing them in a particular part of the brain, where the soul is thought to have her residence, and others placing them in the mind itself. Des Cartes held the first of these opinions; to which Newton seems likewise to have inclined [. . .] But Locke seems to place the ideas of sensible things in the mind: and that Berkeley, and the author of the *Treatise of human nature*, were of the same opinion, is evident. The last makes a very curious application of this doctrine, by endeavouring to prove from it, That the mind either is no substance, or that it is an extended and divisible substance; because the ideas of extension cannot be in a subject which is indivisible and unextended.

I confess I think his reasoning in this, as in most cases, is clear and strong. For whether the idea of extension be only another name for extension itself, as Berkeley and this author assert; or whether the idea of extension be an image and resemblance of extension, as Locke conceived; I appeal to any man of common sense, whether extension, or any image of extension, can be in an unextended and indivisible subject. But while I agree with him in his reasoning, I would make a different application of it. He takes it for granted, that there are ideas of extension in the mind; and thence infers, that if it is at all a substance, it must be an extended and divisible substance. On the contrary, I take it for granted, upon the testimony of common sense, that my mind is a substance, that is, a permanent subject of thought; and my reason convinces me, that it is an unextended and indivisible substance; and hence I infer, that there cannot be in it any thing that resembles extension. If this reasoning had occurred to Berkeley, it would probably have led him to acknowledge, that we may think and reason concerning bodies, without having ideas of them in the mind, as well as concerning spirits.

Part III

Kant's Critique of Rationalism and Empiricism

Introduction

Another voice critical of the empiricist method in philosophy is the German philosopher Immanuel Kant (1724–1804). Kant was equally critical also of what he called the "dogmatic" philosophy of rationalism. Against rationalists who thought it possible to learn important truths about the world merely though reasoning – truths such as "God exists" or "Every event has a cause" – Kant objected in the same way as the empiricists. He said, like them, that human knowledge has its basis always in sense experience. But then against the empiricists Kant raised some of the very same objections raised by rationalists: that knowledge of the world requires applying ideas or concepts not derivable from sense experience alone – concepts such as "substance," "causation," and "necessity."

Perhaps the simplest way to harmonize Kant's seemingly inconsistent challenges to both rationalism and empiricism is to describe his own view by saying that human knowledge always depends on two sources: one conceptual, the other sensory. He believed, first, that the human mind is originally furnished with a limited set of "pure concepts," without which experience itself would be impossible. In this way his theory of knowledge resembles the innatism of rationalist philosophers. Yet Kant also believed, secondly, that those pure concepts have no application in human knowledge apart from sense experience. He therefore agreed with the empiricists in thinking that human knowledge cannot, by means of innate ideas, extend beyond what we can know through the senses.

In the introduction to this volume we discussed Kant's claim that "synthetic a priori knowledge" is possible. *How* it is possible, we saw there, is related to Kant's view of time and space. The point was that time and space are not real, but are ways in which our minds order our experience of the world. Kant explained also that in experiencing the world the human mind employs a set of pure concepts, called "categories of the understanding." One of these categories, "causation," represents the relation of cause–effect. It applies to our experience of the world in the following way: whenever we think of an event, of something happening, we automatically, necessarily, locate that event at some point in time, and we think of a prior time in which another event occurred that was its cause. We do not necessarily identify any prior event that was the cause; but we think at least that something must have happened to have caused the event. Perhaps the following analogy from geometry will help to clarify the point. Our thinking of an event in time is like our thinking of a point on a line; we cannot think of a point on a line without imagining points before it and after it; we join (synthesize) these points into a series to form a line, according to rules of geometry, just as we join events in time to form the causal series of the world, according to laws of nature. The concept of "line" comes to us from geometry, which we apply in order to organize points in space. The concept of "cause" is more fundamental; it is a category employed by the mind as a way of making sense of the series of events that makes up experience.

Another way to understand what Kant is trying to explain with his views on time, space, and the categories is to recognize that, for him, "experience" is not a passive mental process. Empiricists, following Locke, treated the human mind as a blank page upon which sensation writes traces or imprints of reality. The empiricists therefore assumed that philosophers need only reflect upon what sense experience has impressed on the passive mind in order to learn the basic structure of reality. But Kant thought of experience as something more like the mind actively structuring the material presented by sensation, according to its own rules. For Kant, that is, experience is "experiencing"; it is the process of forming a coherent, rule-governed world of objects in time and space out of the "data" presented by sensation. Different human observers will of course experience different sense data. But because human minds all apply the same set of categories, in the same time and space, we can be confident that the reality every human being actively experiences has the same structure. This means, incidentally, that different types of beings from us, who may not experience time and space the way we do, or who may operate with a different set of categories, would experience reality with a different structure.

In this way of looking at human experience, objects we experience are called "appearances," or *phenomena*. These make up what Kant sometimes called the "sensible world." But these same things considered as they are "in themselves," apart from human experience, are called *noumena*, and they belong to what is called an "intelligible world." These things as they really are in themselves are not in time and space, and cannot know them. The mistake of the dogmatic rationalists, Kant claimed, was to suppose that we can know reality as it is in itself, purely through reason. His "Critique" of pure reason was meant to show instead why we can know reality only as it appears to human sense experience. Kant allows us no knowledge of things as they are in themselves; except, of course, that they are unknowable, and that they constitute the basis for the sensible world of human experience.

Now if there must be a difference between things as they appear in time and space and things as they really are, then there could well be a difference between yourself as you appear to yourself in time, and yourself as you really are. This would establish a distinction between the so-called "phenomenal self" and the "noumenal self." Kant's argument for the synthetic *a priori* truth that every event has a cause must apply without exception to all events appearing in time, including all mental events appearing to us in introspection. If we therefore experience ourselves acting, then we can know *a priori* that there was a prior cause of our action-event. Our action's cause may have been a desire; and if so, then we can know *a priori* that this desire had a prior cause as well. If we continue following this regressive sequence of causes and effects we could, theoretically, map out the prior causes of any action all the way back to ancient times. So what sense does it make to hold people morally responsible for their actions? Why praise or blame people for doing things today that are the inevitable effects of ancient causes over which they had absolutely no control?

Kant's distinction between the phenomenal self and the noumenal self is supposed to help solve this difficult philosophical problem. When we view ourselves as acting in time, then we are considering ourselves only as appearances. When viewing ourselves in this way we are also correct to see every one of our actions as caused by prior events that extend back in a causal series well before our birth. But when we consider ourselves as noumena, we do not place ourselves in time, and we therefore cannot see ourselves as caused to act by anything prior. Kant took this basic distinction between the way we appear and the way we are in ourselves to provide the solution to the problem of free will. He claimed that if we think of ourselves as active, noumenal beings, then since there is no time prior to our noumenal action, it must be free. Scholars have not found it easy to understand how this solution is supposed to work, however. In his *Critique of Pure Reason* Kant went only as far as to claim that thoroughgoing causal determinism is at least not inconsistent with freedom of the will, provided we locate determinism in the world of appearances and freedom in the noumenal world. That is, he did not claim we can know we have free will; but only that it is possible that we do. For to *know* we have free will would require knowing something about things in themselves, something that could not be an object of sense experience.

In his later works in moral philosophy, however, Kant went on to claim that we can know, as a "fact of reason," that we are free. Since we recognize that there are actions we ought to do, we can infer that we are therefore free to choose to do them. Even if we desire not to do them, the point is that we are always somehow free to overcome our contrary desires, and to act as we ought. How this freedom is supposed to be explained is, again, a very difficult matter of interpretation. Many recent scholars have settled on an interpretation that says Kant believed we are free because we act on the basis of reasons. We are never caused to act by desires arising through sense experience, they say. If we do act on any desire, it is because we have freely chosen to take that desire as our reason for action. Yet this view makes it difficult to see our choices as events in the temporal world of sense experience, where every event is supposed to have a prior cause. A free action supposedly follows as the effect of freely choosing to take a desire as a reason for doing the action. But then that free-choice event, which must be in time if it is understood as a cause in time, should need its prior cause also; and it is difficult to see what its cause could be, especially if it is supposed to be a *free* choice.

Other scholars have explained that, in distinguishing between things as they appear and as they are in themselves, Kant was describing the difference between a theoretical or scientific perspective on things and a practical or moral perspective on things. They say that if we look at ourselves theoretically, as scientific observers, then we will always expect a prior cause for every event, including every human action. We will not consider free will as providing a suitable explanation for any of our actions. On the other hand, when we look at ourselves practically, as moral decision-makers, we cannot explain our actions otherwise than under the assumption that we are free to choose. As appealing as this interpretation may be, however, it does not seem to cohere with much of what Kant said about the difference between appearances and things in themselves. Absolutely central to that distinction was his view that time is not real, but only a feature of human sense-experience. Yet this is not at all central to the distinction between the theoretical and practical perspectives on our actions. The difference between these two perspectives is merely the difference between explaining what happens and deciding what to do; and understanding this difference, as almost everyone does, requires no views about the reality of time.

Kant, like other philosophers of his day, understood that the possibility of human free will depends on how we explain causation in the world. Those who deny the possibility of free will do so on the basis of how they understand the causal order of nature. Consequently, those who insist that free will is possible must develop a different understanding of nature's causal order. This is what Kant has done: he has explained that the causal order of nature is only a phenomenon, the mere appearance of a reality outside of time. So if we act in that atemporal reality, we are free of determination by natural causes. But what Kant has not done is explain clearly how free actions in that reality are incorporated into the causal order of appearances in nature. Despite this shortcoming, Kant's critique of rationalism and empiricism stands as a fair summary of the inherent weaknesses of each of these philosophical methods; and his constructive attempt to combine the best features of them both ranks as one of the finest achievements of late modern philosophy.

8

Immanuel Kant, *Prolegomena to Any Future Metaphysics* (1783)

Kant's great work of 1781, the *Critique of Pure Reason*, is hard to understand. He hoped therefore to alleviate the difficulty readers were having in comprehending his main ideas by presenting them in a shorter, more accessible book. The word "Prolegomena" in the title suggests that Kant intended to write a kind of "preface" to some future system of metaphysics. He considered metaphysics to be still groping toward becoming a science, so one of the main questions he raised in the *Prolegomena* was: "How is metaphysics as a science possible?" By "science" (*Wissenschaft*), Kant meant an organized body of general truths. He recognized physics and biology as sciences, along with geometry, and hoped that someday metaphysics would become one.

Kant's philosophical vocabulary is unique. He often used *intuition* (*Anschauung*) as a general term meaning, roughly, "sensation." Knowledge based on intuition is therefore empirical knowledge, not some form of mystical insight. But he used *a priori intuition* to refer to time and space as aspects of sensibility presupposed by empirical intuition. One of his central claims was that human knowledge requires intuition, both empirical and *a priori*, as well as concepts of the understanding by which we judge the "objective validity" or reality of what we experience. The understanding's most fundamental concepts are called *categories*: a set of concepts such as "unity," "totality," "substance," and "cause" that are not derived from experience, but actually help make our experience of the world possible. Kant's term *category* must not be confused with *idea*. The understanding provides us with categories for judging experience, but ideas come from reason, and refer to things "beyond" experience, such as the soul, freedom, and God. Things as we know them through intuition and the categories are called *phenomena* or *appearances* in Kant's philosophy. But things as they really are, apart from our intuitions of them, are called *noumena*, or *things in themselves*.

Kant began the *Prolegomena* by assuming we have some "synthetic *a priori*" knowledge (see the general introduction to this volume). So his leading question was: *How is synthetic a priori knowledge possible?* He proceeded to show how it is possible first in mathematics, *and then in* natural science. Turning next to metaphysics, he showed that what makes synthetic *a priori* knowledge possible in mathematics and science does not apply in metaphysics. The reason is that we can have synthetic *a priori* knowledge only where intuition or sense experience is involved; but metaphysical knowledge, by definition, abstracts from all experience. Near the end of the *Prolegomena* Kant suggested that the method for proceeding in metaphysics must be based always on "practical" or moral interests. But he did not develop this further stage of his philosophy here.

Königsberg, East Prussia, was Kant's lifelong home, from his birth in 1724 to his death in 1804. It is now named Kaliningrad, and is in Russia. He taught philosophy and other subjects at the University of Königsberg, where he himself had been a student.

Preface

[. . .]

Since the Essays of *Locke* and *Leibniz*, or rather since the rise of metaphysics as far as the history of it reaches, no event has occurred that could have been more decisive with respect to the fate of this science than the attack made upon it by *David Hume*. He brought no light to this kind of knowledge, but he certainly struck a spark from which a light could well have been kindled, if it had hit some welcoming tinder whose glow had then been carefully kept going and made to grow.

Hume started mainly from a single but important concept in metaphysics, namely, that of the *connection of cause and effect* (and of course also its derivative concepts, of force and action, etc.), and called upon reason, which pretends to have generated this concept in her womb, to give him an account of by what right she thinks: that something could be so constituted that, if it is posited, something else necessarily must thereby be posited as well; for that is what the concept of cause says. He undisputably proved that it is wholly impossible for reason to think such a connection *a priori* and from concepts, because this connection contains necessity; and it is simply not to be seen how it could be, that because something is, something else necessarily must also be, and therefore how the concept of such a connection could be introduced *a priori*. From this he concluded that reason completely and fully deceives herself with this concept, falsely taking it for her own child, when it is really nothing but a bastard of the imagination, which, impregnated by experience, and having brought certain representations under the law of association, passes off the resulting subjective necessity (i.e., habit) for an objective necessity (from insight). From which he concluded that reason has no power at all to think such connections, not even merely in general, because its concepts would then be bare fictions, and all of its cognitions allegedly established *a priori* would be nothing but falsely marked ordinary experiences; which is as much as to say that there is no metaphysics at all, and cannot be any.

As premature and erroneous as his conclusion was, nevertheless it was at least founded on inquiry, and this inquiry was of sufficient value, that the best minds of his time might have come together to solve (more happily if possible) the problem in the sense in which he presented it, from which a complete reform of the science must soon have arisen.

But fate, ever ill-disposed toward metaphysics, would have it that Hume was understood by no one. One cannot, without feeling a certain pain, behold how utterly and completely his opponents, *Reid, Oswald, Beattie,* and finally *Priestley,* missed the point of his problem, and misjudged his hints for improvement – constantly taking for granted just what he doubted, and, conversely, proving with vehemence and, more often than not, with great insolence exactly what it had never entered his mind to doubt – so that everything remained in its old condition, as if nothing had happened. The question was not, whether the concept of cause is right, useful, and, with respect to all cognition of nature, indispensable, for this Hume had never put in doubt; it was rather whether it is thought through reason *a priori*, and in this way has an inner truth independent of all experience, and therefore also a much more widely extended use which is not limited merely to objects of experience: regarding this *Hume* awaited enlightenment. The discussion was only about the origin of this concept, not about its indispensability in use; if the former were only discovered, the conditions of its use and the sphere in which it can be valid would already be given.

In order to do justice to the problem, however, the opponents of this celebrated man would have had to penetrate very deeply into the nature of reason so far as it is occupied solely with pure thought, something that did not suit them. They therefore found a more expedient means to be obstinate without any insight, namely, the appeal to *ordinary common sense*. It is in fact a great gift from heaven to possess right (or, as it has recently been called, plain) common sense. But it must be proven through deeds, by the considered and reasonable things one thinks and says, and not by appealing to it as an oracle when one knows of nothing clever to advance in one's defense. To appeal to ordinary common sense when insight and science run short, and not before, is one of the subtle discoveries of recent times, whereby the dullest windbag can confidently take on the most profound thinker and hold his own with him. So long as a small residue of insight remains, however, one would do well to avoid resorting to this emergency help. And seen in the light of day, this appeal is nothing other than a call to the judgment of the multitude; applause at which the philosopher blushes, but at which the popular wag becomes triumphant and defiant. I should think, however, that *Hume* could lay just as much claim to sound common sense as *Beattie*, and on top of this to something that the latter certainly did not possess, namely, a critical reason, which keeps ordinary common sense in check, so that it doesn't lose itself in speculations, or, if these are the sole topic of discussion, doesn't want to decide anything, since it doesn't understand the justification for its own principles; for only so will it remain sound common sense. Hammer and chisel are perfectly fine for working raw lumber, but for copperplate one must use an etching needle. Likewise, sound common sense and speculative understanding are both useful, but each in its own way; the one, when it is a matter of judgments that find their immediate application in experience, the other, however, when judgments are to be made in a universal mode, out of mere concepts, as in metaphysics, where what calls itself (but often *per antiphrasin*) sound common sense has no judgment whatsoever.

I freely admit that a reminder from *David Hume* was the very thing that many years ago first interrupted my dogmatic slumber and gave a completely different direction to my researches in the field of speculative philosophy. I was very far from listening to him with respect to his conclusions, which arose solely because he did not completely set out his problem but only touched on a part of it, which, without the whole being taken into account, can provide no enlightenment. If we begin from a well-grounded though undeveloped thought that another bequeaths us, then we can well hope, by continued reflection, to take it further than could the sagacious man whom one has to thank for the first spark of this light.

So I tried first whether *Hume's* objection might not be presented in a general manner, and I soon found that the concept of the connection of cause and effect is far from being the only concept through which the understanding thinks connections of things *a priori*; rather, metaphysics consists wholly of such concepts. I sought to ascertain their number, and once I had successfully attained this in the way I wished, namely from a single principle, I proceeded to the deduction of these concepts, from which I henceforth became assured that they were not, as *Hume* had feared, derived from experience, but had arisen from the pure understanding. This deduction, which appeared impossible to my sagacious predecessor, and which had never even occurred to anyone but him, even though everyone confidently made use of these concepts without asking what their objective validity is based on – this deduction, I say, was the most difficult thing that could ever be undertaken on behalf of metaphysics; and the worst thing about it is that metaphysics, as much of it as might be present anywhere at all, could not give me the slightest help with this, because this very deduction must first settle the possibility of a metaphysics. As I had now succeeded in the solution of the Humean problem not only in a single case but with respect to the entire faculty of pure reason, I could therefore take sure, if still always slow, steps toward finally determining, completely and according to universal principles, the entire extent of pure reason with regard to its boundaries as well as its content, which was indeed the very thing that metaphysics requires in order to build its system according to a sure plan.

[. . .]

Preamble

[. . .]

§2
On the Type of Cognition That Alone Can Be Called Metaphysical

(a) On the distinction between synthetic and analytic judgments in general

Metaphysical cognition must contain nothing but judgments a priori, as required by the distinguishing feature of its sources. But judgments may have any origin whatsoever, or be constituted in whatever manner according to their logical form, and yet there is nonetheless a distinction between them according to their content, by dint of which they are either merely *explicative* and add nothing to the content of the cognition, or *ampliative* and augment the given cognition; the first may be called *analytic* judgments, the second *synthetic*.

Analytic judgments say nothing in the predicate except what was actually thought already in the concept of the subject, though not so clearly nor with the same consciousness. If I say: All bodies are extended, then I have not in the least amplified my concept of body, but have merely resolved it, since extension, although not explicitly said of the former concept prior to the judgment, nevertheless was actually thought of it; the judgment is therefore analytic. By contrast, the proposition: Some bodies are heavy, contains something in the predicate that is not actually thought in the general concept of body; it therefore augments my cognition, since it adds something to my concept, and must therefore be called a synthetic judgment.

(b) The common principle of all analytic judgments is the principle of contradiction

All analytic judgments rest entirely on the principle of contradiction and are by their nature *a priori* cognitions, whether the concepts that serve for their material be empirical or not. For since the predicate of an affirmative analytic judgment is already thought beforehand in the concept of the subject, it cannot be denied of that subject without contradiction; exactly so is its opposite necessarily denied of the subject in an analytic, but negative, judgment, and indeed also according to the principle of contradiction. So it stands with the propositions: Every body is extended, and: No body is unextended (simple).

For that reason all analytic propositions are still *a priori* judgments even if their concepts are empirical, as in: Gold is a yellow metal; for in order to know this, I need no further experience outside my concept of gold, which includes that this body is yellow and a metal; for this constitutes my very concept, and I did not have to do anything except analyze it, without looking beyond it to something else.

(c) Synthetic judgments require a principle other than the principle of contradiction

There are synthetic judgments *a posteriori* whose origin is empirical; but there are also synthetic judgments that are *a priori* certain and that arise from pure understanding and reason. Both however agree in this, that they can by no means arise solely from the principle of analysis, namely the principle of contradiction; they demand yet a completely different principle, though they always must be derived from some fundamental proposition, whichever it may be, *in accordance with the Principle of contradiction*; for nothing can run counter to this principle, even though everything cannot be derived from it. I shall first classify the synthetic judgments.

1. *Judgments of experience* are always synthetic. For it would be absurd to base an analytic judgment on experience, since I do not at all need to go beyond my concept in order to formulate the judgment and therefore have no need for any testimony from experience. That a body is extended, is a proposition that stands certain *a priori*, and not a judgment of experience. For before I go to experience, I have all the conditions for my judgment already in the concept, from which I merely extract the predicate in accordance with the principle of contradiction, and by this means can simultaneously become conscious of the *necessity* of the judgment, which experience could never teach me.

2. *Mathematical judgments* are one and all synthetic. This proposition appears to have completely escaped the observations of analysts of human reason up to the present, and indeed to be directly opposed to all of their conjectures, although it is incontrovertibly certain and very important in its consequences. Because they found that the inferences of the mathematicians all proceed in accordance with the principle of contradiction (which, by nature, is required of any apodictic certainty), they were persuaded that the fundamental propositions were also known through the principle of contradiction, in which they were very mistaken; for a synthetic proposition can of course be discerned in accordance with the principle of contradiction, but only insofar as another synthetic propositions is presupposed from which the first can be deduced, never however in itself.

First of all it must be observed: that properly mathematical propositions are always *a priori* and not empirical judgments, because they carry necessity with them, which cannot be taken from experience. But if this will not be granted me, very well, I will restrict my proposition to *pure mathematics*, the concept of which already conveys that it contains not empirical but only pure cognition *a priori*.

One might well at first think: that the proposition $7 + 5 = 12$ is a purely analytical proposition that follows from the concept of a sum of seven and five according to the principle of contradiction. However, upon closer inspection, one finds that the concept of the sum of 7 and 5 contains nothing further than the unification of the two numbers into one, through which by no means is thought what this single number may be that combines the two. The concept of twelve is in no way already thought because I merely think to myself this unification of seven and five, and I may analyze my concept of such a possible sum for as long as may be, still I will not meet with twelve therein. One must go beyond these concepts, in making use of the intuition that corresponds to one of the two, such as one's five fingers, or (like *Segner* in his arithmetic) five points, and in that manner adding the units of the five given in intuition step by step to the concept of seven. One therefore truly amplifies one's concept through this proposition 7 + 5 = 12 and adds to the first concept a new one that was not thought in it; that is, an arithmetical proposition is always synthetic, which can be seen all the more plainly in the case of somewhat larger numbers, for it is then clearly evident that, though we may turn and twist our concept as we like, we could never find the sum through the mere analysis of our concepts, without making use of intuition.

Nor is any fundamental proposition of pure geometry analytic. That the straight line between two points is the shortest is a synthetic proposition. For my concept of the straight contains nothing of magnitude, but only a quality. The concept of the shortest is therefore wholly an addition and cannot be extracted by any analysis from the concept of the straight line. Intuition must therefore be made use of here, by means of which alone the synthesis is possible.

Some other fundamental propositions that geometers presuppose are indeed actually analytic and rest on the principle of contradiction; however, they serve only, like identical propositions, as links in the chain of method and not as principles: e.g., a = a, the whole is equal to itself, or (a + b) > a, i.e., the whole is greater than its part. And indeed even these, although they are valid from concepts alone, are admitted into mathematics only because they can be exhibited in intuition.

It is merely ambiguity of expression which makes us commonly believe here that the predicate of such apodictic judgments already lies in our concept and that the judgment is therefore analytic. Namely, we *are required* to add in thought a particular predicate to a given concept, and this necessity is already attached to the concepts. But the question is not, what we *are required to add in thought* to a given concept, but what we *actually think* in it, even if only obscurely, and then it becomes evident that the predicate attaches to such concepts indeed necessarily, though not immediately, but rather through an intuition that has to be added.

The essential feature of pure *mathematical* cognition, differentiating it from all other *a priori* cognition, is that it must throughout proceed *not from concepts*, but always and only through the construction of concepts (*Critique of Pure Reason*, A713). Because pure mathematical cognition, in its propositions, must therefore go beyond the concept to that which is contained in the intuition corresponding to it, its propositions can and must never arise through the analysis of concepts, i.e., analytically, and so are one and all synthetic.

I cannot, however, refrain from noting the damage that neglect of this otherwise seemingly insignificant and unimportant observation has brought upon philosophy. *Hume*, when he felt the call, worthy of a philosopher, to cast his gaze over the entire field of pure *a priori* cognition, in which the human understanding claims such vast holdings, inadvertently lopped off a whole (and indeed the most considerable) province of the same, namely pure mathematics, by imagining that the nature and so to speak the legal constitution of this province rested on completely different principles, namely solely on the principle of contradiction; and although he had by no means made a classification of propositions so formally and generally, or with such nomenclature, as I have here, it was nonetheless just as if he had said: Pure mathematics contains only *analytic* propositions, but metaphysics contains synthetic propositions *a priori*. Now he erred severely in this, and this error had decisively damaging consequences for his entire conception. For had he not done this, he would have expanded his question about the origin of our synthetic judgments far beyond his metaphysical concept of causality and extended it also to the possibility of *a priori* mathematics; for he would have had to accept mathematics as synthetic as well. But then he would by no means have been able to found his metaphysical propositions on mere experience, for otherwise he would have had to subject the axioms of pure mathematics to experience as well, which he was much too reasonable to do. The good company in which metaphysics would then have come to be situated would have secured it against the danger of scornful mistreatment; for the blows that were intended for the latter would have had to strike the former as well, which was not his intention, and could not have been; and so the acute man would have been drawn into reflections which must have been similar to those with which we are now occupied, but which would have gained infinitely from his inimitably fine presentation.

3. *Properly metaphysical* judgments are one and all synthetic. Judgments belonging *to metaphysics* must be distinguished from properly *metaphysical* judgments. Very many among the former are analytic, but they merely provide the means to metaphysical judgments, toward which the aim of the science is completely directed, and which are always synthetic. For if concepts belong to metaphysics, e.g., that of substance, then necessarily the judgments arising from their mere analysis belong to metaphysics as well, e.g., substance is that which exists only as subject, etc., and through several such analytic judgments we try to approach the definition of those concepts. Since, however, the analysis of a pure concept of the understanding (such as metaphysics contains) does not proceed in a different manner from the analysis of any other, even empirical, concept which does not belong to metaphysics (e.g., air is an elastic fluid, the elasticity of which is not lost with any known degree of cold), therefore the concept may indeed be properly metaphysical, but not the analytic judgment; for this science possesses something special and proper to it in the generation of its *a priori* cognitions, which generation must therefore be distinguished from what this science has in common with all other cognitions of the understanding; thus, e.g., the proposition: All that is substance in things persists, is a synthetic and properly metaphysical proposition.

If one has previously assembled, according to fixed principles, the *a priori* concepts that constitute the material of metaphysics and its tools, then the analysis of these concepts is of great value; it can even be presented apart from all the synthetic propositions that constitute metaphysics itself, as a special part (as it were a *philosophia definitiva*) containing nothing but analytic propositions belonging to metaphysics. For in fact such analyses do not have much use anywhere except in metaphysics, i.e., with a view toward the synthetic propositions that are to be generated from such previously analyzed concepts.

The conclusion of this section is therefore: that metaphysics properly has to do with synthetic propositions *a priori*, and these alone constitute its aim, for which it indeed requires many analyses of its concepts (therefore many analytic judgments), in which analyses, though, the procedure is no different from that in any other type of cognition when one seeks simply to make its concepts clear through analysis. But the *generation* of cognition *a priori* in accordance with both intuition and concepts, ultimately of synthetic propositions *a priori* as well, and specifically in philosophical cognition, forms the essential content of metaphysics.

[. . .]

Main Transcendental Question, First Part
How Is Pure Mathematics Possible?

§6

Here now is a great and proven body of cognition, which is already of admirable extent and promises unlimited expansion in the future, which carries with it thoroughly apodictic certainty (i.e., absolute necessity), hence rests on no grounds of experience, and so is a pure product of reason, but beyond this is thoroughly synthetic. "How is it possible then for human reason to achieve such cognition wholly *a priori*?" Does not this capacity, since it is not, and cannot be, based on experience, presuppose some *a priori* basis for cognition, which lies deeply hidden, but which might reveal itself through these its effects, if their first beginnings were but diligently tracked down?

§7

We find, however, that all mathematical cognition has this distinguishing feature, that it must present its concept beforehand *in intuition* and indeed *a priori*, consequently in an intuition that is not empirical but pure, without which means it cannot take a single step; therefore its judgments are always *intuitive*, in the place of which philosophy can content itself with *discursive* judgments *from mere concepts*, and can indeed exemplify its apodictic teachings through intuition but can never derive them from it. This observation with respect to the nature of mathematics already guides us toward the first and highest condition of its possibility; namely, it must be grounded in some *pure intuition* or other, in which it can present, or, as one calls it, *construct* all of its concepts *in concreto* yet *a priori*. If we could discover this pure intuition and its possibility, then from there it could easily be explained how synthetic *a priori* propositions are possible in pure mathematics, and consequently also how this science itself is possible; for just as empirical intuition makes it possible for us, without difficulty, to amplify (synthetically in experience) the concept we form of an object of intuition through new predicates that are presented by intuition itself, so too will pure intuition do the same only with this difference: that in the latter case the synthetic judgment will be *a priori* certain and apodictic, but in the former only *a posteriori* and empirically certain, because the former contains only what is met with in contingent empirical intuition, while the latter contains what necessarily must be met with in pure intuition, since it is, as intuition *a priori*, inseparably bound with the concept *before all experience* or individual perception.

§8

But with this step the difficulty seems to grow rather than to diminish. For now the question runs: *How is it possible to intuit something* a priori? An intuition is a representation of the sort which would depend immediately on the presence of an object. It therefore seems impossible *originally* to intuit *a priori*, since then the intuition would have to occur without an object being present, either previously or now, to which it could refer, and so it could not be an intuition. Concepts are indeed of the kind that we can quite well form some of them for ourselves *a priori* (namely, those that contain only the thinking of an object in general) without our being in an immediate relation to an object, e.g., the concept of magnitude, of cause, etc.; but even these still require, in order to provide them with signification and sense, a certain use *in concreto*, i.e., application to some intuition or other, by which an object for them is given to us. But how can the *intuition* of an object precede the object itself?

§9

If our intuition had to be of the kind that represented things *as they are in themselves*, then absolutely no intuition *a priori* would take place, but it would always be empirical. For I can only know what may be contained in the object in itself if the object is present and given to me. Of course, even then it is incomprehensible how the intuition of a thing that is present should allow me to cognize it the way it is in itself, since its properties cannot migrate over into my power of representation; but even granting such a possibility, the intuition still would not take place *a priori*, i.e., before the object were presented to me, for without that no basis for the relation of my representation to the object can be conceived; so it would have to be based on inspiration. There is therefore only one way possible for my intuition to precede the actuality of the object and occur as an *a priori* cognition, *namely if it contains nothing else except the form of sensibility, which in me as subject precedes all actual impressions through which I am affected by objects*. For I can know *a priori* that the objects of the senses can be intuited only in accordance with this form of sensibility. From this it follows: that propositions which relate merely to this form of sensory intuition will be possible and valid for objects of the senses; also, conversely, that intuitions which are possible *a priori* can never relate to things other than objects of our senses.

§10

Therefore it is only by means of the form of sensory intuition that we can intuit things *a priori*, though by this means we can cognize objects only as they *appear* to us (to our senses), not as they may be in themselves; and this supposition is utterly necessary, if synthetic propositions *a priori* are to be granted as possible, or, in case they are actually encountered, if their possibility is to be conceived and determined in advance.

Now space and time are the intuitions upon which pure mathematics bases all its cognitions and judgments, which come forward as at once apodictic and necessary; for mathematics must first exhibit all of its concepts in intuition – and pure mathematics in pure intuition – i.e., it must first construct them, failing which (since mathematics cannot proceed analytically, namely, through the analysis of concepts, but only synthetically) it is impossible for it to advance a step, that is, as long as it lacks pure intuition, in which alone the material for synthetic judgments *a priori* can be given. Geometry bases itself on the pure intuition of space. Even arithmetic forms its concepts of numbers through successive addition of units in time, but above all pure mechanics can form its concepts of motion only by means of the representation of time. Both representations are, however, merely intuitions; for, if one eliminates from the empirical intuitions of bodies and their alterations (motion) everything empirical, that is, that which belongs to sensation, then space and time still remain, which are therefore pure intuitions that underlie *a priori* the empirical intuitions, and for that reason can never themselves be eliminated; but, by the very fact that they are pure intuitions *a priori*, they prove that they are mere forms of our sensibility that must precede all empirical intuition (i.e., the perception of actual objects), and in accordance with which objects can be cognized *a priori*, though of course only as they appear to us.

§11

The problem of the present section is therefore solved. Pure mathematics, as synthetic cognition *a priori*, is possible only because it refers to no other objects than mere objects of the senses, the empirical intuition of which is based on a pure and indeed *a priori* intuition (of space and time), and can be so based because this pure intuition is nothing but the mere form of sensibility, which precedes the actual appearance of objects, since it in fact first makes this appearance possible. This faculty of intuiting *a priori* does not, however, concern the matter of appearance – i.e., that which is sensation in the appearance, for that constitutes the empirical – but only the form of appearance, space and time. If anyone wishes to doubt in the slightest that the two are not determinations inhering in things in themselves but only mere determinations inhering in the relation of those things to sensibility, I would very much like to know how he can find it possible to know, *a priori* and therefore before all acquaintance with things, how their intuition must be constituted – which certainly is the case here with space and time. But this is completely comprehensible as soon as the two are taken for nothing more than formal conditions of our sensibility, and objects are taken merely for appearances; for then the form of appearance, i.e., the pure intuition, certainly can be represented from ourselves, i.e., *a priori*.

§12

In order to add something by way of illustration and confirmation, we need only to consider the usual and unavoidably necessary procedure of the geometers. All proofs of the thoroughgoing equality of two given figures (that one can in all parts be put in the place of the other) ultimately come down to this: that they are congruent with one another; which plainly is nothing other than a synthetic proposition based upon immediate intuition; and this intuition must be given pure and *a priori*, for otherwise that proposition could not be granted as apodictically certain but would have only empirical certainty. It would only mean: we observe it always to be so and the proposition holds only as far as our perception has reached until now. That full-standing space (a space that is itself not the boundary of another space) has three dimensions, and that space in general cannot have more, is built upon the proposition that not more than three lines can cut each other at right angles in one point; this proposition can, however, by no means be proven from concepts, but rests immediately upon intuition, and indeed on pure *a priori* intuition, because it is apodictically certain; indeed, that we can require that a line should be drawn to infinity (*in indefinitum*), or that a series of changes (e.g., spaces traversed through motion) should be continued to infinity, presupposes a representation of space and of time that can only inhere in intuition, that is, insofar as the latter is not in itself bounded by anything; for this could never be concluded from concepts. Therefore pure intuitions *a priori* indeed actually do underlie mathematics, and make possible its synthetic and apodictically valid propositions; and consequently our transcendental deduction of the concepts of space and time at the same time explains the possibility of a pure mathematics, a possibility which, without such a deduction, and without our assuming that "everything which our senses may be given (the outer in space, the inner in time) is only intuited by us as it appears to us, not as it is in itself," could indeed be granted, but into which we could have no insight at all.

§13

All those who cannot yet get free of the conception, as if space and time were actual qualities attaching to things in themselves, can exercise their acuity on the following paradox, and, if they have sought its solution in vain, can then, free of prejudice at least for a few moments, suppose that perhaps the demotion of space and of time to mere forms of our sensory intuition may indeed have foundation.

If two things are fully the same (in all determinations belonging to magnitude and quality) in all the parts of each that can always be cognized by itself alone, it should indeed then follow that one, in all cases and respects, can be put in the place of the other, without this exchange causing the least recognizable difference. In fact this is how things stand with plane figures in geometry; yet various spherical figures, notwithstanding this sort of complete inner agreement, nonetheless reveal such a difference in outer relation that one cannot in any case be put in the place of the other; e.g., two spherical triangles from each of the hemispheres, which have an arc of the equator for a common base, can be fully equal with respect to their sides as well as their angles, so that nothing will be found in either, when it is fully described by itself, that is not also in the description of the other, and still one cannot be put in the place of the other (that is, in the opposite hemisphere); and here is then after all an *inner* difference between the triangles that no understanding can specify as inner, and that reveals itself only through the outer relation in space. But I will cite more familiar instances that can be taken from ordinary life.

What indeed can be more similar to, and in all parts more equal to, my hand or my ear than its image in the mirror? And yet I cannot put such a hand as is seen in the mirror in the place of its original; for if the one was a right hand, then the other in the mirror is a left, and the image of the right ear is a left one, which can never take the place of the former. Now there are no inner differences here that any understanding could merely think; and yet the differences are inner as far as the senses teach, for the left hand cannot, after all, be enclosed within the same boundaries as the right (they cannot be made congruent), despite all reciprocal equality and similarity; one hand's glove cannot be used on the other. What then is the solution? These objects are surely not representations of things as they are in themselves, and as the pure understanding would cognize them, rather, they are sensory intuitions, i.e., appearances, whose possibility rests on the relation of certain things, unknown in themselves, to something else, namely our sensibility. Now, space is the form of outer intuition of this sensibility, and the inner determination of any space is possible only through the determination of the outer relation to the whole space of which the space is a part (the relation to outer sense); that is, the part is possible only through the whole, which never occurs with things in themselves as objects of the understanding alone, but well occurs with mere appearances. We can therefore make the difference between similar and equal but nonetheless incongruent things (e.g., oppositely spiralled snails) intelligible through no concept alone, but only through the relation to right-hand and left-hand, which refers immediately to intuition.

Note I

Pure mathematics, and especially pure geometry, can have objective reality only under the single condition that it refers merely to objects of the senses, with regard to which objects, however, the principle remains fixed, that our sensory representation is by no means a representation of things in themselves, but only of the way in which they appear to us. From this it follows, not at all that the propositions of geometry are determinations of a mere figment of our poetic phantasy, and therefore could not with certainty be referred to actual objects, but rather, that they are valid necessarily for space and consequently for everything that may be found in space, because space is nothing other than the form of all outer appearances, under which alone objects of the senses can be given to us. Sensibility, whose form lies at the foundation of geometry, is that upon which the possibility of outer appearances rests; these, therefore, can never contain anything other than what geometry prescribes to them. It would be completely different if the senses had to represent objects as they are in themselves. For then it absolutely would not follow from the representation of space, a representation that serves *a priori*, with all the various properties of space, as foundation for the geometer, that all of this, together with what is deduced from it, must be exactly so in nature. The space of the geometer would be taken for mere fabrication and would be credited with no objective validity, because it is simply not to be seen how things would have to agree necessarily with the image that we form of them by ourselves and in advance. If, however, this image – or, better, this formal intuition – is the essential property of our sensibility by means of which alone objects are given to us, and if this sensibility represents not things in themselves but only their appearances, then it is very easy to comprehend, and at the same time to prove incontrovertibly: that all outer objects of our sensible world must necessarily agree, in complete exactitude, with the propositions of geometry, because sensibility itself, through its form of outer intuition (space), with which the geometer deals, first makes those objects possible, as mere appearances. It will forever remain a remarkable phenomenon in the history of philosophy that there was a time when even mathematicians who were at the same time philosophers began to doubt, not, indeed, the correctness of their geometrical propositions insofar as they related merely to space, but the objective validity and application to nature of this concept itself and all its geometrical determinations, since they were concerned that a line in nature might indeed be composed of physical points, consequently that true space in objects might be composed of simple parts, notwithstanding that the space which the geometer holds in thought can by no means be composed of such things. They did not realize that this space in thought itself makes possible physical space, i.e., the extension of matter; that this space is by no means a property of things in themselves, but only a form of our power of sensory representation; that all objects in space are mere appearances, i.e., not things in themselves but representations of our sensory intuition; and that, since space as the geometer thinks it is precisely the form of sensory intuition which we find in ourselves *a priori* and which contains the ground of the possibility of all outer appearances (with respect to their form), these appearances must of necessity and with the greatest precision harmonize with the propositions of the geometer, which he extracts not from any fabricated concept, but from the subjective foundation of all outer appearances, namely sensibility itself. In this and no other way can the geometer be secured, regarding the indubitable objective reality of his propositions, against all the chicaneries of a shallow metaphysics, however strange this way must seem to such a metaphysics because it does not go back to the sources of its concepts.

Note II

Everything that is to be given to us as object must be given to us in intuition. But all our intuition happens only by means of the senses; the understanding intuits nothing, but only reflects. Now since, in accordance with what has just been proven, the senses never and in no single instance enable us to cognize things in themselves, but only their appearances, and as these are mere representations of sensibility, "consequently all bodies together with the space in which they are found must be taken for nothing but mere representations in us, and exist nowhere else than merely in our thoughts." Now is this not manifest idealism?

Idealism consists in the claim that there are none other than thinking beings; the other things that we believe we perceive in intuition are only representations in thinking beings, to which in fact no object existing outside these beings corresponds. I say in opposition: There are things given to us as objects of our senses existing outside us, yet we know nothing of them as they may be in themselves, but are acquainted only with their appearances, i.e., with the representations that they produce in us because they affect our senses. Accordingly, I by all means avow that there are bodies outside us, i.e., things which, though completely unknown to us as to what they may be in themselves, we know through the representations which their influence on our sensibility provides for us, and to which we give the name of a body – which word therefore merely signifies the appearance of this object that is unknown to us but is nonetheless real. Can this be called idealism? It is the very opposite of it.

That one could, without detracting from the actual existence of outer things, say of a great many of their predicates: they belong not to these things in themselves, but only to their appearances and have no existence of their own outside our representation, is something that was generally accepted and acknowledged long before *Locke's* time, though more commonly thereafter. To these predicates belong warmth, color, taste, etc. That I, however, even beyond these, include (for weighty reasons) also among mere appearances the remaining qualities of bodies, which are called *primarias*: extension, place, and more generally space along with everything that depends on it (impenetrability or materiality, shape, etc.), is something against which not the least ground for uncertainty can be raised; and as little as someone can be called an idealist because he wants to admit colors as properties that attach not to the object in itself, but only to the sense of vision as modifications, just as little can my system be called idealist simply because I find that even more of, *nay, all of the properties that make up the intuition of a body* belong merely to its appearance: for the existence of the thing that appears is not thereby nullified, as with real idealism, but it is only shown that through the senses we cannot cognize it at all as it is in itself.

I would very much like to know how then my claims must be framed so as not to contain any idealism. Without doubt I would have to say: that the representation of space not only is perfectly in accordance with the relation that our sensibility has to objects, for I have said that, but that it is even fully similar to the object; an assertion to which I can attach no sense, any more than to the assertion that the sensation of red is similar to the property of cinnabar that excites this sensation in me.

Note III

From this an easily foreseen but empty objection can now be quite easily rejected: "namely that through the ideality of space and time the whole sensible world would be transformed into sheer illusion." After all philosophical insight into the nature of sensory cognition had previously been perverted by making sensibility into merely a confused kind of representation, through which we might still cognize things as they are but without having the ability to bring everything in this representation of ours to clear consciousness, we showed on the contrary that sensibility consists not in this logical difference of clarity or obscurity, but in the genetic difference of the origin of the cognition itself, since sensory cognition does not at all represent things as they are but only in the way in which they affect our senses, and therefore that through the senses mere appearances, not the things themselves, are given to the understanding for reflection; from this necessary correction an objection arises, springing from an inexcusable and almost deliberate misinterpretation, as if my system transformed all the things of the sensible world into sheer illusion.

If an appearance is given to us, we are still completely free as to how we want to judge things from it. The former, namely the appearance, was based on the senses, but the judgment on the understanding, and the only question is whether there is truth in the determination of the object or not. The difference between truth and dream, however, is not decided through the quality of the representations that are referred to objects, for they are the same in both, but through their connection according to the rules that determine the connection of representations in the concept of an object, and how far they can or cannot stand together in one experience. And then it is not the fault of the appearances at all, if our cognition takes illusion for truth, i.e., if intuition, through which an object is given to us, is taken for the concept of the object, or even for its existence, which only the understanding can think. The course of the planets is represented to us by the senses as now progressive, now retrogressive, and herein is neither falsehood nor truth, because as long as one grants that this is as yet only appearance, one still does not judge at all the objective quality of their motion. Since, however, if the understanding has not taken good care to prevent this subjective mode of representation from being taken for objective, a false judgment can easily arise, one therefore says: they appear to go backwards; but the illusion is not ascribed to the senses, but to the understanding, whose lot alone it is to render an objective judgment from the appearance.

In this manner, if we do not reflect at all on the origin of our representations, and we connect our intuitions of the senses, whatever they may contain, in space and time according to rules for the connection of all cognition in one experience, then either deceptive illusion or truth can arise, according to whether we are heedless or careful; that concerns only the use of sensory representations in the understanding, and not their origin. In the same way, if I take all the representations of the senses together with their form, namely space and time, for nothing but appearances, and these last two for a mere form of sensibility that is by no means to be found outside it in the objects, and I make use of these same representations only in relation to possible experience: then in the fact that I take them for mere appearances is contained not the least illusion or temptation toward error; for they nonetheless can be connected together correctly in experience according to rules of truth. In this manner all the propositions of geometry hold good for space as well as for all objects of the senses, and hence for all possible experience, whether I regard space as a mere form of sensibility or as something inhering in things themselves; though only in the first case can I comprehend how it may be possible to know those propositions *a priori* for all objects of outer intuition; otherwise, with respect to all merely possible experience, everything remains just as if I had never undertaken this departure from the common opinion.

But if I venture to go beyond all possible experience with my concepts of space and time – which is inevitable if I pass them off for qualities that attach to things in themselves (for what should then prevent me from still permitting them to hold good for the very same things, even if my senses might now be differently framed and either suited to them or not?) – then an important error can spring up which rests on an illusion, since I passed off as universally valid that which was a condition for the intuition of things (attaching merely to my subject, and surely valid for all objects of the senses, hence for all merely possible experience), because I referred it to the things in themselves and did not restrict it to conditions of experience.

Therefore, it is so greatly mistaken that my doctrine of the ideality of space and time makes the whole sensible world a mere illusion, that, on the contrary, my doctrine is the only means for securing the application to actual objects of one of the most important bodies of cognition – namely, that which mathematics expounds *a priori* – and for preventing it from being taken for nothing but mere illusion, since without this observation it would be quite impossible to make out whether the intuitions of space and time, which we do not derive from experience but which nevertheless lie *a priori* in our representations, were not mere self-produced fantasies, to which no object at all corresponds, at least not adequately, and therefore geometry itself a mere illusion, whereas we have been able to demonstrate the incontestable validity of geometry with respect to all objects of the sensible world for the very reason that the latter are mere appearances.

Second, it is so greatly mistaken that these principles of mine, because they make sensory representations into appearances, are supposed, in place of the truth of experience, to transform sensory representations into mere illusion, that, on the contrary, my principles are the only means of avoiding the transcendental illusion by which metaphysics has always been deceived and thereby tempted into the childish endeavor of chasing after soap bubbles, because appearances, which after all are mere representations, were taken for things in themselves; from which followed all those remarkable enactments of the antinomy of reason, which I will mention later on, and which is removed through this single observation: that appearance, as long as it is used in experience, brings forth truth, but as soon as it passes beyond the boundaries of experience and becomes transcendent, brings forth nothing but sheer illusion.

Since I therefore grant their reality to the things that we represent to ourselves through the senses, and limit our sensory intuition of these things only to the extent that in no instance whatsoever, not even in the pure intuitions of space and time, does it represent anything more than mere appearances of these things, and never their quality in themselves, this is therefore no thoroughgoing illusion ascribed by me to nature, and my protestation against all imputation of idealism is so conclusive and clear that it would even seem superfluous if there were not unauthorized judges who, being glad to have an ancient name for every deviation from their false though common opinion, and never judging the spirit of philosophical nomenclatures but merely clinging to the letter, were ready to put their own folly in the place of well-determined concepts, and thereby to twist and deform them. For the fact that I have myself given to this theory of mine the name of transcendental idealism cannot justify anyone in confusing it with the empirical idealism of *Descartes* (although this idealism was only a problem, whose insolubility left everyone free, in *Descartes'* opinion, to deny the existence of the corporeal world, since the problem could never be answered satisfactorily) or with the mystical and visionary idealism of *Berkeley* (against which, along with other similar fantasies, our *Critique*, on the contrary, contains the proper antidote). For what I called idealism did not concern the existence of things (the doubting of which, however, properly constitutes idealism according to the received meaning), for it never came into my mind to doubt that, but only the sensory representation of things, to which space and time above all belong; and about these last, hence in general about all *appearances*, I have only shown: that they are not things (but mere modes of representation), nor are they determinations that belong to things in themselves. The word transcendental, however, which with me never signifies a relation of our cognition to things, but only to the *faculty of cognition*, was intended to prevent this misinterpretation. But before it prompts still more of the same, I gladly withdraw this name, and I will have it called critical idealism. But if it is an in fact reprehensible idealism to transform actual things (not appearances) into mere representations, with what name shall we christen that idealism which, conversely, makes mere representations into things? I think it could be named *dreaming* idealism, to distinguish it from the preceding, which may be called *visionary* idealism, both of which were to have been held off by my formerly so-called transcendental, or better, *critical* idealism.

Main Transcendental Question, Second Part
How Is Pure Natural Science Possible?

§14

Nature is the *existence* of things, insofar as that existence is determined according to universal laws. If nature meant the existence of things *in themselves*, we would never be able to cognize it, either *a priori* or *a posteriori*. Not *a priori*, for how are we to know what pertains to things in themselves, inasmuch as this can never come about through the analysis of our concepts (analytical propositions), since I do not want to know what may be contained in my concept of a thing (for that belongs to its logical essence), but what would be added to this concept in the actuality of a thing, and what the thing itself would be determined by in its existence apart from my concept. My understanding, and the conditions under which alone it can connect the determinations of things in their existence, prescribes no rule to the things themselves; these do not conform to my understanding, but my understanding would have to conform to them; they would therefore have to be given to me in advance so that these determinations could be drawn from them, but then they would not be cognized *a priori*.

Such cognition of the nature of things in themselves would also be impossible *a posteriori*. For if experience were supposed to teach me *laws* to which the existence of things is subject, then these laws, insofar as they relate to things in themselves, would have to apply to them *necessarily* even apart from my experience. Now experience teaches me what there is and how it is, but never that it necessarily must be so and not otherwise. Therefore it can never teach me the nature of things in themselves.

§15

Now we are nevertheless actually in possession of a pure natural science, which, *a priori* and with all of the necessity required for apodictic propositions, propounds laws to which nature is subject. Here I need call to witness only that propaedeutic to the theory of nature which, under the title of universal natural science, precedes all of physics (which is founded on empirical principles). Therein we find mathematics applied to appearances, and also merely discursive principles (from concepts), which make up the philosophical part of pure cognition of nature. But indeed there is also much in it that is not completely pure and independent of sources in experience, such as the concept of *motion*, of *impenetrability* (on which the empirical concept of matter is based), of *inertia*, among others, so that it cannot be called completely pure natural science; furthermore it refers only to the objects of the outer senses, and therefore does not provide an example of a universal natural science in the strict sense; for that would have to bring nature in general – whether pertaining to an object of the outer senses or of the inner sense (the object of physics as well as psychology) – under universal laws. But among the principles of this universal physics a few are found that actually have the universality we require, such as the proposition: *that substance remains* and persists, that *everything that Happens* always previously *is determined by a cause* according to constant laws, and so on. These are truly universal laws of nature, that exist fully *a priori*. There is then in fact a pure natural science, and now the question is: *How is it possible?*

§16

The word *nature* assumes yet another meaning, namely one that determines the *object*, whereas in the above meaning it only signified the *conformity to law* of the determinations of the existence of things in general. Nature considered *materialiter* is the *sum total of all objects of experience*. We are concerned here only with this, since otherwise things that could never become objects of an experience if they had to be cognized according to their nature would force us to concepts whose significance could never be given *in concreto* (in any example of a possible experience), and we would therefore have to make for ourselves mere concepts of the nature of those things, the reality of which concepts, i.e., whether they actually relate to objects or are mere beings of thought, could not be decided at all. Cognition of that which cannot be an object of experience would be hyperphysical, and here we are not concerned with such things at all, but rather with that cognition of nature the reality of which can be confirmed through experience, even though such cognition is possible *a priori* and precedes all experience.

§17

The *formal* in nature in this narrower meaning is therefore the conformity to law of all objects of experience, and, insofar as this conformity is cognized *a priori*, the *necessary* conformity to law of those objects. But it has just been shown: that the laws of nature can never be cognized *a priori* in objects insofar as these objects are considered, not in relation to possible experience, but as things in themselves. We are here, however, concerned not with things in themselves (the properties of which we leave undetermined), but only with things as objects of a possible experience, and the sum total of such objects is properly what we here call nature. And now I ask whether, if the discussion is of the possibility of a cognition of nature *a priori*, it would be better to frame the problem in this way: How is it possible to cognize *a priori* the necessary conformity to law *of things* as objects of experience, or: How is it possible in general to cognize *a priori* the necessary conformity to law *of experience* itself with regard to all of its objects?

On closer examination, whether the question is posed one way or the other, its solution will come out absolutely the same with regard to the pure cognition of nature (which is actually the point of the question). For the subjective laws under which alone a cognition of things through experience is possible also hold good for those things as objects of a possible experience (but obviously not for them as things in themselves, which, however, are not at all being considered here). It is completely the same, whether I say: A judgment of perception can never be considered as valid for experience without the law, that if an event is perceived then it is always referred to something preceding from which it follows according to a universal rule; or if I express myself in this way: Everything of which experience shows that it happens must have a cause.

It is nonetheless more appropriate to choose the first formulation. For since we can indeed, *a priori* and previous to any objects being given, have a cognition of those conditions under which alone an experience regarding objects is possible, but never of the laws to which objects may be subject in themselves without relation to possible experience, we will therefore be able to study *a priori* the nature of things in no other way than by investigating the conditions, and the universal (though subjective) laws, under which alone such a cognition is possible as experience (as regards mere form), and determining the possibility of things as objects of experience accordingly; for were I to choose the second mode of expression and to seek the *a priori* conditions under which nature is possible as an *object* of experience, I might then easily fall into misunderstanding and fancy that I had to speak about nature as a thing in itself, and in that case I would be wandering about fruitlessly in endless endeavors to find laws for things about which nothing is given to me.

We will therefore be concerned here only with experience and with the universal conditions of its possibility which are given *a priori*, and from there we will determine nature as the whole object of all possible experience. I think I will be understood: that here I do not mean the rules for the *observation* of a nature that is already given, which presuppose experience already; and so do not mean, how we can learn the laws from nature (through experience), for these would then not be laws *a priori* and would provide no pure natural science; but rather, how the *a priori* conditions of the possibility of experience are at the same time the sources out of which all universal laws of nature must be derived.

§18

We must therefore first of all note: that, although all judgments of experience are empirical, i.e., have their basis in the immediate perception of the senses, nonetheless the reverse is not the case, that all empirical judgments are therefore judgments of experience; rather, beyond the empirical and in general beyond what is given in sensory intuition, special concepts must yet be added, which have their origin completely *a priori* in the pure understanding, and under which every perception can first be subsumed and then, by means of the same concepts, transformed into experience.

Empirical judgments, insofar as they have objective validity, are JUDGMENTS OF EXPERIENCE; those, however, that are *only subjectively valid* I call mere JUDGMENTS OF PERCEPTION. The latter do not require a pure concept of the understanding, but only the logical connection of perceptions in a thinking subject. But the former always demand, in addition to the representations of sensory intuition, special *concepts originally generated in the understanding*, which are precisely what make the judgment of experience *objectively valid*.

All of our judgments are at first mere judgments of perception; they hold only for us, i.e., for our subject, and only afterwards do we give them a new relation, namely to an object, and intend that the judgment should also be valid at all times for us and for everyone else; for if a judgment agrees with an object, then all judgments of the same object must also agree with one another, and hence the objective validity of a judgment of experience signifies nothing other than its necessary universal validity. But also conversely, if we find cause to deem a judgment necessarily, universally valid (which is never based on the perception, but on the pure concept of the understanding under which the perception is subsumed), we must then also deem it objective, i.e., as expressing not merely a relation of a perception to a subject, but a property of an object; for there would be no reason why other judgments necessarily would have to agree with mine, if there were not the unity of the object – an object to which they all refer, with which they all agree, and, for that reason, also must all harmonize among themselves.

§19

Objective validity and necessary universal validity (for everyone) are therefore interchangeable concepts, and although we do not know the object in itself, nonetheless, if we regard a judgment as universally valid and hence necessary, objective validity is understood to be included. Through this judgment we cognize the object (even if it otherwise remains unknown as it may be in itself) by means of the universally valid and necessary connection of the given perceptions; and since this is the case for all objects of the senses, judgments of experience will not derive their objective validity from the immediate cognition of the object (for this is impossible), but merely from the condition for the universal validity of empirical judgments, which, as has been said, never rests on empirical, or indeed sensory conditions at all, but on a pure concept of the understanding. The object always remains unknown in itself; if, however, through the concept of the understanding the connection of the representations which it provides to our sensibility is determined as universally valid, then the object is determined through this relation, and the judgment is objective.

Let us provide examples: that the room is warm, the sugar sweet, the wormwood repugnant, are merely subjectively valid judgments. I do not at all require that I should find it so at every time, or that everyone else should find it just as I do; they express only a relation of two sensations to the same subject, namely myself, and this only in my present state of perception, and are therefore not expected to be valid for the object: these I call judgments of perception. The case is completely different with judgments of experience. What experience teaches me under certain circumstances, it must teach me at every time and teach everyone else as well, and its validity is not limited to the subject or its state at that time. Therefore I express all such judgments as objectively valid; as, e.g., if I say: the air is elastic, then this judgment is to begin with only a judgment of perception; I relate two sensations in my senses only to one another. If I want it to be called a judgment of experience, I then require that this connection be subject to a condition that makes it universally valid. I want therefore that I, at every time, and also everyone else, would necessarily have to conjoin the same perceptions under the same circumstances.

§20

We will therefore have to analyze experience in general, in order to see what is contained in this product of the senses and the understanding, and how the judgment of experience is itself possible. At bottom lies the intuition of which I am conscious, i.e., perception (*perceptio*), which belongs solely to the senses. But, secondly, judging (which pertains solely to the understanding) also belongs here. Now this judging can be of two types: first, when I merely compare the perceptions and conjoin them in a consciousness of my state, or, second, when I conjoin them in a consciousness in general. The first judgment is merely a judgment of perception and has thus far only subjective validity; it is merely a connection of perceptions within my mental state, without reference to the object. Hence it is not, as is commonly imagined, sufficient for experience to compare perceptions and to connect them in one consciousness by means of judging; from that there arises no universal validity and necessity of the judgment, on account of which alone it can be objectively valid and so can be experience.

A completely different judgment therefore occurs before experience can arise from perception. The given intuition must be subsumed under a concept that determines the form of judging in general with respect to the intuition, connects the empirical consciousness of the latter in a consciousness in general, and thereby furnishes empirical judgments with universal validity; a concept of this kind is a pure *a priori* concept of the understanding, which does nothing but simply determine for an intuition the mode in general in which it can serve for judging. The concept of cause being such a concept, it therefore determines the intuition which is subsumed under it, e.g., that of air, with respect to judging in general – namely, so that the concept of air serves, with respect to expansion, in the relation of the antecedent to the consequent in a hypothetical judgment. The concept of cause is therefore a pure concept of the understanding, which is completely distinct from all possible perception, and serves only, with respect to judging in general, to determine that representation which is contained under it and so to make possible a universally valid judgment.

Now before a judgment of experience can arise from a judgment of perception, it is first required: that the perception be subsumed under a concept of the understanding of this kind; e.g., the air belongs under the concept of cause, which determines the judgment about the air as hypothetical with respect to expansion. This expansion is thereby represented not as belonging merely to my perception of the air in my state of perception or in several of my states or in the state of others, but as *necessarily* belonging to it, and the judgment: the air is elastic, becomes universally valid and thereby for the first time a judgment of experience, because certain judgments occur beforehand, which subsume the intuition of the air under the concept of cause and effect, and thereby determine the perceptions not merely with respect to each other in my subject, but with respect to the form of judging in general (here, the hypothetical), and in this way make the empirical judgment universally valid.

If one analyzes all of one's synthetic judgments insofar as they are objectively valid, one finds that they never consist in mere intuitions that have, as is commonly thought, merely been connected in a judgment through comparison, but rather that they would not be possible if, over and above the concepts drawn from intuition, a pure concept of the understanding had not been added under which these concepts had been subsumed and in this way first connected in an objectively valid judgment. Even the judgments of pure mathematics in its simplest axioms are not exempt from this condition. The principle: a straight line is the shortest line between two points, presupposes that the line has been subsumed under the concept of magnitude, which certainly is no mere intuition, but has its seat solely in the understanding and serves to determine the intuition (of the line) with respect to such judgments as may be passed on it as regards the quantity of these judgments, namely plurality (as *judicia plurativa*), since through such judgments it is understood that in a given intuition a homogeneous plurality is contained.

§21

In order therefore to explain the possibility of experience insofar as it rests on pure *a priori* concepts of the understanding, we must first present that which belongs to judgments in general, and the various moments of the understanding therein, in a complete table; for the pure concepts of the understanding – which are nothing more than concepts of intuitions in general insofar as these intuitions are, with respect to one or another of these moments, in themselves determined to judgments and therefore determined necessarily and with universal validity – will come out exactly parallel to them. By this means the *a priori* principles of the possibility of all experience as objectively valid empirical cognition will also be determined quite exactly. For they are nothing other than propositions that subsume all perception (according to certain universal conditions of intuition) under those pure concepts of the understanding.

LOGICAL TABLE
of Judgments

1.
According to Quantity

Universal
Particular
Singular

2.
According to Quality

Affirmative
Negative
Infinite

3.
According to Relation

Categorical
Hypothetical
Disjunctive

4.
According to Modality

Problematic
Assertoric
Apodictic

TRANSCENDENTAL TABLE
of Concepts of the Understanding

1.
According to Quantity

Unity (measure)
Plurality (magnitude)
Totality (the whole)

2.
According to Quality

Reality
Negation
Limitation

3.
According to Relation

Substance
Cause
Community

4.
According to Modality

Possibility
Existence
Necessity

[. . .]

§21[a]

In order to comprise all the preceding in one notion, it is first of all necessary to remind the reader that the discussion here is not about the genesis of experience, but about that which lies in experience. The former belongs to empirical psychology and could never be properly developed even there without the latter, which belongs to the critique of cognition and especially of the understanding.

Experience consists of intuitions, which belong to sensibility, and of judgments, which are solely the understanding's business. Those judgments that the understanding forms solely from sensory intuitions are, however, still not judgments of experience by a long way. For in the one case the judgment would only connect perceptions as they are given in sensory intuition; but in the latter case the judgments are supposed to say what experience in general contains, therefore not what mere perception – whose validity is merely subjective – contains. The judgment of experience must still therefore, beyond the sensory intuition and its logical connection (in accordance with which the intuition has been rendered universal through comparison in a judgment), add something that determines the synthetic judgment as necessary, and thereby as universally valid; and this can be nothing but that concept which represents the intuition as in itself determined with respect to one form of judgment rather than the others, i.e., a concept of that synthetic unity of intuitions which can be represented only through a given logical function of judgments.

§22

To sum this up: the business of the senses is to intuit; that of the understanding, to think. To think, however, is to unite representations in a consciousness. This unification either arises merely relative to the subject and is contingent and subjective, or it occurs without condition and is necessary or objective. The unification of representations in a consciousness is judgment. Therefore, thinking is the same as judging or as relating representations to judgments in general. Judgments are therefore either merely subjective, if representations are related to one consciousness in one subject alone and are united in it, or they are objective, if they are united in a consciousness in general, i.e., are united necessarily therein. The logical moments of all judgments are so many possible ways of uniting representations in a consciousness. If, however, the very same moments serve as concepts, they are concepts of the *necessary* unification of these representations in a consciousness, and so are principles of objectively valid judgments. This unification in a consciousness is either analytic, through identity, or synthetic, through combination and addition of various representations with one another. Experience consists in the synthetic connection of appearances (perceptions) in a consciousness, insofar as this connection is necessary. Therefore pure concepts of the understanding are those under which all perceptions must first be subsumed before they can serve in judgments of experience, in which the synthetic unity of perceptions is represented as necessary and universally valid.

§23

Judgments, insofar as they are regarded merely as the condition for the unification of given representations in a consciousness, are rules. These rules, insofar as they represent the unification as necessary, are *a priori* rules, and provided that there are none above them from which they can be derived, are principles. Now since, with respect to the possibility of all experience, if merely the form of thinking is considered in the experience, no conditions on judgments of experience are above those that bring the appearance (according to the varying form of their intuition) under pure concepts of the understanding (which make the empirical judgment objectively valid), these conditions are therefore the *a priori* principles of possible experience.

Now the principles of possible experience are, at the same time, universal laws of nature that can be cognized *a priori*. And so the problem that lies in our second question, presently before us: *how is pure natural science possible?* is solved. For the systematization that is required for the form of a science is here found to perfection, since beyond the aforementioned formal conditions of all judgments in general, hence of all rules whatsoever furnished by logic, no others are possible, and these form a logical system; but the concepts based thereon, which contain the *a priori* conditions for all synthetic and necessary judgments, for that very reason form a transcendental system; finally, the principles by means of which all appearances are subsumed under these concepts form a physiological system, i.e., a system of nature, which precedes all empirical cognition of nature and first makes it possible, and can therefore be called the true universal and pure natural science.

§24

The first of the physiological principles subsumes all appearances, as intuitions in space and time, under the concept of *magnitude* and is to that extent a principle for the application of mathematics to experience. The second does not subsume the properly empirical – namely sensation, which signifies the real in intuitions – directly under the concept of *magnitude*, since sensation is no intuition *containing* space or time, although it does place the object corresponding to it in both; but there nonetheless is, between reality (sensory representation) and nothing, i.e., the complete emptiness of intuition in time, a difference that has a magnitude, for indeed between every given degree of light and darkness, every degree of warmth and the completely cold, every degree of heaviness and absolute lightness, every degree of the filling of space and completely empty space, ever smaller degrees can be thought, just as between consciousness and total unconsciousness (psychological darkness) ever smaller degrees occur; therefore no perception is possible that would show a complete absence, e.g., no psychological darkness is possible that could not be regarded is a consciousness that is merely outweighed by another, stronger one, and thus it is in all cases of sensation; as a result of which the understanding can anticipate even sensations, which form the proper quality of empirical representations (appearances), by means of the principle that they all without exception, hence the real in all appearance, have degrees – which is the second application of mathematics (*mathesis intensorum*) to natural science.

§25

With respect to the relation of appearances, and indeed exclusively with regard to their existence, the determination of this relation is not mathematical but dynamical, and it can never be objectively valid, hence fit for experience, if it is not subject to *a priori* principles, which first make cognition through experience possible with respect to that determination. Therefore appearances must be subsumed under the concept of substance, which, as a concept of the thing itself, underlies all determination of existence; or second, insofar as a temporal sequence, i.e., an event, is met with among the appearances, they must be subsumed under the concept of an effect in relation to a cause; or, insofar as simultaneous existence is to be cognized objectively, i.e., through a judgment of experience, they must be subsumed under the concept of community (interaction): and so *a priori* principles underlie objectively valid, though empirical, judgments, i.e., they underlie the possibility of experience insofar as it is supposed to connect objects in nature according to existence. These principles are the actual laws of nature, which can be called dynamical.

Finally, there also belongs to judgments of experience the cognition of agreement and connection: not so much of the appearances among themselves in experience, but of their relation to experience in general, a relation that contains either their agreement with the formal conditions that the understanding cognizes, or their connection with the material of the senses and perception, or both united in one concept, and thus possibility, existence, and necessity according to universal laws of nature; all of which would constitute the physiological theory of method (the distinction of truth and hypotheses, and the boundaries of the reliability of the latter).

[. . .]

§27

Here is now the place to dispose thoroughly of the Humean doubt. He rightly affirmed: that we in no way have insight through reason into the possibility of causality, i.e., the possibility of relating the existence of one thing to the existence of some other thing that would necessarily be posited through the first one. I add to this that we have just as little insight into the concept of subsistence, i.e., of the necessity that a subject, which itself cannot be a predicate of any other thing, should underlie the existence of things – nay, that we cannot frame any concept of the possibility of any such thing (although we can point out examples of its use in experience); and I also add that this very incomprehensibility affects the community of things as well, since we have no insight whatsoever into how, from the state of one thing, a consequence could be drawn about the state of completely different things outside it (and vice versa), and into how substances, each of which has its own separate existence, should depend on one another and should indeed do so necessarily. Nonetheless, I am very far from taking these concepts to be merely borrowed from experience, and from taking the necessity represented in them to be falsely imputed and a mere illusion through which long habit deludes us; rather, I have sufficiently shown that they and the principles taken from them stand firm *a priori* prior to all experience, and have their undoubted objective correctness, though of course only with respect to experience.

[. . .]

§29

For having a try at *Hume's* problematic concept (this, his *crux metaphysicorum*), namely the concept of cause, there is first given to me *a priori*, by means of logic: the form of a conditioned judgment in general, that is, the use of a given cognition as ground and another as consequent. It is, however, possible that in perception a rule of relation will be found, which says this: that a certain appearance is constantly followed by another (though not the reverse); and this is a case for me to use hypothetical judgment and, e.g., to say: If a body is illuminated by the sun for long enough, then it becomes warm. Here there is of course not yet a necessity of connection, hence not yet the concept of cause. But I continue on, and say: if the above proposition, which is merely a subjective connection of perceptions, is to be a proposition of experience, then it must be regarded as necessarily and universally valid. But a proposition of this sort would be: The sun through its light is the cause of the warmth. The foregoing empirical rule is now regarded as a law, and indeed as valid not merely of appearances, but of them on behalf of a possible experience, which requires universally and therefore necessarily valid rules. I therefore have quite good insight into the concept of cause, as a concept that necessarily belongs to the mere form of experience, and into its possibility as a synthetic unification of perceptions in a consciousness in general; but I have no insight at all into the possibility of a thing in general as a cause, and indeed have none just because the concept of cause indicates a condition that in no way attaches to things, but only to experience, namely, that experience can be an objectively valid cognition of appearances and their sequence in time only insofar as the antecedent appearance can be conjoined with the subsequent one according to the rule of hypothetical judgments.

§30

Consequently, even the pure concepts of the understanding have no significance at all if they depart from objects of experience and want to be referred to things in themselves (*noumena*). They serve as it were only to spell out appearances, so that they can be read as experience; the principles that arise from their relation to the sensible world serve our understanding for use in experience only; beyond this there are arbitrary conjoinings without objective reality whose possibility cannot be cognized *a priori* and whose relation to objects cannot, through any example, be confirmed or even made intelligible, since all examples can be taken only from some possible experience or other and hence the objects of these concepts can be met with nowhere else but in a possible experience.

This complete solution of the Humean problem, though coming out contrary to the surmise of the originator, thus restores to the pure concepts of the understanding their *a priori* origin, and to the universal laws of nature their validity as laws of the understanding, but in such a way that it restricts their use to experience only, because their possibility is founded solely in the relation of the understanding to experience: not, however, in such a way that they are derived from experience, but that experience is derived from them, a completely reversed type of connection that never occurred to *Hume*.

From this now flows the following result of all the foregoing investigations: "All synthetic *a priori* principles are nothing more than principles of possible experience," and can never be related to things in themselves, but only to appearances as objects of experience. Therefore both pure mathematics and pure natural science can never refer to anything more than mere appearances, and they can only represent either that which makes experience in general possible, or that which, being derived from these principles, must always be able to be represented in some possible experience or other.

[...]

§33

There is in fact something insidious in our pure concepts of the understanding, as regards enticement toward a transcendent use; for so I call that use which goes out beyond all possible experience. It is not only that our concepts of substance, of force, of action, of reality, etc., are wholly independent of experience, likewise contain no sensory appearance whatsoever, and so in fact seem to refer to things in themselves (*noumena*); but also, which strengthens this supposition yet further, that they contain in themselves a necessity of determination which experience never equals. The concept of cause contains a rule, according to which from one state of affairs another follows with necessity; but experience can only show us that from one state of things another state often, or, at best, commonly, follows, and it can therefore furnish neither strict universality nor necessity (and so forth).

Consequently, the concepts of the understanding appear to have much more significance and content than they would if their entire vocation were exhausted by mere use in experience, and so the understanding unheededly builds onto the house of experience a much roomier wing, which it crowds with mere beings of thought, without once noticing that it has taken its otherwise legitimate concepts as far beyond the boundaries of their use.

§34

Two important, nay completely indispensable, though utterly dry investigations were therefore needed, which were carried out in the *Critique*. Through the first of these ["On the Schematism of the Pure Concepts of the Understanding," A137ff.] it was shown that the senses do not supply pure concepts of the understanding *in concreto*, but only the schema for their use, and that the object appropriate to this schema is found only in experience (as the product of the understanding from materials of sensibility). In the second investigation ["On the Basis of the Distinction of All Objects in General into *Phenomena* and *Noumena*," A235ff.] it is shown: that notwithstanding the independence from experience of our pure concepts of the understanding and principles, and even their apparently larger sphere of use, nonetheless, outside the field of experience nothing at all can be thought by means of them, because they can do nothing but merely determine the logical form of judgment with respect to given intuitions; but since beyond the field of sensibility there is no intuition at all, these pure concepts lack completely all significance, in that there are no means through which they can be exhibited *in concreto*, and so all such *noumena*, together with their aggregate – an intelligible world – are nothing but representations of a problem, whose object is in itself perfectly possible, but whose solution, given the nature of our understanding, is completely impossible, since our understanding is no faculty of intuition but only of the connection of given intuitions in an experience; and experience therefore has to contain all the objects for our concepts, whereas apart from it all concepts will be without significance, since no intuition can be put under them.

§36
How Is Nature Itself Possible?

This question, which is the highest point that transcendental philosophy can ever reach, and up to which, as its boundary and completion, it must be taken, actually contains two questions.

FIRST: How is nature possible in general in the *material* sense, namely, according to intuition, as the sum total of appearances; how are space, time, and that which fills them both, the object of sensation, possible in general? The answer is: by means of the constitution of our sensibility, in accordance with which our sensibility is affected in its characteristic way by objects that are in themselves unknown to it and that are wholly distinct from said appearances. This answer is, in the book itself, given in the Transcendental Aesthetic, but here in the *Prolegomena* through the solution of the first main question.

SECOND: How is nature possible in the *formal* sense, as the sum total of the rules to which all appearances must be subject if they are to be thought as connected in one experience? The answer cannot come out otherwise than: it is possible only by means of the constitution of our understanding, in accordance with which all these representations of sensibility are necessarily referred to one consciousness, and through which, first, the characteristic manner of our thinking, namely by means of rules, is possible, and then, by means of these rules, experience is possible – which is to be wholly distinguished from insight into objects in themselves. This answer is, in the book itself, given in the Transcendental Logic, but here in the *Prolegomena*, in the course of solving the second main question.

But how this characteristic property of our sensibility itself may be possible, or that of our understanding and of the necessary apperception that underlies it and all thinking, cannot be further solved and answered, because we always have need of them in turn for all answering and for all thinking of objects.

There are many laws of nature that we can know only through experience, but lawfulness in the connection of appearances, i.e., nature in general, we cannot come to know through any experience, because experience itself has need of such laws, which lie *a priori* at the basis of its possibility.

The possibility of experience in general is thus at the same time the universal law of nature, and the principles of the former are themselves the laws of the latter. For we are not acquainted with nature except as the sum total of appearances, i.e., of the representations in us, and so we cannot get the laws of their connection from anywhere else except the principles of their connection in us, i.e., from the conditions of necessary unification in one consciousness, which unification constitutes the possibility of experience.

Even the main proposition that has been elaborated throughout this entire part, that universal laws of nature can be cognized *a priori*, already leads by itself to the proposition: that the highest legislation for nature must lie in ourselves, i.e., in our understanding, and that we must not seek the universal laws of nature from nature by means of experience, but, conversely, must seek nature, as regards its universal conformity to law, solely in the conditions of the possibility of experience that lie in our sensibility and understanding; for how would it otherwise be possible to become acquainted with these laws *a priori*, since they are surely not rules of analytic cognition, but are genuine synthetic amplifications of cognition? Such agreement, and indeed necessary agreement, between the principles of possible experience and the laws of the possibility of nature, can come about only from one of two causes: either these laws are taken from nature by means of experience, or, conversely, nature is derived from the laws of the possibility of experience in general and is fully identical with the mere universal lawfulness of experience. The first one contradicts itself, for the universal laws of nature can and must be cognized *a priori* (i.e., independently of all experience) and set at the foundation of all empirical use of the understanding; so only the second remains.

We must, however, distinguish empirical laws of nature, which always presuppose particular perceptions, from the pure or universal laws of nature, which, without having particular perceptions underlying them, contain merely the conditions for the necessary unification of such perceptions in one experience; with respect to the latter laws, nature and *possible* experience are one and the same, and since in possible experience the lawfulness rests on the necessary connection of appearances in one experience (without which we would not be able to cognize any object of the sensible world at all), and so on the original laws of the understanding, then, even though it sounds strange at first, it is nonetheless certain, if I say with respect to the universal laws of nature: *the understanding does not draw its* (a priori) *laws from nature, but prescribes them to it.*

[. . .]

Main Transcendental Question, Third Part
How Is Metaphysics in General Possible?

§40

Pure mathematics and pure natural science would not have needed, *for the purpose of their own security* and certainty, a deduction of the sort that we have hitherto accomplished for them both; for the first is supported by its own evidence, whereas the second, though arising from pure sources of the understanding, is nonetheless supported from experience and thoroughgoing confirmation by it – experience being a witness that natural science cannot fully renounce and dispense with, because, as philosophy, despite all its certainty it can never rival mathematics. Neither science had need of the aforementioned investigation for itself, but for another science, namely metaphysics.

Apart from concepts of nature, which always find their application in experience, metaphysics is further concerned with pure concepts of reason that are never given in any possible experience whatsoever, hence with concepts whose objective reality (that they are not mere fantasies) and with assertions whose truth or falsity cannot be confirmed or exposed by any experience; and this part of metaphysics is moreover precisely that which forms its essential end, toward which all the rest is only a means – and so this science needs such a deduction *for its own sake*. The third question, now put before us, therefore concerns as it were the core and the characteristic feature of metaphysics, namely, the preoccupation of reason simply with itself, and that acquaintance with objects which is presumed to arise immediately from reason's brooding over its own concepts without its either needing mediation from experience for such an acquaintance, or being able to achieve such an acquaintance through experience at all.

Without a solution to this question, reason will never be satisfied with itself. The use in experience to which reason limits the pure understanding does not entirely fulfill reason's own vocation. Each individual experience is only a part of the whole sphere of the domain of experience, but the *absolute totality of all possible experience* is not itself an experience, and yet is still a necessary problem for reason, for the mere representation of which reason needs concepts entirely different from the pure concepts of the understanding, whose use is only *immanent*, i.e., refers to experience insofar as such experience can be given, whereas the concepts of reason extend to the completeness, i.e., the collective unity of the whole of possible experience, and in that way exceed any given experience and become *transcendent*.

Hence, just as the understanding needed the categories for experience, reason contains in itself the basis for ideas, by which I mean necessary concepts whose object nevertheless *cannot* be given in any experience. The latter are just as intrinsic to the nature of reason as are the former to that of the understanding; and if the ideas carry with them an illusion that can easily mislead, this illusion is inevitable, although it can very well be prevented "from leading us astray."

Since all illusion consists in taking the subjective basis for a judgment to be objective, pure reason's knowledge of itself in its transcendent (overreaching) use will be the only prevention against the errors into which reason falls if it misconstrues its vocation and, in transcendent fashion, refers to the object in itself that which concerns only its own subject and the guidance of that subject in every use that is immanent.

§41

The distinction of *ideas*, i.e., of pure concepts of reason, from categories, or pure concepts of the understanding, as cognitions of completely different type, origin, and use, is so important a piece of the foundation of a science which is to contain a system of all these cognitions *a priori* that, without such a division, metaphysics is utterly impossible, or at best is a disorderly and bungling endeavor to patch together a house of cards, without knowledge of the materials with which one is preoccupied and of their suitability for one or another end.

[. . .]

§44

In this examination it is in general further noteworthy: that the ideas of reason are not, like the categories, helpful to us in some way in using the understanding with respect to experience, but are completely dispensable with respect to such use, nay, are contrary to and obstructive of the maxims for the cognition of nature through reason, although they are still quite necessary in another respect, yet to be determined. In explaining the appearances of the soul, we can be completely indifferent as to whether it is a simple substance or not; for we are unable through any possible experience to make the concept of a simple being sensorily intelligible, hence intelligible *in concreto*; and this concept is therefore completely empty with respect to all hoped-for insight into the cause of the appearances, and cannot serve as a principle of explanation of that which supplies inner or outer experience. Just as little can the cosmological ideas of the beginning of the world or the eternity of the world (*a parte ante*) help us to explain any event in the world itself. Finally, in accordance with a correct maxim of natural philosophy, we must refrain from all explanations of the organization of nature drawn from the will of a supreme being, because this is no longer natural philosophy but an admission that we have come to the end of it. These ideas therefore have a completely different determination of their use from that of the categories, through which (and through the principles built upon them) experience itself first became possible. Nevertheless our laborious analytic of the understanding would have been entirely superfluous, if our aim had been directed toward nothing other than mere cognition of nature insofar as such cognition can be given in experience; for reason conducts its affairs in both mathematics and natural science quite safely and quite well, even without any such subtle deduction; hence our critique of the understanding joins with the ideas of pure reason for a purpose that lies beyond the use of the understanding in experience, though we have said above that the use of the understanding in this regard is wholly impossible and without object or significance. There must nonetheless be agreement between what belongs to the nature of reason and of the understanding, and the former must contribute to the perfection of the latter and cannot possibly confuse it.

The solution to this question is as follows: Pure reason does not, among its ideas, have in view particular objects that might lie beyond the field of experience, but it merely demands completeness in the use of the understanding in the connection of experience. This completeness can, however, only be a completeness of principles, but not of intuitions and objects. Nonetheless, in order to represent these principles determinately, reason conceives of them as the cognition of an object, cognition of which is completely determined with respect to these rules – though the object is only an idea – so as to bring cognition through the understanding as close as possible to the completeness that this idea signifies.

§45
Preliminary Remark On the Dialectic of Pure Reason

We have shown above (§§33, 34): that the purity of the categories from all admixture with sensory determinations can mislead reason into extending their use entirely beyond all experience to things in themselves; and yet, because the categories are themselves unable to find any intuition that could provide them with significance and sense *in concreto*, they cannot in and of themselves provide any determinate concept of anything at all, though they can indeed, as mere logical functions, represent a thing in general. Now hyperbolical objects of this kind are what are called NOUMENA or pure beings of the understanding (better: beings of thought) – such as, e.g., *substance*, but which is thought *without persistence* in time, or a *cause*, which would however *not* act *in time*, and so on – because such predicates are attributed to these objects as serve only to make the lawfulness of experience possible, and yet they are nonetheless deprived of all the conditions of intuition under which alone experience is possible, as a result of which the above concepts again lose all significance.

There is, however, no danger that the understanding will of itself wantonly stray beyond its boundaries into the field of mere beings of thought, without being urged by alien laws. But if reason, which can never be fully satisfied with any use of the rules of the understanding in experience because such use is always still conditioned, requires completion of this chain of conditions, then the understanding is driven out of its circle, in order partly to represent the objects of experience in a series stretching so far that no experience can comprise the likes of it, partly (in order to complete the series) even to look for NOUMENA entirely outside said experience to which reason can attach the chain and in that way, independent at last of the conditions of experience, nonetheless can make its hold complete. These then are the transcendental ideas, which, although in accordance with the true but hidden end of the natural determination of our reason they may be aimed not at overreaching concepts but merely at the unbounded expansion of the use of concepts in experience, may nonetheless, through an inevitable illusion, elicit from the understanding a *transcendent* use, which, though deceitful, nonetheless cannot be curbed by any resolve to stay within the bounds of experience, but only through scientific instruction and hard work.

§46
I. Psychological Ideas (*Critique*, A341ff.)

It has long been observed that in all substances the true subject – namely that which remains after all accidents (as predicates) have been removed – and hence the *substantial* itself, is unknown to us; and various complaints have been made about these limits to our insight. But it needs to be said that human understanding is not to be blamed because it does not know the substantial in things, i.e., cannot determine it by itself, but rather because it wants to cognize determinately, like an object that is given, what is only an idea. Pure reason demands that for each predicate of a thing we should seek its appropriate subject, but that for this subject, which is in turn necessarily only a predicate, we should seek its subject again, and so forth to infinity (or as far as we get). But from this it follows that we should take nothing that we can attain for a final subject, and that the substantial itself could never be thought by our ever-so-deeply penetrating understanding, even if the whole of nature were laid bare before it; for the specific nature of our understanding consists in thinking everything discursively, i.e., through concepts, hence through mere predicates, among which the absolute subject must therefore always be absent. Consequently, all real properties by which we cognize bodies are mere accidents for which we lack a subject – even impenetrability, which must always be conceived only as the effect of a force.

Now it does appear as if we have something substantial in the consciousness of ourselves (i.e., in the thinking subject), and indeed have it in immediate intuition; for all the predicates of inner sense are referred to the *I* as subject, and this *I* cannot again be thought as the predicate of some other subject. It therefore appears that in this case completeness in referring the given concepts to a subject as predicates is not a mere idea, but that the object, namely the *absolute subject* itself, is given in experience. But this expectation is disappointed. For the I is not a concept at all, but only a designation of the object of inner sense insofar as we do not further cognize it through any predicate; hence although it cannot itself be the predicate of any other thing, just as little can it be a determinate concept of an absolute subject, but as in all the other cases it can only be the referring of inner appearances to their unknown subject. Nevertheless, through a wholly natural misunderstanding, this idea (which, as a regulative principle, serves perfectly well to destroy completely all materialistic explanations of the inner appearances of our soul) gives rise to a seemingly plausible argument for inferring the nature of our thinking being from this presumed cognition of the substantial in it, inasmuch as knowledge of its nature falls completely outside the sum total of experience.

§47

This thinking self (the soul), as the ultimate subject of thinking, which cannot itself be represented as the predicate of another thing, may now indeed be called substance: but this concept nonetheless remains completely empty and without any consequences, if persistence (as that which renders the concept of substances fertile within experience) cannot be proven of it.

Persistence, however, can never be proven from the concept of a substance as a thing in itself, but only for the purposes of experience. This has been sufficiently established in the first Analogy of Experience (*Critique*, A182); and anyone who will not grant this proof can test for themselves whether they succeed in proving, from the concept of a subject that does not exist as the predicate of another thing, that the existence of that subject is persistent throughout, and that it can neither come into being nor pass away, either in itself or through any natural cause. Synthetic *a priori* propositions of this type can never be proven in themselves, but only in relation to things as objects of a possible experience.

§48

If, therefore, we want to infer the persistence of the soul from the concept of the soul as substance, this can be valid of the soul only for the purpose of possible experience, and not of the soul as a thing in itself and beyond all possible experience. But life is the subjective condition of all our possible experience: consequently, only the persistence of the soul during life can be inferred, for the death of a human being is the end of all experience as far as the soul as an object of experience is concerned (provided that the opposite has not been proven, which is the very matter in question). Therefore the persistence of the soul can be proven only during the life of a human being (which proof will doubtless be granted us), but not after death (which is actually our concern) – and indeed then only from the universal ground that the concept of substance, insofar as it is to be considered as connected necessarily with the concept of persistence, can be so connected only in accordance with a principle of possible experience, and hence only for the purpose of the latter.

§49

That our outer perceptions not only do correspond to something real outside us, but must so correspond, also can never be proven as a connection of things in themselves, but can well be proven for the purpose of experience. This is as much as to say: it can very well be proven that there is something outside us of an empirical kind, and hence as appearance in space; for we are not concerned with other objects than those that belong to a possible experience, just because such objects cannot be given to us in any experience and therefore are nothing for us. Outside me empirically is that which is intuited in space; and because this space, together with all the appearances it contains, belongs to those representations whose connection according to laws of experience proves their objective truth, just as the connection of the appearances of the inner sense proves the reality of my soul (as an object of inner sense), it follows that I am, by means of outer appearances, just as conscious of the reality of bodies as outer appearances in space, as I am, by means of inner experience, conscious of the existence of my soul in time – which soul I cognize only as an object of inner sense through the appearances constituting an inner state, and whose being as it is in itself, which underlies these appearances, is unknown to me. Cartesian idealism therefore distinguishes only outer experience from dream, and lawfulness as a criterion of the truth of the former from the disorder and false illusion of the latter. In both cases it presupposes space and time as conditions for the existence of objects and merely asks whether the objects of the outer senses are actually to be found in the space in which we put them while awake, in the way that the object of inner sense, the soul, actually is in time, i.e., whether experience carries with itself sure criteria to distinguish it from imagination. Here the doubt can easily be removed, and we always remove it in ordinary life by investigating the connection of appearances in both space and time according to universal laws of experience, and if the representation of outer things consistently agrees therewith, we cannot doubt that those things should not constitute truthful experience. Because appearances are considered as appearances only in accordance with their connection within experience, material idealism can therefore very easily be removed; and it is just as secure an experience that bodies exist outside us (in space) as that I myself exist in accordance with the representation of inner sense (in time) – for the concept: *outside us*, signifies only existence in space. Since, however, the I in the proposition

I am does not signify merely the object of inner intuition (in time) but also the subject of consciousness, just as body does not signify merely outer intuition (in space) but also the thing *in itself* that underlies this appearance, accordingly the question of whether bodies (as appearances of outer sense) exist *outside my thought* as bodies in nature can without hesitation be answered negatively; but here matters do not stand otherwise for the question of whether I myself *as an appearance of inner sense* (the soul according to empirical psychology) exist in time outside my power of representation, for this question must also be answered negatively. In this way everything is, when reduced to its true signification, conclusive and certain. Formal idealism (elsewhere called transcendental idealism by me) actually destroys material or Cartesian idealism. For if space is nothing but a form of my sensibility, then it is, as a representation in me, just as real as I am myself, and the only question remaining concerns the empirical truth of the appearances in this space. If this is not the case, but rather space and the appearances in it are something existing outside us, then all the criteria of experience can never, outside our perception, prove the reality of these objects outside us.

§50
II. Cosmological Ideas (*Critique,* A405ff.)

This product of pure reason in its transcendent use is its most remarkable phenomenon, and it works the most strongly of all to awaken philosophy from its dogmatic slumber, and to prompt it toward the difficult business of the critique of reason itself.

I call this idea cosmological because it always finds its object only in the sensible world and needs no other world than that whose object is an object for the senses, and so, thus far, is immanent and not transcendent, and therefore, up to this point, is not yet an idea; by contrast, to think of the soul as a simple substance already amounts to thinking of it as an object (the simple) the likes of which cannot be represented at all to the senses. Notwithstanding all that, the cosmological idea expands the connection of the conditioned with its condition (be it mathematical or dynamic) so greatly that experience can never match it, and therefore it is, with respect to this point, always an idea whose object can never be adequately given in any experience whatever.

§51

In the first place, the usefulness of a system of categories is here revealed so clearly and unmistakably that even if there were no further grounds of proof of that system, this alone would sufficiently establish their indispensability in the system of pure reason. There are no more than four such transcendent ideas, as many as there are classes of categories; in each of them, however, they refer only to the absolute completeness of the series of conditions for a given conditioned. In accordance with these cosmological ideas there are also only four kinds of dialectical assertions of pure reason, which show themselves to be dialectical because for each such assertion a contradictory one stands in opposition in accordance with equally plausible principles of pure reason, a conflict that cannot be avoided by any metaphysical art of the most subtle distinctions, but that requires the philosopher to return to the first sources of pure reason itself. This antinomy, by no means arbitrarily contrived, but grounded in the nature of human reason and so inevitable and neverending, contains the following four theses together with their antitheses.

1.

Thesis

The world has, as to time and space,
a beginning (a boundary).

Antithesis

The world is, as to time and space,
infinite.

2.

Thesis

Everything in the world
is constituted out of the
simple.

Antithesis

There is nothing simple,
but everything is
composite.

3.

Thesis

There exist in the world
causes through
freedom.

Antithesis

There is no freedom,
but everything is
nature.

4.

Thesis

In the series of causes in the world there is a
necessary being.

Antithesis

There is nothing necessary in this series, but in it
everything is contingent.

§52a

Here is now the strangest phenomenon of human reason, no other example of which can be pointed to in any of its other uses. If (as normally happens) we think of the appearances of the sensible world as things in themselves, if we take the principles of their connection to be principles that are universally valid for things in themselves and not merely for experience (as is just as common, nay, is inevitable without our *Critique*): then an unexpected conflict comes to light, which can never be settled in the usual dogmatic manner, since both thesis and antithesis can be established through equally evident, clear, and incontestable proofs – for I will vouch for the correctness of all these proofs – and therefore reason is seen to be divided against itself, a situation that makes the skeptic rejoice, but must make the critical philosopher pensive and uneasy.

§52b

One can tinker around with metaphysics in sundry ways without even suspecting that one might be venturing into untruth. For if only we do not contradict ourselves – something that is indeed entirely possible with synthetic, though completely fanciful, propositions – then we can never be refuted by experience in all such cases where the concepts we connect are mere ideas, which can by no means be given (in their entire content) in experience. For how would we decide through experience: Whether the world has existed from eternity, or has a beginning? Whether matter is infinitely divisible, or is constituted out of simple parts? Concepts such as these cannot be given in any experience (even the greatest possible), and so the falsity of the affirmative or negative thesis cannot be discovered through that touchstone.

The single possible case in which reason would reveal (against its will) its secret dialectic (which it falsely passes off as dogmatics) would be that in which it based an assertion on a universally acknowledged principle, and, with the greatest propriety in the mode of inference, derived the direct opposite from another equally accredited principle. Now this case is here actual, and indeed is so with respect to four natural ideas of reason, from which there arise – each with proper consistency and from universally acknowledged principles – four assertions on one side and just as many counterassertions on the other, thereby revealing the dialectical illusion of pure reason in the use of these principles, which otherwise would have had to remain forever hidden.

Here is, therefore, a decisive test, which must necessarily disclose to us a fault that lies hidden in the presuppositions of reason. Of two mutually contradictory propositions, both cannot be false save when the concept underlying them both is itself contradictory; e.g., the two propositions: a square circle is round, and: a square circle is not round, are both false. For, as regards the first, it is false that the aforementioned circle is round, since it is square; but it is also false that it is not round, i.e., has corners, since it is a circle. The logical mark of the impossibility of a concept consists, then, in this: that under the presupposition of this concept, two contradictory propositions would be false simultaneously; and since between these two no third proposition can be thought, through this concept *nothing at all* is thought.

§52c

Now underlying the first two antinomies, which I call mathematical because they concern adding together or dividing up the homogeneous, is a contradictory concept of this type; and by this means I explain how it comes about that thesis and antithesis are false in both.

If I speak of objects in time and space, I am not speaking of things in themselves (since I know nothing of them), but only of things in appearance, i.e., of experience as a distinct way of cognizing objects that is granted to human beings alone. I must not say of that which I think in space or time: that it is in itself in space and time, independent of this thought of mine; for then I would contradict myself, since space and time, together with the appearances in them, are nothing existing in themselves and outside my representations, but are themselves only ways of representing, and it is patently contradictory to say of a mere way of representing that it also exists outside our representation. The objects of the senses therefore exist only in experience; by contrast, to grant them a self-subsistent existence of their own, without experience or prior to it, is as much as to imagine that experience is also real without experience or prior to it.

Now if I ask about the magnitude of the world with respect to space and time, for all of my concepts it is just as impossible to assert that it is infinite as that it is finite. For neither of these can be contained in experience, because it is not possible to have experience either of an *infinite* space or infinitely flowing time, or of a *bounding* of the world by an empty space or by an earlier, empty time; these are only ideas. Therefore the magnitude of the world, determined one way or the other, must lie in itself, apart from all experience. But this contradicts the concept of a sensible world, which is merely a sum total of appearance, whose existence and connection takes place only in representation, namely in experience, since it is not a thing in itself, but is itself nothing but a kind of representation. From this it follows that, since the concept of a sensible world existing for itself is self-contradictory, any solution to this problem as to its magnitude will always be false, whether the attempted solution be affirmative or negative.

The same holds for the second antinomy, which concerns dividing up the appearances. For these appearances are mere representations, and the parts exist only in the representation of them, hence in the dividing, i.e., in a possible experience in which they are given, and the dividing therefore proceeds only as far as possible experience reaches. To assume that an appearance, e.g., of a body, contains within itself, before all experience, all of the parts to which possible experience can ever attain, means: to give to a mere appearance, which can exist only in experience, at the same time an existence of its own previous to experience, which is to say: that mere representations are present before they are encountered in the representational power, which contradicts itself and hence also contradicts every solution to this misunderstood problem, whether that solution asserts that bodies in themselves consist of infinitely many parts or of a finite number of simple parts.

§53

In the first (mathematical) class of antinomy, the falsity of the presupposition consisted in the following: that something self-contradictory (namely, appearance as a thing in itself) would be represented as being unifiable in a concept. But regarding the second, namely the dynamical, class of antinomy, the falsity of the presupposition consists in this: that something that is unifiable is represented as contradictory; consequently, while in the first case both of the mutually opposing assertions were false, here on the contrary the assertions, which are set in opposition to one another through mere misunderstanding, can both be true.

Specifically, mathematical combination necessarily presupposes the homogeneity of the things combined (in the concept of magnitude), but dynamical connection does not require this at all. If it is a question of the magnitude of something extended, all parts must be homogeneous among themselves and with the whole; by contrast, in the connection of cause and effect homogeneity can indeed be found, but is not necessary; for the concept of causality (whereby through one thing, something completely different from it is posited) at least does not require it.

If the objects of the sensible world were taken for things in themselves, and the previously stated natural laws for laws of things in themselves, contradiction would be inevitable. In the same way, if the subject of freedom were represented, like the other objects, as a mere appearance, contradiction could again not be avoided, for the same thing would be simultaneously affirmed and denied of the same object in the same sense. But if natural necessity is referred only to appearances and freedom only to things in themselves, then no contradiction arises if both kinds of causality are assumed or conceded equally, however difficult or impossible it may be to make causality of the latter kind conceivable.

Within appearance, every effect is an event, or something that happens in time; the effect must, in accordance with the universal law of nature, be preceded by a determination of the causality of its cause (a state of the cause), from which the effect follows in accordance with a constant law. But this determination of the cause to causality must also be something *that* occurs or *takes place*; the cause must have *begun* to *act*, for otherwise no sequence in time could be thought between it and the effect. Both the effect and the causality of the cause would have always existed. Therefore the *determination* of the cause *to act* must also have arisen among the appearances, and so must, like its effect, be an event, which again must have its cause, and so on, and hence natural necessity must be the condition in accordance with which efficient causes are determined. Should, by contrast, freedom be a property of certain causes of appearances, then that freedom must, in relation to the appearances as events, be a faculty of starting those events *from itself* (*sponte*), i.e., without the causality of the cause itself having to begin, and hence without need for any other ground to determine its beginning. But then *the cause*, as to its causality, would not have to be subject to temporal determinations of its state, i.e., would *not* have to be *appearance* at all, i.e., would have to be taken for a thing in itself, and only the *effects* would have to be taken for *appearances*. If this sort of influence of intelligible beings on appearances can be thought without contradiction, then natural necessity will indeed attach to every connection of cause and effect in the sensible world, and yet that cause which is itself not an appearance (though it underlies appearance) will still be entitled to freedom, and therefore nature and freedom will be attributable without contradiction to the very same thing, but in different respects, in the one case as appearance, in the other as a thing in itself.

We have in us a faculty that not only stands in connection with its subjectively determining grounds, which are the natural causes of its actions – and thus far is the faculty of a being which itself belongs to appearances – but that also is related to objective grounds that are mere ideas, insofar as these ideas can determine this faculty, a connection that is expressed by *ought*. This faculty is called *reason*, and insofar as we are considering a being (the human being) solely as regards this objectively determinable reason, this being cannot be considered as a being of the senses; rather, the aforesaid property is the property of a thing in itself, and the possibility of that property – namely, how the *ought*, which has never yet happened, can determine the activity of this being and can be the cause of actions whose effect is an appearance in the sensible world – we cannot comprehend at all. Yet the casuality of reason with respect to effects in the sensible world would nonetheless be freedom, insofar as *objective grounds*, which are themselves ideas, are taken to be determining with respect to that causality. For the action of that causality would in that case not depend on any subjective, hence also not on any temporal conditions, and would therefore also not depend on the natural law that serves to determine those conditions, because grounds of reason provide the rule for actions universally, from principles, without influence from the circumstances of time or place.

What I adduce here counts only as an example, for intelligibility, and does not belong necessarily to our question, which must be decided from mere concepts independently of properties that we find in the actual world.

I can now say without contradiction: all actions of rational beings, insofar as they are appearances (are encountered in some experience or other), are subject to natural necessity; but the very same actions, with respect only to the rational subject and its faculty of acting in accordance with bare reason, are free. What, then, is required for natural necessity? Nothing more than the determinability of every event in the sensible world according to constant laws, and therefore a relation to a cause within appearance; whereby the underlying thing in itself and its causality remain unknown. But I say: *the law of nature remains*, whether the rational being be a cause of effects in the sensible world through reason and hence through freedom, or whether that being does not determine such effects through rational grounds. For if the first is the case, the action takes place according to maxims whose effect within appearance will always conform to constant laws; if the second is the case, and the action does not take place according to principles of reason, then it is subject to the empirical laws of sensibility, and in both cases the effects are connected according to constant laws; but we require nothing more for natural necessity, and indeed know nothing more of it. In the first case, however, reason is the cause of these natural laws and is therefore free, in the second case the effects flow according to mere natural laws of sensibility, because reason exercises no influence on them; but, because of this, reason is not itself determined by sensibility (which is impossible), and it is therefore also free in this case. Therefore freedom does not impede the natural law of appearances, any more than this law interferes with the freedom of the practical use of reason, a use that stands in connection with things in themselves as determining grounds.

In this way practical freedom – namely, that freedom in which reason has causality in accordance with objective determining grounds – is rescued, without natural necessity suffering the least harm with respect to the very same effects, as appearances. This can also help elucidate what we have had to say about transcendental freedom and its unification with natural necessity (in the same subject, but not taken in one and the same respect). For, as regards transcendental freedom, any beginning of an action of a being out of objective causes is always, with respect to these determining grounds, a *first beginning*, although the same action is, in the series of appearances, only a *subalternate beginning*, which has to be preceded by a state of the cause which determines that cause, and which is itself determined in the same way by an immediately preceding cause: so that in rational beings (or in general in any beings, provided that their causality is determined in them as things in themselves) one can conceive of a faculty for beginning a series of states spontaneously, without falling into contradiction with the laws of nature. For the relation of an action to the objective grounds of reason is not a temporal relation; here, that which determines the causality does not precede the action as regards time, because such determining grounds do not represent the relation of objects to the senses (and so to causes within appearance), but rather they represent determining causes as things in themselves, which are not subject to temporal conditions. Hence the action can be regarded as a first beginning with respect to the causality of reason, but can nonetheless at the same time be seen as a mere subordinated beginning with respect to the series of appearances, and can without contradiction be considered in the former respect as free, in the latter (since the action is mere appearance) as subject to natural necessity.

As regards the *fourth* antinomy, it is removed in a similar manner as was the conflict of reason with itself in the third. For if only the *cause in the appearances* is distinguished from the *cause of the appearances* insofar as the latter cause can be thought as a *thing in itself*, then these two propositions can very well exist side by side, as follows: that there occurs no cause of the sensible world (in accordance with similar laws of causality) whose existence is absolutely necessary, as also on the other side: that this world is nonetheless connected with a necessary being as its cause (but of another kind and according to another law) – the inconsistency of these two propositions resting solely on the mistake of extending what holds merely for appearances to things in themselves, and in general of mixing the two of these up into one concept.

§54

This then is the statement and solution of the whole antinomy in which reason finds itself entangled in the application of its principles to the sensible world, and of which the former (the mere statement) even by itself would already be of considerable benefit toward a knowledge of human reason, even if the solution of this conflict should not yet fully satisfy the reader, who has here to combat a natural illusion that has only recently been presented to him as such, after he had hitherto always taken that illusion for the truth. One consequence of all this is, indeed, inevitable; namely, that since it is completely impossible to escape from this conflict of reason with itself as long as the objects of the sensible world are taken for things in themselves – and not for what they in fact are, that is, for mere appearances – the reader is obliged, for that reason, to take up once more the deduction of all our cognition *a priori* (and the examination of that deduction which I have provided), in order to come to a decision about it. For the present I do not require more; for if, through this pursuit, he has first thought himself deeply enough into the nature of pure reason, then the concepts by means of which alone the solution to this conflict of reason is possible will already be familiar to him, a circumstance without which I cannot expect full approbation from even the most attentive reader.

§55
III. Theological Idea (*Critique*, A571ff.)

The third transcendental idea, which provides material for the most important among all the uses of reason – but one that, if pursued merely speculatively, is overreaching (transcendent) and thereby dialectical – is the ideal of pure reason. Here reason does not, as with the psychological and the cosmological idea, start from experience and become seduced by the ascending sequence of grounds into aspiring, if possible, to absolute completeness in their series, but instead breaks off entirely from experience and descends from bare concepts of what would constitute the absolute completeness of a thing in general – and so by means of the idea of a supremely perfect first being – to determination of the possibility, hence the reality, of all other things; in consequence, here the bare presupposition of a being that, although not in the series of experiences, is nonetheless thought on behalf of experience, for the sake of comprehensibility in the connection, ordering, and unity of that experience – i.e., the *idea* – is easier to distinguish from the concept of the understanding than in the previous cases. Here therefore the dialectical illusion, which arises from our taking the subjective conditions of our thinking for objective conditions of things themselves and our taking a hypothesis that is necessary for the satisfaction of our reason for a dogma, is easily exposed, and I therefore need mention nothing more about the presumptions of transcendental theology, since what the *Critique* says about them is clear, evident, and decisive.

§56
General Note to the Transcendental Ideas

The objects that are given to us through experience are incomprehensible to us in many respects, and there are many questions to which natural law carries us, which, if pursued to a certain height (yet always in conformity with those laws) cannot be solved at all; e.g., how pieces of matter attract one another. But if we completely abandon nature, or transcend all possible experience in advancing the connection of nature and so lose ourselves in mere ideas, then we are unable to say that the object is incomprehensible to us and that the nature of things presents us with unsolvable problems; for then we are not concerned with nature or in general with objects that are given, but merely with concepts that have their origin solely in our reason, and with mere beings of thought, with respect to which all problems, which must originate from the concepts of those very beings, can be solved, since reason certainly can and must be held fully accountable for its own proceedings. Because the psychological, cosmological, and theological ideas are nothing but pure concepts of reason, which cannot be given in any experience, the questions that reason puts before us with respect to them are not set for us through objects, but rather through mere maxims of reason for the sake of its self-satisfaction, and these questions must one and all be capable of sufficient answer

– which occurs by its being shown that they are principles for bringing the use of our understanding into thoroughgoing harmony, completeness, and synthetic unity, and to that extent are valid only for experience, though in the *totality* of that experience. But although an absolute totality of experience is not possible, nonetheless the idea of a totality of cognition according to principles in general is what alone can provide it with a special kind of unity, namely that of a system, without which unity our cognition is nothing but piecework and cannot be used for the highest end (which is nothing other than the system of all ends); and here I mean not only the practical use of reason, but also the highest end of its speculative use.

Therefore the transcendental ideas express the peculiar vocation of reason, namely to be a principle of the systematic unity of the use of the understanding. But if one looks upon this unity in the manner of cognition as if it were inhering in the object of cognition, if one takes that which really is only *regulative* to be *constitutive*, and becomes convinced that by means of these ideas one's knowledge can be expanded far beyond all possible experience, hence can be expanded transcendently, even though this unity serves only to bring experience in itself as near as possible to completeness (i.e., to have its advance constrained by nothing that cannot belong to experience), then this is a mere misunderstanding in judging the true vocation of our reason and its principles, and it is a dialectic, which partly confounds the use of reason in experience, and partly divides reason against itself.

Part IV

Arguments for the Existence of God

Introduction

Philosophers are interested in arguments for God's existence for various reasons. Some may expect these arguments to have an impact on religious belief, although the reasons people believe in God are usually not based on philosophical argument. In the eighteenth century, Samuel Clarke and William Paley were religious believers who publicly defended the rationality of belief in God. Other philosophers, like Descartes and Berkeley, proposed so-called "theistic proofs" as a means of solving philosophical problems related to human knowledge and causality. Still others argued that belief in the existence of God is essential for sound moral philosophy. While Kant thought morality stood on its own, regardless of the existence of God, he offered a unique argument for the existence of God based on our need to understand morality as a system. Three traditional philosophical "proofs" for God's existence worth noting here are the ontological argument, the cosmological argument, and the teleological argument.

The "ontological argument" attempts to demonstrate the reality of God through the very "idea" or conception of a God that we employ even in wondering whether such a being is real. This argument gets its name from "ontology," the philosophy of "being" or reality, because it purports to show that the reality of God is implied in the very idea of God. It is often referred to as an *a priori* argument for belief in God, since it begins with a definition of God proceeding by reasoning "deductively" to the conclusion that God must exist. The argument purports to show, in other words, that the statement "God does not exist" is a logical contradiction, and hence cannot be true. No factual evidence about the world, nothing known only by experience, is appealed to in this *a priori* argument from the definition of God.

The "cosmological argument" appeals to an undoubted fact about the world of experience, which is that *everything has a cause*. It gets its name from "cosmology," which is the philosophy or science of the world as a whole. It purports to show that since everything that is not eternal must have a cause, the world itself must have a cause, which is the eternal God. In previous readings we have seen how modern philosophers disagreed over our knowledge that everything has a cause. Hume, for example, treated this as something we know only *a posteriori*, or through experience. But Kant disagreed, and attempted to show

how we know it *a priori*. Because of the different views taken on the causal principle, the cosmological argument is sometimes called an *a posteriori* argument, and at other times classified as an *a priori* argument. A further reason for this confusion over different ways the cosmological argument has been classified is that a "deductive," *a priori* argument, if sound, is assumed to provide a conclusion of which we can be absolutely certain. But an "inductive," *a posteriori* argument is usually taken to provide, at best, a conclusion whose truth is only highly probable. Many therefore consider the cosmological argument an *a priori* argument because it purports to show that God's existence is more than highly probable.

The "teleological argument" is the third basic approach philosophers and theologians have taken in proving God's existence. The name comes from "teleology," which is the philosophy or science of purposes. It is sometimes called the "design argument," because of the emphasis it places on intelligent design in nature. This proof is always classified as an *a posteriori* argument. It not only begins from evidence of natural design discovered by experience, but also concludes with nothing more than a strong probability of God's existence. It is usually presented in the form of the following analogy: just as intelligently designed artifacts provide evidence of the existence of their human designers, so intelligent design in nature, including human nature, provides evidence of the existence of a super-human designer.

In his *Meditations on First Philosophy* (1641), Descartes used two arguments to establish the existence of God, which was crucial to his philosophical system. He needed to prove that there was an all-perfect being in order to rule out the possibility that he was continually deceived in the beliefs he formed. Without God, he felt he had no basis for any certainty. The simpler of his two arguments for God's existence is an ontological one, which he derived probably from the medieval philosopher St. Anselm. The argument moves from the concept of God to the conclusion that he exists as follows: (1) I have an idea of God, which is an idea of a supremely perfect being, a being with all perfection. (2) Necessary existence is a perfection (if God did not exist *necessarily*, then he would not be as perfect or great as he is conceived to be). (3) Therefore, God necessarily exists. The very idea of a perfect, surpassingly great God that does not exist is a logical contradiction.

The ontological argument is criticized briefly in the reading selection below from Samuel Clarke, and at length in a selection from Immanuel Kant. Kant argues, basically, that the term or predicate "exists" does not have the same logical function as almost all other predicates, such as "great" or "good" or "glorious." To say that God exists does not modify our conception of him, in the way our conception of him is modified when we say that he is great or good or glorious. We therefore do not contradict ourselves when we think of God as not existing. (This line of objection to the ontological argument seems to be found earlier also in Hume's *Treatise*.)

A version of the cosmological argument is presented here in the short reading selection from Clarke, which is followed by Paley's brief but powerful presentation of the teleological argument. Selections from Hume's *Dialogues concerning Natural Religion* offer different critiques of the design argument and of Clarke's cosmological argument. To the design argument, Hume raised the question whether we can infer anything about the whole world from considering what we find true of its parts. We rightly infer the existence of a designer for the steps of a stairway, since their proportions so perfectly accommodate the climbing of human legs. But is the whole of nature like a part of it? Can what we say of a part be applied to the entirety? Hume's *Dialogues* also raises the issue whether we can draw any justified conclusions about God's attributes. Do we have any reason to think God's mind is like a human mind, so that we can discern God's intentions from examining the world in the way we understand human intentions from examining an artifact of human creation? Hume raised several difficult questions for the cosmological argument as well. How can there be a first cause for a succession of events that goes to eternity? Furthermore, why ask for a cause of the whole succession of events when the individual events in the causal series are seen as explaining one another? Hume's criticisms are devastating, as usual. But we miss his point if we conclude from his objections to these proofs that he was irreligious or even hostile to religious belief. As a philosopher, Hume was primarily interested in the grounds or reasons we have for our beliefs. His other philosophical works constantly encourage us to consider what grounds we have for thinking, say, that one thing causes another; that matter exists apart from the sense impressions; or even that you are the same person now as when you first learned about Hume. If there are good grounds for religious belief, Hume would say, philosophical proofs like the design argument are not among them. Whatever sustains religious belief, it is not philosophy.

Kant also subjected the different arguments for God's existence to severe criticism. They do not work, he concluded; or they do not prove what they purport to prove. But we include here some reading selections from Kant that present a new type of theistic proof, sometimes referred to as the "moral proof." Many have supposed that moral principles must come from the commandments of God, so that our moral duties or obligations would not exist if there were no God. It is often assumed, that is, that belief in God provides a sound basis for moral belief. But Kant's moral proof of God actually runs this line of thinking in reverse. He argued, in effect, that moral belief provides a sound basis for belief in God. Kant would not agree that we need God in order to have morality. Morality, he argued, is something rational beings discover on their own. They do not need God to command how they ought to behave (see the selections from Kant's *Lectures on Ethics* in part VI below). So even if there were no God, our moral beliefs would still be firmly grounded, according to Kant. His moral proof of God's existence says that because we have these moral beliefs insofar as we are rational beings, we must also believe there is some final purpose for morality. That purpose, he concluded, is that in the end each of us should be rewarded with just as much happiness as we deserve, based on our virtue and moral conduct. But the only way this can occur is if there is a God who knows just how virtuous we are, and has the power to make us as happy as we deserve to be. Hence, because we simply cannot deny our moral beliefs, we must also believe in what these beliefs imply: that the soul is immortal; that there is a God; and that good people will receive a final reward.

Samuel Clarke, *A Demonstration of the Being and Attributes of God* (1704)

The proof of God's existence that presents God as the cause of the world is probably the oldest line of rational argument for religious belief. This so-called "cosmological argument" points to the fact that the world around us is populated with "contingent" beings, or with beings whose existence is not necessary. These contingent beings would not exist, the argument says, unless they were caused to exist by a being whose existence is necessary, which is God.

The version of the cosmological argument Clarke provides in this short reading selection emphasizes what can be called the *unthinkability* of there being nothing at all in the universe. The universe supposed as containing nothing would lack even eternity and infinity, or what Clarke refers to as "immensity": the vast totality of space. Following Isaac Newton, Clarke considered space to be a "mode" or "attribute" of the Deity itself ("omnipresence"), and therefore something that would not exist if the divine "substance" upon which it depends were nonexistent. We can easily imagine our immense universe as completely vacant of all material things. But Clarke's point is that we cannot conceive of the universe without its immensity. This idea is as illogical or contradictory as someone's believing that two times two is not four, says Clarke. So if eternity and immensity necessarily exist, there must be something that is eternal and immense, something which contains the ground or basis for its own existence within itself: a self-existent being who is God.

Near the end of this reading selection Clarke is critical of Cartesian philosophers on two points. One is their conception of matter defined as taking up space (extension). From this conception it follows, according to Clarke, that matter is also an eternal, self-existing being. For to remove the world's matter, as extension, would be the same as removing the world's immense space. In his second critical point, although Clarke does not mention Descartes or his followers, he refers to an ontological proof of God's existence once used by Descartes. It is the proof that the very definition of God logically contains the idea of his existence, so that to imagine God as not existing is to imagine something self-contradictory and therefore impossible. Clarke's objection to this line of argument is a common one. It is that we of course cannot think of anything fitting the definition of (an existing) God as being as nonexistent; but we need to be given some additional reason for thinking that *there is* anything fitting this definition of (an existing) God. Clarke thought that his argument here provided just that additional reason.

In 1704 Clarke delivered a set of lectures on the "Being and Attributes of God," which made him widely popular in the learned circles of England. The ten lectures were published in book form shortly thereafter. The short selection below is taken from Lecture III in the series.

III

That unchangeable and independent being which has existed from eternity, without any external cause of its existence, must be self-existent, that is, necessarily existing. For whatever exists must either have come into being out of nothing, absolutely without cause, or it must have been produced by some external cause, or it must be self-existent. Now to arise out of nothing absolutely without any cause has been already shown to be a plain contradiction. To have been produced by some external cause cannot possibly be true of every thing, but something must have existed eternally and independently, as has likewise been shown already. Which remains, therefore, [is] that that being which has existed independently from eternity must of necessity be self-existent. Now to be self-existent is not to be produced by itself, for that is an express contradiction, but it is (which is the only idea we can frame of self-existence, and without which the word seems to have no signification at all) – it is, I say, to exist by an absolute necessity originally in the nature of the thing itself. And this necessity must be antecedent, not indeed in time, to the existence of the being itself (because that is eternal), but it must be antecedent in the natural order of our ideas to our supposition of its being. That is, this necessity must not barely be consequent upon our supposition of the existence of such a being (for then it would not be a necessity absolutely such in itself, nor be the ground or foundation of the existence of anything, being on the contrary only a consequent of it), but it must antecedently force itself upon us whether we will or no, even when we are endeavoring to suppose that no such being exists. For example, when we are endeavoring to suppose that there is no being in the universe that exists necessarily, we always find in our minds (besides the foregoing demonstration of something being self-existent from the impossibility of every thing's being dependent) – we always find in our minds, I say, some ideas, as of infinity and eternity, which to remove (that is, to suppose that there is no being, no substance in the universe to which these attributes or modes of existence are necessarily inherent) is a contradiction in the very terms. For modes and attributes exist only by the existence of the substance to which they belong. Now he that can suppose eternity and immensity, and consequently the substance by whose existence these modes or attributes exist, removed out of the universe, may, if he please, as easily remove the relation of equality between twice two and four.

That to suppose immensity removed out of the universe, or not necessarily eternal, is an express contradiction is intuitively evident to every one who attends to his own ideas and considers the essential nature of things. To suppose any part of space removed is to suppose it removed from and out of itself; and to suppose the whole to be taken away is supposing it to be taken away from itself, that is, to be taken away while it still remains, which is a contradiction in terms. There is no obscurity in the argument but what arises to those who think immense space to be absolutely nothing, which notion is itself likewise an express contradiction. For nothing is that which has no properties or modes whatsoever, that is to say, it is that of which nothing can truly be affirmed and of which every thing can truly be denied, which is not the case of immensity or space.

From this third proposition it follows, first, that the only true idea of a self-existent or necessarily existing being is the idea of a being the supposition of whose not-existing is an express contradiction. For, since it is absolutely impossible but there must be somewhat self-existing, that is, [something] which exists by the necessity of its own nature, it is plain that that necessity cannot be a necessity consequent upon any foregoing supposition (because nothing can be antecedent to that which is self-existent, no not its own will, so as to be the cause or ground of its own existence), but it must be a necessity absolutely such in its own nature. Now a necessity not relatively or consequentially, but absolutely such in its own nature, is nothing else but its being a plain impossibility or implying a contradiction to suppose the contrary. For instance, the relation of equality between twice two and four is an absolute necessity only because it is an immediate contradiction in terms to suppose them unequal. This is the only idea we can frame of an absolute necessity, and to use the word in any other sense seems to be using it without any signification at all.

If any one now asks, what sort of idea the idea of that being is, the supposition of whose not-existing is thus an express contradiction, I answer: it is that first and simplest idea we can possibly frame; an idea necessarily and essentially included or presupposed as a sine qua non in every other idea whatsoever; an idea which (unless we forbear thinking at all) we cannot possibly extirpate or remove out of our minds of a most simple being, absolutely eternal and infinite, original and independent. For, that he who supposes there is no original independent being in the universe supposes a contradiction, has been shown already. And that he who supposes there may possibly be no eternal and infinite being in the universe, supposes likewise a contradiction, is evident from hence (beside that these two attributes do necessarily follow from self-originate independent existence, as shall be shown hereafter), that when he has done his utmost in endeavoring to imagine that no such being exists, he cannot avoid imagining an eternal and infinite nothing. That is, he will imagine eternity and immensity removed out of the universe, and yet that at the same time they still continue there, as has been above distinctly explained.

This argument the Cartesians, who supposed the idea of immensity to be the idea of matter, have been greatly perplexed with. For however in words they have contradicted themselves, yet in reality they have more easily been driven to that most intolerable absurdity of asserting matter to be a necessary being, than being able to remove out of their minds the idea of immensity as existing necessarily and inseparably from eternity. Which absurdity and inextricable perplexity of theirs, in respect of the idea of immensity, shows that they found that indeed to be necessary and impossible to be removed; but in respect of matter it was only a perverse applying [of] an idea to an object whereto it no ways belongs. For, that it is indeed absolutely impossible and contradictory to suppose matter necessarily existing, shall be demonstrated presently.

Secondly, from hence it follows that there is no man whatsoever who makes any use of his reason but may easily become more certain of the being of a supreme independent cause than he can be of any thing else besides his own existence. For how much thought soever it may require to demonstrate the other attributes of such a being, as it may do to demonstrate the greatest mathematical certainties (of which more hereafter), yet, as to its existence, that there is somewhat eternal, infinite, and self-existing, which must be the cause and origin of all other things, this is one of the first and most natural conclusions that any man who thinks at all can frame in his mind; and no man can any more doubt of this than he can doubt whether twice two be equal to four. It is possible indeed a man may in some sense be ignorant of this first and plain truth by being utterly stupid and not thinking at all (for though it is absolutely impossible for him to imagine the contrary, yet he may possibly neglect to conceive this; though no man can possibly think that twice two is not four, yet he may possibly be stupid and never have thought at all whether it be so or not). But this I say: there is no man who thinks or reasons at all but may easily become more certain that there is something eternal, infinite, and self-existing than he can be certain of anything else.

Thirdly, hence we may observe that our first certainty of the existence of God does not arise from this, that in the idea our minds frame of him (or rather in the definition that we make of the word God as signifying a being of all possible perfections) we include self-existence, but from hence, that it is demonstrable both negatively, that neither can all things possibly have arisen out of nothing, nor can they have depended one on another in an endless succession, and also positively, that there is something in the universe actually existing without us, the supposition of whose not existing plainly implies a contradiction. The argument which has by some been drawn from our including self-existence in the idea of God, or our comprehending it in the definition or notion we frame of him, has this obscurity and defect in it: that it seems to extend only to the nominal idea or mere definition of a self-existent being, and does not with a sufficiently evident connection refer and apply that general nominal idea, definition, or notion which we frame in our own mind, to any real particular being actually existing without us. For it is not satisfactory that I have in my mind an idea of the proposition "there exists a being endowed with all possible perfections" or "there is a self-existent being." But I must also have some idea of the thing. I must have an idea of something actually existing without me. And I must see wherein consists the absolute impossibility of removing that idea, and consequently of supposing the non-existence of the thing before I can be satisfied from that idea that the thing actually exists. The bare having an idea of the proposition "there is a self-existent being" proves indeed the thing not to be impossible, for of an impossible proposition there can be no idea. But that it actually is, cannot be proved from the idea unless the certainty of the actual existence of a necessarily existing being follows from the possibility of the existence of such a being, which that it does in this particular case many learned men have indeed thought, and their subtle arguings upon this head are sufficient to raise a cloud not very easy to be seen through.

But it is a much clearer and more convincing way of arguing, to demonstrate that there does actually exist without us a being whose existence is necessary and of itself, by showing the evident contradiction contained in the contrary supposition (as I have before done), and at the same time the absolute impossibility of destroying or removing some ideas, as of eternity and immensity, which therefore must needs be modes or attributes of a necessary being actually existing. For if I have in my mind an idea of a thing, and cannot possibly in my imagination take away the idea of that thing as actually existing any more than I can change or take away the idea of the equality of twice two to four, the certainty of the existence of that thing is the same, and stands on the same foundation, as the certainty of the other relation. For the relation of equality between twice two and four has no other certainty but this, that I cannot, without a contradiction, Change or take away the idea of that relation. We are certain, therefore, of the being of a supreme independent cause because it is strictly demonstrable that there is some thing in the universe actually existing without us, the supposition of whose not-existing plainly implies a contradiction.

10

William Paley, *Natural Theology* (1802)

William Paley (1743–1805) was an English clergyman who for several years at the beginning of his career taught courses in metaphysics, ethics, and New Testament at Cambridge University, his alma mater. He is best known not for any original philosophical work, but as an author of standard textbooks. Paley had a gift for popularly persuasive philosophical rhetoric, which kept his books in the classroom for generations of students.

The full title of the book from which the following reading selection is taken is *Natural Theology: or, Evidences of the Existence and Attributes of the Deity, Collected from the Appearances of Nature*. Natural theology, as opposed to revealed theology, seeks religious knowledge from the study of nature. Revealed theology focuses on what we can learn about God from the revelation provided by Scripture. Paley began his text in natural theology with a classic statement of the "argument from design." Here he honed almost to perfection the famous "watchmaker" analogy, which other thinkers before him had proposed. Upon finding a watch on a deserted island you would not conclude that its pieces of metal and glass had simply fallen together by themselves. Their mechanical precision and mutual adaptation for the purpose of marking time would justify you in believing that the watch had been designed by an intelligent human being. If you subsequently found that the watch was capable of reproducing itself, you could not fail to be impressed by the marvelous intelligence behind its design. We find evidence of similarly marvelous design throughout nature, Paley said. Hence, nature provides us with all the evidence we need for believing in God, its supremely intelligent designer.

One of the world's most famous scientists came under Paley's influence as a student reader of his textbooks. That was Charles Darwin. In his autobiography Darwin reported having been deeply impressed by Paley's thoughts on design and adaptation everywhere in nature. But he eventually found an alternative explanation of nature's apparently intelligent design, through the unintelligent mechanism of natural selection ("survival of the fittest").

In the reading selection that follows this one, David Hume's *Dialogues* present devastating criticisms of the design argument that were published twenty-five years earlier than Paley's *Natural Theology*. Yet in his textbook Paley had nothing to say in response to Hume's already published criticisms. Two reasons perhaps explain this. First, Hume had long been considered an atheistic writer whose ideas need not be taken seriously by Christians. Second,

Paley was, after all, merely an accomplished textbook writer on philosophical and religious subjects. His objective was to present the most persuasive case for religious belief, for the benefit of students. He did not adopt the conscientious philosopher's approach of attempting to reply to all reasonable criticism of his ideas. For this reason Paley is not generally regarded as having contributed substantially to modern philosophy. Were it not for the persuasiveness of the several pages he wrote on the "watchmaker" analogy, Paley would probably now be all but forgotten.

Chapter I
State of the Argument

In crossing a heath, suppose I pitched my foot against a *stone*, and were asked how the stone came to be there; I might possibly answer, that, for any thing I knew to the contrary, it had lain there for ever: nor would it perhaps be very easy to show the absurdity of this answer. But suppose I had found a *watch* upon the ground, and it should be inquired how the watch happened to be in that place; I should hardly think of the answer which I had before given, that, for any thing I knew, the watch might have always been there. Yet why should not this answer serve for the watch as well as for the stone? why is it not as admissible in the second case, as in the first? For this reason, and for no other, viz. that, when we come to inspect the watch, we perceive (what we could not discover in the stone) that its several parts are framed and put together for a purpose, *e.g.* that they are so formed and adjusted as to produce motion, and that motion so regulated as to point out the hour of the day; that, if the different parts had been differently shaped from what they are, of a different size from what they are, or placed after any other manner, or in any other order, than that in which they are placed, either no motion at all would have been carried on in the machine, or none which would have answered the use that is now served by it. To reckon up a few of the plainest of these parts, and of their offices, all tending to one result: – We see a cylindrical box containing a coiled elastic spring, which, by its endeavour to relax itself, turns round the box. We next observe a flexible chain (artificially wrought for the sake of flexure), communicating the action of the spring from the box to the fusee. We then find a series of wheels, the teeth of which catch in, and apply to, each other, conducting the motion from the fusee to the balance, and from the balance to the pointer; and at the same time, by the size and shape of those wheels, so regulating that motion, as to terminate in causing an index, by an equable and measured progression, to pass over a given space in a given time. We take notice that the wheels are made of brass in order to keep them from rust; the springs of steel, no other metal being so elastic; that over the face of the watch there is placed a glass, a material employed in no other part of the work, but in the room of which, if there had been any other than a transparent substance, the hour could not be seen without opening the case. This mechanism being observed (it requires indeed an examination of the instrument, and perhaps some previous knowledge of the subject, to perceive and understand it; but being once, as we have said, observed and understood), the inference, we think, is inevitable, that the watch must have had a maker: that there must have existed, at some time, and at some place or other, an artificer or artificers who formed it for the purpose which we find it actually to answer; who comprehended its construction, and designed its use.

I. Nor would it, I apprehend, weaken the conclusion, that we had never seen a watch made; that we had never known an artist capable of making one; that we were altogether incapable of executing such a piece of workmanship ourselves, or of understanding in what manner it was performed; all this being no more than what is true of some exquisite remains of ancient art, of some lost arts, and, to the generality of mankind, of the more curious productions of modern manufacture. Does one man in a million know how oval frames are turned? Ignorance of this kind exalts our opinion of the unseen and unknown artist's skill, if he be unseen and unknown, but raises no doubt in our minds of the existence and agency of such an artist, at some former time, and in some place or other. Nor can I perceive that it varies at all the inference, whether the question arise concerning a human agent, or concerning an agent of a different species, or an agent possessing, in some respects, a different nature.

II. Neither, secondly, would it invalidate our conclusion, that the watch sometimes went wrong, or that it seldom went exactly right. The purpose of the machinery, the design, and the designer, might be evident, and in the case supposed would be evident, in whatever way we accounted for the irregularity of the movement, or whether we could account for it or not. It is not necessary that a machine be perfect, in order to show with what design it was made: still less necessary, where the only question is, whether it were made with any design at all.

III. Nor, thirdly, would it bring any uncertainty into the argument, if there were a few parts of the watch, concerning which we could not discover, or had not yet discovered, in what manner they conduced to the general effect; or even some parts, concerning which we could not ascertain, whether they conduced to that effect in any manner whatever. For, as to the first branch of the case; if by the loss, or disorder, or decay of the parts in question, the movement of the watch were found in fact to be stopped, or disturbed, or retarded, no doubt would remain in our minds as to the utility or intention of these parts, although we should be unable to investigate the manner according to which, or the connexion by which, the ultimate effect depended upon their action or assistance; and the more complex is the machine, the more likely is this obscurity to arise. Then, as to the second thing supposed, namely, that there were parts which might be spared, without prejudice to the movement of the watch, and that we had proved this by experiment, – these superfluous parts, even if we were completely assured that they were such, would not vacate the reasoning which we had instituted concerning other parts. The indication of contrivance remained, with respect to them, nearly as it was before.

[. . .]

Chapter II
State of the Argument Continued

Suppose, in the next place, that the person who found the watch, should, after some time, discover that, in addition to all the properties which he had hitherto observed in it, it possessed the unexpected property of producing, in the course of its movement, another watch like itself (the thing is conceivable); that it contained within it a mechanism, a system of parts, a mould for instance, or a complex adjustment of lathes, files, and other tools, evidently and separately calculated for this purpose; let us inquire, what effect ought such a discovery to have upon his former conclusion.

I. The first effect would be to increase his admiration of the contrivance, and his conviction of the consummate skill of the contriver. Whether he regarded the object of the contrivance, the distinct apparatus, the intricate, yet in many parts intelligible mechanism, by which it was carried on, he would perceive, in this new observation, nothing but an additional reason for doing what he had already done, – for referring the construction of the watch to design, and to supreme art. If that construction *without* this property, or which is the same thing, before this property had been noticed, proved intention and art to have been employed about it; still more strong would the proof appear, when he came to the knowledge of this further property, the crown and perfection of all the rest.

II. He would reflect, that though the watch before him were, *in some sense*, the maker of the watch, which was fabricated in the course of its movements, yet it was in a very different sense from that, in which a carpenter, for instance, is the maker of a chair; the author of its contrivance, the cause of the relation of its parts to their use. With respect to these, the first watch was no cause at all to the second: in no such sense as this was it the author of the constitution and order, either of the parts which the new watch contained, or of the parts by the aid and instrumentality of which it was produced. We might possibly say, but with great latitude of expression, that a stream of water ground corn: but no latitude of expression would allow us to say, no stretch of conjecture could lead us to think, that the stream of water built the mill, though it were too ancient for us to know who the builder was. What the stream of water does in the affair, is neither more nor less than this; by the application of an unintelligent impulse to a mechanism previously arranged, arranged independently of it, and arranged by intelligence, an effect is produced, viz. the corn is ground. But the effect results from the arrangement. The force of the stream cannot be said to be the cause or author of the effect, still less of the arrangement. Understanding and plan in the formation of the mill were not the less necessary, for any share which the water has in grinding the corn: yet is this share the same, as that which the watch would have contributed to the production of the new watch, upon the supposition assumed in the last section. Therefore,

III. Though it be now no longer probable, that the individual watch, which our observer had found, was made immediately by the hand of an artificer, yet doth not this alteration in anywise affect the inference, that an artificer had been originally employed and concerned in the production. The argument from design remains as it was. Marks of design and contrivance are no more accounted for now, than they were before. In the same thing, we may ask for the cause of different properties. We may ask for the cause of the colour of a body, of its hardness, of its head; and these causes may be all different. We are now asking for the cause of that subserviency to a use, that relation to an end, which we have remarked in the watch before us. No answer is given to this question, by telling us that a preceding watch produced it. There cannot be design without a designer; contrivance without a contriver; order without choice; arrangement, without any thing capable of arranging; subserviency and relation to a purpose, without that which could intend a purpose; means suitable to an end, and executing their office, in accomplishing that end, without the end ever having been contemplated, or the means accommodated to it. Arrangement, disposition of parts, subserviency of means to an end, relation of instruments to a use, imply the presence of intelligence and mind. No one, therefore, can rationally believe, that the insensible, inanimate watch, from which the watch before us issued, was the proper cause of the mechanism we so much admire in it; – could be truly said to have constructed the instrument, disposed its parts, assigned their office, determined their order, action, and mutual dependency, combined their several motions into one result, and that also a result connected with the utilities of other beings. All these properties, therefore, are as much unaccounted for, as they were before.

IV. Nor is any thing gained by running the difficulty farther back, *i.e.* by supposing the watch before us to have been produced from another watch, that from a former, and so on indefinitely. Our going back ever so far, brings us no nearer to the least degree of satisfaction upon the subject. Contrivance is still unaccounted for. We still want a contriver. A designing mind is neither supplied by this supposition, nor dispensed with. If the difficulty were diminished the further we went back, by going back indefinitely we might exhaust it. And this is the only case to which this sort of reasoning applies. Where there is a tendency, or, as we increase the number of terms, a continual approach towards a limit, *there*, by supposing the number of terms to be what is called infinite, we may conceive the limit to be attained: but where there is no such tendency, or approach, nothing is effected by lengthening the series. There is no difference as to the point in question (whatever there may be as to many points), between one series and another; between a series which is finite, and a series which is infinite. A chain, composed of an infinite number of links, can no more support itself, than a chain composed of a finite number of links. And of this we are assured (though we never *can* have tried the experiment), because, by increasing the number of links, from ten for instance to a hundred, from a hundred to a thousand, &c. we make not the smallest approach, we observe not the smallest tendency, towards self-support. There is no difference in this respect (yet there may be a great difference in several respects) between a chain of a greater or less length, between one chain and another, between one that is finite and one that is infinite. This very much resembles the case before us. The machine which we are inspecting, demonstrates, by its construction, contrivance and design. Contrivance must have had a contriver; design, a designer; whether the machine immediately proceeded from another machine or not. That circumstance alters not the case. That other machine may, in like manner, have proceeded from a former machine: nor does that alter the case; contrivance must have had a contriver. That former one from one preceding it: no alteration still; a contriver is still necessary. No tendency is perceived, no approach towards a diminution of this necessity. It is the same with any and every succession of these machines; a succession of ten, of a hundred, of a thousand; with one series, as with another; a series which is finite, as with a series which is infinite. In whatever other respects they may differ, in this they do not. In all equally, contrivance and design are unaccounted for.

The question is not simply, How came the first watch into existence? which question, it may be pretended, is done away by supposing the series of watches thus produced from one another to have been infinite, and consequently to have had no-such *first*, for which it was necessary to provide a cause. This, perhaps, would have been nearly the state of the question, if no thing had been before us but an unorganized, unmechanized substance, without mark or indication of contrivance. It might be difficult to show that such substance could not have existed from eternity, either in succession (if it were possible, which I think it is not, for unorganized bodies to spring from one another), or by individual perpetuity. But that is not the question now. To suppose it to be so, is to suppose that it made no difference whether we had found a watch or a stone. As it is, the metaphysics of that question have no place; for, in the watch which we are examining, are seen contrivance, design; an end, a purpose; means for the end, adaptation to the purpose. And the question which irresistibly presses upon our thoughts, is, whence this contrivance and design? The thing required is the intending mind, the adapting hand, the intelligence by which that hand was directed. This question, this demand, is not shaken off, by increasing a number or succession of substances, destitute of these properties; nor the more, by increasing that number to infinity. If it be said, that, upon the supposition of one watch being produced from another in the course of that other's movements, and by means of the mechanism within it, we have a cause for the watch in my hand, viz. the watch from which it proceeded. I deny, that for the design, the contrivance, the suitableness of means to an end, the adaptation of instruments to a use (all which we discover in the watch), we have any cause whatever. It is in vain, therefore, to assign a series of such causes, or to allege that a series may be carried back to infinity; for I do not admit that we have yet any cause at all of the phænomena, still less any series of causes either finite or infinite. Here is contrivance, but no contriver; proofs of design, but no designer.

V. Our observer would further also reflect, that the maker of the watch before him, was, in truth and reality, the maker of every watch produced from it; there being no difference (except that the latter manifests a more exquisite skill) between the making of another watch with his own hands, by the mediation of files, lathes, chisels, &c. and the disposing, fixing, and inserting of these instruments, or of others equivalent to them, in the body of the watch already made in such a manner, as to form a new watch in the course of the movements which he had given to the old one. It is only working by one set of tools, instead of another.

The conclusion of which the *first* examination of the watch, of its works, construction, and movement, suggested, was, that it must have had, for the cause and author of that construction, an artificer, who understood its mechanism, and designed its use. This conclusion is invincible. A *second* examination presents us with a new discovery. The watch is found, in the course of its movement, to produce another watch, similar to itself; and not only so, but we perceive in it a system or organization, separately calculated for that purpose. What effect would this discovery have, or ought it to have, upon our former inference? What, as hath already been said, but to increase, beyond measure, our admiration of the skill, which had been employed in the formation of such a machine? Or shall it, instead of this, all at once turn us round to an opposite conclusion, viz. that no art or skill whatever has been concerned in the business, although all other evidences of art and skill remain as they were, and this last and supreme piece of art be now added to the rest? Can this be maintained without absurdity? Yet this is atheism.

David Hume, *Dialogues concerning Natural Religion* (1779)

Hume was a lifelong critic of Christianity. Although he was frequently condemned as an "atheist" by the clergy of his native Scotland, it is not so clear that he opposed all religious belief. In an earlier reading selection we saw his argument against religious belief based on miracles – or at least on testimonial evidence of miracles. Here in his *Dialogues concerning Natural Religion* Hume lays out arguments against belief in a Christian God based on evidence of intelligent design in nature.

The three principal characters in these dialogues are Cleanthes, who is impressed by the so-called "design argument"; Philo, who criticizes that argument in ways suggesting that he speaks for Hume; and Demea, who is also critical of Cleanthes. Demea objects to the *a posteriori* or "matter of fact" argument provided by Cleanthes, because it offers, at best, a merely "probable" conclusion. He is convinced that only an *a priori*, "demonstrative" proof is appropriate for belief in God's existence. The final segment of the reading selection below (Part IX) presents Demea's preferred argument. It bears an unmistakable resemblance to one we have already seen in the reading selection from Clarke. But that argument is easily demolished by Cleanthes.

In the first segment we have selected below from the *Dialogues* (Part II), Cleanthes summarizes a design argument similar to the one presented in the preceding reading selection from William Paley. Philo then proceeds to launch a critique of its reasoning. The first point of contention is the strength of the argument's analogy. Cleanthes argues that, just as the obvious intelligent design of an object like a house or a watch is incontrovertible evidence of its human designer, so, by analogy, is the abundant design we find in nature evidence of an intelligent, human-like designer of the world. But Philo is at first skeptical that our experience of designers and their designs within the world should tell us anything about a designer of the whole world. In Part V of the *Dialogues* Philo continues his critique of Cleanthes' design argument with a different line of objection. He asks: do we have any reason to suppose that the purported designer of the world is infinite, supremely wise, and even single-handed in his creation, as Christianity teaches?

Hume worked on the manuscript of his *Dialogues* off and on for over twenty years. He hurriedly finished it only in the last year of his life, when he knew that his death was imminent. It is ironic, then, that at a stage in life when a person might be most receptive to religious belief we find Hume working intently on expressing his criticisms of popular grounds for belief in the existence of a Christian God. Though Hume seems to have found little merit in the reasons most give for religious belief, he probably would have been among the last to say that he had good reasons for accepting atheism. For by what reasoning could he conclude that there is no God? What field of experience could lead him solidly to the conclusion that beyond the world of human experience there is nothing, no wise designer, no creator, nothing? The churchmen of his day seem to have been misguided in charging Hume with atheism.

Part II

[...]

Cleanthes. Not to lose any time in circumlocutions, said *Cleanthes*, addressing himself to *Demea*, much less in replying to the pious declamations of *Philo*, I shall briefly explain how I conceive this matter. Look round the world: Contemplate the whole and every part of it: You will find it to be nothing but one great machine, subdivided into an infinite number of lesser machines, which again admit of subdivisions to a degree beyond what human senses and faculties can trace and explain. All these various machines, and even their most minute parts, are adjusted to each other with an accuracy which ravishes into admiration all men who have ever contemplated them. The curious adapting of means to ends, throughout all nature, resembles exactly, though it much exceeds, the productions of human contrivance; of human design, thought, wisdom, and intelligence. Since therefore the effects resemble each other, we are led to infer, by all the rules of analogy, that the causes also resemble, and that the Author of Nature is somewhat similar to the mind of man, though possessed of much larger faculties, proportioned to the grandeur of the work which he has executed. By this argument *a posteriori*, and by this argument alone, do we prove at once the existence of a Deity and his similarity to human mind and intelligence.

Demea. I shall be so free, *Cleanthes*, said *Demea*, as to tell you that from the beginning I could not approve of your conclusion concerning the similarity of the Deity to men; still less can I approve of the mediums by which you endeavor to establish it. What! No demonstration of the Being of God! No abstract arguments! No proofs *a priori*! Are these which have hitherto been so much insisted on by philosophers all fallacy, all sophism? Can we reach no farther in this subject than experience and probability? I will say not that this is betraying the cause of a Deity; but surely, by this affected candor, you give advantages to atheists which they never could obtain by the mere dint of argument and reasoning.

Philo. What I chiefly scruple in this subject, said *Philo*, is not so much that all religious arguments are by *Cleanthes* reduced to experience, as that they appear not be even the most certain and irrefragable of that inferior kind. That a stone will fall, that fire will burn, that the earth has solidity, we have observed a thousand and a thousand times; and when any new instance of this nature is presented, we draw without hesitation the accustomed infer-ence. The exact similarity of the cases gives us a perfect assurance of a similar event, and a stronger evidence is never desired nor sought after. But wherever you depart, in the least, from the similarity of the cases, you diminish proportionably the evidence; and may at last bring it to a very weak *analogy*, which is confessedly liable to error and uncertainty. After having experienced the circulation of the blood in human creatures, we make no doubt that it takes place in *Titius* and *Maevius*; but from its circulation in frogs and fishes it is only a presumption, though a strong one, from analogy that it takes place in men and other animals. The analogical reasoning is much weaker when we infer the circulation of the sap in vegetables from our experience that the blood circulates in animals; and those who hastily followed that imperfect analogy are found, by more accurate experiments, to have been mistaken.

If we see a house, *Cleanthes*, we conclude, with the greatest certainty, that it had an architect or builder because this is precisely that species of effect which we have experienced to proceed from that species of cause. But surely you will not affirm that the universe bears such a resemblance to a house that we can with the same certainty infer a similar cause, or that the analogy is here entire and perfect. The dissimilitude is so striking that the utmost you can here pretend to is a guess, a conjecture, a presumption concerning a similar cause; and how that pretension will be received in the world, I leave you to consider.

Cleanthes. It would surely be very ill received, replied *Cleanthes*; and I should be deservedly blamed and detested did I allow that the proofs of a Deity amounted to no more than a guess or conjecture. But is the whole adjustment of means to ends in a house and in the universe so slight a resemblance? The economy of final causes? The order, proportion, and arrangement of every part? Steps of a stair are plainly contrived that human legs may use them in mounting; and this inference is certain and infallible. Human legs are also contrived for walking and mounting; and this inference, I allow, is not altogether so certain because of the dissimilarity which you remark; but does it, therefore, deserve the name only of presumption or conjecture?

Demea. Good Cod! cried *Demea*, interrupting him, where are we? Zealous defenders of religion allow that the proofs of a Deity fall short of perfect evidence! And you, *Philo*, on whose assistance I depended in proving the adorable mysteriousness of the Divine Nature, do you assent to all these extravagant opinions of *Cleanthes*? For what other name can I give them? or, why spare my censure when such principles are advanced, supported by such an authority, before so young a man as *Pamphilus*?

Philo. You seem not to apprehend, replied *Philo*, that I argue with *Cleanthes* in his own way, and, by showing him the dangerous consequences of his tenets, hope at last to reduce him to our opinion. But what sticks most with you, I observe, is the representation which *Cleanthes* has made of the argument *a posteriori*; and, finding that that argument is likely to escape your hold and vanish into air, you think it so disguised that you can scarcely believe it to be set in its true light. Now, however much I may dissent, in other respects, from the dangerous principle of *Cleanthes*, I must allow that he has fairly represented that argument, and I shall endeavor so to state the matter to you that you will entertain no further scruples with regard to it.

Were a man to abstract from everything which he knows or has seen, he would be altogether incapable, merely from his own ideas, to determine what kind of scene the universe must be, or to give the preference to one state or situation of things above another. For as nothing which he clearly conceives could be esteemed impossible or implying a contradiction, every chimera of his fancy would be upon an equal footing; nor could he assign any just reason why he adheres to one idea or system, and rejects the others which are equally possible.

Again, after he opens his eyes and contemplates the world as it really is, it would be impossible for him at first to assign the cause of any one event, much less of the whole of things, or of the universe. He might set his fancy a rambling, and she might bring him in an infinite variety of reports and representations. These would all be possible; but, being all equally possible, he would never of himself give a satisfactory account for his preferring one of them to the rest. Experience alone can point out to him the true cause of any phenomenon.

Now, according to this method of reasoning, *Demea*, it follows (and is, indeed, tacitly allowed by *Cleanthes* himself) that order, arrangement, or the adjustment of final causes, is not of itself any proof of design, but only so far as it has been experienced to proceed from that principle. For aught we can know *a priori*, matter may contain the source or spring of order originally within itself, as well as mind does; and there is no more difficulty in conceiving that the several elements, from an internal unknown cause, may fall into the most exquisite arrangement, than to conceive that their ideas, in the great universal mind, from a like internal unknown cause, fall into that arrangement. The equal possibility of both these suppositions is allowed. But, by experience, we find, according to *Cleanthes*, that there is a difference between them. Throw several pieces of steel together, without shape or form; they will never arrange themselves so as to compose a watch. Stone and mortar and wood, without an architect, never erect a house. But the ideas in a human mind, we see, by an unknown, inexplicable economy, arrange themselves so as to form the plan of a watch or house. Experience, there-fore, proves that there is an original principle of order in mind, not in matter. From similar effects we infer similar causes. The adjustment of means to ends is alike in the universe, as in a machine of human contrivance. The causes, therefore, must be resembling.

I was from the beginning scandalized, I must own, with this resemblance which is asserted between the Deity and human creatures, and must conceive it to imply such a degradation of the Supreme Being as no sound theist could endure. With your assistance, therefore, *Demea*, I shall endeavor to defend what you justly call the adorable mysteriousness of the Divine Nature, and shall refute this reasoning of *Cleanthes*, provided he allows that I have made a fair representation of it.

When *Cleanthes* had assented, *Philo*, after a short pause, proceeded in the following manner.

That all inferences, *Cleanthes*, concerning fact are founded on experience, and that all experi-mental reasonings are founded on the supposition that similar causes prove similar effects, and similar effects similar causes, I shall not at present much dispute with you. But observe, I entreat you, with what extreme caution all just reasoners proceed in the transferring of experiments to similar cases. Unless the cases be exactly similar, they repose no perfect confidence in applying their past observation to any particular phenomenon. Every alteration of cir-cumstances occasions a doubt concerning the event; and it requires new experiments to prove certainly that the new circumstances are of no moment or importance. A change in bulk, situation, arrangement, age, disposition of the air, or surrounding bodies; any of these particulars may be attended with the most unexpected consequences. And unless the objects be quite familiar to us, it is the highest temerity to expect with assurance, after any of these changes, an event similar to that which before fell under our observation. The slow and deliberate steps of philosophers here, if anywhere, are distinguished from the precipitate march of the vulgar, who, hurried on by the smallest similitude, are incapable of all discernment or consideration.

But can you think, *Cleanthes*, that your usual phlegm and philosophy have been preserved in so wide a step as you have taken when you compared to the universe houses, ships, furniture, machines; and, from their similarity in some circumstances, inferred a similarity in their causes? Thought, design, intelligence, such as we discover in men and other animals, is no more than one of the springs and principles of the universe, as well as heat or cold, attraction or repulsion, and a hundred others which fall under daily observation. It is an active cause by which some particular parts of nature, we find, produce alterations on other parts. But can a conclusion, with any propriety, be transferred from parts to the whole? Does not the great disproportion bar all comparison and inference? From observing the growth of a hair, can we learn anything concerning the generation of a man? Would the manner of a leaf's blowing, even though perfectly known, afford us any instruction concerning the vegetation of a tree?

But allowing that we were to take the *operations* of one part of nature upon another for the foundation of our judgment concerning the *origin* of the whole (which never can be admitted), yet why select so minute, so weak, so bounded a principle as the reason and design of animals is found to be upon this planet? What peculiar privilege has this little agitation of the brain which we call "thought", that we must thus make it the model of the whole universe? Our partiality in our own favor does indeed present it on all occasions, but sound philosophy ought carefully to guard against so natural an illusion.

So far from admitting, continued *Philo*, that the operations of a part can afford us any just conclusion concerning the origin of the whole, I will not allow any one part to form a rule for another part if the latter be very remote from the former. Is there any reasonable ground to conclude that the inhabitants of other planets possess thought, intelligence, reason, or any-thing similar to these faculties in men? When nature has so extremely diversified her manner of operation in this small globe, can we imagine that she incessantly copies herself through-out so immense a universe? And if thought, as we may well suppose, be confined merely to this narrow corner, and has even there so limited a sphere of action, with what propriety can we assign it for the original cause of all things? The narrow views of a peasant who makes his domestic economy the rule for the government of kingdoms is in comparison a pardonable sophism.

But were we ever so much assured that a thought and reason resembling the human were to be found throughout the whole universe, and were its activity elsewhere vastly greater and more commanding than it appears in this globe; yet I cannot see why the operations of a world constituted, arranged, adjusted, can with any propriety be extended to a world which is in its embryo-state, and is advancing towards that constitution and arrangement. By observa-tion we know somewhat of the economy, action, and nourishment of a finished animal; but we must transfer with great caution that observation to the growth of a foetus in the womb, and still more to the formation of an animalcule in the loins of its male parent. Nature, we find, even from our limited experience, possesses an infinite number of springs and principles which incessantly discover themselves on every change of her position and situation. And what new and unknown principles would actuate her in so new and unknown a situation as that of the formation of a universe, we cannot, without the utmost temerity, pretend to determine.

A very small part of this great system, during a very short time, is very imperfectly dis-covered to us; and do we thence pronounce decisively concerning the origin of the whole?

Admirable conclusion! Stone, wood, brick, iron, brass, have not, at this time, in this minute globe of earth, an order or arrangement without human art and contrivance; therefore, the universe could not originally attain its order and arrangement without something similar to human art. But is a part of nature a rule for another part very wide of the former? Is it a rule for the whole? Is a very small part a rule for the universe? Is nature in one situation a certain rule for nature in another situation vastly different from the former?

[. . .]

Part V

Philo. But to show you still more inconveniences, continued *Philo*, in your anthropomor-phism, please to take a new survey of your principles. *Like effects prove like causes*. This is the experimental argument; and this, you say too, is the sole theological argument. Now it is certain that the liker the effects are which are seen and the liker the causes which are inferred, the stronger is the argument. Every departure on either side diminishes the probability and renders the experiment less conclusive. You cannot doubt of the principle; neither ought you to reject its consequences. [. . .] Now, *Cleanthes*, [. . .] mark the consequences. *First*, by this method of reasoning you renounce all claim to infinity in any of the attributes of the Deity. For, as the cause ought only to be proportioned to the effect, and the effect, so far as it falls under our cognizance, is not infinite: What pretensions have we, upon your suppositions, to ascribe that attribute to the Divine Being? You will still insist that, by removing him so much from all similarity to human creatures, we give in to the most arbitrary hypothesis, and at the same time weaken all proofs of his existence.

Secondly, you have no reason, on your theory, for ascribing perfection to the Deity, even in his finite capacity; or for supposing him free from every error, mistake, or incoherence, in his undertakings. There are many inexplicable difficulties in the works of Nature which, if we allow a perfect author to be proved *a priori*, are easily solved, and become only seeming difficulties from the narrow capacity of man, who cannot trace infinite relations. But according to your method of reasoning, these difficulties become all real; and, perhaps, will be insisted on as new instances of likeness to human art and contrivance. At least, you must acknowledge that it is impossible for us to tell, from our limited views, whether this system contains any great faults or deserves any considerable praise if compared to other possible and even real systems. Could a peasant, if the *Aeneid* were read to him, pronounce that poem to be absolutely faultless, or even assign to it its proper rank among the productions of human wit, he who had never seen any other production?

But were this world ever so perfect a production, it must still remain uncertain whether all the excellences of the work can justly be ascribed to the workman. If we survey a ship, what an exalted idea must we form of the ingenuity of the carpenter who framed so complicated, useful, and beautiful a machine? And what surprise must we feel when we find him a stupid mechanic who imitated others, and copied an art which, through a long succession of ages, after multiplied trials, mistakes, corrections, deliberations, and controversies, had been gradually improving? Many worlds might have been botched and bungled, throughout an eternity, ere this system was struck out; much labor lost; many fruitless trials made; and a slow but continued improvement carried on during infinite ages in the art of world-making. In such subjects, who can determine where the truth, nay, who can conjecture where the probability lies, amidst a great number of hypotheses which may be proposed, and a still greater which may be imagined?

And what shadow of an argument, continued Philo, can you produce from your hypothesis to prove the unity of the Deity? A great number of men join in building a house or ship, in rearing a city, in framing a commonwealth; why may not several deities combine in contriving and framing a world? This is only so much greater similarity to human affairs. By sharing the work among several, we may so much further limit the attributes of each, and get rid of that extensive power and knowledge which must be supposed in one deity, and which, according to you, can only serve to weaken the proof of his existence. And if such foolish, such vicious creatures as man can yet often unite in framing and executing one plan, how much more those deities or demons, whom we may suppose several degrees more perfect?

To multiply causes without necessity is indeed contrary to true philosophy, but this principle applies not to the present case. Were one deity antecedently proved by your theory who were possessed of every attribute requisite to the production of the universe, it would be needless, I own (though not absurd), to suppose any other deity existent. But while it is still a question whether all these attributes are united in one subject or dispersed among several independent beings; by what phenomena in nature can we pretend to decide the controversy? Where we see a body raised in a scale, we are sure that there is in the opposite scale, however concealed from sight, some counterpoising weight equal to it; but it is still allowed to doubt whether that weight be an aggregate of several distinct bodies or one uniform united mass. And if the weight requisite very much exceeds anything which we have ever seen conjoined in any single body, the former supposition becomes still more probable and natural. An intelligent being of such vast power and capacity as is necessary to produce the universe, or, to speak in the language of ancient philosophy, so prodigious an animal, exceeds all analogy and even comprehension.

[. . .]

Part IX

Demea. But if so many difficulties attend the argument *a posteriori*, said *Demea*, had we not better adhere to that simple and sublime argument *a priori* which, by offering to us infallible demonstration, cuts off at once all doubt and difficulty? By this argument, too, we may prove the *Infinity* of the Divine Attributes, which, I am afraid, can never be ascertained with certainty from any other topic. For how can an effect which either is finite or, for aught we know, may be so; how can such an effect, I say, prove an infinite cause? The unity, too, of the Divine Nature it is very difficult, if not absolutely impossible, to deduce merely from contemplating the works of Nature; nor will the uniformity alone of the plan, even were it allowed, give us any assurance of that attribute. Whereas the argument *a priori* . . .

Cleanthes. You seem to reason, *Demea*, interposed *Cleanthes*, as if those advantages and conveniences in the abstract argument were full proofs of its solidity. But it is first proper, in my opinion, to determine what argument of this nature you choose to insist on; and we shall afterwards, from itself, better than from its *useful* consequences, endeavor to determine what value we ought to put upon it.

Demea. The argument, replied *Demea*, which I would insist on is the common one. Whatever exists must have a cause or reason of its existence, it being absolutely impossible for anything to produce itself or be the cause of its own existence. In mounting up, therefore, from effects to causes, we must either go on in tracing an infinite succession, without any ultimate cause at all, or must at last have recourse to some ultimate cause that is *necessarily* existent: Now, that the first supposition is absurd may be thus proved. In the infinite chain or succession of causes and effects, each single effect is determined to exist by the power and efficacy of that cause which immediately preceded; but the whole eternal chain or succession, taken together, is not determined or caused by anything: And yet it is evident that it requires a cause or reason, as much as any particular object which begins to exist in time. The question is still reasonable why this particular succession of causes existed from eternity, and not any other succession or no succession at all. If there be no necessarily existent being, any supposition which can be formed is equally possible; nor is there any more absurdity in nothing's having existed from eternity than there is in that succession of causes which constitutes the universe. What was it, then, which determined something to exist rather than nothing, and bestowed being on a particular possibility, exclusive of the rest? *External causes*, there are supposed to be none. *Chance* is a word without a meaning. Was it *nothing*? But that can never produce anything. We must, therefore, have recourse to a necessarily existent Being who carries the *reason* of his existence in himself; and who cannot be supposed not to exist, without an express contradiction. There is, consequently, such a Being – that is, there is a Deity.

Cleanthes. I shall not leave it to *Philo*, said *Cleanthes* (though I know that the starting objections is his chief delight), to point out the weakness of this metaphysical reasoning. It seems to me so obviously ill-grounded, and at the same time of so little consequence to the cause of true piety and religion, that I shall myself venture to show the fallacy of it.

I shall begin with observing that there is an evident absurdity in pretending to demonstrate a matter of fact, or to prove it by any arguments a priori. Nothing is demonstrable unless the contrary implies a contradiction. Nothing that is distinctly conceivable implies a contradiction. Whatever we conceive as existent, we can also conceive as non-existent. There is no being, therefore, whose non-existence implies a contradiction. Consequently there is no being whose existence is demonstrable. I propose this argument as entirely decisive, and am willing to rest the whole controversy upon it.

It is pretended that the Deity is a necessarily existent being; and this necessity of his existence is attempted to be explained by asserting that, if we knew his whole essence or nature, we should perceive it to be as impossible for him not to exist, as for twice two not to be four. But it is evident that this can never happen, while our faculties remain the same as at present. It will still be possible for us, at any time, to conceive the non-existence of what we formerly conceived to exist; nor can the mind ever lie under a necessity of supposing any object to remain always in being; in the same manner as we lie under a necessity of always conceiving twice two to be four. The words, therefore, "necessary existence" have no meaning; or, which is the same thing, none that is consistent.

But further, why may not the material universe be the necessarily existent Being, according to this pretended explication of necessity? We dare not affirm that we know all the qualities of matter; and, for aught we can determine, it may contain some qualities which, were they known, would make its non-existence appear as great a contradiction as that twice two is five. I find only one argument employed to prove that the material world is not the necessarily existent Being; and this argument is derived from the contingency both of the matter and the form of the world. "Any particle of matter," it is said, "may be *conceived* to be annihilated; and any form may be *conceived* to be altered. Such an annihilation or alteration, therefore, is not impossible" But it seems a great partiality not to perceive that the same argument extends equally to the Deity, so far as we have any conception of him; and that the mind can at least imagine him to be non-existent, or his attributes to be altered. It must be some unknown, inconceivable qualities which can make his non-existence appear impossible or his attributes unalterable: And no reason can be assigned why these qualities may not belong to matter. As they are altogether unknown and inconceivable, they can never be proved incompatible with it.

Add to this that in tracing an eternal succession of objects it seems absurd to inquire for a general cause or first author. How can anything that exists from eternity have a cause, since that relation implies a priority in time and a beginning of existence?

In such a chain, too, or succession of objects, each part is caused by that which preceded it, and causes that which succeeds it. Where then is the difficulty? But the *whole*, you say, wants a cause. I answer that the uniting of these parts into a whole, like the uniting of several distinct countries into one kingdom, or several distinct members into one body, is performed merely by an arbitrary act of the mind, and has no influence on the nature of things. Did I show you the particular causes of each individual in a collection of twenty particles of matter, I should think it very unreasonable should you afterwards ask me what was the cause of the whole twenty. This is sufficiently explained in explaining the cause of the parts.

Philo. Though the reasonings which you have urged, *Cleanthes*, may well excuse me, said *Philo*, from starting any further difficulties; yet I cannot forbear insisting still upon another topic. It is observed by arithmeticians that the products of 9 compose always either 9 or some lesser product of 9 if you add together all the characters of which any of the former products is composed. Thus, of 18, 27, 36, which are products of 9, you make 9 by adding 1 to 8, 2 to 7, 3 to 6. Thus 369 is a product also of 9; and if you add 3, 6, and 9, you make 18, a lesser product of 9. To a superficial observer so wonderful a regularity may be admired as the effect either of chance or design; but a skilful algebraist immediately concludes it to be the work of necessity, and demonstrates that it must forever result from the nature of these numbers. Is it not probable, I ask, that the whole economy of the universe is conducted by a like necessity, though no human algebra can furnish a key which solves the difficulty? And instead of admiring the order of natural beings, may it not happen that, could we penetrate into the intimate nature of bodies, we should clearly see why it was absolutely impossible they could ever admit of any other disposition? So dangerous is it to introduce this idea of necessity into the present question! And so naturally does it afford an inference directly opposite to the religious hypothesis!

But dropping all these abstractions, continued *Philo*, and confining ourselves to more familiar topics, I shall venture to add an observation that the argument *a priori* has seldom been found very convincing, except to people of a metaphysical head who have accustomed themselves to abstract reasoning, and who, finding from mathematics that the understanding frequently leads to truth through obscurity, and contrary to first appearances, have transferred the same habit of thinking to subjects where it ought not to have place. Other people, even of good sense and the best inclined to religion, feel always some deficiency in such arguments, though they are not perhaps able to explain distinctly where it lies, a certain proof that men ever did and ever will derive their religion from other sources than from this species of reasoning.

12

Immanuel Kant, *Critique of Pure Reason* (1781)

By a "Critique" of pure reason Kant understood the project of determining how far we can rely on reason alone to provide us with knowledge of the world, and of what may lie beyond it. His conclusion was that reason, unaided by human sensibility, is not able to provide us with any knowledge of the empirical world, nor with answers to the traditional speculative questions of metaphysics: questions about the reality of human freedom, the immortality of the soul, and the existence of God. Kant's well-known objection to all "ontological proofs" claiming to demonstrate the existence of God by pure reason appears in this work, in a passage where he argues that "existence" is not a "real predicate."

Kant would say that as far as what he called "theoretical reason" is concerned, any attempt to provide a purely rational, *a priori* proof of the existence of God is bound to fail. But when it comes to what he called "practical reason," the story is different. Practical reason concerns itself not with finding out what there is, but with discovering what ought to be. Practical reason is the basis for morality, as Kant saw it. If theoretical reason cannot demonstrate that there is a God, it may well be that practical reason presupposes the existence of God, as an all-knowing, all-powerful creator and issuer of moral commands. Kant believed that in order for the idea of morality as a system of rules of conduct to make sense to us, or to have "a point," we must suppose that there is a God who commands the moral law, and who will reward each of us with a measure of happiness proportionate to our degree of virtue. This means also that our souls will have to be immortal, in order to receive the eternal reward or punishment we deserve. This is Kant's so-called "moral proof" for God's existence.

Scholars today are divided on whether Kant's moral philosophy really needs this appeal to God as the moral governor of the world. Most find that Kant's thinking about practical reason and its relation to morality provides a suitably powerful moral theory on its own. The "back-up" provided by his moral proof is superfluous, many say.

The *Critique of Pure Reason* was first published in 1781 (the "A edition"), and then significantly revised in 1787 (the "B edition"). Although it is primarily a work in theory of knowledge and metaphysics, the "first *Critique*," as it is known, also contains the philosophical basis for Kant's moral philosophy, and for his conception of natural science as an ordered system. It was followed in 1788 by a much shorter *Critique of Practical Reason*, focusing on morality, and in 1790 by a *Critique of Judgment*, where Kant dealt with both aesthetics and teleology, or intelligent design in nature. These three of Kant's major works make up what is commonly known as his "critical philosophy."

On the Impossibility of an Ontological Proof of God's Existence

[. . .]

In all ages one has talked about the *absolutely necessary* being, but has taken trouble not so much to understand whether and how one could so much as think of a thing of this kind as rather to prove its existence. Now a nominal definition of this concept is quite easy, namely that it is something whose non-being is impossible; but through this one becomes no wiser in regard to the conditions that make it necessary to regard the non-being of a thing as absolutely unthinkable, and that are really what one wants to know, namely whether or not through this concept we are thinking anything at all. For by means of the word *unconditional* to reject all the conditions that the understanding always needs in order to regard something as necessary, is far from enough to make intelligible to myself whether through a concept of an unconditionally necessary being I am still thinking something or perhaps nothing at all.

Still more: one believed one could explain this concept, which was ventured upon merely haphazardly, and that one has finally come to take quite for granted through a multiplicity of examples, so that all further demands concerning its intelligibility appeared entirely unnecessary. Every proposition of geometry, e.g., "a triangle has three angles," is absolutely necessary, and in this way one talked about an object lying entirely outside the sphere of our understanding as if one understood quite well what one meant by this concept.

All the alleged examples are without exception taken only from *judgments*, but not from *things* and their existence. The unconditioned necessity of judgments, however, is not an absolute necessity of things. For the absolute necessity of the judgment is only a conditioned necessity of the thing, or of the predicate in the judgment. The above proposition does not say that three angles are absolutely necessary, but rather that under the condition that a triangle exists (is given), three angles also exist (in it) necessarily. Nevertheless the illusion of this logical necessity has proved so powerful that when one has made a concept a priori of a thing that was set up so that its existence was comprehended within the range of its meaning, one believed one could infer with certainty that because existence necessarily pertains to the object of this concept, i.e., under the condition that I posit this thing as given (existing), its existence can also be posited necessarily (according to the rule of identity), and this being itself, therefore, is necessarily, because its existence is thought along with a concept assumed arbitrarily and under the condition that I posit its object.

If I cancel the predicate in an identical judgment and keep the subject, then a contradiction arises; hence I say that the former necessarily pertains to the latter. But if I cancel the subject together with the predicate, then no contradiction arises; for there *is no longer anything* that could be contradicted. To posit a triangle and cancel its three angles is contradictory; but to cancel the triangle together with its three angles is not a contradiction. It is exactly the same with the concept of an absolutely necessary being. If you cancel its existence, then you cancel the thing itself with all its predicates; where then is the contradiction supposed to come from? Outside it there is nothing that would contradict it, for the thing is not supposed to be externally necessary; and nothing internally either, for by cancelling the thing itself, you have at the same time cancelled everything internal. God is omnipotent; that is a necessary judgment. Omnipotence cannot be cancelled if you posit a divinity, i.e., an infinite being, which is identical with that concept. But if you say, *God is not*, then neither omnipotence nor any other of his predicates is given; for they are all cancelled together with the subject, and in this thought not the least contradiction shows itself.

Thus you have seen that if I cancel the predicate of a judgment together with the subject, an internal contradiction can never arise, whatever the predicate might be. Now no escape is left to you except to say: there are subjects that cannot be cancelled at all and thus have to remain. But that would be the same as saying that there are absolutely necessary subjects – just the presupposition whose correctness I have doubted, and the possibility of which you wanted to show me. For I cannot form the least concept of a thing that, if all its predicates were cancelled, would leave behind a contradiction, and without a contradiction, I have through mere pure concepts *a priori* no mark of impossibility.

Against all these general inferences (which no human being can refuse to draw) you challenge me with one case that you set up as a proof through the fact that there is one and indeed only this one concept where the non-being or the cancelling of its object is contradictory within itself, and this is the concept of a most real being. It has, you say, all reality, and you are justified in assuming such a being as possible (to which I have consented up to this point, even though a non-contradictory concept falls far short of proving the possibility of its object). Now existence is also comprehended under all reality: thus existence lies in the concept of something possible. If this thing is cancelled, then the internal possibility of the thing is cancelled, which is contradictory.

I answer: You have already committed a contradiction when you have brought the concept of its existence, under whatever disguised name, into the concept of a thing which you would think merely in terms of its possibility. If one allows you to do that, then you have won the illusion of a victory, but in fact You have said nothing; for you have committed a mere tautology. I ask you: is the proposition, *This or that thing* (which I have conceded to you as possible, whatever it may be) *exists* – is this proposition, I say, an analytic or a synthetic proposition? If it is the former, then with existence you add nothing to your thought of the thing; but then either the thought that is in you must be the thing itself, or else you have presupposed an existence as belonging to possibility, and then inferred that existence on this pretext from its inner possibility, which is nothing but a miserable tautology. The word "reality," which sounds different from "existence" in the concept of the predicate, does not settle it. For if you call all positing (leaving indeterminate what you posit) "reality," then you have already posited the thing with all its predicates in the concept of the subject and assumed it to be actual, and you only repeat that in the predicate. If you concede, on the contrary, as in all fairness you must, that every existential proposition is synthetic, then how would you assert that the predicate of existence may not be cancelled without contradiction? – since this privilege pertains only in the analytic propositions, as resting on its very character.

I would have hoped to annihilate this over-subtle argumentation without any digressions through a precise determination of the concept of existence, if I had not found that the illusion consisting in the confusion of a logical predicate with a real one (i.e., the determination of a thing) nearly precludes all instruction. Anything one likes can serve as a *logical predicate*, even the subject can be predicated of itself; for logic abstracts from every content. But the *determination* is a predicate, which goes beyond the concept of the subject and enlarges it. Thus it must not be included in it already.

Being is obviously not a real predicate, i.e., a concept of something that could add to the concept of a thing. It is merely the positing of a thing or of certain determinations in themselves. In the logical use it is merely the copula of a judgment. The proposition *God is omnipotent* contains two concepts that have their objects: God and omnipotence; the little word *"is"* is not a predicate in it, but only that which posits the predicate *in relation* to the subject. Now if I take the subject (God) together with all his predicates (among which omnipotence belongs), and say *God is*, or there is a God, then I add no new predicate to the concept of God, but only posit the subject in itself with all its predicates, and indeed posit the *object* in relation to my *concept*. Both must contain exactly the same, and hence when I think this object as given absolutely (through the expression, "it is"), nothing is thereby added to the concept, which expresses merely its possibility. Thus the actual contains nothing more than the merely possible. A hundred actual dollars do not contain the least bit more than a hundred possible ones. For since the latter signifies the concept and the former its object and its positing in itself, then, in case the former contained more than the latter, my concept would not express the entire object and thus would not be the suitable concept of it. But in my financial condition there is more with a hundred actual dollars than with the mere concept of them (i.e., their possibility). For with actuality the object is not merely included in my concept analytically, but adds synthetically to my concept (which is a determination of my state); yet the hundred dollars themselves that I am thinking of are not in the least increased through this being outside my concept.

Thus when I think a thing, through whichever and however many predicates I like (even in its thoroughgoing determination), not the least bit gets added to the thing when I posit in addition that this thing *is*. For otherwise what would exist would not be the same as what I had thought in my concept, but more than that, and I could not say that the very object of my concept exists. Even if I think in a thing every reality except one, then the missing reality does not get added when I say the thing exists, but it exists encumbered with just the same defect as I have thought in it; otherwise something other than what I thought would exist. Now if I think of a being as the highest reality (without defect), the question still remains whether it exists or not. For although nothing at all is missing in my concept of the possible real content of a thing in general, something is still missing in the relation to my entire state of thinking, namely that the cognition of this object should also be possible *a posteriori*. And here the cause of the predominant difficulty shows itself. If the issue were an object of sense, then I could not confuse the existence of the thing with the mere concept of the thing. For through its concept, the object would be thought only as in agreement with the universal conditions of a possible empirical cognition in general, but through its existence it would be thought as contained in the context of the entirety of experience; thus through connection with the content of the entire experience the concept of the object is not in the least increased, but our thinking receives more through it, namely a possible perception. If, on the contrary, we tried to think existence through the pure category alone, then it is no wonder that we cannot assign any mark distinguishing it from mere possibility.

Thus whatever and however much our concept of an object may contain, we have to go out beyond it in order to provide it with existence. With objects of sense this happens through the connection with some perception of mine in accordance with empirical laws; but for objects of pure thinking there is no means whatever for cognizing their existence, because it would have to be cognized entirely *a priori*, but our consciousness of all existence (whether immediately through perception or through inferences connecting something with perception) belongs entirely and without exception to the unity of experience, and though an existence outside this field cannot be declared absolutely impossible, it is a presupposition that we cannot justify through anything.

The concept of a highest being is a very useful idea in many respects; but just because it is merely an idea, it is entirely incapable all by itself of extending our cognition in regard to what exists. It is not even able to do so much as to instruct us in regard to the possibility of anything more. The analytic mark of possibility, which consists in the fact that mere positings (realities) do not generate a contradiction, of course, cannot be denied of this concept; since, however, the connection of all real properties in a thing is a synthesis about whose possibility we cannot judge *a priori* because the realities are not given to us specifically – and even if this were to happen no judgment at all could take place because the mark of possibility of synthetic cognitions always has to be sought only in experience, to which, however, the object of an idea can never belong – the famous Leibniz was far from having achieved what he flattered himself he had done, namely, gaining insight *a priori* into the possibility of such a sublime ideal being.

Thus the famous ontological (Cartesian) proof of the existence of a highest being from concepts is only so much trouble and labor lost, and a human being can no more become richer in insight from mere ideas than a merchant could in resources if he wanted to improve his financial state by adding a few zeros to his cash balance.

[. . .]

[Excerpts on the Moral Proof]

Happiness is the satisfaction of all of our inclinations (*extensive*, with regard to their manifoldness, as well as *intensive*, with regard to degree, and also *protensive*, with regard to duration). The practical law from the motive of *happiness* I call pragmatic (rule of prudence); but that which is such that it has no other motive than the *worthiness to be happy* I call moral (moral law). The first advises us what to do if we want to partake of happiness; the second commands how we should behave in order even to be worthy of happiness. The first is grounded on empirical principles; for except by means of experience I can know neither which inclinations there are that would be satisfied nor what the natural causes are that could satisfy them. The second abstracts from inclinations and natural means of satisfying them, and considers only the freedom of a rational being in general and the necessary conditions under which alone it is in agreement with the distribution of happiness in accordance with principles, and thus it at least *can* rest on mere ideas of pure reason and be cognized *a priori*.

I assume that there are really pure moral laws, which determine completely *a priori* (without regard to empirical motives, i.e., happiness) the action and omission, i.e., the use of the freedom of a rational being in general, and that these laws command *absolutely* (not merely hypothetically under the presupposition of other empirical ends), and are thus necessary in every respect. I can legitimately presuppose this proposition by appealing not only to the proofs of the most enlightened moralists but also to the moral judgment of every human being, if he will distinctly think such a law.

Pure reason thus contains – not in its speculative use, to be sure, but yet in a certain practical use, namely the moral use – principles of the *possibility of experience*, namely of those actions in conformity with moral precepts which *could* be encountered in the *history* of humankind. For since they command that these actions ought to happen, they must also be able to happen, and there must therefore be possible a special kind of systematic unity, namely the moral, whereas the systematic unity of nature *in accordance with speculative principles of reason* could not be proved, since reason has causality with regard to freedom in general but not with regard to the whole of nature, and moral principles of reason can produce free actions but not laws of nature. Thus the principles of pure reason have objective reality in their practical use, that is, in the moral use.

I call the world as it would be if it were in conformity with all moral laws (as it *can* be in accordance with the *freedom* of rational beings and *should* be in accordance with the necessary laws of *morality*) a *moral world*. This is conceived thus far merely as an intelligible world, since abstraction is made therein from all conditions (ends) and even from all hindrances to morality in it (weakness or impurity of human nature).

Thus far it is therefore a mere, yet practical, idea, which really can and should have its influence on the sensible world, in order to make it agree as far as possible with this idea. The idea of a moral world thus has objective reality, not as if it pertained to an object of an intelligible intuition (for we cannot even think of such a thing), but as pertaining to the sensible world, although as an object of pure reason in its practical use and a *corpus mysticum* of the rational beings in it, insofar as their free choice under moral laws has thoroughgoing systematic unity in itself as well as with the freedom of everyone else.

This was the reply to the first of the two questions of pure reason that concern the practical interest: *Do that through which you will become worthy to be happy.* Now the second question asks: Now if I behave so as not to be unworthy of happiness, how may I hope thereby to partake of it? For the answer to this question, the issue is whether the principles of pure reason that prescribe the law *a priori* also necessarily connect this hope with it.

I say, accordingly, that just as the moral principles are necessary in accordance with reason in its *practical* use, it is equally necessary to assume in accordance with reason in its *theoretical* use that everyone has cause to hope for happiness in the same measure as he has made himself worthy of it in his conduct, and that the system of morality is therefore inseparably combined with the system of happiness, though only in the idea of pure reason.

Now in an intelligible world, i.e., in the moral world, in the concept of which we have abstracted from all hindrances to morality (of the inclinations), such a system of happiness proportionately combined with morality can also be thought as necessary, since freedom, partly moved and partly restricted by moral laws, would itself be the cause of the general happiness, and rational beings, under the guidance of such principles, would themselves be the authors of their own enduring welfare and at the same time that of others. But this system of self-rewarding morality is only an idea, the realization of which rests on the condition that *everyone* do what he should, i.e., that all actions of rational beings occur as if they arose from a highest will that comprehends all private choice in or under itself. But since the obligation from the moral law remains valid for each particular use of freedom even if others do not conduct themselves in accord with this law, how their consequences will be related to happiness is determined neither by the nature of the things in the world, nor by the causality of actions themselves and their relation to morality; and the necessary connection of the hope of being happy with the unremitting effort to make oneself worthy of happiness that has been adduced cannot be cognized through reason if it is grounded merely in nature, but may be hoped for only if it is at the same time grounded on a *highest reason*, which commands in accordance with moral laws, as at the same time the cause of nature.

I call the idea of such an intelligence, in which the morally most perfect will, combined with the highest blessedness, is the cause of all happiness in the world, insofar as it stands in exact relation with morality (as the worthiness to be happy), *the ideal of the highest good*. Thus only in the ideal of the highest *original* good can pure reason find the ground of the practically necessary connection of both elements of the highest derived good, namely of an intelligible, i.e., *moral* world. Now since we must necessarily represent ourselves through reason as belonging to such a world, although the senses do not present us with anything except a world of appearances, we must assume the moral world to be a consequence of our conduct in the sensible world; and since the latter does not offer such a connection to us, we must assume the former to be a world that is future for us. Thus God and a future life are two presuppositions that are not to be separated from the obligation that pure reason imposes on us in accordance with principles of that very same reason.

Morality in itself constitutes a system, but happiness does not, except insofar as it is distributed precisely in accordance with morality. This, however, is possible only in the intelligible world, under a wise author and regent. Reason sees itself as compelled either to assume such a thing, together with life in such a world, which we must regard as a future one, or else to regard the moral laws as empty figments of the brain, since without that presupposition their necessary success, which the same reason connects with them, would have to disappear. Hence everyone also regards the moral laws as *commands*, which, however, they could not be if they did not connect appropriate consequences with their rule *a priori*, and thus carry with them *promises* and *threats*. This, however, they could not do if they did not lie in a necessary being, as the highest good, which alone can make possible such a purposive unity.

[. . .]

Now this moral theology has the peculiar advantage over the speculative one that it inexorably leads to the concept of a *single, most perfect*, and *rational* primordial being, of which speculative theology could not on objective grounds give us even a *hint*, let alone *convince* us. For neither in speculative nor in natural theology, as far as reason may lead us, do we find even a single significant ground for assuming a single being to set before all natural causes, on which we would at the same time have sufficient cause to make the latter dependent in every way. On the contrary, if, from the standpoint of moral unity, we assess the cause that can alone provide this with the appropriate effect and thus obligating force for us, as a necessary law of the world, then there must be a single supreme will, which comprehends all these laws in itself. For how would we find complete unity of purposes among different wills? This will must be omnipotent, so that all of nature and its relation to morality in the world are subject to it; omniscient, so that it cognizes the inmost dispositions and their moral worth; omnipresent, so that it is immediately ready for every need that is demanded by the highest good for the world; eternal, so that this agreement of nature and freedom is not lacking at any time, etc.

[. . .]

But now when practical reason has attained this high point, namely the concept of a single original being as the highest good, it must not undertake to start out from this concept and derive the moral laws themselves from it, as if it had elevated itself above all empirical conditions of its application and soared up to an immediate acquaintance with new objects. For it was these laws alone whose *inner* practical necessity led us to the presupposition of a self-sufficient cause or a wise world-regent, in order to give effect to these laws, and hence we cannot in turn regard these as contingent and derived from a mere will, especially from a will of which we would have had no concept at all had we not formed it in accordance with those laws. So far as practical reason has the right to lead us, we will not hold actions to be obligatory because they are God's commands, but will rather regard them as divine commands because we are internally obligated to them. We will study freedom under the purposive unity in accordance with principles of reason, and will believe ourselves to be in conformity with the divine will only insofar as we hold as holy the moral law that reason teaches us from the nature of actions themselves, believing ourselves to serve this divine will only through furthering what is best for the world in ourselves and others. Moral theology is therefore only of immanent use, namely for fulfilling our vocation here in the world by fitting into the system of all ends, not for fanatically or even impiously abandoning the guidance of a morally legislative reason in the good course of life in order to connect it immediately to the idea of the highest being, which would provide a transcendental use but which even so, like the use of mere speculation, must pervert and frustrate the ultimate ends of reason.

Part V

Political Philosophy

Introduction

The theory of the social contract, developed by Thomas Hobbes in the seventeenth century, established several focal points for the political philosophy of the next hundred years. Through compelling arguments beginning in metaphysics, epistemology, and human psychology, Hobbes had drawn conclusions about the origin of political obligation – about what makes it *right* or *reasonable* to obey civil authority – that almost no one could accept. The reading selections from Locke, Hume, and Rousseau that follow below each provide alternative accounts of the focal points of social philosophy Hobbes was attempting to explain. If they do not explicitly mention Hobbes as the author of views they are criticizing, it is because they do not need to: his views were immediately recognizable in the eighteenth century. What, then, were the central tenets of Hobbes's political philosophy?

First, that the natural state of human beings, the so-called "state of nature," is a condition of war: all against all. Hobbes began the development of his theory of political obligation by imagining human life without governments, civil authority, or law enforcement. People in that natural state would have a natural right to do whatever they desired, according to Hobbes. Moreover, since the resources for satisfying these desires are usually limited, if not scarce, people living in the state of nature would be in constant competition with one another in their attempts to satisfy their desires. But with no rules to limit their competitive behavior, anything they wanted to do in pursuit of their own interests would be permitted. "All's fair in love and war," as they say; likewise in the Hobbesian state of nature. Yet with so little love for one's fellow man in that state, the state of nature is nothing but a state of war. That is why Hobbes concluded that human life in the state of nature is "solitary, poor, nasty, brutish and short."

Second, because human life in the state of nature is so awful, any reasonable person would take the means required to move out of that condition into a new state. Hobbes speculated that rational people would very soon recognize how they can do this. They would see that a better way of life is possible if people would agree with one another, in a "social contract," to submit themselves to a common political authority. No one would literally "sign" a contract. The assumption is that at some point people would simply make known their willingness to cooperate with one another rather than compete. Gradually, just about everyone would join in the emerging social contract, expecting a more peaceful existence and a better life.

Third, Hobbes explained that the simple terms of the social contract have no meaning whatsoever without a common power to keep everyone "in awe." The contracting parties are understood to be willing to surrender their natural right to do whatever they want, so that they will not need to be constantly on guard against attack from others. Yet this can actually make them all the more vulnerable to attack. Wouldn't faking a willingness to participate in a social contract be the perfect strategy for taking advantage of others? Simply convince a number of people to agree to cooperate with you rather than compete, and then, once they trust you, strike when their defenses are down. Because this strategy would be so effective, no one can really trust anyone else to abide by his or her agreement in the social contract unless there is some "higher power" that will enforce the terms of the agreement. Someone will have to be able to make sure that all those who indicate that they will agree to live peaceably with others will actually do so, or face severe reprisal. So, in attempting to move out of the state of nature, people have no reason agree to a social contract unless there is some powerful neutral party who is able to punish those who would default on their agreement.

This third point is the heart of Hobbes's account of political obligation. We cannot move out of the dreaded state of nature unless there is a neutral party with enough power to ensure that we all keep our promises to live peacefully with others, in social cooperation. So that is why our present submission to the sovereign power of society is right, or reasonable: without it we would simply slip back into the state of nature. Hobbes went on to explain that, by our act of submitting to the sovereign authority, we actually make the sovereign into a kind of "agent" for us all. The sovereign power that enforces the social contract becomes the representative of the "general will" of our society. As a consequence, whatever this person or authority may wish becomes the will of us all. This means too that any conditions or restrictions the sovereign authority wishes to impose upon us as parties to the social contract are conditions or restrictions that we, in effect, impose upon ourselves. It therefore becomes unreasonable, irrational, to disagree with or disobey civil authority, for in doing so we are actually disagreeing with ourselves!

The fourth, most controversial, tenet of Hobbes's social philosophy is that persons holding sovereign authority remain in the state of nature. It has to be this way, said Hobbes, because if the ruler of the society should be a party to the social contract, then, logically, an even more powerful authority will be required to keep him or her "in awe." And then if that superpower is also party to the contract, a still more powerful enforcer will be required, and so on. In short, the final sovereign authority simply must have absolute power, and can be bound by no contractual agreements with anyone under his or her jurisdiction. But many of Hobbes's critics saw this point as a complete *reductio ad absurdum* of his system (an absurd consequence that indicates some mistaken prior assumption). They applied the old saying that "Absolute power corrupts absolutely."

In response to this line of objection Hobbes would say that it is simply impossible for the sovereign authority to become corrupt. Since the sovereign ruler cannot be a party to the social contract, he or she must remain in the state of nature. It is therefore impossible for the sovereign to do anything wrong, since in the state of nature everyone has a right to do whatever they please. According to Hobbes, therefore, wrongful action and corruption can be defined only as some form of disobedience to sovereign authority, and for this reason the sovereign's absolute power can never lead to any type of corruption.

What would it be like to live in a society founded on a social contract and controlled by an absolute dictator? It may not be so bad, Hobbes would answer, especially if the dictator is kind and to some extent respectful of the wishes of the citizens under his or her authority to live in peace. But if not, then still, no matter how disagreeable life may be under the rule of a ruthless tyrant, it has got to be an improvement over its only alternative, which is life in the state of nature. Hobbes would point out that it is better to live in fear of the whims of a sovereign authority than to live in fear of *everyone*, in a war of all against all.

To most of Hobbes's critics this line of thinking seemed to pose a false dilemma. That is, it seemed to propose that our only alternatives are *either* to submit ourselves voluntarily to absolute authority *or* to risk our lives in the constant warfare of the state of nature. Many, like John Locke and Jean-Jacques Rousseau, rejected this false dilemma by objecting to Hobbes's characterization of the natural state of human beings. It was a widespread belief in the eighteenth century that Hobbes had made the following mistake: he had assumed that people in the state of nature would be just like the people living in society now, only not subject to any laws or regulation. The objection was, in other words, that Hobbes had not recognized that human beings *never having lived in society* might be naturally inclined to cooperate with one another, and to sympathize with their fellow human beings. It is not likely that life in the state of nature would be as brutish as Hobbes imagined; consequently, people's motives for leaving their natural state in order to establish a society and political authority by means of a social contract would have been different from what Hobbes assumed. In the reading selections below, John Locke and Jean-Jacques Rousseau each present rather different accounts of people's motives for entering the social contract.

Yet another objection to the theory of the social contract as presented by Hobbes is represented below in a reading selection from David Hume. Hume asks us to consider how plausible it is to assume that the actual societies and governments we know can be traced back to an "original contract." Historical records, which we have every reason to believe, usually present quite different accounts of the origins of societies. Political power often changes hands through intrigue, treachery, betrayal, and even ruthless conquest. What, then, is Hume's alternative explanation of the moral legitimacy of that power? How does he see our obligation emerging to obey political authority if it is not based on our voluntary submission through a social contract? Hume's answer refers to the observable fact that we are creatures of habit. In due time, as people become accustomed to living under a ruling power, they confer upon this power the character of rightness and legitimacy, without ever joining with others in any original social agreement. As stated in the General Introduction to this volume, Hume's view is not that might makes right, but that might tends to become right, as people become accustomed to yielding to it.

As signaled in the introduction also, however, we can look for Rousseau to point out how it takes a tacit agreement for individuals to form a governable "people." In order for political legitimacy to be conferred on a government by the habitual yielding of a people, Rousseau would argue, individuals must originally have become a people through their tacit consent, by an original contract. Hume's survey of historical power struggles notwithstanding, the point is that unless we are talking about the history of peoples having voluntarily united themselves by means of tacit social contracts, we are not talking about political history.

13

John Locke, *Second Treatise on Government* (1690)

John Locke stands out as both an empiricist philosopher and a political philosopher. His best-known political work is his *Second Treatise on Government*, which is excerpted here. Although it was published around the same time as his *Essay concerning Human Understanding*, Locke seems to have completed the manuscript of the *Second Treatise* nearly a decade earlier. Political events in England in the late 1600s made it prudent for him to keep his "liberal" ideas out of circulation for a while. Among the dangerous ideas expounded in the *Second Treatise* are: the freedom and equal rights of all men; the natural right to acquire property; and government by consent of the governed.

In the introduction to this section we surveyed some of Hobbes's ideas on the "state of nature." We indicated also why rational individuals would consent to government by a sovereign political authority, in order to escape the brutal conditions of continuous conflict. But Locke, as we see below, worked with a more idyllic vision of the pre-social state of human beings. As Hobbes had done, Locke also proposed a natural law of reason to govern human behavior in the state of nature: "The state of nature has a law of nature to govern it," wrote Locke, "and reason, which is that law, teaches all mankind, who will but consult it, that being all equal and independent, no one ought to harm another in his life, health, liberty, or possessions." Where Hobbes had traced the motivation for leaving the state of nature to the misery and mutual fear of the combatants in a war of all against all, Locke understood the pre-social human being as a relatively peaceful creature, interested primarily in acquiring property through labor. He would continue in that state indefinitely, perhaps, were it not for the fact that law, impartial trials, and punishment are necessary for the protection of property rights. These protections require the mutual consent of all property holders, by social contract, to leave the state of nature and submit themselves to civil authority.

At the time it may have been irresistible for Locke to imagine the uncivilized parts of the new world of America as a vast state of nature. Generalizing about that state he once concluded: "Thus, in the beginning all the world was America." But for the native inhabitants of the American state of nature, the right to acquire property seems not to have been as self-evident as Locke supposed. Locke, arguably, had made a mistake similar to Hobbes's. The inhabitants of the primal state of nature as he conceived it would think and behave more like the civilized Europeans he knew than like human beings without social experience. This suggests a problem for political philosophies based on the idea of a social contract: without reliable knowledge of human beings in their original, pre-social state, how do we explain their motivation for entering a social contract? And without knowledge of that motivation, how are we to understand the social contract's basic principles? As a set of ideas for guiding social reform in eighteenth-century English society, Locke's political philosophy may well have been sound. But as a set of principles for understanding political authority, Locke's social contract theory shows its limitations.

Chapter Two
Of the State of Nature

4. To understand political power right, and derive it from its original, we must consider what state all men are naturally in, and that is a state of perfect freedom to order their actions and dispose of their possessions and persons as they think fit, within the bounds of the law of nature, without asking leave, or depending upon the will of any other man.

A state also of equality, wherein all the power and jurisdiction is reciprocal, no one having more than another: there being nothing more evident than that creatures of the same species and rank promiscuously born to all the same advantages of nature, and the use of the same faculties, should also be equal one amongst another without subordination or subjection, unless the lord and master of them all should by any manifest declaration of his will set one above another, and confer on him by an evident and clear appointment an undoubted right to dominion and sovereignty.

[. . .]

6. But though this be a state of liberty, yet it is not a state of licence, though man in that state have an uncontrollable liberty to dispose of his person or possessions, yet he has not liberty to destroy himself, or so much as any creature in his possession, but where some nobler use than its bare preservation calls for it. The state of nature has a law of nature to govern it, which obliges everyone. And reason, which is that law, teaches all mankind who will but consult it that, being all equal and independent, no one ought to harm another in his life, health, liberty, or possessions. For men being all the workmanship of one omnipotent and infinitely wise maker, all the servants of one sovereign master, sent into the world by his order and about his business, they are his property whose workmanship they are, made to last during his, not one another's, pleasure. And being furnished with like faculties, sharing all in one community of nature, there cannot be supposed any such subordination among us that may authorize us to destroy one another, as if we were made for one another's uses, as the inferior ranks of creatures are for ours. Everyone, as he is bound to preserve himself, and not to quit his station wilfully, so by the like reason, when his own preservation comes not in competition, ought he, as much as he can, to preserve the rest of mankind, and may not, unless it be to do justice on an offender, take away or impair the life, or what tends to the preservation of the life, liberty, health, limb, or goods of another.

7. And that all men may be restrained from invading others' rights, and from doing hurt to one another, and the law of nature be observed, which willeth the peace and preservation of all mankind, the execution of the law of nature is in that state put into every man's

hands, whereby everyone has a right to punish the transgressors of that law to such a degree as may hinder its violation. For the law of nature would, as all other laws that concern men in this world, be in vain, if there were nobody that in the state of nature had a power to execute that law, and thereby preserve the innocent and restrain offenders, and if anyone in the state of nature may punish another, for any evil he has done, everyone may do so. For in that state of perfect equality, where naturally there is no superiority or jurisdiction of one over another, what any may do in prosecution of that law, everyone must needs have a right to do.

8. And thus in the state of nature, one man comes by a power over another; but yet no absolute or arbitrary power to use a criminal, when he has got him in his hands, according to the passionate heats, or boundless extravagancy of his own will, but only to retribute to him, so far as calm reason and conscience dictates, what is proportionate to his transgression, which is so much as may serve for reparation and restraint. For these two are the only reasons why one man may lawfully do harm to another, which is what we call *punishment*. In transgressing the law of nature the offender declares himself to live by another rule than that of reason and common equity, which is that measure God has set to the actions of men for their mutual security; and so he becomes dangerous to mankind, the tie which is to secure them from injury and violence being slighted and broken by him. Which, being a trespass against the whole species, and the peace and safety of it provided for by the law of nature, every man upon this score, by the right he hath to preserve mankind in general, may restrain, or, where it is necessary, destroy things noxious to them, and so may bring such evil on anyone who hath transgressed that law as may make him repent the doing of it, and thereby deter him, and by his example others, from doing the like mischief. And, in this case and upon this ground, every man hath a right to punish the offender, and be executioner of the law of nature.

9. I doubt not but this will seem a very strange doctrine to some men; but before they condemn it I desire them to resolve me, by what right any prince or state can put to death, or punish, an alien, for any crime he commits in their country. 'Tis certain their laws, by virtue of any sanction they receive from the promulgated will of the legislative, reach not a stranger. They speak not to him, nor, if they did, is he bound to hearken to them. The legislative authority, by which they are in force over the subjects of that commonwealth, hath no power over him. Those who have the supreme power of making laws in England, France, or Holland are to an Indian but like the rest of the world, men without authority; and therefore if by the law of nature every man hath not a power to punish offences against it, as he soberly judges the case to require, I see not how the magistrates of any community can punish an alien of another country, since in reference to him they can have no more power than what every man naturally may have over another.

10. Besides the crime which consists in violating the law, and varying from the right rule of reason, whereby a man so far becomes degenerate, and declares himself to quit the principles of human nature, and to be a noxious creature, there is commonly injury done to some person or other, and some other man receives damage by his transgression, in which case he who hath received any damage has, besides the right of punishment common to him with other men, a particular right to seek reparation from him that has done it. And any other person who finds it just may also join with him that is injured, and assist him in recovering from the offender so much as may make satisfaction for the harm he has suffered.

11. From these two distinct rights, the one of punishing the crime for restraint, and preventing the like offence, which right of punishing is in everybody; the other of taking

reparation, which belongs only to the injured party, comes it to pass that the magistrate, who by being magistrate hath the common right of punishing put into his hands, can often, where the public good demands not the execution of the law, remit the punishment of criminal offences by his own authority, but yet cannot remit the satisfaction due to any private man for the damage he has received. That, he who has suffered the damage has a right to demand in his own name, and he alone can remit. The damnified person has this power of appropriating to himself the goods or service of the offender by right of self-preservation, as every man has a power to punish the crime, to prevent its being committed again, by the right he has of preserving all mankind, and doing all reasonable things he can in order to that end. And thus it is that every man in the state of nature has a power to kill a murderer, both to deter others from doing the like injury, which no reparation can compensate, by the example of the punishment that attends it from everybody, and also to secure men from the attempts of a criminal who, having renounced reason, the common rule and measure God hath given to mankind, hath, by the unjust violence and slaughter he hath committed upon one, declared war against all mankind, and therefore may be destroyed as a lion or a tiger, one of those wild savage beasts with whom men can have no society nor security. And upon this is grounded the great law of nature 'Who so sheddeth man's blood, by man shall his blood be shed' [Genesis 9.6]. And Cain was so fully convinced that everyone had a right to destroy such a criminal that after the murder of his brother he cries out 'Every one that findeth me shall slay me' [Genesis 4.14]; so plain was it writ in the hearts of all mankind.

12. By the same reason may a man in the state of nature punish the lesser breaches of that law. It will perhaps be demanded: With death? I answer: Each transgression may be punished to that degree, and with so much severity, as will suffice to make it an ill bargain to the offender, give him cause to repent, and terrify others from doing the like. Every offence that can be committed in the state of nature may in the state of nature be also punished, equally and as far forth as it may in a commonwealth; for though it would be besides my present purpose to enter here into the particulars of the law of nature, or its measures of punishment, yet it is certain there is such a law, and that too as intelligible and plain to a rational creature, and a studier of that law, as the positive laws of commonwealths; nay possibly plainer, as much as reason is easier to be understood than the fancies and intricate contrivances of men following contrary and hidden interests put into words. For so, truly, are a great part of the municipal laws of countries, which are only so far right as they are founded on the law of nature, by which they are to be regulated and interpreted.

13. To this strange doctrine, viz. that in the state of nature everyone has the executive power of the law of nature, I doubt not but it will be objected that it is unreasonable for men to be judges in their own cases, that self-love will make men partial to themselves and their friends. And, on the other side, that ill-nature, passion, and revenge will carry them too far in punishing others. And hence nothing but confusion and disorder will follow, and that therefore God hath certainly appointed government to restrain the partiality and violence of men. I easily grant that civil government is the proper remedy for the inconveniences of the state of nature, which must certainly be great where men may be judges in their own case, since 'tis easily to be imagined that he who was so unjust as to do his brother an injury will scarce be so just as to condemn himself for it. But I shall desire those who make this objection to remember that absolute monarchs are but men, and if government is to be the remedy of those evils which necessarily follow from men's being judges in their

own cases, and the state of nature is therefore not [to] be endured, I desire to know what kind of government that is, and how much better it is than the state of nature, where one man commanding a multitude has the liberty to be judge in his own case, and may do to all his subjects whatever he pleases, without the least liberty to anyone to question or control those who execute his pleasure? And in whatsoever he doth, whether led by reason, mistake, or passion, must be submitted to? Much better it is in the state of nature, wherein men are not bound to submit to the unjust will of another, and if he that judges judges amiss in his own or any other case, he is answerable for it to the rest of mankind.

14. 'Tis often asked as a mighty objection: Where are or ever were there any men in such a state of nature? To which it may suffice as an answer at present: That since all princes and rulers of independent governments all through the world are in a state of nature, 'tis plain the world never was, nor ever will be, without numbers of men in that state. I have named all governors of independent communities, whether they are, or are not, in league with others. For 'tis not every compact that puts an end to the state of nature between men, but only this one of agreeing together mutually to enter into one community, and make one body politic; other promises and compacts men may make one with another, and yet still be in the state of nature. The promises and bargains for truck etc. between the two men in the desert island mentioned by Garcilaso de la Vega, in his history of Peru, or between a Swiss and an Indian in the woods of America, are binding to them, though they are perfectly in a state of nature in reference to one another. For truth and keeping of faith belongs to men as men, and not as members of society.

[. . .]

Chapter Three
Of the State of War

16. The state of war is a state of enmity and destruction. And, therefore, declaring by word or action, not a passionate and hasty, but a sedate, settled design upon another man's life puts him in a state of war with him against whom he has declared such an intention, and so has exposed his life to the other's power, to be taken away by him, or anyone that joins with him in his defence and espouses his quarrel: it being reasonable and just I should have a right to destroy that which threatens me with destruction. For by the fundamental law of nature – man being to be preserved, as much as possible – when all cannot be preserved the safety of the innocent is to be preferred. And one may destroy a man who makes war upon him, or has discovered an enmity to his being, for the same reason that he may kill a wolf or a lion: because such men are not under the ties of the common law of reason, have no other rule but that of force and violence, and so may be treated as beasts of prey, those dangerous and noxious creatures, that will be sure to destroy him whenever he falls into their power.

17. And hence it is that he who attempts to get another man into his absolute power does thereby put himself into a state of war with him, it being to be understood as a declaration of a design upon his life. For I have reason to conclude that he who would get me into his power without my consent would use me as he pleased when he had got me there, and destroy me too when he had a fancy to it; for nobody can desire to have me in his absolute power, unless it be to compel me by force to that which is against the right of my freedom,

i.e. make me a slave. To be free from such force is the only security of my preservation, and reason bids me look on him as an enemy to my preservation, who would take away that freedom which is the fence to it. So that he who makes an attempt to enslave me thereby puts himself into a state of war with me. He that in the state of nature would take away the freedom that belongs to anyone in that state must necessarily be supposed to have a design to take away everything else, that freedom being the foundation of all the rest; as he that in the state of society would take away the freedom belonging to those of that society or commonwealth must be supposed to design to take away from them everything else, and so be looked on as in a state of war.

18. This makes it lawful for a man to kill a thief who has not in the least hurt him, nor declared any design upon his life, any further than by the use of force so to get him in his power as to take away his money, or what he pleases, from him. Because using force, where he has no right, to get me into his power, let his pretence be what it will, I have no reason to suppose that he, who would take away my liberty, would not when he had me in his power take away everything else. And therefore it is lawful for me to treat him as one who has put himself into a state of war with me, i.e. kill him if I can; for to that hazard does he justly expose himself, whoever introduces a state of war, and is aggressor in it.

19. And here we have the plain difference between the state of nature and the state of war, which, however some men have confounded, are as far distant as a state of peace, good-will, mutual assistance, and preservation, and a state of enmity, malice, violence, and mutual destruction are one from another. Men living together according to reason, without a common superior on earth with authority to judge between them, is properly the state of nature. But force, or a declared design of force upon the person of another, where there is no common superior on earth to appeal to for relief, is the state of war; and 'tis the want of such an appeal gives a man the right of war even against an aggressor, though he be in society and a fellow-subject. Thus a thief, whom I cannot harm but by appeal to the law for having stolen all that I am worth, I may kill when he sets on me to rob me but of my horse or coat. Because the law, which was made for my preservation, where it cannot interpose to secure my life from present force, which, if lost, is capable of no reparation, permits me my own defence, and the right of war, a liberty to kill the aggressor, because the aggressor allows not time to appeal to our common judge, nor the decision of the law for remedy in a case where the mischief may be irreparable. Want of a common judge with authority puts all men in a state of nature; force without right upon a man's person makes a state of war, both where there is and is not a common judge.

[. . .]

21. To avoid this state of war (wherein there is no appeal but to heaven, and wherein every the least difference is apt to end, where there is no authority to decide between the contenders) is one great reason of men's putting themselves into society, and quitting the state of nature. For where there is an authority, a power on earth from which relief can be had by appeal, there the continuance of the state of war is excluded, and the controversy is decided by that power. Had there been any such court, any superior jurisdiction on earth, to determine the right between Jephtha and the Ammonites, they had never come to a state of war, but we see he was forced to appeal to heaven. 'The Lord the Judge,' says he, 'be judge this day between the children of Israel and the children of Ammon' (Judges 11.27), and then prosecuting, and relying on his appeal, he leads out his army to battle. And there-

fore in such controversies, where the question is put: 'Who shall be judge?', it cannot be meant 'Who shall decide the controversy?'; everyone knows what Jephtha here tells us, that the Lord the Judge shall judge. Where there is no judge on earth, the appeal lies to God in heaven. That question then cannot mean 'Who shall judge whether another hath put himself in a state of war with me, and whether I may, as Jephtha did, appeal to heaven in it?' Of that I myself can only be judge in my own conscience, as I will answer it at the great day, to the supreme judge of all men.

[. . .]

Chapter Five
Of Property

[. . .]

27. Though the earth and all inferior creatures be common to all men, yet every man has a property in his own person. This nobody has any right to but himself. The labour of his body, and the work of his hands, we may say, are properly his. Whatsoever, then, he removes out of the state that nature hath provided and left it in, he hath mixed his labour with, and joined to it something that is his own, and thereby makes it his property. It being by him removed from the common state nature placed it in, it hath by this labour something annexed to it that excludes the common right of other men. For this labour being the unquestionable property of the labourer, no man but he can have a right to what that is once joined to, at least where there is enough and as good left in common for others.

28. He that is nourished by the acorns he picked up under an oak, or the apples he gathered from the trees in the wood, has certainly appropriated them to himself. Nobody can deny but the nourishment is his. I ask then, When did they begin to be his? When he digested? Or when he ate? Or when he boiled? Or when he brought them home? Or when he picked them up? And 'tis plain if the first gathering made them not his, nothing else could. That labour put a distinction between them and common. That added something to them more than nature, the common mother of all, had done; and so they became his private right. And will anyone say he had no right to those acorns or apples he thus appropriated, because he had not the consent of all mankind to make them his? Was it a robbery thus to assume to himself what belonged to all in common? If such a consent as that was necessary, man had starved, notwithstanding the plenty God had given him. We see in commons, which remain so by compact, that 'tis the taking any part of what is common, and removing it out of the state nature leaves it in, which begins the property; without which the common is of no use. And the taking of this or that part does not depend on the express consent of all the commoners. Thus the grass my horse has bit, the turfs my servant has cut, and the ore I have digged in any place where I have a right to them in common with others become my property, without the assignation or consent of anybody. The labour that was mine, removing them out of that common state they were in, hath fixed my property in them.

[. . .]

31. It will perhaps be objected to this that if gathering the acorns, or other fruits of the earth, etc. makes a right to them, then anyone may engross as much as he will. To which I answer: Not so. The same law of nature that does by this means give us property, does also bound that property too. 'God has given us all things richly' (I Tim. 6.17) is the voice of reason confirmed by inspiration. But how far has he given it us? To enjoy. As much as anyone can make use of to any advantage of life before it spoils, so much he may by his labour fix a property in. Whatever is beyond this, is more than his share, and belongs to others. Nothing was made by God for man to spoil or destroy. And thus, considering the plenty of natural provisions there was a long time in the world, and the few spenders, and to how small a part of that provision the industry of one man could extend itself, and engross it to the prejudice of others; especially keeping within the bounds, set by reason, of what might serve for his use; there could be then little room for quarrels or contentions about property so established.

32. But the chief matter of property being now not the fruits of the earth, and the beasts that subsist on it, but the earth itself, as that which takes in and carries with it all the rest, I think it is plain that property in that too is acquired as the former. As much land as a man tills, plants, improves, cultivates, and can use the product of, so much is his property. He by his labour does, as it were, enclose it from the common. Nor will it invalidate his right to say 'Everybody else has an equal title to it, and therefore he cannot appropriate, he cannot enclose, without the consent of all his fellow-commoners, all mankind.' God, when he gave the world in common to all mankind, commanded man also to labour, and the penury of his condition required it of him. God and his reason commanded him to subdue the earth, i.e. improve it for the benefit of life, and therein lay out something upon it that was his own, his labour. He that, in obedience to this command of God, subdued, tilled and sowed any part of it, thereby annexed to it something that was his property, which another had no title to, nor could without injury take from him.

33. Nor was this appropriation of any parcel of land, by improving it, any prejudice to any other man, since there was still enough – and as good – left; and more than the yet unprovided could use. So that, in effect, there was never the less left for others because of his enclosure for himself. For he that leaves as much as another can make use of, does as good as take nothing at all. Nobody could think himself injured by the drinking of another man, though he took a good draught, who had a whole river of the same water left him to quench his thirst. And the case of land and water, where there is enough of both, is perfectly the same.

[. . .]

46. The greatest part of things really useful to the life of man, and such as the necessity of subsisting made the first commoners of the world look after, as it doth the Americans now, are generally things of short duration, such as, if they are not consumed by use, will decay and perish of themselves. Gold, silver, and diamonds are things that fancy or agreement hath put the value on, more than real use and the necessary support of life. Now of those good things which nature hath provided in common, everyone had a right (as hath been said) to as much as he could use, and had a property in all that he could affect with his labour. All that his industry could extend to, to alter from the state nature had put it in, was his. He that gathered a hundred bushels of acorns or apples had thereby a property in them; they were his goods as soon as gathered. He was only to look that he used them before they spoiled; else he took more than his share and robbed others. And indeed it was a foolish thing,

as well as dishonest, to hoard up more than he could make use of. If he gave away a part to anybody else, so that it perished not uselessly in his possession, these he also made use of. And if he also bartered away plums that would have rotted in a week for nuts that would last good for his eating a whole year, he did no injury; he wasted not the common stock, destroyed no part of the portion of goods that belonged to others, so long as nothing perished uselessly in his hands. Again, if he would give his nuts for a piece of metal, pleased with its colour, or exchange his sheep for shells, or wool for a sparkling pebble or a diamond, and keep those by him all his life, he invaded not the right of others: he might heap up as much of these durable things as he pleased; the exceeding of the bounds of his just property not lying in the largeness of his possession, but the perishing of anything uselessly in it.

47. And thus came in the use of money, some lasting thing that men might keep without spoiling, and that by mutual consent men would take in exchange for truly useful but perishable supports of life.

48. And as different degrees of industry were apt to give men possessions in different proportions, so this invention of money gave them the opportunity to continue and enlarge them. For supposing an island separate from all possible commerce with the rest of the world, wherein there were but a hundred families, but there were sheep, horses, and cows, with other useful animals, wholesome fruits, and land enough for corn for a hundred thousand times as many, but nothing in the island, either because of its commonness, or perishableness, fit to supply the place of money: what reason could anyone have there to enlarge his possessions beyond the use of his family, and a plentiful supply to its consumption, either in what their own industry produced or they could barter for like perishable, useful commodities with others? Where there is not something both lasting and scarce, and so valuable to be hoarded up, there men will not be apt to enlarge their possessions of land, were it never so rich, never so free for them to take. For I ask, what would a man value ten thousand or an hundred thousand acres of excellent land, ready cultivated and well-stocked too with cattle, in the middle of the inland parts of America, where he had no hopes of commerce with other parts of the world, to draw money to him by the sale of the product? It would not be worth the enclosing, and we should see him give up again to the wild common of nature whatever was more than would supply the conveniences of life to be had there for him and his family.

49. Thus in the beginning all the world was America, and more so than that is now, for no such thing as money was anywhere known. Find out something that hath the use and value of money amongst his neighbours, you shall see the same man will begin presently to enlarge his possessions.

50. But since gold and silver, being little useful to the life of man in proportion to food, raiment, and carriage, has its value only from the consent of men, whereof labour yet makes, in great part, the measure, it is plain that men have agreed to disproportionate and unequal possession of the earth, they having by a tacit and voluntary consent found out a way how a man may fairly possess more land than he himself can use of the product, by receiving in exchange for the overplus gold and silver, which may be hoarded up without injury to anyone, these metals not spoiling or decaying in the hands of the possessor. This partage of things in an inequality of private possessions, men have made practicable out of the bounds of society, and without compact, only by putting a value on gold and silver and tacitly agreeing in the use of money. For in governments the laws regulate the right of property, and the possession of land is determined by positive constitutions.

[. . .]

Chapter Seven
Of Political or Civil Society

[. . .]

87. Man being born, as has been proved, with a title to perfect freedom, and an uncontrolled enjoyment of all the rights and privileges of the law of nature, equally with any other man or number of men in the world, hath by nature a power not only to preserve his property, that is his life, liberty and estate, against the injuries and attempts of other men, but to judge of and punish the breaches of that law in others as he is persuaded the offence deserves, even with death itself in crimes where the heinousness of the fact, in his opinion, requires it. But because no political society can be, nor subsist, without having in itself the power to preserve the property, and in order thereunto punish the offences, of all those of that society; there and there only is political society where every one of the members hath quitted this natural power, resigned it up into the hands of the community in all cases that exclude him not from appealing for protection to the law established by it. And thus all private judgement of every particular member being excluded, the community comes to be umpire, by settled standing rules, indifferent and the same to all parties; and, by men having authority from the community for the execution of those rules, decides all the differences that may happen between any members of that society concerning any matter of right; and punishes those offences which any member hath committed against the society with such penalties as the law has established. Whereby it is easy to discern who are and who are not in political society together. Those who are united into one body, and have a common established law and judicature to appeal to, with authority to decide controversies between them, and punish offenders, are in civil society one with another; but those who have no such common appeal, I mean on earth, are still in the state of nature, each being, where there is no other, judge for himself and executioner; which is, as I have before showed it, the perfect state of nature.

[. . .]

91. For he being supposed to have all, both legislative and executive power in himself alone, there is no judge to be found, no appeal lies open to anyone who may fairly and indifferently, and with authority, decide, and from whose decision relief and redress may be expected of any injury or inconveniency that may be suffered from the prince or by his order. So that such a man, however entitled – Czar, or Grand Signor, or how you please – is as much in the state of nature with all under his dominion as he is with the rest of mankind. For wherever any two men are who have no standing rule and common judge to appeal to on earth for the determination of controversies of right betwixt them, there they are still in the state of nature, and under all the inconveniences of it, with only this woeful difference to the subject, or rather slave, of an absolute prince, that whereas in the ordinary state of nature he has a liberty to judge of his right and, according to the best of his power, to maintain it, now whenever his property is invaded by the will and order of his monarch, he has not only no appeal, as those in society ought to have, but, as if he were degraded from the common state of rational creatures, is denied a liberty to judge of or to defend his right, and so is exposed to all the misery and inconveniences that a man can fear from one who, being in the unrestrained state of nature, is yet corrupted with flattery, and armed with power.

[. . .]

Chapter Eight
Of the Beginning of Political Societies

95. Men being, as has been said, by nature all free, equal and independent, no man can be put out of this estate and subjected to the political power of another without his own consent. The only way whereby anyone divests himself of his natural liberty and puts on the bonds of civil society is by agreeing with other men to join and unite into a community for their comfortable, safe, and peaceable living one amongst another in a secure enjoyment of their properties, and a greater security against any that are not of it. This any number of men may do, because it injures not the freedom of the rest; they are left as they were, in the liberty of the state of nature. When any number of men have so consented to make one community or government, they are thereby presently incorporated, and make one body politic, wherein the majority have a right to act and conclude the rest.

96. For when any number of men have, by the consent of every individual, made a community, they have thereby made that community one body, with a power to act as one body, which is only by the will and determination of the majority. For that which acts any community being only the consent of the individuals of it, and it being necessary to that which is one body to move one way, it is necessary the body should move that way whither the greater force carries it, which is the consent of the majority; or else it is impossible it should act or continue one body, one community, which the consent of every individual that united into it agreed that it should; and so everyone is bound by that consent to be concluded by the majority. And therefore we see that in assemblies empowered to act by positive laws where no number is set by that positive law which empowers them, the act of the majority passes for the act of the whole, and of course determines, as having by the law of nature and reason the power of the whole.

97. And thus every man, by consenting with others to make one body politic under one government, puts himself under an obligation to everyone of that society to submit to the determination of the majority, and to be concluded by it; or else this original compact, whereby he with others incorporates into one society, would signify nothing, and be no compact, if he be left free, and under no other ties than he was in before, in the state of nature. For what appearance would there be of any compact? What new engagement if he were no further tied by any decrees of the society than he himself thought fit and did actually consent to? This would still be as great a liberty as he himself had before his compact, or anyone else in the state of nature hath, who may submit himself and consent to any acts of it if he thinks fit.

98. For if the consent of the majority shall not, in reason, be received as the act of the whole, and conclude every individual, nothing but the consent of every individual can make anything to be the act of the whole. But such a consent is next impossible ever to be had, if we consider the infirmities of health and avocations of business which, in a number though much less than that of a commonwealth, will necessarily keep many away from the public assembly. To which if we add the variety of opinions, and contrariety of interests, which unavoidably happen in all collections of men, the coming into society upon such terms would be only like Cato's coming into the theatre, only to go out again. Such a constitution as this would make the mighty Leviathan of a shorter duration than the feeblest creatures, and not let it outlast the day it was born in; which cannot be supposed till we can think that

rational creatures should desire and constitute societies only to be dissolved. For where the majority cannot conclude the rest, there they cannot act as one body, and consequently will be immediately dissolved again.

99. Whosoever, therefore, out of a state of nature unite into a community, must be understood to give up all the power necessary to the ends for which they unite into society to the majority of the community, unless they expressly agreed in any number greater than the majority. And this is done by barely agreeing to unite into one political society, which is all the compact that is, or needs be, between the individuals that enter into or make up a commonwealth. And thus that which begins and actually constitutes any political society is nothing but the consent of any number of freemen capable of a majority to unite and incorporate into such a society. And this is that, and that only, which did or could give beginning to any lawful government in the world.

[. . .]

119. Every man being, as has been showed, naturally free, and nothing being able to put him into subjection to any earthly power, but only his own consent; it is to be considered, what shall be understood to be a sufficient declaration of a man's consent, to make him subject to the laws of any government. There is a common distinction of an express and a tacit consent, which will concern our present case. Nobody doubts but an express consent, of any man, entering into any society, makes him a perfect member of that society, a subject of that government. The difficulty is what ought to be looked upon as a tacit consent, and how far it binds, i.e. how far anyone shall be looked on to have consented, and thereby submitted to any government, where he has made no expressions of it at all. And to this I say that every man that hath any possession, or enjoyment, of any part of the dominions of any government, doth thereby give his tacit consent, and is as far forth obliged to obedience to the laws of that government, during such enjoyment, as anyone under it; whether this his possession be of land, to him and his heirs for ever, or a lodging only for a week; or whether it be barely travelling freely on the highway; and, in effect, it reaches as far as the very being of anyone within the territories of that government.

120. To understand this the better, it is fit to consider that every man, when he, at first, incorporates himself into any commonwealth, he, by his uniting himself thereunto, annexed also and submits to the community those possessions which he has, or shall acquire, that do not already belong to any other government. For it would be a direct contradiction for anyone to enter into society with others for the securing and regulating of property, and yet to suppose his land, whose property is to be regulated by the laws of the society, should be exempt from the jurisdiction of that government to which he himself, the proprietor of the land, is a subject. By the same act, therefore, whereby anyone unites his person, which was before free, to any commonwealth, by the same he unites his possessions, which were before free, to it also; and they become, both of them, person and possession, subject to the government and dominion of that commonwealth, as long as it hath a being. Whoever, therefore, from thenceforth, by inheritance, purchase, permission, or otherways enjoys any part of the land so annexed to and under the government of that commonwealth, must take it with the condition it is under, that is, of submitting to the government of the commonwealth under whose jurisdiction it is, as far forth as any subject of it.

121. But since the government has a direct jurisdiction only over the land, and reaches the possessor of it (before he has actually incorporated himself in the society) only as he dwells

upon, and enjoys that, the obligation anyone is under, by virtue of such enjoyment, to submit to the government, begins and ends with the enjoyment. So that whenever the owner who has given nothing but such a tacit consent to the government will, by donation, sale, or otherwise, quit the said possession, he is at liberty to go and incorporate himself into any other commonwealth, or to agree with others to begin a new one, *in vacuis locis*, in any part of the world they can find free and unpossessed. Whereas he that has once by actual agreement and any express declaration given his consent to be of any commonwealth, is perpetually and indispensably obliged to be and remain unalterably a subject to it, and can never be again in the liberty of the state of nature, unless by any calamity the government he was under comes to be dissolved; or else by some public act cuts him off from being any longer a member of it.

122. But submitting to the laws of any country, living quietly, and enjoying privileges and protection under them, makes not a man a member of that society. This is only a local protection and homage due to, and from, all those who, not being in a state of war, come within the territories belonging to any government, to all parts whereof the force of its law extends. But this no more makes a man a member of that society, a perpetual subject of that commonwealth, than it would make a man a subject to another in whose family he found it convenient to abide for some time; though, whilst he continued in it, he were obliged to comply with the laws, and submit to the government he found there. And thus we see that foreigners, by living all their lives under another government, and enjoying the privileges and protection of it, though they are bound, even in conscience, to submit to its administration, as far forth as any denizen, yet do not thereby come to be subjects or members of that commonwealth. Nothing can make any man so, but his actually entering into it by positive engagement, and express promise and compact. This is that which I think concerning the beginnings of political societies and that consent which makes anyone a member of any commonwealth.

14

David Hume, "Of the Original Contract" (1748)

In his theory of knowledge, Hume extended the basic principles of Locke's empiricist philosophy. It can even be said that Hume "purified" Locke's empiricism, by rejecting all supernatural, non-experiential grounds for philosophical principles. This purification is nowhere more evident than in Hume's moral and political philosophy, where he set aside Locke's appeals to theological bases for his views, and relied instead solely on evidence provided by sense experience. So naturally, Hume's response to the eighteenth-century theory of the social contract was to inquire about the empirical evidence for its claims. Does history provide any basis for thinking that political power attains its legitimacy through a social contract? Hume's skeptical answer in his essay "Of the Original Contract" was "No." As he observed there: "Were you to preach, in most parts of the world, that political connections are founded altogether on voluntary consent or a mutual promise, the magistrate would soon imprison you as seditious, for loosening the ties of obedience; if your friends did not before shut you up as delirious, for advancing such absurdities."

But besides this straightforward, empirical argument against the contract theory, Hume's essay also probed another of its apparent weaknesses. The theory of the social contract bases our moral obligation to obey civil government on our mutual consent or promise to be governed. Yet it offers no basis for any moral obligation to keep that promise. The political obligation of obedience or *allegiance*, Hume argues, is on the same moral footing as the obligation of promise-keeping or *fidelity*. One cannot be based upon the other; so whatever sanctions the one will also sanction the other. But this then gives rise to the following dilemma. If there is no moral basis for the duty of fidelity to promises, then the contract theory will not be able to give us any moral basis for duties of political obedience. On the other hand, however, if there is a moral basis for the duty of fidelity to promises, then whatever *that* basis may be, it can also provide a moral basis for political obedience, making consent by social contract pointless. If we say, for example, that promise-keeping is morally right because God commands it, then why not say also that political obedience is sanctioned directly by divine command as well?

In 1748 Hume published a short collection of three essays on political themes: "Of National Character"; "Of the Original Contract"; and "Of Passive Obedience." The first of these, which attributed differences in the characters of different peoples and races to "moral" or political causes, contained some scandalous footnotes. Due largely to the influence of the Scottish clergy, Hume had been denied a teaching position at the University of Edinburgh. So it is probably not by coincidence that in a long note to this essay Hume lashed out against the clergy, accusing the profession of hypocrisy, and attributing their actions to motives of ambition and revenge. A later edition of the same essay contains a footnote arguing for white supremacy. But this was an unfortunate and short-sighted afterthought, especially since the point of Hume's essay was to attribute differences between races and nations to ever-variable political causes.

When we consider how nearly equal all men are in their bodily force, and even in their mental powers and faculties, till cultivated by education; we must necessarily allow, that nothing but their own consent could, at first, associate them together, and subject them to any authority. The people, if we trace government to its first origin in the woods and desarts, are the source of all power and jurisdiction, and voluntarily, for the sake of peace and order, abandoned their native liberty, and received laws from their equal and companion. The conditions, upon which they were willing to submit, were either expressed, or were so clear and obvious, that it might well be esteemed superfluous to express them. If this, then, be meant by the *original contract*, it cannot be denied, that all government is, at first, founded on a contract, and that the most ancient rude combinations of mankind were formed chiefly by that principle. In vain, are we asked in what records this charter of our liberties is registered. It was not written on parchment, nor yet on leaves or barks of trees. It preceded the use of writing and all the other civilized arts of life. But we trace it plainly in the nature of man, and in the equality, or something approaching equality, which we find in all the individuals of that species. The force, which now prevails, and which is founded on fleets and armies, is plainly political, and derived from authority, the effect of established government. A man's natural force consists only in the vigour of his limbs, and the firmness of his courage; which could never subject multitudes to the command of one. Nothing but their own consent, and their sense of the advantages resulting from peace and order, could have had that influence.

Yet even this consent was long very imperfect, and could not be the basis of a regular administration. The chieftain, who had probably acquired his influence during the continuance of war, ruled more by persuasion than command; and till he could employ force to reduce the refractory and disobedient, the society could scarcely be said to have attained a state of civil government. No compact or agreement, it is evident, was expressly formed for general submission; an idea far beyond the comprehension of savages: Each exertion of authority in the chieftain must have been particular, and called forth by the present exigencies of the case: The sensible utility, resulting from his interposition, made these exertions become daily more frequent; and their frequency gradually produced an habitual, and, if you please to call it so, a voluntary, and therefore precarious, acquiescence in the people.

But philosophers, who have embraced a party (if that be not a contradiction in terms) are not contented with these concessions. They assert, not only that government in its earliest infancy arose from consent or rather the voluntary acquiescence of the people; but also, that, even at present, when it has attained full maturity, it rests on no other foundation. They affirm, that all men are still born equal, and owe allegiance to no prince or government, unless bound by the obligation and sanction of a *promise*. And as no man, without some equivalent, would forego the advantages of his native liberty, and subject himself to the will of another; this promise is always understood to be conditional, and imposes on him no obligation, unless he meet with justice and protection from his sovereign. These advantages the sovereign promises him in return; and if he fail in the execution, he has broken, on his part, the articles of engagement, and has thereby freed his subject from all obligations to allegiance. Such, according to these philosophers, is the foundation of authority in every government; and such the right of resistance, possessed by every subject.

But would these reasoners look abroad into the world, they would meet with nothing that, in the least, corresponds to their ideas, or can warrant so refined and philosophical a system. On the contrary, we find, every where, princes, who claim their subjects as their property, and assert their independent right of sovereignty, from conquest or succession. We find also, every where, subjects, who acknowledge this right in their prince, and suppose themselves born under obligations of obedience to a certain sovereign, as much as under the ties of reverence and duty to certain parents. These connexions are always conceived to be equally independent of our consent, in PERSIA and CHINA; in FRANCE and SPAIN; and even in HOLLAND and ENGLAND, wherever the doctrines above-mentioned have not been carefully inculcated. Obedience or subjection becomes so familiar, that most men never make any enquiry about its origin or cause, more than about the principle of gravity, resistance, or the most universal laws of nature. Or if curiosity ever move them; as soon as they learn, that they themselves and their ancestors have, for several ages, or from time immemorial, been subject to such a form of government or such a family; they immediately acquiesce, and acknowledge their obligation to allegiance. Were you to preach, in most parts of the world, that political connexions are founded altogether on voluntary consent or a mutual promise, the magistrate would soon imprison you, as seditious, for loosening the ties of obedience; if your friends did not before shut you up as delirious, for advancing such absurdities. It is strange, that an act of the mind, which every individual is supposed to have formed, and after he came to the use of reason too, otherwise it could have no authority; that this act, I say, should be so much unknown to all of them, that, over the face of the whole earth, there scarcely remain any traces or memory of it.

But the contract, on which government is founded, is said to be the *original contract*; and consequently may be supposed too old to fall under the knowledge of the present generation. If the agreement, by which savage men first associated and conjoined their force, be here meant, this is acknowledged to be real; but being so ancient, and being obliterated by a thousand changes of government and princes, it cannot now be supposed to retain any authority. If we would say any thing to the purpose, we must assert, that every particular government, which is lawful, and which imposes any duty of allegiance on the subject, was, at first, founded on consent and a voluntary compact. But besides that this supposes the consent of the fathers to bind the children, even to the most remote generations, (which republican writers will never allow) besides this, I say, it is not justified by history or experience, in any age or country of the world.

Almost all the governments, which exist at present, or of which there remains any record in story, have been founded originally, either on usurpation or conquest, or both, without any pretence of a fair consent, or voluntary subjection of the people. When an artful and bold man is placed at the head of an army or faction, it is often easy for him, by employing, sometimes violence, sometimes false pretences, to establish his dominion over a people a hundred times more numerous than his partizans. He allows no such open communication, that his enemies can know, with certainty, their number or force. He gives them no leisure to assemble together in a body to oppose him. Even all those, who are the instruments of his usurpation, may wish his fall; but their ignorance of each other's intention keeps them in awe, and is the sole cause of his security. By such arts as these, many governments have been established; and this is all the *original contract*, which they have to boast of.

[. . .]

My intention here is not to exclude the consent of the people from being one just foundation of government where it has place. It is surely the best and most sacred of any. I only pretend, that it has very seldom had place in any degree, and never almost in its full extent. And that therefore some other foundation of government must also be admitted.

Were all men possessed of so inflexible a regard to justice, that, of themselves, they would totally abstain from the properties of others; they had for ever remained in a state of absolute liberty, without subjection to any magistrate or political society: But this is a state of perfection, of which human nature is justly deemed incapable. Again; were all men possessed of so perfect an understanding, as always to know their own interests, no form of government had ever been submitted to, but what was established on consent, and was fully canvassed by every member of the society: But this state of perfection is likewise much superior to human nature. Reason, history, and experience shew us, that all political societies have had an origin much less accurate and regular; and were one to choose a period of time, when the people's consent was the least regarded in public transactions, it would be precisely on the establishment of a new government. In a settled constitution, their inclinations are often consulted; but during the fury of revolutions, conquests, and public convulsions, military force or political craft usually decides the controversy.

When a new government is established, by whatever means, the people are commonly dissatisfied with it, and pay obedience more from fear and necessity, than from any idea of allegiance or of moral obligation. The prince is watchful and jealous, and must carefully guard against every beginning or appearance of insurrection. Time, by degrees, removes all these difficulties, and accustoms the nation to regard, as their lawful or native princes, that family, which, at first, they considered as usurpers or foreign conquerors. In order to found this opinion, they have no recourse to any notion of voluntary consent or promise, which, they know, never was, in this case, either expected or demanded. The original establishment was formed by violence, and submitted to from necessity. The subsequent administration is also supported by power, and acquiesced in by the people, not as a matter of choice, but of obligation. They imagine not, that their consent gives their prince a title: But they willingly consent, because they think, that, from long possession, he has acquired a title, independent of their choice or inclination.

Should it be said, that, by living under the dominion of a prince, which one might leave, every individual has given a *tacit* consent to his authority, and promised him obedience; it may be answered, that such an implied consent can only have place, where a man imagines, that the matter depends on his choice. But where he thinks (as all mankind do who are born under established governments) that by his birth he owes allegiance to a certain prince or certain form of government; it would be absurd to infer a consent or choice, which he expressly, in this case, renounces and disclaims.

Can we seriously say, that a poor peasant or artizan has a free choice to leave his country, when he knows no foreign language or manners, and lives from day to day, by the small wages which he acquires? We may as well assert, that a man, by remaining in a vessel, freely consents to the dominion of the master; though he was carried on board while asleep, and must leap into the ocean, and perish, the moment he leaves her.

[. . .]

But would we have a more regular, at least a more philosophical, refutation of this principle of an original contract or popular consent; perhaps, the following observations may
suffice.

All *moral* duties may be divided into two kinds. The *first* are those, to which men are impelled
by a natural instinct or immediate propensity, which operates on them, independent of all
ideas of obligation, and of all views, either to public or private utility. Of this nature
are, love of children, gratitude to benefactors, pity to the unfortunate. When we reflect on
the advantage, which results to society from such humane instincts, we pay them the just
tribute of moral approbation and esteem: But the person, actuated by them, feels their power
and influence, antecedent to any such reflection.

The *second* kind of moral duties are such as are not supported by any original instinct of
nature, but are performed entirely from a sense of obligation, when we consider the necessities of human society, and the impossibility of supporting it, if these duties were neglected.
It is thus *justice* or a regard to the property of others, *fidelity* or the observance of promises,
become obligatory, and acquire an authority over mankind. For as it is evident, that
every man loves himself better than any other person, he is naturally impelled to extend his
acquisitions as much as possible; and nothing can restrain him in this propensity, but
reflection and experience, by which he learns the pernicious effects of that licence, and the
total dissolution of society which must ensue from it. His original inclination, therefore, or
instinct, is here checked and restrained by a subsequent judgment or observation.

The case is precisely the same with the political or civil duty of *allegiance*, as with the
natural duties of justice and fidelity. Our primary instincts lead us, either to indulge ourselves
in unlimited freedom, or to seek dominion over others: And it is reflection only, which
engages us to sacrifice such strong passions to the interests of peace and public order. A small
degree of experience and observation suffices to teach us, that society cannot possibly be
maintained without the authority of magistrates, and that this authority must soon fall into
contempt, where exact obedience is not paid to it. The observation of these general and
obvious interests is the source of all allegiance, and of that moral obligation, which we attribute
to it.

What necessity, therefore, is there to found the duty of *allegiance* or obedience to magistrates on that of *fidelity* or a regard to promises, and to suppose, that it is the consent of each
individual, which subjects him to government; when it appears, that both allegiance and fidelity
stand precisely on the same foundation, and are both submitted to by mankind, on account
of the apparent interests and necessities of human society? We are bound to obey our sovereign,
it is said; because we have given a tacit promise to that purpose. But why are we bound
to observe our promise? It must here be asserted, that the commerce and intercourse of mankind,
which are of such mighty advantage, can have no security where men pay no regard to
their engagements. In like manner, may it be said, that men could not live at all in society,
at least in a civilized society, without laws and magistrates and judges, to prevent the encroach-
ments of the strong upon the weak, of the violent upon the just and equitable. The obligation to allegiance being of like force and authority with the obligation to fidelity, we gain
nothing by resolving the one into the other. The general interests or necessities of society
are sufficient to establish both.

If the reason be asked of that obedience, which we are bound to pay to government, I
readily answer, *because society could not otherwise subsist*: And this answer is clear and intelli-

gible to all mankind. Your answer is, *because we should keep our word*. But besides, that no body, till trained in a philosophical system, can either comprehend or relish this answer: Besides this, I say, you find yourself embarrassed, when it is asked, *why we are bound to keep our word?* Nor can you give any answer, but what would, immediately, without any circuit, have accounted for our obligation to allegiance.

But *to whom is allegiance due? And who is our lawful sovereign?* This question is often the most difficult of any, and liable to infinite discussions. When people are so happy, that they can answer, *Our present sovereign, who inherits, in a direct line, from ancestors, that have governed us for many ages*; this answer admits of no reply; even though historians, in tracing up to the remotest antiquity, the origin of that royal family, may find, as commonly happens, that its first authority was derived from usurpation and violence. It is confessed, that private justice, or the abstinence from the properties of others, is a most cardinal virtue: Yet reason tells us, that there is no property in durable objects, such as lands or houses, when carefully examined in passing from hand to hand, but must, in some period, have been founded on fraud and injustice. The necessities of human society, neither in private nor public life, will allow of such an accurate enquiry: And there is no virtue or moral duty, but what may, with facility, be refined away, if we indulge a false philosophy, in sifting and scrutinizing it, by every captious rule of logic, in every light or position, in which it may be placed.

[. . .]

We shall only observe, before we conclude, that, though an appeal to general opinion may justly, in the speculative sciences of metaphysics, natural philosophy, or astronomy, be deemed unfair and inconclusive, yet in all questions with regard to morals, as well as criticism, there is really no other standard, by which any controversy can ever be decided. And nothing is a clearer proof, that a theory of this kind is erroneous, than to find, that it leads to paradoxes, repugnant to the common sentiments of mankind, and to the practice and opinion of all nations and all ages. The doctrine, which founds all lawful government on an *original contract*, or consent of the people, is plainly of this kind; nor has the most noted of its partizans, in prosecution of it, scrupled to affirm, *that absolute monarchy is inconsistent with civil society, and so can be no form of civil government at all*; and *that the supreme power in a state cannot take from any man, by taxes and impositions, any part of his property, without his own consent or that of his representatives*. What authority any moral reasoning can have, which leads into opinions so wide of the general practice of mankind, in every place but this single kingdom, it is easy to determine.

The only passage I meet with in antiquity, where the obligation of obedience to government is ascribed to a promise, is in PLATO's *Crito*: where SOCRATES refuses to escape from prison, because he had tacitly promised to obey the laws. Thus he builds a *tory* consequence of passive obedience, on a *whig* foundation of the original contract.

New discoveries are not to be expected in these matters. If scarce any man, till very lately, ever imagined that government was founded on compact, it is certain, that it cannot, in general, have any such foundation.

15

Jean-Jacques Rousseau, *On the Social Contract* (1762)

The problem Rousseau sets for himself in *On the Social Contract* is to "Find a form of association which defends and protects with all common forces the person and goods of each associate [while each] nevertheless obeys only himself and remains as free as before." The form of association called the social contract, he says, is this problem's solution. Here Rousseau signals a distinctive strain of contractarian thinking. Posing his problem in this way shows that he will not treat the idea of the social contract as a device explaining the historical foundation of actual societies. He will see it, rather, as an ideal agreement considered to be the basis for legitimate political authority, wherever and whenever it may occur.

Rousseau here begins with the observation that "Man is born free, and everywhere he is in chains." That is, the natural freedom of human beings has been lost or corrupted in the transition from the state of nature to social life. What is needed now, according to Rousseau, is a clearer understanding of a form of "association" by which people can restore their freedom while still enjoying the benefits of society. The people need to take back their freedom by rethinking the fundamental social structure. Rousseau quotes with approval the saying of the Dutch moral and political philosopher Hugo Grotius (1583–1645) that "A people can give itself to a king." But, he adds, this implies a prior political act by which a people becomes a people. That act is, of course, the foundation of all legitimate political authority: the social contract. By means of the original contract the individual parties thereto become collectively a people. They are each subsequently known as *citizens*, insofar as they participate in the sovereign authority of the people, and also as *subjects*, insofar as they are obligated to obey. But the people do not legislate, says Rousseau. Rather, the people, exercising sovereign authority, delegate a form of government for purposes of legislation and law enforcement. In this way the citizens freely choose to become subjects, and through its enforcement of the law their designated government, representing the general will of the united citizenry, forces its subjects to be free.

Rousseau was born in Geneva on June 28, 1712. As a young man in Paris he met influential philosophers and artists, and began his literary career around 1750. In 1762 he published *On the Social Contract*, in four short "books," and shortly thereafter a weighty treatise on education, *Emile*. Rousseau understood just as well as Plato that political philosophy and philosophy of education go hand in hand, since every state depends on the acquired knowledge and virtues of its citizens. Kant would later say of Rousseau's *Emile* that its publication was an event comparable to the French Revolution. But some of Rousseau's ideas were thought controversial, and he felt persecuted for them.

Book I

[. . .]

Chapter I
Subject of the First Book

Man is born free, and everywhere he is in chains. He who believes himself the master of others does not escape being more of a slave than they. How did this change take place? I have no idea. What can render it legitimate? I believe I can answer this question.

Were I to consider only force and the effect that flows from it, I would say that so long as a people is constrained to obey and does obey, it does well. As soon as it can shake off the yoke and does shake it off, it does even better. For by recovering its liberty by means of the same right that stole it, either the populace is justified in getting it back or else those who took it away were not justified in their actions. But the social order is a sacred right which serves as a foundation for all other rights. Nevertheless, this right does not come from nature. It is therefore founded upon convention. Before coming to that, I ought to substantiate what I just claimed.

[. . .]

Chapter III
On the Right of the Strongest

The strongest is never strong enough to be master all the time, unless he transforms force into right and obedience into duty. Hence the right of the strongest, a right that seems like something intended ironically and is actually established as a basic principle. But will no one explain this word to me? Force is a physical power; I fail to see what morality can result from its effects. To give in to force is an act of necessity, not of will. At most, it is an act of prudence. In what sense could it be a duty?

Let us suppose for a moment that there is such a thing as this alleged right. I maintain that all that results from it is an inexplicable mish-mash. For once force produces the right, the effect changes places with the cause. Every force that is superior to the first succeeds to its right. As soon as one can disobey with impunity, one can do so legitimately; and since the strongest is always right, the only thing to do is to make oneself the strongest. For what kind of right is it that perishes when the force on which it is based ceases? If one must obey because of force, one need not do so out of duty; and if one is no longer forced to obey one is no longer obliged. Clearly then, this word "right" adds nothing to force. It is utterly meaningless here.

Obey the powers that be. If that means giving in to force, the precept is sound, but superfluous. I reply it will never be violated. All power comes from God – I admit it – but so does every disease. Does this mean that calling in a physician is prohibited? If a brigand takes me by surprise at the edge of a wooded area, is it not only the case that I must surrender my purse, but even that I am in good conscience bound to surrender it, if I were able to withhold it? After all, the pistol he holds is also a power.

Let us then agree that force does not bring about right, and that one is obliged to obey only legitimate powers. Thus my original question keeps returning.

Chapter IV
On Slavery

Since no man has a natural authority over his fellow man, and since force does not give rise to any right, conventions therefore remain the basis of all legitimate authority among men.

If, says Grotius, a private individual can alienate his liberty and turn himself into the slave of a master, why could not an entire people alienate its liberty and turn itself into the subject of a king? There are many equivocal words here which need explanation, but let us confine ourselves to the word *alienate*. To alienate is to give or to sell. A man who makes himself the slave of someone else does not give himself; he sells himself, at least for his subsistence. But why does a people sell itself? Far from furnishing his subjects with their subsistence, a king derives his own from them alone, and, according to Rabelais, a king does not live cheaply. Do subjects then give their persons on the condition that their estate will also be taken? I fail to see what remains for them to preserve.

It will be said that the despot assures his subjects of civil tranquility. Very well. But what do they gain, if the wars his ambition drags them into, if his insatiable greed, if the oppressive demands caused by his ministers occasion more grief for his subjects than their own dissensions would have done? What do they gain, if this very tranquility is one of their miseries? A tranquil life is also had in dungeons; is that enough to make them desirable? The Greeks who were locked up in the Cyclops' cave lived a tranquil existence as they awaited their turn to be devoured.

To say that a man gives himself gratuitously is to say something absurd and inconceivable. Such an act is illegitimate and null, if only for the fact that he who commits it does not have his wits about him. To say the same thing of an entire populace is to suppose a populace composed of madmen. Madness does not bring about right.

Even if each person can alienate himself, he cannot alienate his children. They are born men and free. Their liberty belongs to them; they alone have the right to dispose of it. Before they have reached the age of reason, their father can, in their name, stipulate conditions for their maintenance and for their well-being. But he cannot give them irrevocably and unconditionally, for such a gift is contrary to the ends of nature and goes beyond the rights of paternity. For an arbitrary government to be legitimate, it would therefore be necessary in each generation for the people to be master of its acceptance or rejection. But in that event this government would no longer be arbitrary.

Renouncing one's liberty is renouncing one's dignity as a man, the rights of humanity and even its duties. There is no possible compensation for anyone who renounces everything. Such a renunciation is incompatible with the nature of man. Removing all morality from his actions is tantamount to taking away all liberty from his will. Finally, it is a vain and contradictory convention to stipulate absolute authority on one side and a limitless obedience on the other. Is it not clear that no commitments are made to a person from whom one has the right to demand everything? And does this condition alone not bring with it, without equivalent or exchange, the nullity of the act? For what right would my slave have against me, given that all he has belongs to me, and that, since his right is my right, my having a right against myself makes no sense?

Grotius and others derive from war another origin for the alleged right of slavery. Since, according to them, the victor has the right to kill the vanquished, these latter can repurchase their lives at the price of their liberty – a convention all the more legitimate, since it turns a profit for both of them.

But clearly this alleged right to kill the vanquished does not in any way derive from the state of war. Men are not naturally enemies, for the simple reason that men living in their original state of independence do not have sufficiently constant relationships among themselves to bring about either a state of peace or a state of war. It is the relationship between things and not that between men that brings about war. And since this state of war cannot come into existence from simple personal relations, but only from real [proprietary] relations, a private war between one man and another can exist neither in the state of nature, where there is no constant property, nor in the social state, where everything is under the authority of the laws.

Fights between private individuals, duels, encounters are not acts which produce a state. And with regard to private wars, authorized by the ordinances of King Louis IX of France and suspended by the Peace of God, they are abuses of feudal government, an absurd system if there ever was one, contrary to the principles of natural right and to all sound polity.

War is not therefore a relationship between one man and another, but a relationship between one state and another. In war private individuals are enemies only incidentally: not as men or even as citizens, but as soldiers; not as members of the homeland but as its defenders. Finally, each state can have as enemies only other states and not men, since there can be no real relationship between things of disparate natures.

This principle is even in conformity with the established maxims of all times and with the constant practice of all civilized peoples. Declarations of war are warnings not so much to powers as to their subjects. The foreigner (be he king, private individual, or a people) who robs, kills or detains subjects of another prince without declaring war on the prince, is not an enemy but a brigand. Even in the midst of war a just prince rightly appropriates to himself everything in an enemy country belonging to the public, but respects the person and goods of private individuals. He respects the rights upon which his own rights are founded. Since the purpose of war is the destruction of the enemy state, one has the right to kill the defenders of that state so long as they bear arms. But as soon as they lay down their arms and surrender, they cease to be enemies or instruments of the enemy. They return to being simply men; and one no longer has a right to their lives. Sometimes a state can be killed without a single one of its members being killed. For war does not grant a right that is unnecessary to its purpose. These principles are not those of Grotius. They are not based on the authority of poets. Rather they are derived from the nature of things; they are based on reason.

As to the right of conquest, the only basis it has is the law of the strongest. If war does not give the victor the right to massacre the vanquished peoples, this right (which he does not have) cannot be the basis for the right to enslave them. One has the right to kill the enemy only when one cannot enslave him. The right to enslave him does not therefore derive from the right to kill him. Hence it is an iniquitous exchange to make him buy his life, to which no one has any right, at the price of his liberty. In establishing the right of life and death on the right of slavery, and the right of slavery on the right of life and death, is it not clear that one falls into a vicious circle?

Even if we were to suppose that there were this terrible right to kill everyone, I maintain that neither a person enslaved during wartime nor a conquered people bears any obligation whatever toward its master, except to obey him for as long as it is forced to do so. In taking the equivalent of his life, the victor has done him no favor. Instead of killing him unprofitably he kills him usefully. Hence, far from the victor having acquired any authority over him beyond force, the state of war subsists between them just as before. Their relationship itself is the effect of war, and the usage of the right to war does not suppose any peace treaty. They have made a convention. Fine. But this convention, far from destroying the state of war, presupposes its continuation.

Thus, from every point of view, the right of slavery is null, not simply because it is illegitimate, but because it is absurd and meaningless. These words, *slavery* and *right*, are contradictory. They are mutually exclusive. Whether it is the statement of one man to another man, or one man to a people, the following sort of talk will always be equally nonsensical. *I make a convention with you which is wholly at your expense and wholly to my advantage; and, for as long as it pleases me, I will observe it and so will you.*

Chapter V
That It Is Always Necessary to Return to a First Convention

Even if I were to grant all that I have thus far refuted, the supporters of despotism would not be any better off. There will always be a great difference between subduing a multitude and ruling a society. If scattered men, however many they may be, were successively enslaved by a single individual, I see nothing there but a master and slaves; I do not see a people and its leader. It is, if you will, an aggregation, but not an association. There is neither a public good nor a body politic there. Even if that man had enslaved half the world, he is always just a private individual. His interest, separated from that of others, is never anything but a private interest. If this same man is about to die, after his passing his empire remains scattered and disunited, just as an oak tree dissolves and falls into a pile of ashes after fire has consumed it.

A people, says Grotius, can give itself to a king. According to Grotius, therefore, a people is a people before it gives itself to a king. This gift itself is a civil act; it presupposes a public deliberation. Thus, before examining the act whereby a people chooses a king, it would be well to examine the act whereby a people is a people. For since this act is necessarily prior to the other, it is the true foundation of society.

In fact, if there were no prior convention, then, unless the vote were unanimous, what would become of the minority's obligation to submit to the majority's choice, and where do one hundred who want a master get the right to vote for ten who do not? The law of majority rule is itself an established convention, and presupposes unanimity on at least one occasion.

Chapter VI
On the Social Compact

I suppose that men have reached the point where obstacles that are harmful to their maintenance in the state of nature gain the upper hand by their resistance to the forces that each individual can bring to bear to maintain himself in that state. Such being the case, that original state cannot subsist any longer, and the human race would perish if it did not alter its mode of existence.

For since men cannot engender new forces, but merely unite and direct existing ones, they have no other means of maintaining themselves but to form by aggregation a sum of forces that could gain the upper hand over the resistance, so that their forces are directed by means of a single moving power and made to act in concert.

This sum of forces cannot come into being without the cooperation of many. But since each man's force and liberty are the primary instruments of his maintenance, how is he going to engage them without hurting himself and without neglecting the care that he owes himself? This difficulty, seen in terms of my subject, can be stated in the following terms:

"Find a form of association which defends and protects with all common forces the person and goods of each associate, and by means of which each one, while uniting with all, nevertheless obeys only himself and remains as free as before?" This is the fundamental problem for which the social contract provides the solution.

The clauses of this contract are so determined by the nature of the act that the least modification renders them vain and ineffectual, that, although perhaps they have never been formally promulgated, they are everywhere the same, everywhere tacitly accepted and acknowledged. Once the social compact is violated, each person then regains his first rights and resumes his natural liberty, while losing the conventional liberty for which he renounced it.

These clauses, properly understood, are all reducible to a single one, namely the total alienation of each associate, together with all of his rights, to the entire community. For first of all, since each person gives himself whole and entire, the condition is equal for everyone; and since the condition is equal for everyone, no one has an interest in making it burdensome for the others.

Moreover, since the alienation is made without reservation, the union is as perfect as possible, and no associate has anything further to demand. For if some rights remained with private individuals, in the absence of any common superior who could decide between them and the public, each person would eventually claim to be his own judge in all things, since he is on some point his own judge. The state of nature would subsist and the association would necessarily become tyrannical or hollow.

Finally, in giving himself to all, each person gives himself to no one. And since there is no associate over whom he does not acquire the same right that he would grant others over himself, he gains the equivalent of everything he loses, along with a greater amount of force to preserve what he has.

If, therefore, one eliminates from the social compact whatever is not essential to it, one will find that it is reducible to the following terms. *Each of us places his person and all his power in common under the supreme direction of the general will; and as one we receive each member as an indivisible part of the whole.*

At once, in place of the individual person of each contracting party, this act of association produces a moral and collective body composed of as many members as there are voices in the assembly, which receives from this same act its unity, its common *self*, its life and its will. This public person, formed thus by union of all the others formerly took the name *city*, and at present takes the name *republic* or *body politic*, which is called *state* by its members when it is passive, *sovereign* when it is active, *power* when compared to others like itself. As to the associates, they collectively take the name *people*; individually they are called *citizens*, insofar as participants in the sovereign authority, and *subjects*, insofar as they are subjected to the laws of the state. But these terms are often confused and mistaken for one another. It is enough to know how to distinguish them when they are used with absolute precision.

Chapter VII
On the Sovereign

This formula shows that the act of association includes a reciprocal commitment between the public and private individuals, and that each individual, contracting, as it were, with himself, finds himself under a twofold commitment: namely as a member of the sovereign to private individuals, and as a member of the state toward the sovereign. But the maxim of civil law that no one is held to commitments made to himself cannot be applied here, for there is a considerable difference between being obligated to oneself, or to a whole of which one is a part.

It must be further noted that the public deliberation that can obligate all the subjects to the sovereign, owing to the two different relationships in which each of them is viewed, cannot, for the opposite reason, obligate the sovereign to itself, and that consequently it is contrary to the nature of the body politic that the sovereign impose upon itself a law it could not break. Since the sovereign can be considered under but one single relationship, it is then in the position of a private individual contracting with himself. Whence it is apparent that there neither is nor can be any type of fundamental law that is obligatory for the people as a body, not even the social contract. This does not mean that the whole body cannot perfectly well commit itself to another body with respect to things that do not infringe on this contract. For in regard to the foreigner, it becomes a simple being, an individual.

However, since the body politic or the sovereign derives its being exclusively from the sanctity of the contract, it can never obligate itself, not even to another power, to do anything that derogates from the original act, such as alienating some portion of itself or submitting to another sovereign. Violation of the act whereby it exists would be self-annihilation, and whatever is nothing produces nothing.

As soon as this multitude is thus united in a body, one cannot harm one of the members without attacking the whole body. It is even less likely that the body can be harmed without the members feeling it. Thus duty and interest equally obligate the two parties to come to one another's aid, and the same men should seek to combine in this two-fold relationship all the advantages that result from it.

For since the sovereign is formed entirely from the private individuals who make it up, it neither has nor could have an interest contrary to theirs. Hence, the sovereign power has no need to offer a guarantee to its subjects, since it is impossible for a body to want to harm all of its members, and, as we will see later, it cannot harm any one of them in particular. The sovereign, by the mere fact that it exists, is always all that it should be.

But the same thing cannot be said of the subjects in relation to the sovereign, for which, despite their common interest, their commitments would be without substance if it did not find ways of being assured of their fidelity.

In fact, each individual can, as a man, have a private will contrary to or different from the general will that he has as a citizen. His private interest can speak to him in an entirely different manner than the common interest. His absolute and naturally independent existence can cause him to envisage what he owes the common cause as a gratuitous contribution, the loss of which will be less harmful to others than its payment is burdensome to him. And in viewing the moral person which constitutes the state as a being of reason because it is not a man, he would enjoy the rights of a citizen without wanting to fulfill the duties of a subject, an injustice whose growth would bring about the ruin of the body politic.

Thus, in order for the social compact to avoid being an empty formula, it tacitly entails the commitment – which alone can give force to the others – that whoever refuses to obey the general will will be forced to do so by the entire body. This means merely that he will be forced to be free. For this is the sort of condition that, by giving each citizen to the homeland, guarantees him against all personal dependence – a condition that produces the skill and the performance of the political machine, and which alone bestows legitimacy upon civil commitments. Without it such commitments would be absurd, tyrannical and subject to the worst abuses.

Chapter VIII
On the Civil State

This passage from the state of nature to the civil state produces quite a remarkable change in man, for it substitutes justice for instinct in his behavior and gives his actions a moral quality they previously lacked. Only then, when the voice of duty replaces physical impulse and right replaces appetite, does man, who had hitherto taken only himself into account, find himself forced to act upon other principles and to consult his reason before listening to his inclinations. Although in this state he deprives himself of several of the advantages belonging to him in the state of nature, he regains such great ones. His faculties are exercised and developed, his ideas are broadened, his feelings are ennobled, his entire soul is elevated to such a height that, if the abuse of this new condition did not often lower his status to beneath the level he left, he ought constantly to bless the happy moment that pulled him away from it forever and which transformed him from a stupid, limited animal into an intelligent being and a man.

Let us summarize this entire balance sheet so that the credits and debits are easily compared. What man loses through the social contract is his natural liberty and an unlimited right to everything that tempts him and that he can acquire. What he gains is civil liberty and the proprietary ownership of all he possesses. So as not to be in error in these compensations, it is necessary to draw a careful distinction between natural liberty (which is limited solely by the force of the individual involved) and civil liberty (which is limited by the general will), and between possession (which is merely the effect of the force or the right of the first occupant) and proprietary ownership (which is based solely on a positive title).

To the preceding acquisitions could be added the acquisition in the civil state of moral liberty, which alone makes man truly the master of himself. For to be driven by appetite alone is slavery, and obedience to the law one has prescribed for oneself is liberty. But I have already said too much on this subject, and the philosophical meaning of the word *liberty* is not my subject here.

[. . .]

Book II

[. . .]

Chapter III
Whether the General Will Can Err

It follows from what has preceded that the general will is always right and always tends toward the public utility. However, it does not follow that the deliberations of the people always have the same rectitude. We always want what is good for us, but we do not always see what it is. The populace is never corrupted, but it is often tricked, and only then does it appear to want what is bad.

There is often a great deal of difference between the will of all and the general will. The latter considers only the general interest, whereas the former considers private interest and is merely the sum of private wills. But remove from these same wills the pluses and minuses that cancel each other out, and what remains as the sum of the differences is the general will.

If, when a sufficiently informed populace deliberates, the citizens were to have no communication among themselves, the general will would always result from the large number of small differences, and the deliberation would always be good. But when intrigues and partial associations come into being at the expense of the large association, the will of each of these associations becomes general in relation to its members and particular in relation to the state. It can be said, then, that there are no longer as many voters as there are men, but merely as many as there are associations. The differences become less numerous and yield a result that is less general. Finally, when one of these associations is so large that it dominates all the others, the result is no longer a sum of minor differences, but a single difference. Then there is no longer a general will, and the opinion that dominates is merely a private opinion.

For the general will to be well articulated, it is therefore important that there should be no partial society in the state and that each citizen make up his own mind. Such was the unique and sublime institution of the great Lycurgus. If there are partial societies, their number must be multiplied and inequality among them prevented, as was done by Solon, Numa and Servius. These precautions are the only effective way of bringing it about that the general will is always enlightened and that the populace is not tricked.

Chapter IV
On the Limits of Sovereign Power

If the state or the city is merely a moral person whose life consists in the union of its members, and if the most important of its concerns is that of its own conservation, it ought to have a universal compulsory force to move and arrange each part in the manner best suited to the whole. Just as nature gives each man an absolute power over all his members, the social compact gives the body politic an absolute power over all its members, and it is the same power which, as I have said, is directed by the general will and bears the name sovereignty.

But over and above the public person, we need to consider the private persons who make it up and whose life and liberty are naturally independent of it. It is, therefore, a question of making a rigorous distinction between the respective rights of the citizens and the sovereign, and between the duties the former have to fulfill as subjects and the natural right they should enjoy as men.

We grant that each person alienates, by the social compact, only that portion of his power, his goods, and liberty whose use is of consequence to the community; but we must also grant that only the sovereign is the judge of what is of consequence.

A citizen should render to the state all the services he can as soon as the sovereign demands them. However, for its part, the sovereign cannot impose on the subjects any fetters that are of no use to the community. It cannot even will to do so, for under the law of reason nothing takes place without a cause, any more than under the law of nature.

The commitments that bind us to the body politic are obligatory only because they are mutual, and their nature is such that in fulfilling them one cannot work for someone else without also working for oneself. Why is the general will always right, and why do all constantly want the happiness of each of them, if not because everyone applies the word *each* to himself and thinks of himself as he votes for all? This proves that the quality of right and the notion of justice it produces are derived from the preference each person gives himself, and thus from the nature of man; that the general will, to be really such, must be general in its object as well as in its essence; that it must derive from all in order to be applied to all; and that it loses its natural rectitude when it tends toward any individual, determinate object. For then, judging what is foreign to us, we have no true principle of equity to guide us.

In effect, once it is a question of a state of affairs or a particular right concerning a point that has not been regulated by a prior, general convention, the issue becomes contentious. It is a suit in which the interested private individuals are one of the parties and the public the other, but in which I fail to see either what law should be followed or what judge should render the decision. In these circumstances it would be ridiculous to want to defer to an express decision of the general will, which can only be the conclusion reached by one of its parts, and which, for the other party, therefore, is merely an alien, particular will, inclined on this occasion to injustice and subject to error. Thus, just as a private will cannot represent the general will, the general will, for its part, alters its nature when it has a particular object; and as general, it is unable to render a decision on either a man or a state of affairs. When, for example, the populace of Athens appointed or dismissed its leaders, decreed that honors be bestowed on one or inflicted penalties on another, and by a multitude of particular decrees, indiscriminately exercised all the acts of government, the people in this case no longer had a general will in the strict sense. It no longer functioned as sovereign but as magistrate. This will appear contrary to commonly held opinions, but I must be given time to present my own.

It should be seen from this that what makes the will general is not so much the number of votes as the common interest that unites them, for in this institution each person necessarily submits himself to the conditions he imposes on others, an admirable accord between interest and justice which bestows on common deliberations a quality of equity that disappears when any particular matter is discussed, for lack of a common interest uniting and identifying the role of the judge with that of the party.

From whatever viewpoint one approaches this principle, one always arrives at the same conclusion, namely that the social compact establishes among the citizens an equality of such a kind that they all commit themselves under the same conditions and should all enjoy the same rights. Thus by the very nature of the compact, every act of sovereignty (that is, every authentic act of the general will) obligates or favors all citizens equally, so that the sovereign knows only the nation as a body and does not draw distinctions between any of those members that make it up. Strictly speaking, then, what is an act of sovereignty? It is not a convention between a superior and an inferior, but a convention of the body with each of its members. This convention is legitimate, because it has the social contract as a basis; equitable, because it is common to all; useful, because it can have only the general good for its object; and solid, because it has the public force and the supreme power as a guarantee. So long as the subjects are subordinated only to such convention, they obey no one but their own will alone. And asking how far the respective rights of the sovereign and the citizens extend is asking how far the latter can commit themselves to one another, each to all and all to each.

We can see from this that the sovereign power, absolute, wholly sacred and inviolable as it is, does not and cannot exceed the limits of general conventions, and that every man can completely dispose of such goods and freedom as has been left to him by these conventions. This results in the fact that the sovereign never has the right to lay more charges on one subject than on another, because in that case the matter becomes particular, no longer within the range of the sovereign's competence.

Once these distinctions are granted, it is so false that there is, in the social contract, any genuine renunciation on the part of private individuals that their situation, as a result of this contract, is really preferable to what it was beforehand; and, instead of an alienation, they have merely made an advantageous exchange of an uncertain and precarious mode of existence for another that is better and surer. Natural independence is exchanged for liberty; the power to harm others is exchanged for their own security; and their force, which others could overcome, for a right which the social union renders invincible. Their life itself, which they have devoted to the state, is continually protected by it; and when they risk their lives for its defense, what are they then doing but returning to the state what they have received from it? What are they doing, that they did not do more frequently and with greater danger in the state of nature, when they would inevitably have to fight battles, defending at the peril of their lives the means of their preservation? It is true that everyone has to fight, if necessary, for the homeland; but it also is the case that no one ever has to fight on his own behalf. Do we not still gain by running, for something that brings about our security, a portion of the risks we would have to run for ourselves once our security is taken away?

[. . .]

Book III

[. . .]

Chapter I
On Government in General

I am warning the reader that this chapter should be read carefully and that I do not know the art of being clear to those who do not want to be attentive.

Every free action has two causes that come together to produce it. The one is moral, namely the will that determines the act; the other is physical, namely the power that executes it. When I walk toward an object, I must first want to go there. Second, my feet must take me there. A paralyzed man who wants to walk or an agile man who does not want to walk will both remain where they are. The body politic has the same moving causes. The same distinction can be made between force and the will; the one under the name *legislative power* and the other under the name *executive power*. Nothing is done and ought to be done without their concurrence.

We have seen that legislative power belongs to the people and can belong to it alone. On the contrary, it is easy to see, by the principles established above, that executive power cannot belong to the people at large in its role as legislator or sovereign, since this power consists solely of particular acts that are not within the province of the law, nor consequently of the sovereign, none of whose acts can avoid being laws.

Therefore the public force must have an agent of its own that unifies it and gets it working in accordance with the directions of the general will, that serves as a means of communication between the state and the sovereign, and that accomplishes in the public person just about what the union of soul and body accomplishes in man. This is the reason for having government in the state, something often badly confused with the sovereign, of which it is merely the minister.

What then is the government? An intermediate body established between the subjects and the sovereign for their mutual communication, and charged with the execution of the laws and the preservation of liberty, both civil and political.

The members of this body are called magistrates or *kings*, that is to say, *governors*, and the entire body bears the name *prince*. Therefore those who claim that the act by which a people submits itself to leaders is not a contract are quite correct. It is absolutely nothing but a commission, an employment in which the leaders, as simple officials of the sovereign, exercise in its own name the power with which it has entrusted them. The sovereign can limit, modify, or appropriate this power as it pleases, since the alienation of such a right is incompatible with the nature of the social body and contrary to the purpose of the association.

Therefore, I call *government* or supreme administration the legitimate exercise of executive power; I call prince or magistrate the man or the body charged with that administration.

In government one finds the intermediate forces whose relationships make up that of the whole to the whole or of the sovereign to the state. This last relationship can be represented as one between the extremes of a continuous proportion, whose proportional mean is the government. The government receives from the sovereign the orders it gives the people, and, for the state to be in good equilibrium, there must, all things considered, be an equality between the output or the power of the government, taken by itself, and the output or power of the citizens, who are sovereigns on the one hand and subjects on the other.

Moreover, none of these three terms could be altered without the simultaneous destruction of the proportion. If the sovereign wishes to govern, or if the magistrate wishes to give laws, or if the subjects refuse to obey, disorder replaces rule, force and will no longer act in concert, and thus the state dissolves and falls into despotism or anarchy. Finally, since there is only one proportional mean between each relationship, there is only one good government possible for a state. But since a thousand events can change the relationships of a people, not only can different governments be good for different peoples, but also for the same people at different times.

In trying to provide an idea of the various relationships that can obtain between these two extremes, I will take as an example the number of people, since it is a more easily expressed relationship.

Suppose the state is composed of ten thousand citizens. The sovereign can only be considered collectively and as a body. But each private individual in his position as a subject is regarded as an individual. Thus the sovereign is to the subject as ten thousand is to one. In other words, each member of the state has as his share only one ten-thousandth of the sovereign authority, even though he is totally in subjection to it. If the populace is made up of a hundred thousand men, the condition of the subjects does not change, and each bears equally the entire dominion of the laws, while his vote, reduced to one hundred-thousandth, has ten times less influence in the drafting of them. In that case, since the subject always remains one, the ratio of the sovereign to the subject increases in proportion to the number of citizens. Whence it follows that the larger the state becomes, the less liberty there is.

When I say that the ratio increases, I mean that it places a distance between itself and equality. Thus the greater the ratio is in the sense employed by geometricians, the less relationship there is in the everyday sense of the word. In the former sense, the ratio, seen in terms of quantity, is measured by the quotient; in the latter sense, ratio, seen in terms of identity, is reckoned by similarity.

Now the less relationship there is between private wills and the general will, that is, between mores and the laws, the more repressive force ought to increase. Therefore, in order to be good, the government must be relatively stronger in proportion as the populace is more numerous.

On the other hand, as the growth of the state gives the trustees of the public authority more temptations and the means of abusing their power, the more the force the government must have in order to contain the people, the more the force the sovereign must have in order to contain the government. I am speaking here not of an absolute force but of the relative force of the various parts of the state.

It follows from this twofold relationship that the continuous proportion between the sovereign, the prince and the people, is in no way an arbitrary idea, but a necessary consequence of the nature of the body politic. It also follows that since one of the extremes, namely the people as subject, is fixed and represented by unity, whenever the doubled ratio increases or decreases, the simple ratio increases or decreases in like fashion, and that as a consequence the middle term is changed. This makes it clear that there is no unique and absolute constitution of government, but that there can be as many governments of differing natures as there are states of differing sizes.

If, in ridiculing this system, someone were to say that in order to find this proportional mean and to form the body of the government, it is necessary merely, in my opinion, to derive the square root of the number of people, I would reply that here I am taking this number only as an example; that the relationships I am speaking of are not measured solely by the number of men, but in general by the quantity of action, which is the combination of a multitude of causes; and that, in addition, if to express myself in fewer words I borrow for the moment the terminology of geometry, I nevertheless am not unaware of the fact that geometrical precision has no place in moral quantities.

The government is on a small scale what the body politic which contains it is on a large scale. It is a moral person endowed with certain faculties, active like the sovereign and passive like the state, and capable of being broken down into other similar relationships whence there arises as a consequence a new proportion and yet again another within this one according to the order of tribunals, until an indivisible middle term is reached; that is, a single leader or supreme magistrate, who can be represented in the midst of this progression as the unity between the series of fractions and that of whole numbers.

Without involving ourselves in this multiplication of terms, let us content ourselves with considering the government as a new body in the state, distinct from the people and sovereign, and intermediate between them.

The essential difference between these two bodies is that the state exists by itself, while the government exists only through the sovereign. Thus the dominant will of the prince is not and should not be anything other than the general will or the law. His force is merely the public force concentrated in him. As soon as he wants to derive from himself some absolute and independent act, the bond that links everything together begins to come loose. If it should finally happen that the prince had a private will more active than that of the sovereign, and that he had made use of some of the public force that is available to him in order to obey this private will, so that there would be, so to speak, two sovereigns – one de jure and the other de facto, at that moment the social union would vanish and the body politic would be dissolved.

However, for the body of the government to have an existence, a real life that distinguishes it from the body of the state, and for all its members to be able to act in concert and to fulfill the purpose for which it is instituted, there must be a particular *self*, a sensibility common to all its members, a force or will of its own that tends toward its preservation. This particular existence presupposes assemblies, councils, a power to deliberate and decide, rights, titles and privileges that belong exclusively to the prince and that render the condition of the magistrate more honorable in proportion as it is more onerous. The difficulties lie in the manner in which this subordinate whole is so organized within the whole, that it in no way alters the general constitution by strengthening its own, that it always distinguishes its particular force, which is intended for its own preservation, from the public force intended for the preservation of the state, and that, in a word, it is always ready to sacrifice the government to the people and not the people to the government.

In addition, although the artificial body of the government is the work of another artificial body and has, in a sense, only a borrowed and subordinate life, this does not prevent it from being capable of acting with more or less vigor or speed, or from enjoying, so to speak, more or less robust health. Finally, without departing directly from the purpose of its institution, it can deviate more or less from it, according to the manner in which it is constituted.

From all these differences arise the diverse relationships that the government should have with the body of the state, according to the accidental and particular relationships by which the state itself is modified. For often the government that is best in itself will become the most vicious, if its relationships are not altered according to the defects of the body politic to which it belongs.

[. . .]

Chapter IX
On the Signs of a Good Government

When the question arises which one is absolutely the best government, an insoluble question is being raised because it is indeterminate. Or, if you wish, it has as many good answers as there are possible combinations in the absolute and relative positions of peoples.

But if it is asked by what sign it is possible to know that a given people is well or poorly governed, this is another matter, and the question of fact could be resolved.

However, nothing is answered, since each wants to answer it in his own way. The subjects praise public tranquillity; the citizens praise the liberty of private individuals. The former prefers the security of possessions; the latter that of persons. The former has it that the best government is the one that is most severe; the latter maintains that the best government is the one that is mildest. This one wants crimes to be punished, and that one wants them prevented. The former think it a good thing to be feared by their neighbors; the latter prefer to be ignored by them. The one is content so long as money circulates; the other demands that the people have bread. Even if agreement were had on these and similar points, would we be any closer to an answer? Since moral quantities do not allow of precise measurement, even if there were agreement regarding the sign, how could there be agreement regarding the evaluation.

For my part, I am always astonished that such a simple sign is overlooked or that people are of such bad faith as not to agree on it. What is the goal of the political association? It is the preservation and prosperity of its members. And what is the surest sign that they are preserved and prospering? It is their number and their population. Therefore do not go looking elsewhere for this much disputed sign. All other things being equal, the government under which, without external means, without naturalizations, without colonies, the citizens become populous and multiply the most, is infallibly the best government. That government under which a populace diminishes and dies out is the worst. Calculators, it is now up to you. Count, measure, compare.

[. . .]

Chapter XVI
That the Institution of Government Is Not a Contract

Once the legislative power has been well established, it is a matter of establishing the executive power in the same way. For this latter, which functions only by means of particular acts, not being of the essence of the former, is naturally separate from it. Were it possible for the sovereign, considered as such, to have the executive power, right and fact would be so completely confounded that we would no longer know what is law and what is not. And the body politic, thus denatured, would soon fall prey to the violence against which it was instituted.

Since the citizens are all equal by the social contract, what everyone should do can be prescribed by everyone. On the other hand, no one has the right to demand that someone else do what he does not do for himself. Now it is precisely this right, indispensable for making the body politic live and move, that the sovereign gives the prince in instituting the government.

Several people have claimed that this act of establishment was a contract between the populace and the leaders it gives itself, a contract by which are stipulated between the two parties the conditions under which the one obliges itself to command and the other to obey. It will be granted, I am sure, that this is a strange way of entering into a social contract! But let us see if this opinion is tenable.

First, the supreme authority cannot be modified any more than it can be alienated; to limit it is to destroy it. It is absurd and contradictory for the sovereign to acquire a superior. To obligate oneself to obey a master is to return to full liberty.

Moreover, it is evident that this contract between the people and some or other persons would be a particular act. Whence it follows that this contract could be neither a law nor an act of sovereignty, and that consequently it would be illegitimate.

It is also clear that the contracting parties would, in relation to one another, be under only the law of nature and without any guarantee of their reciprocal commitments, which is contrary in every way to the civil state. Since the one who has force at his disposal is always in control of its employment, it would come to the same thing if we were to give the name contract to the act of a man who would say to another, "I am giving you all my goods, on the condition that you give me back whatever you wish."

There is only one contract in the state, that of the association, and that alone excludes any other. It is impossible to imagine any public contract that was not a violation of the first contract.

Chapter XVII
On the Institution of the Government

What should be the terms under which we should conceive the act by which the government is instituted? I will begin by saying that this act is complex or composed of two others, namely the establishment of the law and the execution of the law.

By the first, the sovereign decrees that there will be a governing body established under some or other form. And it is clear that this act is a law.

By the second, the people names the leaders who will be placed in charge of the established government. And since this nomination is a particular act, it is not a second law, but merely a consequence of the first and a function of the government.

The problem is to understand how there can be an act of government before a government exists, and how the people, which is only sovereign or subject, can in certain circumstances become prince or magistrate.

Moreover, it is here that we discover one of those remarkable properties of the body politic, by which it reconciles seemingly contradictory operations. For this takes place by a sudden conversion of sovereignty into democracy, so that, without any noticeable change, and solely by a new relation of all to all, the citizens, having become magistrates, pass from general to particular acts, and from the law to its execution.

This change of relation is not a speculative subtlety without exemplification in practice. It takes place everyday in the English Parliament, where the lower chamber on certain occasions turns itself into a committee of the whole in order to discuss better the business of the sovereign court, thus becoming the simple commission of the sovereign court (the latter being what it was the moment before), so that it later reports to itself, as the House of Commons, the result of what it has just settled in the committee of the whole, and deliberates all over again under one title about what it had already settled under another.

The peculiar advantage to democratic government is that it can be established in actual fact by a simple act of the general will. After this, the provisional government remains in power, if this is the form adopted, or establishes in the name of the sovereign the government prescribed by the law; and thus everything is in accordance with the rule. It is not possible to institute the government in any other legitimate way without renouncing the principles established above.

Part VI

Moral Philosophy

Introduction

The central controversy in moral philosophy among philosophers of the eighteenth century was over the source of moral knowledge. Do we distinguish between right and wrong, virtue and vice, by means of the senses, as the empiricists said, or by means of the intellect, as the rationalists held? Empiricist philosophers claimed that moral ideas must enter our consciousness through some sensory avenue. Since we typically care about right and wrong, and since these ideas typically move us to action, empiricists presumed that right and wrong must be connected somehow with feelings of pleasure and pain. Rationalist philosophers, on the other hand, pointed out that everyone recognizes a difference between what is pleasant and what is good, and that everyone understands that sometimes doing the right thing can be unpleasant. Rationalists accordingly pointed to understanding or reason as the source of moral ideas, and often claimed that these ideas themselves have the power to move us to action, regardless of what pleasures or displeasures may be involved in the circumstances. The common assumption of both moral empiricists and moral rationalists of the eighteenth century was that, once we identify the correct source for ideas of right and wrong, we will be able to settle ethical and political controversies with confidence.

In the readings that follow, the empiricist tradition in ethics is represented by selections from the writings of the Scottish moral sentimentalists David Hume and Adam Smith (1723–90), and the English utilitarian thinker Jeremy Bentham (1748–1832). Rationalism in ethics is represented below by selections taken from the writings of Samuel Clarke and Immanuel Kant. Included here also are selections from a few writers mainly critical of moral sentimentalism: Richard Price (1723–91) and Thomas Reid. Mary Wollstonecraft (1759–97), whose ideas harmonize with moral rationalism, shows how ethical thought lends itself naturally to political critique. From a survey of the principle figures of late modern moral philosophy it is possible to identify four general approaches to ethics: moral sentimentalism, moral rationalism, utilitarianism, and virtue theory.

Moral Sentimentalism

Francis Hutcheson (1694–1746) was a professor of moral philosophy at Glasgow University, whose original ideas greatly influenced subsequent thinkers in Scotland and abroad. It was

Hutcheson's idea that moral right and wrong, virtue and vice, are known through a divinely implanted "moral sense," a kind of "sixth sense" for the moral qualities of actions. He believed that human beings are capable of feeling pleasure and displeasure in the contemplation of actions which may have no bearing on their own interests. Imagine two people you do not know, who are also strangers to one another. Suppose also that you meet them in circumstances where the one is doing something to help the other: perhaps the one is saving the other from drowning in a river. You would naturally feel pleasure in thinking about the helping or benevolent action of this hero, Hutcheson said. This is because God has implanted a special "moral sense" in each of us, creating a world in which we are happy when surrounded by benevolently motivated agents.

A good way to understand Hume's thoughts in moral philosophy is to see him as taking on the project of separating Hutcheson's theory of the moral sense from its theological roots. Hume attributed our feelings of pleasure and displeasure as spectators of others' actions to a principle in human nature that he identified as *sympathy*, the ability to experience the same kind of feelings others have. He thought that our moral judgments are, under certain circumstances, based on sympathetic feelings, but that the motivation to act virtuously comes from traits of character (our being benevolent, kind, prudent, and so on). Hume was interested also in developing a theory of justice, since Hutcheson's work had focused on benevolence, and many doubted that justice could be understood correctly as a form of benevolent conduct.

Adam Smith, an admirer of both Hutcheson and Hume, proposed that a natural mechanism of sympathetic feeling is what accounts for our moral behavior toward one another. Human beings naturally share in the feelings and passions of others, he explained, and therefore our conduct is often influenced by how we feel about the feelings of others. This is different from Hume's view insofar as Smith thought that the motivation toward other-regarding actions comes from the mechanism of sympathy itself. Smith believed, therefore, that we do not need to posit a sixth sense, as Hutcheson did, in order to explain why people prefer to benefit strangers when they can, and would rather avoid harming them.

But critics of moral sentimentalism, such as Richard Price, could not agree that the moral qualities of action are like secondary qualities of objects, dependent wholly upon the sensations or feelings of observers. Thomas Reid likewise opposed sentimentalism, arguing that we each know right from wrong though active judgments of our own conscience, and not merely through passive sensations of pleasure or pain. (See the General Introduction to this volume for some of the positive contributions of Price and Reid to moral philosophy.)

Moral Rationalism

Where scientific observation provided the model for empiricists, rationalist philosophers were inspired more by mathematical reasoning, even in moral philosophy. Numbers and figures exhibit eternal relations of proportion and congruence, and people around the world calculate in the same way with common ideas such as equality, multiple, unit, and sum. So rationalists in ethics sometimes found the comparison between moral ideas and concepts of mathematics or logic irresistible. Clarke, for example, emphasized the point that human relations, just like mathematical relations, exhibit "fitness" and "just proportions." In the nature of the relation between God and his creatures, or between king and subject or parent and child, we find moral duties proportioned to each partner's role in the relationship. To act contrary to such duties, said Clarke, is as absurd as believing that the part is greater than the whole, or that the effect is more powerful than the cause.

As we see below in two reading selections from Kant, he claimed that "practical reasoning" gives us moral rules that identify our duties. One selection emphasizes the version of his supreme moral principle (the "categorical imperative") that demands logically consistent willing for all, that is: "Act only on the maxim that you can at the same time will to become a universal law." The second selection emphasizes what Kant took to be an equivalent formula of the supreme moral principle, concerned with the practical logic of choosing means to ends: "So act that you use humanity, whether in your own person or in the person of any other, always at the same time as an end, never merely as a means."

Utilitarianism

The empiricist moral theory most prominent among moral philosophers today is the theory of utilitarianism, which has its modern roots in the writings of Bentham. Bentham's follower John Stuart Mill (1806–73) would later formulate the classical statement of the "Principle of Utility" in this way: "Actions are right in proportion as they tend to produce happiness; wrong as they tend to produce the reverse of happiness. By happiness is intended pleasure and the absence of pain; by unhappiness, pain and the privation of pleasure." It was always the utilitarians' intention to emphasize the consequences of actions or social policies for *overall* happiness. That is why they sometimes called the "Principle of Utility" the "Greatest Happiness Principle," and affirmed the slogan: "The Greatest Happiness for the Greatest Number." Based on Bentham's analysis of the different kinds and degrees of pleasure, which is found in the reading selection below, Mill likewise emphasized a distinction between the "quantity" and "quality" of happiness, pointing out that "It is better to be a human being dissatisfied than a pig satisfied; better to be Socrates dissatisfied than a fool satisfied."

Despite the central importance of pleasure and pain for classical, "hedonistic" utilitarians like Bentham and Mill, their theory encounters a difficulty similar to that of the moral rationalists. How can we expect people to be moved to action by abstract ideas of overall happiness, especially if the principle of utility requires them to sacrifice their own happiness for that of others? Utilitarian thinkers preoccupied with "universal benevolence" have also had difficulties explaining the evident priority of justice over benevolence. Justice seems often to demand actions that may adversely affect overall happiness. Some actions and policies are simply unfair, regardless of whom, and how many, they may benefit. A third line of critique often leveled against utilitarian thinkers has been that the moral qualities of actions are properly seen to be features of those actions themselves, and not to be based on their consequences. Lying, promise-breaking, and punishing the innocent seem to most people to be wrong just in their very nature or conception. But utilitarian theorists tell us instead that no actions are right or wrong by their very nature; right and wrong depend always on consequences. So depending on its consequences, an act of punishing the innocent may well be the right thing to do.

Virtue Theory

In a widely cited article published in 1958 entitled "Modern Moral Philosophy," the British philosopher G. E. M. Anscombe offered a critique of the approaches to ethics that had emerged from the modern period. Since that time, in her view, moral philosophers had been too exclusively interested in ethical concepts such as right action, obligation, duty, and consequences. To do ethics properly, she argued, it would be necessary to return to some "pre-modern," even ancient, approaches that emphasized moral character and virtue. But it would be a mistake to think that philosophers in the modern period were negligent in the theory of virtue.

Hume is an excellent example of a modern moral philosopher taking the virtue approach. His sentimentalist theory lends itself well to making "virtue" the primary ethical concept. As will be seen in the reading selections from Hume below, what initially stimulates our "moral sense" is the attractive or deplorable character traits of the people we observe (including ourselves). That is why, as Hume explained, we approve or disapprove of people's actions always on the basis of their motives; for their motives, to the extent that we can discern them, reveal their inner character.

It was mentioned above that Mary Wollstonecraft's views on ethics tended toward a rationalist approach. But virtue is a primary concern of her critique of contemporary society. She saw how prevailing attitudes and prejudices denied girls and women the opportunity to develop the virtues characteristic of their sex.

In addition to exemplifying the four approaches to ethics just identified, the authors of several of the reading selections below contribute to a controversy of interest to moral philosophers even today. This is a debate over the goodness or moral value of "the motive of duty." Hume had argued near the end of the 1730s that "the sense of duty" was not a very good motive for moral action. But Adam Smith later disagreed. He claimed that, at least in the case of just actions, we expect people to be moved to do them by the thought that it is their duty to do so; but it is not proper, among friends or family, or in the case of beneficent or grateful actions, for people act coldly "from duty." Next in line to oppose Hume's argument on this point was Reid, whose view was that moral actions ought always to be done with a regard to the fact of their being required by duty. This is a position most contemporary philosophers will recognize as having been made famous by Kant. For he claimed that actions have "moral worth" only when they are done from motive of duty *alone*. Bentham took yet a fourth position in this ongoing debate by arguing, on utilitarian grounds, that no motive is by itself either a good one or a bad one.

In selecting the readings below we have been concerned about presenting the writings of the eighteenth-century moral philosophers who have been most influential, while also including briefer selections from less well known thinkers who contributed much to the philosophical climate of their own age. We have also been concerned about presenting texts accessible to students. Fortunately, a good number of writers in this period produced philosophically interesting contributions to ethics that were not technically impenetrable.

Samuel Clarke, *Discourse concerning the Unchangeable Obligations of Natural Religion* (1705)

Among the questions asked by the eighteenth-century moralists were questions about the source of morality and how we discover it. Samuel Clarke argued that there are "eternal and immutable" relations among persons and things in nature, and that these relations establish certain unchangeable duties of persons toward each other. These relationships make some actions a better fit with nature than others. Clarke used analogies to math and geometry to explain what he meant. For example, he wrote, "That God is infinitely superior to Men, is as clear, as that Infinity is larger than a Point, or Eternity longer than a Moment." It is fitting, then, that people honor and obey God, and so they have a duty to do so. Among our duties to one another is the obligation to promote the welfare of all, which is much more befitting our relations with others than our trying to destroy each other. Clarke saw our moral obligations as necessary and certain in the way that mathematics is. Furthermore, while God is not the author of morality on Clarke's view, God's will coincides with its dictates.

It follows from Clarke's theory that any rational person can understand these universal relations and so know the difference between right and wrong. Since he held that reason by itself, without appeal to experience or feeling, can discern moral obligation, he was a moral rationalist. Clarke's ideas about duties based on eternal relations seemed incorrect to Hume, however, so he posed the following kind of counter-proof. If Clarke is correct in basing moral ideas on abstract relations such as those between parent and child, then it should not matter whether human beings or plants or animals stand in such relations. But no one thinks that puppies have moral duties to their parents, and when a tree grows to overshadow and kill its parent we do not charge it with murder! From these examples it follows that moral right and wrong must be based on something other than mere relations and proportions.

Clarke's *Discourse* was originally presented in a famous series of lectures named for the British scientist Robert Boyle, who left in his will an endowment for annual lectures in defense of Christianity against the encroaching discoveries of science.

I. The same necessary and eternal *different relations*, that different things bear one to another; and the same consequent *fitness* or *unfitness* of the application of different things or different relations one to another; with regard to which, the will of God always and necessarily *does* determine itself, to choose to act only what is agreeable to justice, equity, goodness and truth, in order to the welfare of the whole universe; *ought* likewise constantly to determine the wills of all subordinate rational beings, to govern all their actions by the same rules, for the good of the public, in their respective stations. That is; these eternal and necessary differences of things make it *fit and reasonable* for creatures so to act; they cause it to be their *duty*, or lay an *obligation* upon them, so to do; even separate from the consideration of these rules being the *positive will* or *command of God*; and also antecedent to any respect or regard, expectation or apprehension, of any *particular private and personal advantage or disadvantage, reward or punishment*, either present or future; annexed either by natural consequence, or by positive appointment, to the practising or neglecting of those rules.

The several parts of this proposition, may be proved distinctly, in the following manner.

1. That there are differences of things; and different relations, respects or proportions, of some things towards others; is as evident and undeniable, as that one magnitude or number, is greater, equal to, or smaller than another. That from these different relations of different things, there necessarily arises an agreement or disagreement of some things with others, or a fitness or unfitness of the application of different things or different relations one to another; is likewise as plain, as that there is any such thing as proportion or disproportion in geometry and arithmetic, or uniformity or difformity in comparing together the respective figures of bodies. Further, that there is a fitness or suitableness of certain circumstances to certain persons, and an unsuitableness of others; founded in the nature of things and the qualifications of persons, antecedent to all positive appointment whatsoever; also that from the different relations of different persons one to another, there necessarily arises a fitness or unfitness of certain manners of behaviour of some persons towards others: is as manifest, as that the properties which flow from the essences of different mathematical figures, have different congruities or incongruities between themselves; or that, in mechanics, certain weights or powers have very different forces, and different effects one upon another, according to their different distances, or different positions and situations in respect of each other. For instance: that God is infinitely superior to men; is as clear, as that infinity is larger than a point, or eternity longer than a moment. And it is as certainly fit, that men should honour and worship, obey and imitate God, rather than on the contrary in all their actions endeavour to dishonour and disobey him; as it is certainly true, that they have an entire dependence on him, and he on the contrary can in no respect receive any advantage from them; and not only so, but also that his will is as certainly and unalterably just and equitable in giving his commands, as his power is irresistible in requiring submission to it. Again; it is a thing absolutely and necessarily fitter in itself, that the supreme author and creator of the universe, should govern, order, and direct all things to certain constant and regular ends; than that every thing should be permitted to go on at adventures, and produce uncertain effects merely by chance and in the utmost confusion, without any determinate view or design at all. It is a thing manifestly fitter in itself, that the all-powerful governor of the world, should do always what is best in the whole, and what tends most to the universal good of the whole creation; than that he should make the whole continually miserable; or that, to satisfy the unreasonable desires of any particular depraved natures, he should at any time suffer the order of the whole to be altered and perverted. Lastly, it is a thing evidently and infinitely more fit, that any one particular innocent and good being, should by the supreme ruler and disposer of all things, be placed and preserved in an easy and happy estate; than that, without any fault or demerit of its own, it should be made extremely, remedilessly, and endlessly miserable. In like manner; in men's dealing and conversing one with another; it is undeniably

more fit, absolutely and in the nature of the thing itself, that all men should endeavour to promote the universal good and welfare of all; than that all men should be continually contriving the ruin and destruction of all. It is evidently more fit, even before all positive bargains and compacts, that men should deal one with another according to the known rules of justice and equity; than that every man for his own present advantage, should without scruple disappoint the most reasonable and equitable expectations of his neighbours, and cheat and defraud, or spoil by violence, all others without restraint. Lastly, it is without dispute more fit and reasonable in itself, that I should preserve the life of an innocent man, that happens at any time to be in my power; or deliver him from any imminent danger, though I have never made any promise so to do; than that I should suffer him to perish, or take away his life, without any reason or provocation at all.

[. . .]

2. Now what these eternal and unalterable relations, respects, or proportions of things, with their consequent agreements or disagreements, fitnesses or unfitnesses, absolutely and necessarily *are* in themselves; *that* also they *appear to be*, to the *understandings* of all intelligent beings; except those only, who understand things to be what they are not, that is, whose understandings are either very imperfect, or very much depraved. And by this understanding or knowledge of the natural and necessary relations, fitnesses, and proportions of things, the *wills* likewise of all intelligent beings are constantly directed, and must needs be determined to act accordingly; excepting those only, who will things to be what they are not and cannot be; that is, whose wills are corrupted by particular interest or affection, or swayed by some unreasonable and prevailing passion. Wherefore since the *natural* attributes of God, his infinite knowledge, wisdom and power, set him infinitely above all possibility of being deceived by any error, or of being influenced by any wrong affection; it is manifest his divine will cannot but always and necessarily determine itself to choose to do what in the whole is absolutely best and fittest to be done; that is, to act constantly according to the eternal rules of infinite goodness, justice and truth. As I have endeavoured to show distinctly in my former discourse, in deducing severally the *moral* attributes of God.

3. And now, that the same reason of things, with regard to which the will of God always and necessarily *does* determine itself to act in constant conformity to the eternal rules of justice, equity, goodness and truth; *ought* also constantly to determine the wills of all subordinate rational beings, to govern all *their* actions by the same rules; is very evident. For, as it is absolutely impossible in nature, that God should be deceived by any error, or influenced by any wrong affection: so it is very unreasonable and blame-worthy in practice, that any intelligent creatures, whom God has made so far like unto himself, as to endue them with those excellent faculties of reason and will, whereby they are enabled to distinguish good from evil, and to choose the one and refuse the other; should either negligently suffer themselves to be imposed upon and deceived in matters of good and evil, right and wrong; or wilfully and perversely allow themselves to be over-ruled by absurd passions, and corrupt or partial affections, to act contrary to what they know is fit to be done. Which two things, viz. negligent misunderstanding and wilful passions or lusts, are, as I said, the only causes which can make a reasonable creature act contrary to reason, that is, contrary to the eternal rules of justice, equity, righteousness and truth. For, was it not for these inexcusable corruptions and depravations; it is impossible but the same proportions and fitnesses of things, which have so much weight and so much excellency and beauty in them, that the

all-powerful creator and governor of the universe, (who has the absolute and uncontrollable dominion of all things in his own hands, and is accountable to none for what he does, yet) thinks it no diminution of his power to make this reason of things the unalterable rule and law of his own actions in the government of the world, and does nothing by mere will and arbitrariness; it is impossible (I say,) if it was not for inexcusable corruption and depravation, but the same eternal reason of things must much more have weight enough to determine constantly the wills and actions of all subordinate, finite, dependent and accountable beings. For originally and in reality, it is as natural and (morally speaking) necessary, that the will should be determined in every action by the reason of the thing, and the right of the case; as it is natural and (absolutely speaking) necessary, that the understanding should submit to a demonstrated truth. And it is as absurd and blame-worthy, to mistake negligently plain right and wrong, that is, to understand the proportions of things in morality to be what they are not; or wilfully to act contrary to known justice and equity, that is, to will things to be what they are not and cannot be; as it would be absurd and ridiculous for a man in arith-metical matters, ignorantly to believe that twice two is not equal to four; or wilfully and obstinately to contend, against his own clear knowledge, that the whole is not equal to all its parts. The only difference is, that *assent* to a plain speculative truth, is not in a man's power to withhold; but to *act* according to the plain right and reason of things, this he may, by the natural liberty of his will, forbear. But the one he *ought* to do; and it is as much his plain and indispensable *duty*; as the other he *cannot but do*, and it is the *necessity* of his nature to do it. He that wilfully refuses to honour and obey God, from whom he received his being, and to whom he continually owes his preservation; is really guilty of an equal absurdity and incon-sistency in practice; as he that in speculation denies the effect to owe any thing to its cause, or the whole to be bigger than its part. He that refuses to deal with all men equitably, and with every man as he desires they should deal with him: is guilty of the very same un-reasonableness and contradiction in one case; as he that in another case should affirm one number or quantity to be equal to another, and yet that other at the same time not to be equal to the first. Lastly, he that acknowledges himself obliged to the practice of certain *duties* both towards God and towards men, and yet takes no care either to preserve his own being, or at least not to preserve himself in such a state and temper of mind and body, as may best enable him to perform those duties; is altogether as inexcusable and ridiculous, as he that in any other matter should *affirm* one thing at the same time that he *denies* another, without which the former could not possibly be *true*; or *undertake* one thing, at the same time that he obstinately *omits* another, without which the former is by no means *practicable*. Wherefore all rational creatures, whose wills are not constantly and regularly determined, and their actions governed, by right reason and the necessary differences of good and evil, according to the eternal and invariable rules of justice, equity, goodness and truth; but suffer themselves to be swayed by unaccountable arbitrary humours, and rash passions, by lusts, vanity and pride; by private interest, or present sensual pleasures: these, setting up their own unreasonable self-will in opposition to the nature and reason of things, endeavour (as much as in them lies) to make things be what they are not, and cannot be. Which is the highest presumption and greatest insolence, as well as the greatest absurdity, imaginable. It is acting contrary to that understanding, reason and judgement, which God has implanted in their natures on purpose to enable them to discern the difference between good and evil. It is attempting to destroy that order, by which the universe subsists. It is offering the highest affront imaginable to the creator of all things, who made things to be what they are, and governs every thing himself according to the laws of their several natures. In a word; all wilful wickedness and perversion of right, is the very same insolence and absurdity in *moral matters*; as it would be in *natural things*, for a man to pretend to alter the certain proportions of numbers, to take away the demonstrable relations and properties of mathematical figures; to make light darkness, and darkness light; or to call sweet bitter, and bitter sweet.

17

David Hume, *A Treatise of Human Nature* (1739–40)

Hume's moral theory is a response to moral rationalists like Clarke, who argued that right and wrong are determined by a permanent structure in the universe that all rational beings can understand. Hume's arguments for his "sentimentalist" view of morality depend crucially on his theory of motivation. He maintains that the beliefs, whether factual or logical, produced by reason alone are not motives. He thinks that motivation is produced only when we care about something.

Hume then argues that, because our making moral judgments instills motives in us whereas using reason by itself does not, it must be that our moral judgments are based on something besides reason. According to Hume's analysis, we experience a feeling of disapproval, an uncomfortable emotion, when we observe certain actions such as murder. Likewise, we have a feeling of approval, a sort of pleasure, when we observe actions such as someone giving a donation to charity. If no one ever reacted emotionally to actions or actors, no one would make moral judgments; they would just contemplate facts.

Hume inquires why we feel pleasure at the thought of some actions or characters, and pain at the thought of others. In response, he appeals to a natural capacity of ours: sympathy. Sympathy is the ability to turn an idea of the passions of another into an experience of our own. We infer the feelings of others from their behavior. This idea of their feelings takes on a greater forcefulness as we imagine ourselves affected by others' circumstances. However, we are more affected by the feelings of those related to us than by the feelings of strangers. If sympathetic feelings are the foundation of our moral judgments, does it follow that, even though my friend has the same traits as a stranger, I think the former more virtuous than the latter because my feelings of approval are stronger? Hume answers that in order to avoid practical problems arising from conflicting moral judgments, we consider our sympathetic feelings indicative of moral distinctions *only* when we take up a generally shared perspective on an action or character. In so doing, we consider the effects of an action or character in isolation from our personal connections to the actor.

Morality also includes our using notions of the just and the unjust. These notions are different from the others because acts of justice, such as respecting property, are ones we approve, not because the individual acts are pleasurable to the people we sympathize with, but because we approve of the system in which just actions play a part. For instance, repaying a loan from a miser is the right thing to do, but neither the borrower nor the miser may be better off for it. Hume takes on the complicated task of explaining the practical and psychological process by which we constitute the rules of justice and approve of those who follow them.

Book 2
Of the Passions

Part 3
Of the Will and Direct Passions

Section 3
Of the influencing motives of the will

Nothing is more usual in philosophy, and even in common life, than to talk of the combat of passion and reason, to give the preference to reason, and assert that men are only so far virtuous as they conform themselves to its dictates. Every rational creature, tis said, is oblig'd to regulate his actions by reason; and if any other motive or principle challenge the direction of his conduct, he ought to oppose it, till it be entirely subdu'd, or at least brought to a conformity with that superior principle. On this method of thinking the greatest part of moral philosophy, antient and modern, seems to be founded; nor is there an ampler field, as well for metaphysical arguments, as popular declamations, than this suppos'd pre-eminence of reason above passion. The eternity, invariableness, and divine origin of the former have been display'd to the best advantage: The blindness, unconstancy, and deceitfulness of the latter have been as strongly insisted on. In order to show the fallacy of all this philosophy, I shall endeavour to prove *first*, that reason alone can never be a motive to any action of the will; and *secondly*, that it can never oppose passion in the direction of the will.

The understanding exerts itself after two different ways, as it judges from demonstration or probability; as it regards the abstract relations of our ideas, or those relations of objects, of which experience only gives us information. I believe it scarce will be asserted, that the first species of reasoning alone is ever the cause of any action. As its proper province is the world of ideas, and as the will always places us in that of realities, demonstration and volition seem, upon that account, to be totally remov'd, from each other. Mathematics, indeed, are useful in all mechanical operations, and arithmetic in almost every art and profession: But 'tis not of themselves they have any influence. Mechanics are the art of regulating the motions of bodies *to some design'd end or purpose*; and the reason why we employ arithmetic in fixing the proportions of numbers, is only that we may discover the proportions of their influence and operation. A merchant is desirous of knowing the sum total of his accounts with any person: Why? But that he may learn what sum will have the same *effects* in paying his debt, and going to market, as all the particular articles taken together. Abstract or demonstrative reasoning, therefore, never influences any of our actions, but only as it directs our judgment concerning causes and effects; which leads us to the second operation of the understanding.

'Tis obvious, that when we have the prospect of pain or pleasure from any object, we feel a consequent emotion of aversion or propensity, and are carry'd to avoid or embrace what will give us this uneasiness or satisfaction. 'Tis also obvious, that this emotion rests not here, but making us cast our view on every side, comprehends whatever objects are connected with its original one by the relation of cause and effect. Here then reasoning takes place to discover this relation; and according as our reasoning varies, our actions receive a subsequent variation. But 'tis evident in this case, that the impulse arises not from reason, but is only directed by it. 'Tis from the prospect of pain or pleasure that the aversion or propensity arises towards any object: And these emotions extend themselves to the causes and effects of that object, as they are pointed out to us by reason and experience. It can never in the least concern us to know, that such objects are causes, and such others effects, if both the causes and effects be indifferent to us. Where the objects themselves do not affect us, their connexion can never give them any influence; and 'tis plain, that as reason is nothing but the discovery of this connexion, it cannot be by its means that the objects are able to affect us.

Since reason alone can never produce any action, or give rise to volition, I infer, that the same faculty is as incapable of preventing volition, or of disputing the preference with any passion or emotion. This consequence is necessary. 'Tis impossible reason cou'd have the latter effect of preventing volition, but by giving an impulse in a contrary direction to our passion; and that impulse, had it operated alone, wou'd have been able to produce volition. Nothing can oppose or retard the impulse of passion, but a contrary impulse; and if this contrary impulse ever arises from reason, that latter faculty must have an original influence on the will, and must be able to cause, as well as hinder any act of volition. But if reason has no original influence, 'tis impossible it can withstand any principle, which has such an efficacy, or ever keep the mind in suspence a moment. Thus it appears, that the principle, which opposes our passion, cannot be the same with reason, and is only call'd so in an improper sense. We speak not strictly and philosophically when we talk of the combat of passion and of reason. Reason is, and ought only to be the slave of the passions, and can never pretend to any other office than to serve and obey them. As this opinion may appear somewhat extraordinary, it may not be improper to confirm it by some other considerations.

A passion is an original existence, or, if you will, modification of existence, and contains not any representative quality, which renders it a copy of any other existence or modification. When I am angry, I am actually possest with the passion, and in that emotion have no more a reference to any other object, than when I am thirsty, or sick, or more than five foot high. 'Tis impossible, therefore, that this passion can be oppos'd by, or be contradictory to truth and reason; since this contradiction consists in the disagreement of ideas, consider'd as copies, with those objects, which they represent.

What may at first occur on this head, is, that as nothing can be contrary to truth or reason, except what has a reference to it, and as the judgments of our understanding only have this reference, it must follow, that passions can be contrary to reason only so far as they are *accompany'd* with some judgment or opinion. According to this principle, which is so obvious and natural, 'tis only in two senses, that any affection can be call'd unreasonable. *First*, When a passion, such as hope or fear, grief or joy, despair or security, is founded on the supposition of the existence of objects, which really do not exist. *Secondly*, When in exerting any passion in action, we choose means insufficient for the design'd end, and deceive ourselves in our judgment of causes and effects. Where a passion is neither founded on false suppositions, nor chooses means insufficient for the end, the understanding can neither justify nor condemn it. 'Tis not contrary to reason to prefer the destruction of the whole world to the scratching of my finger. 'Tis not contrary to reason for me to choose my total ruin, to prevent the least uneasiness of an *Indian* or person wholly unknown to me. 'Tis as little contrary to reason to prefer even my own acknowledg'd lesser good to my greater, and have a more ardent affection for the former than the latter. A trivial good may, from certain circumstances, produce a desire superior to what arises from the greatest and most valuable enjoyment; nor is there any thing more extraordinary in this, than in mechanics to see one pound weight raise up a hundred by the advantage of its situation. In short, a passion must be accompany'd with some false judgment, in order to its being unreasonable; and even then 'tis not the passion, properly speaking, which is unreasonable, but the judgment.

The consequences are evident. Since a passion can never, in any sense, be call'd unreasonable, but when founded on a false supposition, or when it chooses means insufficient for the design'd end, 'tis impossible, that reason and passion can ever oppose each other, or dispute for the government of the will and actions. The moment we perceive the falshood of any supposition, or the insufficiency of any means our passions yield to our reason without any opposition. I may desire any fruit as of an excellent relish; but whenever you convince me of my mistake, my longing ceases. I may will the performance of certain actions as means of obtaining any desir'd good; but as my willing of these actions is only secondary, and founded on the supposition, that they are causes of the propos'd effect; as soon as I discover the falshood of that supposition, they must become indifferent to me.

'Tis natural for one, that does not examine objects with a strict philosophic eye, to imagine, that those actions of the mind are entirely the same, which produce not a different sensation, and are not immediately distinguishable to the feeling and perception. Reason, for instance, exerts itself without producing any sensible emotion; and except in the more sublime disquisitions of philosophy, or in the frivolous subtilties of the schools, scarce ever conveys any pleasure or uneasiness. Hence it proceeds, that every action of the mind, which operates with the same calmness and tranquillity, is confounded with reason by all those, who judge of things from the first view and appearance. Now 'tis certain, there are certain calm desires and tendencies, which, tho' they be real passions, produce little emotion in the mind, and are more known by their effects than by the immediate feeling or sensation. These desires are of two kinds; either certain instincts originally implanted in our natures, such as benevolence and resentment, the love of life, and kindness to children; or the general appetite to good, and aversion to evil, consider'd merely as such. When any of these passions are calm, and cause no disorder in the soul, they are very readily taken for the determinations of reason, and are suppos'd to proceed from the same faculty, with that, which judges of truth and falshood. Their nature and principles have been suppos'd the same, because their sensations are not evidently different.

Beside these calm passions, which often determine the will, there are certain violent emotions of the same kind, which have likewise a great influence on that faculty. When I receive any injury from another, I often feel a violent passion of resentment, which makes me desire his evil and punishment, independent of all considerations of pleasure and advantage to myself. When I am immediately threaten'd with any grievous ill, my fears, apprehensions, and aversions rise to a great height, and produce a sensible emotion.

The common error of metaphysicians has lain in ascribing the direction of the will entirely to one of these principles, and supposing the other to have no influence. Men often act knowingly against their interest: For which reason the view of the greatest possible good does not always influence them. Men often counter-act a violent passion in prosecution of their interests and designs: 'Tis not therefore the present uneasiness alone, which determines them. In general we may observe, that both these principles operate on the will; and where they are contrary, that either of them prevails, according to the *general* character or *present* disposition of the person. What we call strength of mind, implies the prevalence of the calm passions above the violent; tho' we may easily observe, there is no man so constantly possess'd of this virtue, as never on any occasion to yield to the sollicitations of passion and desire. From these variations of temper proceeds the great difficulty of deciding concerning the actions and resolutions of men, where there is any contrariety of motives and passions.

[. . .]

Book 3
Of MORALS

Part 1
Of Virtue and Vice in General

Section 1
Moral distinctions not deriv'd from reason

There is an inconvenience which attends all abstruse reasoning, that it may silence, without convincing an antagonist, and requires the same intense study to make us sensible of its force, that was at first requisite for its invention. When we leave our closet, and engage in the common affairs of life, its conclusions seem to vanish, like the phantoms of the night on the appearance of the morning; and 'tis difficult for us to retain even that conviction, which we had attain'd with difficulty. This is still more conspicuous in a long chain of reasoning, where we must preserve to the end the evidence of the first propositions, and where we often lose sight of all the most receiv'd maxims, either of philosophy or common life. I am not, however, without hopes, that the present system of philosophy will acquire new force as it advances; and that our reasonings concerning *morals* will corroborate whatever has been said concerning the *understanding* and the *passions*. Morality is a subject that interests us above all others: We fancy the peace of society to be at stake in every decision concerning it; and 'tis evident, that this concern must make our speculations appear more real and solid, than where the subject is, in a great measure, indifferent to us. What affects us, we conclude can never be a chimera; and as our passion is engag'd on the one side or the other, we naturally think that the question lies within human comprehension; which, in other cases of this nature, we are apt to entertain some doubt of. Without this advantage I never shou'd have ventur'd upon a third volume of such abstruse philosophy, in an age, wherein the greatest part of men seem agreed to convert reading into an amusement, and to reject every thing that requires any considerable degree of attention to be comprehended.

It has been observ'd, that nothing is ever present to the mind but its perceptions; and that all the actions of seeing, hearing, judging, loving, hating, and thinking, fall under this denomination. The mind can never exert itself in any action, which we may not comprehend under the term of *perception*; and consequently that term is no less applicable to those judgments, by which we distinguish moral good and evil, than to every other operation of the mind. To approve of one character, to condemn another, are only so many different perceptions.

Now as perceptions resolve themselves into two kinds, viz. *impressions* and *ideas*, this distinction gives rise to a question, with which we shall open up our present enquiry concerning morals, *Whether 'tis by means of our* ideas *or* impressions *we distinguish betwixt vice and virtue, and pronounce an action blameable or praise-worthy?* This will immediately cut off all loose discourses and declamations, and reduce us to something precise and exact on the present subject.

Those who affirm that virtue is nothing but a conformity to reason; that there are eternal fitnesses and unfitnesses of things, which are the same to every rational being that considers them; that the immutable measures of right and wrong impose an obligation, not only on human creatures, but also on the deity himself. All these systems concur in the opinion, that morality, like truth, is discern'd merely by ideas, and by their juxta-position and comparison. In order, therefore, to judge of these systems, we need only consider, whether it be possible, from reason alone, to distinguish betwixt moral good and evil, or whether there must concur some other principles to enable us to make that distinction.

If morality had naturally no influence on human passions and actions, 'twere in vain to take such pains to inculcate it; and nothing wou'd be more fruitless than that multitude of rules and precepts, with which all moralists abound. Philosophy is commonly divided into *speculative* and *practical*; and as morality is always comprehended under the latter division, 'tis suppos'd to influence our passions and actions, and to go beyond the calm and indolent judgments of the understanding. And this is confirm'd by common experience, which informs us, that men are often govern'd by their duties, and are deter'd from some actions by the opinion of injustice, and impell'd to others by that of obligation.

Since morals, therefore, have an influence on the actions and affections, it follows, that they cannot be deriv'd from reason; and that because reason alone, as we have already prov'd, can never have any such influence. Morals excite passions, and produce or prevent actions. Reason of itself is utterly impotent in this particular. The rules of morality, therefore, are not conclusions of our reason.

No one, I believe, will deny the justness of this inference; nor is there any other means of evading it, than by denying that principle, on which it is founded. As long as it is allow'd, that reason has no influence on our passions and actions, 'tis in vain to pretend, that morality is discover'd only by a deduction of reason. An active principle can never be founded on an inactive; and if reason be inactive in itself, it must remain so in all its shapes and appearances, whether it exerts itself in natural or moral subjects, whether it considers the powers of external bodies, or the actions of rational beings.

It wou'd be tedious to repeat all the arguments, by which I have prov'd, that reason is perfectly inert, and can never either prevent or produce any action or affection. 'Twill be easy to recollect what has been said upon that subject. I shall only recal on this occasion one of these arguments, which I shall endeavour to render still more conclusive, and more applicable to the present subject.

Reason is the discovery of truth or falshood. Truth or falshood consists in an agreement or disagreement either to the *real* relations of ideas, or to *real* existence and matter of fact. Whatever, therefore, is not susceptible of this agreement or disagreement, is incapable of being true or false, and can never be an object of our reason. Now 'tis evident our passions, volitions, and actions, are not susceptible of any such agreement or disagreement; being original facts and realities, compleat in themselves, and implying no reference to other passions, volitions, and actions. 'Tis impossible, therefore, they can be pronounc'd either true or false, and be either contrary or conformable to reason.

This argument is of double advantage to our present purpose. For it proves *directly*, that actions do not derive their merit from a conformity to reason, nor their blame from a contrariety to it; and it proves the same truth more *indirectly*, by showing us, that as reason can never immediately prevent or produce any action by contradicting or approving of it, it cannot be the source of the distinction betwixt moral good and evil, which are found to have that influence. Actions may be laudable or blameable; but they cannot be reasonable or unreasonable: Laudable or blameable, therefore, are not the same with reasonable or unreasonable. The merit and demerit of actions frequently contradict, and sometimes controul our natural propensities. But reason has no such influence. Moral distinctions, therefore, are not the offspring of reason. Reason is wholly inactive, and can never be the source of so active a principle as conscience, or a sense of morals.

But perhaps it may be said, that tho' no will or action can be immediately contradictory to reason, yet we may find such a contradiction in some of the attendants of the action, that is, in its causes or effects. The action may cause a judgment, or may be *obliquely* caus'd by one, when the judgment concurs with a passion; and by an abusive way of speaking, which philosophy will scarce allow of, the same contrariety may, upon that account, be ascrib'd to the action. How far this truth or falshood may be the source of morals, 'twill now be proper to consider.

It has been observ'd, that reason, in a strict and philosophical sense, can have an influence on our conduct only after two ways: Either when it excites a passion by informing us of the existence of something which is a proper object of it; or when it discovers the connexion of causes and effects, so as to afford us means of exerting any passion. These are the only kinds of judgment, which can accompany our actions, or can be said to produce them in any manner; and it must be allow'd, that these judgments may often be false and erroneous. A person may be affected with passion, by supposing a pain or pleasure to lie in an object, which has no tendency to produce either of these sensations, or which produces the contrary to what is imagin'd. A person may also take false measures for the attaining his end, and may retard, by his foolish conduct, instead of forwarding the execution of any project. These false judgments may be thought to affect the passions and actions, which are connected with them, and may be said to render them unreasonable, in a figurative and improper way of speaking. But tho' this be acknowledg'd, 'tis easy to observe, that these errors are so far from being the source of all immorality, that they are commonly very innocent, and draw no manner of guilt upon the person who is so unfortunate as to fall into them. They extend not beyond a mistake of *fact*, which moralists have not generally suppos'd criminal, as being perfectly involuntary. I am more to be lamented than blam'd, if I am mistaken with regard to the influence of objects in producing pain or pleasure, or if I know not the proper means of satisfying my desires. No one can ever regard such errors as a defect in my moral character. A fruit, for instance, that is really disagreeable, appears to me at a distance, and thro' mistake I fancy it to be pleasant and delicious. Here is one error. I choose certain means of reaching this fruit, which are not proper for my end. Here is a second error; nor is there any third one, which can ever possibly enter into our reasonings concerning actions. I ask, therefore, if a man, in this situation, and guilty of these two errors, is to be regarded as vicious and criminal, however unavoidable they might have been? Or if it be possible to imagine, that such errors are the sources of all immorality?

And here it may be proper to observe, that if moral distinctions be deriv'd from the truth or falshood of those judgments, they must take place wherever we form the judgments; nor will there be any difference, whether the question be concerning an apple or a kingdom, or whether the error be avoidable or unavoidable. For as the very essence of morality is suppos'd to consist in an agreement or disagreement to reason, the other circumstances are entirely arbitrary, and can never either bestow on any action the character of virtuous or vicious, or deprive it of that character. To which we may add, that this agreement or disagreement, not admitting of degrees, all virtues and vices wou'd of course be equal.

Shou'd it be pretended, that tho' a mistake of *fact* be not criminal, yet a mistake of *right* often is; and that this may be the source of immorality: I wou'd answer, that 'tis impossible such a mistake can ever be the original source of immorality, since it supposes a real right and wrong; that is, a real distinction in morals, independent of these judgments. A mistake, therefore, of right may become a species of immorality; but 'tis only a secondary one, and is founded on some other, antecedent to it.

As to those judgments which are the *effects* of our actions, and which, when false, give occasion to pronounce the actions contrary to truth and reason; we may observe, that our actions never cause any judgment, either true or false, in ourselves, and that 'tis only on others they have such an influence. 'Tis certain, that an action, on many occasions, may give rise to false conclusions in others; and that a person, who thro' a window sees any lewd behaviour of mine with my neighbour's wife, may be so simple as to imagine she is certainly my own. In this respect my action resembles somewhat a lye or falshood; only with this difference, which is material, that I perform not the action with any intention of giving rise to a false judgment in another, but merely to satisfy my lust and passion. It causes, however, a mistake and false judgment by accident; and the falshood of its effects may be ascrib'd, by some odd figurative way of speaking, to the action itself. But still I can see no pretext of reason for asserting, that the tendency to cause such an error is the first spring or original source of all immorality.

Thus upon the whole, 'tis impossible, that the distinction betwixt moral good and evil, can be made by reason; since that distinction has an influence upon our actions, of which reason alone is incapable. Reason and judgment may, indeed, be the mediate cause of an action, by prompting, or by directing a passion: But it is not pretended, that a judgment of this kind, either in its truth or falshood, is attended with virtue or vice. And as to the judgments, which are caus'd by our actions, they can still less bestow those moral qualities on the actions, which are their causes.

But to be more particular, and to show, that those eternal immutable fitnesses and unfitnesses of things cannot be defended by sound philosophy, we may weigh the following considerations.

If the thought and understanding were alone capable of fixing the boundaries of right and wrong, the character of virtuous and vicious either must lie in some relations of objects, or must be a matter of fact, which is discover'd by our reasoning. This consequence is evident. As the operations of human understanding divide themselves into two kinds, the comparing of ideas, and the inferring of matter of fact; were virtue discover'd by the understanding; it must be an object of one of these operations, nor is there any third operation of the understanding, which can discover it. There has been an opinion very industriously propagated by certain philosophers, that morality is susceptible of demonstration; and tho' no one has ever been able to advance a single step in those demonstrations; yet 'tis taken for granted, that this science may be brought to an equal certainty with geometry or algebra. Upon this supposition, vice and virtue must consist in some relations; since 'tis allow'd on all hands, that no matter of fact is capable of being demonstrated. Let us, therefore, begin with examining this hypothesis, and endeavour, if possible, to fix those moral qualities, which have been so long the objects of our fruitless researches. Point out distinctly the relations, which constitute morality or obligation, that we may know wherein they consist, and after what manner we must judge of them.

If you assert, that vice and virtue consist in relations susceptible of certainty and demonstration, you must confine yourself to those *four* relations, which alone admit of that degree of evidence; and in that case you run into absurdities, from which you will never be able to extricate yourself. For as you make the very essence of morality to lie in the relations, and as there is no one of these relations but what is applicable, not only to an irrational, but also to an inanimate object; it follows, that even such objects must be susceptible of merit or demerit. *Resemblance, contrariety, degrees in quality,* and *proportions in quantity and number;* all these relations belong as properly to matter, as to our actions, passions, and volitions. 'Tis unquestionable, therefore, that morality lies not in any of these relations, nor the sense of it in their discovery.

Shou'd it be asserted, that the sense of morality consists in the discovery of some relation, distinct from these, and that our enumeration was not compleat, when we comprehended all demonstrable relations under four general heads: To this I know not what to reply, till some one be so good as to point out to me this new relation. 'Tis impossible to refute a system, which has never yet been explain'd. In such a manner of fighting in the dark, a man loses his blows in the air, and often places them where the enemy is not present.

I must, therefore, on this occasion, rest contented with requiring the two following conditions of any one that wou'd undertake to clear up this system. *First,* As moral good and evil belong only to the actions of the mind, and are deriv'd from our situation with regard to external objects, the relations, from which these moral distinctions arise, must lie only betwixt internal actions, and external objects, and must not be applicable either to internal actions, compar'd among themselves, or to external objects, when plac'd in opposition to other external objects. For as morality is suppos'd to attend certain relations, if these relations cou'd belong to internal actions consider'd singly, it wou'd follow, that we might be guilty of crimes in ourselves, and independent of our situation, with respect to the universe: And in like manner, if these moral relations cou'd be apply'd to external objects, it wou'd follow, that even inanimate beings wou'd be susceptible of moral beauty and deformity. Now it seems difficult to imagine, that any relation can be discover'd betwixt our passions, volitions and actions, compar'd to external objects, which relation might not belong either to these passions and volitions, or to these external objects, compar'd among *themselves.*

But it will be still more difficult to fulfil the *second* condition, requisite to justify this system. According to the principles of those who maintain an abstract rational difference betwixt moral good and evil, and a natural fitness and unfitness of things, 'tis not only suppos'd, that these relations, being eternal and immutable, are the same, when consider'd by every rational creature, but their *effects* are also suppos'd to be necessarily the same; and 'tis concluded they have no less, or rather a greater, influence in directing the will of the deity, than in governing the rational and virtuous of our own species. These two particulars are evidently distinct. 'Tis one thing to know virtue, and another to conform the will to it. In order, therefore, to prove, that the measures of right and wrong are eternal laws, *obligatory* on every rational mind, 'tis not sufficient to show the relations upon which they are founded: We must also point out the connexion betwixt the relation and the will; and must prove that this connexion is so necessary, that in every well-dispos'd mind, it must take place and have its influence; tho' the difference betwixt these minds be in other respects immense and infinite. Now besides what I have already prov'd, that even in human nature no relation can ever alone produce any action; besides this, I say, it has been shown, in treating of the understanding, that there is no connexion of cause and effect, such as this is suppos'd to be, which is discoverable otherwise than by experience, and of which we can pretend to have any security by the simple consideration of the objects. All beings in the universe, consider'd in themselves, appear entirely loose and independent of each other. 'Tis only by experience we learn their influence and connexion; and this influence we ought never to extend beyond experience.

Thus it will be impossible to fulfil the *first* condition requisite to the system of eternal rational measures of right and wrong; because it is impossible to show those relations, upon which such a distinction may be founded: And 'tis as impossible to fulfil the *second* condition; because we cannot prove *a priori*, that these relations, if they really existed and were perceiv'd, wou'd be universally forcible and obligatory.

But to make these general reflections more clear and convincing, we may illustrate them by some particular instances, wherein this character of moral good or evil is the most universally acknowledg'd. Of all crimes that human creatures are capable of committing, the most horrid and unnatural is ingratitude, especially when it is committed against parents, and appears in the more flagrant instances of wounds and death. This is acknowledg'd by all mankind, philosophers as well as the people; the question only arises among philosophers, whether the guilt or moral deformity of this action be discover'd by demonstrative reasoning, or be felt by an internal sense, and by means of some sentiment, which the reflecting on such an action naturally occasions? This question will soon be decided against the former opinion, if we can show the same relations in other objects, without the notion of any guilt or iniquity attending them. Reason or science is nothing but the comparing of ideas, and the discovery of their relations; and if the same relations have different characters, it must evidently follow, that those characters are not discover'd merely by reason. To put the affair, therefore, to this trial, let us choose any inanimate object, such as an oak or elm; and let us suppose, that by the dropping of its seed, it produces a sapling below it, which springing up by degrees, at last overtops and destroys the parent tree: I ask, if in this instance there be wanting any relation, which is discoverable in parricide or ingratitude? Is not the one tree the cause of the other's existence; and the latter the cause of the destruction of the former, in the same manner as when a child murders his parent? 'Tis not sufficient to reply, that a choice or will is wanting. For in the case of parricide, a will does not give rise to any *different* relations, but is only the cause from which the action is deriv'd; and consequently produces the *same* relations, that in the oak or elm arise from some other principles. 'Tis a will or choice, that determines a man to kill his parent; and they are the laws of matter and motion, that determine a sapling to destroy the oak, from which it sprung. Here then the same relations have different causes; but still the relations are the same: And as their discovery is not in both cases attended with a notion of immorality, it follows, that that notion does not arise from such a discovery.

But to choose an instance, still more resembling; I wou'd fain ask any one, why incest in the human species is criminal, and why the very same action, and the same relations in animals have not the smallest moral turpitude and deformity? If it be answer'd, that this action is innocent in animals, because they have not reason sufficient to discover its turpitude; but that man, being endow'd with that faculty, which *ought* to restrain him to his duty, the same action instantly becomes criminal to him; shou'd this be said, I wou'd reply, that this is evidently arguing in a circle. For before reason can perceive this turpitude, the turpitude must exist; and consequently is independent of the decisions of our reason, and is their object more properly than their effect. According to this system, then, every animal that has sense, and appetite, and will; that is, every animal, must be susceptible of all the same virtues and vices, for which we ascribe praise and blame to human creatures. All the difference is, that our superior reason may serve to discover the vice or virtue, and by that means may augment the blame or praise: But still this discovery supposes a separate being in these moral distinctions, and a being, which depends only on the will and appetite, and which, both in thought and reality, may be distinguish'd from the reason. Animals are susceptible of the same relations, with respect to each other, as the human species, and therefore wou'd also be susceptible of the same morality, if the essence of morality consisted in these relations. Their want of a sufficient degree of reason may hinder them from perceiving the duties and obligations of morality, but can never hinder these duties from existing; since they must antecedently exist, in order to their being perceiv'd. Reason must find them, and can never produce them. This argument deserves to be weigh'd, as being, in my opinion, entirely decisive.

Nor does this reasoning only prove, that morality consists not in any relations, that are the objects of science; but if examin'd, will prove with equal certainty, that it consists not in any *matter of fact*, which can be discover'd by the understanding. This is the *second* part of our argument; and if it can be made evident, we may conclude, that morality is not an object of reason. But can there be any difficulty in proving, that vice and virtue are not matters of fact, whose existence we can infer by reason? Take any action allow'd to be vicious: Wilful murder, for instance. Examine it in all lights, and see if you can find that matter of fact, or real existence, which you call *vice*. In which-ever way you take it, you find only certain passions, motives, volitions, and thoughts. There is no other matter of fact in the case. The vice entirely escapes you, as long as you consider the object. You never can find it, till you turn your reflection into your own breast, and find a sentiment of disapprobation, which arises in you, towards this action. Here is a matter of fact; but 'tis the object of feeling, not of reason. It lies in yourself, not in the object. So that when you pronounce any action or character to be vicious, you mean nothing, but that from the constitution of your nature you have a feeling or sentiment of blame from the contemplation of it. Vice and virtue, therefore, may be compar'd to sounds, colours, heat and cold, which, according to modern philosophy, are not qualities in objects, but perceptions in the mind: And this discovery in morals, like that other in physics, is to be regarded as a considerable advancement of the speculative sciences; tho', like that too, it has little or no influence on practice. Nothing can be more real, or concern us more, than our own sentiments of pleasure and uneasiness; and if these be favourable to virtue, and unfavourable to vice, no more can be requisite to the regulation of our conduct and behaviour.

I cannot forbear adding to these reasonings an observation, which may, perhaps, be found of some importance. In every system of morality, which I have hitherto met with, I have always remark'd, that the author proceeds for some time in the ordinary way of reasoning, and establishes the being of a God, or makes observations concerning human affairs; when of a sudden I am surpriz'd to find, that instead of the usual copulations of propositions, *is*, and *is not*, I meet with no proposition that is not connected with an *ought*, or an *ought not*. This change is imperceptible; but is, however, of the last consequence. For as this *ought*, or *ought not*, expresses some new relation or affirmation, 'tis necessary that it shou'd be observ'd and explain'd; and at the same time that a reason shou'd be given, for what seems altogether inconceivable, how this new relation can be a deduction from others, which are entirely different from it. But as authors do not commonly use this precaution, I shall presume to recommend it to the reader; and am perswaded, that this small attention wou'd subvert all the vulgar systems of morality, and let us see, that the distinction of vice and virtue is not founded merely on the relations of objects, nor is perceiv'd by reason.

Section 2
Moral distinctions deriv'd from a moral sense

Thus the course of the argument leads us to conclude, that since vice and virtue are not discoverable merely by reason, or the comparison of ideas, it must be by means of some impression or sentiment they occasion, that we are able to mark the difference betwixt them. Our decisions concerning moral rectitude and depravity are evidently perceptions; and as all perceptions are either impressions or ideas, the exclusion of the one is a convincing argument for the other. Morality, therefore, is more properly felt than judg'd of; tho' this feeling or sentiment is commonly so soft and gentle, that we are apt to confound it with an idea, according to our common custom of taking all things for the same, which have any near resemblance to each other.

The next question is, of what nature are these impressions, and after what manner do they operate upon us? Here we cannot remain long in suspence, but must pronounce the impression arising from virtue, to be agreeable, and that proceeding from vice to be uneasy. Every moment's experience must convince us of this. There is no spectacle so fair and beautiful as a noble and generous action; nor any which gives us more abhorrence than one that is cruel and treacherous. No enjoyment equals the satisfaction we receive from the company of those we love and esteem; as the greatest of all punishments is to be oblig'd to pass our lives with those we hate or contemn. A very play or romance may afford us instances of this pleasure, which virtue conveys to us; and pain, which arises from vice.

Now since the distinguishing impressions, by which moral good or evil is known, are nothing but *particular* pains or pleasures; it follows, that in all enquiries concerning these moral distinctions, it will be sufficient to show the principles, which make us feel a satisfaction or uneasiness from the survey of any character, in order to satisfy us why the character is laudable or blameable. An action, or sentiment, or character is virtuous or vicious; why? because its view causes a pleasure or uneasiness of a particular kind. In giving a reason, therefore, for the pleasure or uneasiness, we sufficiently explain the vice or virtue. To have the sense of virtue, is nothing but to *feel* a satisfaction of a particular kind from the contemplation of a character. The very *feeling* constitutes our praise or admiration. We go no farther; nor do we enquire into the cause of the satisfaction. We do not infer a character to be virtuous, because it pleases: But in feeling that it pleases after such a particular manner, we in effect feel that it is virtuous. The case is the same as in our judgments concerning all kinds of beauty, and tastes, and sensations. Our approbation is imply'd in the immediate pleasure they convey to us.

I have objected to the system, which establishes eternal rational measures of right and wrong, that 'tis impossible to show, in the actions of reasonable creatures, any relations, which are not found in external objects; and therefore, if morality always attended these relations, 'twere possible for inanimate matter to become virtuous or vicious. Now it may, in like manner, be objected to the present system, that if virtue and vice be determin'd by pleasure and pain, these qualities must, in every case, arise from the sensations; and consequently any object, whether animate or inanimate, rational or irrational, might become morally good or evil, provided it can excite a satisfaction or uneasiness. But tho' this objection seems to be the very same, it has by no means the same force, in the one case as in the other. For, *first*, 'tis evident, that under the term *pleasure*, we comprehend sensations, which are very differ-ent from each other, and which have only such a distant resemblance, as is requisite to make them be express'd by the same abstract term. A good composition of music and a bottle of good wine equally produce pleasure; and what is more, their goodness is determin'd merely by the pleasure. But shall we say upon that account, that the wine is harmonious, or the music of a good flavour? In like manner an inanimate object, and the character or sentiments of any person may, both of them, give satisfaction; but as the satisfaction is different, this keeps our sentiments concerning them from being confounded, and makes us ascribe virtue to the one, and not to the other. Nor is every sentiment of pleasure or pain, which arises from characters and actions, of that *peculiar* kind, which makes us praise or condemn. The good qualities of an enemy are hurtful to us; but may still command our esteem and respect. 'Tis only when a character is consider'd in general, without reference to our particular interest, that it causes such a feeling or sentiment, as denominates it morally good or evil. 'Tis true, those sentiments, from interest and morals, are apt to be confounded, and naturally run into one another. It seldom happens, that we do not think an enemy vicious, and can distinguish betwixt his opposition to our interest and real villainy or baseness. But this hinders not, but that the sentiments are, in themselves, distinct; and a man of temper and judgment may preserve himself from these illusions. In like manner, tho' 'tis certain a musical voice is nothing but one that naturally gives a *particular* kind of pleasure; yet 'tis difficult for a man to be sensible, that the voice of an enemy is agreeable, or to allow it to be musical. But a person of a fine ear, who has the command of himself, can separate these feelings, and give praise to what deserves it.

Secondly, We may call to remembrance the preceding system of the passions, in order to remark a still more considerable difference among our pains and pleasures. Pride and humility, love and hatred are excited, when there is any thing presented to us, that both bears a relation to the object of the passion, and produces a separate sensation related to the sensation of the passion. Now virtue and vice are attended with these circumstances. They must necessarily be plac'd either in ourselves or others, and excite either pleasure or uneasiness; and therefore must give rise to one of these four passions; which clearly distinguishes them from the pleasure and pain arising from inanimate objects, that often bear no relation to us: And this is, perhaps, the most considerable effect that virtue and vice have upon the human mind.

It may now be ask'd *in general*, concerning this pain or pleasure, that distinguishes moral good and evil, *From what principles is it deriv'd, and whence does it arise in the human mind?* To this I reply, *first*, that 'tis absurd to imagine, that in every particular instance, these sentiments are produc'd by an *original* quality and *primary* constitution. For as the number of our duties is, in a manner, infinite, 'tis impossible that our original instincts shou'd extend to each of them, and from our very first infancy impress on the human mind all that multitude of precepts, which are contain'd in the compleatest system of ethics. Such a method of proceeding is not conformable to the usual maxims, by which nature is conducted, where a few principles produce all that variety we observe in the universe, and every thing is carry'd on in the easiest and most simple manner. 'Tis necessary, therefore, to abridge these primary impulses, and find some more general principles, upon which all our notions of morals are founded.

But in the *second* place, shou'd it be ask'd, whether we ought to search for these principles in *nature*, or whether we must look for them in some other origin? I wou'd reply, that our answer to this question depends upon the definition of the word, *nature*, than which there is none more ambiguous and equivocal. If *nature* be oppos'd to miracles, not only the distinction betwixt vice and virtue is natural, but also every event, which has ever happen'd in the world, *excepting those miracles, on which our religion is founded*. In saying, then, that the sentiments of vice and virtue are natural in this sense, we make no very extraordinary discovery.

But *nature* may also be oppos'd to rare and unusual; and in this sense of the word, which is the common one, there may often arise disputes concerning what is natural or unnatural; and one may in general affirm, that we are not possess'd of any very precise standard, by which these disputes can be decided. Frequent and rare depend upon the number of examples we have observ'd; and as this number may gradually encrease or diminish, 'twill be impossible to fix any exact boundaries betwixt them. We may only affirm on this head, that if ever there was any thing, which cou'd be call'd natural in this sense, the sentiments of morality certainly may; since there never was any nation of the world, nor any single person in any nation, who was utterly depriv'd of them, and who never, in any instance, show'd the least approbation or dislike of manners. These sentiments are so rooted in our constitution and temper, that without entirely confounding the human mind by disease or madness, 'tis impossible to extirpate and destroy them.

But *nature* may also be oppos'd to artifice, as well as to what is rare and unusual; and in this sense it may be disputed, whether the notions of virtue be natural or not. We readily forget, that the designs, and projects, and views of men are principles as necessary in their operation as heat and cold, moist and dry: But taking them to be free and entirely our own, 'tis usual for us to set them in opposition to the other principles of nature. Shou'd it, therefore, be demanded, whether the sense of virtue be natural or artificial, I am of opinion, that 'tis impossible for me at present to give any precise answer to this question. Perhaps it will appear afterwards, that our sense of some virtues is artificial, and that of others natural. The discussion of this question will be more proper, when we enter upon an exact detail of each particular vice and virtue.

Mean while it may not be amiss to observe from these definitions of *natural* and *unnatural*, that nothing can be more unphilosophical than those systems, which assert, that virtue is the same with what is natural, and vice with what is unnatural. For in the first sense of the word, *nature*, as oppos'd to miracles, both vice and virtue are equally natural; and in the second sense, as oppos'd to what is unusual, perhaps virtue will be found to be the most unnatural. At least it must be own'd, that heroic virtue, being as unusual, is as little natural as the most brutal barbarity. As to the third sense of the word, 'tis certain, that both vice and virtue are equally artificial, and out of nature. For however it may be disputed, whether the notion of a merit or demerit in certain actions be natural or artificial, 'tis evident, that the actions themselves are artificial, and are perform'd with a certain design and intention; otherwise they cou'd never be rank'd under any of these denominations. 'Tis impossible, therefore, that the character of natural and unnatural can ever, in any sense, mark the boundaries of vice and virtue.

Thus we are still brought back to our first position, that virtue is distinguish'd by the pleasure, and vice by the pain, that any action, sentiment or character gives us by the mere view and contemplation. This decision is very commodious; because it reduces us to this simple question, *Why any action or sentiment upon the general view or survey, gives a certain satisfaction or uneasiness?* in order to show the origin of its moral rectitude or depravity, without looking for any incomprehensible relations and qualities, which never did exist in nature, nor even in our imagination, by any clear and distinct conception. I flatter myself I have executed a great part of my present design by a state of the question, which appears to me so free from ambiguity and obscurity.

Part 2
Of Justice and Injustice

Section 1
Justice, whether a natural or artificial virtue?

I have already hinted, that our sense of every kind of virtue is not natural; but that there are some virtues, that produce pleasure and approbation by means of an artifice or contrivance, which arises from the circumstances and necessities of mankind. Of this kind I assert *justice* to be; and shall endeavour to defend this opinion by a short, and, I hope, convincing argument, before I examine the nature of the artifice, from which the sense of that virtue is deriv'd.

'Tis evident, that when we praise any actions, we regard only the motives that produc'd them, and consider the actions as signs or indications of certain principles in the mind and temper. The external performance has no merit. We must look within to find the moral quality. This we cannot do directly; and therefore fix our attention on actions, as on external signs. But these actions are still consider'd as signs; and the ultimate object of our praise and approbation is the motive, that produc'd them.

After the same manner, when we require any action, or blame a person for not performing it, we always suppose, that one in that situation shou'd be influenc'd by the proper motive of that action, and we esteem it vicious in him to be regardless of it. If we find, upon enquiry, that the virtuous motive was still powerful over his breast, tho' check'd in its operation by some circumstances unknown to us, we retract our blame, and have the same esteem for him, as if he had actually perform'd the action, which we require of him.

It appears, therefore, that all virtuous actions derive their merit only from virtuous motives, and are consider'd merely as signs of those motives. From this principle I conclude, that the first virtuous motive, which bestows a merit on any action, can never be a regard to the virtue of that action, but must be some other natural motive or principle. To suppose, that the mere regard to the virtue of the action, may be the first motive, which produc'd the action, and render'd it virtuous, is to reason in a circle. Before we can have such a regard, the action must be really virtuous; and this virtue must be deriv'd from some virtuous motive: And consequently the virtuous motive must be different from the regard to the virtue of the action. A virtuous motive is requisite to render an action virtuous. An action must be virtuous, before we can have a regard to its virtue. Some virtuous motive, therefore, must be antecedent to that regard.

Nor is this merely a metaphysical subtility; but enters into all our reasonings in common life, tho' perhaps we may not be able to place it in such distinct philosophical terms. We blame a father for neglecting his child. Why? because it shows a want of natural affection, which is the duty of every parent. Were not natural affection a duty, the care of children cou'd not be a duty; and 'twere impossible we cou'd have the duty in our eye in the attention we give to our offspring. In this case, therefore, all men suppose a motive to the action distinct from a sense of duty.

Here is a man, that does many benevolent actions; relieves the distress'd, comforts the afflicted, and extends his bounty even to the greatest strangers. No character can be more amiable and virtuous. We regard these actions as proofs of the greatest humanity. This humanity bestows a merit on the actions. A regard to this merit is, therefore, a secondary consideration, and deriv'd from the antecedent principle of humanity, which is meritorious and laudable.

In short, it may be establish'd as an undoubted maxim, *that no action can be virtuous, or morally good, unless there be in human nature some motive to produce it, distinct from the sense of its morality.*

But may not the sense of morality or duty produce an action, without any other motive? I answer, It may: But this is no objection to the present doctrine. When any virtuous motive or principle is common in human nature, a person, who feels his heart devoid of that principle, may hate himself upon that account, and may perform the action without the motive, from a certain sense of duty, in order to acquire by practice, that virtuous principle, or at least, to disguise to himself, as much as possible, his want of it. A man that really feels no gratitude in his temper, is still pleas'd to perform grateful actions, and thinks he has, by that means, fulfill'd his duty. Actions are at first only consider'd as signs of motives: But 'tis usual, in this case, as in all others, to fix our attention on the signs, and neglect, in some measure, the thing signify'd. But tho', on some occasions, a person may perform an action merely out of regard to its moral obligation, yet still this supposes in human nature some distinct principles, which are capable of producing the action, and whose moral beauty renders the action meritorious.

Now to apply all this to the present case; I suppose a person to have lent me a sum of money, on condition that it be restor'd in a few days; and also suppose, that after the expiration of the term agreed on, he demands the sum: I ask, *What reason or motive have I to restore the money?* It will, perhaps, be said, that my regard to justice, and abhorrence of villainy and knavery, are sufficient reasons for me, if I have the least grain of honesty, or sense of duty and obligation. And this answer, no doubt, is just and satisfactory to man in his civiliz'd state, and when train'd up according to a certain discipline and education. But in his rude and more *natural* condition, if you are pleas'd to call such a condition natural, this answer wou'd be rejected as perfectly unintelligible and sophistical. For one in that situation wou'd immediately ask you, *Wherein consists this honesty and justice, which you find in restoring a loan, and abstaining from the property of others?* It does not surely lie in the external action. It must, therefore, be plac'd in the motive, from which the external action is deriv'd. This motive can never be a regard to the honesty of the action. For 'tis a plain fallacy to say, that a virtuous motive is requisite to render an action honest, and at the same time that a regard to the honesty is the motive of the action. We can never have a regard to the virtue of an action, unless the action be antecedently virtuous. No action can be virtuous, but so far as it proceeds from a virtuous motive. A virtuous motive, therefore, must precede the regard to the virtue; and 'tis impossible, that the virtuous motive and the regard to the virtue can be the same.

'Tis requisite, then, to find some motive to acts of justice and honesty, distinct from our regard to the honesty; and in this lies the great difficulty. For shou'd we say, that a concern for our private interest or reputation is the legitimate motive to all honest actions; it wou'd follow, that wherever that concern ceases, honesty can no longer have place. But 'tis certain, that self-love, when it acts at its liberty, instead of engaging us to honest actions, is the source of all injustice and violence; nor can a man ever correct those vices, without correcting and restraining the *natural* movements of that appetite.

But shou'd it be affirm'd, that the reason or motive of such actions is the *regard to public interest*, to which nothing is more contrary than examples of injustice and dishonesty; shou'd this be said, I wou'd propose the three following considerations, as worthy of our attention. *First*, public interest is not naturally attach'd to the observation of the rules of justice; but is only connected with it, after an artificial convention for the establishment of these rules, as shall be shown more at large hereafter. *Secondly*, if we suppose, that the loan was secret, and that it is necessary for the interest of the person, that the money be restor'd in the same manner (as when the lender wou'd conceal his riches), in that case the example ceases, and the public is no longer interested in the actions of the borrower; tho' I suppose there is no moralist, who will affirm, that the duty and obligation ceases. *Thirdly*, experience sufficiently proves, that men, in the ordinary conduct of life, look not so far as the public interest, when they pay their creditors, perform their promises, and abstain from theft, and robbery, and injustice of every kind. That is a motive too remote and too sublime to affect the generality of mankind, and operate with any force in actions so contrary to private interest as are frequently those of justice and common honesty.

In general, it may be affirm'd, that there is no such passion in human minds, as the love of mankind, merely as such, independent of personal qualities, of services, or of relation to ourself. 'Tis true, there is no human, and indeed no sensible, creature, whose happiness or misery does not, in some measure, affect us, when brought near to us, and represented in lively colours: But this proceeds merely from sympathy, and is no proof of such an universal affection to mankind, since this concern extends itself beyond our own species. An affection betwixt the sexes is a passion evidently implanted in human nature; and this passion not only appears in its peculiar symptoms, but also in inflaming every other principle of affection, and raising a stronger love from beauty, wit, kindness, than what wou'd otherwise flow from them. Were there an universal love among all human creatures, it wou'd appear after the same manner. Any degree of a good quality wou'd cause a stronger affection than the same degree of a bad quality wou'd cause hatred; contrary to what we find by experience. Men's tempers are different, and some have a propensity to the tender, and others to the rougher, affections: But in the main, we may affirm, that man in general, or human nature, is nothing but the object both of love and hatred, and requires some other cause, which by a double relation of impressions and ideas, may excite these passions. In vain wou'd we endeavour to elude this hypothesis. There are no phænomena that point out any such kind affection to men, independent of their merit, and every other circumstance. We love company in general; but 'tis as we love any other amusement. An *Englishman* in *Italy* is a friend: A *Europæan* in *China*; and perhaps a man wou'd be belov'd as such, were we to meet him in the moon. But this proceeds only from the relation to ourselves; which in these cases gathers force by being confin'd to a few persons.

If public benevolence, therefore, or a regard to the interests of mankind, cannot be the original motive to justice, much less can *private benevolence*, or a *regard to the interests of the party concern'd*, be this motive. For what if he be my enemy, and has given me just cause to hate him? What if he be a vicious man, and deserves the hatred of all mankind? What if he be a miser, and can make no use of what I wou'd deprive him of? What if he be a profligate debauchee, and wou'd rather receive harm than benefit from large possessions? What if I be in necessity, and have urgent motives to acquire something for my family? In all these cases, the original motive to justice wou'd fail; and consequently the justice itself, and along with it all property, right, and obligation.

A rich man lies under a moral obligation to communicate to those in necessity a share of his superfluities. Were private benevolence the original motive to justice, a man wou'd not be oblig'd to leave others in the possession of more than he is oblig'd to give them. At least the difference wou'd be very inconsiderable. Men generally fix their affections more on what they are possess'd of, than on what they never enjoy'd: For this reason, it wou'd be greater cruelty to dispossess a man of any thing, than not to give it him. But who will assert, that this is the only foundation of justice?

Besides, we must consider, that the chief reason, why men attach themselves so much to their possessions is, that they consider them as their property, and as secur'd to them inviolably by the laws of society. But this is a secondary consideration, and dependent on the preceding notions of justice and property.

A man's property is suppos'd to be fenc'd against every mortal, in every possible case. But private benevolence towards the proprietor is, and ought to be, weaker in some persons, than in others: And in many, or indeed in most persons, must absolutely fail. Private benevolence, therefore, is not the original motive of justice.

From all this it follows, that we have naturally no real or universal motive for observing the laws of equity, but the very equity and merit of that observance; and as no action can be equitable or meritorious, where it cannot arise from some separate motive, there is here an evident sophistry and reasoning in a circle. Unless, therefore, we will allow, that nature has establish'd a sophistry, and render'd it necessary and unavoidable, we must allow, that the sense of justice and injustice is not deriv'd from nature, but arises artificially, tho' necessarily from education, and human conventions.

I shall add, as a corollary to this reasoning, that since no action can be laudable or blameable, without some motives or impelling passions, distinct from the sense of morals, these distinct passions must have a great influence on that sense. 'Tis according to their general force in human nature, that we blame or praise. In judging of the beauty of animal bodies, we always carry in our eye the œconomy of a certain species; and where the limbs and features observe that proportion, which is common to the species, we pronounce them handsome and beautiful. In like manner we always consider the *natural* and *usual* force of the passions, when we determine concerning vice and virtue; and if the passions depart very much from the common measures on either side, they are always disapprov'd as vicious. A man naturally loves his children better than his nephews, his nephews better than his cousins, his cousins better than strangers, where every thing else is equal. Hence arise our common measures of duty, in preferring the one to the other. Our sense of duty always follows the common and natural course of our passions.

To avoid giving offence, I must here observe, that when I deny justice to be a natural virtue, I make use of the word, *natural*, only as oppos'd to *artificial*. In another sense of the word; as no principle of the human mind is more natural than a sense of virtue; so no virtue is more natural than justice. Mankind is an inventive species; and where an invention is obvious and absolutely necessary, it may as properly be said to be natural as any thing that proceeds immediately from original principles, without the intervention of thought or reflection. Tho' the rules of justice be *artificial*, they are not *arbitrary*. Nor is the expression improper to call them *laws of nature*; if by *natural* we understand what is common to any species, or even if we confine it to mean what is inseparable from the species.

Section 2
Of the origin of justice and property

We now proceed to examine two questions, viz. *concerning the manner, in which the rules of justice are establish'd by the artifice of men*; and *concerning the reasons, which determine us to attribute to the observance or neglect of these rules a moral beauty and deformity*. These questions will appear afterwards to be distinct. We shall begin with the former.

Of all the animals, with which this globe is peopl'd, there is none towards whom nature seems, at first sight, to have exercis'd more cruelty than towards man, in the numberless wants and necessities, with which she has loaded him, and in the slender means, which she affords to the relieving these necessities. In other creatures these two particulars generally compensate each other. If we consider the lion as a voracious and carnivorous animal, we shall easily discover him to be very necessitous; but if we turn our eye to his make and temper, his agility, his courage, his arms, and his force, we shall find, that his advantages hold proportion with his wants. The sheep and ox are depriv'd of all these advantages; but their appetites are moderate, and their food is of easy purchase. In man alone, this unnatural conjunction of infirmity, and of necessity, may be observ'd in its greatest perfection. Not only the food, which is requir'd for his sustenance, flies his search and approach, or at least requires his labour to be produc'd, but he must be possess'd of cloaths and lodging, to defend him against the injuries of the weather; tho' to consider him only in himself, he is provided neither with arms, nor force, nor other natural abilities, which are in any degree answerable to so many necessities.

'Tis by society alone he is able to supply his defects, and raise himself up to an equality with his fellow-creatures, and even acquire a superiority above them. By society all his infirmities are compensated; and tho' in that situation his wants multiply every moment upon him, yet his abilities are still more augmented, and leave him in every respect more satisfy'd and happy, than 'tis possible for him, in his savage and solitary condition, ever to become. When every individual person labours apart, and only for himself, his force is too small to execute any considerable work; his labour being employ'd in supplying all his different necessities, he never attains a perfection in any particular art; and as his force and success are not at all times equal, the least failure in either of these particulars must be attended with inevitable ruin and misery. Society provides a remedy for these *three* inconveniencies. By the conjunction of forces, our power is augmented: By the partition of employments, our ability encreases: And by mutual succour we are less expos'd to fortune and accidents. 'Tis by this additional *force*, *ability*, and *security*, that society becomes advantageous.

But in order to form society, 'tis requisite not only that it be advantageous, but also that men be sensible of its advantages; and 'tis impossible, in their wild uncultivated state, that by study and reflection alone, they shou'd ever be able to attain this knowledge. Most fortunately, therefore, there is conjoin'd to those necessities, whose remedies are remote and obscure, another necessity, which having a present and more obvious remedy, may justly be regarded as the first and original principle of human society. This necessity is no other than that natural appetite betwixt the sexes, which unites them together, and preserves their union, till a new tye takes place in their concern for their common offspring. This new concern becomes also a principle of union betwixt the parents and offspring, and forms a more numerous society; where the parents govern by the advantage of their superior strength and wisdom, and at the same time are restrain'd in the exercise of their authority by that natural affection, which they bear their children. In a little time, custom and habit operating on the tender minds of the children, makes them sensible of the advantages, which they may reap from society, as well as fashions them by degrees for it, by rubbing off those rough corners and untoward affections, which prevent their coalition.

For it must be confest, that however the circumstances of human nature may render an union necessary, and however those passions of lust and natural affection may seem to render it unavoidable; yet there are other particulars in our *natural temper*, and in our *outward circumstances*, which are very incommodious, and are even contrary to the requisite conjunction. Among the former, we may justly esteem our *selfishness* to be the most considerable. I am sensible, that, generally speaking, the representations of this quality have been carry'd much too far; and that the descriptions, which certain philosophers delight so much to form of mankind in this particular, are as wide of nature as any accounts of monsters, which we meet with in fables and romances. So far from thinking, that men have no affection for any thing beyond themselves, I am of opinion, that tho' it be rare to meet with one, who loves any single person better than himself; yet 'tis as rare to meet with one, in whom all the kind affections, taken together, do not over-ballance all the selfish. Consult common experience: Do you not see, that tho' the whole expence of the family be generally under the direction of the master of it, yet there are few that do not bestow the largest part of their fortunes on the pleasures of their wives, and the education of their children, reserving the smallest portion for their own proper use and entertainment? This is what we may observe concerning such as have those endearing ties; and may presume, that the case wou'd be the same with others, were they plac'd in a like situation.

But tho' this generosity must be acknowledg'd to the honour of human nature, we may at the same time remark, that so noble an affection, instead of fitting men for large societies, is almost as contrary to them, as the most narrow selfishness. For while each person loves himself better than any other single person, and in his love to others bears the greatest affection to his relations and acquaintance, this must necessarily produce an opposition of passions, and a consequent opposition of actions; which cannot but be dangerous to the new-establish'd union.

'Tis however worth while to remark, that this contrariety of passions wou'd be attended with but small danger, did it not concur with a peculiarity in our *outward circumstances*, which affords it an opportunity of exerting itself. There are three different species of goods, which we are possess'd of; the internal satisfaction of our mind, the external advantages of our body, and the enjoyment of such possessions as we have acquir'd by our industry and good fortune. We are perfectly secure in the enjoyment of the first. The second may be ravish'd from us, but can be of no advantage to him who deprives us of them. The last only are both expos'd to the violence of others, and may be transferr'd without suffering any loss or alteration; while at the same time, there is not a sufficient quantity of them to supply every one's desires and necessities. As the improvement, therefore, of these goods is the chief advantage of society, so the *instability* of their possession, along with their *scarcity*, is the chief impediment.

In vain shou'd we expect to find, in *uncultivated nature*, a remedy to this inconvenience; or hope for any inartificial principle of the human mind, which might controul those partial affections, and make us overcome the temptations arising from our circumstances. The idea of justice can never serve to this purpose, or be taken for a natural principle, capable of inspiring men with an equitable conduct towards each other. That virtue, as it is now understood, wou'd never have been dream'd of among rude and savage men. For the notion of injury or injustice implies an immorality or vice committed against some other person: And as every immorality is deriv'd from some defect or unsoundness of the passions, and as this defect must be judg'd of, in a great measure, from the ordinary course of nature in the constitution of the mind; 'twill be easy to know, whether we be guilty of any immorality, with regard to others, by considering the natural, and usual force of those several affections, which are directed towards them. Now it appears, that in the original frame of our mind, our strongest attention is confin'd to ourselves; our next is extended to our relations and acquaintance; and 'tis only the weakest which reaches to strangers and indifferent persons. This partiality, then, and unequal affection, must not only have an influence on our behaviour and conduct in society, but even on our ideas of vice and virtue; so as to make us regard any remarkable transgression of such a degree of partiality, either by too great an enlargement, or contraction of the affections, as vicious and immoral. This we may observe in our common judgments concerning actions, where we blame a person, who either centers all his affections in his family, or is so regardless of them, as, in any opposition of interest, to give the preference to a stranger, or mere chance acquaintance. From all which it follows, that our natural uncultivated ideas of morality, instead of providing a remedy for the partiality of our affections, do rather conform themselves to that partiality, and give it an additional force and influence.

The remedy, then, is not deriv'd from nature, but from *artifice*; or more properly speaking, nature provides a remedy in the judgment and understanding, for what is irregular and incommodious in the affections. For when men, from their early education in society, have become sensible of the infinite advantages that result from it, and have besides acquir'd a new affection to company and conversation; and when they have observ'd, that the principal disturbance in society arises from those goods, which we call external, and from their looseness and easy transition from one person to another; they must seek for a remedy, by putting these goods, as far as possible, on the same footing with the fix'd and constant advantages of the mind and body. This can be done after no other manner, than by a convention enter'd into by all the members of the society to bestow stability on the possession of those external goods, and leave every one in the peaceable enjoyment of what he may acquire by his fortune and industry. By this means, every one knows what he may safely possess; and the passions are restrain'd in their partial and contradictory motions. Nor is such a restraint contrary to these passions; for if so, it cou'd never be enter'd into, nor maintain'd; but it is only contrary to their heedless and impetuous movement. Instead of departing from our own interest, or from that of our nearest friends, by abstaining from the possessions of others, we cannot better consult both these interests, than by such a convention; because it is by that means we maintain society, which is so necessary to their well-being and subsistence, as well as to our own.

This convention is not of the nature of a *promise*: For even promises themselves, as we shall see afterwards, arise from human conventions. It is only a general sense of common interest; which sense all the members of the society express to one another, and which induces them to regulate their conduct by certain rules. I observe, that it will be for my interest to leave another in the possession of his goods, *provided* he will act in the same manner with regard to me. He is sensible of a like interest in the regulation of his conduct. When this common sense of interest is mutually express'd, and is known to both, it produces a suitable resolution and behaviour. And this may properly enough be call'd a convention or agreement betwixt us, tho' without the interposition of a promise; since the actions of each of us have a reference to those of the other, and are perform'd upon the supposition, that something is to be perform'd on the other part. Two men, who pull the oars of a boat, do it by an agreement or convention, tho' they have never given promises to each other. Nor is the rule concerning the stability of possession the less deriv'd from human conventions, that it arises gradually, and acquires force by a slow progression, and by our repeated experience of the inconveniencies of transgressing it. On the contrary, this experience assures us still more, that the sense of interest has become common to all our fellows, and gives us a confidence of the future regularity of their conduct: And 'tis only on the expectation of this, that our moderation and abstinence are founded. In like manner are languages gradually establish'd by human conventions without any promise. In like manner do gold and silver become the common measures of exchange, and are esteem'd sufficient payment for what is of a hundred times their value.

After this convention, concerning abstinence from the possessions of others, is enter'd into, and every one has acquir'd a stability in his possessions, there immediately arise the ideas of justice and injustice; as also those of *property*, *right*, and *obligation*. The latter are altogether unintelligible without first understanding the former. Our property is nothing but those goods, whose constant possession is establish'd by the laws of society; that is, by the laws of justice. Those, therefore, who make use of the words *property*, or *right*, or *obligation*, before they have explain'd the origin of justice, or even make use of them in that explication, are guilty of a very gross fallacy, and can never reason upon any solid foundation. A man's property is some object related to him. This relation is not natural, but moral, and founded on justice. 'Tis very preposterous, therefore, to imagine, that we can have any idea of property, without fully comprehending the nature of justice, and showing its origin in the artifice and contrivance of men. The origin of justice explains that of property. The same artifice gives rise to both. As our first and most natural sentiment of morals is founded on the nature of our passions, and gives the preference to ourselves and friends, above strangers; 'tis impossible there can be naturally any such thing as a fix'd right or property, while the opposite passions of men impel them in contrary directions, and are not restrain'd by any convention or agreement.

[. . .]

We come now to the *second* question we propos'd, viz. *Why we annex the idea of virtue to justice, and of vice to injustice?* This question will not detain us long after the principles, which we have already establish'd. All we can say of it at present will be dispatch'd in a few words: And for farther satisfaction, the reader must wait till we come to the *third* part of this book. The *natural* obligation to justice, viz. interest, has been fully explain'd; but as to the *moral* obligation, or the sentiment of right and wrong, 'twill first be requisite to examine the natural virtues, before we can give a full and satisfactory account of it.

After men have found by experience, that their selfishness and confin'd generosity, acting at their liberty, totally incapacitate them for society; and at the same time have observ'd, that society is necessary to the satisfaction of those very passions, they are naturally induc'd to lay themselves under the restraint of such rules, as may render their commerce more safe and commodious. To the imposition then, and observance of these rules, both in general, and in every particular instance, they are at first mov'd only by a regard to interest; and this motive, on the first formation of society, is sufficiently strong and forcible. But when society has become numerous, and has encreas'd to a tribe or nation, this interest is more remote; nor do men so readily perceive, that disorder and confusion follow upon every breach of these rules, as in a more narrow and contracted society. But tho' in our own actions we may frequently lose sight of that interest, which we have in maintaining order, and may follow a lesser and more present interest, we never fail to observe the prejudice we receive, either mediately or immediately, from the injustice of others; as not being in that case either blinded by passion, or byass'd by any contrary temptation. Nay when the injustice is so distant from us, as no way to affect our interest, it still displeases us; because we consider it as prejudicial to human society, and pernicious to every one that approaches the person guilty of it. We partake of their uneasiness by *sympathy*; and as every thing, which gives uneasiness in human actions, upon the general survey, is call'd *vice*, and whatever produces satisfaction, in the same manner, is denominated *virtue*; this is the reason why the sense of moral good and evil follows upon justice and injustice. And tho' this sense, in the present case, be deriv'd only from contemplating the actions of others, yet we fail not to extend it even to our own actions. The *general rule* reaches beyond those instances, from which it arose; while at the same time we naturally *sympathize* with others in the sentiments they entertain of us. Thus *self-interest* is the original motive to the *establishment* of justice: But a *sympathy* with *public* interest is the source of the *moral* approbation, which attends that virtue. This latter principle of sympathy is too weak to controul our passions; but has sufficient force to influence our taste, and give us the sentiments of approbation or blame.

[...]

Part 3
Of the Other Virtues and Vices

Section 1
Of the origin of the natural virtues and vices

We come now to the examination of such virtues and vices as are entirely natural, and have no dependance on the artifice and contrivance of men. The examination of these will conclude this system of morals.

The chief spring or actuating principle of the human mind is pleasure or pain; and when these sensations are remov'd, both from our thought and feeling, we are, in a great measure, incapable of passion or action, of desire or volition. The most immediate effects of pleasure and pain are the propense and averse motions of the mind; which are diversify'd into volition, into desire and aversion, grief and joy, hope and fear, according as the pleasure or pain changes its situation, and becomes probable or improbable, certain or uncertain, or is consider'd as out of our power for the present moment. But when along with this, the objects, that cause pleasure or pain, acquire a relation to ourselves or others; they still continue to excite desire and aversion, grief and joy: But cause, at the same time, the indirect passions of pride or humility, love or hatred, which in this case have a double relation of impressions and ideas to the pain or pleasure.

We have already observ'd, that moral distinctions depend entirely on certain peculiar sentiments of pain and pleasure, and that whatever mental quality in ourselves or others gives us a satisfaction, by the survey or reflection, is of course virtuous; as every thing of this nature, that gives uneasiness, is vicious. Now since every quality in ourselves or others, which gives pleasure, always causes pride or love; as every one, that produces uneasiness, excites humility or hatred: It follows, that these two particulars are to be consider'd as equivalent, with regard to our mental qualities, *virtue* and the power of producing love or pride, *vice* and the power of producing humility or hatred. In every case, therefore, we must judge of the one by the other; and may pronounce any *quality* of the mind virtuous, which causes love or pride; and any one vicious, which causes hatred or humility.

If any *action* be either virtuous or vicious, 'tis only as a sign of some quality or character. It must depend upon durable principles of the mind, which extend over the whole conduct, and enter into the personal character. Actions themselves, not proceeding from any constant principle, have no influence on love or hatred, pride or humility; and consequently are never consider'd in morality.

This reflection is self-evident, and deserves to be attended to, as being of the utmost importance in the present subject. We are never to consider any single action in our enquiries concerning the origin of morals; but only the quality or character from which the action proceeded. These alone are *durable* enough to affect our sentiments concerning the person. Actions are, indeed, better indications of a character than words, or even wishes and sentiments; but 'tis only so far as they are such indications, that they are attended with love or hatred, praise or blame.

To discover the true origin of morals, and of that love or hatred, which arises from mental qualities, we must take the matter pretty deep, and compare some principles, which have been already examin'd and explain'd.

We may begin with considering anew the nature and force of *sympathy*. The minds of all men are similar in their feelings and operations; nor can any one be actuated by any affection, of which all others are not, in some degree, susceptible. As in strings equally wound up, the motion of one communicates itself to the rest; so all the affections readily pass from one person to another, and beget correspondent movements in every human creature. When I see the *effects* of passion in the voice and gesture of any person, my mind immediately passes from these effects to their causes, and forms such a lively idea of the passion, as is presently converted into the passion itself. In like manner, when I perceive the *causes* of any emotion, my mind is convey'd to the effects, and is actuated with a like emotion. Were I present at any of the more terrible operations of surgery, 'tis certain, that even before it begun, the preparation of the instruments, the laying of the bandages in order, the heating of the irons, with all the signs of anxiety and concern in the patient and assistants, wou'd have a great effect upon my mind, and excite the strongest sentiments of pity and terror. No passion of another discovers itself immediately to the mind. We are only sensible of its causes or effects. From *these* we infer the passion: And consequently *these* give rise to our sympathy.

Our sense of beauty depends very much on this principle; and where any object has a tendency to produce pleasure in its possessor, it is always regarded as beautiful; as every object, that has a tendency to produce pain, is disagreeable and deform'd. Thus the conveniency of a house, the fertility of a field, the strength of a horse, the capacity, security, and swift-sailing of a vessel, form the principal beauty of these several objects. Here the object, which is denominated beautiful, pleases only by its tendency to produce a certain effect. That effect is the pleasure or advantage of some other person. Now the pleasure of a stranger, for whom we have no friendship, pleases us only by sympathy. To this principle, therefore, is owing the beauty, which we find in every thing that is useful. How considerable a part this is of beauty will easily appear upon reflection. Wherever an object has a tendency to produce pleasure in the possessor, or in other words, is the proper *cause* of pleasure, it is sure to please the spectator, by a delicate sympathy with the possessor. Most of the works of art are esteem'd beautiful, in proportion to their fitness for the use of man, and even many of the productions of nature derive their beauty from that source. Handsome and beautiful, on most occasions, is not an absolute but a relative quality, and pleases us by nothing but its tendency to produce an end that is agreeable.

The same principle produces, in many instances, our sentiments of morals, as well as those of beauty. No virtue is more esteem'd than justice, and no vice more detested than injustice; nor are there any qualities, which go farther to the fixing the character, either as amiable or odious. Now justice is a moral virtue, merely because it has that tendency to the good of mankind; and, indeed, is nothing but an artificial invention to that purpose. The same may be said of allegiance, of the laws of nations, of modesty, and of good-manners. All these are mere human contrivances for the interest of society. The inventors of them had chiefly in view their own interest. But we carry our approbation of them into the most distant countries and ages, and much beyond our own interest. And since there is a very strong sentiment of morals, which has always attended them, we must allow, that the reflecting on the tendency of characters and mental qualities, is sufficient to give us the sentiments of approbation and blame. Now as the means to an end can only be agreeable, where the end is agreeable; and as the good of society, where our own interest is not concern'd, or that of our friends, pleases only by sympathy: It follows, that sympathy is the source of the esteem, which we pay to all the artificial virtues.

Thus it appears, *that* sympathy is a very powerful principle in human nature, *that* it has a great influence on our taste of beauty, and *that* it produces our sentiment of morals in all the artificial virtues. From thence we may presume, that it also gives rise to many of the other virtues; and that qualities acquire our approbation, because of their tendency to the good of mankind. This presumption must become a certainty, when we find that most of those qualities, which we *naturally* approve of, have actually that tendency, and render a man a proper member of society: While the qualities, which we *naturally* disapprove of, have a contrary tendency, and render any intercourse with the person dangerous or disagreeable. For having found, that such tendencies have force enough to produce the strongest sentiment of morals, we can never reasonably, in these cases, look for any other cause of approbation or blame; it being an inviolable maxim in philosophy, that where any particular cause is sufficient for an effect, we ought to rest satisfy'd with it, and ought not to multiply causes without necessity. We have happily attain'd experiments in the artificial virtues, where the tendency of qualities to the good of society, is the *sole* cause of our approbation, without any suspicion of the concurrence of another principle. From thence we learn the force of that principle. And where that principle may take place, and the quality approv'd of is really beneficial to society, a true philosopher will never require any other principle to account for the strongest approbation and esteem.

That many of the natural virtues have this tendency to the good of society, no one can doubt of. Meekness, beneficence, charity, generosity, clemency, moderation, equity, bear the greatest figure among the moral qualities, and are commonly denominated the *social* virtues, to mark their tendency to the good of society. This goes so far, that some philosophers have represented all moral distinctions as the effect of artifice and education, when skilful politicians endeavour'd to restrain the turbulent passions of men, and make them operate to the public good, by the notions of honour and shame. This system, however, is not consistent with experience. For, *first*, there are other virtues and vices beside those which have this tendency to the public advantage and loss. *Secondly*, had not men a natural sentiment of approbation and blame, it cou'd never be excited by politicians; nor wou'd the words *laudable* and *praise-worthy*, *blameable* and *odious*, be any more intelligible, than if they were a language perfectly unknown to us, as we have already observ'd. But tho' this system be erroneous, it may teach us, that moral distinctions arise, in a great measure, from the tendency of qualities and characters to the interest of society, and that 'tis our concern for that interest, which makes us approve or disapprove of them. Now we have no such extensive concern for society but from sympathy; and consequently 'tis that principle, which takes us so far out of ourselves, as to give us the same pleasure or uneasiness in characters which are useful or pernicious to society, as if they had a tendency to our own advantage or loss.

The only difference betwixt the natural virtues and justice lies in this, that the good, which results from the former, arises from every single act, and is the object of some natural passion: Whereas a single act of justice, consider'd in itself, may often be contrary to the public good; and 'tis only the concurrence of mankind, in a general scheme or system of action, which is advantageous. When I relieve persons in distress, my natural humanity is my motive; and so far as my succour extends, so far have I promoted the happiness of my fellow-creatures. But if we examine all the questions, that come before any tribunal of justice, we shall find, that, considering each case apart, it wou'd as often be an instance of humanity to decide contrary to the laws of justice as conformable to them. Judges take from a poor man to give to a rich; they bestow on the dissolute the labour of the industrious; and put into the hands of the vicious the means of harming both themselves and others. The whole scheme, however, of law and justice is advantageous to the society and to every individual; and 'twas with a view to this advantage, that men, by their voluntary conventions, establish'd it. After it is once establish'd by these conventions, it is *naturally* attended with a strong sentiment of morals; which can proceed from nothing but our sympathy with the interests of society. We need no other explication of that esteem, which attends such of the natural virtues, as have a tendency to the public good.

I must farther add, that there are several circumstances, which render this hypothesis much more probable with regard to the natural than the artificial virtues. 'Tis certain, that the imagination is more affected by what is particular, than by what is general; and that the sentiments are always mov'd with difficulty, where their objects are, in any degree, loose and undetermin'd: Now every particular act of justice is not beneficial to society, but the whole scheme or system: And it may not, perhaps, be any individual person, for whom we are concern'd, who receives benefit from justice, but the whole society alike. On the contrary, every particular act of generosity, or relief of the industrious and indigent, is beneficial; and is beneficial to a particular person, who is not undeserving of it. 'Tis more natural, therefore, to think, that the tendencies of the latter virtue will affect our sentiments, and command our approbation, than those of the former; and therefore, since we find, that the approbation of the former arises from their tendencies, we may ascribe, with better reason, the same cause to the approbation of the latter. In any number of similar effects, if a cause can be discover'd for one, we ought to extend that cause to all the other effects, which can be accounted for by it: But much more, if these other effects be attended with peculiar circumstances, which facilitate the operation of that cause.

Before I proceed farther, I must observe two remarkable circumstances in this affair, which may seem objections to the present system. The first may be thus explain'd. When any quality, or character, has a tendency to the good of mankind, we are pleas'd with it, and approve of it; because it presents the lively idea of pleasure; which idea affects us by sympathy, and is itself a kind of pleasure. But as this sympathy is very variable, it may be thought, that our sentiments of morals must admit of all the same variations. We sympathize more with persons contiguous to us, than with persons remote from us: With our acquaintance, than with strangers: With our countrymen, than with foreigners. But notwithstanding this variation of our sympathy, we give the same approbation to the same moral qualities in *China* as in *England*. They appear equally virtuous, and recommend themselves equally to the esteem of a judicious spectator. The sympathy varies without a variation in our esteem. Our esteem, therefore, proceeds not from sympathy.

To this I answer: The approbation of moral qualities most certainly is not deriv'd from reason, or any comparison of ideas; but proceeds entirely from a moral taste, and from certain sentiments of pleasure or disgust, which arise upon the contemplation and view of particular qualities or characters. Now 'tis evident, that these sentiments, whence-ever they are deriv'd, must vary according to the distance or contiguity of the objects; nor can I feel the same lively pleasure from the virtues of a person, who liv'd in *Greece* two thousand years ago, that I feel from the virtues of a familiar friend and acquaintance. Yet I do not say, that I esteem the one more than the other: And therefore, if the variation of the sentiment, without a variation of the esteem, be an objection, it must have equal force against every other system, as against that of sympathy. But to consider the case aright, it has no force at all; and 'tis the easiest matter in the world to account for it. Our situation, with regard both to persons and things, is in continual fluctuation; and a man, that lies at a distance from us, may, in a little time, become a familiar acquaintance. Besides, every particular man has a peculiar position with regard to others; and 'tis impossible we cou'd ever converse together on any reasonable terms, were each of us to consider characters and persons, only as they appear from his peculiar point of view. In order, therefore, to prevent those continual *contradictions*, and arrive at a more *stable* judgment of things, we fix on some *steady* and *general* points of view; and always, in our thoughts, place ourselves in them, whatever may be our present situation. In like manner, external beauty is determin'd merely by pleasure; and 'tis evident, a beautiful countenance cannot give so much pleasure, when seen at the distance of twenty paces, as when it is brought nearer us. We say not, however, that it appears to us less beautiful: Because we know what effect it will have in such a position, and by that reflection we correct its momentary appearance.

In general, all sentiments of blame or praise are variable, according to our situation of nearness or remoteness, with regard to the person blam'd or prais'd, and according to the present disposition of our mind. But these variations we regard not in our general decisions, but still apply the terms expressive of our liking or dislike, in the same manner, as if we remain'd in one point of view. Experience soon teaches us this method of correcting our sentiments, or at least, of correcting our language, where the sentiments are more stubborn and inalterable. Our servant, if diligent and faithful, may excite stronger sentiments of love and kindness than *Marcus Brutus*, as represented in history; but we say not upon that account, that the former character is more laudable than the latter. We know, that were we to approach equally near to that renown'd patriot, he wou'd command a much higher degree of affection and admiration. Such corrections are common with regard to all the senses; and indeed 'twere impossible we cou'd ever make use of language, or communicate our sentiments to one another, did we not correct the momentary appearances of things, and overlook our present situation.

'Tis therefore from the influence of characters and qualities, upon those who have an intercourse with any person, that we blame or praise him. We consider not whether the persons, affected by the qualities, be our acquaintance or strangers, countrymen or foreigners. Nay, we over-look our own interest in those general judgments; and blame not a man for opposing us in any of our pretensions, when his own interest is particularly concern'd. We make allowance for a certain degree of selfishness in men; because we know it to be inseparable from human nature, and inherent in our frame and constitution. By this reflection we correct those sentiments of blame, which so naturally arise upon any opposition.

But however the general principle of our blame or praise may be corrected by those other principles, 'tis certain, they are not altogether efficacious, nor do our passions often correspond entirely to the present theory. 'Tis seldom men heartily love what lies at a distance from them, and what no way redounds to their particular benefit; as 'tis no less rare to meet with persons, who can pardon another any opposition he makes to their interest, however justifiable that opposition may be by the general rules of morality. Here we are contented with saying, that reason requires such an impartial conduct, but that 'tis seldom we can bring ourselves to it, and that our passions do not readily follow the determination of our judgment. This language will be easily understood, if we consider what we formerly said concerning that *reason*, which is able to oppose our passion; and which we have found to be nothing but a general calm determination of the passions, founded on some distant view or reflection. When we form our judgments of persons, merely from the tendency of their characters to our own benefit, or to that of our friends, we find so many contradictions to our sentiments in society and conversation, and such an uncertainty from the incessant changes of our situation, that we seek some other standard of merit and demerit, which may not admit of so great variation. Being thus loosen'd from our first station, we cannot afterwards fix ourselves so commodiously by any means as by a sympathy with those, who have any commerce with the person we consider. This is far from being as lively as when our own interest is concern'd, or that of our particular friends; nor has it such an influence on our love and hatred: But being equally conformable to our calm and general principles, 'tis said to have an equal authority over our reason, and to command our judgment and opinion. We blame equally a bad action, which we read of in history, with one perform'd in our neighbourhood the other day: The meaning of which is, that we know from reflection, that the former action wou'd excite as strong sentiments of disapprobation as the latter, were it plac'd in the same position.

I now proceed to the *second* remarkable circumstance, which I propos'd to take notice of. Where a person is possess'd of a character, that in its natural tendency is beneficial to society, we esteem him virtuous, and are delighted with the view of his character, even tho' particular accidents prevent its operation, and incapacitate him from being serviceable to his friends and country. Virtue in rags is still virtue; and the love, which it procures, attends a man into a dungeon or desart, where the virtue can no longer be exerted in action, and is lost to all the world. Now this may be esteem'd an objection to the present system. Sympathy interests us in the good of mankind; and if sympathy were the source of our esteem for virtue, that sentiment of approbation cou'd only take place, where the virtue actually attain'd its end, and was beneficial to mankind. Where it fails of its end, 'tis only an imperfect means; and therefore can never acquire any merit from that end. The goodness of an end can bestow a merit on such means alone as are compleat, and actually produce the end.

To this we may reply, that where any object, in all its parts, is fitted to attain any agreeable end, it naturally gives us pleasure, and is esteem'd beautiful, even tho' some external circumstances be wanting to render it altogether effectual. 'Tis sufficient if every thing be compleat in the object itself. A house, that is contriv'd with great judgment for all the commodities of life, pleases us upon that account; tho' perhaps we are sensible, that no one will ever dwell in it. A fertile soil, and a happy climate, delight us by a reflection on the happiness which they wou'd afford the inhabitants, tho' at present the country be desart and uninhabited. A man, whose limbs and shape promise strength and activity, is esteem'd handsome, tho' condemn'd to perpetual imprisonment. The imagination has a set of passions belonging to it, upon which our sentiments of beauty much depend. These passions are mov'd by degrees of liveliness and strength, which are inferior to *belief*, and independent of the real existence of their objects. Where a character is, in every respect, fitted to be beneficial to society, the imagination passes easily from the cause to the effect, without considering that there are still some circumstances wanting to render the cause a compleat one. *General rules* create a species of probability, which sometimes influences the judgement, and always the imagination.

18

Richard Price, *A Review of the Principal Questions in Morals* (1758)

In the history of moral philosophy, Richard Price is recognized as a critic of the "moral sense theory" popularized in Britain chiefly by Francis Hutcheson, David Hume, and Adam Smith. He objected to their moral sentimentalism primarily on epistemological grounds, pointing out that if moral ideas are sense-based, then the actions we consider right and wrong cannot be right and wrong *in themselves*. He reasoned that if we assume moral qualities depend on the feelings or sensations of observers, then we must think of them as qualities comparable to the colors and temperatures of objects. But just as no object is *by nature* green or cold, so no action would be *by nature* right or wrong. Price took this to mean also that God could have no good reason for having created us so that we generally abhor cheating or stealing, and admire kind or selfless people. If there is really nothing wrong with cheating or selfishness *in themselves*, then God could have created us so that we always feel sentiments of admiration for cheaters and for selfish people. This was a logical consequence of sentimentalist moral theories that Price could not accept.

In opposition to empiricism in general, Price insisted that human understanding itself can be a source of general ideas – for instance "equality." He assures us in the reading selections that follow that it is not by *sense* that we recognize two lines as equal, but by applying our understanding's idea of equality to the material provided by our senses. Something similar is true of moral ideas, he held. Even if our sentiments always approve of actions we judge to be right, they do so only because of our prior, "intuitive" understanding of the essential rightness of those actions. Nor do we understand the rightness of actions or virtues of characters in terms of their effects on the public good, as sentimentalists sometimes supposed. Imagine two worlds of roughly equal overall happiness, one where the virtuous are continually oppressed by the wicked, and one where the virtuous enjoy life and the wicked suffer. No one "unbiased," says Price, can regard these two arrangements as equally good from a moral point of view.

Price was born in Wales in 1723, and became a clergyman like his father, though he rejected many of the latter's more conservative views. He was perhaps best known in his lifetime for his writings in support of the American Revolution. But he also made contributions to the mathematics of probability, which were useful for establishing life insurance rates and benefits, and he was even invited by the fledgling American Congress to advise it on financial matters. Shortly before his death in 1791 Price preached a controversial sermon in support of the French Revolution that inspired vigorous public debate. Edmund Burke wrote in opposition to Price's ideas, and Mary Wollstonecraft, who was a member of Price's congregation, published a pamphlet entitled *A Vindication of the Rights of Man* in Price's defense.

Chapter I
Of the Origin of our Ideas of Right and Wrong

[. . .]

Section I
The Question Stated Concerning the Foundation of Morals

Some actions we all feel ourselves irresistibly determined to approve, and others to disapprove. Some actions we cannot but think *right*, and others *wrong*, and of all actions we are led to form some opinion, as either *fit* to be performed or *unfit*; or neither fit nor unfit to be performed; that is, *indifferent*. What the power within us is, which thus determines, is the question to be considered.

A late very distinguished writer, Dr. Hutcheson, deduces our moral ideas from a *moral sense*; meaning by this *sense*, a power within us, different from reason, which renders certain actions pleasing and others displeasing to us. As we are so made, that certain impressions on our bodily organs shall excite certain ideas in our minds, and that certain outward forms, when presented to us, shall be the necessary occasions of pleasure or pain. In like manner, according to Dr. Hutcheson, we are so made, that certain affections and actions of moral agents shall be the necessary occasions of agreeable or disagreeable sensations in us, and procure our love or dislike of them. He has indeed well shown, that we have a faculty determining us *immediately* to approve or disapprove actions, abstracted from all views of private advantage; and that the highest pleasures of life depend upon this faculty. Had he proceeded no farther, and intended nothing more by the *moral sense*, than our *moral faculty* in general, little room would have been left for any objections: but then he would have meant by it nothing *new*, and he could not have been considered as the *discoverer* of it. From the term *sense*, which he applies to it, from his rejection of all the arguments that have been used to prove it to be an intellectual power, and from the whole of his language on this subject; it is evident, he considered it as the effect of a *positive constitution* of our minds, or as an *implanted* and *arbitrary* principle, by which a *relish* is given us for certain moral objects and forms and aversion to others, similar to the relishes and aversions created by any of our other senses. In other words; our ideas of morality, if this account is right, have the same origin with our ideas of the sensible qualities of bodies, the harmony of sounds, or the beauties of painting or sculpture; that is, the mere good pleasure of our Maker adapting the mind and its organs in a particular manner to certain objects. Virtue (as those who embrace this scheme say) is an affair of taste. Moral right and wrong, signify nothing *in the objects themselves* to which they are applied, any more than agreeable and harsh; sweet and bitter; pleasant and painful; but only *certain effects in us*. Our perception of *right*, or moral good, in actions, is that agreeable *emotion*, or feeling, which certain actions produce in us; and of *wrong*, or moral evil, the contrary. They are particular modifications of our minds, or impressions which they are made to receive from the contemplation of certain actions, which the contrary actions *might* have occasioned, had the Author of nature so pleased; and which to suppose to belong to these actions themselves, is as absurd as to ascribe the pleasure or uneasiness, which the observation of a particular form gives us, to the form itself. It is therefore, by this account, improper to say of an action, that it *is right*, in much the same sense that it is improper to say of an object of taste, that it is *sweet*; or of *pain*, that it is *in* fire.

The present inquiry therefore is; whether this be a true account of virtue or not; whether it *has* or *has not* a foundation in the *nature* of its object; whether *right* and *wrong* are real characters of *actions*, or only qualities of our *minds*; whether, in short, they denote what actions *are*, or only *sensations* derived from the particular frame and structure of our natures.

[. . .]

Section II
Of the Origin of our Ideas in General

SENSATION and REFLECTION have been commonly reckoned the sources of all our ideas: and Mr. Locke has taken no small pains to prove this. How much soever, on the whole, I admire his excellent *Essay*, I cannot think him sufficiently clear or explicit on this subject. It is hard to determine exactly what he meant by *sensation* and *reflection*. If by the former we understand, the effects arising from the impressions made on our minds by external objects; and by the latter, the notice the mind takes of its own operations; it will be impossible to derive some of the most important of our ideas from them. This is the explanation Mr. Locke gives of them in the beginning of his *Essay*. But it seems probable that what he chiefly meant, was, that all our ideas are either derived *immediately* from these two sources, or ultimately *grounded* upon ideas so derived; or, in other words, that they furnish us with all the subjects, materials, and occasions of knowledge, comparison, and internal perception. This, however, by no means renders them in any proper sense, the sources of all our ideas: nor indeed does it appear, notwithstanding all he has said of the operations of the mind about its ideas, that he thought we had any faculty different from sensation and reflection which could give rise to any *simple ideas*; or that was capable of more than compounding, dividing, abstracting, or enlarging ideas previously in the mind. But be this as it may, what I am going to observe, will, I believe, be found true.

The power, I assert, that *understands*; or the faculty within us that discerns *truth*, and that compares all the objects of thought, and *judges* of them, is a spring of new ideas.

As, perhaps, this has not been enough attended to, and as the question to be discussed, is; whether our *moral ideas* are derived from the *understanding* or from a *sense*; it will be necessary to state distinctly the different natures and provinces of sense and reason.

To this purpose we may observe, first, that the power which judges of the perceptions of the senses, and contradicts their decisions; which discovers the nature of the sensible qualities of objects, inquires into their causes, and distinguishes between what is real and what is not real in them, must be a power within us which is superior to sense.

Again, it is plain that one sense cannot judge of the objects of another; the eye, for instance, of harmony, or the ear of colours. The faculty therefore which views and compares the objects of *all* the senses, cannot be sense. When, for instance, we consider sound and colour together, we observe in them *essence, number, identity, diversity*, etc. and determine their reality to consist, not in being properties of *external substances*, but in being modifications of *our souls*.

The power which takes cognizance of all this, and gives rise to these notions, must be a power capable of subjecting all things alike to its inspection, and of acquainting itself with necessary truth and existence.

Sense consists in the obtruding of certain impressions upon us, independently of our wills; but it cannot perceive what they are, or whence they are derived. It lies prostrate under its object, and is only a capacity in the soul of having its own state altered by the influence of particular causes. It must therefore remain a stranger to the objects and causes affecting it.

Were not *sense* and *knowledge* entirely different, we should rest satisfied with sensible impressions, such as light, colours, and sounds, and inquire no farther about them, at least when the impressions are strong and vigorous: whereas, on the contrary, we necessarily desire some farther acquaintance with them, and can never be satisfied till we have subjected them to the survey of reason. – Sense presents *particular* forms to the mind; but cannot rise to any *general* ideas. It is the intellect that examines and compares the presented forms, that rises above individuals to universal and abstract ideas; and thus looks downward upon objects, takes in at one view an infinity of particulars, and is capable of discovering general truths. – Sense sees only the *outside* of things, reason acquaints itself with their *natures*. – Sensation is only a mode of feeling in the mind; but knowledge implies an active and vital energy of the mind. Feeling pain, for example, is the effect of sense; but the understanding is employed when pain itself is made an object of the mind's reflection, or held up before it, in order to discover its nature and causes. Mere sense can perceive nothing in the most exquisite work of art; suppose a plant, or the body of an animal; but what is painted in the eye, or what might be described on paper. It is the intellect that must perceive in it order and proportion; variety and regularity; design, connection, art, and power; aptitudes, dependencies, correspondencies, and adjustment of parts so as to subserve an end, and compose one perfect whole; things which can never be represented on a sensible organ, and the ideas of which cannot be passively communicated, or stamped on the mind by the operation of external objects. – Sense cannot perceive any of the modes of thinking beings; these can be discovered only by the mind's survey of itself.

In a word, it appears that *sense* and *understanding* are faculties of the soul totally different: the one being conversant only about *particulars*; the other about *universals*: the one not *discerning*, but *suffering*; the other not *suffering*, but *discerning*; and signifying the soul's *power* of surveying and examining all things, in order to judge of them; which *power*, perhaps, can hardly be better defined, than by calling it, in Plato's language, the power in the soul to which belongs κατάληψις τοῦ ὄντος, or the apprehension of TRUTH.

But, in order farther to show how little a way mere sense (and let me add *imagination*, a faculty nearly allied to *sense*) can go, and how far we are dependent on our higher reasonable powers for many of our fundamental ideas; I would instance in the following particulars.

The idea of *solidity* has been generally reckoned among the ideas we owe to sense; and yet perhaps it would be difficult to prove, that we ever had actual experience of that *impenetrability* which we include in it, and consider as essential to all bodies.

[. . .]

Section III
Of the Origin of our Ideas of Moral Right and Wrong

Let us now return to our first inquiry, and apply the foregoing observations to our ideas of *right* and *wrong* in particular.

It is a very necessary previous observation, that our ideas of *right* and *wrong* are simple ideas, and must therefore be ascribed to some power of *immediate* perception in the human mind. He that doubts this, need only try to give definitions of them, which shall amount to more than synonymous expressions. Most of the confusion in which the question concerning the foundation of morals has been involved has proceeded from inattention to this remark. There are, undoubtedly, some actions that are *ultimately* approved, and for justifying which no reason can be assigned; as there are some ends, which are *ultimately* desired, and for choosing which no reason can be given. Were not this true; there would be an infinite progression of reasons and ends, and therefore nothing could be at all approved or desired.

Supposing then, that we have a power *immediately* perceiving right and wrong: the point I am now to endeavour to prove, is, that this power is the *understanding*, agreeably to the assertion at the end of the *first* section. I cannot but flatter myself, that the main obstacle to the acknowledgement of this, has been already removed, by the observations made in the preceding section, to show that the understanding is a power of immediate perception, which gives rise to new original ideas; nor do I think it possible that there should have been many disputes on this subject had this been properly considered.

But, in order more explicitly and distinctly to evince what I have asserted (in the only way the nature of the question seems capable of) let me,

First, observe, that it implies no absurdity, but evidently *may* be true. It is undeniable, that many of our ideas are derived from our INTUITION of truth, or the discernment of the natures of things by the understanding. This therefore *may* be the source of our moral ideas. It is at least *possible*, that *right* and *wrong* may denote what we *understand* and *know* concerning certain objects, in like manner with proportion and disproportion, connection and repugnancy, contingency and necessity, and the other ideas before-mentioned. – I will add, that nothing has been offered which has any tendency to prove the contrary. All that can appear, from the objections and reasonings of the author of the *Inquiry into the original of our ideas of beauty and virtue*, is only, what has been already observed, and what does not in the least affect the point in debate: namely, that the words *right* and *wrong*, *fit* and *unfit*, express simple and undefinable ideas. But that the power perceiving them is properly a *sense* and not *reason*; that these ideas denote nothing *true* of actions, nothing in the *nature* of actions; this, he has left entirely without proof. He appears, indeed, to have taken for granted, that if virtue and vice are *immediately* perceived, they must be perceptions of an *implanted* sense. But no conclusion could have been more hasty. For will any one take upon him to say, that all powers of immediate perception must be arbitrary and implanted; or that there can be no simple ideas denoting any thing besides the qualities and passions of the mind? – In short. Whatever some writers have said to the contrary, it is certainly a point not yet decided, that virtue is wholly factitious, and to be *felt*, not *understood*.

As there are some propositions, which, when attended to, necessarily determine all minds to *believe* them: and as (which will be shown hereafter) there are some ends, whose natures are such, that, when perceived, all beings immediately and necessarily *desire* them: so is it very credible, that, in like manner, there are some actions whose natures are such, that, when observed, all rational beings immediately and necessarily *approve* them.

I do not at all care what follows from Mr. Hume's assertion, that all our ideas are either *impressions, or copies of impressions*; or from Mr. Locke's assertion that they are all *deducible from* SENSATION *and* REFLECTION. – The first of these assertions is, I think, destitute of all proof; supposes, when applied in this as well as many other cases, the point in question; and, when pursued to its consequences, ends in the destruction of all truth and the subversion of our intellectual faculties. – The other wants much explication to render it consistent with any tolerable account of the original of our moral ideas: nor does there seem to be any thing necessary to convince a person, that all our ideas are not deducible from sensation and reflection, except taken in a very large and comprehensive sense, besides considering how Mr. Locke derives from them our *moral ideas*. He places them among our ideas of relations, and represents *rectitude* as signifying the conformity of actions to some rules or laws; which rules or laws, he says, are either *the will of God*, the *decrees of the magistrate, or the fashion of the country*: from whence it follows, that it is an absurdity to apply *rectitude* to rules and laws themselves; to suppose the *divine* will to be directed by it; or to consider it as *itself* a rule and law. But, it is undoubted, that this great man would have detested these consequences; and, indeed, it is sufficiently evident, that he was strangely embarrassed in his notions on this, as well as some other subjects. But,

Secondly, I know of no better way of determining this point, than by referring those who doubt about it to common sense, and putting them upon considering the nature of their own perceptions. – Could we suppose a person, who, when he perceived an external object, was at a loss to determine whether he perceived it by means of his organs of sight or touch; what better method could be taken to satisfy him? There is no possibility of doubting in any such cases. And it seems not more difficult to determine in the present case.

Were the question; what that perception is, which we have of number, diversity, causation or proportion; and whether our ideas of them signify truth and reality perceived by the understanding, or impressions made by the objects to which we ascribe them, on our minds; were, I say, this the question; would it not be sufficient to appeal to every man's consciousness? – These perceptions seem to me to have no greater pretence to be denominated perceptions of the understanding, than *right* and *wrong*.

It is true, some impressions of pleasure or pain, satisfaction or disgust, generally attend our perceptions of virtue and vice. But these are merely their effects and concomitants, and not the perceptions themselves, which ought no more to be confounded with them, than a particular truth (like that for which Pythagoras offered a hecatomb) ought to be confounded with the pleasure that may attend the discovery of it. Some emotion or other accompanies, perhaps, all our perceptions; but more remarkably our perceptions of right and wrong. And this, as will be again observed in the next chapter, is what has led to the mistake of making them to signify nothing but impressions, which error some have extended to all objects of knowledge; and thus have been led into an extravagant and monstrous scepticism.

But to return; let any one compare the ideas arising from our *powers of sensation*, with those arising from our *intuition of the natures of things*, and inquire which of them his ideas of right and wrong most resemble. On the issue of such a comparison may we safely rest this question. It is scarcely conceivable that any one can impartially attend to the nature of his own perceptions, and determine that, when he thinks gratitude or beneficence to be *right*, he perceives nothing *true* of them, and *understands* nothing, but only receives an impression from a *sense*. Was it possible for a person to question, whether his idea of *equality* was gained from sense or intelligence; he might soon be convinced, by considering, whether he is not sure, that certain lines or figures are *really* equal, and that their equality must be perceived by all minds, as soon as the objects themselves are perceived. – In the same manner may we satisfy ourselves concerning the origin of the idea of *right*: for have we not a like consciousness, that we discern the one, as well as the other, *in* certain objects? Upon what possible grounds can we pronounce the one to be *sense*, and the other *reason*? Would not a being purely intelligent, having happiness within his reach, *approve* of securing it for himself?

Would not he *think* this right; and would it not *be* right? When we contemplate the happiness of a species, or of a world, and pronounce concerning the actions of reasonable beings which promote it, that they are *right*; is this judging erroneously? Or is it no determination of judgement at all, but a species of mental taste? – Are not such actions *really right*? Or is every apprehension of rectitude in them false and delusive, just as the like apprehension is concerning the effects of external and internal sensation, when taken to belong to the causes producing them?

It seems beyond contradiction certain, that every being must *desire* happiness for himself; and can those natures of things, from which the *desire* of happiness and *aversion* to misery necessarily arise, leave, at the same time, a rational nature totally indifferent as to any *approbation* of actions procuring the one, or preventing the other? Is there nothing that any *understanding* can perceive to be amiss in a creature's bringing upon himself, or others, calamities and ruin? Is there nothing truly wrong in the absolute and eternal misery of an innocent being? – 'It *appears* wrong to us.' – And what reason can you have for doubting, whether it appears what *it is*? – Should a being, after being flattered with hopes of bliss, and having his expectations raised by encouragements and promises, find himself, without reason, plunged into irretrievable torments; would he not *justly* complain? Would he want a *sense* to cause the idea of *wrong* to arise in his mind? – Can goodness, gratitude, and veracity, appear to any mind under the same characters, with cruelty, ingratitude, and treachery? – Darkness may as soon appear to be light.

It would, I doubt, be to little purpose to plead further here, the natural and universal apprehensions of mankind, that our ideas of right and wrong belong to the understanding, and denote real characters of actions; because it will be easy to reply, that they have a like opinion of the *sensible qualities* of bodies; and that nothing is more common than for men to mistake their own sensations for the properties of the objects producing them, or to apply to the object itself, what they find always accompanying it, whenever observed. Let it therefore be observed,

Thirdly, that if right and wrong denote effects of sensation, it must imply the greatest absurdity to suppose them applicable to actions: that is; the ideas of *right* and *wrong* and of *action*, must in this, case be incompatible; as much so, as the idea of pleasure and a regular form, or of pain and the collisions of bodies. – All sensations, as such, are modes of consciousness, or feelings of a sentient being, which must be of a nature totally different form the particular causes which produce them. A *coloured body*, if we speak accurately, is the same absurdity with a *square sound*. We need no experiments to prove that heat, cold, colours, tastes, etc. are not real qualities of bodies; because the ideas of matter and of these qualities, are incompatible. – But is there indeed any such incompatibility between *actions* and *right*? Or any such absurdity in affirming the one of the other? – Are the ideas of them as different as the idea of a sensation, and its cause?

How strange would it be to maintain, that there is no possibility of *mistaking* with respect to right and wrong; that the apprehensions of all beings, on this subject, are alike just, since all sensation must be alike *true* sensation? – Is there a greater absurdity, than to suppose, that the *moral rectitude* of an action is nothing absolute and unvarying; but capable, like all the modifications of pleasure and pain, of being intended and remitted, of increasing and lessening, of rising and sinking with the force and liveliness of our feelings? Would it be less ridiculous to suppose this of the relations between given quantities, of the equality of numbers, or the figure of bodies?

In the last place; let it be considered, that all actions, undoubtedly, have a *nature*. That is, *some character* certainly belongs to them, and somewhat there is to be *truly* affirmed of them. This may be, that some of them are right, others wrong. But if this is not allowed; if no actions are, *in themselves*, either right or wrong, or any thing of a moral and obligatory nature, which can be an object to the understanding; it follows, that, in themselves, they *are* all indifferent. This is what is essentially true of them, and this is what all understandings, that perceive right, must perceive them to be. But are we not conscious, that we perceive the contrary? And have we not as much reason to believe the contrary, as to believe or trust at all our own discernment?

[. . .]

Chapter IV
Of our Ideas of Good and Ill Desert

It is needless to say any thing to show that the ideas of good and ill desert necessarily arise in us upon considering certain actions and characters; or, that we conceive virtue as always *worthy*, and vice as the contrary. These ideas are plainly a species of the ideas of right and wrong. There is, however, the following difference between them, which may be worth mentioning. The epithets, *right* and *wrong*, are, with strict propriety, applied only to *actions*; but *good* and *ill desert* belong rather to the *agent*. It is the *agent* alone, that is capable of happiness or misery; and, therefore, it is he alone that properly can be said to *deserve* these.

I apprehend no great difficulty in explaining these ideas. They suppose virtue practised, or neglected; and regard the treatment due to beings in consequence of this. They signify the propriety which there is in making virtuous agents happy, and in discountenancing the vicious. When we say, a man *deserves* well, we mean, that his character is such, that we *approve* of showing him *favour*; or that it is *right* he should be happier than if he had been of a contrary character. We cannot but love a virtuous agent, and desire his happiness above that of others. Reason determines at once, that he *ought* to be the better for his virtue. – A vicious being, on the contrary, as such, we cannot but hate and condemn. Our concern for his happiness is necessarily diminished; nor can any truth appear more self-evidently to our minds, than that it is improper he should prosper in his wickedness, or that happiness should be conferred on him to the same degree that it is on others of worthy characters; or that it would have been conferred on himself, had he been virtuous.

Different characters require different treatment. Virtue affords a *reason* for communicating happiness to the agent. Vice is a *reason* for withdrawing favour, and for punishing. – This seems to be very intelligible. But in order farther to explain this point, it is necessary to observe particularly, that the *whole* foundation of the sentiments now mentioned is by no means this; 'the tendency of virtue to the happiness of the world, and of vice to its misery; or the public utility of the one, and perniciousness of the other.' – We have an *immediate* approbation of making the virtuous happy, and discouraging the vicious, abstracted from all consequences. Were there but two beings in the universe, one of whom was virtuous, the other vicious; or, were we to conceive two such beings, in other respects alike, governed apart from the rest of the world, and removed for ever from the notice of all other creatures; we should still approve of a different treatment of them. That the good being should be less happy, or a greater sufferer, than his evil fellow-being, would appear to us wrong.

The moral worth or MERIT of an agent, then, is, 'his virtue considered as implying the fitness, that good should be communicated to him preferably to others; and as disposing all observers to esteem, and love him, and study his happiness.' – Virtue naturally, and of itself, recommends to favour and happiness, qualifies for them, and renders the being possessed of it the proper object of encouragement and reward. It is, in a like sense, we say that a person, who has been a benefactor to another, *deserves* well of him; that benefits received ought to be acknowledged and recompensed; and, that the person who bestows them is, preferably to others, the proper object of our regard and benevolence.

I deny not, but that one circumstance of great importance, upon which is grounded the fitness of countenancing virtue and discountenancing vice among reasonable beings, is, the manifest tendency of this to prevent misery, and to preserve order and happiness in the world. What I assert is, that it is not *all* that renders such a procedure right; but that, setting aside the consideration of public interest, it would still remain right to make a distinction between the lots of the virtuous and vicious. Vice is of ESSENTIAL DEMERIT; and virtue is *in itself rewardable*. For, once more, let us imagine an order of reasonable beings made to pass through a particular stage of existence, at the end of which they are annihilated: among whom, during the period they existed, no distinction was made on account of their different characters: virtue was not favoured, nor vice punished: happiness and misery were distributed promiscuously; the guilty often prosperous, and flourishing; the good, as often afflicted and distressed, and sometimes brought to untimely ends by the oppression of their more happy, though wicked fellow-beings: the *most* wicked, generally, the *least* sufferers; and the *most* upright, the *least* happy. Notwithstanding all this, the quantity of happiness enjoyed may be conceived to exceed the ill. But will any one say, that, were there no connection between such beings and the rest of the universe, there would be nothing in the disposition of its affairs that would be wrong? – It will be said, for nothing else can be said, 'that such a state of reasonable beings cannot be approved because there would have been *more* happiness among them, had their different lots been ordered agreeably to the rules of distributive justice.' But is it so unavoidable to see this, that every one's disapprobation must be always immediately determined by it? Is there no other kind of wrong in so governing a system of beings, than in producing a *smaller* quantity of happiness rather than a *greater*? Or can the view of such beings give as much satisfaction to an unbiased mind, as if there had been among them, upon the whole, the same quantity of happiness, but distributed with a regard to their moral characters?

In the case of a single, solitary evil being, it may perhaps be very true, that the only thing that could justify putting him into a state of absolute misery, would be its conduciveness to his reformation. But the reason why we approve of using methods to accomplish his reformation, is not merely this; 'that it is expedient to his happiness.' For were this true, it would, in a moral view, be indifferent whether he was made happy in consequence of being *punished* and thus reformed, or in consequence of such an extraordinary communication of advantages as should counteract and overbalance any sufferings necessarily occasioned by his vices. Can we equally approve these opposite methods of treating such a being? Supposing the same quantity of happiness enjoyed, is it indifferent whether a being enjoys it in a course of wickedness, or of virtue? – It would be extravagant to assert, that there is no *possible* method whereby a being can, in any degree, escape the hurtful effects of his vices, or lose the beneficial effects of his virtue. We see enough in the present world to convince us of the contrary.

19

Adam Smith, *The Theory of Moral Sentiments* (1759)

Although he is best known today as an economist, Adam Smith was a professor of moral philosophy at the University of Glasgow. In that post he succeeded his own professor, the influential moral-sense theorist Francis Hutcheson. But Smith departed from Hutcheson's teachings on the central point of the existence of a divinely implanted moral sense, by which we judge the virtue and vice of actions and characters. Smith's view was that our approbation or disapproval of conduct and character arise instead through a natural mechanism of sympathetic feeling.

In isolation from society, Smith held, every human being would concern himself with nothing other than the objects of his own passions and his own self-interest. But in the company of others, human beings naturally sympathize with the passions of those they observe, always mirroring their feelings to some degree. This is how we feel sorrow at the misfortune of others, and joy in their success. By the same mechanism we also hate the injustice that causes harm to others, and approve actions of gratitude or benevolence that benefit them. Smith accordingly found in these innate human tendencies toward selfless sentiments a basis for explaining morality. When we survey our own character and conduct we cannot help wanting to comport ourselves so as to inspire pleasing sentiments in others, pleasing sentiments that, through the mechanism of sympathy, we can expect to feel ourselves.

In agreement with other sentimentalists Smith admired, he said that we approve of actions as virtuous or vicious on the basis of the motives of their agents. But this raises a question whether we approve of actions as virtuous when they are motivated by the agent's regard to their rightness. David Hume had argued that the "sense of duty" cannot be approved as a virtuous motive for action; but Smith disagreed. Smith's view was that we certainly do not approve of many actions when they are motivated by the sense of duty: for example, actions called for by gratitude, or by love. The cold sense of duty is out of place here. Yet we do expect the sense of duty to motivate actions of justice, Smith held. He argued that since the general rules of justice admit precise formulations, whereas the rules or precepts for the other virtues must always remain vague and approximate, we expect the motives for just actions to adhere strictly to the rule that determines their justice; but we cannot expect this same regard to rules in the other virtues.

Born in Scotland in 1723, Smith graduated from the University of Glasgow and went on to study at Oxford. His reputation in moral philosophy was based on his *The Theory of Moral Sentiments*; but the work responsible for his still enduring fame was his treatise in economics, *An Inquiry into the Nature and Causes of the Wealth of Nations* (1776). Smith died in 1790, after having served briefly as rector of the University of Edinburgh, and then as commissioner of Scottish Customs.

Part I
Of the Propriety of Action

Section I
Of the Sense of Propriety

Chapter 1
Of sympathy

How selfish soever man may be supposed, there are evidently some principles in his nature, which interest him in the fortune of others, and render their happiness necessary to him, though he derives nothing from it, except the pleasure of seeing it. Of this kind is pity or compassion, the emotion which we feel for the misery of others, when we either see it, or are made to conceive it in a very lively manner. That we often derive sorrow from the sorrow of others, is a matter of fact too obvious to require any instances to prove it; for this sentiment, like all the other original passions of human nature, is by no means confined to the virtuous and humane, though they perhaps may feel it with the most exquisite sensibility. The greatest ruffian, the most hardened violator of the laws of society, is not altogether without it.

As we have no immediate experience of what other men feel, we can form no idea of the manner in which they are affected, but by conceiving what we ourselves should feel in the like situation. Though our brother is upon the rack, as long as we ourselves are at our ease, our senses will never inform us of what he suffers. They never did, and never can, carry us beyond our own person, and it is by the imagination only that we can form any conception of what are his sensations. Neither can that faculty help us to this any other way, than by representing to us what would be our own, if we were in his case. It is the impressions of our own senses only, not those of his, which our imaginations copy. By the imagination we place ourselves in his situation, we conceive ourselves enduring all the same torments, we enter as it were into his body, and become in some measure the same person with him, and thence form some idea of his sensations, and even feel something which, though weaker in degree, is not altogether unlike them. His agonies, when they are thus brought home to ourselves, when we have thus adopted and made them our own, begin at last to affect us, and we then tremble and shudder at the thought of what he feels. For as to be in pain or distress of any kind excites the most excessive sorrow, so to conceive or to imagine that we are in it, excites some degree of the same emotion, in proportion to the vivacity or dulness of the conception.

That this is the source of our fellow-feeling for the misery of others, that it is by changing places in fancy with the sufferer, that we come either to conceive or to be affected by what he feels, may be demonstrated by many obvious observations, if it should not be thought sufficiently evident of itself. When we see a stroke aimed, and just ready to fall upon the leg or arm of another person, we naturally shrink and draw back our own leg or our own arm; and when it does fall, we feel it in some measure, and are hurt by it as well as the sufferer. The mob, when they are gazing at a dancer on the slack rope, naturally writhe and twist and balance their own bodies as they see him do, and as they feel that they themselves must do if in his situation. Persons of delicate fibres and a weak constitution of body complain, that in looking on the sores and ulcers which are exposed by beggars in the streets, they are apt to feel an itching or uneasy sensation in the corresponding part of their own bodies. The horror which they conceive at the misery of those wretches affects that particular part in themselves more than any other; because that horror arises from conceiving what they themselves would suffer, if they really were the wretches whom they are looking upon, and if that particular part in themselves was actually affected in the same miserable manner. The very force of this conception is sufficient, in their feeble frames, to produce that itching or uneasy sensation complained of. Men of the most robust make, observe that in looking upon sore eyes they often feel a very sensible soreness in their own, which proceeds from the same reason; that organ being in the strongest man more delicate than any other part of the body is in the weakest.

Neither is it those circumstances only, which create pain or sorrow, that call forth our fellow-feeling. Whatever is the passion which arises from any object in the person principally concerned, an analogous emotion springs up, at the thought of his situation, in the breast of every attentive spectator. Our joy for the deliverance of those heroes of tragedy or romance who interest us, is as sincere as our grief for their distress, and our fellow-feeling with their misery is not more real than that with their happiness. We enter into their gratitude towards those faithful friends who did not desert them in their difficulties; and we heartily go along with their resentment against those perfidious traitors who injured, abandoned, or deceived them. In every passion of which the mind of man is susceptible, the emotions of the bystander always correspond to what, by bringing the case home to himself, he imagines should be the sentiments of the sufferer.

Pity and compassion are words appropriated to signify our fellow-feeling with the sorrow of others. Sympathy, though its meaning was, perhaps, originally the same, may now, however, without much impropriety, be made use of to denote our fellow-feeling with any passion whatever.

Upon some occasions sympathy may seem to arise merely from the view of a certain emotion in another person. The passions, upon some occasions, may seem to be transfused from one man to another, instantaneously, and antecedent to any knowledge of what excited them in the person principally concerned. Grief and joy, for example, strongly expressed in the look and gestures of any person, at once affect the spectator with some degree of a like painful or agreeable emotion. A smiling face is, to everybody that sees it, a cheerful object; as a sorrowful countenance, on the other hand, is a melancholy one.

This, however, does not hold universally, or with regard to every passion. There are some passions of which the expressions excite no sort of sympathy, but, before we are acquainted with what gave occasion to them, serve rather to disgust and provoke us against them. The furious behaviour of an angry man is more likely to exasperate us against himself than against his enemies. As we are unacquainted with his provocation, we cannot bring his case home to ourselves, nor conceive any thing like the passions which it excites. But we plainly see what is the situation of those with whom he is angry, and to what violence they may be exposed from so enraged an adversary. We readily, therefore, sympathize with their fear or resentment, and are immediately disposed to take part against the man from whom they appear to be in danger.

If the very appearances of grief and joy inspire us with some degree of the like emotions, it is because they suggest to us the general idea of some good or bad fortune that has befallen the person in whom we observe them: and in these passions this is sufficient to have some little influence upon us. The effects of grief and joy terminate in the person who feels those emotions, of which the expressions do not, like those of resentment, suggest to us the idea of any other person for whom we are concerned, and whose interests are opposite to his. The general idea of good or bad fortune, therefore, creates some concern for the person who has met with it; but the general idea of provocation excites no sympathy with the anger of the man who has received it. Nature, it seems, teaches us to be more averse to enter into this passion, and, till informed of its cause, to be disposed rather to take part against it.

Even our sympathy with the grief or joy of another, before we are informed of the cause of either, is always extremely imperfect. General lamentations, which express nothing but the anguish of the sufferer, create rather a curiosity to enquire into his situation, along with some disposition to sympathize with him, than any actual sympathy that is very sensible. The first question which we ask is, What has befallen you? Till this be answered, though we are uneasy both from the vague idea of his misfortune, and still more from torturing ourselves with conjectures about what it may be, yet our fellow-feeling is not very considerable.

Sympathy, therefore, does not arise so much from the view of the passion, as from that of the situation which excites it. We sometimes feel for another, a passion of which he himself seems to be altogether incapable; because, when we put ourselves in his case, that passion arises in our breast from the imagination, though it does not in his from the reality. We blush for the impudence and rudeness of another, though he himself appears to have no sense of the impropriety of his own behavior; because we cannot help feeling with what confusion we ourselves should be covered, had we behaved in so absurd a manner.

Of all the calamities to which the condition of mortality exposes mankind, the loss of reason appears, to those who have the least spark of humanity, by far the most dreadful; and they behold that last stage of human wretchedness with deeper commiseration than any other. But the poor wretch, who is in it, laughs and sings, perhaps, and is altogether insensible to his own misery. The anguish which humanity feels, therefore, at the sight of such an object, cannot be the reflection of any sentiment of the sufferer. The compassion of the spectator must arise altogether from the consideration of what he himself would feel if he was reduced to the same unhappy situation, and, what perhaps is impossible, was at the same time able to regard it with his present reason and judgment.

[. . .]

Chapter 4
The same subject continued*

We may judge of the propriety or impropriety of the sentiments of another person by their correspondence or disagreement with our own, upon two different occasions; either, first, when the objects which excite them are considered without any peculiar relation, either to ourselves or to the person whose sentiments we judge of; or, secondly, when they are considered as peculiarly affecting one or other of us.

1. With regard to those objects which are considered without any peculiar relation either to ourselves or to the person whose sentiments we judge of; wherever his sentiments entirely

---

* Smith's title for this chapter refers to the subject of his previous chapter, entitled: *"Of the manner in which we judge of the propriety or impropriety of the affections of other men, by their concord or dissonance with our own."*

correspond with our own, we ascribe to him the qualities of taste and good judgment. The beauty of a plain, the greatness of a mountain, the ornaments of a building, the expression of a picture, the composition of a discourse, the conduct of a third person, the proportions of different quantities and numbers, the various appearances which the great machine of the universe is perpetually exhibiting, with the secret wheels and springs which produce them; all the general subjects of science and taste, are what we and our companions regard as having no peculiar relation to either of us. We both look at them from the same point of view, and we have no occasion for sympathy, or for that imaginary change of situations from which it arises, in order to produce, with regard to these, the most perfect harmony of sentiments and affections. If, notwithstanding, we are often differently affected, it arises either from the different degrees of attention which our different habits of life allow us to give easily to the several parts of those complex objects, or from the different degrees of natural acuteness in the faculty of the mind to which they are addressed.

When the sentiments of our companion coincide with our own in things of this kind, which are obvious and easy, and in which, perhaps, we never found a single person who differed from us, though we, no doubt, must approve of them, yet he seems to deserve no praise or admiration on account of them. But when they not only coincide with our own, but lead and direct our own; when, in forming them, he appears to have attended to many things which we had overlooked, and to have adjusted them to all the various circumstances of their objects; we not only approve of them, but wonder and are surprised at their uncommon and unexpected acuteness and comprehensiveness, and he appears to deserve a very high degree of admiration and applause. For approbation, heightened by wonder and surprise, constitutes the sentiment which is properly called admiration, and of which applause is the natural expression. The decision of the man who judges that exquisite beauty is preferable to the grossest deformity, or that twice two are equal to four, must certainly be approved of by all the world, but will not, surely, be much admired. It is the acute and delicate discernment of the man of taste, who distinguishes the minute, and scarce perceptible differences of beauty and deformity; it is the comprehensive accuracy of the experienced mathematician, who unravels with ease the most intricate and perplexed proportions; it is the great leader in science and taste, the man who directs and conducts our own sentiments, the extent and superior justness of whose talents astonish us with wonder and surprise, who excites our admiration, and seems to deserve our applause; and upon this foundation is grounded the greater part of the praise which is bestowed upon what are called the intellectual virtues.

The utility of these qualities, it may be thought, is what first recommends them to us; and, no doubt, the consideration of this, when we come to attend to it, gives them a new value. Originally, however, we approve of another man's judgment, not as something useful, but as right, as accurate, as agreeable to truth and reality; and it is evident we attribute those qualities to it for no other reason but because we find that it agrees with our own. Taste, in the same manner, is originally approved of, not as useful, but as just, as delicate, and as precisely suited to its object. The idea of the utility of all qualities of this kind is plainly an afterthought, and not what first recommends them to our approbation.

2. With regard to those objects, which affect in a particular manner either ourselves or the person whose sentiments we judge of, it is at once more difficult to preserve this harmony and correspondence, and, at the same time, vastly more important. My companion does not naturally look upon the misfortune that has befallen me, or the injury that has been done me, from the same point of view in which I consider them. They affect me much more nearly. We do not view them from the same station, as we do a picture, or a poem, or a

system of philosophy; and are therefore apt to be very differently affected by them. But I can much more easily overlook the want of this correspondence of sentiments with regard to such indifferent objects as concern neither me nor my companion, than with regard to what interests me so much as the misfortune that has befallen me, or the injury that has been done me. Though you despise that picture, or that poem, or even that system of philosophy which I admire, there is little danger of our quarrelling upon that account. Neither of us can reasonably be much interested about them. They ought all of them to be matters of great indifference to us both; so that, though our opinions may be opposite, our affections may still be very nearly the same. But it is quite otherwise with regard to those objects by which either you or I are particularly affected. Though your judgments in matters of speculation, though your sentiments in matters of taste, are quite opposite to mine, I can easily overlook this opposition; and if I have any degree of temper, I may still find some entertainment in your conversation, even upon those very subjects. But if you have either no fellow-feeling for the misfortunes I have met with, or none that bears any proportion to the grief which distracts me; or if you have either no indignation at the injuries I have suffered, or none that bears any proportion to the resentment which transports me, we can no longer converse upon these subjects. We become intolerable to one another. I can neither support your company, nor you mine. You are confounded at my violence and passion, and I am enraged at your cold insensibility and want of feeling.

In all such cases, that there may be some correspondence of sentiments between the spectator and the person principally concerned, the spectator must, first of all, endeavour as much as he can to put himself in the situation of the other, and to bring home to himself every little circumstance of distress which can possibly occur to the sufferer. He must adopt the whole case of his companion, with all its minutest incidents; and strive to render as perfect as possible that imaginary change of situation upon which his sympathy is founded.

After all this, however, the emotions of the spectator will still be very apt to fall short of the violence of what is felt by the sufferer. Mankind, though naturally sympathetic, never conceive, for what has befallen another, that degree of passion which naturally animates the person principally concerned. That imaginary change of situation, upon which their sympathy is founded, is but momentary. The thought of their own safety, the thought that they themselves are not really the sufferers, continually intrudes itself upon them; and though it does not hinder them from conceiving a passion somewhat analogous to what is felt by the sufferer, hinders them from conceiving any thing that approaches to the same degree of violence. The person principally concerned is sensible of this, and at the same time passionately desires a more complete sympathy. He longs for that relief which nothing can afford him but the entire concord of the affections of the spectators with his own. To see the emotions of their hearts in every respect beat time to his own, in the violent and disagreeable passions, constitutes his sole consolation. But he can only hope to obtain this by lowering his passion to that pitch, in which the spectators are capable of going along with him. He must flatten, if I may be allowed to say so, the sharpness of its natural tone, in order to reduce it to harmony and concord with the emotions of those who are about him. What they feel will, indeed, always be in some respects different from what he feels, and compassion can never be exactly the same with original sorrow; because the secret consciousness that the change of situations, from which the sympathetic sentiment arises, is but imaginary, not only lowers it in degree, but in some measure varies it in kind, and gives it a quite different modification. These two sentiments, however, may, it is evident, have such a correspondence with one another, as is sufficient for the harmony of society. Though they will never be unisons, they may be concords, and this is all that is wanted or required.

In order to produce this concord, as nature teaches the spectators to assume the circumstances of the person principally concerned, so she teaches this last in some measure to assume those of the spectators. As they are continually placing themselves in his situation, and thence conceiving emotions similar to what he feels; so he is as constantly placing himself in theirs, and thence conceiving some degree of that coolness about his own fortune, with which he is sensible that they will view it. As they are constantly considering what they themselves would feel, if they actually were the sufferers, so he is constantly led to imagine in what manner he would be affected if he was only one of the spectators of his own situation. As their sympathy makes them look at it in some measure with his eyes, so his sympathy makes him look at it, in some measure, with theirs, especially when in their presence, and acting under their observation: and, as the reflected passion which he thus conceives is much weaker than the original one, it necessarily abates the violence of what he felt before he came into their presence, before he began to recollect in what manner they would be affected by it, and to view his situation in this candid and impartial light.

The mind, therefore, is rarely so disturbed, but that the company of a friend will restore it to some degree of tranquillity and sedateness. The breast is, in some measure, calmed and composed the moment we come into his presence. We are immediately put in mind of the light in which he will view our situation, and we begin to view it ourselves in the same light; for the effect of sympathy is instantaneous. We expect less sympathy from a common acquaintance than from a friend; we cannot open to the former all those little circumstances which we can unfold to the latter; we assume, therefore, more tranquillity before him, and endeavour to fix our thoughts upon those general outlines of our situation which he is willing to consider. We expect still less sympathy from an assembly of strangers, and we assume, therefore, still more tranquillity before them, and always endeavour to bring down our passion to that pitch, which the particular company we are in may be expected to go along with. Nor is this only an assumed appearance; for if we are at all masters of ourselves, the presence of a mere acquaintance will really compose us, still more than that of a friend; and that of an assembly of strangers, still more than that of an acquaintance.

Society and conversation, therefore, are the most powerful remedies for restoring the mind to its tranquillity, if, at any time, it has unfortunately lost it; as well as the best preservatives of that equal and happy temper, which is so necessary to self-satisfaction and enjoyment. Men of retirement and speculation, who are apt to sit brooding at home over either grief or resentment, though they may often have more humanity, more generosity, and a nicer sense of honour, yet seldom possess that equality of temper which is so common among men of the world.

[. . .]

Part III
Of the Foundation of our Judgments concerning our own Sentiments and Conduct, and of the Sense of Duty

Chapter 1
Of the principle of self-approbation and of self-disapprobation

In the two foregoing parts of this discourse, I have chiefly considered the origin and foundation of our judgments concerning the sentiments and conduct of others. I come now to consider more particularly the origin of those concerning our own.

The principle by which we naturally either approve or disapprove of our own conduct, seems to be altogether the same with that by which we exercise the like judgments concerning the conduct of other people. We either approve or disapprove of the conduct of another man according as we feel that, when we bring his case home to ourselves, we either can or cannot entirely sympathize with the sentiments and motives which directed it. And, in the same manner, we either approve or disapprove of our own conduct, according as we feel that, when we place ourselves in the situation of another man, and view it, as it were, with his eyes and from his station, we either can or cannot entirely enter into and sympathize with the sentiments and motives which influenced it. We can never survey our own sentiments and motives, we can never form any judgment concerning them; unless we remove ourselves, as it were, from our own natural station, and endeavour to view them as at a certain distance from us. But we can do this in no other way than by endeavouring to view them with the eyes of other people, or as other people are likely to view them. Whatever judgment we can form concerning them, accordingly, must always bear some secret reference, either to what are, or to what, upon a certain condition, would be, or to what, we imagine, ought to be the judgment of others. We endeavour to examine our own conduct as we imagine any other fair and impartial spectator would examine it. If, upon placing ourselves in his situation, we thoroughly enter into all the passions and motives which influenced it, we approve of it, by sympathy with the approbation of this supposed equitable judge. If otherwise, we enter into his disapprobation, and condemn it.

Were it possible that a human creature could grow up to manhood in some solitary place, without any communication with his own species, he could no more think of his own character, of the propriety or demerit of his own sentiments and conduct, of the beauty or deformity of his own mind, than of the beauty or deformity of his own face. All these are objects which he cannot easily see, which naturally he does not look at, and with regard to which he is provided with no mirror which can present them to his view. Bring him into society, and he is immediately provided with the mirror which he wanted before. It is placed in the countenance and behaviour of those he lives with, which always mark when they enter into, and when they disapprove of his sentiments; and it is here that he first views the propriety and impropriety of his own passions, the beauty and deformity of his own mind. To a man who from his birth was a stranger to society, the objects of his passions, the external bodies which either pleased or hurt him, would occupy his whole attention. The passions themselves, the desires or aversions, the joys or sorrows, which those objects excited, though of all things the most immediately present to him, could scarce ever be the objects of his thoughts. The idea of them could never interest him so much as to call upon his attentive consideration. The consideration of his joy could in him excite no new joy, nor that of his sorrow any new sorrow, though the consideration of the causes of those passions might often excite both. Bring him into society, and all his own passions will immediately become the causes of new passions. He will observe that mankind approve of some of them, and are disgusted by others. He will be elevated in the one case, and cast down in the other; his desires and aversions, his joys and sorrows, will now often become the causes of new desires and new aversions, new joys and new sorrows: they will now, therefore, interest him deeply, and often call upon his most attentive consideration.

Our first ideas of personal beauty and deformity, are drawn from the shape and appearance of others, not from our own. We soon become sensible, however, that others exercise the same criticism upon us. We are pleased when they approve of our figure, and are disobliged when they seem to be disgusted. We become anxious to know how far our appearance deserves either their blame or approbation. We examine our persons limb by limb, and by placing ourselves before a looking-glass, or by some such expedient, endeavour, as much as possible, to view ourselves at the distance and with the eyes of other people. If, after this examination, we are satisfied with our own appearance, we can more easily support the most disadvantageous judgments of others. If, on the contrary, we are sensible that we are the natural objects of distaste, every appearance of their disapprobation mortifies us beyond all measure. A man who is tolerably handsome, will allow you to laugh at any little irregularity in his person; but all such jokes are commonly unsupportable to one who is really deformed. It is evident, however, that we are anxious about our own beauty and deformity, only upon account of its effect upon others. If we had no connexion with society, we should be altogether indifferent about either.

In the same manner our first moral criticisms are exercised upon the characters and conduct of other people; and we are all very forward to observe how each of these affects us. But we soon learn, that other people are equally frank with regard to our own. We become anxious to know how far we deserve their censure or applause, and whether to them we must necessarily appear those agreeable or disagreeable creatures which they represent us. We begin, upon this account, to examine our own passions and conduct, and to consider how these must appear to them, by considering how they would appear to us if in their situation. We suppose ourselves the spectators of our own behaviour, and endeavour to imagine what effect it would, in this light, produce upon us. This is the only looking-glass by which we can, in some measure, with the eyes of other people, scrutinize the propriety of our own conduct. If in this view it pleases us, we are tolerably satisfied. We can be more indifferent about the applause, and, in some measure, despise the censure of the world, secure that, however misunderstood or misrepresented, we are the natural and proper objects of approbation. On the contrary, if we are doubtful about it, we are often, upon that very account, more anxious to gain their approbation, and, provided we have not already, as they say, shaken hands with infamy, we are altogether distracted at the thoughts of their censure, which then strikes us with double severity.

When I endeavour to examine my own conduct, when I endeavour to pass sentence upon it, and either to approve or condemn it, it is evident that, in all such cases, I divide myself, as it were, into two persons; and that I, the examiner and judge, represent a different character from that other I, the person whose conduct is examined into and judged of. The first is the spectator, whose sentiments with regard to my own conduct I endeavour to enter into, by placing myself in his situation, and by considering how it would appear to me, when seen from that particular point of view. The second is the agent, the person whom I properly call myself, and of whose conduct, under the character of a spectator, I was endeavouring to form some opinion. The first is the judge; the second the person judged of. But that the judge should, in every respect, be the same with the person judged of, is as impossible, as that the cause should, in every respect, be the same with the effect.

To be amiable and to be meritorious; that is, to deserve love and to deserve reward, are the great characters of virtue; and to be odious and punishable, of vice. But all these characters have an immediate reference to the sentiments of others. Virtue is not said to be amiable, or to be meritorious, because it is the object of its own love, or of its own gratitude; but because it excites those sentiments in other men. The consciousness that it is the object of such favourable regards, is the source of that inward tranquillity and self-satisfaction with which it is naturally attended, as the suspicion of the contrary gives occasion to the torments of vice. What so great happiness as to be beloved, and to know that we deserve to be beloved? What so great misery as to be hated, and to know that we deserve to be hated?

[. . .]

Chapter 6
In what cases the sense of duty ought to be the sole principle of our conduct; and in what cases it ought to concur with other motives

[. . .]

The decision of this question, which cannot, perhaps, be given with any very great accuracy, will depend upon two different circumstances; first, upon the natural agreeableness or deformity of the sentiment or affection which would prompt us to any action independent of all regard to general rules; and, secondly, upon the precision and exactness, or the looseness and inaccuracy, of the general rules themselves.

1. First, I say, it will depend upon the natural agreeableness or deformity of the affection itself, how far our actions ought to arise from it, or entirely proceed from a regard to the general rule.

All those graceful and admired actions to which the benevolent affections would prompt us, ought to proceed as much from the passions themselves as from any regard to the general rules of conduct. A benefactor thinks himself but ill requited if the person upon whom he has bestowed his good offices repays them merely from a cold sense of duty, and without any affection to his person. A husband is dissatisfied with the most obedient wife, when he imagines her conduct is animated by no other principle besides her regard to what the relation she stands in requires. Though a son should fail in none of the offices of filial duty, yet if he wants that affectionate reverence which it so well becomes him to feel, the parent may justly complain of his indifference. Nor could a son be quite satisfied with a parent who, though he performed all the duties of his situation, had nothing of that fatherly fondness which might have been expected from him. With regard to all such benevolent and social affections, it is agreeable to see the sense of duty employed rather to restrain than to enliven them, rather to hinder us from doing too much, than to prompt us to do what we ought. It gives us pleasure to see a father obliged to check his own fondness, a friend obliged to set bounds to his natural generosity, a person who has received a benefit, obliged to restrain the too sanguine gratitude of his own temper.

The contrary maxim takes place with regard to the malevolent and unsocial passions. We ought to reward from the gratitude and generosity of our own hearts, without any reluctance, and without being obliged to reflect how great the propriety of rewarding; but we ought always to punish with reluctance, and more from a sense of the propriety of punishing than from any savage disposition to revenge. Nothing is more graceful than the behaviour of the man who appears to resent the greatest injuries, more from a sense that they deserve, and are the proper objects of resentment, than from feeling himself the furies of that disagreeable passion; who, like a judge, considers only the general rule, which determines what vengeance is due for each particular offence; who, in executing that rule, feels less for what himself has suffered, than for what the offender is about to suffer; who, though in wrath, remembers mercy, and is disposed to interpret the rule in the most gentle and favourable manner, and to allow all the alleviations which the most candid humanity could, consistently with good sense, admit of.

[. . .]

2. Secondly, I say it will depend partly upon the precision and exactness, or the looseness and inaccuracy of the general rules themselves, how far our conduct ought to proceed entirely from a regard to them.

The general rules of almost all the virtues, the general rules which determine what are the offices of prudence, of charity, of generosity, of gratitude, of friendship, are in many respects loose and inaccurate, admit of many exceptions, and require so many modifications, that it is scarce possible to regulate our conduct entirely by a regard to them. The common pro-verbial maxims of prudence, being founded in universal experience, are perhaps the best general rules which can be given about it. To affect, however, a very strict and literal adher-ence to them, would evidently be the most absurd and ridiculous pedantry. Of all the virtues I have just now mentioned, gratitude is that, perhaps, of which the rules are the most precise, and admit of the fewest exceptions. That as soon as we can we should make a return of equal, and, if possible, of superior value to the services we have received, would seem to be a pretty plain rule, and one which admitted of scarce any exceptions. Upon the most superficial examination, however, this rule will appear to be in the highest degree loose and inaccurate, and to admit of ten thousand exceptions. If your benefactor attended you in your sickness, ought you to attend him in his? or can you fulfil the obligation of gratitude by mak-ing a return of a different kind? If you ought to attend him, how long ought you to attend him? The same time which he attended you, or longer, and how much longer?

[. . .]

There is, however, one virtue, of which the general rules determine, with the greatest exactness, every external action which it requires. This virtue is Justice. The rules of justice are accurate in the highest degree, and admit of no exceptions or modifications but such as may be ascertained as accurately as the rules themselves, and which generally, indeed, flow from the very same principles with them. If I owe a man ten pounds, justice requires that I should precisely pay him ten pounds, either at the time agreed upon, or when he demands it. What I ought to perform, how much I ought to perform, when and where I ought to perform it, the whole nature and circumstances of the action prescribed, are all of them pre-cisely fixed and determined. Though it may be awkward and pedantic, therefore, to affect too strict an adherence to the common rules of prudence or generosity, there is no pedantry in sticking fast by the rules of justice. On the contrary, the most sacred regard is due to them; and the actions which this virtue requires are never so properly performed as when the chief motive for performing them is a reverential and religious regard to those general rules which require them. In the practice of the other virtues, our conduct should rather be directed by a certain idea of propriety, by a certain taste for a particular tenor of conduct, than by any regard to a precise maxim or rule; and we should consider the end and foundation of the rule more than the rule itself. But it is otherwise with regard to justice: the man who in that refines the least, and adheres with the most obstinate stedfastness to the general rules them-selves, is the most commendable, and the most to be depended upon. Though the end of the rules of justice be to hinder us from hurting our neighbour, it may frequently be a crime to violate them, though we could pretend, with some pretext of reason, that this particular violation could do no hurt. A man often becomes a villain the moment he begins, even in his own heart, to chicane in this manner. The moment he thinks of departing from the most staunch and positive adherence to what those inviolable precepts prescribe to him, he is no longer to be trusted, and no man can say what degree of guilt he may not arrive at. The thief imagines he does no evil when he steals from the rich, what he supposes they may easily want, and what possibly they may never even know has been stolen from them. The adulterer imagines he does no evil when he corrupts the wife of his friend, provided he covers his intrigue from the suspicion of the husband, and does not disturb the peace of the family. When once we begin to give way to such refinements, there is no enormity so gross of which we may not be capable.

The rules of justice may be compared to the rules of grammar; the rules of the other virtues to the rules which critics lay down for the attainment of what is sublime and elegant in composition. The one are precise, accurate, and indispensable. The others are loose, vague, and indeterminate, and present us rather with a general idea of the perfection we ought to aim at, than afford us any certain and infallible directions for acquiring it. A man may learn to write grammatically by rule, with the most absolute infallibility; and so, perhaps, he may be taught to act justly. But there are no rules whose observance will infallibly lead us to the attainment of elegance or sublimity in writing: though there are some which may help us, in some measure, to correct and ascertain the vague ideas which we might otherwise have entertained of those perfections. And there are no rules by the knowledge of which we can infallibly be taught to act upon all occasions with prudence, with just magnanimity, or proper beneficence: though there are some which may enable us to correct and ascertain, in several respects, the imperfect ideas which we might otherwise have entertained of those virtues.

[. . .]

As a person may act wrong by following a wrong sense of duty, so nature may some-times prevail, and lead him to act right in opposition to it. We cannot in this case be displeased to see that motive prevail, which we think ought to prevail, though the person himself is so weak as to think otherwise. As his conduct, however, is the effect of weakness, not principle, we are far from bestowing upon it any thing that approaches to complete appro-bation. A bigotted Roman Catholic, who, during the massacre of St. Bartholomew, had been so overcome by compassion, as to save some unhappy Protestants whom he thought it his duty to destroy, would not seem to be entitled to that high applause which we should have bestowed upon him, had he exerted the same generosity with complete self-approbation. We might be pleased with the humanity of his temper, but we should still regard him with a sort of pity, which is altogether inconsistent with the admiration that is due to perfect virtue. It is the same case with all the other passions. We do not dislike to see them exert them-selves properly, even when a false notion of duty would direct the person to restrain them. A very devout Quaker, who upon being struck upon one cheek, instead of turning up the other, should so far forget his literal interpretation of our Saviour's precept, as to bestow some good discipline upon the brute that insulted him, would not be disagreeable to us. We should laugh, and be diverted with his spirit, and rather like him the better for it. But we should by no means regard him with that respect and esteem which would seem due to one who, upon a like occasion, had acted properly from a just sense of what was proper to be done. No action can properly be called virtuous, which is not accompanied with the sentiment of self-approbation.

20

Immanuel Kant, *Lectures on Ethics* (ca. 1775)

Kant criticized both empiricism and rationalism in ethics. Although his own ethical theory is appropriately classified as rationalist, it seems to avoid the difficulties he pointed out for other rationalist theories. The reading selection that follows begins with his classification of all ethical theories as either empiricist or "intellectualist." Among empirical principles he listed the moral sense theory of Francis Hutcheson and the conventionalism of Thomas Hobbes. His primary objection to such theories is that he did not see how any empirical (or "pathological") principle can adequately capture the universality or necessity of moral obligation. We know that we ought to tell the truth, for example. Yet it is merely a contingent fact that human sentiments and conventions disapprove of lying. According to moral sense theories, Kant argued, someone who happened not to feel displeasure at the thought of lying would have no moral obligation to tell the truth; according to conventionalism, in a society or culture that happened not to condemn lying, there would be no moral reason not to lie. Kant observed that all empirical moral theories propose some object or condition as the basis for moral obligation. The result, however, is that their moral principles are always *hypothetical* or *conditional* in form. For example: if you care about your own happiness (the public good, tradition, a heavenly reward, etc.), then do not lie!

Only rationalist moral theories can accommodate what Kant took to be the true, *categorical* form of moral principles, such as "Thou shalt not lie!" He thought that such theories tended to be excessively theological, however, often basing the morality of actions simply on the commands of God. Kant's theory, in contrast, purports to derive moral principles in categorical form from the authority of reason itself. (In the reading selection below, Kant does not distinguish between "reason" and "understanding," as he does in later works.) The way to derive moral principles from reason, he believed, is to recognize immoral actions as involving some kind of logical impossibility when projected universally. "Consider, for instance, the case of telling a lie in order to gain a large fortune. If this were made a universal principle, it would be impossible to maintain it, because the end would be known to everyone. That action is immoral whose intent cancels and destroys itself when it is made a universal rule."

Despite his rationalist commitments, Kant is far from denying that morality has a "sensible" or empirical side. His view, as expressed in these lectures, was that moral feeling provides the motive for moral action. That is why a person who understands that his action is wrong may perform it anyway, due to weakness in his moral feeling. This point may seem contrary to Kant's published writings, however, where moral feeling is often treated merely as a side-effect of moral motivation.

Kant taught philosophy for forty years. Several sets of handwritten notes from his ethics lectures have survived, whose similarity and comprehensiveness suggest that they were produced by professional copyists in attendance. The following selections from those notes for students present Kant's main thoughts on ethics without much of the technical vocabulary and argumentation found in his published writings for professional philosophers.

The General Principle of Morality

Having considered the ideal of the highest moral perfection, we must now see wherein the general principle of morality consists. So far we have said no more than that it rests upon the goodness of the free will. We must now investigate what it essentially is. To establish the general principle of science is by no means easy, particularly if the sciences have already reached a certain stage of development. Thus, for instance, it is difficult to establish the general principle of law or of mechanics. But as we all need a basis for our moral judgments, a principle by which to judge with unanimity what is morally good and what bad, we apprehend that there must exist a single principle having its source in our will. We must therefore set ourselves to discover this principle, upon which we establish morality, and through which we are able to discriminate between what is moral and what immoral. However capable and talented a man may be, we still ask about his character. However great his qualities, we still ask about his moral quality. What then is the one principle of morality, the criterion by which to judge everything and in which lies the distinction between moral goodness and all other goodness? Before we decide these questions we must cite and classify the various points of view which lead to the definition of this principle in various ways.

The theoretical concept (not yet a theory, but merely a concept from which a theory can be constructed) is that morality has either an empirical or an intellectual basis, and that it must be derived either from empirical or from intellectual principles. Empirical grounds are derived from the senses, in so far as the senses find satisfaction in them. Intellectual grounds are those in which all morality is derived from the conformity of our actions to the laws of reason. Accordingly, *systema morale est vel empiricum vel intellectuale*.

If an ethical system is based upon empirical grounds, those may be either inner or outer grounds, as they are drawn from the objects of the inner or of the outer sense. The ethics derived from inner grounds gives us the first part of the empirical system; ethics derived from outer grounds, the second part. Those who derive ethics from the inner grounds of the empirical principle, presuppose a feeling, either physical or ethical.

The physical feeling which they take is self-love, which has two constituents, vanity and self-interest. Its aim is advantage to self; it is selfish and aims at satisfying our senses. It is a principle of prudence. Writers who follow the principle of self-love are, among the ancients, Epicurus (who grounds his philosophy in general upon an intuitional principle), and, among the moderns, Helvetius and Mandeville.

The second principle of the inner ground of the empirical system appears when the ground is placed in the ethical feeling whereby we discriminate between good and evil. Among those who build on this basis the foremost are Shaftesbury and Hutcheson.

To the empirical system of the theoretical concept of ethics belong, in the second place, outer grounds. Philosophers who base ethics on these argue that all morality rests upon two things, education and government, which in turn are a matter of custom; we judge all actions in a customary way by what we have been taught or by what the law tells us. Example or legal precept are thus the sources of the moral judgment. While Hobbes takes precept as his thesis and argues that the sovereign power may permit or prohibit any act, Montaigne bases himself on example and points out that in matters of morality men differ with environment, and that the morality of one locality is not that of another. He quotes as instances the permission of theft in Africa, that in China parents may desert their children with impunity, that the Eskimos strangle them, and that in Brazil children are buried alive.

On these grounds it is not permissible for reason to pass ethical judgments on actions. Instead, we act by reference to customary example and the commands of authority, from which it follows that there is no ethical principle, unless it be one borrowed from experience.

But now, in the empirical system, the first principle of ethics is based upon contingent grounds. In the case of self-love, contingent circumstances decide the nature of the action which will advantage or harm us. Where ethical feeling is the basis, and we judge actions by liking or disliking, by repugnance, or in general by taste, the grounds of judgment are again contingent, for what may please one individual may disgust another. (Thus a savage will turn from wine with abhorrence, while we drink it with pleasure.) It is the same with the outer grounds of education and government.

In the second *Systema morale*, which is the intellectual, the philosopher judges that the ethical principle has its ground in the understanding and can be completely apprehended à priori. We say, for instance: 'Thou shalt not lie.' On the principle of self-love this would mean: 'Thou shalt not lie if it harm thee; if it advantage thee then thou mayest lie.' If ethical feeling were the basis, then a person so devoid of a refined ethical feeling, that in him lying evoked no disgust, would be at liberty to lie. If it depended on up-bringing and government, then, if we were brought up to telling lies and if the Government so ordained, it would be open to us to tell lies. But if the principle lies in the understanding we say simply: 'Thou shalt not lie, be the circumstances what they may.' This, if I look into my free will, expresses the consistency of my free will with itself and with that of others; it is a necessary law of the free will. Such principles, which are universal, constant and necessary, have their source in pure reason; they cannot be derived from experience. Every ethical law expresses a categorical necessity, not one drawn from experience, and as every necessary rule must be established à priori, the principles of morality must be intellectual. The moral judgment never occurs at all in virtue of sensuous or empirical principles, for the ethical is never an object of the senses, but purely of the understanding.

The intellectual principle may be of two kinds:

1. Internal – if it depends on the inner nature of the action as apprehended by the understanding.
2. External – where our actions bear some relation to an external being.

But just as we have an ethical theology, so we have theological ethics, and the external intellectual principle is of that kind; but it is false, because discrimination between moral good and evil does not depend on any relation to another being. It follows, therefore, that the basic moral principle is of the first (i.e. the internal) of the above two kinds of intellectual principle. *Principium morale est intellectuale internum.* Our aim in what follows will be to discern and determine its constitution; but this can only be done gradually.

[. . .]

The Supreme Principle of Morality

In this connexion we must first notice that there are two points to consider; the principle of the discrimination of our obligation and the principle of its performance or execution. We must distinguish between measuring-rod and mainspring. The measuring-rod is the principle of discrimination; the mainspring is the principle of the performance of our obligation. Confusion between these has led to complete falsity in the sphere of ethics. If we ask, 'What is morally good and what is not?' it is the principle of discrimination which is in question, in terms of which I decide the goodness of the action. But if we ask, 'What is it that moves me to act in accordance with the laws of morality?' we have a question which concerns the principle of the motive. The equity of the action is the objective ground, but is still not the subjective ground. The *motiva subjective moventia* are what moves me to do that which the understanding tells me I ought to do.

The supreme principle of all moral judgment lies in the understanding: that of the moral incentive to action lies in the heart. This motive is moral feeling. We must guard against confusing the principle of the judgment with the principle of the motive. The first is the norm; the second the incentive. The motive cannot take the place of the rule. Where the motive is wanting, the error is practical; but when the judgment fails the error is theoretical.

We shall now proceed to indicate shortly and negatively what does not constitute the principle of morality. Firstly, there is nothing pathological about it. It would be pathological if it were derived from subjective grounds, from our inclination and feeling. There is no pathological principle in ethics because its laws are objective, and deal with what we ought to do, not with what we desire to do. Ethics is no analysis of inclination but a prescription which is contrary to all inclination. A pathological principle of morality would consist in an instruction to satisfy all our desires, and this would constitute a bestial, not the real, Epicureanism.

We can conceive two *principia pathologica* of morality, the one aiming at the satisfaction of all our inclinations, the other at the satisfaction of one particular inclination, the inclination to morality. The aim of the first would be merely physical feeling; the second would be based on an intellectual inclination. But an intellectual inclination is a contradiction in terms; for a feeling for objects of the understanding is in itself an absurdity, so that a moral feeling resulting from an intellectual inclination is also an absurdity and is, therefore, impossible. A feeling cannot be regarded as something ideal; it cannot belong both to our intellectual and to our sensuous nature; and even if it were possible for us to feel morality, it would still not be possible to establish a system of rules on this principle. For a moral law states categorically what ought to be done, whether it pleases us or not. It is, therefore, not a case of satisfying an inclination. If it were, there would be no moral law, but every one might act according to his own feeling. Even if we assumed that all men had a like degree of feeling, there would still be no Obligation to act according to feeling, for we could not then say that we *ought* to do what pleases us, but only that so-and-so might do such-and-such *because* it pleased him. The moral law, however, commands categorically. Morality cannot, therefore, be based on any pathological principle, neither on a physical nor yet on a moral feeling. Moreover, to have recourse to feeling in the case of a practical rule is quite contrary to philosophy. Every feeling has only a private validity, and no man's feeling can be apprehended by another. If a man argues that 'he feels in himself that it is so', his argument is a tautology. His feeling can have no value for others, and the man who once appeals to his feelings forswears all rational grounds. There is, therefore, no such thing as a pathological principle of morality, and there must accordingly be an intellectual principle in the sense that it must be derived from the understanding. This principle will consist in a rule of the understanding, either because the understanding provides us with the means so to direct our actions that they conform to our inclinations or because the ground of morality is immediately apprehended by the understanding. If the former, the principle is no doubt intellectual, inasmuch as the understanding provides the means; it is nevertheless evidently rooted in inclination. Such a pseudo-intellectual principle is pragmatic, and depends on the capacity of the rule to satisfy our inclinations. This principle of prudence is the true Epicurean principle. To be told that we ought to promote our happiness is in effect to be told that we ought to employ our understanding to discover the means for satisfying our inclinations and our desire for pleasure. This principle is intellectual in so far as it requires the understanding to provide the rules for the employment of the means to promote our happiness. But as this happiness consists in the satisfaction of all our inclinations, the pragmatic principle is dependent on the inclinations. Morality is, however, independent of all inclination, and it is not, therefore, grounded in any pragmatic principle. Were it so grounded, there could be no agreement amongst men in regard to morality, as every individual would seek to satisfy his own inclinations. Morality cannot, however, be based on the subjective laws of men's inclinations, and so it follows that the principle of morality cannot be pragmatic. It must, to be sure, be intellectual, but not, as in the case of the pragmatic principle, mediately so; it must be an unmediated principle of morality in the sense that the ground of morality is apprehended immediately by the mind. The ethical principle is, therefore, a sheerly intellectual principle of the pure reason. But this pure intellectual principle must not be tautologous. It must not consist in the tautology of pure reason as does, for example, Wolff's rule, 'do good and eschew evil', which, as we have already shown, is empty and unphilosophic.

Another tautological principle is that enunciated by Cumberland. It is the principle of truth. Cumberland asserts that we all seek perfection, that we are misled by appearance, but that ethics shows us the truth.

A third is that of Aristotle, the principle of the mean, which is consequently tautologous.

The pure intellectual principle cannot, however, be a *principium externum*, in terms of the relation of our actions to a foreign being. It does not, therefore, depend on the divine will. It cannot, for instance, take the form: 'Thou shalt not lie, because lying is forbidden.' Accordingly, as it cannot be external, it cannot be tautological. There are those who argue that we must first have God and then morality – a very convenient principle; but ethics and theology are neither of them a principle of the other. It is true that theology cannot subsist without ethics and vice versa. We are not, however, discussing here the fact that theology is a motive for ethics – which it is, but we are investigating whether the principle of ethical discrimination is theological – and it cannot be that. Were it so, then before a nation could have any concept of duties it would first have to know God. Consequently, nations which had no right concept of God would have no duties, and this is not the case. Nations had a right idea of their duties, and were aware that lies were detestable, without having the proper concept of God. Other peoples, besides, have constructed for themselves concepts of God which were merely sacred, and erroneous, who yet had proper concepts of the duties. Duties must, therefore, be derived from another source. Men have derived morality from the divine will because the moral laws are expressed in the form 'thou shalt', and this has led to the belief that a third being must have promulgated the command. But whilst it is true that the moral laws are commands, and whilst they may be commandments of the divine will, they do not originate in the commandment. God has commanded this or that because it is a moral law, and because His will coincides with the moral law. Moreover, it would seem as though there were no obligations but such as had reference to an obligator; that Obligation itself implied a reference to a being *universaliter obligans*, and that God, therefore, was the obligator of the moral laws. It is true that in the matter of performance we must have a third being to make it necessary for us to do that which is morally good, but for the judging of morality no third being is needed. Moral laws can be right without a third being, but in the absence of such a being to make their performance necessary they would be empty. Men were right, therefore, in recognising that the absence of a supreme judge would make all moral laws ineffectual. There would be no incentive, no reward and no punishment. Knowledge of God is, therefore, necessary to make the moral laws effective, but it is not necessary for the mere apprehension of those laws. For this latter purpose it is not necessary to presuppose the existence of a third being. How do we know the divine will? None of us feels it in his heart; we cannot know the moral law from any revelation; for if we did so know it, then would those who had no revelation be wholly ignorant of it, and Paul himself asserts that the latter are guided by their reason. It is by our reason that we apprehend the divine will. We imagine God as possessing the most holy and the most perfect will. But what then is the most perfect will? The moral law shows us what it is, and herein we find the whole of ethics. We say that the divine will accords with the moral law and is, therefore, the holiest and the most perfect. Thus we recognize the perfection of the divine will from the moral law. God wills all that is morally good and proper and His will is, therefore, the most holy and the most perfect. But what is it that is morally good? Ethics supplies the answer to this question.

The more corrupt the moral concepts, the more corrupt are the theological concepts. If the ethical concepts in theology and religion were pure and holy, no man would strive to please God in a human and improper manner. Every one imagines God in terms of that concept which is most familiar to himself. We may, for instance, imagine Him as a great and mighty lord, something beyond the mightiest of the lords of this earth. Each man, therefore, forms for himself a concept of morality which corresponds to his concept of God. As a consequence, men endeavour to find favour with God, by testifying in His favour and by singing His praises; they extol Him as a great lord, than whom there can be no greater; they recognize their faults, and think that all men have such faults that none is able to do anything good; they take all their sins and lay them at God's feet, and sigh, and think thereby they honour God; they fail to see that such mean and petty eulogy from worms such as we are is but a reproach to God. They do not see that man cannot praise and eulogize God. To honour God is to obey His commandments with a willing heart, not to sing songs of praise to Him. An upright man who strives from an inner impulse to give expression to the moral law on account of the inner goodness of such action, who keeps God's commandments with a willing heart, – such a one honours God. If, however, we do as God has commanded because He has commanded it and because He is so mighty that He can force us to it, we act under orders, from fear and fright, not appreciating the propriety of our actions and not knowing *why* we should do as God has commanded nor *why* we should obey Him. Might cannot constitute a *vis obligandi*. Threats do not impose an obligation, they extort. If then we comply with the moral law from fear of punishment and of the power of God, and for no other reason than that God has so commanded, we act not from duty and obligation, but from fear and fright. Such conduct does not make the heart better. But if we act from inner principles, if we do a thing simply because it is good in itself and do it with a liking, such conduct is truly pleasing in the sight of God. God looks to our dispositions, and these derive only from a principle within us. If we do a thing with a liking, we do it from a good disposition. We cannot even give a proper exposition of divine revelation except on the inner principle of morality. Theology may regard willingness as piety, but it is not so: virtue consists in moral conduct; and moral conduct in accordance with the divine, beneficent will becomes piety.

Having examined what the principle of morality is not, we must now examine what it is. Now the principle of morality is *intellectuale internum*, and must, therefore, be sought in the action itself by the pure reason. Wherein then does it consist? Morality is the harmony of actions with the universally valid law of the free will: it is always the relation in which actions stand to the general rule. In all our actions that which is called moral is regular. It conforms to a rule. The essence of morality is that our actions are motivated by a general rule, that is, that the reasons for the actions are to be found in such a rule. If we make it the foundation of our conduct that our actions shall be consistent with the universal rule, which is valid at all times and for every one, then our actions have their source in the principle of morality. Take, for example, the keeping of a promise. To break a promise as it please our sensibility is not moral, for if no man were willing to keep his promise simply in terms of the original proposal promises would in the long run become useless. But I may judge the matter in terms of the understanding, to discover whether it is a universal rule that promises should be kept. I then find that as I wish that all others should keep their promises to me, I must keep my promises to others. My action then conforms to the universal rule of will in general. Take again the practice of benevolence. Assume that I meet a man who is in the most distressed circumstances, and though I have the wherewithal to assist him, I am indifferent to his sufferings and prefer to spend my money on my own pleasures. Let me test this by my understanding; let me see whether my conduct can be a universal rule; let me see whether such indifference on the part of another, if I were in distress, would accord with my will; and what do I find? I find that it would not. Such conduct, therefore, is not moral.

Every immoral man has his maxims. While a precept is an objective law in accordance with which we ought to act, a maxim is a subjective law in accordance with which we actually do act. Every one regards the moral law as something, which he can publicly profess, but his maxims as something which must be concealed because they are contrary to morality and cannot serve as a universal rule. Take, for example, a man whose maxim is to become rich. He cannot and will not declare it, or else he would fail in his purpose. If it came to be used as a general rule, every one would want to grow rich, and then it would be impossible to become rich, because everyone would know about it and everyone would want to be so. Examples from the sphere of duties towards oneself are the least well known and are, therefore, somewhat more difficult to understand. They are often confused with the pragmatic rules (of which more anon) for promoting one's well-being. May a man, for instance, mutilate his body for profit? May he sell a tooth? May he surrender himself at a price to the highest bidder? What is the moral aspect of such questions as these? I apply my understanding to investigate whether the intent of the action is of such a nature that it could be a universal rule. What is that intent in these cases? It is to gain material advantage. It is obvious, therefore, that in so acting man reduces himself to a thing, to an instrument of animal amusements. We are, however, as human beings, not things but persons, and by turning ourselves into things we dishonour human nature in our own persons. The same applies to suicide. By the rules of prudence there might be cases in which, in order to have done with misery, one might commit suicide, but not so by rules of morality. Suicide is immoral; for the intention is to rid oneself of all pains and discomforts attendant upon one's state by sacrificing that state, and this subordinates human nature to animal nature and brings the understanding under the control of animal impulses. In doing this I contradict myself, if I still desire to possess the rights of man.

In all moral judgments the idea which we frame is this, 'What is the character of the action taken by itself.' If the intent of the action can without self-contradiction be universalized, it is morally possible; if it cannot be so universalized without contradicting itself, it is morally impossible. Consider, for instance, the case of telling a lie in order to gain a large fortune. If this were made a universal principle, it would be impossible to maintain it, because the end would be known to every one. That action is immoral whose intent cancels and destroys itself when it is made a universal rule. It is moral, if the intent of the action is in harmony with itself when it is made a universal rule. Understanding is the faculty of the rule of our actions, and actions which are in harmony with the universal rule are in harmony with the understanding, and thus their impulsive grounds are in the understanding. If then an action is done because it harmonizes with the universal rule of the understanding, it has its source in the *principium moralitatis purum intellectuale internum*. As, therefore, the understanding is the faculty of the rule and of judgment, morality is the subordination of actions in general to the principle of the understanding. How the understanding can contain a principle of action is somewhat difficult to apprehend. In no sense does the understanding contain the *end* of action; rather, morality is constituted by the universal *form* of the understanding (which is purely intellectual), the action being taken, in fact, universally, so as to constitute a rule. And it is here that the distinction we have drawn above between the objective principle of discrimination and the subjective principle of performance comes in. Of these two principles it is the objective principle of judgment that we are here concerned with. We have already, in another connexion, rejected the subjective principle, moral feeling, which is the motive of action. Moral feeling is the capacity to be affected by a moral judgment. My understanding may judge that an action is morally good, but it need not follow that I shall do that action which I judge morally good: from understanding to performance is still a far cry. If this judgment were to move me to do the deed, it would be moral feeling; but it is quite incomprehensible that the mind should have a motive force to judge. The understanding, obviously, can judge, but to give to this judgment of the understanding a compelling force, to make it an incentive that can move the will to perform the action – this is the philosopher's stone!

The understanding takes account of everything which has a bearing on its rule. It accepts all those things which conform to the rule and opposes those which conflict with it. But immoral actions conflict with the rule; they cannot be made a universal rule; the understanding is, therefore, hostile to them, as they are hostile to its principle. Thus in a sense a motive force is embedded in the understanding in virtue of its own nature. All action ought, therefore, to be so constituted that it agrees with the universal form of the understanding; it must be such that it can at all times become a universal rule; if it is so constituted, it is moral. Does it then depend on the mind that any particular action is immoral, or does it depend on the will? If it is the understanding that is at fault in the discrimination of the action, that is, when it is badly instructed, the action is morally imperfect; but the depravity or wickedness of an action is not constituted by discrimination, and so does not lie in the understanding; it consists in the motive of the will. Having learnt to discriminate actions, man still lacks the incentive to perform the actions. An action is, therefore, immoral not because the understanding is at fault, but because the will or the heart is depraved. The will is depraved if the sensibility overpowers the motive force of the understanding. The understanding has no *elateres animi*, though it possesses impulsive force and *motiva*, but these are not capable of overpowering the *elateres* of the sensibility. A sensibility in harmony with the impulsive force of the understanding would be moral feeling. It is true that we cannot feel the goodness of an action; but the understanding sets itself against an evil action because it runs contrary to the rule. This opposition of the understanding is the impulsive ground. If this impulsive ground of understanding could move the sensibility to conformity and induce motives in it, this would constitute moral feeling. On what then does man's possession of such a moral feeling depend? Anyone can see that an action is disgusting, but only the man who feels disgust at it has moral feeling. The understanding sees that a thing is disgusting and is hostile to it, but it cannot be disgusted: it is only the sensibility which is disgusted. If then the sensibility is disgusted with that which the mind sees to be disgusting, we have moral feeling. It is quite impossible to make any man feel disgust at vice. We can only tell him what our understanding apprehends and bring him to the point of apprehending it also, but if his sensibility is dull we cannot make him feel disgust. He recognizes that the action is abhorrent; he wishes that all actions were so, if only he could make profit from them thereby; he feels it better to have something in his purse. So nothing is achieved in general by such methods. Man is not so delicately made that he can be moved by objective grounds; he is not endowed by nature with a spring which could be wound up to produce the desired result. But we can produce a *habitus*, which is not natural, but takes the place of nature, and is produced by imitation and oft-repeated practice. The various methods, however, for making us regard vice with abhorrence are falsely conceived. From its earliest infancy we ought to instil in the child an immediate hate and disgust of hateful and disgusting actions; an immediate, not a mediated abhorrence, which has only a pragmatic usefulness; an action should, therefore, be represented to the child not as forbidden or harmful but as in itself detestable. For instance, a child which tells lies should not be punished, but shamed: it should feel ashamed, contemptible, nauseated as though it had been bespattered with dirt. By repeated doses of such treatment we can inspire the child with such an abhorrence of vice as will become in him a *habitus*. If, however, he is punished instead – say, at school – he thinks to himself that once out of school he runs no risk of being punished and he will also try by jesuitical tricks to escape punishment. Again, some old people conceive the notion of becoming converted towards the end of their lives and think that they can thereby make amends for all past misdeeds and place themselves in the same position as if they had lived morally all their lives. Such people consider sudden death as the greatest misfortune. Education and religion ought, therefore, to aim at instilling an immediate aversion from evil conduct and an immediate predilection for moral conduct.

Immanuel Kant, *Groundwork of the Metaphysics of Morals* (1785)

In ethics, Kant began with the assumption that moral duties or obligations must be seen as commands indicating what ought to be done, regardless of how we might feel, and regardless of what else we may want to do. In his technical vocabulary, this means that moral duties are expressed in "categorical imperatives" such as "Thou shalt not lie!" and not in "hypothetical imperatives," that is, not in imperatives that command what ought to be done *in order to attain something else*. In the previous reading selection Kant explained one way his supreme moral principle can be formulated, emphasizing the idea of "universal law." The following selection begins by repeating Kant's objections to empirical approaches to ethics, and proceeds to present a new, equivalent formulation of his supreme moral principle. This second version of the categorical imperative commands that in all our actions we respect humanity: *"So act that you use humanity, whether in your own person or in the person of any other, always at the same time as an end, never merely as a means."*

Kant argued for this principle by claiming first that individual human beings see themselves as ends in all their actions. By this he seems to have meant that, no matter what else we may value, we could not value it without first valuing ourselves. Yet the esteem that we each have for ourselves is our esteem for the rational abilities shared by all rational beings. So from this it follows that the value we recognize in human rationality is the very condition of everything else we value. Hence, to use a human person as a means to achieve any other purpose is to spend something of "absolute worth" in order to attain something of lesser, merely "relative," worth. That is why it is irrational to use humanity merely as a means, as expressed in Kant's second formulation of the categorical imperative.

In four examples Kant provided further clarification of how this principle applies to particular moral questions. One example shows us that it is wrong to commit suicide, since in doing so we would treat our humanity as something disposable merely in order to avoid continued misery. In another example, Kant showed why it is wrong to make lying promises: in doing so we manipulate the person we deceive like a puppet, in order to achieve our secret end.

Scholars have been fascinated by Kant's bold attempt in his *Groundwork* to derive the whole of commonsense morality simply from concepts like "universal law," and "humanity as an end in itself." It is probably correct to say that no one today accepts Kant's main theses in ethics without qualification; yet there is hardly anyone who would reject all that Kant has contributed to ethical thought. His work has certainly inspired more progress among contemporary moral and political philosophers than any other writer of the eighteenth century.

We have therefore shown at least this much: that if duty is a concept that is to contain significance and real lawgiving for our actions it can be expressed only in categorical imperatives and by no means in hypothetical ones; we have also – and this is already a great deal – set forth distinctly and as determined for every use the content of the categorical imperative, which must contain the principle of all duty (if there is such a thing at all). But we have not yet advanced so far as to prove a priori that there really is such an imperative, that there is a practical law, which commands absolutely of itself and without any incentives, and that the observance of this law is duty.

For the purpose of achieving this it is of the utmost importance to take warning that we must not let ourselves think of wanting to derive the reality of this principle from the *special property of human nature*. For, duty is to be practical unconditional necessity of action and it must therefore hold for all rational beings (to which alone an imperative can apply at all) and *only because of this* be also a law for all human wills. On the other hand, what is derived from the special natural constitution of humanity – what is derived from certain feelings and propensities and even, if possible, from a special tendency that would be peculiar to human reason and would not have to hold necessarily for the will of every rational being – that can indeed yield a maxim for us but not a law; it can yield a subjective principle on which we might act if we have the propensity and inclination, but not an objective principle on which we would be *directed* to act even though every propensity, inclination, and natural tendency of ours were against it – so much so that the sublimity and inner dignity of the command in a duty is all the more manifest the fewer are the subjective causes in favor of it and the more there are against it, without thereby weakening in the least the necessitation by the law or taking anything away from its validity.

Here, then, we see philosophy put in fact in a precarious position, which is to be firm even though there is nothing in heaven or on earth from which it depends or on which it is based. Here philosophy is to manifest its purity as sustainer of its own laws, not as herald of laws that an implanted sense or who knows what tutelary nature whispers to it, all of which – though they may always be better than nothing at all – can still never yield basic principles that reason dictates and that must have their source entirely and completely a priori and, at the same time, must have their commanding authority from this: that they expect nothing from the inclination of human beings but everything from the supremacy of the law and the respect owed it or, failing this, condemn the human being to contempt for himself and inner abhorrence.

Hence everything empirical, as an addition to the principle of morality, is not only quite inept for this; it is also highly prejudicial to the purity of morals, where the proper worth of an absolutely good will – a worth raised above all price – consists just in the principle of action being free from all influences of contingent grounds, which only experience can furnish. One cannot give too many or too frequent warnings against this laxity, or even mean cast of mind, which seeks its principle among empirical motives and laws; for, human reason in its weariness gladly rests on this pillow and in a dream of sweet illusions (which allow it to embrace a cloud instead of Juno) it substitutes for morality a bastard patched up from limbs of quite diverse ancestry, which looks like whatever one wants to see in it but not like virtue for him who has once seen virtue in her true form.

The question is therefore this: is it a necessary law *for all rational beings* always to appraise their actions in accordance with such maxims as they themselves could will to serve as universal laws? If there is such a law, then it must already be connected (completely a priori) with the concept of the will of a rational being as such. But in order to discover this connection we must, however reluctantly, step forth, namely into metaphysics, although into a domain of it that is distinct from speculative philosophy, namely into metaphysics of morals. In a practical philosophy, where we have to do not with assuming grounds for what *happens* but rather laws for what *ought to happen* even if it never does, that is, objective practical laws, we do not need to undertake an investigation into the grounds on account of which something pleases or displeases; how the satisfaction of mere sensation differs from taste, and whether the latter differs from a general satisfaction of reason; upon what the feeling of pleasure or displeasure rests, and how from it desires and inclinations arise, and from them, with the cooperation of reason, maxims; for all that belongs to an empirical doctrine of the soul, which would constitute the second part of the doctrine of nature when this is regarded as *philosophy of nature* insofar as it is based *on empirical laws*. Here, however, it is a question of objective practical laws and hence of the relation of a will to itself insofar as it determines itself only by reason; for then everything that has reference to the empirical falls away of itself, since if reason entirely by itself determines conduct (and the possibility of this is just what we want now to investigate), it must necessarily do so a priori.

The will is thought as a capacity to determine itself to acting in conformity with the *representation of certain laws*. And such a capacity can be found only in rational beings. Now, what serves the will as the objective ground of its self-determination is an end, and this, if it is given by reason alone, must hold equally for all rational beings. What, on the other hand, contains merely the ground of the possibility of an action the effect of which is an end is called a *means*. The subjective ground of desire is an *incentive*; the objective ground of volition is a *motive*; hence the distinction between subjective ends, which rest on incentives, and objective ends, which depend on motives, which hold for every rational being. Practical principles are *formal* if they abstract from all subjective ends, whereas they are *material* if they have put these, and consequently certain incentives, at their basis. The ends that a rational being proposes at his discretion as *effects* of his actions (material ends) are all only relative; for only their mere relation to a specially constituted faculty of desire on the part of the subject gives them their worth, which can therefore furnish no universal principles, no principles valid and necessary for all rational beings and also for every volition, that is, no practical laws. Hence all these relative ends are only the ground of hypothetical imperatives.

But suppose there were something the *existence of which in itself* has an absolute worth, something which as *an end in itself* could be a ground of determinate laws; then in it, and in it alone, would lie the ground of a possible categorical imperative, that is, of a practical law.

Now I say that the human being and in general every rational being *exists* as an end in itself, *not merely as a means* to be used by this or that will at its discretion; instead he must in all his actions, whether directed to himself or also to other rational beings, always be regarded *at the same time as an end*. All objects of the inclinations have only a conditional worth; for, if there were not inclinations and the needs based on them, their object would be without worth. But the inclinations themselves, as sources of needs, are so far from having an absolute worth, so as to make one wish to have them, that it must instead be the universal wish of every rational being to be altogether free from them. Thus the worth of any object *to be acquired* by our action is always conditional. Beings the existence of which rests not on our will but on nature, if they are beings without reason, still have only a relative worth, as means, and are therefore called *things*, whereas rational beings are called *persons* because their nature already marks them out as an end in itself, that is, as something that may not be used merely as a means, and hence so far limits all choice (and is an object of respect). These, therefore, are not merely subjective ends, the existence of which as an effect of our action has a worth *for us*, but rather *objective ends*, that is, beings the existence of which is in itself an end, and indeed one such that no other end, to which they would serve *merely* as means, can be put in its place, since without it nothing of *absolute worth* would be found anywhere; but if all worth were conditional and therefore contingent, then no supreme practical principle for reason could be found anywhere.

If, then, there is to be a supreme practical principle and, with respect to the human will, a categorical imperative, it must be one such that, from the representation of what is necessarily an end for everyone because it is an *end in itself*, it constitutes an *objective* principle of the will and thus can serve as a universal practical law. The ground of this principle is: *rational nature exists as an end in itself*. The human being necessarily represents his own existence in this way; so far it is thus a *subjective* principle of human actions. But every other rational being also represents his existence in this way consequent on just the same rational ground that also holds for me; thus it is at the same time an *objective* principle from which, as a supreme practical ground, it must be possible to derive all laws of the will. The practical imperative will therefore be the following: *So act that you use humanity, whether in your own person or in the person of any other, always at the same time as an end, never merely as a means.* We shall see whether this can be carried out.

To keep to the preceding examples:

First, as regards the concept of necessary duty to oneself, someone who has suicide in mind will ask himself whether his action can be consistent with the idea of humanity *as an end in itself*. If he destroys himself in order to escape from a trying condition he makes use of a person *merely as a means* to maintain a tolerable condition up to the end of life. A human being, however, is not a thing and hence not something that can be used *merely* as a means, but must in all his actions always be regarded as an end in itself. I cannot, therefore, dispose of a human being in my own person by maiming, damaging or killing him. (I must here pass over a closer determination of this principle that would prevent any misinterpretation, e.g., as to having limbs amputated in order to preserve myself, or putting my life in danger in order to preserve my life, and so forth; that belongs to morals proper.)

Second, as regards necessary duty to others or duty owed them, he who has it in mind to make a false promise to others sees at once that he wants to make use of another human being *merely as a means*, without the other at the same time containing in himself the end. For, he whom I want to use for my purposes by such a promise cannot possibly agree to my way of behaving toward him, and so himself contain the end of this action. This conflict with the principle of other human beings is seen more distinctly if examples of assaults on the freedom and property of others are brought forward. For then it is obvious that he who transgresses the rights of human beings intends to make use of the person of others merely as means, without taking into consideration that, as rational beings, they are always to be valued at the same time as ends, that is, only as beings who must also be able to contain in themselves the end of the very same action.

Third, with respect to contingent (meritorious) duty to oneself, it is not enough that the action does not conflict with humanity in our person as an end in itself; it must also *harmonize with it*. Now there are in humanity predispositions to greater perfection, which belong to the end of nature with respect to humanity in our subject; to neglect these might admittedly be consistent with the *preservation* of humanity as an end in itself but not with the *furtherance* of this end.

Fourth, concerning meritorious duty to others, the natural end that all human beings have is their own happiness. Now, humanity might indeed subsist if no one contributed to the happiness of others but yet did not intentionally withdraw anything from it; but there is still only a negative and not a positive agreement with *humanity as an end in itself* unless everyone also tries, as far as he can, to further the ends of others. For, the ends of a subject who is an end in itself must as far as possible be also *my* ends, if that representation is to have its *full* effect in me.

This principle of humanity, and in general of every rational nature, *as an end in itself* (which is the supreme limiting condition of the freedom of action of every human being) is not borrowed from experience; first because of its universality, since it applies to all rational beings as such and no experience is sufficient to determine anything about them; second because in it humanity is represented not as an end of human beings (subjectively), that is, not as an object that we of ourselves actually make our end, but as an objective end that, whatever ends we may have, ought as law to constitute the supreme limiting condition of all subjective ends, so that the principle must arise from pure reason. That is to say, the ground of all practical lawgiving lies (in accordance with the first principle) *objectively in the rule* and the form of universality which makes it fit to be a law (possibly a law of nature); *subjectively*, however, it lies in the *end*; but the subject of all ends is every rational being as an end in itself (in accordance with the second principle); from this there follows now the third practical principle of the will, as supreme condition of its harmony with universal practical reason, the idea *of the will of every rational being as a will giving universal law.*

22

Thomas Reid, *Essays on the Active Powers of the Human Mind* (1788)

In ethics, Reid was content to attribute our knowledge of right and good conduct to a "moral sense." But he understood that the more renowned moral-sense theorists of his day, such as Francis Hutcheson and David Hume, would not share his understanding of sensation. As seen in earlier excerpts from his writings (see part II of this volume), Reid thought of sensation as an active, judging faculty, whereas the modern empiricists typically considered the senses to be merely passive. Consequently, for Reid, there is no real distinction to be drawn between operations of the moral sense and judgments of conscience. Sometimes our conscience may be misguided, to be sure; just as we sometimes misperceive sensory objects. But there is no reason, in principle, why disagreements in matters of conscience cannot be resolved. Just as perceptual disagreements can be resolved, and misperceptions corrected, so also can disagreements of conscience be resolved.

What therefore sets the standard for correct judgments of conscience? To answer this question Reid appealed to common sense. In all languages, he wrote, human beings speak about rational grounds for belief, just as much as rational grounds for action. Just as it is universally expected that we form beliefs according to reason, so we are expected to conform our conduct to reason. Reason gives us two general guides for conduct, according to Reid: our interest and our duty (on this point, see the General Introduction to this volume).

We have seen how Smith disagreed with Hume over whether a regard for an action's rightness, or the "sense of duty," should be the agent's motive in acts of justice. But Reid staked out a position even further removed from Hume when he argued that "those actions only can truly be called virtuous, or deserving of moral approbation, which the agent believed to be right, and to which he was influenced, more or less, by that belief." Hume had claimed that an agent's regard for the virtue or rightness of an action can never make it virtuous. Something besides the sense of duty is required for this; belief in an action's virtue cannot make it so. But Reid disagreed, pointing out a sense in which the moral quality of an action can be determined by the agent's belief or intention in performing it. Is it not still dishonest for a man to tell what he believes is a lie, even when what he says turns out to be the truth? Reid proposed that we distinguish between the goodness of an action in the abstract, and its goodness as done by the agent. Whether an action in the former, abstract sense is truly kind, for example, will always depend upon facts about its beneficial effects.

But whether an agent's action is kind in the latter sense will depend entirely on its motive and the belief that influenced the agent in performing it. In the latter sense, an agent's beliefs and motives may be sufficient to make her action kind, virtuous, and dutiful, even if her action is, in the abstract, truly harmful, the worst that could be done, and directly contrary to duty.

Essay III
Of the Principles of Action

Part III
Of the Rational Principles of Action

Chapter I
There are rational principles of action in man

[...]

That talent which we call *reason*, by which men that are adult and of a sound mind, are distinguished from brutes, idiots, and infants, has, in all ages, among the learned and unlearned, been conceived to have two offices, to regulate our belief, and to regulate our actions and conduct.

Whatever we believe, we think agreeable to reason, and, on that account, yield our assent to it. Whatever we disbelieve, we think contrary to reason, and, on that account, dissent from it. Reason therefore is allowed to be the principle by which our belief and opinions ought to be regulated.

But reason has been no less universally conceived to be a principle, by which our actions ought to be regulated.

To act reasonably, is a phrase no less common in all languages, than to judge reasonably. We immediately approve of a man's conduct, when it appears that he had good reason for what he did. And every action we disapprove, we think unreasonable, or contrary to reason.

A way of speaking so universal among men, common to the learned and the unlearned in all nations, and in all languages, must have a meaning. To suppose it to be words without meaning, is to treat, with undue contempt, the common sense of mankind.

Supposing this phrase to have a meaning, we may consider in what way reason may serve to regulate human conduct, so that some actions of men are to be denominated reasonable, and others unreasonable.

I take it for granted, that there can be no exercise of reason without judgment, nor, on the other hand, any judgment of things abstract and general, without some degree of reason.

If, therefore, there be any principles of action in the human constitution, which, in their nature, necessarily imply such judgment, they are the principles which we may call rational, to distinguish them from animal principles, which imply desire, and will, but not judgment.

Every deliberate human action must be done either as the means, or as an end; as the means to some end, to which it is subservient, or as an end, for its own sake, and without regard to any thing beyond it.

That it is a part of the office of reason to determine, what are the proper means to any end which we desire, no man ever denied. But some philosophers, particularly Mr. Hume, think that it is no part of the office of reason to determine the ends we ought to pursue, or the preference due to one end above another. This, he thinks, is not the office of reason, but of taste or feeling.

If this be so, reason cannot, with any propriety, be called a principle of action. Its office can only be to minister to the principles of action, by discovering the means of their gratification. Accordingly, Mr. Hume maintains, that reason is no principle of action; but that it is, and ought to be, the servant of the passions.

I shall endeavour to show, that, among the various ends of human actions, there are some, of which, without reason, we could not even form a conception; and that, as soon as they are conceived, a regard to them is, by our constitution, not only a principle of action, but a leading and governing principle, to which all our animal principles are subordinate, and to which they ought to be subject.

These I shall call *rational* principles; because they can exist only in beings endowed with reason, and because, to act from these principles, is what has always been meant by acting according to reason.

The ends of human actions I have in view, are two, to wit, what is good for us upon the whole, and what appears to be our duty. They are very strictly connected, lead to the same course of conduct, and co-operate with each other; and, on that account, have commonly been comprehended under one name, that of *reason*. But as they may be disjoined, and are really distinct principles of action, I shall consider them separately.

Chapter V
Of the notion of duty, rectitude, moral obligation

A being endowed with the animal principles of action only, may be capable of being trained to certain purposes by discipline, as we see many brute animals are, but would be altogether incapable of being governed by law.

The subject of law must have the conception of a general rule of conduct, which, without some degree of reason, he cannot have. He must likewise have a sufficient inducement to obey the law, even when his strongest animal desires draw him the contrary way.

This inducement may be a sense of interest, or a sense of duty, or both concurring.

These are the only principles I am able to conceive which can reasonably induce a man to regulate all his actions according to a certain general rule, or law. They may therefore be justly called the *rational* principles of action, since they can have no place but in a being endowed with reason, and since it is by them only, that man is capable either of political or of moral government.

[...]

With regard to the notion or conception of duty, I take it to be too simple to admit of a logical definition.

We can define it only by synonymous words or phrases, or by its properties and necessary concomitants; as when we say that it is what we ought to do, what is fair and honest, what is approvable, what every man professes to be the rule of his conduct, what all men praise, and what is in itself laudable, though no man should praise it.

I observe, in the *next* place, that the notion of duty cannot be resolved into that of interest, or what is most for our happiness.

Every man may be satisfied of this who attends to his own conceptions, and the language of all mankind shows it. When I say this is my interest, I mean one thing; when I say it is my duty, I mean another thing. And though the same course of action, when rightly understood, may be both my duty and my interest, the conceptions are very different. Both are reasonable motives to action, but quite distinct in their nature.

I presume it will be granted, that in every man of real worth, there is a principle of honor, a regard to what is honorable or dishonorable, very distinct from a regard to his interest. It is folly in a man to disregard his interest, but to do what is dishonorable is baseness. The first may move our pity, or, in some cases, our contempt, but the last provokes our indignation.

As these two principles are different in their nature, and not resolvable into one, so the principle of honor is evidently superior in dignity to that of interest.

No man would allow him to be a man of honor, who should plead his interest to justify what he acknowledged to be dishonorable; but to sacrifice interest to honor never costs a blush.

It likewise will be allowed by every man of honor, that this principle is not to be resolved into a regard to our reputation among men, otherwise the man of honor would not deserve to be trusted in the dark. He would have no aversion to lie, or cheat, or play the coward, when he had no dread of being discovered.

I take it for granted, therefore, that every man of real honor feels an abhorrence of certain actions, because they are in themselves base, and feels an obligation to certain other actions, because they are in themselves what honor requires, and this, independently of any consideration of interest or reputation.

This is an immediate moral obligation. This principle of honor, which is acknowledged by all men who pretend to character, is only another name for what we call a regard to duty, to rectitude, to propriety of conduct. It is a moral obligation which obliges a man to do certain things because they are right, and not to do other things because they are wrong.

Ask the man of honor, why he thinks himself obliged to pay a debt of honor? The very question shocks him. To suppose that he needs any other inducement to do it but the principle of honor, is to suppose that he has no honor, no worth, and deserves no esteem.

There is therefore a principle in man, which, when he acts according to it, gives him a consciousness of worth, and when he acts contrary to it, a sense of demerit.

From the varieties of education, of fashion, of prejudices, and of habits, men may differ much in opinion with regard to the extent of this principle, and of what it commands and forbids; but the notion of it, as far as it is carried, is the same in all. It is that which gives a man real worth, and is the object of moral approbation.

[...]

Chapter VI
Of the sense of duty

We are next to consider, how we learn to judge and determine, that this is right, and that is wrong.

The abstract notion of moral good and ill would be of no use to direct our life, if we had not the power of applying it to particular actions, and determining what is morally good, and what is morally ill.

Some philosophers, with whom I agree, ascribe this to an original power or faculty in man, which they call the *moral sense*, the *moral faculty*, *conscience*. Others think, that our moral sentiments may be accounted for without supposing any original sense or faculty appropriated to that purpose, and go into very different systems to account for them.

I am not, at present, to take any notice of those systems, because the opinion first mentioned seems to me to be the truth, to wit, that, by an original power of the mind, when we come to years of understanding and reflection, we not only have the notions of right and wrong in conduct, but perceive certain things to be right, and others to be wrong.

The name of the *moral sense*, though more frequently given to conscience since lord Shaftesbury and Dr. Hutcheson wrote, is not new. The *sensus recti et honesti* is a phrase not unfrequent among the ancients, neither is the *sense of duty* among us.

It has got this name of *sense*, no doubt, from some analogy which it is conceived to bear to the external senses. And if we have just notions of the office of the external senses, the analogy is very evident, and I see no reason to take offence, as some have done, at the name of the *moral sense*.

The offence taken at this name seems to be owing to this, that philosophers have degraded the senses too much, and deprived them of the most important part of their office.

We are taught, that by the senses, we have only certain ideas which we could not have otherwise. They are represented as powers by which we have sensations and ideas, not as powers by which we judge.

This notion of the senses I take to be very lame, and to contradict what nature and accurate reflection teach concerning them.

A man who has totally lost the sense of seeing, may retain very distinct notions of the various colours; but he cannot judge of colours, because he has lost the sense by which alone he could judge. By my eyes I not only have the ideas of a square and a circle, but I perceive this surface to be a square, that to be a circle.

By my ear, I not only have the idea of sounds, loud and soft, acute and grave, but I immediately perceive and judge this sound to be loud, that to be soft, this to be acute, that to be grave. Two or more synchronous sounds I perceive to be concordant, others to be discordant.

These are judgments of the senses. They have always been called and accounted such, by those whose minds are not tinctured by philosophical theories. They are the immediate testimony of nature by our senses; and we are so constituted by nature, that we must receive their testimony, for no other reason but because it is given by our senses.

In vain do skeptics endeavour to overturn this evidence by metaphysical reasoning. Though we should not be able to answer their arguments, we believe our senses still, and rest our most important concerns upon their testimony.

If this be a just notion of our external senses, as I conceive it is, our moral faculty may, I think, without impropriety, be called the *moral sense*.

In its dignity it is, without doubt, far superior to every other power of the mind; but there is this analogy between it and the external senses, that, as by them we have not only the original conceptions of the various qualities of bodies, but the original judgments that this body has such a quality, that such another; so by our moral faculty, we have both the original conceptions of right and wrong in conduct, of merit and demerit, and the original judgments that this conduct is right, that is wrong; that this character has worth, that, demerit.

The testimony of our moral faculty, like that of the external senses, is the testimony of nature, and we have the same reason to rely upon it.

The truths immediately testified by the external senses are the first principles from which we reason, with regard to the material world, and from which all our knowledge of it is deduced.

The truths immediately testified by our moral faculty, are the first principles of all moral reasoning, from which all our knowledge of our duty must be deduced.

[. . .]

Essay V

Chapter IV
Whether an action deserving moral approbation, must be done with the belief of its being morally good

[. . .]

Every question about what is or is not the proper object of moral approbation, belongs to practical morals, and such is the question now under consideration: Whether actions deserving moral approbation must be done with the belief of their being morally good? Or, Whether an action, done without any regard to duty or to the dictates of conscience, can be entitled to moral approbation?

In every action of a moral agent, his conscience is either altogether silent, or it pronounces the action to be good, or bad, or indifferent. This, I think, is a complete enumeration. If it be perfectly silent, the action must be very trifling, or appear so. For conscience, in those who have exercised it, is a very pragmatical faculty, and meddles with every part of our conduct, whether we desire its counsel or not. And what a man does in perfect simplicity, without the least suspicion of its being bad, his heart cannot condemn him for, nor will he that knows the heart condemn him. If there was any previous culpable negligence or inattention which led him to a wrong judgment, or hindered his forming a right one, that I do not exculpate. I only consider the action done, and the disposition with which it was done, without its previous circumstances. And in this there appears nothing that merits disapprobation. As little can it merit any degree of moral approbation, because there was neither good nor ill intended. And the same may be said when conscience pronounces the action to be indifferent.

If, in the *second* place, I do what my conscience pronounces to be bad, or dubious, I am guilty to myself, and justly deserve the disapprobation of others. Nor am I less guilty in this case, though what I judged to be bad, should happen to be good or indifferent. I did it believing it to be bad, and this is an immorality.

Lastly, If I do what my conscience pronounces to be right and my duty, either I have some regard to duty, or I have none. The last is not supposable; for I believe there is no man so abandoned, but that he does what he believes to be his duty, with more assurance and alacrity upon that account. The more weight the rectitude of the action has in determining me to do it, the more I approve of my own conduct. And if my worldly interest, my appetites, or inclinations, draw me strongly the contrary way, my following the dictates of my conscience, in opposition to these motives, adds to the moral worth of the action.

When a man acts from an erroneous judgment, if his error be invincible, all agree that he is inculpable: but if his error be owing to some previous negligence or inattention, there seems to be some difference among moralists. This difference, however, is only seeming, and not real. For wherein lies the fault in this case? It must be granted by all, that the fault lies in this, and solely in this, that he was not at due pains to have his judgment well informed. Those moralists, therefore, who consider the action and the previous conduct that led to it as one whole, find something to blame in the whole; and they do so most justly. But those who take this whole to pieces, and consider what is blameable and what is right in each part, find all that is blameable in what preceded this wrong judgment, and nothing but what is approveable in what followed it.

Let us suppose, for instance, that a man believes that God has indispensably required him to observe a very rigorous fast in Lent; and that, from a regard to this supposed Divine command, he fasts in such manner as is not only a great mortification to his appetite, but even hurtful to his health.

His superstitious opinion may be the effect of a culpable negligence, for which he can by no means be justified. Let him, therefore, bear all the blame upon this account that he deserves. But now, having this opinion fixed in his mind, shall he act according to it or against it? Surely we cannot hesitate a moment in this case. It is evident, that in following the light of his judgment, he acts the part of a good and pious man, whereas, in acting contrary to his judgment, he would be guilty of wilful disobedience to his Maker.

If my servant, by mistaking my orders, does the contrary of what I commanded, believing, at the same time, that he obeys my orders, there may be some fault in his mistake, but to charge him with the crime of disobedience, would be inhuman and unjust.

These determinations appear to me to have intuitive evidence, no less than that of mathematical axioms. A man who is come to years of understanding, and who has exercised his faculties in judging of right and wrong, sees their truth as he sees day-light. Metaphysical arguments brought against them have the same effect as when brought against the evidence of sense: they may puzzle and confound, but they do not convince. It appears evident, therefore, that those actions only can truly be called virtuous, or deserving of moral approbation, which the agent believed to be right, and to which he was influenced, more or less, by that belief.

If it should be objected, that this principle makes it to be of no consequence to a man's morals, what his opinions may be, providing he acts agreeably to them, the answer is easy.

Morality requires, not only that a man should act according to his judgment, but that he should use the best means in his power that his judgment be according to truth. If he fail in either of these points, he is worthy of blame; but, if he fail in neither, I see not wherein he can be blamed.

When a man must act, and has no longer time to deliberate, he ought to act according to the light of his conscience, even when he is an error. But, when he has time to deliberate, he ought surely to use all the means in his power to be rightly informed. When he has done so, he may still be in an error; but it is an invincible error, and cannot justly be imputed to him as a fault.

A *second* objection is, that we immediately approve of benevolence, gratitude, and other primary virtues, without inquiring whether they are practised from a persuasion that they are our duty. And the laws of God place the sum of virtue in loving God and our neighbour, without any provision that we do it from a persuasion that we ought to do so.

The answer to this objection is, that the love of God, the love of our neighbour, justice, gratitude, and other primary virtues, are, by the constitution of human nature, necessarily accompanied with a conviction of their being morally good. We may therefore safely presume, that these things are never disjoined, and that every man who pratises these virtues does it with a good conscience. In judging of men's conduct, we do not suppose things which cannot happen, nor do the laws of God give decisions upon impossible cases, as they must have done, if they supposed the case of a man who thought it contrary to his duty to love God or to love mankind.

But if we wish to know how the laws of God determine the point in question, we ought to observe their decision with regard to such actions as may appear good to one man and ill to another. And here the decisions of scripture are clear: *Let every man be persuaded in his own mind. He that doubteth is condemned if he eat, because he eateth not of faith; for whatsoever is not of faith is sin. To him that esteemeth any thing to be unclean, it is unclean.* The scripture often places the sum of virtue in *living in all good conscience*, in acting so *that our hearts condemn us not.*

The last objection I shall mention is a metaphysical one urged by Mr Hume.

It is a favourite point in his system of morals, that justice is not a natural but an artificial virtue. To prove this, he has exerted the whole strength of his reason and eloquence. And as the principle we are considering stood in his way, he takes pains to refute it.

[. . .]

1st, If we could not loose this metaphysical knot, I think we might fairly and honestly cut it, because it fixes an absurdity upon the clearest and most indisputable principles of morals and of common sense. For I appeal to any man whether there be any principle of morality, or any principle of common sense, more clear and indisputable than that which we just now quoted from the Apostle Paul, that although a thing be not unclean in itself, yet to him that esteemeth it to be unclean, to him it is unclean. But the metaphysical argument makes this absurd. For, says the metaphysician, if the thing was not unclean in itself, you judged wrong in esteeming it to be unclean; and what can be more absurd, than that your esteeming a thing to be what it is not, should make it what you erroneously esteem it to be?

Let us try the edge of this argument in another instance. Nothing is more evident, than that an action does not merit the name of benevolent, unless it be done from a belief that it tends to promote the good of our neighbour. But this is absurd, says the metaphysician. For, if it be not a benevolent action in itself, your belief of its tendency cannot change its nature. It is absurd, that your erroneous belief should make the action to be what you believe it to be. Nothing is more evident, than that a man who tells the truth, believing it to be a lie, is guilty of falsehood; but the metaphysician would make this to be absurd.

In a word, if there be any strength in this argument, it would follow, that a man might be in the highest degree virtuous, without the least regard to virtue; that he might be very benevolent, without ever intending to do a good office; very malicious, without ever intending any hurt; very revengeful, without ever intending to retaliate an injury; very grateful, without ever intending to return a benefit; and a man of strict veracity, with an intention to lie. We might, therefore, reject this reasoning, as repugnant to self-evident truths, though we were not able to point out the fallacy of it.

2dly, But let us try, in the *second* place, whether the fallacy of this argument may not be discovered.

We ascribe moral goodness to actions considered abstractly, without any relation to the agent. We likewise ascribe moral goodness to an agent on account of an action he has done; we call it a good action, though, in this case, the goodness is properly in the man, and is only by a figure ascribed to the action. Now, it is to be considered, whether *moral goodness,* when applied to an action considered abstractly, has the same meaning as when we apply it to a man on account of that action; or whether we do not unawares change the meaning of the word, according as we apply it to the one or to the other.

The action, considered abstractly, has neither understanding nor will; it is not accountable, nor can it be under any moral obligation. But all these things are essential to that moral goodness which belongs to a man; for, if a man had not understanding and will, he could have no moral goodness. Hence it follows necessarily, that the moral goodness which we ascribe to an action considered abstractly, and that which we ascribe to a person for doing that action, are not the same. The meaning of the word is changed when it is applied to these different subjects.

This will be more evident, when we consider what is meant by the moral goodness which we ascribe to a man for doing an action, and what by the goodness which belongs to the action considered abstractly. A good action in a man is that in which he applied his intellectual powers properly, in order to judge what he ought to do, and acted according to his best judgment. This is all that can be required of a moral agent; and in this his moral goodness, in any good action, consists. But is this the goodness which we ascribe to an action considered abstractly? No, surely. For the action, considered abstractly, is neither endowed with judgment nor with active power; and, therefore, can have none of that goodness which we ascribe to the man for doing it.

But what do we mean by goodness in an action considered abstractly? To me it appears to lie in this, and and in this only, that it is an action which ought to be done by those who have the power and opportunity, and the capacity of perceiving their obligation to do it. I would gladly know of any man, what other moral goodness can be in an action considered abstractly. And this goodness is inherent in its nature, and inseparable from it. No opinion or judgment of an agent can in the least alter its nature.

Suppose the action to be that of relieving an innocent person out of great distress. This surely has the moral goodness that an action considered abstractly can have. Yet it is evident, that an agent, in relieving a person in distress, may have no moral goodness, may have great merit, or may have great demerit.

Suppose, 1st, that mice cut the cords which bound the distressed person, and so bring him relief. Is there moral goodness in this act of the mice?

Suppose, 2dly, that a man maliciously relieves the distressed person, in order to plunge him into greater distress. In this action there is surely no moral goodness, but much malice and inhumanity.

If, in the *last* place, we suppose a person, from real sympathy and humanity, to bring relief to the distressed person, with considerable expense or danger to himself; here is an action of real worth, which every heart approves and every tongue praises. But wherein lies the worth? Not in the action considered by itself, which was common to all the three, but in the man who, on this occasion, acted the part which became a good man. He did what his heart approved, and therefore he is approved by God and man.

Upon the whole, if we distinguish between that goodness which may be ascribed to an action considered by itself, and that goodness which we ascribe to a man when he puts it in execution, we shall find a key to this metaphysical lock. We admit, that the goodness of an action, considered abstractly, can have no dependence upon the opinion or belief of an agent, any more than the truth of a proposition depends upon our believing it to be true. But, when a man exerts his active power well or ill, there is a moral goodness or turpitude, which we figuratively impute to the action, but which is truly and properly imputable to the man only;

and this goodness or turpitude depends very much upon the intention of the agent, and the opinion he had of his action.

This distinction has been understood in all ages by those who gave any attention to morals, though it has been variously expressed. The Greek moralists gave the name of καθῆκον to an action good in itself; such an action might be done by the most worthless. But an action done with a right intention, which implies real worth in the agent, they called κατ᾽οζὗωμα. The distinction is explained by Cicero in his offices. He calls the first *officium medium*, and the second *officium perfectum*, or *rectum*. In the scholastic ages, an action good in itself was said to be *materially* good, and an action done with a right intention was called *formally* good. This last way of expressing the distinction is still familiar among theologians; but Mr. Hume seems not to have attended to it, or to have thought it to be words without any meaning.

Mr. Hume, in the section already quoted, tells us with great assurance, "In short, it may be established as an undoubted maxim, that no action can be virtuous or morally good, unless there be in human nature some motive to produce it distinct from the sense of its morality." And upon this maxim he founds many of his reasonings on the subject of morals.

Whether it be consistent with Mr. Hume's own system, that an action may be produced merely from the sense of its morality, without any motive of agreeableness or utility, I shall not now inquire. But, if it be true, and I think it evident to every man of common understanding, that a judge or an arbiter acts the most virtuous part when his sentence is produced by no other motive but a regard to justice and a good conscience; nay, when all other motives distinct from this are on the other side: if this, I say, be true, then that undoubted maxim of Mr. Hume must be false, and all the conclusions built upon it must fall to the ground.

23

Jeremy Bentham, *An Introduction to the Principles of Morals and Legislation* (1789)

Jeremy Bentham was the greatest "utilitarian" thinker of the eighteenth century. William Paley advocated a theological version of utilitarianism, and the moral-sense theories of Francis Hutcheson and David Hume at least tended toward utilitarian principles. But it was Bentham who offered the utilitarian definition of "good" and "bad" strictly in terms of pleasure and pain, and who identified the moral obligations of both private individuals and of legislators as the promotion of pleasure and the general happiness: "the greatest happiness for the greatest number."

Two types of moral system stand in opposition to utilitarianism, Bentham wrote in the reading selection below: the "ascetic" system, and the system of "sympathy and antipathy." According to the former, pleasure is mistakenly identified with evil. According to the latter, actions are designated good just insofar as we are inclined to admire or reward them, and designated bad just insofar as we are inclined to deplore or punish them. It is not difficult to see that Bentham would rank the moral sentimentalists of his day as proponents of the latter system. Their common mistake, he argued, lay in ignoring all objective, external considerations, like the pleasant or painful consequences of actions, while focusing exclusively on the subjective feelings of spectators. To his way of thinking these systems were especially vulnerable on the morality of punishment, since they maintained, in Bentham's words, that "whatever you find in yourself a propensity to condemn, it is wrong for that very reason. For the same reason it is also meet for punishment ... if you hate much, punish much; if you hate little, punish little: punish as you hate."

Another common tenet of sentimentalist theories to which Bentham objected was the moral evaluation of actions always on the basis of their agent's good or bad motives. After analyzing the multiple meanings of "motive" near the end of the selection that follows, Bentham draws the conclusion that "A motive is substantially nothing other than pleasure or pain, operating in a certain manner." This is because pleasure serves as a motive by prompting us to act to enjoy something, while pain prompts us to act to avoid something. From this it follows in turn that no motive can be considered in itself bad; for all motives have some tendency to produce pleasure or avert its opposite, and therefore all motives, in the utilitarian system, are good.

Bentham was born in London in 1748, the son of an established attorney. He would later become a critic and reformer of the English legal system, and a founding member of a group of philosophical radicals that included the father of the greatest utilitarian thinker of the nineteenth century, John Stuart Mill. Noteworthy among Bentham's radical interests were prison reform, democratic government, the abolition of slavery, animal welfare, the decriminalization of homosexuality, and equal rights for women. Following his death in 1832, the terms of his will called for his body to be preserved at University College London, where it remains today as an "auto-icon," with a wax head, dressed and seated in a display cabinet.

Chapter I
Of the Principle of Utility

I

Nature has placed mankind under the governance of two sovereign masters, *pain* and *pleasure*. It is for them alone to point out what we ought to do, as well as to determine what we shall do. On the one hand the standard of right and wrong, on the other the chain of causes and effects, are fastened to their throne. They govern us in all we do, in all we say, in all we think: every effort we can make to throw off our subjection, will serve but to demonstrate and confirm it. In words a man may pretend to abjure their empire: but in reality he will remain subject to it all the while. The *principle of utility* recognises this subjection, and assumes it for the foundation of that system, the object of which is to rear the fabric of felicity by the hands of reason and of law. Systems which attempt to question it, deal in sounds instead of sense, in caprice instead of reason, in darkness instead of light.

But enough of metaphor and declamation: it is not by such means that moral science is to be improved.

II

The principle of utility is the foundation of the present work: it will be proper therefore at the outset to give an explicit and determinate account of what is meant by it. By the principle of utility is meant that principle which approves or disapproves of every action whatsoever, according to the tendency which it appears to have to augment or diminish the happiness of the party whose interest is in question: or, what is the same thing in other words, to promote or to oppose that happiness. I say of every action whatsoever; and therefore not only of every action of a private individual, but of every measure of government.

III

By utility is meant that property in any object, whereby it tends to produce benefit, advantage, pleasure, good, or happiness, (all this in the present case comes to the same thing) or (what comes again to the same thing) to prevent the happening of mischief, pain, evil, or unhappiness to the party whose interest is considered: if that party be the community in general, then the happiness of the community: if a particular individual, then the happiness of that individual.

IV

The interest of the community is one of the most general expressions that can occur in the phraseology of morals: no wonder that the meaning of it is often lost. When it has a meaning, it is this. The community is a fictitious *body*, composed of the individual persons who are considered as constituting as it were its *members*. The interest of the community then is, what? – the sum of the interests of the several members who compose it.

V

It is in vain to talk of the interest of the community, without understanding what is the interest of the individual. A thing is said to promote the interest, or to be *for* the interest, of an individual, when it tends to add to the sum total of his pleasures: or, what comes to the same thing, to diminish the sum total of his pains.

VI

An action then may be said to be conformable to the principle of utility, or, for shortness sake, to utility, (meaning with respect to the community at large) when the tendency it has to augment the happiness of the community is greater than any it has to diminish it.

VII

A measure of government (which is but a particular kind of action, performed by a particular person or persons) may be said to be conformable to or dictated by the principle of utility, when in like manner the tendency which it has to augment the happiness of the community is greater than any which it has to diminish it.

VIII

When an action, or in particular a measure of government, is supposed by a man to be conformable to the principle of utility, it may be convenient, for the purposes of discourse, to imagine a kind of law or dictate, called a law or dictate of utility: and to speak of the action in question, as being conformable to such law or dictate.

IX

A man may be said to be a partizan of the principle of utility, when the approbation or disapprobation he annexes to any action, or to any measure, is determined by and proportioned to the tendency which he conceives it to have to augment or to diminish the happiness of the community: or in other words, to its conformity or unconformity to the laws or dictates of utility.

X

Of an action that is conformable to the principle of utility, one may always say either that it is one that ought to be done, or at least that it is not one that ought not to be done. One may say also, that it is right it should be done; at least that it is not wrong it should be done: that it is a right action; at least that it is not a wrong action. When thus interpreted, the words *ought*, and *right* and *wrong*, and others of that stamp, have a meaning: when otherwise, they have none.

[. . .]

Chapter II
Of Principles Adverse to that of Utility

I

If the principle of utility be a right principle to be governed by, and that in all cases, it follows from what has been just observed, that whatever principle differs from it in any case must necessarily be a wrong one. To prove any other principle, therefore, to be a wrong one, there needs no more than just to show it to be what it is, a principle of which the dictates are in some point or other different from those of the principle of utility: to state it is to confute it.

II

A principle may be different from that of utility in two ways: 1. By being constantly opposed to it: this is the case with a principle which may be termed the principle of *asceticism*. 2. By being sometimes opposed to it, and sometimes not, as it may happen: this is the case with another, which may be termed the principle of *sympathy* and *antipathy*.

III

By the principle of asceticism I mean that principle, which, like the principle of utility, approves or disapproves of any action, according to the tendency which it appears to have to augment or diminish the happiness of the party whose interest is in question; but in an inverse manner: approving of actions in as far as they tend to diminish his happiness; disapproving of them in as far as they tend to augment it.

[. . .]

IX

The principle of asceticism seems originally to have been the reverie of certain hasty speculators, who having perceived, or fancied, that certain pleasures, when reaped in certain circumstances, have, at the long run, been attended with pains more than equivalent to them, took occasion to quarrel with every thing that offered itself under the name of pleasure. Having then got thus far, and having forgot the point which they set out from, they pushed on, and went so much further as to think it meritorious to fall in love with pain. Even this, we see, is at bottom but the principle of utility misapplied.

X

The principle of utility is capable of being consistently pursued; and it is but tautology to say, that the more consistently it is pursued, the better it must ever be for human-kind. The principle of asceticism never was, nor ever can be, consistently pursued by any living creature. Let but one tenth part of the inhabitants of this earth pursue it consistently, and in a day's time they will have turned it into a hell.

XI

Among principles adverse to that of utility, that which at this day seems to have most influence in matters of government, is what may be called the principle of sympathy and antipathy. By the principle of sympathy and antipathy, I mean that principle which approves or disapproves of certain actions, not on account of their tending to augment the happiness, nor yet on account of their tending to diminish the happiness of the party whose interest is in question, but merely because a man finds himself disposed to approve or disapprove of them: holding up that approbation or disapprobation as a sufficient reason for itself, and disclaiming the necessity of looking out for any extrinsic ground. Thus far in the general department of morals: and in the particular department of politics, measuring out the quantum (as well as determining the ground) of punishment, by the degree of the disapprobation.

XII

It is manifest, that this is rather a principle in name than in reality: it is not a positive principle of itself, so much as a term employed to signify the negation of all principle. What one expects to find in a principle is something that points out some external consideration, as a means of warranting and guiding the internal sentiments of approbation and disapprobation: this expectation is but ill fulfilled by a proposition, which does neither more nor less than hold up each of those sentiments as a ground and standard for itself.

XIII

In looking over the catalogue of human actions (says a partizan of this principle) in order to determine which of them are to be marked with the seal of disapprobation, you need but to take counsel of your own feelings: whatever you find in yourself a propensity to condemn, is wrong for that very reason. For the same reason it is also meet for punishment: in what proportion it is adverse to utility, or whether it be adverse to utility at all, is a matter that makes no difference. In that same *proportion* also is it meet for punishment: if you hate much, punish much: if you hate little, punish little: punish as you hate. If you hate not at all, punish not at all: the fine feelings of the soul are not to be overborne and tyrannized by the harsh and rugged dictates of political utility.

XIV

The various systems that have been formed concerning the standard of right and wrong, may all be reduced to the principle of sympathy and antipathy. One account may serve for all of them. They consist all of them in so many contrivances for avoiding the obligation of appealing to any external standard, and for prevailing upon the reader to accept of the author's sentiment or opinion as a reason for itself. The phrases different, but the principle the same.

XV

It is manifest, that the dictates of this principle will frequently coincide with those of utility, though perhaps without intending any such thing. Probably more frequently than not: and hence it is that the business of penal justice is carried on upon that tolerable sort of footing upon which we see it carried on in common at this day. For what more natural or more general ground of hatred to a practice can there be, than the mischievousness of such practice? What all men are exposed to suffer by, all men will be disposed to hate. It is far yet, however, from being a constant ground: for when a man suffers, it is not always that he knows what it is he suffers by. A man may suffer grievously, for instance, by a new tax, without being able to trace up the cause of his sufferings to the injustice of some neighbour, who has eluded the payment of an old one.

XVI

The principle of sympathy and antipathy is most apt to err on the side of severity. It is for applying punishment in many cases which deserve none: in many cases which deserve some, it is for applying more than they deserve. There is no incident imaginable, be it ever so trivial, and so remote from mischief, from which this principle may not extract a ground of punishment. Any difference in taste: any difference in opinion: upon one subject as well as upon another. No disagreement so trifling which perseverance and altercation will not render serious. Each becomes in the other's eyes an enemy, and, if laws permit, a criminal. This is one of the circumstances by which the human race is distinguished (not much indeed to its advantage) from the brute creation.

XVII

It is not, however, by any means unexampled for this principle to err on the side of lenity. A near and perceptible mischief moves antipathy. A remote and imperceptible mischief, though not less real, has no effect.

[. . .]

Chapter IV
Value of a Lot of Pleasure or Pain, How To Be Measured

I

Pleasures then, and the avoidance of pains, are the *ends* which the legislator has in view: it behoves him therefore to understand their *value*. Pleasures and pains are the *instruments* he has to work with: it behoves him therefore to understand their force, which is again, in other words, their value.

II

To a person considered *by himself*, the value of a pleasure or pain considered *by itself*, will be greater or less, according to the four following circumstances:

1. Its *intensity*.
2. Its *duration*.
3. Its *certainty* or *uncertainty*.
4. Its *propinquity* or *remoteness*.

III

These are the circumstances which are to be considered in estimating a pleasure or a pain considered each of them by itself. But when the value of any pleasure or pain is considered for the purpose of estimating the tendency of any *act* by which it is produced, there are two other circumstances to be taken into the account; these are,

5. Its *fecundity,* or the chance it has of being followed by sensations of the *same* kind: that is, pleasures, if it be a pleasure: pains, if it be a pain.
6. Its *purity,* or the chance it has of *not* being followed by sensations of the *opposite* kind: that is, pains, if it be a pleasure: pleasures, if it be a pain.

These two last, however, are in strictness scarcely to be deemed properties of the pleasure or the pain itself; they are not, therefore, in strictness to be taken into the account of the value of that pleasure or that pain. They are in strictness to be deemed properties only of the act, or other event, by which such pleasure or pain has been produced; and accordingly are only to be taken into the account of the tendency of such act or such event.

IV

To a *number* of persons, with reference to each of whom the value of a pleasure or a pain is considered, it will be greater or less, according to seven circumstances: to wit, the six preceding ones; *viz.*

1. Its *intensity.*
2. Its *duration.*
3. Its *certainty* or *uncertainty.*
4. Its *propinquity* or *remoteness.*
5. Its *fecundity.*
6. Its *purity.*
And one other; to wit:
7. Its *extent;* that is, the number of persons to whom it *extends;* or (in other words) who are affected by it.

V

To take an exact account then of the general tendency of any act, by which the interests of a community are affected, proceed as follows. Begin with any one person of those whose interests seem most immediately to be affected by it: and take an account,

1. Of the value of each distinguishable *pleasure* which appears to be produced by it in the *first* instance.
2. Of the value of each *pain* which appears to be produced by it in the *first* instance.
3. Of the value of each pleasure which appears to be produced by it *after* the first. This constitutes the *fecundity* of the first *pleasure* and the *impurity* of the first *pain.*
4. Of the value of each *pain* which appears to be produced by it after the first. This constitutes the *fecundity* of the first *pain,* and the *impurity* of the first pleasure.

5. Sum up all the values of all the *pleasures* on the one side, and those of all the pains on the other. The balance, if it be on the side of pleasure, will give the *good* tendency of the act upon the whole, with respect to the interests of that *individual* person; if on the side of pain, the *bad* tendency of it upon the whole.

6. Take an account of the *number* of persons whose interests appear to be concerned; and repeat the above process with respect to each. *Sum up* the numbers expressive of the degrees of *good* tendency, which the act has, with respect to each individual, in regard to whom the tendency of it is *good* upon the whole: do this again with respect to each individual, in regard to whom the tendency of it is *good* upon the whole: do this again with respect to each individual, in regard to whom the tendency of it is *bad* upon the whole. Take the *balance*; which, if on the side of *pleasure*, will give the general *good tendency* of the act, with respect to the total number or community of individuals concerned; if on the side of pain, the general *evil tendency*, with respect to the game community.

VI

It is not to be expected that this process should be strictly pursued previously to every moral judgment, or to every legislative or judicial operation. It may, however, be always kept in view: and as near as the process actually pursued on these occasions approaches to it, so near will such process approach to the character of an exact one.

VII

The same process is alike applicable to pleasure and pain, in whatever shape they appear: and by whatever denomination they are distinguished: to pleasure, whether it be called *good* (which is properly the cause or instrument of pleasure) or *profit* (which is distant pleasure, or the cause or instrument of distant pleasure,) or *convenience*, or *advantage, benefit, emolument, happiness*, and so forth: to pain, whether it be called *evil*, (which corresponds to *good*) or *mischief*, or *inconvenience*, or *disadvantage*, or *loss*, or *unhappiness*, and so forth.

VIII

Nor is this a novel and unwarranted, any more than it is a useless theory. In all this there is nothing but what the practice of mankind, wheresoever they have a clear view of their own interest, is perfectly conformable to. An article of property, an estate in land, for instance, is valuable, on what account? On account of the pleasures of all kinds which it enables a man to produce, and what comes to the same thing the pains of all kinds which it enables him to avert. But the value of such an article of property is universally understood to rise or fall according to the length or shortness of the time which a man has in it: the certainty or uncertainty of its coming into possession: and the nearness or remoteness of the time at which, if at all, it is to come into possession. As to the *intensity* of the pleasures which a man may derive from it, this is never thought of, because it depends upon the use which each particular person may come to make of it; which cannot be estimated till the particular pleasures he may come to derive from it, or the particular pains he may come to exclude by means of it, are brought to view. For the same reason, neither does he think of the *fecundity* or *purity* of those pleasures.

Chapter X
Of Motives

§1. Different senses of the word motive

I

It is an acknowledged truth, that every kind of act whatever, and consequently every kind of offence, is apt to assume a different character, and be attended with different effects, according to the nature of the *motive* which gives birth to it. This makes it requisite to take a view of the several motives by which human conduct is liable to be influenced.

II

By a motive, in the most extensive sense in which the word is ever used with reference to a thinking being, is meant any thing that can contribute to give birth to, or even to prevent, any kind of action. Now the action of a thinking being is the act either of the body, or only of the mind: and an act of the mind is an act either of the intellectual faculty, or of the will. Acts of the intellectual faculty will sometimes rest in the understanding merely, without exerting any influence in the production of any acts of the will. Motives, which are not of a nature to influence any other acts than those, may be styled purely *speculative* motives, or motives resting in speculation. But as to these acts, neither do they exercise any influence over external acts, or over their consequences, nor consequently over any pain or any pleasure that may be in the number of such consequences. Now it is only on account of their tendency to produce either pain or pleasure, that any acts can be material. With acts, therefore, that rest purely in the understanding, we have not here any concern: nor therefore with any object, if any such there be, which, in the character of a motive, can have no influence on any other acts than those.

III

The motives with which alone we have any concern, are such as are of a nature to act upon the will. By a motive then, in this sense of the word, is to be understood any thing whatsoever, which, by influencing the will of a sensitive being, is supposed to serve as a means of determining him to act, or voluntarily to forbear to act, upon any occasion. Motives of this sort, in contradistinction to the former, may be styled *practical* motives, or motives applying to practice.

IV

Owing to the poverty and unsettled state of language, the word *motive* is employed indiscriminately to denote two kinds of objects, which, for the better understanding of the subject, it is necessary should be distinguished. On some occasions it is employed to denote any of those really existing incidents from whence the act in question is supposed to take its rise. The sense it bears on these occasions may be styled its literal or *unfigurative* sense. On other occasions it is employed to denote a certain fictitious entity, a passion, an affection of the mind, an ideal being which upon the happening of any such incident is considered as operating upon the mind, and prompting it to take that course, towards which it is impelled by the influence of such incident. Motives of this class are Avarice, Indolence, Benevolence, and so forth; as we shall see more particularly farther on. This latter may be styled the *figura-tive* sense of the term *motive*.

V

As to the real incidents to which the name of motive is also given, these too are of two very different kinds. They may be either, 1. The *internal* perception of any individual lot of pleasure or pain, the expectation of which is looked upon as calculated to determine you to act in such or such a manner; as the pleasure of acquiring such a sum of money, the pain of exerting yourself on such an occasion, and so forth: Or, 2. Any *external* event, the happening whereof is regarded as having a tendency to bring about the perception of such pleasure or such pain: for instance, the coming up of a lottery ticket, by which the posses-sion of the money devolves to you; or the breaking out of a fire in the house you are in, which makes it necessary for you to quit it. The former kind of motives may be termed interior, or internal: the latter exterior, or external.

VI

Two other senses of the term *motive* need also to be distinguished. Motive refers necessarily to action. It is a pleasure, pain, or other event, that prompts to action. Motive then, in one sense of the word, must be previous to such event. But, for a man to be governed by any motive, he must in every case look beyond that event which is called his action; he must look to the consequences of it: and it is only in this way that the idea of pleasure, of pain, or of any other event, can give birth to it. He must look, therefore, in every case, to some event posterior to the act in contemplation: an event which as yet exists not, but stands only in prospect. Now, as it is in all cases difficult, and in most cases unnecessary, to distinguish between objects so intimately connected, as the posterior possible object which is thus looked forward to, and the present existing object or event which takes place upon a man's look-ing forward to the other, they are both of them spoken of under the same appellation, *motive*. To distinguish them, the one first mentioned may be termed a motive in *prospect,* the other a motive in *esse*: and under each of these denominations will come as well exterior as inter-nal motives. A fire breaks out in your neighbour's house: you are under apprehension of its extending to your own: you are apprehensive, that if you stay in it, you will be burnt: you accordingly run out of it. This then is the act: the others are all motives to it. The event of the fire's breaking out in your neighbour's house is an external motive, and that in *esse*: the idea or belief of the probability of the fire's extending to your own house, that of your being burnt if you continue, and the pain you feel at the thought of such a catastrophe, are all so many internal events, but still in *esse*: the event of the fire's actually extending to your own house, and that of your being actually burnt by it, external motives in prospect: the pain you would feel at seeing your house a burning, and the pain you would feel while you yourself were burning, internal motives in prospect: which events, according as the matter turns out, may come to be in *esse*: but then of course they will cease to act as motives.

VII

Of all these motives, which stand nearest to the act, to the production of which they all contribute, is that internal motive in *esse* which consists in the expectation of the internal motive in prospect: the pain or uneasiness you feel at the thoughts of being burnt. All other motives are more or less remote: the motives in prospect, in proportion as the period at which they are expected to happen is more distant from the period at which the act takes place, and consequently later in point of time: the motives in *esse*, in proportion as they also are more distant from that period, and consequently earlier in point of time.

VIII

It has already been observed, that with motives of which the influence terminates altogether in the understanding, we have nothing here to do. If then, amongst objects that are spoken of as motives with reference to the understanding, there be any which concern us here, it is only in as far as such objects may, through the medium of the understanding, exercise an influence over the will. It is in this way, and in this way only, that any objects, in virtue of any tendency they may have to influence the sentiment of belief, may in a practical sense act in the character of motives. Any objects, by tending to induce a belief concerning the existence, actual, or probable, of a practical motive; that is, concerning the probability of a motive in prospect, or the existence of a motive in *esse*; may exercise an influence on the will, and rank with those other motives that have been placed under the name of practical. The pointing out of motives such as these, is what we frequently mean when we talk of giving *reasons*. Your neighbour's house is on fire as before. I observe to you, that at the lower part of your neighbour's house is some wood-work, which joins on to your's; that the flames have caught this wood-work, and so forth; which I do in order to dispose you to believe as I believe, that if you stay in your house much longer you will be burnt. In doing this, then, I suggest motives to your understanding; which motives, by the tendency they have to give birth to or strengthen a pain, which operates upon you in the character of an internal motive in *esse*, join their force, and act as motives upon the will.

§2. No motives either constantly good, or constantly bad

IX

In all this chain of motives, the principal or original link seems to be the last internal motive in prospect; it is to this that all the other motives in prospect owe their materiality: and the immediately acting motive its existence. This motive in prospect, we see, is always some pleasure, or some pain; some pleasure, which the act in question is expected to be a means of continuing or producing: some pain which it is expected to be a means of discontinuing or preventing. A motive is substantially nothing more than pleasure or pain, operating in a certain manner.

X

Now, pleasure is in *itself* a good: nay, even setting aside immunity from pain, the only good: pain is in itself an evil; and, indeed, without exception, the only evil; or else the words good and evil have no meaning. And this is alike true of every sort of pain, and of every sort of pleasure. It follows, therefore, immediately and incontestibly, that *there is no such thing as any sort of motive that is in itself a bad one.*

24

Mary Wollstonecraft, *A Vindication of the Rights of Woman* (1792)

Mary Wollstonecraft's *A Vindication of the Rights of Woman* is a moral critique of the status of women in eighteenth-century England and Europe. The book followed the publication in 1790 of her *A Vindication of the Rights of Man*, which was a reaction to Edmund Burke's conservative critique of the French Revolution. In *The Rights of Woman* Wollstonecraft is often critical also of Rousseau's recommendations for the education of girls, in his *Emile* (1762).

Commonly known as the "first feminist" or the "mother of feminism," Wollstonecraft believed God's having created women in a subservient role to men would be inconsistent with divine justice. She believed, consequently, that society should be structured so that independent individuals of both sexes could have the potential to develop their respective talents and virtues. "A truly benevolent legislator," she wrote, "always endeavours to make it the interest of each individual to be virtuous; and thus private virtue becoming the cement of public happiness, an orderly whole is consolidated by the tendency of all the parts towards a common centre." Although Wollstonecraft did not intend to offer her readers a moral theory, she nevertheless based her social critique on theoretical assumptions about morality. Beginning *The Rights of Woman* with an acknowledgment of simple first principles, she wrote that "the perfection of our nature and capability of happiness, must be estimated by the degree of reason, virtue, and knowledge, that distinguish the individual, and direct the laws which bind society: and that from the exercise of reason, knowledge and virtue naturally flow, is equally undeniable, if mankind be viewed collectively."

With this and similar statements Wollstonecraft declared her allegiance to either common sense or moral rationalism, rejecting sentimentalism and utilitarianism. Reason, she seems to say, provides criteria for both knowledge and virtue. Subordinating sentiment to reason, she wrote: "Nature has wisely attached affections to duties, to sweeten toil, and to give that vigour to the exertions of reason which only the heart can give", and in almost direct opposition to utilitarian thinkers she claimed: "True happiness, I mean all the contentment, and virtuous satisfaction, that can be snatched in [humanity's] imperfect state, must arise from well regulated affections; and an affection includes a duty."

Mary Wollstonecraft was born in London in 1759, and as a young adult helped establish a school for girls. She wrote often on education, morality, and politics, usually on behalf of women. In 1797 she married the writer William Godwin, and died the same year in child-birth. Her daughter grew up to become Mary Wollstonecraft Shelley, author of *Frankenstein*.

Chapter 9
Of the Pernicious Effects which Arise from the Unnatural Distinctions Established in Society

From the respect paid to property flow, as from a poisoned fountain, most of the evils and vices which render this world such a dreary scene to the contemplative mind. For it is in the most polished society that noisome reptiles and venomous serpents lurk under the rank herbage; and there is voluptuousness pampered by the still sultry air, which relaxes every good disposition before it ripens into virtue.

One class presses on another; for all are aiming to procure respect on account of their property: and property, once gained, will procure the respect due only to talents and virtue. Men neglect the duties incumbent on man, yet are treated like demi-gods; religion is also separated from morality by a ceremonial veil, yet men wonder that the world is almost, literally speaking, a den of sharpers or oppressors.

There is a homely proverb, which speaks a shrewd truth, that whoever the devil finds idle he will employ. And what but habitual idleness can hereditary wealth and titles produce? For man is so constituted that he can only attain a proper use of his faculties by exercising them, and will not exercise them unless necessity, of some kind, first set the wheels in motion. Virtue likewise can only be acquired by the discharge of relative duties; but the importance of these sacred duties will scarcely be felt by the being who is cajoled out of his humanity by the flattery of sycophants. There must be more equality established in society, or morality will never gain ground, and this virtuous equality will not rest firmly even when founded on a rock, if one half of mankind be chained to its bottom by fate, for they will be continually undermining it through ignorance or pride.

It is vain to expect virtue from women till they are, in some degree, independent of men; nay, it is vain to expect that strength of natural affection, which would make them good wives and mothers. Whilst they are absolutely dependent on their husbands they will be cunning, mean, and selfish, and the men who can be gratified by the fawning fondness of spaniel-like affection, have not much delicacy, for love is not to be bought, in any sense of the words, its silken wings are instantly shrivelled up when any thing beside a return in kind is sought. Yet whilst wealth enervates men; and women live, as it were, by their personal charms, how can we expect them to discharge those ennobling duties which equally require exertion and self-denial. Hereditary property sophisticates the mind, and the unfortunate victims to it, if I may so express myself, swathed from their birth, seldom exert the loco-motive faculty of body or mind; and, thus viewing every thing through one medium, and that a false one, they are unable to discern in what true merit and happiness consist. False, indeed, must be the light when the drapery of situation hides the man, and makes him stalk in masquerade, dragging from one scene of dissipation to another the nerveless limbs that hang with stupid listlessness, and rolling round the vacant eye which plainly tells us that there is no mind at home.

I mean, therefore, to infer that the society is not properly organized which does not compel men and women to discharge their respective duties, by making it the only way to acquire that countenance from their fellow-creatures, which every human being wishes some way to attain. The respect, consequently, which is paid to wealth and mere personal charms, is a true north-east blast, that blights the tender blossoms of affection and virtue. Nature has wisely attached affections to duties, to sweeten toil, and to give that vigour to the exertions of reason which only the heart can give. But, the affection which is put on merely because it is the appropriated insignia of a certain character, when its duties are not fulfilled, is one of the empty compliments which vice and folly are obliged to pay to virtue and the real nature of things.

To illustrate my opinion, I need only observe, that when a woman is admired for her beauty, and suffers herself to be so far intoxicated by the admiration she receives, as to neglect to discharge the indispensable duty of a mother, she sins against herself by neglecting to cultivate an affection that would equally tend to make her useful and happy. True happiness, I mean all the contentment, and virtuous satisfaction, that can be snatched in this imperfect state, must arise from well regulated affections; and an affection includes a duty. Men are not aware of the misery they cause, and the vicious weakness they cherish, by only inciting women to render themselves pleasing; they do not consider that they thus make natural and artificial duties clash, by sacrificing the comfort and respectability of a woman's life to voluptuous notions of beauty, when in nature they all harmonize.

Cold would be the heart of a husband, were he not rendered unnatural by early debauchery, who did not feel more delight at seeing his child suckled by its mother, than the most artful wanton tricks could ever raise; yet this natural way of cementing the matrimonial tie, and twisting esteem with fonder recollections, wealth leads women to spurn. To preserve their beauty, and wear the flowery crown of the day, which gives them a kind of right to reign for a short time over the sex, they neglect to stamp impressions on their husbands' hearts, that would be remembered with more tenderness when the snow on the head began to chill the bosom, than even their virgin charms. The maternal solicitude of a reasonable affectionate woman is very interesting, and the chastened dignity with which a mother returns the caresses that she and her child receive from a father who has been fulfilling the serious duties of his station, is not only a respectable, but a beautiful sight. So singular, indeed, are my feelings, and I have endeavoured not to catch factitious ones, that after having been fatigued with the sight of insipid grandeur and the slavish ceremonies that with cumberous pomp supplied the place of domestic affections, I have turned to some other scene to relieve my eye by resting it on the refreshing green every where scattered by nature. I have then viewed with pleasure a woman nursing her children, and discharging the duties of her station with, perhaps, merely a servant maid to take off her hands the servile part of the household business. I have seen her prepare herself and children, with only the luxury of cleanliness, to receive her husband, who returning weary home in the evening found smiling babes and a clean hearth. My heart has loitered in the midst of the group, and has even throbbed with sympathetic emotion, when the scraping of the well known foot has raised a pleasing tumult.

Whilst my benevolence has been gratified by contemplating this artless picture, I have thought that a couple of this description, equally necessary and independent of each other, because each fulfilled the respective duties of their station, possessed all that life could give. – Raised sufficiently above abject poverty not to be obliged to weigh the consequence of every farthing they spend, and having sufficient to prevent their attending to a frigid system of oeconomy, which narrows both heart and mind. I declare, so vulgar are my conceptions, that I know not what is wanted to render this the happiest as well as the most respectable situation in the world, but a taste for literature, to throw a little variety and interest into social converse, and some superfluous money to give to the needy and to buy books. For it is not pleasant when the heart is opened by compassion and the head active in arranging plans of usefulness, to have a prim urchin continually twitching back the elbow to prevent the hand from drawing out an almost empty purse, whispering at the same time some prudential maxim about the priority of justice.

Destructive, however, as riches and inherited honours are to the human character, women are more debased and cramped, if possible, by them, than men, because men may still, in some degree, unfold their faculties by becoming soldiers and statesmen.

As soldiers, I grant, they can now only gather, for the most part, vain glorious laurels, whilst they adjust to a hair the European balance, taking especial care that no bleak north-ern nook or sound incline the beam. But the days of true heroism are over, when a citizen fought for his country like a Fabricius or a Washington, and then returned to his farm to let his virtuous fervour run in a more placid, but not a less salutary, stream. No, our British heroes are oftener sent from the gaming table than from the plow; and their passions have been rather inflamed by hanging with dumb suspense on the turn of a die, than sublimated by panting after the adventurous march of virtue in the historic page.

The statesman, it is true, might with more propriety quit the Faro Bank, or card-table, to guide the helm, for he has still but to shuffle and trick. The whole system of British politics, if system it may courteously be called, consisting in multiplying dependents and contriving taxes which grind the poor to pamper the rich; thus a war, or any wild goose chace, is, as the vulgar use the phrase, a lucky turn-up of patronage for the minister, whose chief merit is the art of keeping himself in place. It is not necessary then that he should have bowels for the poor, so he can secure for his family the odd trick. Or should some shew of respect, for what is termed with ignorant ostentation an Englishman's birth-right, be expedient to bubble the gruff mastiff that he has to lead by the nose, he can make an empty shew, very safely, by giving his single voice, and suffering his light squadron to file off to the other side. And when a question of humanity is agitated he may dip a sop in the milk of human kind-ness, to silence Cerberus, and talk of the interest which his heart takes in an attempt to make the earth no longer cry for vengeance as it sucks in its children's blood, though his cold hand may at the very moment rivet their chains, by sanctioning the abominable traffick. A minister is no longer a minister, than while he can carry a point, which he is determined to carry. – Yet it is not necessary that a minister should feel like a man, when a bold push might shake his seat.

But, to have done with these episodical observations, let me return to the more specious slavery which chains the very soul of woman, keeping her for ever under the bondage of ignorance.

The preposterous distinctions of rank, which render civilization a curse, by dividing the world between voluptuous tyrants, and cunning envious dependents, corrupt, almost equally, every class of people, because respectability is not attached to the discharge of the relative duties of life, but to the station, and when the duties are not fulfilled the affections cannot gain sufficient strength to fortify the virtue of which they are the natural reward. Still there are some loop-holes out of which a man may creep, and dare to think and act for himself; but for a woman it is an herculean task, because she has difficulties peculiar to her sex to overcome, which require almost super-human powers.

A truly benevolent legislator always endeavours to make it the interest of each individual to be virtuous; and thus private virtue becoming the cement of public happiness, an orderly whole is consolidated by the tendency of all the parts towards a common centre. But, the private or public virtue of woman is very problematical; for Rousseau, and a numerous list of male writers, insist that she should all her life be subjected to a severe restraint, that of propriety. Why subject her to propriety – blind propriety, if she be capable of acting from a nobler spring, if she be an heir of immortality? Is sugar always to be produced by vital blood? Is one half of the human species, like the poor African slaves, to be subject to prejudices that brutalize them, when principles would be a surer guard, only to sweeten the cup of man? Is not this indirectly to deny woman reason? for a gift is a mockery, if it be unfit for use.

Women are, in common with men, rendered weak and luxurious by the relaxing pleasures which wealth procures; but added to this they are made slaves to their persons, and must render them alluring that man may lend them his reason to guide their tottering steps aright. Or should they be ambitious, they must govern their tyrants by sinister tricks, for without rights there cannot be any incumbent duties. The laws respecting woman, which I mean to discuss in a future part, make an absurd unit of a man and his wife; and then, by the easy transition of only considering him as responsible, she is reduced to a mere cypher.

The being who discharges the duties of its station is independent; and, speaking of women at large, their first duty is to themselves as rational creatures, and the next, in point of importance, as citizens, is that, which includes so many, of a mother. The rank in life which dispenses with their fulfilling this duty, necessarily degrades them by making them mere dolls. Or, should they turn to something more important than merely fitting drapery upon a smooth block, their minds are only occupied by some soft platonic attachment; or, the actual management of an intrigue may keep their thoughts in motion; for when they neglect domestic duties, they have it not in their power to take the field and march and counter-march like soldiers, or wrangle in the senate to keep their faculties from rusting.

I know that, as a proof of the inferiority of the sex, Rousseau has exultingly exclaimed, How can they leave the nursery for the camp! – And the camp has by some moralists been termed the school of the most heroic virtues; though, I think, it would puzzle a keen casuist to prove the reasonableness of the greater number of wars that have dubbed heroes. I do not mean to consider this question critically; because, having frequently viewed these freaks of ambition as the first natural mode of civilization, when the ground must be torn up, and the woods cleared by fire and sword, I do not choose to call them pests; but surely the present system of war has little connection with virtue of any denomination, being rather the school of *finesse* and effeminacy, than of fortitude.

Yet, if defensive war, the only justifiable war, in the present advanced state of society, where virtue can shew its face and ripen amidst the rigours which purify the air on the mountain's top, were alone to be adopted as just and glorious, the true heroism of antiquity might again animate female bosoms. – But fair and softly, gentle reader, male or female, do not alarm thyself, for though I have compared the character of a modern soldier with that of a civilized woman, I am not going to advise them to turn their distaff into a musket, though I sincerely wish to see the bayonet converted into a pruning-hook. I only recreated an imagination, fatigued by contemplating the vices and follies which all proceed from a feculent stream of wealth that has muddied the pure rills of natural affection, by supposing that society will some time or other be so constituted, that man must necessarily fulfil the duties of a citizen, or be despised, and that while he was employed in any of the departments of civil life, his wife, also an active citizen, should be equally intent to manage her family, educate her children, and assist her neighbours.

But, to render her really virtuous and useful, she must not, if she discharge her civil duties, want, individually, the protection of civil laws; she must not be dependent on her husband's bounty for her subsistence during his life, or support after his death – for how can a being be generous who has nothing of its own? or, virtuous, who is not free? The wife, in the present state of things, who is faithful to her husband, and neither suckles nor educates her children, scarcely deserves the name of a wife, and has no right to that of a citizen. But take away natural rights, and duties become null.

Women then must be considered as only the wanton solace of men, when they become so weak in mind and body, that they cannot exert themselves, unless to pursue some frothy pleasure, or to invent some frivolous fashion. What can be a more melancholy sight to a thinking mind, than to look into the numerous carriages that drive helter-skelter about this metropolis in a morning full of pale-faced creatures who are flying from themselves. I have often wished, with Dr. Johnson, to place some of them in a little shop with half a dozen children looking up to their languid countenances for support. I am much mistaken, if some latent vigour would not soon give health and spirit to their eyes, and some lines drawn by the exercise of reason on the blank cheeks, which before were only undulated by dimples, might restore lost dignity to the character, or rather enable it to attain the true dignity of its nature. Virtue is not to be acquired even by speculation, much less by the negative supineness that wealth naturally generates.

Besides, when poverty is more disgraceful than even vice, is not morality cut to the quick? Still to avoid misconstruction, though I consider that women in the common walks of life are called to fulfil the duties of wives and mothers, by religion and reason, I cannot help lamenting that women of a superiour cast have not a road open by which they can pursue more extensive plans of usefulness and independence. I may excite laughter, by dropping an hint, which I mean to pursue, some future time, for I really think that women ought to have representatives, instead of being arbitrarily governed without having any direct share allowed them in the deliberations of government.

But, as the whole system of representation is now, in this country, only a convenient handle for despotism, they need not complain, for they are as well represented as a numerous class of hard working mechanics, who pay for the support of royalty when they can scarcely stop their children's mouths with bread. How are they represented whose very sweat supports the splendid stud of an heir apparent, or varnishes the chariot of some female favourite who looks down on shame? Taxes on the very necessaries of life, enable an endless tribe of idle princes and princesses to pass with stupid pomp before a gaping crowd, who almost worship the very parade which costs them so dear. This is mere gothic grandeur, something like the barbarous useless parade of having sentinels on horseback at Whitehall, which I could never view without a mixture of contempt and indignation.

How strangely must the mind be sophisticated when this sort of state impresses it! But, till these monuments of folly are levelled by virtue, similar follies will leaven the whole mass. For the same character, in some degree, will prevail in the aggregate of society: and the refinements of luxury, or the vicious repinings of envious poverty, will equally banish virtue from society, considered as the characteristic of that society, or only allow it to appear as one of the stripes of the harlequin coat, worn by the civilized man.

In the superiour ranks of life, every duty is done by deputies, as if duties could ever be waved, and the vain pleasures which consequent idleness forces the rich to pursue, appear so enticing to the next rank, that the numerous scramblers for wealth sacrifice every thing to tread on their heels. The most sacred trusts are then considered as sinecures, because they were procured by interest, and only sought to enable a man to keep *good company*. Women, in particular, all want to be ladies. Which is simply to have nothing to do, but listlessly to go they scarcely care where, for they cannot tell what.

But what have women to do in society? I may be asked, but to loiter with easy grace; surely you would not condemn them all to suckle fools and chronicle small beer! No. Women might certainly study the art of healing, and be physicians as well as nurses. And midwifery, decency seems to allot to them, though I am afraid the word midwife, in our dictionaries, will soon give place to *accoucheur*, and one proof of the former delicacy of the sex be effaced from the language.

They might, also, study politics, and settle their benevolence on the broadest basis; for the reading of history will scarcely be more useful than the perusal of romances, if read as mere biography; if the character of the times, the political improvements, arts, &c. be not observed. In short, if it be not considered as the history of man; and not of particular men, who filled a niche in the temple of fame, and dropped into the black rolling stream of time, that silently sweeps all before it, into the shapeless void called – eternity. – For shape, can it be called, 'that shape hath none'?

Business of various kinds, they might likewise pursue, if they were educated in a more orderly manner, which might save many from common and legal prostitution. Women would not then marry for a support, as men accept of places under government, and neglect the implied duties; nor would an attempt to earn their own subsistence, a most laudable one! sink them almost to the level of those poor abandoned creatures who live by prostitution. For are not milliners and mantua-makers reckoned the next class? The few employments open to women, so far from being liberal, are menial; and when a superiour education enables them to take charge of the education of children as governesses, they are not treated like the tutors of sons, though even clerical tutors are not always treated in a manner calculated to render them respectable in the eyes of their pupils, to say nothing of the private comfort of the individual. But as women educated like gentlewomen, are never designed for the humiliating situation which necessity sometimes forces them to fill; these situations are considered in the light of a degradation; and they know little of the human heart, who need to be told, that nothing so painfully sharpens sensibility as such a fall in life.

Some of these women might be restrained from marrying by a proper spirit or delicacy, and others may not have had it in their power to escape in this pitiful way from servitude; is not that government then very defective, and very unmindful of the happiness of one half of its members, that does not provide for honest, independent women, by encouraging them to fill respectable stations? But in order to render their private virtue a public benefit, they must have a civil existence in the state, married or single; else we shall continually see some worthy woman, whose sensibility has been rendered painfully acute by undeserved contempt, droop like 'the lily broken down by a plow-share.'

It is a melancholy truth; yet such is the blessed effect of civilization! the most respectable women are the most oppressed; and, unless they have understandings far superiour to the common run of understandings, taking in both sexes, they must, from being treated like contemptible beings, become contemptible. How many women thus waste life away the prey of discontent, who might have practised as physicians, regulated a farm, managed a shop, and stood erect, supported by their own industry, instead of hanging their heads surcharged with the dew of sensibility, that consumes the beauty to which it at first gave lustre; nay, I doubt whether pity and love are so near akin as poets feign, for I have seldom seen much compassion excited by the helplessness of females, unless they were fair; then, perhaps, pity was the soft handmaid of love, or the harbinger of lust.

How much more respectable is the woman who earns her own bread by fulfilling any duty, than the most accomplished beauty! – beauty did I say? – so sensible am I of the beauty of moral loveliness, or the harmonious propriety that attunes the passions of a well-regulated mind, that I blush at making the comparison; yet I sigh to think how few women aim at attaining this respectability by withdrawing from the giddy whirl of pleasure, or the indolent calm that stupifies the good sort of women it sucks in.

Proud of their weakness, however, they must always be protected, guarded from care, and all the rough toils that dignify the mind. – If this be the fiat of fate, if they will make themselves insignificant and contemptible, sweetly to waste 'life away,' let them not expect to be valued when their beauty fades, for it is the fate of the fairest flowers to be admired and pulled to pieces by the careless hand that plucked them. In how many ways do I wish, from the purest benevolence, to impress this truth on my sex; yet I fear that they will not listen to a truth that dear bought experience has brought home to many an agitated bosom, nor willingly resign the privileges of rank and sex for the privileges of humanity, to which those have no claim who do not discharge its duties.

Those writers are particularly useful, in my opinion, who make man feel for man, independent of the station he fills, or the drapery of factitious sentiments. I then would fain convince reasonable men of the importance of some of my remarks; and prevail on them to weigh dispassionately the whole tenor of my observations. – I appeal to their understandings; and, as a fellow-creature, claim, in the name of my sex, some interest in their hearts. I entreat them to assist to emancipate their companion, to make her a *help meet* for them!

Would men but generously snap our chains, and be content with rational fellowship instead of slavish obedience, they would find us more observant daughters, more affectionate sisters, more faithful wives, more reasonable mothers – in a word, better citizens. We should then love them with true affection, because we should learn to respect ourselves; and the peace of mind of a worthy man would not be interrupted by the idle vanity of his wife, nor the babes sent to nestle in a strange bosom, having never found a home in their mother's.

Suggestions for Further Reading

A majority of the books we recommend are introductory and appropriate for university students. Some, however, including the general books on eighteenth-century thought at the top of this list, are more scholarly works that we hope will repay the effort of study.

Brown, Stuart. 1996. *British Philosophy and the Age of Enlightenment*. London: Routledge.

Kors, Alan Charles. 2002. *Encyclopedia of the Enlightenment*. New York: Oxford University Press.

Stewart, M. A., ed. 1990. *Studies in the Philosophy of the Scottish Enlightenment*. New York: Oxford University Press.

Waithe, Mary Ellen, ed. 1991. *Modern Women Philosophers, 1600–1900*. Vol. 3 in *History of Women Philosophers*. 3 vols. Dordrecht: Kluwer Academic Publishers.

Yolton, John. 1984. *Perceptual Acquaintance from Descartes to Reid*. Oxford: Basil Blackwell and University of Minnesota Press.

I. EMPIRICISM

Aune, Bruce. 1970. *Rationalism, Empiricism, and Pragmatism: An Introduction*. New York: Random House.

Bennett, Jonathan. 1971. *Locke, Berkeley, Hume: Central Themes*. Oxford: Oxford University Press.

LOCKE

Ayers, Michael. 1999. *Locke: The Arguments of the Philosophers*. London: Routledge.

Jolley, Nicholas. 1999. *Locke: His Philosophical Thought*. Oxford: Oxford University Press.

Lowe, E. J. 1995. *Routledge Philosophy Guidebook to Locke on Human Understanding*. New York: Routledge.

Lowe, E. J. 2005. *Locke*. London: Routledge.

Yolton, John W. 1985. *Locke: An Introduction*. Oxford: Basil Blackwell.

BERKELEY

Dancy, Jonathan. 1987. *Berkeley: An Introduction*. Oxford: Basil Blackwell.

Flage, Daniel E. 1987. *Berkeley's Doctrine of Notions*. New York: St. Martin's Press.

Fogelin, Robert J. 2001. *Routledge Philosophy Guidebook to Berkeley and Principles of Human Knowledge*. New York: Routledge.

Pappas, George. 2000. *Berkeley's Thought*. Ithaca: Cornell University Press.
Pitcher, George. 1977. *Berkeley: The Arguments of the Philosophers*. London: Routledge & Kegan Paul.
Winkler, Kenneth. 1989. *Berkeley: An Interpretation*. Oxford: Clarendon Press.

HUME

Dicker, Georges. 1998. *Hume's Epistemology and Metaphysics: An Introduction*. London: Routledge.
Fogelin, Robert. 1985. *Hume's Scepticism in the* Treatise of Human Nature. London: Routledge & Kegan Paul.
Noonan, Harold. 1999. *Routledge Philosophy Guidebook to Hume on Knowledge*. New York: Routledge.
Penelhum, Terence. 1992. *David Hume: An Introduction to his Philosophical System*. West Lafayette, IN: Purdue University Press.
Radcliffe, Elizabeth S. 2000. *On Hume*. Wadsworth Philosophers Series. Belmont, CA: Wadsworth.
Stroud, Barry. 1978. *Hume: The Arguments of the Philosophers*. London: Routledge & Kegan Paul.

II. CRITICS OF EMPIRICISM

Gallie, Roger. 1989. *Thomas Reid and "The Way of Ideas"*. Dordrecht: Kluwer.
Jolley, Nicholas. 1984. *Leibniz and Locke: A Study of the New Essays on Human Understanding*. Oxford: Clarendon Press.
Jolley, Nicholas. 2005. *Leibniz*. London: Routledge.
Lehrer, Keith. 1989. *Thomas Reid: The Arguments of the Philosophers*. London: Routledge.
Mates, Benson. 1986. *The Philosophy of Leibniz*. New York: Oxford University Press.
Vailati, Ezio. 1997. *Leibniz and Clarke: A Study of their Correspondence*. New York: Oxford University Press.

III. KANT'S CRITIQUE OF RATIONALISM AND EMPIRICISM

Dicker, Georges. 2004. *Kant's Theory of Knowledge: An Analytical Introduction*. Oxford: Oxford University Press.
Hoffe, Otfried. 1994. *Immanuel Kant*. Trans. Marshall Farrier. Albany, NY: State University of New York Press.
Scruton, Roger. 2001. *Kant: A Very Short Introduction*. Oxford: Oxford University Press.
Walker, Ralph C. S. 1978. *Kant: The Arguments of the Philosophers*. London: Routledge & Kegan Paul.
Wood, Allen. 2005. *Kant*. Great Minds Series. Oxford: Blackwell Publishing.

IV. ARGUMENTS FOR THE EXISTENCE OF GOD

Clarke, M. L. 1974. *Paley: Evidences for the Man*. Toronto: University of Toronto Press; London: SPCK.
Gaskin, J. C. A. 1988. *Hume's Philosophy of Religion*. 2nd edn. Basingstoke: Macmillan.
Michalson, Gordon E. 1999. *Kant and the Problem of God*. Oxford: Basil Blackwell.
O'Connor, David. 2001. *Routledge Philosophy Guidebook to Hume on Religion*. London: Routledge.
Penelhum, Terence. 1983. *God and Skepticism*. Dordrecht: Reidel.
Sessions, William Ladd. 2002. *Reading Hume's Dialogues: A Veneration for True Religion*. Bloomington: Indiana University Press.
Smart, J. J. C., and Haldane, J. J. 1996. *Atheism and Theism*. Oxford: Basil Blackwell.

V. POLITICAL PHILOSOPHY

Haakonssen, Knud. 1981. *The Science of a Legislator: The Natural Jurisprudence of David Hume and Adam Smith*. Cambridge: Cambridge University Press.
O'Hagan, Timothy. 1999. *Rousseau*. Arguments of the Philosophers. New York: Routledge.

Plant, Raymond. 1991. *Modern Political Thought*. Oxford: Basil Blackwell.

Thomas, David Lloyd. 1995. *Routledge Philosophy Guidebook to Locke on Government*. New York: Routledge.

Tully, James. 1993. *An Approach to Political Philosophy: Locke in Context*. Cambridge: Cambridge University Press.

Wokler, Robert. 2001. *Rousseau: A Very Short Introduction*. Oxford: Oxford University Press.

VI. MORAL PHILOSOPHY

Anscombe, G. E. M. 1958. "Modern Moral Philosophy." *Philosophy*, 33: 1–19.

HUME

Ballie, James. 2000. *The Routledge Guidebook to Hume on Morality*. New York: Routledge.

Harrison, Jonathan. 1976. *Hume's Moral Epistemology*. Oxford: Clarendon Press.

Mackie, J. L. 1980. *Hume's Moral Theory*. London: Routledge.

Norton, David Fate. 1982. *David Hume: Common-Sense Moralist, Sceptical Metaphysician*. Princeton: Princeton University Press.

SMITH

Campbell, T. D. 1971. *Adam Smith's Science of Morals*. London: Allen & Unwin.

Griswold, Charles L. 1999. *Adam Smith and the Virtues of Enlightenment*. New York: Cambridge University Press.

Weinstein, Jack Russell. 2000. *On Adam Smith*. Wadsworth Philosophers Series. Belmont, CA: Wadsworth.

KANT

Aune, Bruce. 1979. *Kant's Theory of Morals*. Princeton, NJ: Princeton University Press.

Sullivan, Roger J. 1994. *An Introduction to Kant's Ethics*. Cambridge: Cambridge University Press.

Wood, Allen. 1999. *Kant's Ethical Thought*. New York: Cambridge University Press.

REID; PRICE

Gallie, Roger D. 1998. *Thomas Reid: Ethics, Aesthetics and the Anatomy of the Self*. Dordrecht: Kluwer Academic Publishers.

Hudson, W. D. 1970. *Reason and Right: A Critical Examination of Richard Price's Moral Philosophy*. San Francisco: Freeman, Cooper.

BENTHAM

Crimmins, James E. 2004. *On Bentham*. Wadsworth Philosophers Series. Belmont, CA: Wadsworth.

Harrison, Ross. 1983. *Bentham: The Arguments of the Philosophers*. London: Routledge & Kegan Paul.

Rosen, Frederick. 2003. *Classical Utilitarianism from Hume to Mill*. London: Routledge.

WOLLSTONECRAFT

Johnson, Patricia Altenbernd. 2000. *On Wollstonecraft*. Wadsworth Philosophers Series. Belmont, CA: Wadsworth.

Taylor, Barbara. 2003. *Mary Wollstonecraft and the Feminist Imagination*. Cambridge: Cambridge University Press.

Index

*Index compiled by Meg Davies (Fellow of the Society
of Indexers)*